Lecture Notes in Computer Science 8880

Commenced Publication in 1973
Founding and Former Series Editors:
Gerhard Goos, Juris Hartmanis, and Jan van Leeuwen

Lecture Notes in Computer Science   8880

Atul Prakash   Rudrapatna Shyamasundar (Eds.)

Information Systems Security

10th International Conference, ICISS 2014
Hyderabad, India, December 16-20, 2014
Proceedings

 Springer

Volume Editors

Atul Prakash
University of Michigan
Department of EECS
Ann Arbor, MI, USA
E-mail: aprakash@umich.edu

Rudrapatna Shyamasundar
Tata Institute of Fundamental Research
Faculty of Technology and Computer Science
Mumbai, India
E-mail: shyam@tifr.res.in

ISSN 0302-9743   e-ISSN 1611-3349
ISBN 978-3-319-13840-4   e-ISBN 978-3-319-13841-1
DOI 10.1007/978-3-319-13841-1
Springer Cham Heidelberg New York Dordrecht London

Library of Congress Control Number: 2014955999

LNCS Sublibrary: SL 4 – Security and Cryptology

Typesetting: Camera-ready by author, data conversion by Scientific Publishing Services, Chennai, India

Printed on acid-free paper

Springer is part of Springer Science+Business Media (www.springer.com)

Message from the General Chairs

It has been a truly delightful experience for us to be associated with the organization of the 10th International Conference on Information Systems Security (ICISS 2014) hosted by the Institute for Development and Research in Banking Technology (IDRBT), Hyderabad, India, during December 16–20, 2014. Over the last 10 years, the ICISS conference has made significant progress to establish itself as one of the premier conferences in the field of information systems security. This has been possible in part due to the emphasis on quality of the selected research papers. The number of submissions as well as the spread of the participating countries has been steadily growing with record numbers being achieved this year.

Our special thanks and gratitude are due to Atul Prakash and R.K. Shyamasundar, and their Program Committee of 40 international experts in the field, for ensuring a high-quality technical program. We are grateful to Herbert Bos, Sushil Jajodia, Zhenkai Liang, and Vyas Sekar for agreeing to deliver keynote talks, thereby adding luster to the conference proceedings. This has been possible largely due to the persistent efforts of R. Sekar and N. Raghukishore.

We would like to express our sincere appreciation to N. Subramanian and V. Ravi for organizing a whole suite of topical tutorials, U.B. Desai and V.N. Sastri for organizing the doctoral symposium, and Pavel Gladyshev and M.V.N.K. Prasad for organizing the short talks. We duly acknowledge the efforts of G. Raghuraj, M.V. Sivakumaran, Vijay Belurgikar, Aditya Bagchi, G.R. Gangadharan, Ratna Kumar, V. Radha, N.P. Dhavale, and Lalit Mohan in helping out with the various non-technical aspects of the conference including logistics, publicity and sponsorship.

Finally, we take this opportunity to thank IDRBT management for their unstinted support and guidance without which this conference would not be the same.

Venu Govindaraju
B.M. Mehtre

Preface

This volume contains the papers presented at the 10th International Conference on Information System Security (ICISS 2014), held during December 16–20, 2014, in Hyderabad. The conference initiated in 2005 to cater to cyber security research in India has successfully entered its tenth edition and has been providing an attractive international forum on information system security for academics, industry, business, and government.

This year, the conference attracted 129 submissions from 21 countries. Given the high quality of the submissions, the Program Committee (PC) accepted 20 full papers and five short papers after a rigorous review process with multiple reviews for each paper. We thank all the expert reviewers for their invaluable support. We are grateful to the PC members who put in enormous efforts in reviewing and selecting the papers. Without the untiring efforts of the PC members/reviewers and the contributions of the authors of 129 papers, the conference would not have been possible.

The entire process of submission, refereeing, e-meetings of the PC for selecting the papers, and compiling the proceedings was done through the EasyChair system. Thanks go to the artchitects of EasyChair for providing a highly configurable conference management system.

One of the hallmarks of the ICISS conference series is the high quality of plenary/invited presentations. This year we were fortunate to have four eminent speakers give invited presentations: Herbert Bos (Vrije Universiteit Amsterdam), Sushil Jajodia (George Mason University), Zhenkai Liang (National University of Singapore), and Vyas Sekar (Carnegie Mellon University). It is indeed a great pleasure for us to thank the invited speakers who agreed to present at the conference coming from from far off places in mid-December. Three of the invited speakers have also contributed to the volume by providing their papers/extended abstracts. We are grateful to them for their time and efforts.

Due to the keen interest in information system security, the conference also included several tutorials on various topics in cyber security and also short talks to facilitate discussion on emerging topics.

We thank all the members of the Steering Committee and the Organizing Committee for making all the arrangements for the conference. We are grateful to IDRBT for all the support provided for running the conference. In particular, Dr. Mehtre, Dr. Venu Govindaraju, and Dr. Sushil Jajodia helped us at key points with the logistics of running the PC.

It is our pleasure to acknowledge Srirangaraj Setlur (SUNY, Buffalo) for all his untiring efforts in preparing the proceedings. Last but not least thanks go to Alfred Hofmann from Springer for readily agreeing to publish the proceedings in the LNCS series. Thanks go to his team and in particular Anna Kramer in preparing the proceedings meticulously and in time for the conference.

December 2014   Atul Prakash
                                                          Rudrapatna Shyamasundar

Organization

Executive Chairs

B. Sambamurthy   IDRBT, Hyderabad, India
A.S. Ramasastri   IDRBT, Hyderabad, India

General Chairs

Venu Govindaraju   SUNY Buffalo, USA
B.M. Mehtre   IDRBT, Hyderabad, India

Program Chairs

Atul Prakash   University of Michigan, Ann Arbor, USA
Rudrapatna Shyamasundar   Tata Institute of Fundamental Research, India

Keynote Chairs

R. Sekar   SUNY Stonybrook, USA
N. Raghukishore   IDRBT, Hyderabad, India

Publication Chairs

Srirangaraj Setlur   SUNY Buffalo, USA
Rajarshi Pal   IDRBT, Hyderabad, India
S. Rashmi Dev   IDRBT, Hyderabad, India

Tutorial Chairs

N. Subramanian   C-DAC, India
V. Ravi   IDRBT, Hyderabad, India

Doctoral Forum Chairs

Uday B. Desai   Indian Institute of Technology, Hyderabad, India
V.N. Sastry   IDRBT, Hyderabad, India

Short Talk Chairs

Pavel Gladyshev   University College, Dublin, Ireland
M.V.N.K. Prasad   IDRBT, Hyderabad, India

Awards Committee

B.L. Deekshatulu	IDRBT, Hyderabad, India
D. Manjunath	Indian Institute of Technology, Hyderabad, India
Atul Negi	University of Hyderabad, India

Logistics and Finance Committee

G. Raghuraj	IDRBT, Hyderabad, India
Vijay Belurgikar	IDRBT, Hyderabad, India
M.V. Sivakumaran	IDRBT, Hyderabad, India

Publicity Committee

Aditya Bagchi	Indian Statistical Institute, Kolkata, India
V. Radha	IDRBT, Hyderabad, India
G.R. Gangadharan	IDRBT, Hyderabad, India
Ratna Kumar	IDRBT, Hyderabad, India

Sponsorship Committee

N.P. Dhavale	IDRBT, Hyderabad, India
Patrick Kishore	IDRBT, Hyderabad, India
S. Lalit Mohan	IDRBT, Hyderabad, India

Steering Committee

Aditya Bagchi	Indian Statistical Institute, Kolkata, India
Sushil Jajodia	George Mason University, USA
Somesh Jha	University of Wisconsin, USA
Arun Kumar Majumdar	Indian Institute of Technology, Kharagpur, India
Anish Mathuria	DA-IICT, India
Chandan Mazumdar	Jadavpur University, India
Atul Prakash	University of Michigan, Ann Arbor, USA
Gulshan Rai	DIT, Government of India
Sriram K. Rajamani	Microsoft Research, India
A.S. Ramasastri	IDRBT, Hyderabad, India
Pierangela Samarati	University of Milan, India
Venkat Venkatakrishnan	University of Illinois, Chicago, India

Program Committee

Vijay Atluri	Rutgers University, USA
Aditya Bagchi	Indian Statistical Institute, Kolkata, India

Additional Reviewers

Ahmed, Ferdous
Albanese, Massimiliano
Alcaraz, Cristina
Bhattacharjee, Anup
Bhattacharyya, Rishiraj
Carminati, Michele
Chatterjee, Ayantika
Chitukuri, Architha
Colombo, Edoardo
Davidson, Drew
De Capitani Di Vimercati, Sabrina
De Carli, Lorenzo
De, Sourya
Dutta, Ratna
Eshete, Birhanu
Fernandez, Carmen
Foresti, Sara
Fredrikson, Matt
Fu, Zhang
Ghosh, R.K.
Gokhale, Amruta
Gondi, Kalpana
Harris, William
Jha, Susmit
Kim, Daeyoung
Li, Yan
Luchaup, Daniel

Matsuda, Takahiro
Mehta, Anil
Monshizadeh, Maliheh
N.P., Narendra
Naskar, Ruchira
Nguyen, Hai
Nieto, Ana
Nuñez, David
Papini, Davide
Paraboschi, Stefano
Peddinti, Sai Teja
Phuong Ha, Nguyen
Polino, Mario
Quarta, Davide
Ruj, Sushmita
Sarkar, Santanu
Sen Gupta, Sourav
Sinha, Rohit
Spagnuolo, Michele
Tan, Wei Yang
Tupsamudre, Harshal
Vadnala, Praveen Kumar
Vaidyanathan, Shivaramakrishnan
Vora, Poorvi
Wang, Daibin
Zhang, Lei

A Decade of ICISS Conference Series

A Reflection

Manu V.T. and Babu M. Mehtre

Information systems security is an area that deals with protecting data from intrusions, malwares, frauds and any criminal activities that are surfacing in systems to maintain non-repudiation, confidentiality and integrity of data. In the present day world, as the systems are more inter-connected and networked, information systems security has become a huge challenge due to various vulnerabilities. This challenge has evoked the interest of the researchers in this area.

Information systems security research continued to gain importance over the years and gradually India also joined the process. Thus the inception of an international conference series in the area of information systems security came into the picture.

The objectives of this conference series were to discuss in depth the current state of research and practices in information systems security, provide a platform for the researchers to share and disseminate the research results.

In the initial stages of the conference series, the country wise participation was less. But gradually it drew attention from many more interested countries. From the number of participating countries in the latest edition of the conference, it is evident that it has achieved global recognition. The acceptance rate of the conference series has been consistently low. This forces the contributors to ensure the quality of work and to give upmost focus on quality in the areas concerned.

The acceptance rate has constantly within the range 0.25 to 0.4. There was only a single occurrence of acceptance rate value reaching 0.4, except this, it has been around 0.25.

Google Scholar Metrics provide an easy way for authors to quickly gauge the visibility and influence of recent articles in scholarly publications. It summarizes recent citations to many publications, to help authors as they consider where to publish their new research.

The h5-index and h5-median of a publication are, respectively, the h-index and h-median of only those of its articles that were published in the last five complete calendar years.

The Google Scholar Metrics results for the ICISS conference series returned the value of h5-index = 12 and h5-median = 16 which seems promising. The various aspects of the conferences including paper contributing countries, acceptance rate and google metrics were analyzed.

The participation from across the globe gives a picture of the success and global outreach of the conferences series.

Table 1. Participation from Different Countries

Year	Countries			
2005	- Italy - USA - India	- Korea - Singapore	- France - Japan	- England - Australia - China
2006	- Italy - USA - Germany	- France - Iran - Spain	- Australia - Korea - Austria	- Israel - India - New Zealand
2007	- USA - China - India	- Germany - France	- Italy - Australia - Iran	- Korea - Japan
2008	- USA - India - Germany	- Italy - Poland	- France - United Kingdom	- Australia
2009	- Canada - Mexico - France	- Singapore - Australia - Korea	- China - United Kingdom - Belgium	- Italy - USA - India
2010	- Singapore - France - Italy	- Iran - Belgium - China	- Luxembourg - USA - Sweden	- Saudi Arabia - Japan - India
2011	- Germany - USA - France	- Saudi Arabia - India - United Kingdom	- Italy - Iran	- Sweden - Netherlands
2012	- USA - Estonia - India	- Jordan - Egypt	- Belgium - Iran	- Spain
2013	- United Kingdom - Germany - India	- USA - Japan	- France - Iran	- Belgium
2014	- Australia - Belgium - Brazil - United Kingdom - UAE	- Saudi Arabia - Singapore - South Africa - USA	- France - Germany - Iceland - China - Italy	- Spain - Canada - Viet Nam - Japan - New Zealand - India

Manu.V.T. and Babu M. Mehtre
Center for Information Assurance & Management,
Institute for Development and Research in Banking Technology, India.

Invited Talks

Adversarial and Uncertain Reasoning for Adaptive Cyber Defense: Building the Scientific Foundation*

George Cybenko[1], Sushil Jajodia[2], Michael P. Wellman[3], and Peng Liu[4]

[1] Thayer School of Engineering, Dartmouth College, Hanover, NH 03755
`george.cybenko@dartmouth.edu`
[2] Center for Secure Information Systems, George Mason University, Fairfax,
VA 22030-4422
`jajodia@gmu.edu`
[3] Department of Electrical Engineering and Computer Science,
University of Michigan, Ann Arbor, MI 48109-2122
`wellman@umich.edu`
[4] College of Information Sciences and Technology, Pennsylvania State University,
University Park, PA
`pliu@ist.psu.edu`

Abstract. Today's cyber defenses are largely static. They are governed
by slow deliberative processes involving testing, security patch deployment, and human-in-the-loop monitoring. As a result, adversaries can
systematically probe target networks, pre-plan their attacks, and ultimately persist for long times inside compromised networks and hosts.
A new class of technologies, called Adaptive Cyber Defense (ACD),
is being developed that presents adversaries with optimally changing
attack surfaces and system configurations, forcing adversaries to continually re-assess and re-plan their cyber operations. Although these approaches (e.g., moving target defense, dynamic diversity, and bio-inspired
defense) are promising, they assume stationary and stochastic, but non-
adversarial, environments. To realize the full potential, we need to build
the scientific foundations so that system resiliency and robustness in adversarial settings can be rigorously defined, quantified, measured, and
extrapolated in a rigorous and reliable manner.

* This work was supported by the Army Research Office under grant W911NF-13-1-
0421.

SNIPS: A Software-Defined Approach for Scaling Intrusion Prevention Systems via Offloading

Victor Heorhiadi[1], Seyed Kaveh Fayaz[2], Michael K. Reiter[1], and Vyas Sekar[2]

[1] UNC Chapel Hill
[2] Carnegie Mellon University

Abstract. Growing traffic volumes and the increasing complexity of attacks pose a constant scaling challenge for network intrusion prevention systems (NIPS). In this respect, *offloading* NIPS processing to compute clusters offers an immediately deployable alternative to expensive hardware upgrades. In practice, however, NIPS offloading is challenging on three fronts in contrast to passive network security functions: (1) NIPS offloading can impact other traffic engineering objectives; (2) NIPS offloading impacts user perceived latency; and (3) NIPS actively change traffic volumes by dropping unwanted traffic. To address these challenges, we present the SNIPS system. We design a formal optimization framework that captures tradeoffs across scalability, network load, and latency. We provide a practical implementation using recent advances in software-defined networking without requiring modifications to NIPS hardware. Our evaluations on realistic topologies show that SNIPS can reduce the maximum load by up to 10× while only increasing the latency by 2%.

Application Architectures for Critical Data Isolation

Zhenkai Liang

Department of Computer Science
School of Computing
National University of Singapore

Data in applications are not equally important. Certain data, such as passwords and credit card numbers, are critical to application security. Protecting the confidentiality and integrity of this class of critical data is the key requirement for security. However, applications usually lack the abstraction to handle critical data separately. As a result, regardless of their sensitivity, critical data are mixed with non-critical data, and are unnecessarily exposed to many components of an application, such as third-party libraries. To tighten protection of critical data, the contact surface of such data within applications should be minimized.

In this talk, we introduce our work on new application architectures for critical data isolation. We rethink the trust-based, monolithic model of handing critical data, and advocate to provide critical data protection as first-class abstractions in application security mechanisms. In our design, the notion of data owners is made explicit in applications, which is associated with critical data. Based on data ownership, critical data are cryptographically isolated from the rest of application data. To support rich operations on critical data, we enable operations on critical data from authenticated parties through dedicated engines. This design offers data-oriented protection using a much smaller trusted computing base (TCB), which gives strong security guarantees.

We instantiated the new application architecture design on the web platform and the Android mobile platform. On the web platform, we designed a data abstraction and browser primitive, and developed the Webkit-based CRYPTONOS [1] to offer strong isolation of critical data in web applications. On the Android platform, we created DroidVault [2], a data safe based on the TrustZone architecture. It isolates and processes critical data without relying trust of the Android system. We will discuss the design and experience with both systems.

References

1. Dong, X., Chen, Z., Siadati, H., Tople, S., Saxena, P., Liang, Z.: Protecting sensitive web content from client-side vulnerabilities with CRYPTONS. In: Proceedings of the 14th ACM Conference on Computer and Communications Security, CCS (2013)
2. Li, X., Hu, H., Bai, G., Jia, Y., Liang, Z., Saxena., P.: Droidvault: A trusted data vault for android devices. In: Proceedings of the 19th International Conference on Engineering of Complex Computer Systems, ICECCS (2014)

Table of Contents

Invited Talks

Adversarial and Uncertain Reasoning for Adaptive Cyber Defense:
Building the Scientific Foundation 1
  George Cybenko, Sushil Jajodia, Michael P. Wellman, and Peng Liu

SNIPS: A Software-Defined Approach for Scaling Intrusion Prevention
Systems via Offloading 9
  *Victor Heorhiadi, Seyed Kaveh Fayaz, Michael K. Reiter,
  and Vyas Sekar*

Contributed Papers

Security Inferences

Inference-Proof Data Publishing by Minimally Weakening a Database
Instance 30
  Joachim Biskup and Marcel Preuß

Extending Dolev-Yao with Assertions 50
  R. Ramanujam, Vaishnavi Sundararajan, and S.P. Suresh

Inferring Accountability from Trust Perceptions 69
  Koen Decroix, Denis Butin, Joachim Jansen, and Vincent Naessens

Client Side Web Session Integrity as a Non-interference Property 89
  *Wilayat Khan, Stefano Calzavara, Michele Bugliesi,
  Willem De Groef, and Frank Piessens*

Security Policies

Impact of Multiple t-t SMER Constraints on Minimum User
Requirement in RBAC 109
  Arindam Roy, Shamik Sural, and Arun Kumar Majumdar

Temporal RBAC Security Analysis Using Logic Programming in the
Presence of Administrative Policies 129
  *Sadhana Jha, Shamik Sural, Jaideep Vaidya,
  and Vijayalakshmi Atluri*

A Formal Methodology for Modeling Threats to Enterprise Assets 149
  Jaya Bhattacharjee, Anirban Sengupta, and Chandan Mazumdar

A Novel Approach for Searchable CP-ABE with Hidden
Ciphertext-Policy 167
  Mukti Padhya and Devesh Jinwala

Security User Interfaces

Towards a More Democratic Mining in Bitcoins 185
  Goutam Paul, Pratik Sarkar, and Sarbajit Mukherjee

Authentication Schemes - Comparison and Effective Password Spaces ... 204
  Peter Mayer, Melanie Volkamer, and Michaela Kauer

A Security Extension Providing User Anonymity and Relaxed Trust
Requirement in Non-3GPP Access to the EPS 226
  Hiten Choudhury, Basav Roychoudhury, and Dilip Kr. Saikia

A Usage-Pattern Perspective for Privacy Ranking of Android Apps
(Short Paper) 245
  Xiaolei Li, Xinshu Dong, and Zhenkai Liang

Security Attacks

Privacy Leakage Attacks in Browsers by Colluding Extensions 257
  Anil Saini, Manoj Singh Gaur, Vijay Laxmi, Tushar Singhal,
  and Mauro Conti

CORP: A Browser Policy to Mitigate Web Infiltration Attacks 277
  Krishna Chaitanya Telikicherla, Venkatesh Choppella,
  and Bruhadeshwar Bezawada

An Improved Methodology towards Providing Immunity against Weak
Shoulder Surfing Attack 298
  Nilesh Chakraborty and Samrat Mondal

Catching Classical and Hijack-Based Phishing Attacks 318
  Tanmay Thakur and Rakesh Verma

Malware Detection

PMDS: Permission-Based Malware Detection System 338
  Paolo Rovelli and Ýmir Vigfússon

Efficient Detection of Multi-step Cross-Site Scripting Vulnerabilities 358
  Alexandre Vernotte, Frédéric Dadeau, Franck Lebeau,
  Bruno Legeard, Fabien Peureux, and François Piat

CliSeAu: Securing Distributed Java Programs by Cooperative Dynamic
Enforcement 378
    Richard Gay, Jinwei Hu, and Heiko Mantel

Automatic Generation of Compact Alphanumeric Shellcodes for x86
(Short Paper) 399
    Aditya Basu, Anish Mathuria, and Nagendra Chowdary

Forensics

Analysis of Fluorescent Paper Pulps for Detecting Counterfeit Indian
Paper Money 411
    Biswajit Halder, Rajkumar Darbar, Utpal Garain,
    and Abhoy Ch. Mondal

A Vein Biometric Based Authentication System (Short Paper) 425
    Puneet Gupta and Phalguni Gupta

Digital Forensic Technique for Double Compression Based JPEG Image
Forgery Detection (Short Paper) 437
    Pankaj Malviya and Ruchira Naskar

Location Based Security Services

Preserving Privacy in Location-Based Services Using Sudoku
Structures 448
    Sumitra Biswal, Goutam Paul, and Shashwat Raizada

Location Obfuscation Framework for Training-Free Localization
System (Short Paper) 464
    Thong M. Doan, Han N. Dinh, Nam T. Nguyen, and Phuoc T. Tran

Author Index 477

Adversarial and Uncertain Reasoning for Adaptive Cyber Defense: Building the Scientific Foundation[*]

George Cybenko[1], Sushil Jajodia[2], Michael P. Wellman[3], and Peng Liu[4]

[1] Thayer School of Engineering, Dartmouth College, Hanover, NH 03755
george.cybenko@dartmouth.edu
[2] Center for Secure Information Systems, George Mason University, Fairfax,
VA 22030-4422
jajodia@gmu.edu
[3] Department of Electrical Engineering and Computer Science, University of Michigan,
Ann Arbor, MI 48109-2122
wellman@umich.edu
[4] College of Information Sciences and Technology, Pennsylvania State University,
University Park, PA 16802
pliu@ist.psu.edu

Abstract. Today's cyber defenses are largely static. They are governed by slow deliberative processes involving testing, security patch deployment, and human-in-the-loop monitoring. As a result, adversaries can systematically probe target networks, pre-plan their attacks, and ultimately persist for long times inside compromised networks and hosts. A new class of technologies, called Adaptive Cyber Defense (ACD), is being developed that presents adversaries with optimally changing attack surfaces and system configurations, forcing adversaries to continually re-assess and re-plan their cyber operations. Although these approaches (e.g., moving target defense, dynamic diversity, and bio-inspired defense) are promising, they assume stationary and stochastic, but non-adversarial, environments. To realize the full potential, we need to build the scientific foundations so that system resiliency and robustness in adversarial settings can be rigorously defined, quantified, measured, and extrapolated in a rigorous and reliable manner.

1 Introduction

The computer systems, software applications, and network technologies that we use today were developed in user and operator contexts that greatly valued standardization, predictability, and availability. Performance and cost-effectiveness were the main market drivers. It is only relatively recently that security and resilience (not to be confused with fault tolerance) have become equally desirable properties of cyber systems.

As a result, the first generation of cyber security technologies were largely based on system hardening through improved software security engineering (to reduce

---

[*] This work was supported by the Army Research Office under grant W911NF-13-1-0421.

A. Prakash and R. Shyamasundar (Eds.): ICISS 2014, LNCS 8880, pp. 1–8, 2014.

vulnerabilities and attack surfaces) and layering security through defense-in-depth (by adding encryption, access controls, firewalls, intrusion detection systems, and malware scanners, for example). These security technologies sought to respect the homogeneity, standardization, and predictability that have been so valued by the market. Consequently, most of our cyber defenses are static today. They are governed by slow and deliberative processes such as testing, episodic penetration exercises, security patch deployment, and human-in-the-loop monitoring of security events.

Adversaries benefit greatly from this situation because they can continuously and systematically probe targeted networks with the confidence that those networks will change slowly if at all. Adversaries can afford the time to engineer reliable exploits and pre-plan their attacks because their targets are essentially fixed and almost identical. Moreover, once an attack succeeds, adversaries persist for long times inside compromised networks and hosts because the hosts, networks, and services—largely designed for availability and homogeneity—do not reconfigure, adapt or regenerate except in deterministic ways to support maintenance and uptime requirements.

2   Adaptation Techniques

In response to this situation, researchers in recent years have started to investigate various methods that make networked information systems less homogeneous and less predictable. The basic idea of Adaptation Techniques (AT) is to engineer systems that have homogeneous functionalities but randomized manifestations. By Adaptation Techniques, we include concepts such as Moving Target Defenses (MTD) [1, 2] as well as artificial diversity [3, 4] and bio-inspired defenses [5] to the extent that they involve system adaption for security and resiliency purposes.

Homogeneous functionality allows authorized use of networks and services in predictable, standardized ways while randomized manifestations make it difficult for attackers to engineer exploits remotely, let alone parlay one exploit into successful attacks against a multiplicity of hosts. Ideally, each compromise would require the same, significant effort by the attacker.

Examples of Adaptation Techniques (AT) include [1, 2]:

- Randomized network addressing and layout;
- Obfuscated OS types and services;
- Randomized instruction set and memory layout;
- Randomized compiling;
- Just-in-time compiling and decryption;
- Dynamic virtualization;
- Workload and service migration;
- System regeneration.

Each of these techniques has a performance and/or maintenance cost associated with it. For example, randomized instruction set and memory layout clearly limit the extent to which a single buffer overflow based exploit can be used to compromise a collection of hosts. However, it also makes it more difficult for system administrators and software vendors to debug and update hosts because all the binaries are different. Furthermore, randomized instruction set and memory layout techniques will not make it more difficult for an attacker to determine a network's layout and its available services.

Similar analyses are possible for each of the techniques listed above. For example, randomizing network addresses makes it more difficult for an adversary to perform reconnaissance on a target network remotely but does not make it more difficult for the attacker to exploit a specific host once it is identified and reachable (bearing in mind that many exploits are quite small and fit into one packet so the required exploiting sessions are short).

The point is that while a variety of different AT techniques exist, the contexts in which they are useful and their added costs (in terms of performance and maintainability) to the defenders can vary significantly. In fact, the majority of AT research has been focused on developing specific new techniques as opposed to understanding their overall operational costs, when they are most useful, and what their possible inter-relationships might be. In fact, while each AT approach might have some engineering rigor, the overall discipline is largely ad hoc when it comes to understanding the totality of AT methods and their optimized application.

A graphical depiction of the situation is shown in Figure 1 below.

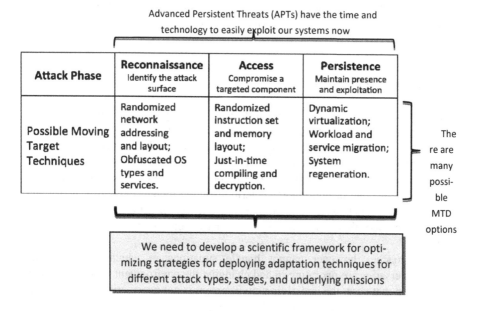

Fig. 1. Attack Phases and Possible Moving Target Techniques

As shown in Figure 1, adaptation techniques are typically aimed at defeating different stages of possible attacks although there is certainly overlap. On the other hand, different defense missions can have different Confidentiality, Integrity, and Availability (CIA) requirements.

For example, an Army patrol that escalates into a firefight might increase availability requirements (for calling up air, reinforcement, and medical support) at the expense of confidentiality (because the opposing side knows much about where and what the patrol is currently doing). Accordingly, if a cyber attack on availability were determined to be present or imminent, adaptation techniques for maintaining availability would be prioritized over techniques for enhancing confidentiality or integrity.

For a different example, a mission such as the generation of a daily Air Tasking Order (ATO) could prioritize confidentiality and integrity (to protect details of future sorties) over availability (because the ATO generation may not be time critical) so that network layout and addressing could be used aggressively to confound possible attackers, at the expense of network performance.

We note that some AT techniques, such as address space layout randomization (ASLR) are typically performed offline at application code compile time so that a decision to deploy ASLR is open-loop in the control sense.

It is clear from these examples and their analyses that there are a variety of possible tradeoffs when taking into account the underlying mission, the perceived attack type, and the system adaptations available through AT techniques. Things get more complex when considering attack scenarios that extend over time, as depicted in Figure 1.

3   Adversarial Reasoning

The situation described above calls for a decision-making solution. The overall system is in some estimated state, there is an objective or utility to optimize, and there are a variety of possible actions that can be selected. What is the right action to take?

If the environment were stationary and non-adversarial, control theory (or, for example, planning in Artificial Intelligence terminology) would provide a classical solution. Whether discrete or continuous, deterministic or stochastic, control theory and its variants instruct us how to compute plans (sequences of actions) that are optimal with respect to maximizing an objective providing the environment is not conspiring against us.

Such approaches however cannot handle situations in which rational, self-interested adversaries are operating in and changing the environment at odds with our own goals. In that case, the underlying environment is not necessarily stationary and treating adversaries as mere stochastic elements is not adequate.

The difference is profound as we go from control theory (modeling everything in the environment as stochastic) to game theory (modeling environmental actors as rational). Solution concepts in control theory are typically defined by optima (maxima or minima) whereas in game theory they are defined by equilibria (in the adversarial case, saddle points) because different agents will have competing objectives that must be optimized with respect to the other agents' concurrent attempts to optimize their own competing goals.

To illustrate how such a situation can arise in the context of cyber operations, suppose we have implemented an automated system regeneration technology (an AT technology) that reboots servers when there is a perceived attempt by an adversary to attack integrity. A secure boot will bring the server back into a known trusted state, defeating any code corruption that might have occurred (such as the installation of a rootkit or other Trojan).

Aggressive rebooting of servers in this manner will affect availability because systems will shut down and the secure boot computes time-consuming hashes to ensure trust in the re-instantiated software base. An attacker whose goal is to compromise availability could aggressively feign integrity attack attempts resulting in repeated regenerations and an effective denial-of-service attack on the servers.

This example illustrates that planning and control in the presence of an intelligent adversary requires different kinds of analysis. If we know the structure of the competitive environment (the game's possible moves and rules), the preferences or utilities of the various parties, and an appropriate solution concept (such as Nash Equilibrium or minmax) then game theory provides a framework for formulating the problem and computing candidate solutions.

Applying the framework, however, requires some knowledge of the opponents, their objectives, and the game structure including possible moves and game states. In cyber operations, that kind of information is not given a priori and must be learned or inferred from historical data (from the kinds of attack behaviors that have been exhibited in the past and by which assumed adversaries) and out-of-band information about adversary types, capabilities, and objectives (which might include the broader strategic context of a conflict including kinetic operations and intelligence about training, tactics, and procedures obtained covertly or through open-source about an adversary).

Another well-known challenge arising in game theory is the computational complexity of solving large games where large can refer to the number of players (e.g., network games), the number/depth of possible moves (e.g., chess) and/or the amount of uncertainty in the game state (e.g., poker). We believe that adversarial models of cyber operations can potentially involve all of these scalability challenges.

4   The Proposed ACD Framework

In a project funded by the Army Research Office, we have developed an ACD framework that has several novel features. See Figure 2. It uses adversarial reasoning to address several fundamental limitations of traditional game-theoretic analysis such as empirically defining the game and the players. ACD uses control-theoretic analysis to bootstrap game analysis and to quantify the robustness of candidate actions. By integrating game-theoretic and control-theoretic analyses for tradeoff analysis, ACD quantifies resilience and observability in an innovative and powerful way.

The proposed ACD framework consists of four thrusts. The goal of Thrust 1 is to design and implement a subsystem that takes two inputs: a) streaming observations of the networked system and; b) external intelligence about possible adversaries and the ambient threat environment and condition. Thrust 1's subsystem will output to Thrust 2 partial models of the perceived adversaries, including estimates of their objectives and capabilities (the Adversary Modeling piece), together with a classically computed set of plans (based on control theory models and analysis) that act as seeds for the Thrust 2 subsystem.

Based on these inputs, Thrust 2 employs empirical methods (simulation, machine learning) to induce a game model from which it derives strategically optimized defense actions (those taken in equilibrium, for example) based on the seed actions and plans it received. Since the value of a defense strategy (such as an adaptation technique defense) depends on the class of attack, Thrust 2 analysis ranges across attack classes and considers a spectrum of game scenarios.

Since Thrust 2 analysis depends significantly on the adaptation mechanisms available to the defense strategy space, Thrust 3 is focused on identifying and adding innovative adaptation mechanisms into the defense strategy space.

Finally, Thrust 4 seeks to perform *tradeoff analysis* and *decision making* through integrated game-theoretic and control-theoretic analysis. The tradeoff analysis will not only consider functionality, performance, usability, and exploitation, but also consider robustness, stability, observability, and resilience. Based on the analysis results, the decision maker may further optimize the strategies generated by Thrust 2 through a feedback loop. Thrust 4 applies the actions to the environment with the OODA-type loop operating continuously.

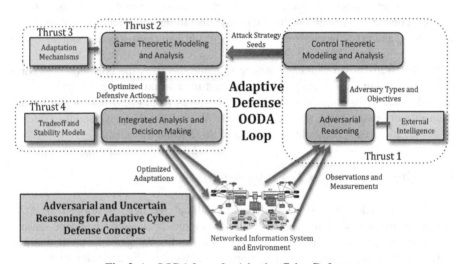

Fig. 2. An OODA Loop for Adaptive Cyber Defense

In the first year of the project, the team focused on identifying the key problems to be addressed, developing a common understanding of the issues, and defining a strategy to collaboratively tackle the challenges at hand. The unifying theme of this initial effort is represented by the objective to quantify several aspects of cyber defenses, and understand game-theoretic and control-theoretic aspects of adaptive cyber defenses [6-15]. First, we defined a framework for modeling, evaluating, and countering an attacker's reconnaissance effort. The proposed defensive strategy consists of controlling how the attacker perceives the attack surface of the target system. Second, we started to develop the quantification of moving target defenses needed for control and game models. Analysis of such defenses has led to the conclusion that moving target defenses are the most effective defenses against well designed botnets. Third, we developed a general (supervisory) control-theoretic formulation of a dynamic cyber-security problem, from the perspective of a defender aiming to maximize its worst-case performance. Fourth, we designed and implemented a simulation model of the basic adaptive cyber-defense scenario, and commenced game-theoretic analysis of this model. Fifth, we developed a control theory based framework for comparing cost-effectiveness of different MTD techniques. Finally, we developed reinforcement learning algorithms for adaptive cyber defense against Heartbleed attack and a novel probabilistic approach to detect and shield Heartbleed attacks.

5   Conclusion

We believe that we need a new scientific foundation and the corresponding technologies that can handle truly adaptive and dynamic cyber operations in the presence of capable adversaries. Without such a foundation, the effectiveness of any cyber defense system adaptation technology cannot be quantified in a rigorous or reliable manner. Consequently, performance estimates based solely on empirical evaluations and tests can only claim an adaptation technology's effectiveness under those very specific test conditions. In order to confidently extrapolate or generalize to other scenarios, a principled scientific foundation as envisioned here is needed.

References

1. Jajodia, S., Ghosh, A.K., Swarup, V., Wang, C., Wang, X.S. (eds.): Moving Target Defense: Creating Asymmetric Uncertainty for Cyber Threats, Berlin. Springer Advances in Information Security, vol. 54, 183 p. (2011) ISBN 978-1-4614-0976-2
2. Jajodia, S., Ghosh, A.K., Subrahmanian, V.S., Swarup, V., Wang, C., Wang, X.S. (eds.): Moving Target Defense II: Application of Game Theory and Adversarial Modeling, Berlin. Springer Advances in Information Security, vol. 100, 203 p. (2013) ISBN 978-1-4614-5415-1
3. Birman, K.P., Schneider, F.B.: The monoculture risk put into context. IEEE Security & Privacy 7(1), 14–17 (2009)
4. Forrest, S., Somayaji, A., Ackley, D.H.: Building diverse computer systems. In: Proc. 6th Workshop on Hot Topics in Operating Systems, pp. 67–72 (1997)

5. Meisel, M., Pappas, V., Zhang, L.: A taxonomy of biologically inspired research in computer networking. Computer Networks 54(6), 901–916 (2010)
6. Albanese, M., Battista, E., Jajodia, S., Casola, V.: Manipulating the Attacker's View of a System's Attack Surface. To Appear in Proc. of the 2nd IEEE Conference on Communications and Network Security (IEEE CNS 2014), San Francisco, California, USA, October 29-31 (2014)
7. Wang, L., Zhang, M., Jajodia, S., Singhal, A., Albanese, M.: Modeling Network Diversity for Evaluating the Robustness of Networks against Zero-Day Attacks. In: Kutyłowski, M., Vaidya, J. (eds.) ICAIS 2014, Part II. LNCS, vol. 8713, pp. 494–511. Springer, Heidelberg (2014)
8. Shakarian, P., Paulo, D., Albanese, M., Jajodia, S.: Keeping Intruders at Large: A Graph-Theoretic Approach to Reducing the Probability of Successful Network Intrusions. In: Proc. 11th International Conference on Security and Cryptography (SECRYPT 2014), Vienna, Austria, August 28-30, pp. 19–30 (2014)
9. Hughes, J., Cybenko, G.: Three tenets for secure cyber-physical system design and assessment. In: Proc. SPIE Cyber Sensing 2014 (May 2014)
10. Xu, J., Guo, P., Zhao, M., Erbacher, R.F., Zhu, M., Liu, P.: Comparing Different Moving Target Defense Techniques. In: Prof. ACM MTD Workshop 2014, in Association with CCS 2014 (November 2014)
11. Zhu, M., Hu, Z., Liu, P.: Reinforcement learning algorithms for adaptive cyber defense against Heartbleed. In: Proc. ACM MTD Workshop 2014, in Association with CCS 2014 (November 2014)
12. Vorobeychik, Y., An, B., Tambe, M., Singh, S.: Computing solutions in infinite-horizon discounted adversarial patrolling games. In: Proc. 24th International Conference on Automated Planning and Scheduling (ICAPS 2014) (June 2014)
13. Rasouli, M., Miehling, E., Teneketzis, D.: A supervisory control approach to dynamic cyber-security. In: Poovendran, R., Saad, W. (eds.) GameSec 2014. LNCS, vol. 8840, pp. 99–117. Springer, Heidelberg (2014)
14. Wellman, M.P., Prakash, A.: Empirical game-theoretic analysis of an adaptive cyber-defense scenario (Preliminary report). In: Poovendran, R., Saad, W. (eds.) GameSec 2014. LNCS, vol. 8840, pp. 43–58. Springer, Heidelberg (2014)
15. Sun, K., Jajodia, S.: Protecting enterprise networks through attack surface expansion. In: Scottsdale, A.Z. (ed.) Proc. SafeConfig 2014: Cyber Security Analytics and Automation (short paper), Scottsdale, AZ (November 3, 2014)

SNIPS: A Software-Defined Approach for Scaling Intrusion Prevention Systems via Offloading

Victor Heorhiadi[1], Seyed Kaveh Fayaz[2], Michael K. Reiter[1], and Vyas Sekar[2]

[1] UNC Chapel Hill, Chapel Hill, NC, USA
[2] Carnegie Mellon University, Pittsburgh, PA, USA

Abstract. Growing traffic volumes and the increasing complexity of attacks pose a constant scaling challenge for network intrusion prevention systems (NIPS). In this respect, *offloading* NIPS processing to compute clusters offers an immediately deployable alternative to expensive hardware upgrades. In practice, however, NIPS offloading is challenging on three fronts in contrast to passive network security functions: (1) NIPS offloading can impact other traffic engineering objectives; (2) NIPS offloading impacts user perceived latency; and (3) NIPS actively change traffic volumes by dropping unwanted traffic. To address these challenges, we present the SNIPS system. We design a formal optimization framework that captures tradeoffs across scalability, network load, and latency. We provide a practical implementation using recent advances in software-defined networking without requiring modifications to NIPS hardware. Our evaluations on realistic topologies show that SNIPS can reduce the maximum load by up to $10\times$ while only increasing the latency by 2%.

1 Introduction

Network intrusion prevention systems (NIPS) are an integral part of today's network security infrastructure [38]. However, NIPS deployments face a constant battle to handle increasing volumes and processing requirements. Today, network operators have few options to tackle NIPS overload – overprovisioning, dropping traffic, or reducing fidelity of the analysis. Unfortunately, none of these options are attractive in practice. Thus, NIPS scaling has been, and continues to be, an active area of research in the intrusion detection community with several efforts on developing better hardware and algorithms (e.g., [32, 34, 36, 39]). While these efforts are valuable, they require significant capital costs and face deployment delays as networks have 3–5 year hardware refresh cycles.

A promising alternative to expensive and delayed hardware upgrades is to *offload* packet processing to locations with spare compute capacity. Specifically, recent work has considered two types of offloading opportunities:

- *On-path offloading* exploits the natural replication of a packet on its route to distribute processing load [27, 28].

- *Off-path offloading* utilizes dedicated clusters or cloud providers to exploit the economies of scale and elastic scaling opportunities [9, 29].

Such offloading opportunities are appealing as they flexibly use existing network hardware and provide the ability to dynamically scale the deployment. Unfortunately,

A. Prakash and R. Shyamasundar (Eds.): ICISS 2014, LNCS 8880, pp. 9–29, 2014.

current solutions either explicitly focus on passive monitoring applications such as flow monitors and NIDS [9, 28] and ignore NIPS-induced effects, e.g., on traffic volumes [23,27,29]. Specifically, we observe three new challenges in NIPS offloading that fall outside the scope of these prior solutions:

- **Interaction with traffic engineering:** Offloading NIPS to a datacenter means that we are effectively *rerouting* the traffic. This may affect network congestion and other traffic engineering objectives.

- **Impact on latency:** NIPS lie on the *critical forwarding path* of traffic. Delays introduced by overloaded NIPS or the additional latency induced by offloading can thus affect the *latency* for user applications.

- **Traffic volume changes:** NIPS *actively* change the traffic volume routed through the network. Thus, the load on a NIPS node is dependent on the processing actions of the upstream nodes along the packet forwarding path.

To address these challenges and deliver the benefits of offloading to NIPS deployments, we present the SNIPS system. SNIPS takes a first-principles approach to capture the above effects and balance the tradeoffs across scalability, latency increase, and network congestion. Perhaps counterintuitively, we show that it is feasible to capture these complex requirements and effects through a linear programming (LP) formulation that is amenable to fast computation using off-the-shelf solvers. As we show in §7, the computation takes ≤2 seconds, for a variety of real topologies enabling SNIPS to react in near-real-time to network dynamics. The design of SNIPS is quite general and it can be used in many deployment settings and the ideas may also be applicable to other network functions virtualization (NFV) applications [17].

We leverage *software-defined networking* (SDN) mechanisms to implement the optimal strategy derived from the LP formulation. A key benefit of SDN is that it does not require modifications to the NIPS hardware or software unlike prior work [9,27]. Using trace-driven simulations and emulations, we show that SNIPS can reduce the maximum load by up to $10\times$ while only increasing the latency by 2%.

Contributions: In summary, this paper makes four contributions:

- Identifying challenges in applying offloading to NIPS deployments (§3);
- Designing formal models to capture new effects (e.g., rerouting, latency, traffic changes) (§5);
- Addressing practical challenges in an SDN-based implementation (§6); and
- A detailed evaluation showing that SNIPS imposes low overhead and offers significant advantages (§7).

2   Related Work

On-Path Offloading: The key difference between SNIPS and prior work on on-path offloading [27, 28] is three-fold: (1) they focus only on on-path monitoring; (2) these assume that the traffic volume does not change inside the network; and (3) they are not concerned with latency. As a result, the models from these efforts do not apply as we highlight in the next section. SNIPS considers a generalized model of both on- and off-path offloading, models the impact of rerouting on latency, and captures effects of NIPS actively changing the traffic volume. In terms of implementation, these efforts modify software platforms such as the yaf flow monitor and the Bro IDS [20]. In contrast, SNIPS leverages software-defined networking (SDN) to provide an in-network offloading solution that does not require access to the NIPS software source or the hardware platform. Thus, SNIPS can accommodate legacy and proprietary NIPS solutions.

Off-Path Offloading: Recent efforts make the case for virtualizing NIPS-like functions [7] and demonstrate the viability of off-path offloading using public cloud providers [29]. Our work shares the motivation to exploit elastic scaling and reduce capital/operating expenses. However, these efforts focus more on the high-level vision and viability. As such they do not provide formal models like SNIPS to capture trade-offs across scalability, network bandwidth costs, and user-perceived latency and incorporating the effects of active traffic dropping by NIPS. The closest work in off-path offloading is our prior work [9]. However, the focus there was on NIDS or *passive monitoring* and thus the traffic is simply replicated to clusters. As such, this prior work does not model rerouting or the impact on user-perceived latency. Furthermore, this implementation requires running a Click-based shim layer [12] below the NIDS, and thus cannot work with legacy NIDS/NIPS hardware. As discussed earlier, SNIPS provides an in-network solution via SDN that accommodates legacy NIPS.

Traditional NIPS/NIDS Scaling: There are several complementary approaches for scaling NIPS, including algorithmic improvements [32], using specialized hardware such as TCAMs (e.g., [15, 39]), FPGAs (e.g., [14]), or GPUs (e.g., [10, 35]). These are orthogonal to SNIPS as they improve single NIPS throughput, while SNIPS focuses on network-wide NIPS resource management.

Distributed NIPS: Prior work in distributed NIDS and NIPS [2, 13, 21] focus on correlating events, combining alerts from different vantage points, and extracting useful information from multiple vantage points. Our framework, in contrast, focuses on distribution primarily for scalability.

SDN and Security: Recent work has recognized the potential of SDN for security tasks; e.g., FRESCO uses SDN to simplify botnet or scan detection [31]. SIMPLE [23] and SoftCell [11] use SDN for steering traffic through a desired sequence of waypoints. These do not, however, model the impact of altering the traffic volume as in SNIPS. In addition, there are subtle issues in ensuring stateful processing and load balancing that these works do not address (see §6). Shin et al. highlight security concerns where reactive controllers that set up forwarding rules dynamically per-flow can get overloaded [30]. SNIPS uses proactive rule installation and is immune to such attacks.

3 Motivation and Challenges

We begin by briefly describing the idea of offloading for scaling *passive monitoring* solutions. Then, we highlight the challenges in using this idea for NIPS deployments that arise as a result of NIPS-specific aspects: NIPS *actively* modify the traffic volume and NIPS placement impacts the *end-to-end latency*.

3.1 Case for Offloading

Avoiding overload is an important part of NIPS management. Some NIPS processing is computationally intensive, and under high traffic loads, CPU resources become scarce. Modern NIPS offer two options for reacting to overload: dropping packets or suspending expensive analysis modules. Neither is an attractive option. For example, Snort by default drops packets when receiving more traffic than it can process — in tests in our lab, Snort dropped up to 30% of traffic when subjected to more traffic than it had CPU to analyze — which can adversely impact end-user performance (especially for TCP traffic). Suspending analysis modules decreases detection coverage. In fact, this behavior under overload can be used to evade NIPS [19]. As such, network operators today have few choices but to provision their NIDS/NIPS to handle maximum load. For example, they can upgrade their NIPS nodes with specialized hardware accelerators (e.g., using TCAM, GPUs, or custom ASICs). While this is a valid (if expensive) option, practical management constraints restrict network appliance upgrades to a 3–5 year cycle.

A practical alternative to avoid packet drops or loss in detection coverage is by exploiting opportunities for *offloading* the processing. Specifically, prior work has exploited this idea in the context of passive monitoring in two ways: (1) *on-path* offloading to other monitoring nodes on the routing path [27, 28] and (2) *off-path* offloading by replicating traffic to a remote datacenter [9, 29].

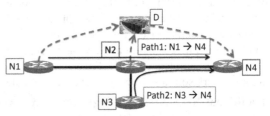

Fig. 1. An example to explain the on- and off-path offloading opportunities that have been proposed in prior work for passive monitoring solutions

To make these more concrete, consider the example network in Figure 1 with 4 nodes N1–N4, with traffic flowing on two end-to-end paths P1:N1 → N4 and P2:N3 → N4.[1] In a traditional deployment, each packet is processed at its *ingress* on each path: N1 monitors traffic on P1 and N3 monitors traffic on P2. An increase in the load on P1 or P2 can cause drops or detection misses

With on-path offloading, we can balance the processing load across the path (i.e., N1, N2, and N4 for P1 and N2, N3, and N4 for P2) to use spare capacity at N2 and N4 [27, 28]. This idea can be generalized to use processing capacity at off-path locations; e.g., N1 and N2 can offload some of their load to the datacenter; e.g., a NIDS cluster [34] or cloudbursting via public clouds [29].

3.2 Challenges in Offloading NIPS

Our goal is to extend the benefits of offloading to NIPS deployments. Unlike passive monitoring solutions, however, NIPS need to be *inline* on the forwarding path and they *actively drop* traffic. This introduces new dimensions for both on-path and off-path offloading that falls outside the scope of the aforementioned prior work.

---

[1] For brevity, in this section we use an abstract notion of a "node" that includes both the NIDS/NIPS functionality and the switching/routing function.

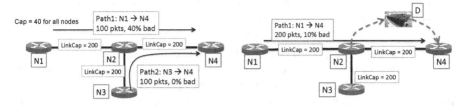

Fig. 2. Need to model the impact of inline traffic modifications

Fig. 3. Impact of rerouting to remote locations

Suppose we have a network administrator who wants to distribute the processing load across the different nodes to: (1) operate within the provisioned capacity of each node; (2) meet traffic engineering objectives w.r.t. link loads (e.g., ensure that no link is loaded to more than 30%); (3) minimize increased latency due to rerouting; and (4) ensures that the unwanted traffic is dropped as close to the origin as possible subject to (1), (2), and (3). We extend the example topology from earlier to highlight the key challenges that arise in meeting these goals

NIPS Change Traffic Patterns: In Figure 2, each NIPS N1–N4 can process 40 packets and each link has a capacity to carry 200 packets. Suppose P1 and P2 carry a total of 100 packets and the volume of unwanted traffic on P1 is 40%; i.e., if we had no NIPS resource constraints, we would drop 40% of the traffic on P1. In order to meet the NIPS load balancing and traffic engineering objectives, we need to model the effects of the traffic being dropped by each NIPS node. If we simply use the formulations for passive monitoring systems and ignore the traffic drop rate, we may incorrectly infer that there is no feasible solution—the total offered load of 200 packets exceeds the total NIPS capacity (160). Because P1 drops 40 packets, there is actually a feasible solution.

Rerouting: Next, let us consider the impact of off-path offloading to a datacenter. Here, we see a key difference between NIDS and NIPS offloading. With NIDS, we *replicate* traffic to the datacenter D. With NIPS, however, we need to actively *reroute* the traffic. In Figure 3, the traffic on P1 exceeds the total NIPS capacity even after accounting for the drop rate. In this case, we

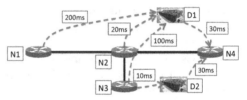

Fig. 4. Need to carefully select offload locations in order to account for the latency for user connections

need to reroute a fraction of the traffic on P1 to the datacenter from N2. If we were replicating the traffic, then the load on the link N2-N4 would be unaltered. With rerouting, however, we are reducing the load on N2-N4 and introducing additional load on the links between N2 and D (and also between D and N4). This has implications for traffic engineering as we need to account for the impact of rerouting on link loads.

Latency Addition Due to Offloading: NIDS do not actively impact user-perceived performance. By virtue of being on the critical forwarding path, however, NIPS offloading to remote locations introduces extra latency to and from the datacenter(s). In Figure 4, naively offloading traffic from N1 to D1 or from N3 to D1 can add hundreds of milliseconds of additional latency. Because the latency is critical for interactive and web applications (e.g., [8]), we need systematic ways to model the impact of rerouting to minimize the impact on user experience.

Conflict with Early Dropping: Naive offloading may also increase the *footprint* of unwanted traffic as traffic that could have been dropped may consume extra network resources before it is eventually dropped. Naturally, operators would like to minimize this impact. Let us extend the previous scenario to case where the link loads are low, and D1 and D2 have significantly higher capacity than the on-path NIPS. From a pure load perspective, we might want to offload most of the traffic to D1 and D2. However, this is in conflict with the goal of dropping unwanted traffic early.

Together, these examples motivate the need for a systematic way to capture NIPS-specific aspects in offloading including: (1) changes to traffic patterns due to NIPS actions; (2) accounting for the impact of rerouting in network load; (3) modeling the impact of off-path offloading on latency for users; and (4) balancing the tension between load balancing and dropping unwanted traffic early.

4   SNIPS System Overview

In order to address the challenges from the previous section, we present the design of the SNIPS system. Figure 5 shows a high-level view of the system. The design of SNIPS is general and can be applied to several contexts: enterprise networks, datacenter networks, and ISPs, though the most common use-case (e.g., as considered by past network security literature) is typically for enterprise networks.

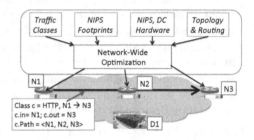

Fig. 5. Overview of the SNIPS architecture for NIPS offloading

We envision a logically centralized *controller* that manages the NIPS deployment as shown, analogous to many recent network management efforts (e.g., [3]). Network administrators specify high-level objectives such as bounds on acceptable link congestion or user-perceived latency. The controller runs a network-wide optimization and translates these high-level goals into physical data plane configurations.

This network-wide optimization is run periodically (e.g., every 5 minutes) or triggered by routing or traffic changes to adapt to network dynamics. To this end, it uses information about the current traffic patterns and routing policies using data feeds that are routinely collected for other network management tasks [5]. Based on these inputs, the controller runs the optimization procedures (described later) to assign NIPS processing responsibilities. We begin by describing the main inputs to this NIPS controller.

- **Traffic Classes:** Each *traffic class* is identified by a specific application-level port (e.g., HTTP, IRC) and network ingress and egress nodes. Each class is associated with some type of NIPS analysis that the network administrator wants to run. We use the variable c to identify a specific class. We use $c.in$ and $c.out$ to denote the ingress and egress nodes for this traffic class; in particular, we assume that a traffic class has exactly one of each. For example, in Figure 5 we have a class c consisting of HTTP traffic entering at $c.in = $ N1 and exiting at $c.out = $ N3. Let $S(c)$ and $B(c)$ denote the (expected) volume of traffic in terms of the number of sessions and bytes, respectively. We use $Match(c)$ to denote the expected rate of unwanted traffic (which, for simplicity, we assume to be the same in sessions or bytes) on the class c, which can be estimated from summary statistics exported by the NIPS.

- **Topology and Routing:** The path traversed by traffic in a given class (before any rerouting due to offloading) is denoted by $c.path$. For clarity, we assume that the routing in the network is symmetric; i.e., the path $c.path = Path(c.in, c.out)$ is identical to the reverse of the path $Path(c.out, c.in)$. In our example, $c.path = \langle$N1, N2, N3$\rangle$. Our framework could be generalized to incorporate asymmetric routing as well. For simplicity, we restrict the presentation of our framework to assume symmetric routing.

  We use the notation $N_j \in Path(src, dst)$ to denote that the NIPS node N_j is *on the routing path* between the source node src and the destination node dst. In our example, this means that N1, N2, N3 $\in Path($N1, N3$)$. Note that some nodes (e.g., a dedicated cluster such as D1 in Figure 5) are off-path; i.e., these do not observe traffic unless we explicitly re-route traffic to them. Similarly, we use the notation $l \in Path(src, dst)$ to denote that the link l is on the path $Path(src, dst)$. We use $|Path(src, dst)|$ to denote the latency along a path $Path(src, dst)$. While our framework is agnostic to the units in which latency is measured, we choose hop-count for simplicity.

- **Resource Footprints:** Each class c may be subject to different types of NIPS analysis. For example, HTTP sessions may be analyzed by a payload signature engine and through web firewall rules. We model the cost of running the NIPS for each class on a specific *resource* r (e.g., CPU cycles, memory) in terms of the expected per-session resource footprint F_c^r, in units suitable for that resource (F_c^r for *Footprint* on r). These values can be obtained either via NIPS vendors' datasheets or estimated using offline benchmarks [4].

- **Hardware Capabilities:** Each NIPS hardware device N_j is characterized by its resource capacity Cap_j^r in units suitable for the resource r. In the general case, we assume that hardware capabilities may be different because of upgraded hardware running alongside legacy equipment.

We observe that each of these inputs (or the instrumentation required to obtain them) is already available in most network management systems. For instance, most centralized network management systems today keep a network information base (NIB) that has the current topology, traffic patterns, and routing policies [5]. Similarly, the hardware capabilities and resource footprints of the different traffic classes can be obtained with simple *offline* benchmarking tools [4]. Note that our assumption on the availability of these inputs is in line with existing work in the network management literature. The only additional input that SNIPS needs is $Match(c)$, which is the expected drop rate for the NIPS functions. These can be estimated using historical logs reported by the NIPS; anecdotal evidence from network administrators suggests that the match rates are typically quite stable [1]. Furthermore, SNIPS can provide significant benefits even with coarse estimates. In this respect, our guiding principle is to err on the conservative side; e.g., we prefer to overestimate resource footprints and underestimate the drop rates.

Note that SNIPS does not compromise the security of the network relative to a traditional ingress-based NIPS deployment. That is, any malicious traffic that would be dropped by an ingress NIPS will also be dropped in SNIPS; this drop may simply occur elsewhere in the network as we will see.

Given this setup, we describe the optimization formulations for balancing the trade-off between the load on the NIPS nodes and the latency and congestion introduced by offloading.

5 SNIPS Optimization

Given the inputs from the previous section, our goal is to optimally distribute the NIPS processing through the network. To this end, we present a linear programming (LP) formulation. While LP-based solutions are commonly used in traffic engineering [6, 28], NIPS introduce new dimensions that make this model significantly different and more challenging compared to prior work [9, 28]. Specifically, rerouting and active manipulation make it challenging to systematically capture the effective link and NIPS loads using the optimization models from prior work, and thus we need a first-principles approach to model the NIPS-specific aspects.

Our formulation introduces decision variables that capture the notion of *processing and offloading fractions*. These variables, defined for each node along a routing path, control the number of flows processed at each node. Let $p_{c,j}$ denote the fraction of traffic on class c that the router N_j processes locally and let $o_{c,j,d}$ denote the fraction of traffic on class c that the NIPS node N_j offloads to the datacenter d. For clarity of pre-

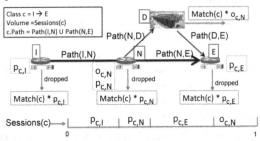

Fig. 6. An example to highlight the key concepts in our formulation and show modeling of the additional latency due to rerouting

sentation, we assume there is a single datacenter d and thus drop the d subscript; it is easy to generalize this formulation to multiple datacenters, though we omit the details here due to space considerations.

Intuitively, we can imagine the set of traffic sessions belonging to class c entering the network (i.e., before any drops or rerouting) as being divided into non-overlapping buckets, e.g., either using hashing or dividing the traffic across prefix ranges [28,34,37]. The fractions $p_{c,j}$ and $o_{c,j}$ represent the length of these buckets as shown in Figure 6.

Figure 7 shows the optimization framework we use to systematically balance the trade-offs involved in NIPS offloading. We illustrate the key aspects of this formulation using the example topology in Figure 6 with a single class c of traffic flowing between

Minimize: $(1 - \alpha - \beta) \times NLdCost + \alpha \times HopsUnwanted + \beta \times LatencyInc$, subject to:

$$\forall c: \sum_{N_j \in c.path} p_{c,j} + o_{c,j} = 1 \quad (1) \qquad \forall r: \sum_c \sum_{N_j \in c.path} o_{c,j} \times S(c) \times F_c^r \leq DCap^r \quad (4)$$

$$\forall r, j: NLd_{j,r} = \sum_{c: N_j \in c.path} p_{c,j} \times S(c) \times F_c^r \quad (2) \qquad \forall r, j: NLdCost \geq NLd_{j,r} \quad (5)$$

$$\forall r, j: NLd_{j,r} \leq Cap_j^r \quad (3) \qquad \forall l: BG_l = \sum_{c: l \in c.path} B(c) \quad (6)$$

$$\forall l: LLd_l \leq MaxLLd \times LCap_l \quad (7)$$

$$LatencyInc = \sum_c \sum_{N_j \in c.path} o_{c,j} \times S(c) \times \left(\begin{array}{c} |Path(N_j, d)| + |Path(d, c.out)| \\ -|Path(N_j, c.out)| \end{array} \right) \quad (8)$$

$$HopsUnwanted = \sum_c \sum_{N_j \in c.path} p_{c,j} \times S(c) \times Match(c) \times |Path(c.in, N_j)|$$

$$+ \sum_c \sum_{N_j \in c.path} o_{c,j} \times S(c) \times Match(c) \times \left(\begin{array}{c} |Path(c.in, N_j)| \\ + |Path(N_j, d)| \end{array} \right) \quad (9)$$

$$\forall l: LLd_l = BG_l + \sum_c \sum_{\substack{N_j: N_j \in c.path \\ \wedge\, l \in Path(N_j, d)}} o_{c,j} \times B(c)$$

$$+ \sum_{c: l \in Path(d, c.out)} \sum_{N_j \in c.path} o_{c,j} \times B(c) \times (1 - Match(c))$$

$$- \sum_c \sum_{N_j \prec_c l} o_{c,j} \times B(c) - \sum_c \sum_{N_j \prec_c l} p_{c,j} \times B(c) \times Match(c) \quad (10)$$

Fig. 7. Formulation for balancing the scaling, latency, and footprint of unwanted traffic in network-wide NIPS offloading

the ingress I and egress E. This toy topology has a single data center D and traffic being offloaded to D from a given node N.

Goals: As discussed earlier, NIPS offloading introduces several new dimensions: (1) ensure that the NIPS hardware is not overloaded; (2) keep all the links at reasonable loads to avoid unnecessary network congestion; (3) add minimal amount of extra latency for user applications; and (4) minimize the network footprint of unwanted traffic. Of these, we model (2) as a *constraint* and model the remaining factors as a multi-criterion objective.[2]

Note that these objectives could possibly be in conflict and thus we need to systematically model the trade-offs between these objectives. For instance, if are not worried about the latency impact, then the optimal solution is to always offload traffic to the datacenter. To this end, we model our objective function as a weighted combination of factors (1), (3), and (4). Our goal here is to devise a general framework rather than

---

[2] The choice of modeling some requirement as a strict constraint vs. objective may differ across deployments; as such, our framework is quite flexible. We use strict bounds on the link loads to avoid congestion.

mandate specific values of the weights. We discuss some natural guidelines for selecting these weights in §7.

Coverage (Eqn. 1): Given the process and offload variables, we need to ensure that every session in each class is processed somewhere in the network. Eqn. 1 captures this coverage requirement and ensures that for each class c the traffic is analyzed by some NIPS on that path or offloaded to the datacenter. In our example, this means that $p_{c,I}$, $p_{c,N}$, $p_{c,E}$, and $o_{c,N}$ should sum up to 1.

Resource Load (Eqn. 2–Eqn. 5): Recall that F_c^r is the per-session processing cost of running the NIPS analysis for traffic on class c. Given these values, we model the load on a node as the product of the processing fraction $p_{c,j}$, the traffic volume along these classes and the resource footprint F_c^r. That is, the load on node N_j due to traffic processed on c is $S(c) \times p_{c,j} \times F_c^r$. Since our goal is to have all nodes operating within their capacity, we add the constraint in Eqn. 3 to ensure that no node exceeds the provisioned capacity. The load on the datacenter depends on the total traffic offloaded to it, which is determined by the $o_{c,j}$ values, i.e., $o_{c,N}$ in our example of Figure 6. Again, this must be less than the capacity of the datacenter, as shown in Eqn. 4. Furthermore, since we want to minimize resource load, Eqn. 5 captures the maximum resource consumption across all nodes (except the datacenter).[3]

Latency Penalty due to Rerouting (Eqn. 8): Offloading means that traffic takes a detour from its normal path to the datacenter (and then to the egress). Thus, we need to compute the latency penalty caused by such rerouting. For any given node N_j, the original path $c.path$ can be treated as the logical concatenation of the path $Path(in, N_j)$ from ingress in to node N_j and the path $Path(N_j, out)$ from N_j to the egress out. When we offload to the datacenter, the additional cost is the latency from this node to the datacenter and datacenter to the egress. However, since this traffic does not traverse the path from N_j to the egress, we can subtract out that latency. In Figure 6, the original latency is $|Path(I, N)| + |Path(N, E)|$; the offloaded traffic incurs a latency of $|Path(I, N)| + |Path(N, D)| + |Path(D, E)|$ which results in a latency increase of $|Path(N, D)| + |Path(D, E)| - |Path(N, E)|$. This models the latency increase for a given class; the accumulated latency across all traffic is simply the sum over all classes (Eqn. 8).

Unwanted Footprint (Eqn. 9): Ideally, we want to drop unwanted traffic as early as possible to avoid unnecessarily carrying such traffic. To capture this, we compute the total "network footprint" occupied by unwanted traffic. Recall that the amount of unwanted traffic on class c is $Match(c) \times B(c)$. If the traffic is processed locally at router N_j, then the network distance traversed by the unwanted traffic is simply $|Path(c.in, N_j)|$. If the traffic is offloaded to the datacenter by N_j, however, then the network footprint incurred will be $|Path(c.in, N_j)| + |Path(N_j, d)|$. Given a reasonable bucketing function, we can assume that unwanted traffic will get mapped uniformly across the different logical buckets corresponding to the process and offload

---

[3] At first glance, it may appear that this processing load model does not account for reduction in processing load due to traffic being dropped upstream. Recall, however, that $p_{c,j}$ and $o_{c,j}$ are defined as fractions of original traffic that enters the network. Thus, traffic dropped upstream will not impact the processing load model.

variables. In our example, the volume of unwanted traffic dropped at N is simply $Match(c) \times B(c) \times p_{c,N}$. Given this, we can compute the network footprint of the unwanted traffic as a combination of the locally processed and offloaded fractions as shown in Eqn. 9.

Due to the processing coverage constraint, we can guarantee that SNIPS provides the same the security functionality as provided by a traditional ingress NIPS deployment. That is, any malicious traffic that should be dropped will be dropped *somewhere* under SNIPS. (And conversely, no legitimate traffic will be dropped.)

Link Load (Eqn. 6, Eqn. 7, Eqn. 10): Last, we come to the trickiest part of the formulation — modeling the link loads. To model the link load, we start by considering the baseline volume that a link will see if there were no traffic being dropped and if there were no offloading. This is the background traffic that is normally being routed. Starting with this baseline, we notice that NIPS offloading introduces both positive and negative components to link loads.

First, rerouting can induce additional load on a given link if it lies on a path between a router and the datacenter; either on the forward path to the datacenter or the return path from the data center to the egress. These are the additional positive contributions shown in Eqn. 10. In our example, any link that lies on the path $Path(N, D)$ will see additional load proportional to the offload value $o_{c,N}$. Similarly, any link on the path from the data center will see additional induced load proportional to $o_{c,N} \times (1 - Match(c))$ because some of the traffic will be dropped.

NIPS actions and offloading can also reduce the load on some links. In our example, the load on the link N-E is lower because some of the traffic has been offloaded from N; this is captured by the first negative term in Eqn. 10. There is also some traffic dropped by the NIPS processing at the upstream nodes. That is, the load on link N-E will be lowered by an amount proportional to $(p_{c,I} + p_{c,N}) \times Match(c)$. We capture this effect with the second negative term in Eqn. 10 where we use the notation $N_j \prec_c l$ to capture routers that are upstream of l along the path $c.path$.

Together, we have the link load on each link expressed as a combination of three factors: (1) baseline background load; (2) new positive contributions if the link lies on the path to/from the datacenter, and (3) negative contributions due to traffic dropped upstream and traffic being rerouted to the data center. Our constraint is to ensure that no link is overloaded beyond a certain fraction of its capacity; this is a typical traffic engineering goal to ensure that there is only a moderate level of congestion at any time.

Solution: Note that our objective function and all the constraints are *linear* functions of the decision variables. Thus, we can leverage commodity linear programming (LP) solvers such as CPLEX to efficiently solve this constrained optimization problem. In §6 we discuss how we map the output of the optimization (fractional $p_{c,j}$ and $o_{c,j}$ assignments) into *data plane* configurations to load balance and offload the traffic.

We note that this basic formulation can be extended in many ways. For instance, administrators may want different types of guarantees on NIPS failures: fail-open (i.e., allow some bad traffic), fail-safe (i.e., no false negatives but allow some benign traffic to be dropped), or strictly correct. SNIPS can be extended to support such policies; e.g., modeling redundant NIPS or setting up forwarding rules to allow traffic to pass through.

6 Implementation Using SDN

In this section, we describe how we implement SNIPS using software-defined network-ing (SDN). At a high-level, an SDN architecture consists of a network controller and SDN-enabled switches [3]. The controller installs rules on the switches using an open API such as OpenFlow [18] to specify forwarding actions for different flow match pat-terns. The flow match patterns are exact or wildcard expressions over packet header fields. This ability to programmatically set up forwarding actions enables a *network-layer* solution for NIPS offloading that does not require NIPS modifications and can thus work with legacy/proprietary NIPS hardware.

SNIPS Using SDN/OpenFlow: We want to set up forwarding rules to steer traffic to the different NIPSes. That is, given the $p_{c,j}$ and $o_{c,j}$ values, we need to ensure that each NIPS receives the designated amount of traffic. In order to decouple the formulation from the implementation, our goal is to translate *any* configuration into a correct set of forwarding rules.

As discussed in §4, each traffic class c is identified by application-level ports and net-work ingress/egress. Enterprise networks typically use structured address assignments; e.g., each site may be given a dedicated IP subnet. Thus, in our prototype we iden-tify the class using the IP addresses (and TCP/UDP port numbers). Note that we do not constrain the addressing structure; the only requirement is that hosts at different locations are assigned addresses from non-overlapping IP prefix ranges and that these assignments are known.

For clarity, we assume that each NIPS is connected to a single SDN-enabled switch. In the context of our formulation, each abstract node N_j can be viewed as consisting of a SDN switch S_j connected to the NIPS $NIPS_j$.[4]

6.1 Challenges in Using SDN

While SDN is indeed an enabler, there are three practical challenges that arise in our context. We do not claim that these are fundamental limitations of SDN. Rather, SNIPS induces new requirements outside the scope of traditional SDN/OpenFlow applica-tions [3] and prior SDN use cases [23, 24].

Stateful Processing: NIPS are *stateful* and must observe both forward and reverse flows of a TCP/UDP session for correct operation. In order to pin a session to a specific node, prior solutions for NIDS load balancing use bidirectional hash functions [9, 34]. However, such capabilities do not exist in OpenFlow and we need to explicitly ensure stateful semantics.

To see why this is a problem, consider the example in Figure 8 with class c1 (c1.*in*=S1 and c1.*out* = S2) with $p_{c1,NIPS1}=p_{c1,NIPS2}=0.5$. Suppose hosts with gate-ways S1 and S2 are assigned IP addresses from prefix ranges $Prefix_1=10.1/16$ and $Prefix_2=10.2/16$ respectively. Then, we set up forwarding rules so that pack-ets with $src = 10.1.0/17$, $dst=10.2/16$ are directed to NIPS NIPS1 and those with

---

[4] For "inline" NIPS deployments, the forwarding rules need to be on the switch immediately upstream of the NIPS and the NIPS needs to be configured to act in "bypass" mode to allow the remaining traffic to pass through untouched.

src=10.1.128/17, dst=10.2/16 are directed to NIPS2 as shown in the top half of Figure 8. Thus, the volume of traffic each NIPS processed matches the SNIPS optimization. Note that we need two rules, one for each direction of traffic. [5]

There is, however, a subtle problem. Consider a different class c2 whose $c2.in = S2$ and $c2.out = S1$. Suppose $p_{c2,NIPS1} = 0.25$ and $p_{c2,NIPS2} = 0.75$. Without loss of generality, let the split be $src = 10.2.0/18$, $dst = 10.1/16$ for NIPS1 and rest to NIPS2 as shown in bottom half of Figure 8.

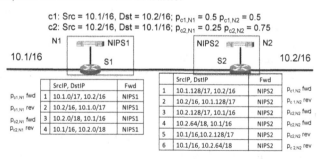

Fig. 8. Potentially conflicting rules with bidirectional forwarding rules for stateful processing. The solution in this case is to logically merge these conflicting classes.

Unfortunately, these new rules will create conflict. Consider a bidirectional session $src = 10.1.0.1$, $dst = 10.2.0.1$. This session will match two sets of rules; e.g., the forward flow of this session matches rule 1 on S1 while the reverse flow matches rule 4 (a reverse rule for c2) on S2. Such ambiguity could violate the stateful processing requirement if the forward and reverse directions of a session are directed to different NIPS.

Skewed Volume Distribution: While class merging ensures stateful processing, using prefix-based partitions may not ensure that the load on the NIPS matches the optimization result. To see why, consider Figure 9 with a single class and two NIPS, NIPS1 and NIPS2, with an equal split. The straw man solution steers traffic be-

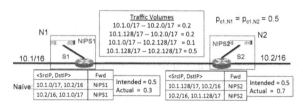

Fig. 9. NIPS loads could be violated with a non-uniform distribution of traffic across different prefix subranges. The solution in this case is a weighted volume-aware split

tween 10.1.0/17–10.2/16 to NIPS1 and the remaining (10.1.128/17–10.2/16) to NIPS2. While this splits the prefix space equally, the actual load may be skewed if the volume is distributed as shown. The actual load on the NIPS nodes will be 0.3 and 0.7 instead of the intended 0.5:0.5. This non-uniform distribution could happen for several reasons; e.g., hotspots of activity or unassigned regions of the address space.

Potential Routing Loops: Finally, there is a corner case if the same switch is on the path to/from the data center. Consider the route: $\langle in, \ldots, S_{offload}, \ldots, S_i, S_j, \ldots, S_d,$ $d, S_d, \ldots, S_i, S_j, \ldots, out\rangle$. With flow-based forwarding rules, S_j cannot decide if a

---

[5] For clarity, the example only shows forwarding rules relevant to NIPS; there are other basic routing rules that are not shown.

packet needs to be sent toward the datacenter d or toward egress out. (Note that this is not a problem for S_d itself; it can use the input interface on which the packet arrived to determine the forwarding action.)

We could potentially address some of these issues by modifying the optimization (e.g., choose a loop-free offload point for (2) or rewrite the optimization w.r.t merged classes for (1).) Our goal is to decouple the formulation from the implementation path. That is, we want to provide a correct SDN-based realization of SNIPS without making assumptions about the structure of the optimization solution or routing strategies.

6.2   Our Approach

Next, we discuss our approaches to address the above challenges. At a high-level, our solution builds on and extends concurrent ideas in the SDN literature [11,23,24]. However, to the best of our understanding, these current solutions do not handle conflicts due to stateful processing or issues of load imbalance across prefixes.

Class Merging for Stateful Processing: Fortunately, there is a simple yet effective solution to avoid such ambiguity. We identify such conflicting classes—i.e., classes c_1 and c_2 with $c_1.in = c_2.out$ and vice versa[6]—and logically *merge* them. We create a merged class c' whose $p_{c',j}$ and $o_{c',j}$ are (weighted) combinations of the original responsibilities so that the load on each NIPS $NIPS_j$ matches the intended loads. Specifically, if the resource footprints $F_{c_1}^r$ and $F_{c_2}^r$ are the same for each resource r, then it suffices to set $p_{c',j} = \frac{S(c_1) \times p_{c_1,j} + S(c_2) \times p_{c_2,j}}{S(c_1) + S(c_2)}$. In Figure 8, if the volumes for c1 and c2 are equal, the effective fractions are $p_{c',\text{NIPS1}} = \frac{0.5+0.25}{2}$ and $p_{c',\text{NIPS2}} = \frac{0.5+0.75}{2}$. We can similarly compute the effective offload values as well. If the resource footprints $F_{c_1}^r$ and $F_{c_2}^r$ are not the same for each resource r, however, then an appropriate combination can be computed using an LP (not shown for brevity).

Volume-Aware Partitioning: A natural solution to this problem is to account for the volumes contributed by different prefix ranges. While this problem is theoretically hard (being reducible to knapsack-style problems), we use a simple heuristic described below that performs well in practice, and is quite efficient.

Let $PrefixPair_c$ denote the IP subnet pairs for the (merged) class c. That is, if $c.in$ is the set $Prefix_{in}$ and $c.out$ is the set $Prefix_{out}$, then $PrefixPair_c$ is the cross product of $Prefix_{in}$ and $Prefix_{out}$. We partition $PrefixPair_c$ into non-overlapping blocks $PrefAtom_{c,1} \ldots PrefAtom_{c,n}$. For instance, if each block is a $/24 \times /24$ subnet and the original $PrefixPair$ is a $/16 \times /16$, then the number of blocks is $n = \frac{2^{16} \times 2^{16}}{2^8 \times 2^8} = 65536$. Let $S(k)$ be the volume of traffic in the kth block.[7] Then, the fractional weight for each block is $w_k = \frac{S(k)}{\sum_{k'} S(k')}$.

We discretize the weights so that each block has weight either δ or zero, for some suitable $0 < \delta < 1$. For any given δ, we choose a suitable partitioning granularity so that

---

[6] If the classes correspond to different well-known application ports, then we can use the port fields to disambiguate the classes. In the worst case, they may share some sets of application ports and so we could have sessions whose port numbers overlap.

[7] These can be generated from flow monitoring reports or statistics exported by the OpenFlow switches themselves.

the error due to this discretization is minimal. Next, given the $p_{c,j}$ and $o_{c,j}$ assignments, we run a pre-processing step where we also "round" each fractional value to be an integral multiple of δ.

Given these rounded fractions, we start from the first assignment variable (some $p_{c,j}$ or $o_{c,j}$) and block $PrefAtom_{c,1}$. We *assign* the current block to the current fractional variable until the variable's demand is satisfied; i.e., if the current variable, say $p_{c,j}$, has the value 2δ, then it is assigned two non-zero blocks. The only requirement for this procedure to be correct is that each variable value is satisfied by an integral number of blocks; this is true because each weight is 0 or δ and each variable value is an integral multiple of δ. With this assignment, the volume of traffic meets the intended $p_{c,j}$ and $o_{c,j}$ values (modulo rounding errors).

Handling Loops Using Packet Tagging: To handle loops, we use *packet tags* similar to prior work [11, 23]. Intuitively, we need the switches on the path from the datacenter to the egress to be able determine that a packet has already been forwarded. Because switches are stateless, we add tags so that the packet itself carries the relevant "state" information. To this end, we add an OpenFlow rule at S_d to set a *tag bit* to packets that are entering *from* the datacenter. Downstream switches on the path to *out* use this bit (in conjunction with other packet header fields) to determine the correct forwarding action. In the above path, S_j will forward packets with tag bit 0 toward d and packets with bit 1 toward *out*.

6.3   Putting it Together

Given these building blocks we translate the LP solution into an SDN configuration in three steps:

1. Identify conflicting classes and merge them.

2. Use a weighted scheme to partition the prefix space for each (merged) class so that the volume matches the load intended by the optimization solution.

3. Check for possible routing loops in offloaded paths and add corresponding tag addition rules on the switches.

We implement these as custom modules in the POX SDN controller [22]. We choose POX mostly due to our familiarity; these extensions can be easily ported to other platforms. One additional concern is how packets are handled during SNIPS rule updates to ensure stateful processing. To address this we can borrow known techniques from the SDN literature [25].

7   Evaluation

In evaluating SNIPS, we focus on two key aspects:

- System benchmarks using our SDN implementation (§7.1).
- Performance benefits over other NIPS architectures (§7.2).

Setup: We use a combination of custom trace-driven simulations, a real system emulation using Mininet [16], and optimization-driven analysis. We use OpenvSwitch as the SDN switch and use Snort as the NIPS.

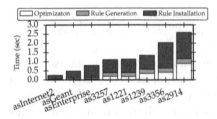
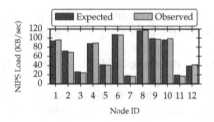

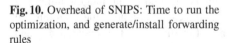

Fig. 10. Overhead of SNIPS: Time to run the optimization, and generate/install forwarding rules

Fig. 11. Validating that our SDN implementation faithfully realizes the SNIPS optimization on the Internet2 topology

We use realistic network topologies from educational backbones, ISPs [33], and an enterprise network; these topologies range in size between 11 and 70 nodes. Due to the absence of public traffic data, we use a *gravity model* based on location populations [26] to generate the traffic matrix specifying the volume of traffic between every pair of network nodes for the AS-level topologies. For the enterprise topology, we obtained the enterprise's empirical traffic matrix. For simplicity, we consider only one application-level class and assume there is a single datacenter located at the node that observes the largest volume of traffic.

We configure the node and link capacities as follows. We assume a baseline *ingress* deployment (without offloading or on-path distribution) where all NIPS processing occurs at the ingress of each end-to-end path. Then, we compute the maximum load across all ingress NIPS and set the capacity of each NIPS to this value and the datacenter capacity to be $10\times$ this node capacity. For link capacities, we simulate the effect of routing traffic without any offloading or NIPS-induced packet drops, and compute the maximum volume observed on the link. Then, we configure the link capacities such that the maximum loaded link is at $\approx 35\%$ load.

7.1   System Benchmarks

Computation Overhead: A potential concern with centralized management is the time to recompute the network configurations, especially in reaction to network dynamics. The SNIPS system has three potential overheads: solving the linear program using CPLEX; translating the LP solution to OpenFlow rules; and rule dissemination. Figure 10 shows the breakdown of these three components for the different topologies. Even with the largest topology (AS2914) with 70 nodes, the total time for configuration is only 2.6 seconds. Given that typical network reconfiguration tasks need to be performed every few minutes, this overhead is quite low [5].

Validation: We validated that our SDN implementation faithfully matches the load distribution intended by the optimization. Figure 11 shows this validation result in terms of the normalized NIPS loads (measured in total volume of traffic) for the Internet2 topology. (We have verified this for other topologies but do not show it for brevity.) Nodes 1–11 are the local NIPS and Node 12 is the data center. We use the LP solution to generate the expected load using the original traffic matrix. The result shows that the observed load closely tracks the intended load.[8] In this specific configuration, the volume of traffic offloaded to the datacenter (node 12) is small, but as we will see in the following sections, in other topologies the datacenter can help significantly.

7.2   Benefits of SNIPS

Next, we evaluate the performance benefits of SNIPS. We start with a baseline result with a simple configuration before evaluating the sensitivity to different parameters. For the baseline, we set the SNIPS parameters $\beta = \alpha = 0.333$; i.e., all three factors (latency, unwanted hops, load) are weighted equally in the optimization. We fix the fraction of unwanted traffic to be 10%. For all results, the maximum allowable link load is 40%.

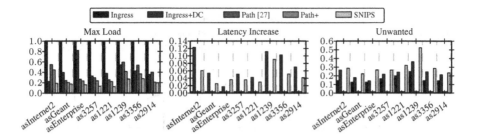

Fig. 12. Trade-offs between current deployments and SNIPS

Improvement Over Current NIPS Architectures: We compare the performance of SNIPS against today's *Ingress* NIPS deployments. As an intermediary point, we also consider three other deployments: 1) *Ingress+DC* deployment, where all processing/offloading happens at the ingress of each path and the datacenter. 2) *Path* deployment, modeling the on-path deployment described in [27]; and 3) *Path+*: identical to *Path* except each node has an increased capacity of $DCap^r/N$.

Figure 12 shows three normalized metrics for the topologies: load, added latency, and unwanted footprint. For ease of presentation, we normalize each metric by the maximum possible value for a specific topology so that it is between 0 and 1.[9] Higher values indicate less desirable configurations (e.g., higher load or latency).

By definition, the Ingress deployment introduces no additional latency and unwanted footprint is low[10], since all of the processing is at the edge of the network. Such a deployment, however, can suffer overload problems as shown in the result. SNIPS offers a more flexible trade-off: a small increase in latency and unwanted footprint for a significant reduction in the maximum compute load. We reiterate that SNIPS does not affect the security guarantees; it will drop *all* unwanted traffic, but it may choose to do so after a few extra hops. In some topologies (e.g., AS3356) SNIPS can reduce the maximum load by $10\times$ compared to a naive ingress deployment while only increasing the latency

---

[8] The small discrepancies are due to the variability in flow sizes.

[9] Hence the values could be different across topologies even for the ingress deployment.

[10] It is impossible for this footprint to be 0, since unwanted traffic enters the network and must be flagged as such.

by 2%. Similarly, SNIPS can provide a $4\times$ reduction in load without increasing latency over the Ingress+DC deployment (e.g., AS3257). Note that these benefits arise with a very simple equi-weighted trade-off across the three objective components; the benefits could be even better with other configurations.

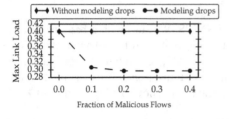
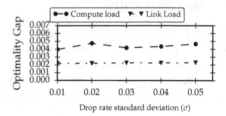

Fig. 13. Link load as a function of fraction of "unwanted" traffic

Fig. 14. Compute and link load optimality gap as functions of drop rate deviation; estimated drop rate = distribution mean $\mu = 0.1$

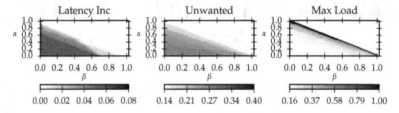

Fig. 15. Visualizing trade-offs in choosing different weight factors on Internet2 topology

Impact of Modeling Traffic Drops: SNIPS provides a higher fidelity model compared to past works in NIDS offloading because it explicitly incorporates the impact of traffic drops. We explore the impact of modeling these effects. For this result, we choose the Internet2 topology and use our simulator to vary the fraction of malicious flows in the network. Figure 13 shows the maximum observed link loads, averaged over 50 simulation runs. In addition to directly using the SNIPS-recommended strategy, we also consider a naive setup that does not account for such drops.

There are two key observations. First, the max link load is significantly lower with SNIPS which means that SNIPS can exploit more opportunities to offload under overload compared to the naive model. Second, by assuming no drops, "no drop" setup ignores the *HopsUnwanted* factor, thus potentially obstructing the link to the datacenter with unwanted traffic that could have been dropped at an earlier point in the network (this effect is represented in Figure 13).

7.3   Sensitivity Analysis

Sensitivity to Weights: As an illustrative result, we show the result of varying the weighting factors for the Internet2 topology in Figure 15. (We show only one topology due to space limitations). In the figure, darker regions depict higher values, which are less desirable. Administrators can use such visualizations to customize the weights to suit their network topology and traffic patterns and avoid undesirable regions. In particular, our equi-weighted configuration is a simple but reasonable choice (e.g., mostly low shades of gray in this graph).

Sensitivity to Estimation Errors: We also show that the parameter estimation (such as drop rate) for our framework need not be precise. For this, we choose to run a number of simulations with imperfect knowledge of the drop rate. In that case, the drop rate is sampled from a Gaussian distribution with mean of 0.1 (the estimated drop rate) and changing standard deviation σ. Figure 14 shows the relative gap for compute and link loads, between values predicted by the optimization with exact drop rate knowledge and the simulated values. This result shows that even with large noise levels the difference in load on links and nodes is insignificant.

8 Conclusions

Offloading has recently emerged as an appealing alternative to traditional approaches for scaling in-network processing. The goal of this paper is to bring the benefits of offloading to NIPS deployments. As we discussed, NIPS create new dimensions—active dropping, rerouting, and user-perceived latency—that fall outside the purvey of prior offloading systems that apply to passive monitoring solutions. To address these challenges, we presented the design and implementation of SNIPS. We presented a linear programming framework to model the new effects and trade-offs and addressed practical challenges in an SDN-based implementation. We showed that SNIPS offers greater scalability and flexibility with respect to current NIPS architectures; it imposes low overhead; and is robust to variations in operating parameters.

Acknowledgments. This work was supported in part by grant number N00014-13-1-0048 from the Office of Naval Research; NSF awards 1040626, 1330599, 1440056, and 1440065; and an NSF Graduate Research Fellowship.

References

1. Private communication with UNC administrators (2013)
2. Abraham, A., Jain, R., Thomas, J., Han, S.Y.: D-SCIDS: Distributed soft computing intrusion detection system. Journal of Network and Computer Applications 30 (2007)
3. Casado, M., et al.: Ethane: Taking control of the enterprise. ACM SIGCOMM (2007)
4. Dreger, H., Feldmann, A., Paxson, V., Sommer, R.: Predicting the resource consumption of network intrusion detection systems. In: Lippmann, R., Kirda, E., Trachtenberg, A. (eds.) RAID 2008. LNCS, vol. 5230, pp. 135–154. Springer, Heidelberg (2008)
5. Feldmann, A., et al.: Deriving traffic demands for operational IP networks: methodology and experience. In: Proc. SIGCOMM (2000)
6. Fortz, B., Rexford, J., Thorup, M.: Traffic engineering with traditional IP routing protocols. IEEE Communications Magazine 40 (2002)
7. Gibb, G., Zeng, H., McKeown, N.: Outsourcing network functionality. In: ACM SIGCOMM Workshop on Hot Topics in Software Defined Networking (2012)
8. Google Research: No Mobile Site = Lost Customers, http://goo.gl/f8lBbR

9. Heorhiadi, V., Reiter, M.K., Sekar, V.: New opportunities for load balancing in network-wide intrusion detection systems. ACM CoNEXT (2012)
10. Jamshed, M.A., Lee, J., Moon, S., Yun, I., Kim, D., Lee, S., Yi, Y., Park, K.: Kargus: a highly-scalable software-based intrusion detection system. In: ACM CCS (2012)
11. Jin, X., Li, L.E., Vanbever, L., Rexford, J.: SoftCell: Scalable and Flexible Cellular Core Network Architecture. In: Proc. CoNext (2013)
12. Kohler, E., Morris, R., Chen, B., Jannotti, J., Kaashoek, M.F.: The Click modular router. TOCS 18, 263–297 (2000)
13. Kreibich, C., Sommer, R.: Policy-controlled event management for distributed intrusion detection. In: Distributed Computing Systems Workshops (2005)
14. Lee, J., et al.: A high performance NIDS using FPGA-based regular expression matching. In: ACM Symposium on Applied Computing (2007)
15. Meiners, C.R., et al.: Fast regular expression matching using small TCAMs for network intrusion detection and prevention systems. In: USENIX Security Symposium (2010)
16. Mininet, http://www.mininet.org
17. Network functions virtualisation – introductory white paper, http://portal.etsi.org/NFV/NFV_White_Paper.pdf
18. Openflow standard, http://www.openflow.org/
19. Papadogiannakis, A., Polychronakis, M., Markatos, E.P.: Tolerating Overload Attacks Against Packet Capturing Systems. In: USENIX Annual Technical Conference (2012)
20. Paxson, V.: Bro: a system for detecting network intruders in real-time. In: Proc. USENIX Security (1998)
21. Porras, P.A., Neumann, P.G.: EMERALD: Event monitoring enabling response to anomalous live disturbances. In: National Information Systems Security Conference (1997)
22. POX Controller, http://www.noxrepo.org/pox/about-pox/
23. Qazi, Z., Tu, C.-C., Chiang, L., Miao, R., Sekar, V., Yu, M.: Simple-fying middlebox policy enforcement using sdn. In: Proc. SIGCOMM (2013)
24. Wang, R., Butnariu, D., Rexford, J.: Openflow-based server load balancing gone wild. In: Proc. Hot-ICE (2011)
25. Reitblatt, M., Foster, N., Rexford, J., Schlesinger, C., Walker, D.: Abstractions for network update. In: ACM SIGCOMM (2012)
26. Roughan, M.: Simplifying the synthesis of internet traffic matrices. ACM CCR, 35 (2005)
27. Sekar, V., Krishnaswamy, R., Gupta, A., Reiter, M.K.: Network-wide deployment of intrusion detection and prevention systems. In: ACM CoNEXT (2010)
28. Sekar, V., Reiter, M.K., Willinger, W., Zhang, H., Kompella, R.R., Andersen, D.G.: CSAMP: a system for network-wide flow monitoring. In: Proc. NSDI (2008)
29. Sherry, J., et al.: Making middleboxes someone else's problem: Network processing as a cloud service. In: ACM SIGCOMM (2012)
30. Shin, S., Gu, G.: Attacking Software-Defined Networks: A First Feasibility Study. In: ACM SIGCOMM Workshop on Hot Topics in Software Defined Networking (2013)
31. Shin, S., Porras, P., Yegneswaran, V., Fong, M., Gu, G., Tyson, M.: FRESCO: Modular composable security services for software-defined networks. In: Proc. NDSS (2013)
32. Smith, R., Estan, C., Jha, S.: XFA: Faster signature matching with extended automata. In: IEEE Symposium on Security and Privacy (2008)
33. Spring, N., Mahajan, R., Wetherall, D.: Measuring ISP topologies with rocketfuel. In: ACM SIGCOMM (2002)
34. Vallentin, M., Sommer, R., Lee, J., Leres, C., Paxson, V., Tierney, B.: The NIDS cluster: Scalable, stateful network intrusion detection on commodity hardware. In: Kruegel, C., Lippmann, R., Clark, A. (eds.) RAID 2007. LNCS, vol. 4637, pp. 107–126. Springer, Heidelberg (2007)

35. Vasiliadis, G., Polychronakis, M., Antonatos, S., Markatos, E.P., Ioannidis, S.: Regular expression matching on graphics hardware for intrusion detection. In: Kirda, E., Jha, S., Balzarotti, D. (eds.) RAID 2009. LNCS, vol. 5758, pp. 265–283. Springer, Heidelberg (2009)
36. Vasiliadis, G., Polychronakis, M., Ioannidis, S.: MIDeA: a multi-parallel intrusion detection architecture. In: ACM CCS (2011)
37. Wang, R., Butnariu, D., Rexford, J.: Openflow-based server load balancing gone wild. In: Proc. Hot-ICE (2011)
38. World intrusion detection and prevention markets, http://goo.gl/j3QPX3
39. Yu, F., et al.: SSA: a power and memory efficient scheme to multi-match packet classification. In: ACM ANCS (2005)

Inference-Proof Data Publishing
by Minimally Weakening a Database Instance[*]

Joachim Biskup and Marcel Preuß

Technische Universität Dortmund, Dortmund, Germany
{biskup,preuss}@ls6.cs.tu-dortmund.de

Abstract. Publishing of data is usually only permitted when complying
with a confidentiality policy. To this end, this work proposes an approach
to weaken an original database instance: within a logic-oriented modeling definite knowledge is replaced by disjunctive knowledge to introduce
uncertainty about confidential information. This provably disables an
adversary to infer this confidential information, even if he employs his
a priori knowledge and his knowledge about the protection mechanism.
As evaluated based on a prototype implementation, this approach can
be made highly efficient. If a heuristic – resulting only in a slight loss of
availability – is employed, it can be even used in interactive scenarios.

Keywords: A Priori Knowledge, Confidentiality Policy, Data Publishing, Disjunctive Knowledge, First-Order Logic, Inference-Proofness, Information Dissemination Control, k-Anonymity, Weakening.

1 Introduction

Nowadays, data publishing is ubiquitous. Governments are often legally obliged
to provide data about matters of public concern, companies release project-
related data to partners and even in most peoples' private lifes the sharing of data
plays a major role. But usually only certain portions of some data are appropriate
for being shared, as data often contains sensitive information. This applies in
particular to data containing personal information, as surveyed in [11,23].

In the area of relational databases the logic-oriented framework of Controlled
Interaction Execution (CIE) can assist a database owner in ensuring that each
of his interaction partners can only obtain a so-called "inference-proof view" on
the owner's data [3]. An inference-proof view does not contain information to be
kept confidential from the respective partner, even if this partner is an adversary
trying to deduce confidential information by drawing inferences based on his a
priori knowledge and his general awareness of the protection mechanism.

An example of such a protection mechanism creating inference-proof materialized views – which are suitable for data publishing – by modifying a minimum
number of truth-values of database tuples has been developed in [7]. This approach is rather versatile as it is based on an expressive fragment of first-order

---

[*] This work has been supported by the DFG under grant SFB 876/A5.

A. Prakash and R. Shyamasundar (Eds.): ICISS 2014, LNCS 8880, pp. 30–49, 2014.

logic, but also suffers from this expressiveness because of its high computational complexity. Moreover, there might also be some ethical concerns as the modification of truth-values means that a user's view on the database contains lies.

This work introduces a novel approach within the framework of CIE creating *inference-proof materialized views* suitable for data publishing and thereby *provably* enforcing a confidentiality policy without modifying any truth-values: instead, harmful database tuples are replaced by weaker knowledge in the form of disjunctions formed by ground atoms stemming from the policy (each of which logically represents a database tuple). These disjunctions contain only true information, but weaken an adversary's possible gain in information such that the adversary is provably not able to infer protected sensitive information.

This approach is first developed in a *purely generic* way in the sense that non-trivial disjunctions of any length ≥ 2 might be employed. Then a possible instantiation of this generic approach is presented, which aims at *maximizing availability* in the sense that only disjunctions of length 2 are seen to be admissible. For this instantiation an algorithmic treatment based on graph clustering is given, which fully specifies the approach except for an admissibility criterion expressing which subsets of potential secrets might possibly form a disjunction. This criterion should be tailored to the needs of each specific application and can be easily specified by employing query languages of relational databases.

To be able to fully implement the availability-maximizing flavor to experimentally demonstrate its high efficiency – which can be even raised by employing a heuristic resulting only in a slight loss of availability – an example for such an admissibility criterion called *interchangeability* is provided and evaluated. Interchangeability admits only disjunctions formed by ground atoms which all pairwise differ in the same single position and do not differ in any other position. This local restriction of distortion preserves definite information about all but one position of each ground atom and *generalizes* each distorted value to a wider set of possible values. Moreover, extensions of the generic approach dealing with policies (and hence disjunctions) of existentially quantified atoms and also coping with a basic kind of an adversary's a priori knowledge are outlined.

As an adversary is aware of which values are weakened by simply considering the disjunctions, particular attention must be paid to eliminate so-called *meta-inferences* (cf. [3,5]). A deduction of sensitive information is called a meta-inference, if it is obtained by excluding all possible alternative settings, under which this sensitive information is *not* valid, by simulating these alternative settings as inputs for the algorithm generating the inference-proof views and by being able to distinguish the outputs resulting from each alternative setting from the published one. In this work meta-inferences are eliminated by imposing a total order on the sentences of weakened instances.

The generalization of values to a wider set of possible values is similarly used in the approaches of k-anonymization and ℓ-diversification [10,16,21]. These approaches aim at preventing the re-identification of individuals based on so-called quasi-identifiers, which describe some of the individuals' properties, by generalizing these quasi-identifiers. We could model k-anonymization and ℓ-diversification as a special case within an extensions of our work, which deals with confidentiality policies containing disjunctions of existentially quantified atoms.

As the suppression of a value corresponds to its maximum generalization, this work is also related to the approach developed in [2], which aims at achieving confidentiality by replacing certain values of certain database tuples by null-values. But – in contrast to our work – this approach relies on the assumption that an adversary is *not* aware of which values are perturbed.

Moreover, there are other approaches clustering the vertices of a graph into sets of vertices to be made indistinguishable to achieve privacy [9,12]. But these approaches aim at preventing structural re-identification of the graph itself, while the approach presented in our work aims at achieving indistinguishability based on disjunctions induced from the clustering of the vertices of a graph.

In the remainder of this article, Sect. 2 provides the basic ideas of achieving inference-proofness by weakening a database instance. Sect. 3 then extends these ideas to also work with confidentiality policies of an arbitrary number of ground atoms, thereby balancing availability and confidentiality requirements. Subsequently, an overall algorithm – which is formally proved to comply with a declarative definition of inference-proofness – is presented in Sect. 4 and a prototype implementation of this algorithm is evaluated with respect to its efficiency in Sect. 5. Before concluding this work with Sect. 7, the algorithm is again extended in Sect. 6 to also deal with confidentiality policies containing existentially quantified atoms and to moreover consider an adversary's a priori knowledge.

2   Basic Ideas: Inference-Proofness by Weakening

The approach developed in this work is located within the area of relational databases. For simplicity, all data is supposed to be represented within a single database instance r over a relational schema $\langle R | \mathcal{A}_R | SC_R \rangle$ with relational symbol R and the set $\mathcal{A}_R = \{A_1, \ldots, A_n\}$ of attributes. Furthermore, all attributes are assumed to have the same *fixed but infinite* domain Dom of constants (cf. [4,15]) and the set SC_R contains some semantic (database) constraints (cf. [1]), which must be satisfied by the relational instance r. For now, these semantic constraints are neglected (i.e., $SC_R = \emptyset$), but they will become of interest in Sect. 6.

Each considered (original) instance r is supposed to represent *complete information*. Thus, the instance contains only a finite set of valid tuples and each constant combination c of the infinite set Dom^n with $c \notin r$ is assumed to be *not* valid by Closed World Assumption (CWA). This is exemplified in Fig. 1(a).

In compliance with CIE (cf. [3,4,7,6,5]), a database instance is modeled logic-orientedly. Therefore, a language $\mathcal{L}$ of first-order logic containing the predicate symbol R of arity $|\mathcal{A}_R| = n$ and the binary predicate symbol $\equiv$ for expressing equality is set up. The fixed but infinite domain Dom is taken as the set of constant symbols of $\mathcal{L}$ and the variables of an infinite set Var can be used to build sentences (i.e., closed formulas) in the natural fashion [15].

This syntactic specification is complemented with a semantics reflecting the characteristics of databases by means of so-called DB-Interpretations [4,7,15]:

r	$+$	$-$
	(a,b,c)	(a,a,a)
	(a,c,c)	(a,a,b)
	(b,a,c)	(a,a,c)
		$\vdots$

(a) Complete instance r

$R(a,b,c),\ R(a,c,c),\ R(b,a,c)$

$(\forall X)(\forall Y)(\forall Z)\ [$
$(X \equiv a \wedge Y \equiv b \wedge Z \equiv c)\ \vee$
$(X \equiv a \wedge Y \equiv c \wedge Z \equiv c)\ \vee$
$(X \equiv b \wedge Y \equiv a \wedge Z \equiv c)\ \vee$
$\neg R(X,Y,Z)$ $]$

(b) Logic-oriented modeling of r

Fig. 1. Example of a logic-oriented modeling of a complete database instance

Definition 1 (DB-Interpretation). *Given the language $\mathscr{L}$ with the set Dom of constant symbols, an interpretation $\mathcal{I}$ is a DB-Interpretation for $\mathscr{L}$ iff*

(i) Dom is the universe of $\mathcal{I}$ and $\mathcal{I}(v) = v$ holds for each $v \in Dom$,
(ii) predicate symbol R is interpreted by a finite relation $\mathcal{I}(R) \subset Dom^n$,
(iii) predicate symbol $\equiv$ is interpreted by $\mathcal{I}(\equiv) = \{(v,v) \mid v \in Dom\}$.

A DB-Interpretation $\mathcal{I}_r$ is induced by a complete database instance r, if its relation $\mathcal{I}_r(R)$ is instantiated by r, i.e., $\mathcal{I}_r(R) = \{\mathbf{c} \in Dom^n \mid \mathbf{c} \in r\}$.

The notion of *satisfaction/validity* of formulas in $\mathscr{L}$ by a DB-Interpretation is the same as in usual first-order logic. A set $\mathcal{S} \subseteq \mathscr{L}$ of sentences *implies/entails* a sentence $\Phi \in \mathscr{L}$ (written as $\mathcal{S} \models_{DB} \Phi$) iff each DB-Interpretation $\mathcal{I}$ satisfying $\mathcal{S}$ (written as $\mathcal{I} \models_M \mathcal{S}$) also satisfies Φ (written as $\mathcal{I} \models_M \Phi$).

A logic-oriented modeling of the complete instance r of Fig. 1(a) is given in Fig. 1(b). Each valid tuple $\mathbf{c} \in r$ is modeled as a ground atom $R(\mathbf{c})$ of $\mathscr{L}$ and the infinite set of invalid tuples – which is not explicitly enumerable – is expressed implicitly by a so-called completeness sentence (cf. [4]) having a universally quantified variable X_j for each attribute $A_j \in \mathcal{A}_R$. This completeness sentence expresses that every constant combination $(c_1, \ldots, c_n) \in Dom^n$ (substituting the universally quantified variables $X_1, \ldots, X_n$) is either explicitly excluded from being invalid or satisfies the sentence $\neg R(c_1, \ldots, c_n)$. By construction, this completeness sentence is satisfied by the DB-Interpretation $\mathcal{I}_r$ induced by r.

To achieve confidentiality, a confidentiality policy containing so-called potential secrets [3] is set up. This policy is supposed to be known by an adversary trying to recover an original instance r unknown to him based on his knowledge about a weakened variant of r and his further (a priori) knowledge.

Definition 2 (Confidentiality Policy). *A potential secret Ψ is a sentence of $\mathscr{L}$ and a confidentiality policy psec is a finite set of potential secrets. A complete database instance r obeys a potential secret $\Psi \in psec$, if $\mathcal{I}_r \not\models_M \Psi$. Moreover, this instance r obeys the confidentiality policy psec, if r obeys each $\Psi \in psec$.*

For now – until Sect. 6 – only potential secrets in the form of ground atoms are considered. To enforce a given confidentiality policy *psec*, an incomplete weakened variant $weak(r, psec)$ of a complete original instance r over $\langle R|\mathcal{A}_R|\emptyset\rangle$ is constructed by a weakening algorithm such that

$R(b, a, c)$

$R(a, b, c) \vee R(a, c, c)$

$(\forall X)(\forall Y)(\forall Z)\ [$
$(X \equiv a \wedge Y \equiv b \wedge Z \equiv c)\ \vee$
$(X \equiv a \wedge Y \equiv c \wedge Z \equiv c)\ \vee$
$(X \equiv b \wedge Y \equiv a \wedge Z \equiv c)\ \vee$
$\neg R(X, Y, Z) \qquad\qquad]$

(a) Weakening $weak(r, psec)$ obeying the policy $psec = \{R(a, \underline{b}, c), R(a, \underline{c}, c)\}$

$R(a, c, c),\ R(b, a, c)$

$R(a, b, c) \vee R(a, b, d)$

$(\forall X)(\forall Y)(\forall Z)\ [$
$(X \equiv a \wedge Y \equiv b \wedge Z \equiv c)\ \vee$
$(X \equiv a \wedge Y \equiv b \wedge Z \equiv d)\ \vee$
$(X \equiv a \wedge Y \equiv c \wedge Z \equiv c)\ \vee$
$(X \equiv b \wedge Y \equiv a \wedge Z \equiv c)\ \vee$
$\neg R(X, Y, Z) \qquad\qquad]$

(b) Weakening $weak(r, psec')$ obeying the policy $psec' = \{R(a, b, \underline{c}), R(a, b, \underline{d})\}$

Fig. 2. Possible inference-proof weakenings of the example instance of Fig. 1

- $weak(r, psec)$ contains only true information, i.e., $\mathcal{I}_r \models_M weak(r, psec)$, and
- for each potential secret $\Psi \in psec$ the existence of a complete alternative instance r^{Ψ} over $\langle R | \mathcal{A}_R | \emptyset \rangle$ is guaranteed such that
- this instance r^{Ψ} obeys Ψ, i.e., $\mathcal{I}_{r^{\Psi}} \not\models_M \Psi$, and the weakening of r^{Ψ} is indistinguishable from the weakening of r, i.e., $weak(r^{\Psi}, psec) = weak(r, psec)$.

Given an original instance r and a *simple* policy $psec = \{\Psi_1, \Psi_2\}$, such a weakening $weak(r, psec)$ can be easily computed: provided that Ψ_1 is *not* obeyed by r or (and, respectively) Ψ_2 is *not* obeyed by r, each knowledge about the constant combinations of Ψ_1 and Ψ_2 is removed from instance r and replaced by the weaker *disjunctive knowledge* that Ψ_1 or Ψ_2 is valid.

In contrast to the original instance r, a total order is supposed to be defined on the sentences that might occur in a weakened instance $weak(r, psec)$ (cf. [4]). This guarantees that an alternative instance r^{Ψ} with $\mathcal{I}_{r^{\Psi}} \models_M weak(r, psec)$ is *not* distinguishable from r based on a different arrangement of the sentences of its weakened instance $weak(r^{\Psi}, psec)$ compared to $weak(r, psec)$. Otherwise, an adversary might be able to draw the meta-inference (cf. Sect. 1) that r^{Ψ} is *not* the original instance of his interest because of $weak(r^{\Psi}, psec) \neq weak(r, psec)$.

To exemplify the simple case, consider the potential secrets $\Psi_1 = R(a, b, c)$ and $\Psi_2 = R(a, c, c)$ both *not* obeyed by instance r of Fig. 1. Both Ψ_1 and Ψ_2 can be protected by weakening r as depicted in Fig. 2(a). From an adversary's point of view both alternative instances $r^{(1)} = \{(a, c, c), (b, a, c)\}$ obeying Ψ_1 and $r^{(2)} = \{(a, b, c), (b, a, c)\}$ obeying Ψ_2 are indistinguishable from the "real" original instance because of $weak(r, psec) = weak(r^{(1)}, psec) = weak(r^{(2)}, psec)$.

Similarly, the potential secrets $\Psi_1' = R(a, b, c)$ *not* obeyed by r and $\Psi_2' = R(a, b, d)$ obeyed by r can be protected by weakening r as depicted in Fig. 2(b). In this case the completeness sentence known from Fig. 1(b) is extended by the disjunct $(X \equiv a \wedge Y \equiv b \wedge Z \equiv d)$ to ensure $\mathcal{I}_{r^{(1)'}} \models_M weak(r, psec')$ for the alternative instance $r^{(1)'} = \{(a, b, d), (b, a, c)\}$ obeying Ψ_1' as the constant combination (a, b, d) is not excluded from being invalid in r. The alternative instance obeying Ψ_2' is simply r itself.

As a last and easy case, consider a confidentiality policy $psec'' = \{\Psi_1'', \Psi_2''\}$ obeyed by r. Here no weakening of r is required, i.e., $weak(r, psec'') = r$.

3   Treating Non-simple Sets of Potential Secrets

In Sect. 2 the basic ideas to create inference-proof weakenings protecting simple confidentiality policies have been introduced. Now, these basic ideas are extended to be able to deal with *non-simple* policies containing an arbitrary number of ground atoms. So, given a non-simple policy *psec*, the challenge is to construct a set of disjunctions consisting of potential secrets of *psec* such that availability and confidentiality requirements are suitably balanced.

3.1   A First Generic Approach

A first *generic approach* is to partition the policy *psec* into disjoint subsets called *clusters*. Then, for each cluster C a disjunction $\bigvee_{\Psi \in C} \Psi$ is constructed, provided that at least one potential secret of C is *not* obeyed by the original instance.

Note that a disjunction of length k is satisfied by $2^k - 1$ DB-Interpretations. Consequently, if $\mathcal{C}$ is the set of clusters, there are up to $\prod_{C \in \mathcal{C}} (2^{|C|} - 1)$ different (alternative) database instances, whose induced DB-Interpretations satisfy the weakened instance. From the point of view of an adversary only knowing the weakened instance, each of these instances is indistinguishable from the original one. Therefore, in terms of confidentiality it is desirable to construct large clusters to maximize the number of these instances, while in terms of availability small clusters are favored to minimize the number of these instances.

To also achieve a meaningful clustering of a policy *psec* regarding a specific application, an additional notion of *admissible indistinguishabilities* specifying all *admissible clusters* – i.e., all acceptable possibilities of making potential secrets of *psec* indistinguishable by disjunctions – should be provided. These admissible clusters need *not* be pairwise disjoint: the construction of a disjoint clustering $\mathcal{C}$, each of whose clusters is admissible, is the task of a *clustering algorithm*.

In some cases it might not be possible to construct such a clustering $\mathcal{C}$ and to moreover guarantee that each of its clusters has a certain minimum size k^*. As clusters of a suitable minimum size are inevitable to guarantee a wanted degree of confidentiality, one obvious approach is to *extend* each too small cluster $C \in \mathcal{C}$ of size $|C| < k^*$ by $k^* - |C|$ additional (i.e., artificial) potential secrets, thereby constructing an extended clustering $\mathcal{C}^*$ based on $\mathcal{C}$. But as each additional potential secret Ψ^A reduces availability, the goal is to find a clustering $\mathcal{C}$ for whose extension only a minimum number of additional potential secrets is needed.

For the quality of a weakening it is of crucial importance that the employed notion of admissible indistinguishabilities fits to the specific application considered: in terms of confidentiality all alternatives provided by a disjunction should be equally probable from an adversary's point of view and in terms of availability each disjunction should still provide as much useful information as possible.

Obviously, no generally valid approach to find such a notion for each possible specific application can be given. But as it is not desirable – and for policies of realistic size usually even impossible – to let a security officer manually design sets of admissible disjunctions, a generic method to construct admissible disjunctions based on a high level specification language is needed.

As a confidentiality policy should be usually managed by a database system, one possible approach to construct admissible clusters of size k (with $k \geq k^*$) is to compute a series of $k-1$ self-joins on the policy table – resulting in combinations each of which contains k pairwise different potential secrets. In this case well-known query languages such as SQL or relational algebra [19] let a security officer implement his concrete notion of admissible indistinguishabilities with the help of a corresponding join condition.

To allow the extension of too small clusters of size $k < k^*$, a notion of admissible indistinguishabilities might require that for some potential secrets of a confidentiality policy up to $k^* - 1$ additional potential secrets can be constructed with a deterministic (and preferably efficient) algorithm. Such a construction only uses a finite subset of the domain Dom of constant symbols. So although favoring an *infinite* domain in theory (cf. Sect. 2) to avoid combinatorial effects possibly leading to harmful inferences, a "sufficiently large" *finite* domain is adequate in practice.

Definition 3 (Well-Defined Indistinguishability). *Given a confidentiality policy psec, the domain Dom of $\mathscr{L}$ and a minimum size k^* of clusters, a notion of admissible indistinguishabilities is* well-defined, *if there is a set $\mathcal{C}^*$ such that*

(i) *for each $\Psi \in psec$ the set $\mathcal{C}^*$ contains a cluster $C_\Psi = \{\Psi, \Psi_{I_1}, \ldots, \Psi_{I_{k^*-1}}\}$ (possibly extended) such that $\Psi \neq \Psi_{I_i}$ for $1 \leq i \leq k^* - 1$ and $\Psi_{I_i} \neq \Psi_{I_j}$ for $1 \leq i < j \leq k^* - 1$ and $\bigvee_{\bar{\Psi} \in C_\Psi} \bar{\Psi}$ is an admissible indistinguishability,*

(ii) *$C_\Psi \cap C_{\Psi'} = \emptyset$ holds for all clusters $C_\Psi, C_{\Psi'} \in \mathcal{C}^*$ with $C_\Psi \neq C_{\Psi'}$,*

(iii) *there is a deterministic algorithm creating each (additional) Ψ^A of $\mathcal{C}^*$ with $\Psi^A \notin psec$, thereby (finitely) augmenting the active domain of psec and*

(iv) *the active domain of $\mathcal{C}^*$ is contained in Dom.*

Note that an extension of clusters is generated independently of any database instance. As an adversary is moreover supposed to know the confidentiality policy as well as the deterministic algorithms employed, he is able to determine all additional potential secrets himself by simulating the corresponding algorithms.

3.2 Algorithmic Treatment of an Availability-Maximizing Flavor

In this subsection a possible instantiation of the generic approach aiming at *maximizing availability* – and hence keeping the size of clusters as small as possible – is developed. To be able to enforce confidentiality, for each potential secret Ψ the existence of at least one alternative instance obeying Ψ must be ensured (cf. Sect. 2 and Theorem 1 below). As clusters of size 2 – which are the smallest clusters complying with this requirement – correspond to binary relations, all admissible indistinguishabilities can be represented by a so-called indistinguishability-graph, whose edges represent all admissible clusters.

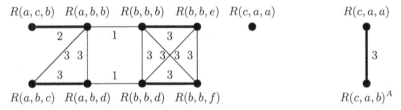

(a) Indistinguishability-graph with (bold) matching edges   (b) Matching extension

Fig. 3. Graph with a clustering of potential secrets and a matching extension

Definition 4 (Indistinguishability-Graph). *Given a confidentiality policy* psec *and a well-defined notion of admissible indistinguishabilities, an* indistinguishability-graph *is an undirected graph* $G = (V, E)$ *such that*

(i) $V := psec$ *is the set of vertices of* G, *and the set of edges of* G *is*
(ii) $E := \{\ \{\Psi_1, \Psi_2\} \in V \times V \mid \Psi_1 \vee \Psi_2$ *is an admissible indistinguishability* $\}$.

An example of an indistinguishability-graph for a non-simple policy is given in Fig. 3(a). Note that for now the edge labelings are not of importance. On such a graph a maximum set of pairwise (vertex-)disjoint clusters of size 2 (i.e., edges) can then be computed efficiently with well-known maximum matching algorithms for general (i.e., not necessarily bipartite) graphs [14,17].

Definition 5 (Maximum Matching). *Let* $G = (V, E)$ *be an undirected graph (without loops). A subset* $M \subseteq E$ *is a* matching *on* G, *if* $\{\Psi_1, \Psi_2\} \cap \{\bar{\Psi}_1, \bar{\Psi}_2\} = \emptyset$ *for each pair of different matching edges* $\{\Psi_1, \Psi_2\}, \{\bar{\Psi}_1, \bar{\Psi}_2\} \in M$. *A matching* M *on* G *is a* maximum matching, *if* $|M'| \leq |M|$ *for each matching* $M' \subseteq E$ *on* G. *A maximum matching* M *on* G *is a* perfect matching, *if each vertex* $\Psi \in V$ *is* covered *by* M, *i.e., there is exactly one* $\{\Psi_1, \Psi_2\} \in M$ *with* $\Psi \in \{\Psi_1, \Psi_2\}$.

In Fig. 3(a) the subset of bold edges constitutes a maximum matching. As demonstrated, a maximum matching is not necessarily a perfect matching. Even given a connected graph with an even number of vertices, several vertices might remain uncovered by a maximum matching. To ensure that each potential secret is assigned to a cluster of size 2, additional potential secrets are created.

Definition 6 (Matching Extension). *Let* psec *be a confidentiality policy and let* M *be a maximum matching on the indistinguishability-graph of* psec. *A* matching extension M^* *of* M *and* psec *initially contains each matching edge* $\{\Psi_1, \Psi_2\} \in M$ *and subsequently, one after another, for each* $\Psi \in psec$ *uncovered by* M *an edge* $\{\Psi, \Psi^A\}$ *is added to* M^*. *Thereby* Ψ^A *is an additional potential secret, i.e., a deterministically created sentence* $\Psi^A \notin psec$ *of* $\mathscr{L}$ *such that* $\Psi \vee \Psi^A$ *is an admissible indistinguishability and* $\Psi^A \notin \{\Psi_1, \Psi_2\}$ *for each* $\{\Psi_1, \Psi_2\} \in M^*$.

In Fig. 3(b) such a matching extension in terms of the running example is given. Note that a matching extension M^* is always a valid matching: initially $M^* = M$ holds and then $\{\Psi, \Psi^A\} \cap \{\Psi_1, \Psi_2\} = \emptyset$ is guaranteed in any subsequent iteration for each $\{\Psi_1, \Psi_2\} \in M^*$ before adding $\{\Psi, \Psi^A\}$ to M^*.

As each matching extension M^* is a perfect matching on the indistinguishability-graph for the set $psec^*$ of all potential secrets of M^*, each potential secret is in exactly one cluster of size 2. Moreover, in terms of availability, only a minimum number of additional potential secrets are created as a maximum matching M already covers as many potential secrets of the original policy $psec$ as possible.

3.3   Admissible Indistinguishabilities Based on Local Distortion

Until now, the clustering of policy elements is based on a purely abstract notion of admissible indistinguishabilities – which must be tailored to the needs of each specific application as argued in Sect. 3.1. An example for an easy to implement and moreover well-defined indistinguishability property, which locally restricts distortion within a disjunction, is the so-called *interchangeability*, which is applicable for *each* confidentiality policy consisting of ground atoms.

Definition 7 (Interchangeability). *The ground atoms* $\Psi_1 = R(c_1, \ldots, c_n)$ *and* $\Psi_2 = R(d_1, \ldots, d_n)$ *are interchangeable, if there is a single differing position* $m \in \{1, \ldots, n\}$ *with* $c_m \neq d_m$ *and* $c_i = d_i$ *for each* $i \in \{1, \ldots, n\} \setminus \{m\}$. *A set* C *of ground atoms over* R *is interchangeable, if all* $\Psi_i, \Psi_j \in C$ *with* $\Psi_i \neq \Psi_j$ *are pairwise interchangeable (and thus all differ at the same single position* m).

The indistinguishability-graph given in Fig. 3(a) is constructed based on the property of interchangeability and each of its edges is labeled with the single differing position of its incident potential secrets. Note that all indistinguishability-graphs resulting from this property have the structure known from a graph introduced by Knuth in [13] and further analyzed in [20], whose vertices are words of fixed length, which are neighbored if they differ in exactly one position.

A disjunction $\bigvee_{i \in \{1, \ldots, k\}} R(c_1, \ldots, c_{m-1}, \tilde{c}_m^{(i)}, c_{m+1}, \ldots, c_n)$ only consisting of pairwise interchangeable potential secrets has the advantage that the constant combinations of each of its disjuncts all only differ at the same single position m. Hence, it locally restricts distortion within this disjunction – and thus captures another aspect of maximizing availability – by providing definite information about all but the m-th columns in the sense that the original instance contains at least one tuple of the form $(c_1, \ldots, c_{m-1}, \Box, c_{m+1}, \ldots, c_n)$ and by only hiding with which of the values $\tilde{c}_m^{(1)}, \ldots, \tilde{c}_m^{(k)}$ this tuple is combined.

If a total order with a successor function $succ(\cdot)$ is supposed to exist on the set Dom of constant symbols, the creation of an additional potential secret Ψ^A for an arbitrary potential secret $R(c_1, \ldots, c_n)$ is easy to define for the interchangeability property. Choose a differing position $m \in \{1, \ldots, n\}$ arbitrarily and initially set $\Psi^A := R(c_1, \ldots, \tilde{c}_m, \ldots, c_n)$ with $\tilde{c}_m := succ(c_m)$. As long as Ψ^A is in $psec$ or Ψ^A is equal to an already constructed additional potential secret, iteratively set $\tilde{c}_m := succ(\tilde{c}_m)$. Note that – demanding clusters of a minimum size of k^* – in a worst case scenario at most $(k^* - 1) \cdot |psec|$ additional constants are needed to create $k^* - 1$ additional potential secrets for each of the $|psec|$ many policy elements. Hence, this indistinguishability property is well-defined.

A disadvantage of this kind of indistinguishability clearly is that it only provides a suitable number of possible disjunctions if the majority of policy elements consist of constant combinations not differing much from each other. If this is not the case, a large number of additional potential secrets is needed and hence employing this kind of indistinguishability may result in a loss of availability. This is exemplified in Sect. 5 and demonstrates that the task of suitably defining admissible disjunctions crucially depends on the specific application considered.

4   Creation of Inference-Proof Weakenings

Before the overall algorithm creating an inference-proof weakening $weak(r, psec)$ of a complete database instance r and a confidentiality policy $psec$ can be developed, the construction of such a weakened instance must be defined. As motivated in Sect. 2, a weakened instance is a totally ordered sequence of sentences.

Definition 8 (Weakened Instance). *Suppose that r is a complete database instance over schema $\langle R | \mathcal{A}_R | \emptyset \rangle$ and $\mathcal{C}_r^*$ is an (extended) clustering of a confidentiality policy psec such that for each cluster $C \in \mathcal{C}_r^*$ there is a potential secret $\Psi \in C$ with $\mathcal{I}_r \models_M \Psi$. Then the incomplete weakened instance $weak(r, psec)$ is constructed as the following three totally ordered sequences of sentences of $\mathcal{L}$:*

(i) *Positive knowledge $weak(r, psec)^+$: Each tuple $c \in r$ with $R(c) \not\models_{DB} \Psi$ for each $\Psi \in \bigcup_{C \in \mathcal{C}_r^*} C$ is modeled as a ground atom $R(c)$. All of these ground atoms are sorted lexicographically according to the order on Dom.*

(ii) *Disjunctive knowledge $weak(r, psec)^\vee$: For each cluster $C \in \mathcal{C}_r^*$ the disjunction $\bigvee_{\Psi \in C} \Psi$ is constructed. First, for each of these disjunctions its disjuncts are sorted lexicographically according to the order on Dom and then all of these disjunctions are sorted in the same way.*

(iii) *Negative knowledge $weak(r, psec)^-$: A completeness sentence (cf. Sect. 2) having a universally quantified variable X_j for each attribute $A_j \in \mathcal{A}_R$ is constructed. It has a disjunct ($\bigwedge_{i \in \{1, \ldots, n\}}$ with $t_i \in Dom$ $X_i \equiv t_i$) for each ground atom $R(t_1, \ldots, t_n)$ of $weak(r, psec)^+$ and for each (existentially quantified) atom[1] $(\exists X) R(t_1, \ldots, t_n)$ of a disjunction of $weak(r, psec)^\vee$. The above mentioned disjuncts are sorted in the same way as the disjunctions of $weak(r, psec)^\vee$. As a last disjunct $\neg R(X_1, \ldots, X_n)$ is added.*

An example of such a weakened instance is given in Fig. 4(c). Each weakened instance $weak(r, psec)$ contains only true information, i.e., $\mathcal{I}_r \models_M weak(r, psec)$, as for each ground atom $R(c)$ of $weak(r, psec)^+$ the tuple c is valid in r; each

---

[1] This definition is generalized to be compatible to Sect. 6. If a potential secret is a ground atom, "$(\exists X)$" is dropped and each t_i is a constant symbol of Dom.

r	$+$	$-$
	(a,b,a)	(a,a,a)
	(a,b,b)	(a,a,b)
	(a,c,b)	$\vdots$
	(c,a,b)	

(a) Original instance r

$\{R(a,\underline{b},b),\ R(a,\underline{c},b)\ \}$,
$\{R(c,a,\underline{a}),\ R(c,a,\underline{b})^{A}\}$

(b) Clusters of a set C_r^* with a potential secret satisfied by $\mathcal{I}_r$

$R(a,b,a)$

$R(a,b,b) \lor R(a,c,b)$

$R(c,a,a) \lor R(c,a,b)$

$(\forall X)(\forall Y)(\forall Z)\ [$
$(X \equiv a \land Y \equiv b \land Z \equiv a)\ \lor$
$(X \equiv a \land Y \equiv b \land Z \equiv b)\ \lor$
$(X \equiv a \land Y \equiv c \land Z \equiv b)\ \lor$
$(X \equiv c \land Y \equiv a \land Z \equiv a)\ \lor$
$(X \equiv c \land Y \equiv a \land Z \equiv b)\ \lor$
$\neg R(X,Y,Z)$ $]$

(c) Weakening $weak(r,psec)$ based on C_r^* obeying the policy of Fig. 3(a)

Fig. 4. Example of an inference-proof weakening obeying the policy of Fig. 3

disjunction of $weak(r,psec)^{\lor}$ contains a disjunct Ψ_i with $\mathcal{I}_r \models_M \Psi_i$ by construction of C_r^*; and for each constant combination $c \in Dom^n$, for which $\neg R(c)$ holds by the completeness sentence of $weak(r,psec)^-$, the tuple c is invalid in r.

Now that all basic operations are known, the overall algorithm generating an inference-proof weakened instance is presented.

Algorithm 1 (Inference-Proof Weakening). *Given a complete database instance r over $\langle R|\mathcal{A}_R|\ \emptyset\ \rangle$, a confidentiality policy psec of ground atoms of $\mathcal{L}$, a minimum size k^* of clusters and a well-defined notion of admissible indistinguishabilities, a weakened instance $weak(r,psec)$ is created as follows:*

- **Stage 1** (independent of r): Disjoint clustering of potential secrets
  - (i) *Generate all admissible clusters with a minimum size of k^* (e.g., an indistinguishability-graph $G = (V,E)$ of psec (Def. 4))*
  - (ii) *Compute a disjoint clustering C based on the admissible clusters (e.g., a maximum matching $M \subseteq E$ on G (Def. 5))*
  - (iii) *Create C^* from C by extending each too small cluster of C to size k^* (e.g., by a matching extension M^* of M and psec (Def. 6))*
- **Stage 2** (dependent on r): Creation of weakened instance
  - (iv) *Create the subset $C_r^* := \{\ C \in C^* \mid \mathcal{I}_r \models_M \bigvee_{\Psi \in C} \Psi\ \}$ of (extended) clusters containing a potential secret not obeyed by $\mathcal{I}_r$*
  - (v) *Create the weakened instance $weak(r,psec)$ based on r and C_r^* (Def. 8)*

An example of a weakened instance created by the *availability-maximizing* flavor of Algorithm 1 for the original instance of Fig. 4(a) is depicted in Fig. 4(c). The confidentiality policy, the corresponding indistinguishability-graph – constructed based on the *interchangeability* property – and the extended matching on which the set C_r^* of clusters given in Fig. 4(b) is based on is known from Fig. 3.

To understand the importance of *disjoint* clusters, consider the instance $r = \{c_1\}$ and the *non-disjoint* clusters $C_1 = \{R(c_1), R(c_2)\}$ and $C_2 = \{R(c_2), R(c_3)\}$

with $c_1, c_2, c_3 \in Dom^n$. Then, $weak(r, psec)$ consists of $weak(r, psec)^+ = \emptyset$ and $weak(r, psec)^\vee = \{R(c_1) \vee R(c_2)\}$. Moreover, because of $R(c_2) \vee R(c_3) \notin weak(r, psec)^\vee$ and by construction of the completeness sentence, an adversary knows $\mathcal{I}_r \not\models_M R(c_2)$. Hence, he can infer that $\mathcal{I}_r \models_M weak(r, psec)^\vee$ can only hold, if $\mathcal{I}_r \models_M R(c_1)$, thereby violating the potential secret $R(c_1)$ of C_1.

Theorem 1 (Inference-Proofness of Weakenings). *Given the inputs of Algorithm 1 (i.e., r over $\langle R|\mathcal{A}_R|\, \emptyset \,\rangle$, psec, k^*, and well defined indistinguishabilities), this algorithm generates an inference-proof weakened instance $weak(r, psec)$ such that for each potential secret $\Psi \in psec$ the existence of a complete alternative instance r^Ψ over $\langle R|\mathcal{A}_R|\emptyset\rangle$ is guaranteed. This alternative instance r^Ψ obeys Ψ, i.e., $\mathcal{I}_{r^\Psi} \not\models_M \Psi$, and the weakening $weak(r^\Psi, psec)$ generated by Algorithm 1 is indistinguishable from $weak(r, psec)$, i.e., $weak(r^\Psi, psec) = weak(r, psec)$.*

Proof. Consider an arbitrary potential secret $\tilde{\Psi} \in psec$ and suppose that Stage 1 generated a (possibly extended) disjoint clustering $\mathcal{C}^*$ with clusters of a minimum size of $k^* \geq 2$. Assume that $\tilde{\Psi}$ is in the cluster $\tilde{C} = \{\tilde{\Psi}, \tilde{\Psi}_{I_1}, \dots, \tilde{\Psi}_{I_{k-1}}\} \in \mathcal{C}^*$.

If $\mathcal{I}_r \not\models_M \bigvee_{\Psi \in \tilde{C}} \Psi$, the complete alternative instance $r^{\tilde{\Psi}}$ is r itself, i.e., $r^{\tilde{\Psi}} := r$. This implies $\mathcal{I}_{r^{\tilde{\Psi}}} \not\models_M \bigvee_{\Psi \in \tilde{C}} \Psi$ and consequently $r^{\tilde{\Psi}}$ obeys $\tilde{\Psi}$, i.e., $\mathcal{I}_{r^{\tilde{\Psi}}} \not\models_M \tilde{\Psi}$, because of $\mathcal{I}_{r^{\tilde{\Psi}}} \models_M \neg(\bigvee_{\Psi \in \tilde{C}} \Psi) = \bigwedge_{\Psi \in \tilde{C}} (\neg \Psi)$. As a direct consequence of $r^{\tilde{\Psi}} = r$ the property of indistinguishability holds, i.e., $weak(r^{\tilde{\Psi}}, psec) = weak(r, psec)$.

If $\mathcal{I}_r \models_M \bigvee_{\Psi \in \tilde{C}} \Psi$ with $\tilde{\Psi} = R(c_{\tilde{\Psi}}) \in \tilde{C}$ and a $\tilde{\Psi}_{I_m} = R(c_{\tilde{\Psi}_{I_m}}) \in \tilde{C}$, the complete alternative instance is $r^{\tilde{\Psi}} := (r \setminus \{c_{\tilde{\Psi}}\}) \cup \{c_{\tilde{\Psi}_{I_m}}\}$. Hence, $r^{\tilde{\Psi}}$ obeys $\tilde{\Psi}$, i.e., $\mathcal{I}_{r^{\tilde{\Psi}}} \not\models_M \tilde{\Psi}$, and $\mathcal{I}_{r^{\tilde{\Psi}}} \models_M \bigvee_{\Psi \in \tilde{C}} \Psi$ because of $\mathcal{I}_{r^{\tilde{\Psi}}} \models_M \tilde{\Psi}_{I_m}$. For each other cluster $C \in M^*$ with $C \neq \tilde{C}$ the corresponding disjunction $\bigvee_{\Psi \in C} \Psi$ is satisfied by $\mathcal{I}_{r^{\tilde{\Psi}}}$ if and only if it is satisfied by $\mathcal{I}_r$ because of $r^{\tilde{\Psi}} \setminus \{c_{\tilde{\Psi}}, c_{\tilde{\Psi}_{I_m}}\} = r \setminus \{c_{\tilde{\Psi}}, c_{\tilde{\Psi}_{I_m}}\}$ and because of $\tilde{\Psi} \notin C$ and $\tilde{\Psi}_{I_m} \notin C$ by the disjoint clustering.

This implies $\mathcal{C}^*_{r^{\tilde{\Psi}}} = \mathcal{C}^*_r$ and hence also $weak(r^{\tilde{\Psi}}, psec)^\vee = weak(r, psec)^\vee$. As $r^{\tilde{\Psi}}$ and r only differ in $c_{\tilde{\Psi}}$ and $c_{\tilde{\Psi}_{I_m}}$ and as $\tilde{C}$ with $R(c_{\tilde{\Psi}}), R(c_{\tilde{\Psi}_{I_m}}) \in \tilde{C}$ is a cluster of both $\mathcal{C}^*_{r^{\tilde{\Psi}}}$ and $\mathcal{C}^*_r$, also $weak(r^{\tilde{\Psi}}, psec)^+ = weak(r, psec)^+$ holds. By construction of the completeness sentence, $weak(r^{\tilde{\Psi}}, psec)^- = weak(r, psec)^-$ directly follows and so the property of indistinguishability, i.e., $weak(r^{\tilde{\Psi}}, psec) = weak(r, psec)$, holds, provided that the sentences of both of these sequences are arranged in the same order. □

5 Efficiency of the Approach

After developing Algorithm 1, a prototype implementation of the *availability-maximizing* instantiation of this algorithm (cf. Sect. 3.2) is now sketched and evaluated theoretically as well as experimentally. Thereby *interchangeability* (cf. Def. 7) is employed as a well-defined indistinguishability property.

Within Stage 1 of Algorithm 1 the indistinguishability-graph is constructed efficiently with a flavor of the merge-join algorithm (cf. Sect. 3.1), which is well-known from relational databases [19]. In typical scenarios the runtime of this algorithm is significantly better than its worst-case complexity $O(|psec|^2)$ [19].

To next compute a maximum matching (cf. [14,17]), the prototype benefits from the "Boost"-library [8]. Although a maximum matching on a general graph $G = (V, E)$ can be computed in $O(\sqrt{|V|} \cdot |E|)$ (cf. [22]), common implementations as provided by "LEDA" [18] or "Boost" [8] prefer an algorithm performing in $O(|V| \cdot |E| \cdot \alpha(|E|, |V|))$ with $\alpha(|E|, |V|) \leq 4$ for any feasible input.

Stage 1 finally computes a matching extension M^* and in a worst-case scenario $|psec|$ different additional potential secrets – whose creation in the case of interchangeability is sketched in Sect. 3.3 – are needed. Provided that binary search is employed to check collisions of tentatively constructed additional potential secrets, M^* is constructed in $O(|psec|^2 \cdot \log(|psec|))$. But note that this upper bound is purely theoretic and usually not even approached.

Stage 2 of Algorithm 1 first creates the subset C_r^* of clusters based on M^* in $O(|psec| \cdot \log(|r|))$ by employing binary search to check which potential secrets in the form of ground atoms are satisfied by the original instance. Finally, the weakened instance is constructed. Again using binary search, $weak(r, psec)^+$ is constructed in $O(|r| \cdot \log(|psec|))$ and sorted in $O(|r| \cdot \log(|r|))$; $weak(r, psec)^\vee$ is constructed in $O(|psec|)$ and sorted in $O(|psec| \cdot \log(|psec|))$; and $weak(r, psec)^-$ is constructed in $O(|r| + |psec|)$ and sorted in $O((|r| + |psec|) \cdot \log(|r| + |psec|))$.

The prototype is implemented in Java 7, except for the C++ implementation of the matching algorithm (see above). All experiments were run under Ubuntu 14.04 on an "Intel Core i7-4770" machine with 32 GB of main memory and each published result is based on the average results of 100 experiments.

To generate the input data for a first test setup, for each experiment a particular finite set $\mathcal{D} \subseteq Dom$ of constant symbols is available for the construction of the constant combinations of all database tuples and potential secrets, which are all supposed to be of arity 4. As the cardinality of $\mathcal{D}$ varies over the experiments from $|\mathcal{D}| = 10$ to $|\mathcal{D}| = 20$, the cardinality of the set $constComb(\mathcal{D}) := \mathcal{D}^n$ of all possible constant combinations varies from $10^4 = 10\,000$ to $20^4 = 160\,000$.

To evaluate Stage 1 of Algorithm 1, for each of the possible cardinalities of $\mathcal{D}$ a randomly chosen subset of $constComb(\mathcal{D})$ is selected to construct a random confidentiality policy $psec$ as input data for an experiment. Thereby, the fraction of tuples of $constComb(\mathcal{D})$ contained in the policy is stepwise increased from 10% to 70% of all tuples of $constComb(\mathcal{D})$. Hence, the average vertex degree of the corresponding indistinguishability-graphs is also stepwise increased.

As depicted in Fig. 5(a), even for large policies Stage 1 of Algorithm 1 performs very well in constructing clusterings of the policies. If an even faster computation is needed, the matching heuristic presented in [17] – which performs in time linear to the size of the graph – can be employed. As depicted in Fig. 5(b), the usage of this heuristic significantly improves the runtime of Stage 1 and usually looses only a negligible fraction of matching edges in relation to a optimum solution, as demonstrated in Fig. 5(c). Hence, using this heuristic results only in a slight

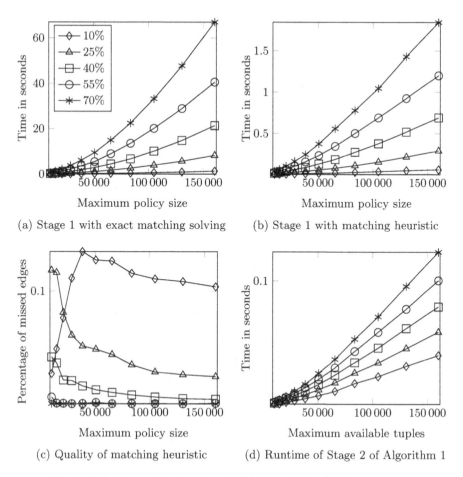

(a) Stage 1 with exact matching solving   (b) Stage 1 with matching heuristic

(c) Quality of matching heuristic   (d) Runtime of Stage 2 of Algorithm 1

Fig. 5. Experimental evaluation of Algorithm 1 for the first test setup

loss of availability, as an additional potential secret is needed for each vertex uncovered by the matching.

To evaluate Stage 2 of Algorithm 1, for each of the possible cardinalities of $\mathcal{D}$ two randomly chosen subsets of $constComb(\mathcal{D})$ are selected to construct a random database instance r as well as a random confidentiality policy $psec$. The fraction of tuples of $constComb(\mathcal{D})$ contained in r is stepwise increased from 10% to 70% of all tuples of $constComb(\mathcal{D})$ while the fraction of tuples contained in $psec$ is fixed to 40%. According to Fig. 5(d), the runtime of Stage 2 needed to construct a weakening based on a given clustering is negligible.

At first glance, input instances constructed based on 20 or even just 10 available constants might look like "toy examples", but note that for a clustering of fully random potential secrets based on the interchangeability property these instances are the expensive inputs: the relatively small number of available constants leads

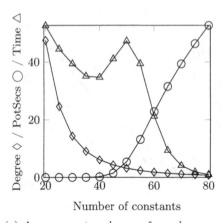

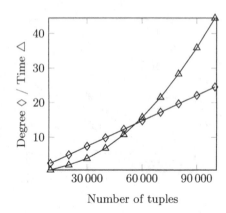

(a) Average vertex *degree* of graph, number of additional *potential secrets* in thousands, and *runtime* of Stage 1 in seconds for 100 000 random tuples of arity 4 constructed for a varying number of constants

(b) Average vertex *degree* of graph, and *runtime* of Stage 1 in seconds for a fixed number of 25 constants and for a number of tuples of arity 4 varying from 10 000 to 100 000

Fig. 6. Evaluation of the interchangeability property within the first test setup

to constant combinations which are likely not to differ much from each other and hence the corresponding indistinguishability-graphs have a large number of edges making the computation of a maximum matching expensive.

This is demonstrated by experiments always constructing 100 000 fully random tuples for a number of available constants varying from 20 to 80. As shown in Fig. 6(a), increasing the number of available constants leads to a decreasing of the average vertex degree of the indistinguishability-graphs. In the end the graphs decompose into a large number of small connected components and as hence the clustering becomes trivial the runtime of Stage 1 also declines. These results are also verified by a second experiment fixing the number of constants to 25 and linearly increasing the number of constructed potential secrets from 10 000 to 100 000. As shown in Fig. 6(b), this leads to an also linearly increasing average vertex degree while the runtime of Stage 1 increases much stronger.

As very low average vertex degrees moreover lead to a large number of additional potential secrets (plotted in thousands in Fig. 6(a)), the interchangeability property only provides suitably high availability, if the majority of policy elements consist of constant combinations not differing much from each other. This demonstrates that the task of finding a suitable notion of admissible indistinguishabilities crucially depends on the specific application considered.

Next, a second test setup is initiated, which is supposed to be more practical than the fully random setup. This second setup – only considering Stage 1 as the runtime of Stage 2 is now known to be negligible – is based on a set of objects, each of which has two attributes: the first attribute has a domain, whose cardinality k is stepwise increased from 2 to 32, and the second attribute has a domain of cardinality 100. Considering binary relations between some of

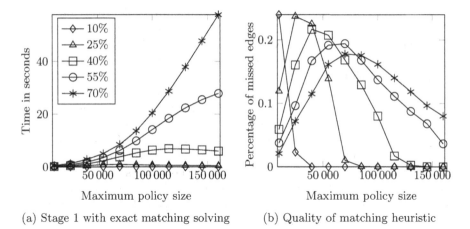

(a) Stage 1 with exact matching solving   (b) Quality of matching heuristic

Fig. 7. Experimental evaluation of Algorithm 1 for the second test setup

these objects, each constructible object is paired with 50 randomly chosen other constructible objects – resulting in $k \cdot 100 \cdot 50$ tuples of arity 4, i.e., the number of available constant combinations again varies from $10\,000$ (for $k = 2$) to $160\,000$ (for $k = 32$). Similarly to the first test setup, for each value of k the confidentiality policy is created as a randomly chosen subset of all available constant combinations, whose cardinality is stepwise increased from 10% to 70%.

For this second test setup the exact computation of Stage 1 performs better than using the first test setup (cf. Fig. 7(a)) as the resulting graphs have a lower but non-trivial average vertex degree. The runtime of the heuristic computation is as good as known from the fully random setup, but the number of lost matching edges is slightly higher compared to the first test setup (cf. Fig. 7(b)) as the graphs resulting from the second test setup often have a lower but non-trivial average vertex degree leading to slightly weaker but still very decent results.

6 Extending the Approach

So far, only potential secrets in the form of ground atoms have been considered. To improve the expressiveness of confidentiality policies, potential secrets are from now on so-called *existentially quantified atoms* known from [5]. Intuitively, an existentially quantified potential secret $\Psi = (\exists Z)\, R(a, b, Z)$ states that an adversary *must not* get to know that a tuple $(a, b, \tilde{c})$ with an arbitrary constant symbol $\tilde{c} \in Dom$ is valid in the original instance r considered.

Definition 9 (Existentially Quantified Atom). *A sentence of $\mathscr{L}$ is an existentially quantified atom if it is of the form $(\exists X)\, R(t_1, \ldots, t_n)$ and*

(i) each term t_i is either a constant symbol of Dom or a variable of X,
(ii) the set X of existentially quantified variables is $X = \{t_1, \ldots, t_n\} \setminus Dom$,
(iii) each variable can only occur once, i.e., $t_i \neq t_j$ for all $t_i, t_j \in X$ with $i \neq j$.

Though implication is generally hard (if not even impossible) to decide within first-order logic [4], under DB-Semantics (cf. Def. 1) it is easy to decide for existentially quantified atoms [5]: $(\exists \boldsymbol{X})\,R(t_1,\ldots,t_n) \models_{DB} (\exists \boldsymbol{Y})\,R(\bar{t}_1,\ldots,\bar{t}_n)$ iff for each term $\bar{t}_i$, which is a constant symbol of Dom, the term t_i is also a constant symbol of Dom such that $t_i = \bar{t}_i$.

Now, suppose that an instance $r = \{R(a,b,c)\}$ and a confidentiality policy $psec = \{(\exists Z)\,R(a,b,Z),\,(\exists Z)\,R(b,b,Z),\,R(a,b,c),\,R(a,b,d)\}$ are inputs for a flavor of Algorithm 1 creating the clusters $C_1 = \{(\exists Z)\,R(a,b,Z),\,(\exists Z)\,R(b,b,Z)\}$ and $C_2 = \{R(a,b,c),\,R(a,b,d)\}$. The weakened instance $weak\,(r,psec)$ then contains the disjunction $R(a,b,\underline{c}) \vee R(a,b,\underline{d})$ and hence directly implies the knowledge $(\exists Z)\,R(a,b,Z)$ which itself is protected by a potential secret of $psec$.

The preceding example indicates that this flavor of Algorithm 1 could create a weakened instance which contains disjunctions implying knowledge protected by potential secrets. So, this implied (and hence weaker) knowledge is still too strong. To avoid the construction of too strong disjunctions, the algorithm must clean the given confidentiality policy in a preprocessing step, i.e., the policy is reduced to its weakest sentences. Moreover, adding the constructed additional potential secrets to this set must not violate the properties of a cleaned set.

Definition 10 (Cleaned Set). *Let S be a set of sentences of $\mathscr{L}$. Its cleaned set $\hat{S}$ is a maximum subset of weakest sentences of S such that no pair of different sentences of $\hat{S}$ is semantically equivalent. $\Psi \in S$ is a weakest sentence of S, if for each sentence $\Psi' \in S$ either $\Psi' \models_{DB} \Psi$ or both $\Psi' \not\models_{DB} \Psi$ and $\Psi \not\models_{DB} \Psi'$.*

Reconsidering the example, $\widehat{psec} = \{(\exists Z)\,R(a,b,Z),\,(\exists Z)\,R(b,b,Z)\}$ is the cleaned policy. Assuming that $\{\widehat{psec}\}$ is the created clustering, the weakening $weak\,(r,\widehat{psec})$ only contains the disjunction $(\exists Z)\,R(a,b,Z) \vee (\exists Z)\,R(b,b,Z)$ not implying any (weaker) knowledge which itself is protected.

In particular, even the potential secrets $R(a,b,c)$ and $R(a,b,d)$ only contained in the original policy $psec$ are protected by $weak\,(r,\widehat{psec})$: from an adversary's point of view an alternative instance r' with $\mathcal{I}_{r'} \models_M weak\,(r,\widehat{psec})$ and $\mathcal{I}_{r'} \not\models_M (\exists Z)\,R(a,b,Z)$ is possible and for this instance also $\mathcal{I}_{r'} \not\models_M R(a,b,c)$ and $\mathcal{I}_{r'} \not\models_M R(a,b,d)$ holds. This implicit protection of all removed policy elements $psec \setminus \widehat{psec}$ by the cleaned policy $\widehat{psec}$ can be generalized as follows.

Lemma 1 (Implicit Protection). *Let Ψ_S and Ψ_W be sentences of $\mathscr{L}$ such that Ψ_W is weaker than Ψ_S, i.e., $\Psi_S \models_{DB} \Psi_W$, and let $\mathcal{I}_r$ be a DB-Interpretation with $\mathcal{I}_r \not\models_M \Psi_W$. Then Ψ_S is not satisfied by $\mathcal{I}_r$ either, i.e., $\mathcal{I}_r \not\models_M \Psi_S$.*

In many real-world scenarios an adversary is supposed to also have some *a priori knowledge* in addition to the knowledge provided by the database (cf. [3]). A priori knowledge is then modeled as a finite set *prior* of sentences of $\mathscr{L}$ and usually includes the set SC_R of semantic constraints (cf. Sect. 2), i.e., $SC_R \subseteq prior$. All sentences of *prior* are supposed to be satisfied by the original instance r, i.e., $\mathcal{I}_r \models_M prior$, and furthermore do not directly compromise the confidentiality policy $psec$, i.e., $prior \not\models_{DB} \Psi$ for each potential secret $\Psi \in psec$. To make a first step towards the handling of a priori knowledge, an adversary is now supposed to be also aware of such a set *prior* of ground atoms of $\mathscr{L}$.

Similar to Def. 3, a notion of admissible indistinguishabilities might require that for some potential secrets of the cleaned policy $\widehat{psec}$ up to $k^* - 1$ additional potential secrets can be constructed. To moreover ensure that all non-implications provided by cleaning the policy are not affected by combinatorial effects, the domain Dom must contain at least one "fresh" constant symbol not occurring in a potential secret of $psec$ or a constructed additional potential secret. In terms of the credibility of these non-implications from an adversary's point of view, a much larger supply of these "fresh" constant symbols is of course highly desirable.

Definition 11 (Well-Defined Indistinguishability Ext.). *Given a cleaned confidentiality policy $\widehat{psec}$, an adversary's a priori knowledge prior, the domain Dom of $\mathcal{L}$ and a minimum size k^* of clusters, a notion of admissible indistinguishabilities is* well-defined, *if there is a set $\mathcal{C}^*$ such that*

(i) for each $\Psi \in \widehat{psec}$ the set $\mathcal{C}^*$ contains a cluster $C_\Psi = \{\Psi, \Psi_{I_1}, \ldots, \Psi_{I_{k^*-1}}\}$ (possibly extended) such that $\Psi \neq \Psi_{I_i}$ for $1 \leq i \leq k^* - 1$ and $\Psi_{I_i} \neq \Psi_{I_j}$ for $1 \leq i < j \leq k^* - 1$ and $\bigvee_{\bar{\Psi} \in C_\Psi} \bar{\Psi}$ is an admissible indistinguishability,
(ii) $C_\Psi \cap C_{\Psi'} = \emptyset$ holds for all clusters $C_\Psi, C_{\Psi'} \in \mathcal{C}^*$ with $C_\Psi \neq C_{\Psi'}$,
(iii) $\bigcup_{C \in \mathcal{C}^*} C$ is a cleaned set,
(iv) prior $\not\models_{DB} \Psi^A$ for each (additional) Ψ^A of $\mathcal{C}^*$ with $\Psi^A \notin \widehat{psec}$,
(v) there is a deterministic algorithm creating each (additional) Ψ^A of $\mathcal{C}^*$ with $\Psi^A \notin \widehat{psec}$, thereby (finitely) augmenting the active domain of $psec$,
(vi) the active domain of $\mathcal{C}^*$ is contained in Dom and
(vii) Dom contains at least one constant not in the active domain of $\mathcal{C}^*$.

As a direct consequence of this extension of Def. 3, no well-defined notion of indistinguishability can be found, if the policy $psec$ contains a potential secret Ψ_W which is semantically equivalent to the weakest possible potential secret $(\exists \boldsymbol{X})\, R(\boldsymbol{X})$ without any constant symbols. In this case the cleaned policy $\widehat{psec}$ only contains Ψ_W and no additional potential secret Ψ_W^A can be found for Ψ_W as $\{\Psi_W, \Psi_W^A\}$ cannot be a cleaned set because of $\Psi_W^A \models_{DB} \Psi_W$.

Based on the thoughts presented so far, Algorithm 1 can be extended. Its inference-proofness can be basically proved as known from Theorem 1, but each "secure" alternative instance must furthermore satisfy an adversary's a priori knowledge to be credible from this adversary's point of view [3].

Theorem 2 (Inference-Proofness of Weakenings). *Let r be a complete instance over $\langle R|\mathcal{A}_R|SC_R\rangle$; $psec$ be a policy of existentially quantified atoms; k^* be the minimum size of clusters; and assume that a well-defined notion of indistinguishabilities is given. Moreover, prior (with $SC_R \subseteq prior$) is a priori knowledge of ground atoms such that $\mathcal{I}_r \models_M prior$ and prior $\not\models_{DB} \Psi$ for each $\Psi \in psec$.*

The extended algorithm then creates an inference-proof weakened instance[2] $weak(r, psec)$ such that for each potential secret $\Psi \in psec$ the existence of a complete alternative instance r^Ψ over $\langle R|\mathcal{A}_R|SC_R\rangle$ is guaranteed. This alternative

---

[2] Though the weakening of an instance now also depends on *prior*, for convenience the weakening-operator $weak(\cdot, \cdot)$ is not extended to explicitly reflect this third input.

instance r^Ψ *obeys* Ψ, *i.e.*, $\mathcal{I}_{r^\Psi} \not\models_M \Psi$, *satisfies the a priori knowledge prior,* *i.e.*, $\mathcal{I}_{r^\Psi} \models_M prior$, *and the weakening* $weak(r^\Psi, psec)$ *is indistinguishable from* $weak(r, psec)$, *i.e.*, $weak(r^\Psi, psec) = weak(r, psec)$.

The detailed proof of Theorem 2 is omitted for lack of space.

7   Conclusion and Future Work

We developed a generic approach provably protecting sensitive information specified by a confidentiality policy consisting of ground atoms – even if an adversary employs inferences. This is achieved by weakening a database instance by means of disjunctions. Furthermore, an algorithm for an availability-maximizing flavor of this approach has been proposed and an implementation of this algorithm based on interchangeability has been shown to be highly efficient. Moreover, the generic approach has also been extended to protect more expressive confidentiality policies while also considering an adversary's a priori knowledge.

But a priori knowledge restricted to ground atoms does not allow for modeling commonly used semantic database constraints such as the well-known classes of Equality Generating and Tuple Generating Dependencies (cf. [1]). Examples for achieving inference-proofness under versatile subclasses of these semantic constraints are given in [6,7] and should be transferred to the current approach.

Moreover, the definition of inference-proofness underlying this work only guarantees the existence of at least one "secure" alternative instance from an adversary's point of view (cf. Theorem 1 and Theorem 2). But in terms of enhancing confidentiality it might be desirable to strengthen this definition to always guarantee a certain number k of different "secure" alternative instances. As discussed for the generic approach, this can be achieved by increasing the length of disjunctions (cf. Sect. 3.1). Hence, algorithms constructing availability-maximizing clusters of size ≥ 3 should be developed on the operational level.

As known from Sect. 3.3, each disjunction of pairwise interchangeable disjuncts preserves definite information about all but one position of each ground atom and *generalizes* each distorted value to a wider set of possible values. This idea of generalizing values is similarly used for k-anonymization and ℓ-diversification [10,16,21]. So, it might be worthwhile to extend our approach to deal with confidentiality policies already containing disjunctions and to then model k-anonymization and ℓ-diversification within such an extension.

References

1. Abiteboul, S., Hull, R., Vianu, V.: Foundations of Databases. Addison-Wesley, Reading (1995)
2. Bertossi, L.E., Li, L.: Achieving data privacy through secrecy views and null-based virtual updates. IEEE Transactions on Knowledge and Data Engineering 25(5), 987–1000 (2013)
3. Biskup, J.: Inference-usability confinement by maintaining inference-proof views of an information system. International Journal of Computational Science and Engineering 7(1), 17–37 (2012)

4. Biskup, J., Bonatti, P.A.: Controlled query evaluation with open queries for a decidable relational submodel. Annals of Mathematics and Artificial Intelligence 50(1-2), 39–77 (2007)
5. Biskup, J., Hartmann, S., Link, S., Lochner, J.-H., Schlotmann, T.: Signature-based inference-usability confinement for relational databases under functional and join dependencies. In: Cuppens-Boulahia, N., Cuppens, F., Garcia-Alfaro, J. (eds.) DBSec 2012. LNCS, vol. 7371, pp. 56–73. Springer, Heidelberg (2012)
6. Biskup, J., Preuß, M.: Database fragmentation with encryption: Under which semantic constraints and a priori knowledge can two keep a secret? In: Wang, L., Shafiq, B. (eds.) DBSec 2013. LNCS, vol. 7964, pp. 17–32. Springer, Heidelberg (2013)
7. Biskup, J., Wiese, L.: A sound and complete model-generation procedure for consistent and confidentiality-preserving databases. Theoretical Computer Science 412(31), 4044–4072 (2011)
8. Boost Graph Library: Maximum cardinality matching (2014), http://www.boost.org/doc/libs/1_55_0/libs/graph/doc/maximum_matching.html
9. Campan, A., Truta, T.M.: Data and structural k-anonymity in social networks. In: Bonchi, F., Ferrari, E., Jiang, W., Malin, B. (eds.) PinKDD 2008. LNCS, vol. 5456, pp. 33–54. Springer, Heidelberg (2009)
10. Ciriani, V., De Capitani di Vimercati, S., Foresti, S., Samarati, P.: k-Anonymity. In: Yu, T., Jajodia, S. (eds.) Secure Data Management in Decentralized Systems. Advances in Information Security, vol. 33, pp. 323–353. Springer, New York (2007)
11. Fung, B.C., Wang, K., Fu, A.W.C., Yu, P.S.: Introduction to Privacy-Preserving Data Publishing: Concepts and Techniques. Data Mining and Knowledge Discovery. CRC Press, Boca Raton (2011)
12. Hay, M., Miklau, G., Jensen, D., Towsley, D.F., Li, C.: Resisting structural re-identification in anonymized social networks. VLDB Journal 19(6), 797–823 (2010)
13. Knuth, D.E.: The Stanford GraphBase: A Platform for Combinatorial Computing. ACM Press, New York (1993)
14. Korte, B., Vygen, J.: Combinatorial Optimization: Theory and Algorithms, 5th edn. Algorithms and Combinatorics. Springer, Heidelberg (2012)
15. Levesque, H.J., Lakemeyer, G.: The Logic of Knowledge Bases. The MIT Press, Cambridge (2000)
16. Machanavajjhala, A., Kifer, D., Gehrke, J., Venkitasubramaniam, M.: ℓ-diversity: Privacy beyond k-anonymity. ACM Transactions on Knowledge Discovery from Data 1(1) (2007)
17. Magun, J.: Greedy matching algorithms: An experimental study. ACM Journal of Experimental Algorithmics 3(6) (1998)
18. Mehlhorn, K., Näher, S.: LEDA: A platform for combinatorial and geometric computing. Cambridge University Press, Cambridge (1999)
19. Ramakrishnan, R., Gehrke, J.: Database Management Systems, 3rd edn. McGraw-Hill, Boston (2003)
20. Stiege, G.: Playing with Knuth's words.dat. Tech. Rep. 1/12, Department of Computer Science, University of Oldenburg, Germany (May 2012)
21. Sweeney, L.: k-anonymity: A model for protecting privacy. International Journal of Uncertainty, Fuzziness and Knowledge-Based Systems 10(5), 557–570 (2002)
22. Vazirani, V.V.: A theory of alternating paths and blossoms for proving correctness of the $O(\sqrt{|V|} \cdot |E|)$ general graph maximum matching algorithm. Combinatorica 14(1), 71–109 (1994)
23. Wong, R.C.W., Fu, A.W.C.: Privacy-Preserving Data Publishing – An Overview. Synthesis Lectures on Data Management. Morgan & Claypool Publishers, San Rafael (2010)

Extending Dolev-Yao with Assertions*

R. Ramanujam[1], Vaishnavi Sundararajan[2], and S.P. Suresh[2]

[1] Institute of Mathematical Sciences Chennai, India
jam@imsc.res.in
[2] Chennai Mathematical Institute, Chennai, India
{vaishnavi,spsuresh}@cmi.ac.in

Abstract. Cryptographic protocols often require principals to send certifications asserting partial knowledge of terms (for instance, that an encrypted secret is 0 or 1). Such certificates are themselves modelled by cryptographic primitives or sequences of communications. For logical analysis of such protocols based on the Dolev-Yao model [12], we suggest that it is useful to separate terms and assertions about them in communications. We propose a perfect assertion assumption by which the underlying model ensures the correctness of the assertion when it is generated. The recipient may then rely on the certificate but may only forward it as second-hand information. We use a simple propositional modal assertion language involving disjunction (for partial knowledge) and formulas of the form *A says α* (for delegation). We study the complexity of the term derivability problem and *safety checking* in the presence of an active intruder (for bounded protocols). We show that assertions add complexity to verification, but when they involve only boundedly many disjunctions, the complexity is the same as that of the standard Dolev-Yao model.

1 Motivation

1.1 Assertions as Certification

Formal verification of cryptographic protocols requires an abstract model of agents' capabilities and communications, and the **Dolev-Yao model** [12] has been the bulwark of such modelling. Its central elements are a *message abstraction* that views the message space as a term algebra and *term derivation rules* that specify how an agent derives new terms from old.

This model and its various extensions have been the object of study for the last 30 years. Typical extensions cater to more complex cryptographic operations like homomorphic encryption, blind signatures etc., that are useful in applications like e-voting and contract signing [15,6,11]. The interaction between the operators can have significant impact on term derivability, and forms an important line of theoretical research [9,15,10].

An important feature of the Dolev-Yao model is that it treats terms as tokens that can be copied and passed along. A recipient of a term "owns" it and can send it to others

---

* We thank A. Baskar for discussions and comments on many ideas in the paper. We also thank the reviewers for many suggestions that improved the paper.

A. Prakash and R. Shyamasundar (Eds.): ICISS 2014, LNCS 8880, pp. 50–68, 2014.

in its own name. On the other hand, cryptographic protocols often use *certificates* that can be verified but not "owned", i.e., an agent B which receives a certificate from A cannot later send the same certificate to C in its own name. Zero-knowledge protocols, for example, often involve agents certifying (via zero-knowledge proofs) that the terms they send to other agents possess certain properties, without revealing the entire terms. The recipient, if malicious, might try to forward this term to some other agent in its own name – however, the fact that the agent is required to have access to the entire term in order to construct the requisite certificate disallows it from being forwarded. Here are a few scenarios that illustrate the use of such certification, or *assertions*.

- A server S generates a session key k for A and B, and also certifies that the key is "good" for use by them.
- An agent A sends a vote v (encrypted) to B, along with a certificate that the vote is valid, i.e. v takes on only a few (pre-specified) values. It is not possible for B to forward this encrypted vote to someone else, and convince the receiver of its being valid, since a proof of validity might – and almost always will – require B to have access to the vote v. (Refer to [17] for more examples of this kind.)
- A passes on to B an assertion α made by S about a key k, but stating explicitly that S *says* α. (Assertions of this kind are used in [7].)

Such certification is expressed in the Dolev-Yao model in a variety of ways.

- In some cases, one relies on conventions and features of the framework, and does not explicitly model assertions in the protocol at all. Examples would be assertions about the goodness of keys, freshness of nonces etc.
- In other cases, one uses cryptographic devices like zero knowledge proofs, bit-commitment schemes etc. to make partial secrecy assertions. For example, a voter V might post an encrypted vote v along with a zero knowledge proof that v is either 0 or 1. This allows an authority to check that the voter and the vote are legitimate, without knowing the value of the vote.
- Sometimes one uses ad hoc conventions specific to a protocol to model some assertions. For instance, a term that models an assertion α might be paired (or tagged) with the agent name S to signify S *says* α.

In this paper, we propose an extension to the Dolev-Yao model in which agents have the ability to communicate assertions explicitly, rather than via an encoding. The fact that the above examples can be expressed in the Dolev-Yao model via various methods of translation seems to suggest that this ability does not add any expressive power. However, communicating both data and assertions gives significant flexibility for formal specification and reasoning about such protocols. In fact, the need for formal methods in security protocols goes beyond verification and includes ways of structuring protocols [1,2], and a syntactic separation of the term algebra and an associated logical language of assertions should be seen in this light.

A natural question would be: how are such assertions to be verified? Should the agent generating the assertion construct a proof and pass it along as well? This is the approach followed in protocols using zero-knowledge proofs [4]. In which case, should the proof thus sent be verified by the recipient?

While such an approach is adopted in models that view assertions as terms, in this work, the syntactic separation of terms and assertions allows us an abstraction similar to the perfect encryption assumption in the Dolev-Yao model. We call it the *perfect assertion assumption*: the model ensures the correctness of assertions at the point of generation, and honest principals assume such correctness and proceed. Thus the onus of verification shifts from the receiver of the assertion to the underlying system. This can be realized as a trusted third party (TTP) model, which verifies any proof that is sent out by any agent into the system. Note that since the adversary monitors the network, it can also see the proof sent by any agent to the TTP and replay assertions in agents' names, and therefore, adversary capabilities are not restricted much. Also note that the TTP is not a principal but an operational realisation of the network's capability to verify every proof that is sent out by agents. Thus we model assertions as signed by the sender, but not encrypted with any key (including that of the TTP). This will be explained further after we define the operational semantics of protocols, in Section 2.4.

How are assertions in our model contrasted with those with zero-knowledge primitives as in [3] or with those in which terms encode zero-knowledge proofs? Consider a simple example of an encrypted vote $\{v\}_k$, where v is either 0 or 1, and the recipient does not know k (or its inverse). In order to assert this using terms, one would present a one-out-of-2-encryption proof for v belonging to $\{0, 1\}$, as presented in [17]. In the model in [3], this would be coded up as $zk_{2,1,\beta_1 = enc(\alpha_1,\alpha_2) \wedge (\alpha_1 = 0 \vee \alpha_1 = 1)}(v, k; \{v\}_k)$. In our model, it is simply represented by the assertion $\{0 \prec \{v\}_k \vee 1 \prec \{v\}_k\}$.

1.2 Assertions in Protocols, and Possible Attacks

We now present a few example protocols illustrating how our model can be used. We also present some attacks where the malicious intruder targets the fact that assertions are transmitted, and tries to gain more information than she is entitled to. This motivates the need for studying the verification problem for protocols with assertions.

Example 1. An agent A sends two encrypted votes to a tallier T, one choice for each of two 'positions', and accompanies each vote with a disjunctive assertion about it. The disjunction may be thought of as expressing that the vote is for one of two possible candidates interested in the position. The tallier checks these assertions, and on confirming that they are indeed true, sends a confirmation c_A to A. Otherwise it sends a 0.

- $A \rightarrow T : \{v_1\}_{k_A},\ \{(a\ occurs\ in\ \{v_1\}_k) \vee (b\ occurs\ in\ \{v_1\}_k)\}$
- $A \rightarrow T : \{v_2\}_{k_A},\ \{(c\ occurs\ in\ \{v_2\}_k) \vee (d\ occurs\ in\ \{v_2\}_k)\}$
- If T confirms these two assertions, $T \rightarrow A : c_A$. Otherwise, $T \rightarrow A : 0$.

Now consider the situation where a particular candidate, say candidate a, is interested in both positions, i.e., $c = a$ in the above protocol. Now, if agent A votes for candidate a (i.e. $v_1 = v_2 = a$) for both positions, he/she sends the same term $\{a\}_{k_A}$ twice, with two disjunctive assertions about it. The intruder can now perform disjunction elimination on these assertions to know the fact that A's vote is for candidate a.

Example 2. An agent B sends an assertion as a response to a communication by another agent A.

- $A \rightarrow B : \{m\}_{pk(B)}$
- $B \rightarrow C : \{m\}_{pk(B)}, \big\{(a \ occurs \ in \ \{m\}_{pk(B)}) \vee (b \ occurs \ in \ \{m\}_{pk(B)})\big\}$

A sends *B* a term which is an encrypted nonce, about which *B* generates an assertion, and then passes on both the term and the assertion to agent *C*. *B*, while generating this disjunction, takes the actual assertion (say *a occurs in* $\{m\}_{pk(B)}$), and adds a disjunct of the form *r occurs in* $\{m\}_{pk(B)}$, where $r \neq a$ is chosen at random from the constants of the protocol. This allows the intruder an attack, whereby she begins a new session with *B* by replaying the same term $\{m\}_{pk(B)}$ from the session of *A* with *B*. Now *B* sends to *C* the same term with a new assertion $\big\{(a \ occurs \ in \ \{m\}_{pk(B)}) \vee (r' \ occurs \ in \ \{m\}_{pk(B)})\big\}$, where r' is another random constant of the protocol. In the earlier session, *B* sent *C* $\big\{(a \ occurs \ in \ \{m\}_{pk(B)}) \vee (r \ occurs \ in \ \{m\}_{pk(B)})\big\}$. By disjunction elimination, the intruder (and *C*) can infer that *a* occurs in $\{m\}_{pk(B)}$.

Example 3. Here is a scenario that might occur in contract signing protocols. Agents *A* and *S* are interested in buying and selling an object, respectively. *A* commits to a value *a*, by sending *S* a term $\{v_a\}_{k(A,S)}$ and an accompanying assertion of the form *a occurs in* $\{v_a\}_{k(A,S)}$, where *a* is his bid for the object. *S*, however, is not interested in honouring *A*'s commitment, and, without responding to *A*, sends agent *B* the assertion *A says* $\{a \ occurs \ in \ \{v_a\}_{k(A,S)}\}$. *B*, who is interested in buying this object at any cost, now quotes a price higher than what *A* quotes, and the seller *S* thereby gets an unfair advantage.

1.3 Logicization and Challenges

The above examples motivate the formal study of Dolev-Yao with assertions. But there are several questions that need to be addressed in building a formal model, and several consequences of the choices we make. We discuss some of them here.

Much as the Dolev-Yao model is a minimal term algebra with its derivation rules, we consider the extension with assertions also as a minimal logic with its associated derivation rules. We suggest a propositional modal language, with highly restricted use of negation and modalities, inspired by *infon logic* [14,5] (which reasons about access control). A priori, certification in cryptographic protocols reveals partial information about hidden (encrypted) terms, and hence we need assertions that achieve this. We use atomic assertions about term structure and disjunctions to make the revelations partial. For instance, (0 *occurs in t*) $\vee$ (1 *occurs in t*) can be seen as a *partial secrecy assertion*. Note that background knowledge of the Dolev-Yao model offers implicit atomic negation: 0 *occurs in* $\{m\}_k$ where *m* is atomic may exclude the assertion 1 *occurs in* $\{m\}_k$. With conjunctions to bundle assertions together, we have a restricted propositional language.

The modality we study is one that refers to agents passing assertions along, and has the flavour of *delegation*: *A* sending α to *B* allows *B* to send *A says* α to other agents, without requiring *B* to be able to derive α. Many papers which view assertions as terms work with assertions similar to the ones used here. For instance, [8] presents a new cryptographic primitive for partial information transmission, while [13] deals with delegation and signatures, although there the focus is more on anonymity and group signatures.

We conduct a proof theoretic investigation of passive intruder capabilities, and we also illustrate the use of these assertions for exploring active intruder attacks. The passive intruder deduction problem (or the term derivability problem) is co-NP-hard even for the simple language that we work with, and has a PSPACE upper bound. The high complexity is mainly due to the presence of disjunctions, but we rarely need an unbounded number of disjunctions. When we bound the number of disjunctions, the term derivability problem is in polynomial time. We also explore the complexity of security verification for the active intruder case, and provide a PSPACE upper bound for protocols with boundedly many sessions, with an NP upper bound when the number of disjunctions is bounded as well.

2 Model

2.1 The Term Model

Fix countable sets Ag, $\mathcal{N}$ and $\mathcal{K}$, denoting the set of *agents*, *nonces* and *keys*, respectively. The set of *basic terms* is $\mathscr{B} = Ag \cup \mathcal{N} \cup \mathcal{K}$. For each $A, B \in Ag$, assume that $sk(A)$, $pk(A)$ and $k(A, B)$ are keys. Further, each $k \in \mathcal{K}$ has an *inverse* defined as follows: $inv(pk(A)) = sk(A)$, $inv(sk(A)) = pk(A)$ and $inv(k) = k$ for the other keys. The set $\mathscr{T}$ of Dolev-Yao terms is given by the following syntax (where $m \in \mathscr{B}$ and $k \in \mathcal{K}$):

$$t := m \mid (t_1, t_2) \mid \{t\}_k$$

For $X \subseteq_{\text{fin}} \mathscr{T}$, we define $\overline{X}$, the *closure* of X, to be the smallest $Y \subseteq \mathscr{T}$ such that (i) $X \subseteq Y$, (ii) $(t, t') \in Y$ iff $\{t, t'\} \subseteq Y$, (iii) if $\{t, k\} \subseteq Y$ then $\{t\}_k \in Y$, and (iv) if $\{\{t\}_k, inv(k)\} \subseteq Y$ then $t \in Y$. We use the notation $X \vdash_{dy} t$ to denote that $t \in \overline{X}$, and $X \vdash_{dy} T$ to denote that $T \subseteq \overline{X}$, for a set of terms T.

We use $st(t)$ to denote the set of *subterms* of t and $st(X) = \bigcup_{t \in X} st(t)$ in Proposition 4, which is a well-known fact about the basic Dolev-Yao model [18].

Proposition 4. *Given $X \subseteq \mathscr{T}$ and $t \in \mathscr{T}$, it can be decided whether $X \vdash_{dy} t$ in time linear in $|st(X \cup \{t\})|$.*

2.2 The Assertion Language

The set of assertions, $\mathscr{A}$, is given by the following syntax:

$$\alpha := m \prec t \mid t = t' \mid \alpha_1 \vee \alpha_2 \mid \alpha_1 \wedge \alpha_2$$

where $m \in \mathscr{B}$ and $t, t' \in \mathscr{T}$. The assertion $m \prec t$ is to be read as *m occurs in t*. The set of *subformulas* of a formula α is denoted $sf(\alpha)$.

The proof rules for assertions are presented as **sequents** of the form $X, \Phi \vdash \alpha$, where X and Φ are finite sets of terms and assertions respectively, and α is an assertion. For ease of presentation, we present the rules in two parts. Figure 1 gives the rules pertaining to propositional reasoning with assertions. The rules capture basic reasoning with conjunction and disjunction, and $\perp$ is a restricted contradiction rule.

$$\frac{}{X, \Phi \cup \{\alpha\} \vdash \alpha} \ ax_1 \qquad \frac{X, \Phi \vdash m \prec \{b\}_k \quad X, \Phi \vdash n \prec \{b\}_k}{X, \Phi \vdash \alpha} \perp \ (m \neq n; \ b \in \mathscr{B})$$

$$\frac{X, \Phi \vdash \alpha_1 \quad X, \Phi \vdash \alpha_2}{X, \Phi \vdash \alpha_1 \wedge \alpha_2} \ \wedge i \qquad \frac{X, \Phi \vdash \alpha_1 \wedge \alpha_2}{X, \Phi \vdash \alpha_i} \ \wedge e$$

$$\frac{X, \Phi \vdash \alpha_i}{X, \Phi \vdash \alpha_1 \vee \alpha_2} \ \vee i \qquad \frac{X, \Phi \vdash \alpha_1 \vee \alpha_2 \quad X, \Phi \cup \{\alpha_1\} \vdash \beta \quad X, \Phi \cup \{\alpha_2\} \vdash \beta}{X, \Phi \vdash \beta} \ \vee e$$

Fig. 1. The rules for deriving assertions: propositional fragment

We next present the rules for atomic assertions of the form $m \prec t$ and $t = t$ in Figure 2. Note that all these rules require X to be nonempty, and some of the rules refer to derivations in the Dolev-Yao theory. For an agent to derive an assertion about a term t, it should know the entire structure of t, which is modelled by saying that from X one can learn (in the Dolev-Yao theory) all basic terms occurring in t. For example, in the *split* rule, suppose the agent can derive from X all of $st(t_i) \cap \mathscr{B}$, and that m is not a basic term in t. The agent can now derive $m \prec t_{1-i}$ from $m \prec (t_0, t_1)$.

$$\frac{X \vdash_{dy} m}{X, \Phi \vdash m \prec m} \ ax_2 \qquad \frac{X \vdash_{dy} st(t) \cap \mathscr{B}}{X, \Phi \vdash t = t} \ eq$$

$$\frac{X \vdash_{dy} \{t\}_k \quad X \vdash_{dy} k \quad X, \Phi \vdash m \prec t}{X, \Phi \vdash m \prec \{t\}_k} \ enc \qquad \frac{X \vdash_{dy} inv(k) \quad X, \Phi \vdash m \prec \{t\}_k}{X, \Phi \vdash m \prec t} \ dec$$

$$\frac{X \vdash_{dy} (t_0, t_1) \quad X, \Phi \vdash m \prec t_i \quad X \vdash_{dy} st(t_{1-i}) \cap \mathscr{B}}{X, \Phi \vdash m \prec (t_0, t_1)} \ pair$$

$$\frac{X, \Phi \vdash m \prec (t_0, t_1) \cdot \quad X \vdash_{dy} st(t_i) \cap \mathscr{B} \quad m \notin st(t_i)}{X, \Phi \vdash m \prec t_{1-i}} \ split$$

Fig. 2. The rules for atomic assertions

We denote by $X, \Phi \vdash_{alp} \alpha$ (resp. $X, \Phi \vdash_{alat} \alpha$; $X, \Phi \vdash_{al} \alpha$) the fact that there is a derivation of $X, \Phi \vdash \alpha$ using the rules in Figure 1 (resp. ax_1 and the rules in Figure 2; the rules in Figures 1 and 2).

2.3 The Protocol Model

Protocols are typically specified as sequences of communications, but in formal analysis, it is convenient to consider a protocol Pr as a pair $(const, R)$ where $const \subseteq \mathscr{B}$ is a set of constants of Pr and R is a finite set of *roles*. For an agent A, an A-role is a sequence of A-actions. A-actions include send actions of the form $A!B:[(M)t, \{\alpha\}_{sd(A)}]$, and receive actions of the form $A?B:[t, \{\alpha\}_{sd(B)}]$. Here $B \in Ag$, $t \in \mathscr{T}$, $M \subseteq \mathscr{N}$, $\alpha \in \mathscr{A}$, and $\{\alpha\}_{sd(A)}$ denotes the assertion α signed by A. In the send action above, B is merely the intended recipient, and in the receive action, B is merely the purported sender, since we assume the presence of an intruder who can block or forge messages, and can see every communication on the network. For simplicity, we assume that all send and receive actions deal with one term and one assertion. $(M)t$ denotes that the set M contains the nonces used in t, in the context of a protocol run, which are *fresh*, i.e., not used till that point in the run. An additional detail is that *assertions* in sends are always signed by the actual sender, and assertions in receives are signed by the purported sender. Thus, when the intruder I sends an assertion $\{\alpha\}_{sd(A)}$ to someone, it is either replaying an earlier communication from A, or $A = I$ and it can construct α.

We admit two other types of actions in our model, *confirm* and *deny*, to capture conditional branching in protocol specifications. An agent A might, at some stage in a protocol, perform action a_1 if a condition is verified to be true, and a_2 otherwise. For simplicity, we let any assertion be a condition. The behaviour of A in a protocol, in the presence of a branch on condition α, is represented by two sequences of actions, one in which A confirms α and one in which it denies α. These actions are denoted by $A : confirm\ \alpha$ and $A : deny\ \alpha$.

A *knowledge state* ks is of the form $((X_A)_{A \in Ag}, \Phi, SD)$. Here, $X_A \subseteq \mathscr{T}$ is the set of terms accumulated by A in the course of a protocol run till the point under consideration. $\Phi \subseteq \mathscr{A}$ is the set of assertions that have been communicated by any agent (and stored by the intruder). Similarly, $SD \subseteq \{\{\alpha\}_{sd(B)} \mid B \in Ag, \alpha \in \mathscr{A}\}$ is the set of signed assertions communicated by any agent and stored by the intruder.

The *initial knowledge state* of a protocol Pr is $((X_A)_{A \in Ag}, \varnothing, \varnothing)$ where, for each A, $X_A = const(Pr) \cup Ag \cup \{sk(A)\} \cup \{pk(B), k(A, B) \mid B \in Ag\}$.

Let $ks = ((X_A)_{A \in Ag}, \Phi, SD)$ and $ks' = ((X'_A)_{A \in Ag}, \Phi', SD')$ be two knowledge states and a be a send or a receive action. We now describe the conditions under which the execution of a changes ks to ks', denoted $ks \xrightarrow{a} ks'$.

- $a = A!B:[(M)t, \{\alpha\}_{sd(A)}]$
  - a is enabled at ks iff
    * $M \cap X_C = \varnothing$ for all C,
    * $X_A \cup M \vdash_{dy} t$, and
    * $X_A \cup M, \varnothing \vdash_{al} \alpha$.
  - $ks \xrightarrow{a} ks'$ iff
    * $X'_A = X_A \cup M$, $X'_I = X_I \cup \{t\}$,
    * $\Phi' = \Phi \cup \{\alpha\}$, and
    * $SD' = SD \cup \{\{\alpha\}_{sd(A)}\}$.
- $a = A?B:[t, \{\alpha\}_{sd(B)}]$
  - a is enabled at ks iff
    * $\{\alpha\}_{sd(B)}$ is verified as signed by B,
    * $X_I \vdash_{dy} t$, and
    * either $B = I$ and $X_I, \Phi \vdash_{al} \alpha$, or $\{\alpha\}_{sd(B)} \in SD$.
  - $ks \xrightarrow{a} ks'$ iff
    * $X'_A = X_A \cup \{t\}$.

- $a = A : confirm\ \alpha$ is enabled at ks iff $X_A, \varnothing \vdash_{al} \alpha$, and $ks \overset{a}{\to} ks'$ iff $ks = ks'$.
- $a = A : deny\ \alpha$ is enabled at ks iff $X_A, \varnothing \nvdash_{al} \alpha$, and $ks \overset{a}{\to} ks'$ iff $ks = ks'$.

We see that when an agent A sends an assertion α, the intruder stores α in its set of assertions, as well as storing $\{\alpha\}_{sd(A)}$ for possible replay, but honest agents only get to send assertions that they themselves generate from scratch.

A substitution σ is a homomorphism on $\mathscr{T}$ such that $\sigma(Ag) \subseteq Ag$, $\sigma(\mathscr{N}) \subseteq \mathscr{N}$ and $\sigma(\mathscr{K}) \subseteq \mathscr{K}$. σ is said to be suitable for a protocol $Pr = (const, R)$ if $\sigma(m) = m$ for all $m \in const$.

A *role instance* of a protocol Pr is a tuple $ri = (\eta, \sigma, lp)$, where η is a role of Pr, σ is a substitution suitable for Pr, and $0 \leq lp \leq |\eta|$. $ri = (\eta, \sigma, 0)$ is said to be an *initial role instance*. The set of role instances of Pr is denoted by $RI(Pr)$. $IRI(Pr)$ is the set of initial role instances of Pr. For $ri = (\eta, \sigma, lp)$, $ri + 1 = (\eta, \sigma, lp + 1)$. If $ri = (\eta, \sigma, lp)$, $lp \geq 1$ and $\eta = a_1 \cdots a_\ell$, $act(ri) = \sigma(a_{lp})$. For $S, S' \subseteq RI(Pr)$ and $ri \in RI(Pr)$, we say that $S \overset{ri}{\to} S'$ iff $ri \in S$, $ri + 1 \in RI(Pr)$ and $S' = (S \setminus \{ri\}) \cup \{ri + 1\}$.

A **protocol state** of Pr is a pair $s = (ks, S)$ where ks is a knowledge state of Pr and $S \subseteq RI(Pr)$. $s = (ks, S)$ is an initial protocol state if ks is initial and $S \subseteq IRI(Pr)$. For two protocol states $s = (ks, S)$ and $s' = (ks', S')$, and an action a, we say that $s \overset{a}{\to} s'$ iff there is $ri \in S$ such that $act(ri+1) = a$ and $S \overset{ri}{\to} S'$, and $ks \overset{a}{\to} ks'$. The states, initial states, and transitions defined above induce a transition system on protocol states, denoted $TS(Pr)$. A **run** of a protocol Pr is any run of $TS(Pr)$.

2.4   Comments on the Transition Rules

The rules for transitioning from a knowledge state, ks, to another, ks', on an action a, deserve some explanation. The change pertaining to the X_A is easily justified by an operational model in which the intruder can snoop on the entire network, but agents are allowed to send only messages they generate. We have extended the same logic to assertions as well, but there is the extra complication of signing the assertions. The intruder typically has access only to its own signature. Thus we posit that the intruder can *replay* assertions signed by another agent A (in case it is passing something in A's name), or that it can generate assertions and sign them in its own name.

As an operational justification for why the honest agents cannot use assertions sent by other agents, we can imagine the following concrete model. There is a trusted third party verifier (TTP) that allows assertions to be transmitted at large only after the sender provides a justification to the TTP. This means that an honest agent B who receives an assertion α from A cannot pass it on to others, because the TTP will demand a justification for this, which B cannot provide. The intruder, though, can snoop on the network, so it has the bits that A sent as justification for α to the TTP, and can thus produce it whenever demanded. Thus the intruder gets to store α in its local database.

2.5   Example Protocol

Recall Example 2 and the attack on it from Section 1.2, reproduced below. We formalize the attack using the transition rules given in Section 2.3.

- $A \rightarrow B : \{m\}_{pk(B)}$
- $B \rightarrow C : \{m\}_{pk(B)}, \{(a < \{m\}_{pk(B)}) \vee (b < \{m\}_{pk(B)})\}_{sd(B)}$

The attack is informally presented below and is formalized in Figure 3.

1. $A \rightarrow B : \{m\}_{pk(B)}$
2. $B \rightarrow C : \{m\}_{pk(B)}, \{(a < \{m\}_{pk(B)}) \vee (r < \{m\}_{pk(B)})\}_{sd(B)}$
3. $I \rightarrow B : \{m\}_{pk(B)}$
4. $B \rightarrow C : \{m\}_{pk(B)}, \{(a < \{m\}_{pk(B)}) \vee (r' < \{m\}_{pk(B)})\}_{sd(B)}$

η_1 : A-role, $\sigma_1(m) = 1$
a_{11} : $A!B$: $\{m\}_{pk(B)}$
η_2 : B-role, $\sigma_2(m) = 1$, $\sigma_2(a) = 1$, $\sigma_2(r) = 3$
a_{21} : $B?A$: $\{m\}_{pk(B)}$
a_{22} : $B!C$: $\{m\}_{pk(B)}, \{(a < \{m\}_{pk(B)}) \vee (r < \{m\}_{pk(B)})\}_{sd(B)}$
η_3 : C-role, $\sigma_3(m) = 1$, $\sigma_3(a) = 1$, $\sigma_3(r) = 3$
a_{31} : $C?B$: $\{m\}_{pk(B)}, \{(a < \{m\}_{pk(B)}) \vee (r < \{m\}_{pk(B)})\}_{sd(B)}$
η_4 : A-role, $\sigma_4(m) = 1$, $\sigma_4(A) = I$
a_{41} : $A!B$: $\{m\}_{pk(B)}$
η_5 : B-role, $\sigma_5(m) = 1$, $\sigma_5(a) = 1$, $\sigma_5(r) = 2$, $\sigma_5(A) = I$
a_{51} : $B?A$: $\{m\}_{pk(B)}$
a_{52} : $B!C$: $\{m\}_{pk(B)}, \{(a < \{m\}_{pk(B)}) \vee (r < \{m\}_{pk(B)})\}_{sd(B)}$
η_6 : C-role, $\sigma_6(m) = 1$, $\sigma_6(a) = 1$, $\sigma_6(r) = 2$
a_{61} : $C?B$: $\{m\}_{pk(B)}, \{(a < \{m\}_{pk(B)}) \vee (r < \{m\}_{pk(B)})\}_{sd(B)}$

Fig. 3. The attack, formalized

In the formalized attack, note that only the actions a_{22} and a_{52} send assertions. It can be seen by applying the given substitutions to these actions, and using the appropriate update actions from the criteria for the change of the knowledge states (as stated earlier), that at the end of this sequence of actions, $\Phi = \{\alpha \vee \beta, \alpha \vee \gamma\}$, where $\alpha = 1 < \{1\}_{pk(B)}$, $\beta = 2 < \{1\}_{pk(B)}$ and $\gamma = 3 < \{1\}_{pk(B)}$.

The intruder can now use these assertions in Φ to perform disjunction elimination, as illustrated in the following proof, and thereby gain the information that the term sent by A is actually $\{1\}_{pk(B)}$, which was supposed to be 'secret'. Thus we see that this protocol admits a run in which there is a reachable state where the intruder is able to learn a secret. This can be thought of as a violation of safety. We elaborate on this idea of safety checking in Section 4.

$$
\cfrac{
  \cfrac{
    \cfrac{}{\Phi \vdash \alpha \vee \beta}\ ax_1
    \qquad
    \cfrac{}{\Phi, \alpha \vdash \alpha}\ ax_1
    \qquad
    \cfrac{
      \cfrac{}{\Phi, \beta \vdash \alpha \vee \gamma}\ ax_1
      \qquad
      \cfrac{}{\Phi, \beta, \alpha \vdash \alpha}\ ax_1
      \qquad
      \cfrac{
        \cfrac{}{\Phi, \beta, , \gamma \vdash \beta}\ ax_1
        \qquad
        \cfrac{
          \cfrac{}{\Phi, \beta, \gamma \vdash \gamma}\ ax_1
        }{\Phi, \beta, \gamma \vdash \alpha}\ \bot
      }{\Phi, \beta, \gamma \vdash \alpha}\ \vee e
    }{\Phi, \beta \vdash \alpha}\ \vee e
  }{}
}{\Phi \vdash \alpha}\ \vee e
$$

3 The Derivability Problem and Its Complexity

The **derivability problem** (or the **passive intruder deduction problem**) is the following: given $X \subseteq \mathcal{T}$, $\Phi \subseteq \mathcal{A}$ and $\alpha \in \mathcal{A}$, determine if $X, \Phi \vdash_{al} \alpha$. In this section, we provide a lower bound and an upper bound for this problem, and also some optimizations to the derivability algorithm.

3.1 Properties of the Proof System

The following is a useful property that will be crucially used in the lower bound proof. The proof can be found in [16].

Proposition 5. $X, \Phi \cup \{\alpha \vee \beta\} \vdash_{al} \delta$ iff $X, \Phi \cup \{\alpha\} \vdash_{al} \delta$ and $X, \Phi \cup \{\beta\} \vdash_{al} \delta$.

Among the rules, *split*, *dec*, $\wedge e$ and $\vee e$ are the **elimination rules**. The rules ax_1, ax_2, *eq*, *split*, *dec* and $\wedge e$ are the **safe rules**, and the rest are the **unsafe rules**. A **normal derivation** is one where no elimination rule has as its major premise the conclusion of an unsafe rule. The following fundamental theorem is on standard lines, and is provided in [16].

Theorem 6. *If there is a derivation of* $X, \Phi \vdash \alpha$ *then there is a normal derivation of* $X, \Phi \vdash \alpha$.

The following corollaries easily follow by a simple case analysis on derivations.

Corollary 7. *If* π *is a normal derivation of* $X, \Phi \vdash \alpha$ *and if the formula* β *occurs in* π, *then* $\beta \in sf(\Phi \cup \{\alpha\})$.

Corollary 8. *If* $\varnothing, \Phi \vdash_{al} \alpha$ *and* Φ *consists only of atomic assertions, then there is a derivation of the sequent* $\varnothing, \Phi \vdash \alpha$ *consisting of only the ax,* $\wedge i$, $\vee i$ *and* $\perp$ *rules.*

A set of atomic assertions Φ is said to be *contradictory* if there exist distinct nonces m, n, and a nonce b and key k such that both $m \prec \{b\}_k$ and $n \prec \{b\}_k$ are in Φ. Otherwise Φ is *non-contradictory*.

Corollary 9. *If* $\varnothing, \Phi \vdash_{al} \alpha$ *and* Φ *is a non-contradictory set of atomic assertions, then there is a derivation of* $\varnothing, \Phi \vdash \alpha$ *consisting of only the ax,* $\wedge i$ *and* $\vee i$ *rules.*

Definition 10 (Derivability Problem). *Given* $X \subseteq_{fin} \mathcal{T}$, $\Phi \subseteq_{fin} \mathcal{A}$, $\alpha \in \mathcal{A}$, *is it the case that* $X, \Phi \vdash_{al} \alpha$?

We first show that the problem is co-NP-hard, and then go on to provide a PSPACE decision procedure. In fact, the hardness result holds even for the propositional fragment of the proof system (consisting of the rules in Figure 1).

3.2 Lower Bound

The hardness result is obtained by reducing the validity problem for propositional logic to the derivability problem. In fact, it suffices to consider the validity problem for propositional formulas in disjunctive normal form for our reduction. We show how to define for each formula φ in disjunctive normal form a set of assertions S_φ and an assertion $\overline{\varphi}$ such that $\varnothing, S_\varphi \vdash \overline{\varphi}$ iff φ is a tautology.

Let $\{p_1, p_2, \ldots\}$ be the set of all propositional variables. Fix infinitely many nonces $n_1, n_2, \ldots$ and a key k. We define $\overline{\varphi}$ as follows, by induction.

- $\overline{p_i} = (1 \prec \{n_i\}_k)$
- $\overline{\neg p_i} = (0 \prec \{n_i\}_k)$
- $\overline{\varphi \vee \psi} = \overline{\varphi} \vee \overline{\psi}$
- $\overline{\varphi \wedge \psi} = \overline{\varphi} \wedge \overline{\psi}$

Suppose $\{p_1, \ldots, p_n\}$ is the set of all propositional variables occurring in φ. Then $S_\varphi = \{\overline{p_1 \vee \neg p_1}, \ldots, \overline{p_n \vee \neg p_n}\}$.

Lemma 11. $\varnothing, S_\varphi \vdash_{al} \overline{\varphi}$ *iff* φ *is a tautology.*

Proof.   For $v \subseteq \{p_1, \ldots, p_n\}$, define $S_v = \{\overline{p_i} \mid p_i \in v\} \cup \{\overline{\neg p_i} \mid p_i \notin v\}$. Note that S_v is a non-contradictory set of atomic assertions.

By repeated appeal to Proposition 5, it is easy to see that $\varnothing, S_\varphi \vdash_{al} \overline{\varphi}$ iff for all valuations v over $\{p_1, \ldots, p_n\}$, $\varnothing, S_v \vdash_{al} \overline{\varphi}$. We now show that $\varnothing, S_v \vdash_{al} \overline{\varphi}$ iff $v \models \varphi$. The statement of the lemma follows immediately from this.

- We first show by induction on $\psi \in sf(\varphi)$ that $\varnothing, S_v \vdash_{al} \overline{\psi}$ whenever $v \models \psi$.
  - If $\psi = p_i$ or $\psi = \neg p_i$, then $\varnothing, S_v \vdash_{al} \overline{\psi}$ follows from the ax_1 rule.
  - If $\psi = \psi_1 \wedge \psi_2$, then it is the case that $v \models \psi_1$ and $v \models \psi_2$. But then, by induction hypothesis, $\varnothing, S_v \vdash_{al} \overline{\psi_1}$ and $\varnothing, S_v \vdash_{al} \overline{\psi_2}$. Hence, by using $\wedge i$, it follows that $\varnothing, S_v \vdash_{al} \overline{\psi_1 \wedge \psi_2}$.
  - If $\psi = \psi_1 \vee \psi_2$, then it is the case that either $v \models \psi_1$ or $v \models \psi_2$. But then, by induction hypothesis, $\varnothing, S_v \vdash_{al} \overline{\psi_1}$ or $\varnothing, S_v \vdash_{al} \overline{\psi_2}$. In either case, by using $\vee i$, it follows that $\varnothing, S_v \vdash_{al} \overline{\psi_1 \vee \psi_2}$.
- We now show that if $\varnothing, S_v \vdash_{al} \overline{\varphi}$, then $v \models \varphi$. Suppose $\varnothing, S_v \vdash_{al} \overline{\varphi}$. Since S_v is a non-contradictory set of atomic assertions, by Corollary 8, there is a derivation π of $\varnothing, S_v \vdash \overline{\varphi}$ that consists of only the ax, $\wedge i$ and $\vee i$ rules. We now show by induction that for all subproofs π' of π with conclusion $\varnothing, S_v \vdash \overline{\psi}$ that $v \models \psi$.
  - Suppose the last rule of π' is ax_1. Then $\overline{\psi} \in S_v$, and for some $i \leq n$, $\psi = p_i$ or $\psi = \neg p_i$. It can be easily seen by definition of S_v that $v \models \psi$.
  - Suppose the last rule of π' is $\wedge i$. Then $\overline{\psi} = \overline{\psi_1} \wedge \overline{\psi_2}$, and $\varnothing, S_v \vdash_{al} \overline{\psi_1}$ and $\varnothing, S_v \vdash_{al} \overline{\psi_2}$. Thus, by induction hypothesis, $v \models \psi_1$ and $v \models \psi_2$. Therefore $v \models \psi$.
  - Suppose the last rule of π' is $\vee i$. Then $\overline{\psi} = \overline{\psi_1} \vee \overline{\psi_2}$, and either $\varnothing, S_v \vdash_{al} \overline{\psi_1}$ or $\varnothing, S_v \vdash_{al} \overline{\psi_2}$. Thus, by induction hypothesis, either $v \models \psi_1$ or $v \models \psi_2$. Therefore $v \models \psi$.   ⊣

Theorem 12. *The derivability problem is co-NP-hard.*

3.3 Upper Bound

Fix X_0, Φ_0 and α_0. Let $\mathsf{sf} = sf(\Phi_0 \cup \{\alpha_0\})$, $|\mathsf{sf}| = N$, and st be the set of all terms occurring in all assertions in sf. To check whether $X_0, \Phi_0 \vdash \alpha_0$, we check whether α_0 is in the set $deriv(X_0, \Phi_0) = \{\alpha \in \mathsf{sf} \mid X_0, \Phi_0 \vdash \alpha\}$. Below we describe a general procedure to compute $deriv(X, \Phi)$ for any $X \subseteq \mathsf{st}$ and $\Phi \subseteq \mathsf{sf}$.

For $X \subseteq \mathsf{st}$ and $\Phi \subseteq \mathsf{sf}$, define

$deriv'(X, \Phi) = \{\alpha \in \mathsf{sf} \mid X, \Phi \vdash \alpha$ has a derivation which does not use the $\vee e$ rule $\}$

Lemma 13. *$deriv'(X, \Phi)$ is computable in time polynomial in N.*

Proof.   Let $Y = \{t \in \mathsf{st} \mid X \vdash_{dy} t\}$. Start with $S = \Phi$ and repeatedly add $\alpha \in \mathsf{sf}$ to S whenever α is the conclusion of a rule *other than* $\vee e$ all of whose premises are in $S \cup Y$. Since there are at most N formulas to add to S, and at each step it takes at most N^2 time to check to add a formula, the procedure runs in time polynomial in N.   ⊣

We now present the algorithm to compute $deriv(X, \Phi)$. It is presented as two mutually recursive functions f and g, where $g(X, \Phi)$ captures the effect of one application of $\vee e$ for each formula $\alpha_1 \vee \alpha_2 \in \Phi$, and f iterates g appropriately.

```
1: function g(X, Φ)
2:     S ← Φ
3:     for all α₁ ∨ α₂ ∈ S do
4:         if α₁ ∉ S and α₂ ∉ S then
5:             T ← {β ∈ f(X, S ∪ {α₁})}
6:             U ← {β ∈ f(X, S ∪ {α₂})}
7:             S ← S ∪ (T ∩ U)
8:         end if
9:     end for
10:    return deriv'(X, S)
11: end function
```

```
1: function f(X, Φ)
2:     S ← Φ
3:     while S ≠ g(X, S) do
4:         S ← g(X, S)
5:     end while
6:     return S
7: end function
```

The following theorem asserts the correctness of the algorithm, and its proof follows from Propositions 20 (Soundness) and 21 (Completeness), presented in Appendix A.

Theorem 14. *For $X \subseteq \mathsf{st}$ and $\Phi \subseteq \mathsf{sf}$, $f(X, \Phi) = deriv(X, \Phi)$.*

3.4 Analysis of the Algorithm

The nesting depth of recursion in the function f is at most $2N$. We can therefore show that $f(X, \Phi)$ can be computed in $O(N^2)$ space; the proof idea is presented below.

Modify the algorithm for $deriv(X, \Phi)$ using $3N$ global variables S_i, T_i, U_i (i ranging from 0 to $N - 1$), each a bit vector of length N. The procedures f and g take a third argument i, representing the depth of the call in the call tree of $f(X, \Phi, 0)$. $f(\cdot, \cdot, i)$ and $g(\cdot, \cdot, i)$ use the variables S_i, T_i, U_i. Further, $f(\cdot, \cdot, i)$ makes calls to $g(\cdot, \cdot, i)$ and $g(\cdot, \cdot, i)$ makes calls to $f(\cdot, \cdot, i + 1)$. Since the nesting depth is at most $2N$, the implicit variables on the call stack for arguments and return values are also $O(N)$ in number, so the overall space used is $O(N^2)$.

Theorem 15. *The derivability problem is in PSPACE.*

3.5 Optimization: Bounded Number of Disjunctions

Since the complexity in the algorithm resides mainly in handling $\vee e$, it is worth considering the problem restricted to p disjunctions (independent of N). In this case, the height of the call tree is bounded by $2p$, and since each $f(\cdot, \cdot, i)$ makes at most N calls to $g(\cdot, \cdot, i)$ and each $g(\cdot, \cdot, i)$ makes at most N calls to $f(\cdot, \cdot, i+1)$, it follows that the total number of calls to f and g is at most N^{2p}. Since $deriv'$ (used by g) can be computed in polynomial time, we have the following theorem.

Theorem 16. *The derivability problem with bounded number of disjunctions is solvable in PTIME.*

As a finer optimization, $deriv'(X, \Phi)$ can be computed in time $O(N)$ by a graph marking algorithm of the kind presented in [14]. This gives an even better running time for the derivability problem in general.

4 Safety Checking

The previous section concentrated on the derivability problem, which pertains to a passive intruder that only derives new terms and assertions from its store of terms and assertions, without engaging with other agents actively. But the important verification problem to study is to *determine the presence of attacks in a protocol*. An attack is typically a sequence of actions conforming to a protocol, with the intruder actively orchestrating communications of the other principals. Formally, an attack on Pr is a run of $TS(Pr)$ that leads to an undesirable system state. The concept is formalized below.

Definition 17 (Safety checking and bounded safety checking). *Let Safe be an arbitrary, but fixed safety predicate (i.e. a set of protocol states).*

Safety Checking: Given a protocol Pr, is some protocol state $s \notin$ Safe reachable in TS(Pr) from an initial protocol state?

k-bounded safety checking: Given Pr, is some protocol state $s \notin$ Safe with at most k-role instances reachable in TS(Pr) from an initial protocol state?

Theorem 18. 1. *If membership in Safe is decidable in PSPACE, the k-bounded safety checking w.r.t. Safe is solved in PSPACE.*
2. *If membership in Safe is decidable in NP, the k-bounded safety checking w.r.t. Safe is in NP if we restrict our attention to protocols with at most p disjunctions, for a fixed p.*

Proof.

1. A run of Pr starting from an initial state with at most k role instances is of length linear in the sum of the lengths of all roles in Pr. A PSPACE algorithm can go through all such runs to see if an unsafe protocol state is reachable. To check that each action is enabled at the appropriate protocol state along a run, we need to solve linearly many instances of the derivability problem, which runs in PSPACE. Thus the problem is in PSPACE.

2. One can guess a sequence of protocol states and actions of length linear in the size of Pr and verify that all the actions are enabled at the appropriate states. Since we are considering a protocol with at most p disjunctions for a fixed p, along each run we consider, there will be at most $k * p$ disjunctions, which is still independent of the size of the input. To check that actions are enabled at the appropriate states, we need to solve linearly many instances of the derivability problem (with bounded number of disjunctions this time) which can be done in polynomial time. Thus the problem is in NP. ⊣

5 Extending the Assertion Language

The assertion language presented in 2.2 used disjunction to achieve transmission of partial knowledge. It should be noted that the assertion language used is not constrained to be the same as that one, and various operators and modalities may be added to achieve other desirable properties. In this section, we demonstrate one such addition, namely the *says* modality.

5.1 Assertion Language with *says*

The set of assertions, $\mathscr{A}$, is now given by the following syntax:

$$\alpha := m \prec t \mid t = t' \mid \alpha_1 \vee \alpha_2 \mid \alpha_1 \wedge \alpha_2 \mid A \textit{ says } \alpha$$

The *says* modality captures the flavour of delegation. An agent B, upon sending agent C the assertion A *says* α, conveys to C that he has obtained this assertion α from the agent A, and that while he himself has no proof of α, A does. A has, in essence, allowed him to transmit this assertion to other agents.

$$\frac{X, \Phi \vdash \sigma : (m \prec \{b\}_k) \quad X, \Phi \vdash \sigma : (n \prec \{b\}_k)}{X, \Phi \vdash \sigma : \alpha} \perp (m \neq n)$$

$$\frac{X, \Phi \vdash \sigma : \alpha_1 \quad X, \Phi \vdash \sigma : \alpha_2}{X, \Phi \vdash \sigma : (\alpha_1 \wedge \alpha_2)} \wedge i \qquad \frac{X, \Phi \vdash \sigma : (\alpha_1 \wedge \alpha_2)}{X, \Phi \vdash \sigma : \alpha_i} \wedge e \qquad \frac{X, \Phi \vdash \sigma : \alpha_i}{X, \Phi \vdash \sigma : (\alpha_1 \vee \alpha_2)} \vee i$$

$$\frac{X, \Phi \vdash \sigma : (\alpha_1 \vee \alpha_2) \quad X, \Phi \cup \{\sigma : \alpha_1\} \vdash \sigma : \beta \quad X, \Phi \cup \{\sigma : \alpha_2\} \vdash \sigma : \beta}{X, \Phi \vdash \sigma : \beta} \vee e$$

Fig. 4. The rules for *says* assertions

Figure 4 gives rules for assertions of the form A *says* α. For $\sigma = A_1 A_2 \cdots A_n$, $\sigma : \alpha$ denotes A_1 *says* (A_2 *says* $\cdots$ (A_n *says* α) $\cdots$), and $\sigma : \Phi = \{\sigma : \alpha \mid \alpha \in \Phi\}$. These rules are direct generalizations of the propositional rules in Figure 1, and permit propositional reasoning in a modal context.

Like earlier, we denote by $X, \Phi \vdash_{als} \alpha$ the fact that there is a derivation of $X, \Phi \vdash \alpha$ using ax_1 and the rules in Figure 4. We now amend the notation $X, \Phi \vdash_{al} \alpha$ to denote the fact that there is a derivation of $X, \Phi \vdash \alpha$ using the rules in Figures 1, 2 and 4).

5.2 Protocol Model

We now outline the modifications to the protocol model occasioned by the *says* modality. The definitions of actions is extended to accommodate the new assertions. However, only *non-modal* assertions are allowed as testable conditions in the *confirm* and *deny* actions.

As regards the transition rules, the addition of the *says* modality allows us one major departure from the definitions specified earlier in 2.3 – agents can reason nontrivially using received assertions. An agent B, on receiving an assertion α from A, can store A *says* α in its state, and use it in further derivations. Thus a knowledge state ks is now a tuple of the form $((X_A, \Phi_A)_{A \in Ag}, SD)$.

Let $ks = ((X_A, \Phi_A)_{A \in Ag}, SD)$ and $ks' = ((X'_A, \Phi'_A)_{A \in Ag}, SD')$ be two knowledge states and a be a send or a receive action. We now describe the conditions under which the execution of a changes ks to ks', denoted $ks \xrightarrow{a} ks'$. (These are minor modifications of the rules presented earlier, but presented in full for the convenience of the reader).

- $a = A!B : [(M)t, \{\alpha\}_{sd(A)}]$
    - a is enabled at ks iff
        * $M \cap X_C = \varnothing$ for all C,
        * $X_A \cup M \vdash_{dy} t$, and
        * $X_A \cup M, \Phi_A \vdash_{al} \alpha$.
    - $ks \xrightarrow{a} ks'$ iff
        * $X'_A = X_A \cup M$, $X'_I = X_I \cup \{t\}$,
        * $\Phi'_I = \Phi_I \cup \{\alpha, A \text{ says } \alpha\}$, and
        * $SD' = SD \cup \{\{\alpha\}_{sd(A)}\}$.
- $a = A?B : [t, \{\alpha\}_{sd(B)}]$
    - a is enabled at ks iff
        * $\{\alpha\}_{sd(B)}$ is verified as signed by B,
        * $X_I \vdash_{dy} t$, and
        * either $B = I$ and $X_I, \Phi_I \vdash_{al} \alpha$, or $\{\alpha\}_{sd(B)} \in SD$.
    - $ks \xrightarrow{a} ks'$ iff
        * $X'_A = X_A \cup \{t\}$, and
        * $\Phi'_A = \Phi_A \cup \{B \text{ says } \alpha\}$.
- $a = A : confirm\ \alpha$ is enabled at ks iff $X_A, \varnothing \vdash_{al} \alpha$, and $ks \xrightarrow{a} ks'$ iff $ks = ks'$.
- $a = A : deny\ \alpha$ is enabled at ks iff $X_A, \varnothing \nvdash_{al} \alpha$, and $ks \xrightarrow{a} ks'$ iff $ks = ks'$.

We see that on receipt of an assertion α, honest agents always store A *says* α in their state, whereas the intruder is allowed to store α itself (along with A *says* α).

The rest of the definitions extend without any modification.

5.3 Example Protocol

A generates a vote, which it wants principals B and C to agree to, and then send to the trusted third party T. However, A does not want B and C to know exactly what the vote is. If a principal agrees to this vote, it prepends its identifier to the term sent to it, encrypts the whole term with the key it shares with T, and sends it to the next agent. Otherwise it merely sends the original term to the next agent. We show the specification where everyone agrees to the vote. $B : A : \alpha$ denotes B *says* A *says* α, and $t = \{v_T\}_k$.

- $A \rightarrow B : t, \ \{(a < t) \vee (b < t)\}_{sd(A)}$
- $B \rightarrow C : \{(B, t)\}_{k(B,T)}, \ \{A : \{(a < t) \vee (b < t)\}\}_{sd(B)}$
- $C \rightarrow T : \{(C, \{(B, t)\}_{k(B,T)}\}_{k(C,T)}, \ \{B : A : \{(a < t) \vee (b < t)\}\}_{sd(C)}$
- If the nested term is signed by both B and C, and $v_T = a$ or $v_T = b$, $T \rightarrow A : ack$.
  Otherwise, $T \rightarrow A : 0$.

We now demonstrate an attack. Suppose there is a session S_1 where a and b take values a_1 and b_1, where B agrees to the vote. Suppose now there is a later session S_2 with a taking value a_1 (or b taking value b_1) again. The intruder can now replay the term from B's message to C in S_2 from S_1, although B might not wish to agree in S_2.

5.4 Derivability Problem

The basic properties of derivability, including normalization and subformula property, still holds for the expanded language. The lower bound result also carried over without modification, since the formulas featuring in the proof do not involve the *says* modality at all. As regards the upper bound, the procedure g needs to be modified slightly. The modified version is presented below. The proof of correctness is in the appendix.

```
 1: function g(X, Φ)
 2:     S ← Φ
 3:     for all σ : (α₁ ∨ α₂) ∈ S do
 4:         if σ : α₁ ∉ S and σ : α₂ ∉ S then
 5:             T ← {σ : β ∈ f(X, S ∪ {σ : α₁})}
 6:             U ← {σ : β ∈ f(X, S ∪ {σ : α₂})}
 7:             S ← S ∪ (T ∩ U)
 8:         end if
 9:     end for
10:     return deriv'(X, S)
11: end function
```

An optimization can also be considered, where the functions f and g are modified to take another argument, σ, which provides the **modal context**. Since an application of $\vee e$ on an assertion $\sigma : (\alpha_1 \vee \alpha_2)$ yields only formulas of the form $\sigma : \beta$ in the conclusion, the function $g(\sigma, \cdot, \cdot, i)$ need only make recursive calls to $f(\sigma, \cdot, \cdot, i + 1)$, concentrating only on assertions with prefix σ. Also $f(\sigma, \cdot, \cdot, i)$ need only make recursive calls to $g(\sigma, \cdot, \cdot, i)$ whenever $\sigma \neq \varepsilon$. This has the advantage that the recursion depth is linearly bounded by the maximum number of disjunctions with the *same prefix*. In summary, it is possible to solve the derivability problem efficiently in practical cases.

6 Conclusions

We have argued that it is worthwhile to extend the Dolev-Yao model of security protocols so that agents have the capability to communicate assertions about terms in addition to terms. These assertions play the same role as certificates that may be verified but cannot be generated by the recipient. We have suggested that such an abstraction allows us to model a variety of such certificate mechanisms. As a contribution to the theory of security protocols, we delineate the complexity of the derivability problem and provide a decision procedure. We study the safety checking problem (which involves the active intruder).

We would like to emphasize here that the main thrust of the paper is the overall framework, rather than a specific assertion language. We use a minimal logic for assertions, and many extensions by way of connectives or modalities are possible; however, it is best to drive extensions by applications that require them.

What we would like to see is to arrive at a 'programming methodology' for the structured use of assertions in protocol specifications. As an instance, consider the fact that in our model terms and assertions are bundled together: we communicate (t, α) where binding them requires the same term t to be used in α. Better structuring would use a quantifier *this* in assertions so that references to terms in assertions are contextually bound to communications. This would ensure that in different instantiations (sessions), the assertion would refer to different concrete terms. A more general approach would involve variables in assertions and scoping rules for their instantiations. This raises interesting technical issues and offers further scope for investigation.

References

1. Abadi, M., Needham, R.M.: Prudent engineering practices for cryptographic protocols. IEEE Transactions on Software Engineering 22, 6–15 (1996)
2. Anderson, R., Needham, R.: Robustness principles for public key protocols. In: Coppersmith, D. (ed.) CRYPTO 1995. LNCS, vol. 963, pp. 236–247. Springer, Heidelberg (1995)
3. Backes, M., Hriţcu, C., Maffei, M.: Type-checking zero-knowledge. In: ACM Conference on Computer and Communications Security, pp. 357–370 (2008)
4. Backes, M., Maffei, M., Unruh, D.: Zero-Knowledge in the Applied Pi-calculus and Automated Verification of the Direct Anonymous Attestation Protocol. In: IEEE Symposium on Security and Privacy, pp. 202–215 (2008)
5. Baskar, A., Naldurg, P., Raghavendra, K.R., Suresh, S.P.: Primal Infon Logic: Derivability in Polynomial Time. In: Proceedings of FSTTCS 2013. LIPIcs, vol. 24, pp. 163–174 (2013)
6. Baskar, A., Ramanujam, R., Suresh, S.P.: A DEXPTIME-complete dolev-yao theory with distributive encryption. In: Hliněný, P., Kučera, A. (eds.) MFCS 2010. LNCS, vol. 6281, pp. 102–113. Springer, Heidelberg (2010)
7. Burrows, M., Abadi, M., Needham, R.M.: A logic of authentication. ACM Transactions on Computer Systems 8(1), 18–36 (1990)
8. Benaloh, J.: Cryptographic capsules: A disjunctive primitive for interactive protocols. In: Odlyzko, A.M. (ed.) CRYPTO 1986. LNCS, vol. 263, pp. 213–222. Springer, Heidelberg (1987)
9. Comon, H., Shmatikov, V.: Intruder Deductions, Constraint Solving and Insecurity Decisions in Presence of Exclusive or. In: Proceedings of LICS 2003, pp. 271–280 (June 2003)
10. Cortier, V., Delaune, S., Lafourcade, P.: A survey of algebraic properties used in cryptographic protocols. Journal of Computer Security 14(1), 1–43 (2006)
11. Delaune, S., Kremer, S., Ryan, M.D.: Verifying privacy-type properties of electronic voting protocols. Journal of Computer Security 17(4), 435–487 (2009)

12. Dolev, D., Yao, A.: On the Security of public-key protocols. IEEE Transactions on Information Theory 29, 198–208 (1983)
13. Fuchsbauer, G., Pointcheval, D.: Anonymous consecutive delegation of signing rights: Unifying group and proxy signatures. In: Cortier, V., Kirchner, C., Okada, M., Sakurada, H. (eds.) Formal to Practical Security. LNCS, vol. 5458, pp. 95–115. Springer, Heidelberg (2009)
14. Gurevich, Y., Neeman, I.: Infon logic: the propositional case. ACM Transactions on Computational Logic 12(2), 9:1–9:28 (2011)
15. Lafourcade, P., Lugiez, D., Treinen, R.: Intruder deduction for the equational theory of abelian groups with distributive encryption. Information and Computation 205(4), 581–623 (2007)
16. Ramanujam, R., Sundararajan, V., Suresh, S.P.: Extending Dolev-Yao with assertions. Technical Report (2014), http://www.cmi.ac.in/~spsuresh/dyassert.pdf
17. Rjaskova, Z.: Electronic voting schemes. Master's Thesis, Comenius University (2002)
18. Rusinowitch, M., Turuani, M.: Protocol Insecurity with Finite Number of Sessions and Composed Keys is NP-complete. Theoretical Computer Science 299, 451–475 (2003)

Appendix

A Algorithm for Derivability: Correctness Proof

For a fixed X, define $f_X : \wp(\mathsf{sf}) \to \wp(\mathsf{sf})$ to be the function that maps Φ to $f(X, \Phi)$. Similarly, $g_X(\Phi)$ is defined to be $g(X, \Phi)$.

Lemma 19. *1. $\Phi \subseteq deriv'(X, \Phi) \subseteq deriv(X, \Phi)$.*
2. $deriv'(X, deriv(X, \Phi)) = deriv(X, deriv(X, \Phi)) = deriv(X, \Phi)$.
3. If $\Phi \subseteq \Psi$ then $g_X(\Phi) \subseteq g_X(\Psi)$ and $f_X(\Phi) \subseteq f_X(\Psi)$.
4. $\Phi \subseteq g_X(\Phi) \subseteq g_X^2(\Phi) \subseteq \cdots \subseteq \mathsf{sf}$.
5. $f_X(\Phi) = g_X^m(\Phi)$ for some $m \leq N$.

The last fact is true because $|\mathsf{sf}| = N$ and the $g_X^i(\Phi)$s form a non-decreasing sequence.

Proposition 20 (Soundness). *For $X \subseteq \mathsf{st}$, $\Phi \subseteq \mathsf{sf}$ and $m \geq 0$, $g_X^m(\Phi) \subseteq deriv(X, \Phi)$.*

Proof. We shall assume that

$$g_X^n(\Psi) \subseteq deriv(X, \Psi) \text{ for all } \Psi \subseteq \mathsf{sf}, n \geq 0 \text{ s.t. } (N - |\Psi|, n) <_{\text{lex}} (N - |\Phi|, m)$$

and prove that

$$g_X^m(\Phi) \subseteq deriv(X, \Phi).$$

Now if $m = 0$, then $g_X^m(\Phi) = \Phi \subseteq deriv(X, \Phi)$. Suppose $m > 0$, Let $Z = g_X^{m-1}(\Phi)$ and let $S \subseteq \mathsf{sf}$ be such that $\alpha \in S$ iff one of the following conditions hold:

- $\alpha \in Z$
- α is of the form $\sigma : \beta$ and there is some $\sigma : (\alpha_1 \vee \alpha_2) \in Z$ such that $\sigma : \alpha_i \notin Z$ and $\alpha \in f_X(Z \cup \{\sigma : \alpha_1\}) \cap f_X(Z \cup \{\sigma : \alpha_2\})$.

Observe that since $(N - |\Phi|, m - 1) <_{\text{lex}} (N - |\Phi|, m)$, by induction hypothesis, $Z = g_X^{m-1}(\Phi) \subseteq \text{deriv}(X, \Phi)$. To conclude that $g_X^m(\Phi) \subseteq \text{deriv}(X, \Phi)$, it suffices to prove that $S \subseteq \text{deriv}(X, \Phi)$, since then we have

$$g_X^m(\Phi) = \text{deriv}'(X, S) \subseteq \text{deriv}'(X, \text{deriv}(X, \Phi)) = \text{deriv}(X, \Phi).$$

Now if $\alpha \in S$, then there are two cases:

- $\alpha \in Z$. But $Z \subseteq \text{deriv}(X, \Phi)$, and so $\alpha \in \text{deriv}(X, \Phi)$.
- α is of the form $\sigma : \beta$ and $\alpha \in f_X(Z \cup \{\sigma : \alpha_1\}) \cap f_X(Z \cup \{\sigma : \alpha_2\})$ for some $\sigma : (\alpha_1 \vee \alpha_2) \in Z$. For any Ψ, $f_X(\Psi) = g_X^n(\Psi)$ for some $n \leq N$, and for any n, $(N - |Z \cup \{\sigma : \alpha_i\}|, n) <_{\text{lex}} (N - |\Phi|, m)$. Thus, by induction hypothesis, $f_X(Z \cup \{\sigma : \alpha_i\}) \subseteq \text{deriv}(X, Z \cup \{\sigma : \alpha_i\})$. In other words, $X, Z \cup \{\sigma : \alpha_1\} \vdash_{al} \sigma : \beta$ and $X, Z \cup \{\sigma : \alpha_2\} \vdash_{al} \sigma : \beta$ and $X, Z \vdash_{al} \sigma : (\alpha_1 \vee \alpha_2)$. By an application of the $\vee e$ rule, we conclude that $X, Z \vdash_{al} \sigma : \beta$. Thus

$$\alpha \in \text{deriv}(X, Z) \subseteq \text{deriv}(X, \text{deriv}(X, \Phi)) = \text{deriv}(X, \Phi).$$

This proves that $S \subseteq \text{deriv}(X, \Phi)$, and we are done.   ⊣

Proposition 21 (Completeness). *For $X \subseteq \text{st}$, $\Phi \subseteq \text{sf}$ and $\alpha \in \text{deriv}(X, \Phi)$, there is $m \geq 0$ such that $\alpha \in g_X^m(\Phi)$.*

Proof.   Suppose $\alpha \in \text{deriv}(X, \Phi)$. Then there is a normal derivation π of $X, \Phi \vdash \alpha$. We now prove the desired claim by induction on the structure of π.

- Suppose the last rule r of π is not $\vee e$. If r is ax_1, $\alpha \in \Phi = g_X^0(\Phi)$. If not, let $S = \{\beta \mid X, \Phi \vdash \beta \text{ is a premise of r}\}$. Since each $\beta \in S$ is the conclusion of a subproof of π, by induction hypothesis, there is an m such that $\beta \in g_X^m(\Phi)$. It follows that there is n such that $S \subseteq g_X^n(\Phi)$. Since for any Ψ, $\text{deriv}'(X, \Psi) \subseteq g_X(\Psi)$, it follows that $\alpha \in \text{deriv}'(X, S) \subseteq \text{deriv}'(X, g_X^n(\Phi)) \subseteq g_X^{n+1}(\Phi)$.
- Suppose the last rule of π is $\vee e$. Then α is of the form $\sigma : \beta$ (where σ could also be ε) and there are subproofs of π with conclusions $X, \Phi \vdash \sigma : (\alpha_1 \vee \alpha_2)$, $X, \Phi \cup \{\sigma : \alpha_1\} \vdash \sigma : \beta$ and $X, \Phi \cup \{\sigma : \alpha_2\} \vdash \sigma : \beta$. By induction hypothesis, there are m, n, p such that $\sigma : (\alpha_1 \vee \alpha_2) \in g_X^m(\Phi)$, $\sigma : \beta \in g_X^n(\Phi \cup \{\alpha_1\})$ and $\sigma : \beta \in g_X^p(\Phi \cup \{\alpha_2\})$. Since $g_X^q(\Psi) \subseteq f_X(\Psi)$ for any Ψ and $q \geq 0$, it follows that $\sigma : \beta \in f_X(\Phi \cup \alpha_1\}) \cap f_X(\Phi \cup \alpha_2\})$. Thus $\sigma : \beta \in g_X^{m+1}(\Phi)$.   ⊣

Inferring Accountability from Trust Perceptions

Koen Decroix[1], Denis Butin[2], Joachim Jansen[3], and Vincent Naessens[1]

[1] KU Leuven, Technology Campus Ghent, Department of Computer Science
Gebroeders Desmetstraat 1, 9000 Ghent, Belgium
{koen.decroix,vincent.naessens}@cs.kuleuven.be
[2] Inria, Université de Lyon, France
denis.butin@inria.fr
[3] Department of Computer Science, KU Leuven, Belgium
joachim.jansen@cs.kuleuven.be

Abstract. Opaque communications between groups of data processors leave individuals out of touch with the circulation and use of their personal information. Empowering individuals in this regard requires supplying them — or auditors on their behalf — with clear data handling guarantees. We introduce an inference model providing individuals with global (organization-wide) accountability guarantees which take into account user expectations and varying levels of usage evidence, such as data handling logs. Our model is implemented in the IDP knowledge base system and demonstrated with the scenario of a surveillance infrastructure used by a railroad company. We show that it is flexible enough to be adapted to any use case involving communicating stakeholders for which a trust hierarchy is defined. Via auditors acting for them, individuals can obtain global accountability guarantees, providing them with a trust-dependent synthesis of declared and proven data handling practices for an entire organization.

Keywords: Accountability, IDP, Trust, Privacy, Surveillance.

1 Context and Motivation

Contemporary situations involving the exchange of personal data for services often leave individuals oblivious as to the actual processing of their data. While privacy policies are widely used by organizations across the world, they often constitute mere declarations of intent. Individuals generally cannot check whether actual processing is in line with such ex ante statements. Furthermore, privacy policies often remain purposely vague while users demand concrete promises about the retention of their data, the purposes for which it is used, obligations in terms of third party forwarding and so on.

The rise of individuals' expectations about data handling transparency, combined with the growing imbalance of power between them and data processing organizations, has made the principle of *accountability* a key component of the discourse over privacy protection. While the concept of accountability was already mentioned in this context in the eighties [24], it appears more prominently

A. Prakash and R. Shyamasundar (Eds.): ICISS 2014, LNCS 8880, pp. 69–88, 2014.
© Springer International Publishing Switzerland 2014

these days. In particular, the upcoming European General Data Protection Regulation [12] cites accountability explicitly. Organizations will therefore increasingly be legally required to be accountable for their data handling practices to data subjects.

A downside of this concept's popularity is that its meaning has been diluted due to frequent use in different contexts. Lawyers often focus on procedural aspects of accountability [7, 25]. Computer scientists often tackle specific security properties — such as non-repudiation [2] — or specific technical contexts like cloud environments [15]. Because of these varied interpretations, no universal definition of accountability can be given. However, it normally refers to the necessity of surpassing mere compliance to achieve demonstration of compliance. By putting the burden of proof of good behavior on the data controller, accountability measures increase pressure on organizations to be transparent and fair in their data handling practices.

In real-world situations, data shared by an individual does often not remain within the realm of a single entity but it disseminated among communicating subsystems that may even be geographically distant. Since subcontractors may belong to different corporations than the organization that collected personal data in the first place, different data handling policies may apply. The initial data controller may fulfill its promises as long as data remains in its initial location, but offer no guarantees about processing by other stakeholders. Such situations leave individuals blind to the whereabouts of their data.

Even if all involved entities publish clear data handling policies, the end result is opaque to individuals. Technical privacy policies may be very detailed and the number of entities may be large. It is useful for individuals to understand the resulting global (organization- or system-wide) guarantees that apply to their personal data. If individuals have defined personal privacy preferences for themselves once and for all, they would also like to know whether the overall processing of their data by an organization and its subcontractors is in conflict with those preferences.

This paper introduces a model capable of inferring global accountability guarantees from the point of view of a trusted auditor. This auditor acts on behalf of the user and represents his interests. In practice, the auditor could be a member of a Data Protection Authority or a third-party, accredited auditing organization. The framework allows the hierarchical representation of entities in an organization, thereby modeling trust relationships: an individual may only trust a given component in an organization, or may trust an entity higher in the hierarchy, thereby trusting all components operating by that entity. These trust assumptions (i.e. user expectations) influence the computation of the global accountability guarantees. We distinguish between three levels of users: a naive user, a regular one and a privacy-aware one. The level of privacy-awareness of a user influences the kind of evidence this user assumes to be trustworthy.

In addition to these different types of users, data handling statements carry different levels of evidence. Each entity subcontracting for an organization has its own data handling statements. At the lowest level, statements are merely declarations of intent with no additional evidence. This level of evidence is akin to a detailed, technical privacy policy. Other statements are provided together with system traces of data handling operations, i.e. logs. These logs are assumed to be trustworthy, but they have not been inspected. Therefore, it may not be obvious at first glance that a data processor has misbehaved, even though a trace of misbehavior is assumed to exist in the logs. The situation where logs cannot be checked easily is realistic because logs are not standardized in general, many organizations use very specific formats and because semantics are often unavailable. The highest level of evidence features statements that are accompanied by logs that have been verified and found to be compliant. Here, it is again assumed that the logs are trustworthy, i.e. reflect actual system execution, and that the log analysis software is sound and accurate.

The three levels of user privacy-awareness and three levels of statement evidence are combined to compute fine-grained global accountability guarantees. The auditor, on behalf of the user, can both inspect those global guarantees or detect potential conflicts by providing the privacy preferences of the individual.

Our framework is implemented in IDP, a knowledge base system [11]. We demonstrate it through the scenario of a surveillance infrastructure managed by a railroad company and involving a third-party security service company, operators such as a surveillance guard and an image processor, and components used by these operators. This kind of scenario demonstrates the typical situation where an individual shares his data with only one entity initially, after which the entity processes and disseminates the data among several subcontractors. Assuming individuals are monitored via cameras, one can distinguish between several categories of personal data which can be collected, processed and distributed. Depending on image quality and on pan-tilt-zoom functionality, cameras may record full body pictures with insufficient quality to distinguish faces, full body pictures with blurred faces, faces only or even record behavior patterns while discarding body images.

As mentioned above, we assume logs (when they exist) to be trustworthy: they are accurate and cannot be forged by entities. In practice, this requires techniques such as forward integrity [3] to guarantee the security of logs, and partial formal modeling or trusted computing to ensure unforgeability. While these criteria are important, they are outside of the scope of this work: here, we suppose that logs reflect actual system execution and therefore embody meaningful evidence. Furthermore, we presume that personal data is categorized in a standardized way, so that individuals and organizations use the same terminology for categories of personal data.

We continue with some technical background on the IDP system, a knowledge base system based on an extension of typed first-order logic (§2). The approach is illustrated by the running example of a railroad surveillance infrastructure, presented informally at first (§3). We then introduce the building blocks of the accountability inference framework and apply it to this scenario (§4). After evaluating the results of this implementation of the model (§5), we discuss related work on formalizations of accountability and privacy (§6), including existing models for privacy reasoning realized with IDP. The paper concludes with a discussion of the potential, limitations and future of the framework (§7).

2 IDP

IDP [16, 29] is a state-of-the-art knowledge base system [8] developed by the Knowledge Representation and Reasoning (KRR) group at KU Leuven. We briefly introduce IDP and how it can be used as a tool to manage an accountability framework, focusing on the parts of the system relevant for this paper. More interested readers can find IDP documentation and source code here [16], and some examples here [17]. In this text we use IDP to refer to IDP^3, the current version of the IDP system. One of the main focuses of IDP is knowledge representation: allowing users to formulate their knowledge in a intuitive manner. To this end the FO($\cdot$) language framework, an extension of First Order Logic (FO), was developed. Using this language, users can model their data (in this case, which organizations or data categories to analyze), as well their knowledge (here, accountability across organizations) in a formal way using logical formulas (constraints) and definitions. This model can be used to solve problems by applying one of the many *inferences* IDP provides. For this paper we will need *(optimal) model expansion*: given a partial assignment for data, find a complete (optimal) assignment such that all expressed constraints and definitions hold. The initial, partial assignment corresponds to the setting of our framework: a hierarchical network of organizations and the accountability guarantees they offer. The outcome of the model expansion inference then corresponds to a complete assignment: a listing of which information is used in what places and what kinds of accountability guarantees it offers. This will later be called the Global Accountability Profile (GAP).

There exists a variety of declarative modeling systems, such as Alloy [19,20] or ASP solvers [13,22]. We chose to use IDP as our modeling tool for two reasons. First, the language it uses is expressive and intuitive: it supports extended first order constraints as well as definitions under well-founded semantics [26]. Second, it is implemented as an extension in Lua [18], which means there is support for procedural integration. This allows us to determine the way in which we want to use our declarative model in a flexible way.

3 A Railway Station Surveillance Scenario

To illustrate the model, we consider the scenario of video camera surveillance in a railway station. Since individuals are filmed by cameras, the collected categories of personal data are related to images (we assume the cameras do not record sound). Several categories of personal data can be inferred from camera recordings, such as identification through face detection [27], gait recognition [21], behavioral tracking [23] and many others. Signs inform passersby that the *Railway Company* installed *Cameras* for video surveillance. The cameras provide the railway's *Monitors* in the control room with real-time video feeds containing

Blurred Faces and *Gaits* of travelers. Furthermore, detailed images of individuals' *Full Body* and *Gait* are stored in the railway's *Image Database* serving as *Evidence* in legal investigations. Only authorized *Image Processors* employed by the railway company have access to it. Additionally, surveillance *Guards* employed by a third-party *Security Company* patrol in the station. They are authorized to view real-time images on the monitors, and carry a *Mobile Device* for registering *Contextual Data* (e.g. time and location) in case of incidents. These devices are connected with the *Status Database*, property of the security company. It is only accessible for the security company's *Status Processors* upon request of legal institutions for collecting *Evidence*.

The trusted auditor (acting on behalf of a filmed individual) is external to the model and we focus on data handling statements from the entities collecting personal data, listed in Tab. 1.

4   Components of the Accountability Inference Model

Having set the stage for both our model and the tool that will be used to evaluate it, we now describe the framework's building blocks (depicted in Fig. 1) in detail. Entities, all related to a core organization, provide individual statements about their data handling practices. These statements can be provided together with unverified logs, verified logs, or exist on their own without companion evidence. Different categories of personal data can be modeled. As a consequence, statements are fine-grained enough to express different guarantees about various types of personal data. The data subject is represented by a trusted auditor. This auditor takes into account the subject's trust perceptions. Global accountability guarantees are automatically computed using the computation rules in the *System Independent Part* of the framework. These guarantees are represented by the *Global Accountability Profile* (GAP) that is automatically inferred, using a *Knowledge Base System* (IDP), from the *System Model* and the *User Model*, both part of the framework's *Input Model*. The former models the individual statements, the relations between the entities expressing the statements, and the level of evidence characterizing the statements. The latter includes the level of trust of the user. As a consequence, the global accountability guarantees take into account both factual evidence and subjective appreciations of privacy risks. This combination reflects the fact that different data subjects demand different levels of proof to be satisfied. The model provides data subjects with an overview of the accountability guarantees resulting from a set of interacting entities. In addition, it allows them (or the auditor, on their behalf) to check whether their personal privacy preferences are compatible with this global accountability panorama. The remainder of this section further details the framework's elements.

4.1   Personal Data

Organizations collect personal data of data subjects that interact with systems owned by these organizations. Being accountable to data subjects involves clarifying which types of their personal data are harvested and used. These categories

Table 1. Camera surveillance data handling statements. Entity statements are (D)eclarative, (L)ogged-unverified or Logged-and-(V)erified.

(R)ailway Company, (C)amera, (M)onitor, (I)mage Database Statements		
Stat R.1	(L)	Full body pictures with blurred or clear faces, gaits, heights, and behavior are recorded for incident detection.
Stat R.2	(D)	Collected pictures containing evidence of incidents can be forwarded to legal authorities upon their request.
Stat R.3	(L)	Pictures are never collected for commercial purposes.
Stat R.4	(L)	The maximal retention time for any category of collected personal data is 60 days.
Stat C.1	(L)	Cameras in the station record full body pictures with blurred or clear faces, gaits, heights, and behaviors of travelers for incident detection purposes.
Stat M.1	(L)	Guards monitor in real-time full body pictures with blurred faces, gaits, heights, and behaviors of travelers in the station for incident detection purposes.
Stat I.1	(L)	Full body pictures with clear faces are stored as evidence of possible incidents.
Stat I.2	(V)	Access to stored full body pictures with clear faces is only granted to the image processor upon request of the legal authorities.
Stat I.3	(V)	Full body pictures with clear faces, gaits, heights, and behavior are never processed for the purpose of identification.
Stat I.4	(D)	Stored images are deleted after 30 days, unless they are being used as evidence in legal cases.

(S)ecurity Company, M(O)bile Device, Status (D)atabase Statements		
Stat S.1	(D)	Time and location of incidents are collected as evidence.
Stat S.2	(L)	Time and location of incidents are only forwarded to legal authorities upon request.
Stat O.1	(V)	Surveillance guards collect time and location as evidence in case of incidents.
Stat D.1	(V)	Time and location of incidents are collected as evidence.
Stat D.2	(V)	Access to stored time and location of incidents is granted to status processors for gathering evidence.
Stat D.3	(V)	The time and location of incidents are deleted after 90 days unless they are being used as legal evidence.

are represented by the *DataCategory* type. All categories of collected personal data involved in a given scenario must be spelled out in the input model as the contents of *DataCategory*.

One can define hierarchies of personal data categories. This models the fact that categories of personal data can be subsets of other categories, e.g. the age of an individual gives strictly more information than a predicate on whether the individual is over 18. The data category hierarchy is represented using *Data-CategoryOf(DataCategory,DataCategory)*, which deduces hierarchical knowledge

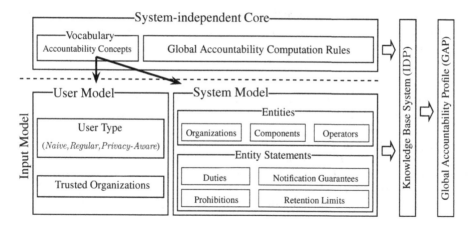

Fig. 1. Structure of the global accountability inference model

from the initial specifications. Listing 1 depicts the IDP input model for the personal data and their hierarchy of the camera surveillance scenario.

type DataCategory = { *PersData; Face; BlurredFace; Gait; Height; Behavior;*
            Location; Time, PictureIncident }
DataCategoryOf(DataCategory, DataCategory) = {
            Face, PictureIncident; BlurredFace, PictureIncident; Gait,
            PictureIncident; Height, PictureIncident; Behavior, PictureIncident }

IDP Listing 1. Partial user model representing personal data categories and hierarchies in the video surveillance scenario.

4.2   Entities

Data subjects and the auditors that act on their behalf are not explicitly modeled since their point of view is external. An arbitrary number of active entities can be modeled in the framework's system model. Active entities are those that handle personal data of the subjects and provide some degree of accountability, i.e. declarations (with or without proof) about the data processing they perform. A distinction is made between *Stakeholders* and *Components*. A stakeholder is either an *Organization*, or an *Operator* acting on behalf of exactly one organization. An organization can employ more than one operator. Components are constituents of data processing systems. A component belongs to exactly one organization, but can be used by multiple operators.

Components process personal data under the responsibility of the organizations that own them. Organizations or authorities may restrict access to the data categories that a given component is capable of collecting. Authorized categories for a given component are specified using *ComponentCanCollect(Component, DataCategory)*. Listing 2 depicts the IDP specification of the entities involved in the camera surveillance scenario.

type Entity = { *RailwayCompany; SecurityCompany; LegalAuthority; Camera;*
        Monitor; MobileDevice; SurveilanceGuard; ImageProcessor;
        StatusProcessor; ImageDB; StatusDB }
type Stakeholder isa Entity = { *RailwayCompany; SecurityCompany;*
        LegalAuthority; SurveilanceGuard; ImageProcessor; StatusProcessor }
type Component isa Entity = { *Camera; Monitor; MobileDevice; ImageDB;*
        StatusDB }
type Organization isa Stakeholder = { *RailwayCompany; SecurityCompany;*
        LegalAuthority }
type Operator isa Stakeholder = { *SurveilanceGuard; ImageProcessor;*
        StatusProcessor }
ComponentOf(Component) : Organization = { *Camera → RailwayCompany;*
        Monitor → RailwayCompany; ImageDB → RailwayCompany;
        StatusDB → SecurityCompany; MobileDevice → SecurityCompany }
EmployeeOf(Operator) : Organization = {
        SurveilanceGuard → SecurityCompany;
        StatusProcessor → SecurityCompany;
        ImageProcessor → RailwayCompany }
OperatorOf(Operator, Component) = { *SurveilanceGuard, Monitor;*
        SurveilanceGuard, MobileDevice; ImageProcessor, ImageDB;
        StatusProcessor, StatusDB }
ComponentCanCollect(Component, DataCategory) = { *Camera, Face;*
        Camera, BlurredFace; Camera, PictureIncident; Camera, Gait;
        Camera, Height; Camera, Behavior; Monitor, Face; Monitor,
        BlurredFace; Monitor, PictureIncident; Monitor, Gait; Monitor, Height;
        Monitor, Behavior; ImageDB, Face; ImageDB, BlurredFace;
        ImageDB, PictureIncident; ImageDB, Gait; ImageDB, Height;
        ImageDB, Behavior; ImageDB, Time; ImageDB, Location; StatusDB,
        Time; StatusDB, Location; MobileDevice, Time; MobileDevice,
        Location }

IDP Listing 2. Partial system model representing the entities and their relationships in the video surveillance scenario.

4.3 Statements and Local Accountability Statements

All entities involved in data handling relevant to a given data subject are assumed to exhibit some level of accountability of practice, i.e. they publish precise declarations about their intended personal data handling practices. In general, each entity publishes a different data handling statement. A one-to-one mapping between entities and data handling statements is assumed, and is modeled using function *StatementFrom(Statement) : Entity*. Listing 3 shows the part of the system model that defines a subset of the *statements* of the *railway company* listed in Tab. 1 [1]. Those statements include the following aspects:

- Purposes of use, i.e. the list of finalities for which the collected personal data may be used (for instance statistics or direct marketing) — this is modeled using *StatementPurpose(Statement, Purpose)*. Multiple purposes can be defined for a statement.
- The category of personal data that is used, i.e. the collection of personal identifiable information. Possibly, multiple subject data categories exist for a statement — this is modeled using predicate *StatementSubject(Statement, DataCategory)*.
- Global retention limits, i.e. the period of time after which the personal data will be deleted by the entity (e.g. 30 days) — this limit is expressed using a partial function (i.e. not every statement expresses a retention limit) *StatementRetentionLimit(Statement) : Duration*.
- *Obligations* built from a *Condition* and an *Action*. These are modeled using partial functions *StatementCondtion(Statement) : Condition* and *StatementAction(Statement) : Action)*. Both are partial functions because not all statements are linked to actions (e.g. retention limits), and unconditional obligations are modeled by only modeling the actions of statements.
- Personal data may be forwarded to organizations. In the model, this is expressed using *StatementDestination(Statement, Organization)*. Possibly, a statement has multiple destinations.

Obligations are flexible and can be used to express a variety of constraints. Conditions are events that trigger a reaction, e.g. the personal data is accessed or the data subject has requested an update. Actions are the resulting events, for instance the update of his personal data or its forwarding.

Statements guaranteeing the sending of a notification (to a user) when a specific event occurs (e.g. when a specific category of personal data is accessed by the entity) are expressed using *StatementNotificationGuarantee(Statement)*.

Accountability occurs at different levels. Some entities may merely declare their intended practices, without providing any companion evidence. Other entities provide data handling logs. In the model this is denoted using function *StatementProof(Statement) : StatementEvidence*. It may not always be possible to check the compliance of data handling logs with obligations. Logs can be in a format which is not standardized, or semantics may not be provided by the entity. We therefore distinguish between three levels of assurance (*StatementEvidence*) for data handling statements:

1. A statement is (purely) *Declarative* if data handling logs relevant to the statement are not made available by the entity publishing the statement.
2. If data handling logs are provided together with the statement but cannot be checked straight away, the statement obtains the status *LoggedUnverified*.

---

[1] For the complete model of the statements, see
https://code.google.com/p/inferring-accountability/.

3. If a statement is provided together with logs that have been checked for compliance (e.g. through a trusted log analysis software), the statement is said to be *LoggedVerified*. This is the highest level of accountability for a data handling statement, since actual behavior has both been recorded and shown to be compliant with the statement.

```
type Statement = { StatR1; StatR2; StatR3; StatR4; ... }
type Purpose = { Evidence; DetectIncident; Commerce; Identification }
type Condition = { RequestLegalAuthority; NoLegalInvestigation }
type Action = { Collecting; Monitoring; Storing; Forwarding; Accessing }
type Duration isa int = { 30; 60; 90 }
type Permission constructed from { Always; Never }
type StatementEvidence constructed from { Declarative;
        LoggedUnverified; LoggedVerified  }
StatementFrom(Statement) : Entity = { StatR1 → RailwayCompany;
        StatR2 → RailwayCompany; StatR3 → RailwayCompany;
        StatR4 → RailwayCompany; ... }
StatementSubject(Statement, DataCategory) = { StatR1, Face;
        StatR1, BlurredFace; StatR1, Gait; StatR1, Height; StatR1, Behavior;
        StatR2, PictureIncident; StatR3, PictureIncident; StatR4, PersData;
        ... }
StatementPurpose(Statement, Purpose) = { StatR1, DetectIncident; StatR2,
        Evidence; StatR3, Commerce; ... }
partial StatementCondtion(Statement) : Condition = {
        StatR2 → RequestLegalAuthority; ... }
StatementPermission(Statement) : Permission = { StatR1 → Always;
        StatR2 → Always; StatR3 → Never; StatR4 → Always; ... }
partial StatementAction(Statement) : Action = { StatR1 → Collecting;
        StatR2 → Forwarding; StatR3 → Collecting; ... }
StatementDestination(Statement, Organization) = {
        StatR2, LegalAuthority; ... }
partial StatementRetentionLimit(Statement) : Duration = {
        StatR4 → 60; ... }
StatementNotificationGuarantee(Statement) = {   }
StatementProof(Statement) : StatementEvidence = {
        StatR1 → LoggedUnverified; StatR2 → Declarative;
        StatR3 → LoggedUnverified; StatR4 → LoggedUnverified; ... }
```

IDP Listing 3. Partial system model representing the statements of the entities involved in the video surveillance scenario.

4.4 Trust Perception and Global Accountability Inference

While organizations may feature complex hierarchies with heterogeneous data handling practices, individuals care about what happens to their personal data globally. A panoramic overview of the worst-case scenario in terms of data processing (i.e. *what are the weakest global guarantees?*) is relevant to individuals, since they must often decide whether to interact with an entire organization. Most of the time, they cannot cherry-pick with which subcontractors to share their data with.

Global accountability inference is a central feature of this framework that builds such a synthetic statement for data subjects. It deduces global guarantees from the local accountability statements of all entities involved in the system. These (subjective) guarantees depend on trust perceptions of data subjects.

Individuals display different levels of trust in the entities that handle their personal data. The framework's user model reflects this socio-technical aspect by modeling three levels of trust, corresponding to three typical types of individuals:

- *Naive* individuals always trust data handling statements, even if statements are purely declarative (i.e. no evidence in the form of a log is provided);
- *Regular* individuals only trust statements co-occurring with relevant data handling logs;
- *Privacy-aware* individuals are most skeptical and trust only statements for which verified logs have been provided by issuing entities.

Furthermore, the user model includes *UserTrust(Organization)*, the user's high-level trust perception towards organizations. It represents his trust in declared data handling practices of related organizations. This also implies that all operators they employ and components they own are trusted by him. The modeled video surveillance scenario features the aforementioned three user models: naive (*U1*), regular (*U2*) and privacy-aware (*U3*). It also assumes that no organization is trusted, i.e. *UserTrust(Organization)* is the empty set.

This impact of these user trust models on the perception of global accountability guarantees is shown in Tab. 2. For instance, a *naive user* considers he is guaranteed that merely declared statements of an entity *E*, owned or employed by organization *O*, correspond with actual data handling practices. By contrast, a *regular user* only considers merely declared statements to be guaranteed if he trusts *O* (i.e. *UserTrust(O)*), and assumes statements provided together with logs to be guaranteed, whether these logs are checked for compliance or not.

Table 2. Global statement evidence deduction rules — the global evidence for the statement *S* by the entity *E* owned by the organization *O* is *(U)ncertain* or *(G)uaranteed* for the modeled user

$StatementProof(S)=$	Declared	Logged-unverified	Logged-and-verified
Naive user	G	G	G
Regular user	$F(E) : \{G, U\}^\star$	G	G
Privacy-aware user	$F(E) : \{G, U\}^\star$	$F(E) : \{G, U\}^\star$	G

$^\star F(E) =' G' \Leftrightarrow UserTrust(O) \wedge (ComponentOf(E) = O \vee EmployeeOf(E) = O)$
$^\star F(E) =' U' \Leftrightarrow \neg UserTrust(O) \wedge (ComponentOf(E) = O \vee EmployeeOf(E) = O)$

Global statement computations are performed differently for *duties* (i.e. statements featuring *Always*) and for *prohibitions* (i.e. statements featuring *Never*).

Beside these categories, models also include statements expressing *notification guarantees* and *global retention limits*. Comparable with duties, these also feature *Always*. Nevertheless, these are treated differently in computations.

Global statements are expressed in terms of *global data categories* (i.e. users are concerned what happens to their personal data). Let S be an individual statement of entity E, *CanCollect(E,DC)* a data category DC that can be collected by an entity E, and *Sub(S,DC)* representing that data category DC is a subject of S. Tab. 3 summarizes the worst-case deduction rules that depend on the *global statement evidence* for the computation of *GlobalDataCategory(S,DC)*, the global data categories derived from S.

Table 3. Worst-case computation rules for deducing *GlobalDataCategory(S,DC)*, the global data categories DC deduced from the individual statement S of entity E, with *Sub(S,DC)* the subject DC of statement S, and *CanCollect(E, DC)* the data categories collectable by E

Global statement evidence of S:	Uncertain	Guaranteed
$Duty(S)$	$CanCollect(E, DC)$	$\psi(S, E, DC)^*$
$Prohibition(S)$	$\psi(S, E, DC)^*$	$Sub(S, DC)$
$NotificationGuarantee(S)$	$Sub(S, DC)$	$\psi(S, E, DC)^*$
$RetentionLimit(S)$	$Sub(S, DC)$	$\psi(S, E, DC)^*$

$^*\psi(S, E, DC) \equiv CanCollect(E, DC) \wedge Sub(S, DC)$

Duties. Global statements using *Always* are built as follows:

- The *global purposes of use* for a global data category are constructed from the union of all purposes of (individual) duties S, with *GlobalDataCategory(S,DC)*. These represent worst-case global purposes which are conjunctive. For instance, personal data is collected for commercial and statistical reasons. If no purpose is explicitly specified, then all purposes are assumed to be permitted globally.
- The *global conditions of use* for a data category are constructed from the disjunction of all conditions of duties S, with *GlobalDataCategory(S,DC)*. If at least one unconditional statement exists, no overall conditional statement is generated.
- The *global actions* for a data category are built from the union of all actions of individual duties S, with *GlobalDataCategory(S,DC)*.
- The *global level of assurance* (i.e. global evidence) for a data category is *Uncertain* if at least one uncertain statement (in the sense of Tab. 3) exists for this data category. Else, the global statement is considered *Guaranteed*.
- The *global notification guarantee* for events relative to a data category is built from the conjunction of all individual notification guarantees S relative to that data category, with *GlobalDataCategory(S,DC)*.

- The *global retention limit* for a data category is the maximum of all retention limts S existing for the data category, with *GlobalDataCategory(S,DC)*.

Prohibitions. Global statements using *Never* are built as follows:

- The *global purposes of use* for a global data category are constructed from the union of all purposes of individual prohibitions S, with *GlobalDataCategory(S,DC)*. These represent worst-case global purposes which are disjunctive. For instance, personal data is never collected for commercial or statistical reasons. Individual prohibitions without explicit purpose are omitted during the deduction of global purposes (i.e. worst-case).
- The *global conditions of use* for a data category are constructed from the conjunction of all conditions of prohibitions S, with *GlobalDataCategory(S,DC)*. Unconditional statements are omitted.
- The *global actions* for a data category is computed as for duties, *mutatis mutandis*.
- The *global level of assurance* for a data category is computed as for duties, *mutatis mutandis*.

In global statements, trust is expressed in a binary way (i.e. *GAPEvidence*): statements are, from the point of view of the data subject, either *Uncertain* or *Guaranteed*. Both global notification guarantees and global retention limits, part of the GAP, are expressed as duties. Global statements present guarantees as a function of categories of personal data. Once global statements have been computed, they are represented as in Listing 4. They are categorized as follows:

- *Global duties about collecting personal data* — declaring actions about the use, collection, or storage of personal data.
- *Global duties about distributing personal data* — declaring actions that forward data to external organizations.
- *Global prohibitions for collecting personal data* — expressing that the use, collection, or storage of personal data is forbidden.
- *Global prohibitions for distributing personal data* — forbidding the forwarding of personal data to an organization.
- *Global notification guarantees* — declaring the sending of a notification upon the occurrence of a specific event.
- *Global retention limits* — expressing the time limit after which all categories of personal data must be deleted.

5   Computation and Evaluation

We illustrate a possible use of the framework with an IDP realization [2]. Our realization infers the GAPs of the user models *U1*, *U2*, and *U3* described earlier,

---

[2] A detailed IDP realization — together with the output containing the GAPs for the three user models — can be found at https://code.google.com/p/inferring-accountability/

```
type GAPEvidence constructed from { Uncertain; Guaranteed }

GAPCollectData(DataCategory)
GAPCollectDataAction(DataCategory, Action)
GAPCollectDataForPurposeOf(DataCategory, Purpose)
GAPCollectDataCondition(DataCategory, Condition)
GAPCollectDataProof(DataCategory, GAPEvidence)

GAPForwardDataTo(DataCategory, Organization)
GAPForwardDataAction(DataCategory, Action)
GAPForwardDataForPurposeOf(DataCategory, Purpose)
GAPForwardDataCondition(DataCategory, Condition)
GAPForwardDataProof(DataCategory, GAPEvidence)

GAPNeverCollectData(DataCategory)
GAPNeverCollectDataForPurposeOf(DataCategory, Purpose)
GAPNeverCollectDataCondition(DataCategory, Condition)
GAPNeverCollectDataProof(DataCategory, GAPEvidence)

GAPNeverForwardDataTo(DataCategory, Organization)
GAPNeverForwardDataForPurposeOf(DataCategory, Purpose)
GAPNeverForwardDataCondition(DataCategory, Condition)
GAPNeverForwardDataProof(DataCategory, GAPEvidence)

GAPNotificationGuarantee(DataCategory)
GAPNotificationGuaranteeCondition(DataCategory, Condition)
GAPNotificationGuaranteeProof(DataCategory, GAPEvidence)

GAPRetentionLimit(DataCategory, Duration)
GAPRetentionLimitCondition(DataCategory, Condition)
GAPRetentionLimitProof(DataCategory, GAPEvidence)
```

IDP Listing 4. Modeling concepts representing the GAP

representing individuals under video surveillance in a railway station. The model was generated in less than a second on a personal computer. We first compare the resulting profiles for naive, regular, and privacy-aware data subjects. Next, we discuss how the statements of entities and users are modeled.

5.1 Trust-Dependent GAP Inference

First, given the type of user and his trust perception toward organizations, we deduce for each entity the user's global statement evidence using the rules of Tab. 2. For instance, $U2$ (i.e. regular user) is sufficiently guaranteed that data practices comply with declared ones if they are merely logged. Instead, $U3$ is satisfied when statements are *logged and verified* by an auditor or just logged in case organizations are trusted by him. This global evidence is then used for the deduction of the GAP using the rules of Tab. 3. The inferred GAPs are summarized in Tab. 4. None of these contain global prohibitions. However, individual statements of entities include two prohibitions (i.e. *R.3* and *I.3*). The reason for this is that worst-case computation rules give priority to global duties containing data categories that are subject of both duties and prohibitions. Semantically, this corresponds to a user who is more concerned about the categories of data used rather than about the unused ones.

Global duties for collecting data are perceived differently by *U1*, *U2*, and *U3*. Since *U1* is satisfied with statements that are purely declarative, he believes that data collection duties are respected by the organizations. Having the same guarantees *U2* is only partially convinced, since he requires at least data handling logs while the security company's duty *S.1* is purely declarative. Therefore, *Time* and *Location*, subjects of *S.1*, are considered as global duty data categories that are uncertain. *U3* needs the strongest guarantees. He is not convinced for any of the data categories part of the GAP. He expects for all data collection duties that logs exist and that they are verified by an auditor. For instance, because duty *R.1* is *logged-unverified*, the duty subjects, such as *Face* and *BlurredFace*, are not sufficiently guaranteed for *U3*. Furthermore, due to *R.1* an additional data category *PictureIncident* is deduced in *U3*'s GAP. This follows from the computation rule in Tab. 3 for duties with global evidence that is uncertain for *U3*, and the given railway station's camera capability *Component-CanCollect(Camera,PictureIncident)*. Also, comparing the GAP of *U3* with the others, more purposes for collecting data are deduced. In particular, besides that *BlurredFace* and *Gait* are collected for incident detection (i.e. *DetectIncident*), these are used as *Evidence* of incidents as well.

Global data forward duties are computed from the declarative duty *R.2* and the merely logged duty *S.2*. Both duties declare to forward data to other stakeholders in the system. The results show that *U1* is satisfied with the guarantees provided that the system respects data forwarding declarations. The same guarantees are too weak to convince *U2* and *U3*. Both doubt that actual data practices correspond with declared ones. At first glance, one could expect that *U2* assumes that *Time* and *Location*, part of the GAP, are used as declared by *S.2*. However, *S.2* is redundant with the purely declared duty *R.2* because *Time* and *Location* are subjects of *R.2* as well. This can be deduced using the computation rules of Tab. 3 and from the railway company's image database capabilities, namely *ComponentCanCollect(ImageDB,Time)* and *ComponentCanCollect(ImageDB,Location)*.

Global retention limits are computed from *R.4*, *I.4*, and *D.3*. Results show that retention limits are conditional (i.e. *NoLegalInvestigation*) for all data categories in the GAP of *U1* and *U2*. The GAP of *U3* shows an additional unconditional retention limit for data category *PersData* (i.e. personal data). This is deduced from *R.4*, which provided evidence not fulfilling *U3*'s expectations. Indeed, *R.4* is just logged, and not verified. Furthermore, *U2* only has partial guarantees for *Time* and *Location* since evidence of *R.3* sufficiently guarantees him. In case of

Table 4. Inferred GAP synthesizing global accountability in the camera surveillance system for user models *U1* (1), *U2* (2), and *U3* (3). The numbers in the table indicate the user models for which the statements in the left column, represented relatively to the different data categories, are valid.

	Picture	Incident	Face	BlurredFace	Gait	Height	Behavior	Time	Location	PersData
Global Collection duties										
Actions										
Collecting	3	1,2,3	1,2,3		1,2,3	1,2,3	1,2,3	1,2,3	1,2,3	
Accessing		1,2,3						1,2,3	1,2,3	
Storing	3	1,2,3	3		3	3	3	1,2,3	1,2,3	
Monitoring	3	3		1,2,3	1,2,3	1,2,3	1,2,3	3	3	
Purposes										
All		1,2,3								
DetectIncident	3		1,2,3		1,2,3	1,2,3	1,2,3	3	3	
Evidence	3		3		3	3	3	1,2,3	1,2,3	
Conditions										
Unconditional	3	1,2,3	1,2,3		1,2,3	1,2,3	1,2,3	1,2,3	1,2,3	
Guaranteed		1,2	1,2		1,2	1,2	1,2	1	1	
Global Forward duties										
Actions										
Forwarding										
to *LegalAuthority*	1,2,3	1,2,3	1,2,3		1,2,3	1,2,3	1,2,3	1,2,3	1,2,3	
Purposes										
Evidence	1,2,3	1,2,3	1,2,3		1,2,3	1,2,3	1,2,3	1,2,3	1,2,3	
Conditions										
RequestLegalAuthority	1,2,3	1,2,3	1,2,3		1,2,3	1,2,3	1,2,3	1,2,3	1,2,3	
Guaranteed	1	1	1		1	1	1	1	1	
Global Retention Limits										
Duration (days)										
60 days	1,2,3	1,2,3	1,2,3		1,2,3	1,2,3	1,2,3			3
90 days								1,2	1,2	
Conditions										
UnConditional										3
NoLegalInvestigation	1,2,3	1,2,3	1,2,3		1,2,3	1,2,3	1,2,3	1,2,3	1,2,3	
Guaranteed	1	1	1		1	1	1	1,2	1,2	

U3, R.3 provides insufficient evidence. Hence, usage of *Time* and *Location* are not sufficiently guaranteed according to *U3*'s GAP.

5.2 Statements Modeling and User Models

The statements presented in the scenario are atomic declarations, i.e. they consist of single actions on subject data categories. Concepts in the framework were defined for modeling atomic statements. However, statements may contain multiple declarations. The concepts defined lack expressiveness for modeling these. These statements must be represented by the atomic parts from which they are composed. For instance, the image database is associated with a declarative statement announcing the storage of personal data of categories *blurred face* and *gait* for a maximum of 30 days and for the purpose of statistics and marketing. This is modeled as (*a*) a *duty* declaring that data categories *blurred face* and *gait* are *stored,* and (*b*) a *retention limit* specifying that data is kept for a maximum of 30 days. In the model, these items correspond to separate elements of the

Statement domain. Though both statements have the same purposes, these must be expressed separately. In particular, *StatementPurpose(Statement,Purpose)* relates the purposes *statistics* and *marketing* to the *duty* and *retention limit* with *2 statements* × *2 purposes* relations. Decomposing combined statements may imply that statement relations grow combinatorially. Similarly, each *Statement* element must be related to the *Entity "ImageDatabase"*, the *Permission "Always"*, and to the *StatementEvidence "Declarative"*. Furthermore, each duty is related to the *Action "Store"*.

Users model. The coarse-grained user categorization we use facilitates user modeling since modelers only need to specify user types via a single constant, for instance *TypeOfUser* = *NaiveUser*. The model's user types intuitively represent typical real-world users, determining how data subjects appreciate statements and evidence from organizations. They reflect the fact that skeptical users are more difficult to convince of the compliance of actual data handling with declared practices. The user model also addresses the high-level trust perception of users. Namely, *UserTrust(O)* expresses that a user trusts the organization *O*.

Reusing framework components. The framework consists of modular components, making possible isolated changes to one part while leaving the others intact. A given system model (e.g. the railway station camera surveillance scenario) is unaffected when new types of users are introduced. Similarly, if an auditor collects different samples of statement evidence, only changes to the evidence in the statement model are required.

Detecting conflicts. The user model could be extended with user privacy preferences containing prohibitions. This aspect could be used by auditors wanting to verify e.g. whether a system, run by a commercial organization, is not collecting sensitive health information. The individual statements of system entities are another flexible facet. Typically, these statements form a large set of opaque and potentially inconsistent declarations. Automated verification can be added to the system-independent part of the framework for easy conflict detection.

6   Related Work

A privacy evaluation framework based on trust assumptions is introduced in [9]. Like our model, it involves multiple stakeholders. This framework was later implemented in IDP [10]. A distinction is made between storage-trusted and distribution-trusted organizations. The privacy analysis focuses on which data is needed for access to services, and how personal data is distributed between interacting services. By contrast, this paper's model targets interactions between organizations, not services, and investigates how statements about personal data handling, backed with varying levels of evidence, combine with trust perceptions to yield assumptions about the processing of personal data.

The approach of using standardized privacy policies to enable accountability by clarifying obligations is widespread. In particular, the idea of combining privacy policies with data handling logs to automatically check compliance ex post appears in [28]. The question of the gap between system event logs and logs at the level of abstraction of privacy policies is addressed in [5]. The consequences of log design choices for log analysis and accountability are addressed in [4]. Adequate log design for compliance checking is tricky because of the numerous possible semantic ambiguities. Both papers presume a single data controller rather than the setting of this paper — a constellation of interacting data processors with different, potentially incompatible privacy policies.

Beyond computer science, the scope of application of accountability is a vividly debated issue in the privacy regulation debate [14]. A key question related to our work is how far data controllers should be required to go to demonstrate compliance. Distinctions are sometimes [6] made between different levels of accountability, ranging from public declarations of intent to full technical transparency, such as the one that we advocate here. The adequacy of procedures, i.e. organizational measures, is often discussed. Privacy Impact Assessments are often advocated [30] and can be seen as a bridge between accountability of procedures and accountability of practice if the assessment is conducted in sufficient detail. The question of privacy-preserving surveillance infrastructures is addressed in particular in the PARIS project [1], with an interdisciplinary angle.

7   Conclusions

We described an accountability inference model and its realization in the IDP knowledge base system. Trust perceptions are taken into account to compute global accountability statements from the individual statements made by interacting entities. We distinguish between different levels of proof for the individual statements, again influencing the resulting global accountability statements. Our approach is illustrated with a scenario involving stakeholders in a railway surveillance infrastructure. The framework is not tied to any particular scenario and can be extended easily. Our representation of data handling evidence is only implicit, and therefore coarse-grained. A more refined approach would model the semantics of log compliance explicitly. This level of detail seems difficult to implement within a first-order logic-based framework. In the current version of the framework, the auditor acting on behalf of an individual is not notified of privacy policy conflicts automatically. Including this aspect would remove the need for manual compatibility checking.

Acknowledgement. This work was funded by the Flemish agency for Innovation by Science and Technology (IWT), the European project PARIS / FP7-SEC-2012-1 and the Inria Project Lab CAPPRIS.

References

1. PrivAcy pReserving Infrastructure for Surveillance (PARIS),
   http://www.paris-project.org
2. Bella, G., Paulson, L.C.: Accountability Protocols: Formalized and Verified. ACM Trans. Inf. Syst. Secur. 9(2), 138–161 (2006)
3. Bellare, M., Yee, B.S.: Forward Integrity for Secure Audit Logs. Tech. rep., University of California at San Diego (1997)
4. Butin, D., Chicote, M., Le Métayer, D.: Log Design for Accountability. In: 2013 IEEE Security & Privacy Workshop on Data Usage Management, pp. 1–7. IEEE Computer Society (2013)
5. Butin, D., Le Métayer, D.: Log Analysis for Data Protection Accountability. In: Jones, C., Pihlajasaari, P., Sun, J. (eds.) FM 2014. LNCS, vol. 8442, pp. 163–178. Springer, Heidelberg (2014)
6. Bennett, C.J.: Implementing Privacy Codes of Practice. Canadian Standards Association (1995)
7. De Hert, P.: Accountability and System Responsibility: New Concepts in Data Protection Law and Human Rights Law. In: Managing Privacy through Accountability, pp. 193–232. Palgrave Macmillan (2012)
8. De Pooter, S., Wittocx, J., Denecker, M.: A Prototype of a Knowledge-based Programming Environment. In: Proceedings of the 19th International Conference on Applications of Declarative Programming and Knowledge Management (INAP 2011), pp. 191–196 (2011)
9. Decroix, K., Lapon, J., De Decker, B., Naessens, V.: A Formal Approach for Inspecting Privacy and Trust in Advanced Electronic Services. In: Jürjens, J., Livshits, B., Scandariato, R. (eds.) ESSoS 2013. LNCS, vol. 7781, pp. 155–170. Springer, Heidelberg (2013)
10. Decroix, K., Lapon, J., De Decker, B., Naessens, V.: A Framework for Formal Reasoning about Privacy Properties Based on Trust Relationships in Complex Electronic Services. In: Bagchi, A., Ray, I. (eds.) ICISS 2013. LNCS, vol. 8303, pp. 106–120. Springer, Heidelberg (2013)
11. Denecker, M.: A Knowledge Base System Project for FO(.). In: Hill, P.M., Warren, D.S. (eds.) ICLP 2009. LNCS, vol. 5649, p. 22. Springer, Heidelberg (2009)
12. European Commission: Regulation of the European Parliament and of the Council on the protection of individuals with regard to the processing of personal data and on the free movement of such data (General Data Protection Regulation), inofficial consolidated version after LIBE committee vote (2013)
13. Gebser, M., Kaufmann, B., Schaub, T.: Conflict-Driven Answer Set Solving: From Theory to Practice. Artif. Intell. 187, 52–89 (2012)
14. Guagnin, D., Hempel, L., Ilten, C.: Managing Privacy Through Accountability. Palgrave Macmillan (2012)
15. Haeberlen, A.: A Case for the Accountable Cloud. Operating Systems Review 44(2), 52–57 (2010)
16. The IDP system (2014), http://dtai.cs.kuleuven.be/krr/idp
17. KRR Software: IDP examples (2014),
    http://dtai.cs.kuleuven.be/krr/software/idp-examples
18. Ierusalimschy, R., de Figueiredo, L.H., Celes, W.: Lua – an extensible extension language. Software: Practice and Experience 26(6), 635–652 (1996)
19. Jackson, D.: Alloy: A Lightweight Object Modelling Notation. ACM Transactions on Software Engineering and Methodology (TOSEM 2002) 11(2), 256–290 (2002)

20. Jackson, D.: Alloy: a language & tool for relational models (2012),
    http://alloy.mit.edu/alloy/
21. Lee, L., Grimson, W.E.L.: Gait Analysis for Recognition and Classification. In:
    IEEE International Conference on Automatic Face and Gesture Recognition,
    pp. 148–155 (2002)
22. Leone, N., Pfeifer, G., Faber, W., Eiter, T., Gottlob, G., Perri, S., Scarcello, F.:
    The DLV system for knowledge representation and reasoning. ACM Trans. Comput.
    Log. 7(3), 499–562 (2006)
23. Mecocci, A., Pannozzo, M., Fumarola, A.: Automatic detection of anomalous be-
    havioural events for advanced real-time video surveillance. In: IEEE International
    Symposium on Computational Intelligence for Measurement Systems and Applica-
    tions (CIMSA 2003), pp. 187–192 (2003)
24. Organisation for Economic Co-operation and Development: OECD Guidelines on
    the Protection of Privacy and Transborder Flows of Personal Data (1980)
25. Raab, C.: The Meaning of 'Accountability' in the Information Privacy Context. In:
    Managing Privacy through Accountability, pp. 15–32. Palgrave Macmillan (2012)
26. Van Gelder, A., Ross, K.A., Schlipf, J.S.: The Well-Founded Semantics for General
    Logic Programs. Journal of the ACM 38(3), 620–650 (1991)
27. Viola, P., Jones, M.: Robust Real-Time Face Detection. International Journal of
    Computer Vision 57(2), 137–154 (2004)
28. Weitzner, D.J., Abelson, H., Berners-Lee, T., Feigenbaum, J., Hendler, J., Sussman,
    G.J.: Information accountability. Commun. ACM 51(6), 82–87 (2008)
29. Wittocx, J., Mariën, M., Denecker, M.: The IDP system: A model expansion system
    for an extension of classical logic. In: Denecker, M. (ed.) Proceedings of the 2nd
    Workshop on Logic and Search, Logic and Search, pp. 153–165. ACCO (2008)
30. Wright, D., de Hert, P.: Introduction to Privacy Impact Assessment. In: Wright,
    D., Hert, P. (eds.) Privacy Impact Assessment, pp. 3–32. Springer (2012)

Client Side Web Session Integrity
as a Non-interference Property

Wilayat Khan[1], Stefano Calzavara[1], Michele Bugliesi[1],
Willem De Groef[2], and Frank Piessens[2]

[1] Ca' Foscari University of Venice, Italy
[2] iMinds-DistriNet, KU Leuven, Belgium

Abstract. Sessions on the web are fragile. They have been attacked successfully in many ways, by network-level attacks, by direct attacks on session cookies (the main mechanism for implementing the session concept) and by application-level attacks where the integrity of sessions is violated by means of cross-site request forgery or malicious script inclusion. This paper defines a variant of non-interference – the classical security notion from information flow security – that can be used to formally define the notion of client-side application-level web session integrity. The paper also develops and proves correct an enforcement mechanism. Combined with state-of-the-art countermeasures for network-level and cookie-level attacks, this enforcement mechanism gives very strong assurance about the client-side preservation of session integrity for authenticated sessions.

Keywords: web security, information flow control.

1 Introduction

Because of the stateless nature of the HTTP protocol, web applications that need to maintain state over multiple interactions with a client have to implement some form of *session management*: the server needs to know to which ongoing session (if any) incoming HTTP requests belong. Sessions are usually implemented by means of *session cookies*. The server generates an unpredictable random identifier at the start of a session, and sends it to the browser as a cookie. All subsequent requests from the same client will carry this cookie, and this tells the server which session incoming requests belong to. Session management is an important but vulnerable part of the modern web, in particular because client authentication is usually tied to sessions: the client is authenticated using either a password, a single-sign-on system or some multi-factor scheme, and if authentication is successful, the server marks the *session* as authenticated. Hence, attacks against session management can be used to impersonate clients to the server.

Sessions can be attacked at many layers. First, at the network layer, network sniffing or man-in-the-middle attacks can break the confidentiality or integrity of web sessions. This is a well-understood problem with well-understood solutions: by appropriate use of transport level security techniques such as SSL/TLS, these

A. Prakash and R. Shyamasundar (Eds.): ICISS 2014, LNCS 8880, pp. 89–108, 2014.

attacks can be stopped. Second, at the session implementation layer, script injection or again network level attacks can be used to steal a session cookie and hijack the session, or to impose a session cookie on a client (a so-called session fixation attack [19,15]). Again, this is a well-understood problem: ensuring that sessions only run over SSL/TLS, prohibiting script access to session cookies (by setting the HttpOnly and Secure attributes on session cookies), and enforcing renewal of a session on authentication, are appropriate countermeasures to such attacks. Third, sessions can be attacked at the application layer: since cookies are attached to HTTP requests by the browser automatically – without any web application involvement – any page in the browser can send malicious requests to any of the servers that the browser currently has a session with, and that request will automatically get the session cookie attached and hence will be considered as part of a (possibly authenticated) session by the server. If the page sending the malicious request is from a different origin, such attacks are called CSRF (cross-site request forgery) attacks [4]. But malicious requests can also be sent by scripts included in – or injected by an attacker into – a page from the same origin. Since both inclusions of third-party scripts [23] and script injection vulnerabilities are common [18], these are important attack vectors.

The focus of this paper is on *client-side protection against application-level attacks against sessions*. We assume that state-of-the-art countermeasures are in place for network-level and session management-level attacks, and our objective is to formally define the notion of *client-side session integrity* and to develop provably secure countermeasures for application-level attacks. While point solutions exist to protect against various forms of CSRF and script injection, the problem of application-level session integrity is not yet well-understood. There are two existing formalizations of the notion of web session integrity: Akhawe et al. [2] develop an Alloy model of the web platform and define session integrity as the property that *no attacker is in the causal chain of any HTTP request belonging to the session*. This is an excellent definition for the purpose of studying CSRF attacks and countermeasures, but the underlying model does not have a sufficiently detailed representation of scripts to study other application-level session integrity issues. In a very recent paper, Bugliesi et al. [10] are the first to provide a formal definition of session integrity that is browser-centric and amenable for client-side enforcement. They define how an attacker can influence execution traces of the browser, and then define session integrity as the property that the attacker has no effective way of interfering with an authenticated session. Based on this definition, they also design an access control/tainting mechanism that enforces session integrity at the client side.

The main objectives of this paper are (1) to refine the definition of Bugliesi et al. to a classical non-interference property [25], under the assumption that appropriate defenses against both network-level and cookie-level attacks are put in place, and (2) to design an information flow control technique that can enforce session integrity in a more permissive and fine-grained way than access control mechanisms can. This is crucial to foster the usability of the client-side protection mechanism and support collaborative web scenarios, like e-payment.

In summary, the main contributions of this paper are:

- the development of *login history dependent* non-interference for reactive systems, a variant of non-interference where the security labeling function is execution history dependent.
- the application of login history dependent non-interference to web session integrity: we show how this notion of non-interference captures the peculiarities and complexities of web session integrity.
- the development of a mechanism for enforcing login history dependent non-interference by means of secure multi-execution, with a formal proof of security.
- the design of additional improvements to this mechanism for the web context.
- a prototype implementation of the mechanism as an extension of the FlowFox information flow secure web browser.

The remainder of this paper is structured as follows. First, in Section 2, we give an informal overview of the problem of application-level session integrity and the idea of login history dependent non-interference. We formalize this in Section 3, where we define an enforcement mechanism and prove it secure. Then, in Section 4 we show how this applies to web session integrity, and in Section 5 we describe a few extensions to the formal model to make the enforcement mechanism more compatible with the web. In Section 6 we describe our prototype implementation. Sections 7 and 8 discuss related work and conclude.

2   Informal Overview

Consider a user using his web browser to interact with a number of web sites. With some of these web sites, the user has an ongoing authenticated session (for instance with his web mail provider M and with a social networking site S). Other sites have been opened in the browser by casually surfing the web, and the user has no authenticated session with them. Both pages from more trusted sites (like M or S) and less trusted sites (e.g., a web site O) might themselves consist of content retrieved from a variety of origins. A page served by M might include scripts, images and other resources from anywhere on the web.

The problem we consider in this paper is the following one: how can we make sure that the browser protects the integrity of the authenticated sessions that it has, for instance, with M, in the sense that no other web site than M itself can influence authenticated HTTP requests from the browser to M. Even if we assume (as we do in this paper) that network communication and session cookies are adequately protected, the following example attacks are still possible:

- CSRF: Pages from O can send HTTP requests to M or S, for instance by including an image or a script from these sites, or (in some cases) by sending an XHR request. The browser will automatically attach cookies to these requests, including the session cookie, and hence such requests are treated by the server as belonging to the authenticated session.

- Malicious resource inclusions: if M includes a script from some script provider (e.g. an advertisement network, a JavaScript library provider, or a web analytics company) then that script can send arbitrary authenticated HTTP requests to M.
- Client-side or reflected XSS: Pages from O can load pages from M and use a mal-formed fragment identifier or URL parameter that trigger a client-side (DOM-based) or reflected XSS vulnerability. The injected script can then send arbitrary authenticated requests to M.

A common way to formalize integrity properties such as the one above is based on concepts from information flow security. One defines a partially ordered set of security labels that represent integrity levels (in the simplest case, two labels $\top$ and $\bot$ for high, respectively low, integrity). All inputs and outputs from the program under consideration (in our case, the browser) are labeled. Inputs are labeled $\top$ if they come from a trustworthy source, and $\bot$ otherwise. Outputs are labeled $\top$ if their integrity is important and $\bot$ otherwise. A program is information flow secure (non-interferent) if low integrity inputs do not influence high integrity outputs (i.e. no information flows from low integrity sources to high integrity targets).

A complication in the case of web session integrity is that both the set of integrity labels, as well as the labeling function, evolve over time as the user logs into more sites. The same message sent by site O to site M (for instance if the page from O sends a request to load a resource from M) will be of low integrity level if the browser is currently not logged into M, and it will be of a higher integrity level if the browser *is* logged into M. This kind of login history dependent non-interference is exactly what we will formalize and then instantiate to the web context in the following sections.

3 Login History Dependent Non-interference: Definition and Enforcement

Following Bohannon et al. [9,8,7], we model a browser as a *reactive system*. Then we introduce the property of *login history dependent reactive non-interference* and an enforcement mechanism for it.

3.1 Reactive System

A reactive system is a constrained labeled transition system that transforms input events into sequences of output events.

Definition 1 (Reactive System). *A reactive system is a tuple* $(\mathcal{C}, \mathcal{P}, \mathcal{I}, \mathcal{O}, \longrightarrow)$, *where* $\mathcal{C}$ *and* $\mathcal{P}$ *are disjoint sets of consumer and producer states respectively,* $\mathcal{I}$ *and* $\mathcal{O}$ *are disjoint sets of input and output events respectively. The last component,* $\longrightarrow$, *is a labeled transition relation over the set of states* $\mathcal{S} \triangleq \mathcal{C} \cup \mathcal{P}$ *and the set of labels* $\mathcal{A} \triangleq \mathcal{I} \cup \mathcal{O}$, *subject to the following constraints:*

1. $C \in \mathcal{C}$ and $C \xrightarrow{\alpha} Q$ imply $\alpha \in \mathcal{I}$ and $Q \in \mathcal{P}$;
2. $P \in \mathcal{P}$, $Q \in \mathcal{S}$ and $P \xrightarrow{\alpha} Q$ imply $\alpha \in \mathcal{O}$;
3. $C \in \mathcal{C}$ and $i \in \mathcal{I}$ imply $\exists P \in \mathcal{P} : C \xrightarrow{i} P$;
4. $P \in \mathcal{P}$ implies $\exists o \in \mathcal{O}, \exists Q \in \mathcal{S} : P \xrightarrow{o} Q$.

We limit our attention in this paper to deterministic reactive systems.

We assume given a set of web domains $\mathcal{D}$, and we stipulate that the set of input events $\mathcal{I}$ contains an event $\mathsf{login}(d)$ for all $d \in \mathcal{D}$. This event models a successful login of the browser into domain d. We assume the set of output events $\mathcal{O}$ contains an event $\cdot$ that represents a *silent* output, i.e. an internal computation step of the reactive system. A stream is defined by the coinductive interpretation of the grammar $S ::= [] \mid s :: S'$, where s ranges over individual stream elements. Bohannon et al. define the behaviour of a reactive system in a state Q as a relation between input and output streams. To handle login history dependence, we instead define it as a relation between input streams and event streams that contain both input and output events, appropriately interleaved:

Definition 2 (Reactive Behaviour). *A reactive system state Q generates the event stream S from the input stream I if the judgment $Q(I) \rightsquigarrow S$ holds, where this judgment is coinductively defined by:*

$$\frac{}{C([]) \rightsquigarrow []} \qquad \frac{C \xrightarrow{i} P \qquad P(I) \rightsquigarrow S}{C(i :: I) \rightsquigarrow i :: S} \qquad \frac{P \xrightarrow{o} Q \qquad Q(I) \rightsquigarrow S}{P(I) \rightsquigarrow o :: S}$$

3.2 Login History Dependent Non-interference

The lattice of possible integrity levels $\mathcal{L}$ has elements $\top$ (highest integrity), $\bot$ (lowest integrity), and d for all $d \in \mathcal{D}$ (integrity level of authenticated communication with domain d). Since higher integrity information can flow to lower integrity levels but not vice-versa, we define the ordering relation on $\mathcal{L}$ as $\top \leq d \leq \bot$, and for different d and d', d and d' are incomparable.

The key idea of login history dependent non-interference (LHDNI) is to make the labeling function that assigns integrity levels to events dependent on the login events that have occurred. Initially, all network events are low integrity ($\bot$), but after a $\mathsf{login}(d)$ event, network communication with d will have level d. This models the behaviour of a web browser: because of the automatic attaching of cookies (including the session cookie), the integrity of network communication to domain d becomes more important after a login to d. It also models our assumption that the server will be more careful with HTTP responses for authenticated sessions (integrity level of these responses is higher).

The login history is represented as a finite sub-lattice L of $\mathcal{L}$, where L is initially $\{\top, \bot\}$, and L evolves with inputs processed as follows (where we write $L \oplus d$ for extending L with element d):

$$\begin{array}{cc} (\tau\text{-LOGIN}) & (\tau\text{-NIL}) \\ i = \mathsf{login}(d) & i \neq \mathsf{login}(d) \\ \hline L \xrightarrow{i} L \oplus d & L \xrightarrow{i} L \end{array}$$

In words, whenever the user logs into a domain d, label d is added to the set of integrity labels L.

The function $lbl_L(e) : \mathcal{I} \uplus \mathcal{O} \to \mathcal{L}$ that labels events depends on the login history L. The intuition is that interactions that belong to a session with a domain d will get label d iff $d \in L$, otherwise they get label $\perp$, i.e. once logged in to d, we care about the integrity of messages to d. We stipulate that $lbl_L(\mathsf{login}(d)) = d$ for any d.

We use the notation $L^{|l}$ for the list of labels $l' \in L$ such that $l \le l'$ and $L_{|l}$ for the list of labels $l' \in L$ such that $l' \le l$. For an input i, for simplicity, we write $L^{|lbl_L(i)}$ as just $L^{|i}$.

LHDNI is defined in terms of the relation *LHD-similarity*, which defines when two streams look the same to an observer at level l while taking the login history into consideration.

Definition 3 (LHD-similarity). *Under login history L, two streams S and S' are LHD-similar at level l if the judgment $L \vdash S \approx_l S'$ holds, where this judgment is coinductively defined by:*

$$\frac{}{L \vdash [] \approx_l []} \text{(ID-NIL)} \qquad \frac{s = \mathsf{login}(d) \quad d \le l \quad L \oplus d \vdash S \approx_l S'}{L \vdash s :: S \approx_l s :: S'} \text{(ID-LOGIN)}$$

$$\frac{s \ne \mathsf{login}(d) \quad lbl_L(s) \le l \quad L \vdash S \approx_l S'}{L \vdash s :: S \approx_l s :: S'} \text{(ID-SIM)} \qquad \frac{lbl_L(s) \not\le l \quad L \vdash S \approx_l S'}{L \vdash s :: S \approx_l S'} \text{(ID-L)}$$

$$\frac{lbl_L(s) \not\le l \quad L \vdash S \approx_l S'}{L \vdash S \approx_l s :: S'} \text{(ID-R)}$$

Now, a state is LHDNI if l-similar inputs lead to l-similar outputs:

Definition 4 (LHDNI). *A state Q of a reactive system is LHDNI if $Q(I) \rightsquigarrow S$ and $Q(I') \rightsquigarrow S'$ imply that $\forall l \in \mathcal{L}, \emptyset \vdash I \approx_l I' \Rightarrow \emptyset \vdash S \approx_l S'$.*

Notice that it is important that we compare S and S', the event streams that contain interleaved input and output events, because of the history dependence of the definition of LHD-similarity. If we would only consider the output events, as classic non-interference definitions do, then there would be no login event present in the output streams; but we have to keep the login events there, because they influence the labeling function.

3.3   Enforcement

We now build an enforcement mechanism based on secure multi-execution (SME) [16,6,24]. The basic idea is to construct a new reactive system that is a wrapper around multiple copies (sub-executions) of the original reactive system, one for each level in the login history L. When the wrapper consumes an input event, it is passed to the copies at or higher than the level of the input. When a sub-execution produces an output, if its level matches the level of the execution, the output is produced by the wrapper, otherwise it is suppressed.

A state of the wrapper is a triple (L, R, L_q), where

- L is the login history,
- R is a function mapping security labels in L to states, i.e. $R(l)$ is the sub-execution at level l, and
- L_q is a waiting queue of levels that still need to process the last input consumed. It is initially empty and when an input is consumed it is set to all levels that should process this input. We order these from low integrity to high integrity such that the sub-execution at level $\bot$ is always executed first.

States $(L, R, [])$ are consumer states, and states (L, R, L_q) with $L_q \neq []$ are producer states. The initial state of the wrapper is a state $(\{\top, \bot\}, R, [])$ with $R(\top)$ and $R(\bot)$ being the initial state of the original reactive system.

(LOGIN)
$$\frac{i = \mathsf{login}(d) \quad d \notin L \quad L' = L \oplus d \quad L_q = L'^{|d}}{R(l) \xrightarrow{i} P_l \quad R'(d) = P_\top \quad R'(l) = P_l \text{ for } l \in L_q \setminus \{d\} \quad R'(l) = R(l) \text{ for } l \notin L_q} $$
$$\frac{}{(L, R, []) \xrightarrow{i} (L', R', L_q)}$$

(LOAD)
$$\frac{i \neq \mathsf{login}(d) \vee (i = \mathsf{login}(d) \text{ with } d \in L)}{R(l) \xrightarrow{i} P_l \quad L_q = L^{|i} \quad R'(l) = P_l \text{ for } l \in L_q \quad R'(l) = R(l) \text{ for } l \notin L_q}$$
$$\frac{}{(L, R, []) \xrightarrow{i} (L, R', L_q)}$$

(OUT-P)
$$\frac{R(l) \xrightarrow{o} P \quad lbl_L(o) = l}{(L, R, l :: L_q) \xrightarrow{o} (L, R[l \mapsto P], l :: L_q)}$$

(OUT-C)
$$\frac{R(l) \xrightarrow{o} C \quad lbl_L(o) = l}{(L, R, l :: L_q) \xrightarrow{o} (L, R[l \mapsto C], L_q)}$$

(DROP-P)
$$\frac{R(l) \xrightarrow{o} P \quad lbl_L(o) \neq l}{(L, R, l :: L_q) \rightarrow (L, R[l \mapsto P], l :: L_q)}$$

(DROP-C)
$$\frac{R(l) \xrightarrow{o} C \quad lbl_L(o) \neq l}{(L, R, l :: L_q) \rightarrow (L, R[l \mapsto C], L_q)}$$

Fig. 1. Basic semantics for secure multi-execution of a reactive system

The semantics is shown in Figure 1. The main extension with respect to standard SME for reactive systems [6] is the way in which login events are handled: these update the login history L, and hence also the number of sub-executions in the wrapper, and (implicitly) the labeling function lbl_L. Note how the newly created sub-execution at level d is initialized: $P_\top$ is the resulting state after giving i to $R(\top)$, i.e. we essentially clone the sub-execution at level $\top$ and feed it i. This is the right thing to do, as we want the newly created sub-execution to have seen all the events of higher integrity than d. The (LOAD) rule handles other input events than initial login events. It essentially feeds the input to all sub-executions with a level $\leq lbl_L(i)$, by updating the appropriate sub-executions in R to a state where they have received i, and by setting the waiting queue to contain all levels that have to process this input event. The other four rules implement the SME output rules, making sure that output of level l is only performed by the execution at level l. They also make sure that, as sub-executions return to a producer state, the next sub-execution in the waiting queue gets a chance to run.

These rules effectively block all cross-origin requests to authenticated domains. For instance, if a page received from an unauthenticated domain (a $\bot$ event) loads an image from an authenticated domain d, the corresponding HTTP request (a d-level event) will be suppressed.

We can do substantially better: instead of dropping such requests, we can strip the session cookie from the request as in other client-side CSRF protection systems [10,14]. We assume the existence of a function $strip^L(o)$ that for any o with $lbl_L(o) = d$ (for some d) strips the session cookies from o, and for all other o returns o.

We define the projection functions π_l^L as follows:

$$\pi_l^L(o) = \begin{cases} strip^L(o) & \text{if } l = \bot \\ o & \text{otherwise} \end{cases}$$

We assume that the event labeling function lbl_L checks for the presence of an authentication cookie to deem a network output as a high integrity event. Hence $lbl_L(strip^L(o))$ is always $\bot$.

(OUT-P)
$$\frac{R(l) \xrightarrow{o} P \qquad release_{L,l,L_q}(o)}{(L,R,l :: L_q) \xrightarrow{\pi_l^L(o)} (L, R[l \mapsto P], l :: L_q)}$$

(OUT-C)
$$\frac{R(l) \xrightarrow{o} C \qquad release_{L,l,L_q}(o)}{(L,R,l :: L_q) \xrightarrow{\pi_l^L(o)} (L, R[l \mapsto C], L_q)}$$

(DROP-P)
$$\frac{R(l) \xrightarrow{o} P \qquad \neg release_{L,l,L_q}(o)}{(L,R,l :: L_q) \xrightarrow{} (L, R[l \mapsto P], l :: L_q)}$$

(DROP-C)
$$\frac{R(l) \xrightarrow{o} C \qquad \neg release_{L,l,L_q}(o)}{(L,R,l :: L_q) \xrightarrow{} (L, R[l \mapsto C], L_q)}$$

Fig. 2. Semantics for secure multi-execution of a reactive system (updated)

The basic semantics (Figure 1) released an output o from a sub-execution at level l only if $lbl_L(o) = l$. We can now generalize this: a sub-execution at level l can release $\pi_l^L(o)$ if the following predicate holds:

$$release_{L,l,L_q}(o) \quad = \quad lbl_L(o) = l \vee (l = \bot \wedge lbl_L(o) \notin L_q)$$

That is, an output is *released* from a sub-execution if its label matches the label l of the sub-execution, or when $l = \bot$ and there is no sub-execution at the level of the output in the waiting queue. Since we process sub-executions in the order from low integrity to high integrity, this means that this output is being sent in response to an input that was *not* of level $lbl_L(o)$, and hence is a cross-domain request to an authenticated domain. We show the updated rules in Figure 2.

3.4 Security

We now show that the enforcement mechanism defined above guarantees LHDNI. All the proofs of lemmas and theorems are given in the full version [21].

Theorem 1 (Security). *All the initial states of the wrapper are LHDNI.*

We prove the theorem using Bohannon's ID-bisimulation proof technique [9]. It suffices to prove that there exists an ID-bisimulation $\approx_l$ such that for every state of the wrapper (L, R, L_q), we have $(L, R, L_q) \approx_l (L, R, L_q)$. The proof of security consists of two steps: first we have to define the relation $\approx_l$ and then we need to show that it is indeed an ID-bisimulation relation. Note the overloading of the $\approx_l$ notation. When used between streams, it is interpreted as LHD-similarity (Definition 3), when used between reactive system states, it refers to the definition below.

Definition 5 (*l-similarity* relation $\approx_l$). *The state (L_1, R_1, L_{q1}) is l-similar to the state (L_2, R_2, L_{q2}) (written $(L_1, R_1, L_{q1}) \approx_l (L_2, R_2, L_{q2})$) iff:*

- $L_{1|l} = L_{2|l}$, *and*
- $R_1 \approx_l R_2$, *meaning* $\forall l' \leq l: R_1(l') = R_2(l')$, *and*
- $L_{q1|l} = L_{q2|l}$.

Lemma 1. *The l-similarity relation is an ID-bisimulation relation.*

4   Instantiation to Web Session Integrity

In this section, we show by example how LHDNI protects browsers from typical attacks on session integrity. Recall that we assume that best practices for session security (i.e. the use of SSL/TLS and the use of the Secure and HttpOnly attributes on session cookies) are in place. We assume that login events are recognizable by the browser; they are triggered for instance by a bookmarklet or password manager, and the response page of the site that one is logging into is shown in a separate top-level frame (tab) in the browser. The browser should enforce that logins to these known and trusted domains *must* happen through these bookmarklets, to avoid attacks such as login CSRF [4].

We show by example how remaining attacks such as classic CSRF and malicious script inclusion are countered by our enforcement mechanism. A similar example can be constructed for client-side or reflected XSS.

Applying the enforcement mechanism described by the semantics in Figure 2 to web browsers requires us to define the sets of input and output events for a browser. We limit our attention to a simple set of events that can model the attacks we care about. These events are described in Table 1 (the first 4 events are input events, the last 4 are output events). The table also shows the value of the lbl_L function.

All these events are standard browser events and easy to recognize by the browser (for the $\mathsf{login}(d)$ event because of the assumptions we made above).

Table 1. User actions, input/output events and their labels

User actions	I/O events	lbl_L	
		$d \in L$	$d \notin L$
typing URL to domain d in the address bar	$\mathsf{ui\_load}(d)$	$\top$	$\top$
network response from domain d with header h	$\mathsf{net\_resp}(d, h)$	d	$\perp$
clicking link on the page from domain d	$\mathsf{ui\_link\_click}(d)$	d	$\perp$
entering password on the page from domain d	$\mathsf{login}(d)$	d	d
network request to domain d (incl. cookie)	$\mathsf{net\_req}(d)$	d	$\perp$
network request to domain d (no cookie)	$\mathsf{net\_req}(d)$	$\perp$	$\perp$
loading a page at the screen	$\mathsf{ui\_page\_loaded}$	$\perp$	$\perp$
dummy	$\cdot$	$\perp$	$\perp$

CSRF. Figure 3 gives a schematic overview of a classic CSRF attack. The user signs into web site A (messages 1-4) and opens a page in another tab from malicious web site E (messages 5-8), which implicitly sends a cross-origin request to load remote content (e.g. an image) from A (message 9). As the browser will attach all the cookies with this request to A, it will lead to a CSRF attack on A.

Figure 4 shows an encoding of this attack in our browser model, and shows how our enforcement mechanism stops the attack. Each line of the encoding is of the form $(E, [Rule]) : (L, R, []) \xrightarrow{n} (L', R', L_q)$, where E is the input or output event, $Rule$ is the semantics rule (Figure 2), (L, R, L_q) represents the state of the wrapper and n is the message number in the corresponding interaction diagram figure. Outputs are shown slightly indented, so that it is easy to see by which input event they are caused. We write L_0 for the set $\{\perp, \top\}$, and L_A for the set $\{\perp, A, \top\}$. For simplicity, the finite list $l_1 :: l_2 :: []$ is denoted with $l_1 :: l_2$. If we do not care about a specific component of the browser state, we write $\_$.

Events and semantics rules corresponding to each event in Figure 3 are shown in Figure 4. In this scenario, using a standard web browser, the attack would happen in message 9, where the request to A (initiated in response from E) would include cookies. However, under the wrapper, the attack is prevented. Specifically, the basic semantics in Figure 1 would drop the request, since a low integrity sub-execution is not allowed to send A-labeled requests; the updated

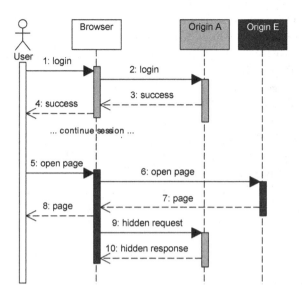

Fig. 3. Classic CSRF

semantics in Figure 2, instead, would strip the cookies from the request for the very same reason. Both options are secure, but the second option will break less existing web sites.

Malicious script inclusion. Figure 5 gives a schematic overview of a script inclusion attack. The user signs into web site A (messages 1-4) and then opens a page (messages 5-6). This page includes a script tag that will include a third party script from E. When the page from A is being rendered (messages 7-8), the remote script is loaded from the web site E (message 9-10). The script can then for instance install an event handler that will trigger an (authenticated) request to A at a later time.

This example is encoded in Figure 6. The response input from E (message 10) gets a $\perp$ label, hence is fed only into the low integrity sub-execution. All the requests to A initiated by the user (in the context of A) or directly by input from A are released from the sub-execution at level A, and hence are not affected by the script injected to the sub-execution at $\perp$. Requests released from the $\perp$ sub-execution may be affected but as those outputs do not include cookies, they are safe. In the example, the request to A (message 12) as the result of the user input (message 11) is released from the execution at $\perp$ (release line 12 in Figure 6). The sub-execution at A label never received the script from E, so it will not react to the link click, and just output a silent event ($\cdot$).

1. $(\mathsf{login}(A), [\mathrm{LOGIN}])$: $(L_0, \lrcorner, [\,]) \xrightarrow{1} (L_A, \lrcorner, \perp :: A)$
   2. suppress $(\mathsf{net\_req}(A), [\mathrm{DROP\text{-}C}])$: $(L_A, \lrcorner, \perp :: A) \dashrightarrow (L_A, \lrcorner, A)$
   2. release $(\mathsf{net\_req}(A), [\mathrm{OUT\text{-}C}])$: $(L_A, \lrcorner, A) \xrightarrow{2} (L_A, \lrcorner, [\,])$
2. $(\mathsf{net\_resp}(A, h), [\mathrm{LOAD}])$: $(L_A, \lrcorner, [\,]) \xrightarrow{3} (L_A, \lrcorner, \perp :: A)$
   4. release $(\mathsf{ui\_page\_loaded}, [\mathrm{OUT\text{-}C}])$: $(L_A, \lrcorner, \perp :: A) \xrightarrow{4} (L_A, \lrcorner, A)$
   4. suppress $(\mathsf{ui\_page\_loaded}, [\mathrm{DROP\text{-}C}])$: $(L_A, \lrcorner, A) \dashrightarrow (L_A, \lrcorner, [\,])$
3. $(\mathsf{ui\_load}(u_E), [\mathrm{LOAD}])$: $(L_A, \lrcorner, [\,]) \xrightarrow{5} (L_A, \lrcorner, \perp :: A :: \top)$
   6. release $(\mathsf{net\_req}(E), [\mathrm{OUT\text{-}C}])$: $(L_A, \lrcorner, \perp :: A :: \top) \xrightarrow{6} (L_A, \lrcorner, A :: \top)$
   6. suppress $(\mathsf{net\_req}(E), [\mathrm{DROP\text{-}C}])$: $(L_A, \lrcorner, A :: \top) \dashrightarrow (L_A, \lrcorner, \top)$
   6. suppress $(\mathsf{net\_req}(E), [\mathrm{DROP\text{-}C}])$: $(L_A, \lrcorner, \top) \dashrightarrow (L_A, \lrcorner, [\,])$
4. $(\mathsf{net\_resp}(E, h), [\mathrm{LOAD}])$: $(L_A, \lrcorner, [\,]) \xrightarrow{7} (L_A, \lrcorner, \perp)$
   8. release $(\mathsf{ui\_page\_loaded}, [\mathrm{OUT\text{-}P}])$: $(L_A, \lrcorner, \perp) \xrightarrow{8} (L_A, \lrcorner, \perp)$
   9. release w/o cookies $(\mathsf{net\_req}(A), [\mathrm{OUT\text{-}C}])$: $(L_A, \lrcorner, \perp) \xrightarrow{9} (L_A, \lrcorner, [\,])$

Fig. 4. Classic CSRF attack encoding and prevention

5 Extensions

The enforcement mechanism described by the formal semantics in Figure 2 enforces security policies to protect against attacks on session integrity, but by doing so it does break some common web scenarios that technically violate session integrity, but do so without malicious purposes. These scenarios can be handled in our approach by means of *endorsement* (the integrity variant of *declassification* [24,28]).

Endorsements will typically have to be declared by the web site that the browser has an authenticated session with. In the two approaches below, these declarations are done by means of request headers, similar to how Content Security Policy (CSP) [27] policies are communicated to the browser.

Endorsing script inclusions. A first, simple and common kind of endorsement is for script inclusion. The script inclusion example in Figure 5 is commonly *not* an attack: web site A includes the script from E intentionally and trusts it to influence the session. While some scripts can be usefully included without having the possibility to influence the session (e.g. analytics scripts), inclusion of other scripts is only useful when these scripts have the right to influence the session (e.g. the jQuery library).

Fortunately, endorsing script inclusions is straightforward. The server A declares in a HTTP header which origins can provide trusted scripts, and the browser uses this information to label outgoing and incoming requests to these white-listed origins from A's pages as being of level A. One could even argue that this should be the default interpretation of the CSP policy directives that allow script inclusions (e.g. the `script-src` directive).

Endorsements for collaborating applications. Endorsements are also required for collaborating web applications such as e-payment systems (e.g. Paypal). Con-

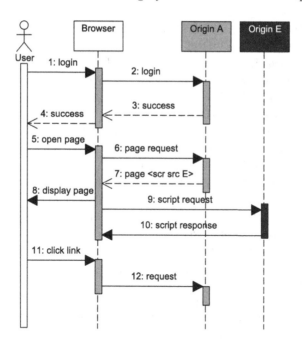

Fig. 5. Script inclusion attack

sider, for example, a user who wants to buy an airline ticket at web site A and pay via *paypal.com* (Figure 7).

The user opens a page from web site A where he clicks the *buy* button and then the user confirms the payment on the *paypal.com* web site. Messages 3-4 and 15-17 of Figure 7 are encoded in our model in Figure 8. We assume the user is logged into both A and P (Paypal), i.e. L contains both A and P.

The message 17 (*GET: confirmed*) is a cross-origin request to A and hence the wrapper will release it from the execution at $\bot$. As all the session cookies are erased, the payment operation will fail.

To support such collaborating web applications, endorsement is needed. For these cases, we propose the use of a response header, used by the web site to specify allowed entry points from different origins. A web site s (source of white-list) sends a list of URLs *url* pointing to s specifying that another site w (white-listed site) is allowed to send cross-origin requests to these URLs, by setting a *connect-destination (cd)* header $<cd: \{ W{:}w, U{:}url\}>$ in the response.

The wrapper will keep track of these headers by updating a set ω of key-value pairs of the form (w, url), where w is the white-listed web site (the *who* part) and *url* is the list of URLs (the *how* part) specified as the allowed entry points white-listed for the w. The list of URLs *url* can also include URLs with wildcard character $*$ such as *s.com/$*$*, where the web site w can send cross-origin (authenticated) requests to any URL of the site *s.com*.

As a simple example, assume two web sites A and B send the endorsement headers $<cd: \{ W{:}P, U{:}[a.com/*]\}>$ and $<cd: \{ W{:}P, U{:}[b.com/u1, b.com/u2]\}>$

1. $(\mathsf{login}(A), [\text{LOGIN}])$: $(L_0, \text{-}, [\,]) \xrightarrow{1} (L_A, \text{-}, \perp :: A)$
   2. suppress $(\mathsf{net\_req}(A), [\text{DROP-C}])$: $(L_A, \text{-}, \perp :: A) \to (L_A, \text{-}, A)$
   2. release $(\mathsf{net\_req}(A), [\text{OUT-C}])$: $(L_A, \text{-}, A) \xrightarrow{2} (L_A, \text{-}, [\,])$
3. $(\mathsf{net\_resp}(A, h), [\text{LOAD}])$: $(L_A, \text{-}, [\,]) \xrightarrow{3} (L_A, \text{-}, \perp :: A)$
   4. release $(\mathsf{ui\_page\_loaded}, [\text{OUT-C}])$: $(L_A, \text{-}, \perp :: A) \xrightarrow{4} (L_A, \text{-}, A)$
   4. suppress $(\mathsf{ui\_page\_loaded}, [\text{DROP-C}])$: $(L_A, \text{-}, A) \to (L_A, \text{-}, [\,])$
5. $(\mathsf{ui\_link\_click}(A), [\text{LOAD}])$: $(L_A, \text{-}, [\,]) \xrightarrow{5} (L_A, \text{-}, \perp :: A)$
   6. suppress $(\mathsf{net\_req}(A), [\text{DROP-C}])$: $(L_A, \text{-}, \perp :: A) \to (L_A, \text{-}, A)$
   6. release $(\mathsf{net\_req}(A), [\text{OUT-C}])$: $(L_A, \text{-}, A) \xrightarrow{6} (L_A, \text{-}, [\,])$
7. $(\mathsf{net\_resp}(A, h), [\text{LOAD}])$: $(L_A, \text{-}, [\,]) \xrightarrow{7} (L_A, \text{-}, \perp :: A)$
   8. release $(\mathsf{ui\_page\_loaded}, [\text{OUT-P}])$: $(L_A, \text{-}, \perp :: A) \xrightarrow{8} (L_A, \text{-}, \perp :: A)$
   9. release $(\mathsf{net\_req}(E), [\text{OUT-C}])$: $(L_A, \text{-}, \perp :: A) \xrightarrow{9} (L_A, \text{-}, A)$
   8. suppress $(\mathsf{ui\_page\_loaded}, [\text{DROP-P}])$: $(L_A, \text{-}, A) \to (L_A, \text{-}, A)$
   9. suppress $(\mathsf{net\_req}(E), [\text{DROP-C}])$: $(L_A, \text{-}, A) \to (L_A, \text{-}, [\,])$
10. $(\mathsf{net\_resp}(E, h), [\text{LOAD}])$: $(L_A, \text{-}, [\,]) \xrightarrow{10} (L_A, \text{-}, \perp)$
    release $(\cdot, [\text{DROP-C}])$: $(L_A, \text{-}, \perp) \to (L_A, \text{-}, [\,])$
11. $(\mathsf{ui\_link\_click}(A), [\text{LOAD}])$: $(L_A, \text{-}, [\,]) \xrightarrow{11} (L_A, \text{-}, \perp :: A)$
    12. suppress $(\mathsf{net\_req}(A), [\text{DROP-C}])$: $(L_A, \text{-}, \perp :: A) \to (L_A, \text{-}, A)$
    12. release $(\cdot, [\text{OUT-C}])$: $(L_A, \text{-}, A) \to (L_A, \text{-}, [\,])$

Fig. 6. Script inclusion attack encoding and prevention

in their responses. Initially, when the response from A is received, the wrapper will store in ω an entry $(P, [a.com/*])$ and when the other response from B is received, it will add the two URLs to the value bound to P, hence ω will become $(P, [a.com/*, b.com/u1, b.com/u2])$. The URL $a.com/*$ represents all the URLs of web site A.

Now we have the required information to decide if a cross-origin request should be endorsed. After receiving the example headers above, an output from P to any URL of A or to any of the two URLs $b.com/u1$ and $b.com/u2$ of web site B should include cookies. On receipt of an input event i with label d, the wrapper will compute the set of URLs that d is allowed to send cross-origin requests to by looking it up in ω. Let us call the resulting set U_i.

We generalize the *release* predicate so that it takes U_i into account. An output is *released* from a state if (1) its label matches the label l of the current sub-execution or, (2) when $l = \perp$ and there is no sub-execution at the level of the output and the request URL is not white-listed, or (3) when $l \neq \perp$, and the request URL is white-listed. The predicate $release_{L,l,L_q}(o, u, U_i)$ is defined as follows:

$$l = lbl_L(o) \lor (l = \perp \land lbl_L(o) \notin L_q \land u \notin U_i) \lor (l \neq \perp \land u \in U_i).$$

We can now show that the Paypal example (Figure 7) works. We show an encoding in our model in Figure 9. (We show ω and U_i as the third and fourth component of the tuple representing the extended browser state.)

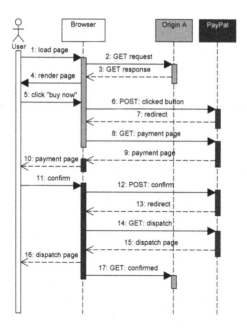

Fig. 7. E-payment scenario

Assume the site A sends the header $<cd:\ \{W{:}P,\ U{:}[a.com/*]\}>$ in the response input (message 3, Figure 7) and the wrapper creates the entry $\omega = (P, [a.com/*])$. Later on, when the input in message 15 is received from P, the corresponding list of URLs for P is retrieved, that is, $U_i = [a.com/*]$. The encoding in Figure 8 will now change as shown in Figure 9. The *GET: confirmed* cross-origin (legitimate) request to web site A is now sent from the sub-execution at label P *with* its authentication cookie.

6   Implementation

Our prototype implementation is constructed as a modification of the FlowFox browser [12,13]. Crucial for our implementation is the ability to keep track of all sites a user is logged into and to make sure that the labelling of JavaScript API calls can be dependent on this login history.

The biggest modification to FlowFox's core is the addition of a shared state variable, shared between all browser windows. This variable contains the login history log of the browser. This history log is a list of strings and contains all domain names for which the browser has established an authenticated session. In our prototype, authentication to a web site has to happen by means of a bookmarklet that interacts with this login history log to add authenticated domains.

The second modification is in the policy library that comes with FlowFox. This library now offers an API to query the login history log so that the labelling of

3. (net_resp(A, h), [LOAD]): $(L, \_, []) \xrightarrow{3} (L, \_, \perp :: A)$

   4. release (ui_page_loaded, [OUT-C]): $(L, \_, \perp :: A) \xrightarrow{4} (L, \_, A)$

   4. suppress (ui_page_loaded, [DROP-C]): $(L, \_, A) \dashrightarrow (L, \_, [])$

...

(user clicks "buy" button, and confirms payment)

...

15. (net_resp(P, h), [LOAD]): $(L, R, []) \xrightarrow{15} (L, \_, \perp :: P)$

  16. release (ui_page_loaded, [OUT-P]): $(L, \_, \perp :: P) \xrightarrow{16} (L, R, \perp :: P)$

  17. release w/o cookies (net_req(u_A), [OUT-C]): $(L, \_, \perp :: P) \xrightarrow{17} (L, R, P)$

  16. suppress (ui_page_loaded, [DROP-P]): $(L, \_, P) \dashrightarrow (L, \_, P)$

  17. suppress (net_req(u_A), [DROP-C]): $(L, \_, P) \dashrightarrow (L, \_, [])$

Fig. 8. E-payment application encoding

...

15. (net_resp(P, h), [LOAD]): $(L, \_, \omega, [], []) \xrightarrow{15} (L, \_, \omega, [a.com/*], \perp :: P)$

  16. release (ui_page_loaded, [OUT-P]):

     $(L, \_, \omega, [a.com/*], \perp :: P) \xrightarrow{16} (L, \_, \omega, [a.com/*], \perp :: P)$

  17. suppress (net_req(u_A), [DROP-C]):

     $(L, \_, \omega, [a.com/*], \perp :: P) \dashrightarrow (L, \_, \omega, [a.com/*], P)$

  16. suppress (ui_page_loaded, [OUT-P]):

     $(L, \_, \omega, [a.com/*], P) \dashrightarrow (L, \_, \omega, [a.com/*], P)$

  17. release (net_req(u_A), [OUT-C]):

     $(L, \_, \omega, [a.com/*], P) \xrightarrow{17} (L, \_, \omega, [a.com/*], [])$

Fig. 9. E-payment application encoding (updated)

JavaScript API calls can depend on this information. We illustrate in a small example how the extended FlowFox can be used.

New top level windows exist only in the low integrity copy of the browser, *unless* the new window is created by a login bookmarklet. In that case, the new window will exist in two levels of the browser: the $\perp$ level, and the level of the authenticated origin.

Consider again the classic CSRF scenario from Figure 3. This executes in our prototype as follows. First, the user starts an authenticated session with `mail.com` by selecting the appropriate bookmarklet. This bookmarklet posts the correct login credentials (stored in the bookmarklet) over HTTPS to `mail.com`. The bookmarklet also interacts with FlowFox's core to store `mail.com` in the login history log. Next, the user loads a page from the `attacker.com` site, and a script on this page tries to influence the current session with `mail.com` by crafting an XMLHttpRequest.

For this example, we configure FlowFox with the policy that makes calls to XMLHttpRequest of d integrity if they go to a domain d in the login history log, and low integrity ($\perp$) otherwise.

When the user visits `attacker.com`, and the script performs an XHR request to `mail.com`, the window containing `attacker.com` exists only in the $\perp$ level of the browser, and the policy above causes the request to be suppressed. Hence, this policy effectively prevents the classic CSRF attack as described in Fig. 3. Requests that go to other sites (with no open authenticated session) would be left untouched. Blocking a request is done by making sure that the `skipCall` primitive used internally by FlowFox (it is hidden from the policy writer by the policy library, which is in fact a domain specific language on top of those primitives) returns the appropriate value.

The current protoype is just a proof-of-concept, and has important limitations. The most important one is that FlowFox only performs multi-execution of JavaScript code, and hence no policies can be enforced on network requests that are not triggered by scripts. If `attacker.com` tries to influence the session with `mail.com` via other means, e.g., an embedded image tag, thereby not relying on any JavaScript code, we have no way to intercept this in FlowFox. Removing this limitation is possible by multi-executing the entire browser, as proposed by Bielova et al. [6], but that would require a major overhaul of FlowFox and hence a substantial implementation effort. Despite this limitation, we believe the prototype is evidence of the feasibility of our proposed mechanism in real browsers.

Our prototype implementation is available online at `http://distrinet.cs.kuleuven.be/software/FlowFox/` .

7   Related Work

There has been a wide variety of work on web session integrity over the past decade. The lines of work most closely related to our contributions are: (1) formal models of web session integrity, (2) countermeasures against CSRF, and (3) information flow control for the web.

7.1   Formal Models of Web Session Integrity

Bohannon et al. [9] propose reactive non-interference, a non-interference property for reactive programs such as web scripts that is proposed to replace the Same Origin Policy in browsers. This was a direct inspiration for our notion of login history dependent non-interference. Later, Bohannon and Pierce [8] developed Featherweight Firefox, a formal model of a simple browser, with the purpose of formally studying confidentiality and integrity policies for browsers, including reactive non-interference policies. This browser model did not yet model session management, and very recently Bugliesi et al. [10] developed Flyweight Firefox, a variant of Featherweight Firefox, and provided a formal definition of web session integrity as well as a provably sound enforcement mechanism. The advantage of our approach is that, by providing information flow control instead of access control, we can more precisely enforce session integrity.

An alternative approach to formally model session integrity was taken by Akhawe et al. [2]. They develop a coarse grained model of the entire web platform in Alloy, and use bounded model checking to find flaws in proposed web security techniques. They model the entire web platform, whereas in our approach we focus on modeling the browser only. Hence, their model is better suited to evaluate security techniques that span client and server, whereas our model is more suitable for pure client-side enforcement techniques.

7.2 Countermeasures against CSRF

CSRF is the most important session integrity attack that is not handled by just protecting the session implementation layer. Server-side countermeasures against CSRF are well-understood. The most widely deployed countermeasure is the use of anti-CSRF tokens. We limit our attention to related work on client-side enforcement. Client-side enforcement of CSRF protection was pioneered by RequestRodeo [20]. This system interposed a proxy between client and server, and stripped authentication information from suspicious requests. Many variants of RequestRodeo have been proposed [14,26,1], differing in (1) how suspicious requests are detected, (2) how suspicious requests are handled (either dropping them or stripping session cookies, or just detecting the attack), and (3) the implementation technique (as a proxy or as a browser extension). All these variants are useful but heuristic solutions, that provide no formal assurance. The only system that provides some formal guarantees is CsFire [14]: it was formally validated through bounded model checking to defend against CSRF in the formal model of the web developed by Akhawe et al. [2].

Our approach for endorsements, where the server tunes or sets a browser policy, is closely related to existing server-driven policies on the web, like Content Security Policies [27], or Allowed Referrer Lists [11].

7.3 Information Flow Control for the Web

Information flow control in web scripts is usually proposed by means of dynamic mechanisms [22] due to the dynamic nature of the JavaScript language, the de facto programming language on the client side web applications. Our work is directly based on existing information flow secure browsers that use the mechanism of secure multi-execution [16] for information flow control. The theoretical development is based on Bielova et al. [6], whereas the implementation extends the FlowFox browser [12,13]. Alternative dynamic information flow control mechanisms for browser scripts are usually monitors. Austin and Flanagan [3] and Hedin and Sabelfeld [17] study runtime monitors for non-interference in JavaScript-like languages. Bichhawat et al. [5] formalize and develop an information flow monitor at the level of JavaScript bytecode in the WebKit engine.

8   Conclusions

Web session security is a key cornerstone of web security. We have shown how client-side application-level web session integrity can be understood as a non-interference property. To make this possible, we introduce LHDNI, login-history-dependent non-interference, and show how this notion captures client-side web session integrity. We also developed and proved correct an enforcement mechanism based on secure multi-execution. A prototype implementation in the Flow-Fox browser is available online.

There are many avenues for future work. While we have formally proven security of our enforcement mechanism, we believe the mechanism has several other interesting properties that deserve a formal study. In particular we believe it to be *precise* in the sense that it does not impact the observable behaviour of the browser as long as the browser is only visiting secure sites. In other words, security is not overapproximating: the enforcement mechanism only does something observable if the browser is definitely behaving insecurely. We also believe that we can prove compatibility results saying that – under some conditions – behaviour of existing sites is preserved, even if they do something insecure; our approach of stripping session cookies instead of blocking requests could allow us to show that such sites behave *as if the browser was not logged into other sites*.

Acknowledgments. This research is partially funded by the Research Fund KU Leuven, by the IWT project SPION, and by the MIUR projects ADAPT and CINA. Willem De Groef holds a PhD grant from the Agency for Innovation by Science and Technology in Flanders (IWT).

References

1. https://www.requestpolicy.com/security.html
2. Akhawe, D., Barth, A., Lam, P.E., Mitchell, J., Song, D.: Towards a formal foundation of web security. In: CSF (2010)
3. Austin, T.H., Flanagan, C.: Multiple Facets for Dynamic Information Flow. In: Proc. of the ACM SIGPLAN-SIGACT Symposium on Principles of Programming Languages, pp. 165–178 (2012)
4. Barth, A., Jackson, C., Mitchell, J.C.: Robust defenses for cross-site request forgery. In: Proceedings of the 15th ACM Conference on Computer and Communications Security, pp. 75–88 (2008)
5. Bichhawat, A., Rajani, V., Garg, D., Hammer, C.: Information flow control in webKit's javaScript bytecode. In: Abadi, M., Kremer, S. (eds.) POST 2014 (ETAPS 2014). LNCS, vol. 8414, pp. 159–178. Springer, Heidelberg (2014)
6. Bielova, N., Devriese, D., Massacci, F., Piessens, F.: Reactive non-interference for a browser model. In: Proc. of the International Conference on Network and System Security, pp. 97–104 (2011)
7. Bohannon, A.: Foundations of web script security. Ph.D. thesis, University of Pennsylvania (2012)
8. Bohannon, A., Pierce, B.C.: Featherweight firefox: Formalizing the core of a web browser. In: Proceedings of the 2010 USENIX Conference on Web Application Development, WebApps 2010, pp. 11–11. USENIX Association, Berkeley (2010)
9. Bohannon, A., Pierce, B.C., Sjöberg, V., Weirich, S., Zdancewic, S.: Reactive Noninterference. In: Proceedings of the ACM Conference on Computer and Communications Security, pp. 79–90 (2009)

10. Bugliesi, M., Calzavara, S., Focardi, R., Khan, W., Tempesta, M.: Provably sound browser-based enforcement of web session integrity. In: CSF 2014 (2014)
11. Czeskis, A., Moshchuk, A., Kohno, T., Wang, H.J.: Lightweight server support for browser-based csrf protection. In: Proceedings of the 22nd International Conference on World Wide Web, pp. 273–284 (2013)
12. De Groef, W., Devriese, D., Nikiforakis, N., Piessens, F.: FlowFox: a Web Browser with Flexible and Precise Information Flow Control. In: Proc. of the ACM Conference on Computer and Communications Security, pp. 748–759 (2012)
13. De Groef, W., Devriese, D., Nikiforakis, N., Piessens, F.: Secure multi-execution of web scripts: Theory and practice. Journal of Computer Security (2014)
14. De Ryck, P., Desmet, L., Joosen, W., Piessens, F.: Automatic and precise client-side protection against CSRF attacks. In: Atluri, V., Diaz, C. (eds.) ESORICS 2011. LNCS, vol. 6879, pp. 100–116. Springer, Heidelberg (2011)
15. De Ryck, P., Nikiforakis, N., Desmet, L., Piessens, F., Joosen, W.: SERENE: Self-reliant client-side protection against session fixation. In: Göschka, K.M., Haridi, S. (eds.) DAIS 2012. LNCS, vol. 7272, pp. 59–72. Springer, Heidelberg (2012)
16. Devriese, D., Piessens, F.: Noninterference Through Secure Multi-Execution. In: Proc. of the IEEE Symposium on Security and Privacy, pp. 109–124 (2010)
17. Hedin, D., Sabelfeld, A.: Information-Flow Security for a Core of JavaScript. In: Proc. of the IEEE Computer Security Foundations Symposium, pp. 3–18 (2012)
18. Johns, M.: On JavaScript Malware and Related Threats - Web Page Based Attacks Revisited. Journal in Computer Virology 4(3), 161–178 (2008)
19. Johns, M., Braun, B., Schrank, M., Posegga, J.: Reliable protection against session fixation attacks. In: Proceedings of the 2011 ACM Symposium on Applied Computing, pp. 1531–1537 (2011)
20. Johns, M., Winter, J.: Proceedings of the OWASP Europe 2006 Conference, pp. 5–17 (2006)
21. Khan, W., Calzavara, S., Bugliesi, M., De Groef, W., Piessens, F.: Client side web session integrity as a non-interference property: Extended version with proofs, http://www.cs.kuleuven.be/publicaties/rapporten/cw/CW674.abs.html
22. Le Guernic, G.: Confidentiality Enforcement Using Dynamic Information Flow Analyses. Ph.D. thesis, Kansas State University (2007)
23. Nikiforakis, N., Invernizzi, L., Kapravelos, A., Van Acker, S., Joosen, W., Kruegel, C., Piessens, F., Vigna, G.: You Are What You Include: Large-scale Evaluation of Remote JavaScript Inclusions. In: Proc. of the ACM Conference on Computer and Communications Security, pp. 736–747 (2012)
24. Rafnsson, W., Sabelfeld, A.: Secure multi-execution: Fine-grained, declassification-aware, and transparent. In: CSF (2013)
25. Sabelfeld, A., Myers, A.C.: Language-Based Information-Flow Security. IEEE Journal on Selected Areas of Communications 21(1), 5–19 (2003)
26. Shahriar, H., Zulkernine, M.: Client-side detection of cross-site request forgery attacks. In: 2010 IEEE 21st International Symposium on Software Reliability Engineering (ISSRE), pp. 358–367 (November 2010)
27. Stamm, S., Sterne, B., Markham, G.: Reining in the web with content security policy. In: Proceedings of the 19th International Conference on World Wide Web, pp. 921–930. ACM (2010)
28. Vanhoef, M., De Groef, W., Devriese, D., Piessens, F., Rezk, T.: Stateful declassification policies for event-driven programs. In: CSF (2014)

Impact of Multiple t-t SMER Constraints on Minimum User Requirement in RBAC

Arindam Roy[1], Shamik Sural[2], and Arun Kumar Majumdar[3]

[1] Advanced Technology Development Centre,
[2] School of Information Technology,
[3] Department of Computer Science and Engineering,
Indian Institute of Technology, Kharagpur, India
{arindam.roy,shamik}@sit.iitkgp.ernet.in, akmj@cse.iitkgp.ernet.in

Abstract. Separation of Duty (SoD) constraints are widely used to specify Role Based Access Control (RBAC) policies in commercial applications. It has been shown previously that efficient implementation of SoD policies in RBAC can be done using t-t Statically Mutually Exclusive Roles (SMER) constraints. In this paper, we present a method for finding the minimum number of users required under multiple t-t SMER constraints. The problem is shown to be NP-complete. We model the general problem using graphs, and present a two-step method for solving it. In the first step, a greedy algorithm is proposed that selects a graph which is likely to have the minimum chromatic number out of a set of graphs. The second step uses a known chromatic number finding algorithm for determining the chromatic number of the graph selected in the first step. Results for different values of the number of roles and the number of constraints as well as for different values of t have been reported.

Keywords: Statically Mutually Exclusive Roles (SMER) constraint, Role Based Access Control (RBAC), Graph, Chromatic number, Greedy algorithm.

1 Introduction

Access control models can be broadly classified as Discretionary Access Control (DAC) [11], Mandatory Access Control (MAC) [1], Role Based Access Control (RBAC) [17] and Attribute Based Access Control [12]. In recent years, RBAC has emerged as the *de facto* standard for access control and has been adopted by many operating systems, database management systems and commercial applications. Separation of Duty (SoD), introduced by Clark and Wilson [4], is accepted as a fundamental principle for security in commercial information systems. If a sensitive task takes n steps to complete, according to the principle of separation of duty, it must require the cooperation of at least k distinct users.

Kuhn first identified how an SoD constraint can be enforced in an RBAC system in terms of mutual exclusion of roles [13]. Furthermore, it has been shown

A. Prakash and R. Shyamasundar (Eds.): ICISS 2014, LNCS 8880, pp. 109–128, 2014.

that while directly enforcing SoD policies in RBAC is intractable, their implementation can be done efficiently using Statically Mutually Exclusive Roles (SMER) constraints [14]. Each SMER constraint specifies the maximum number of roles to which a user can belong out of a given set of roles. Static SoDs (SSoDs) are pre-specified constraints that do not change with RBAC sessions. In this paper, we consider only static SoD constraints and refer to them simply as SoD constraints.

Given that a system is currently using direct user-permission assignment, tools like role mining are used to determine the set of roles, so that the system's access control policies can be migrated to RBAC. Extensive work has been done on developing efficient role mining algorithms [8,10,20]. On the other hand, for organizations setting up RBAC from scratch and also for start-ups, the requirement is different. They have a pre-defined set of roles. The applicable constraints in the system are also known, so that the problem is to determine the minimum number of users needed to fully realize the system without violating the constraints along with the corresponding user-role assignments. Another important application of this work is in estimating the number of administrative users required and their assignment to administrative roles [16] in large RBAC deployments. Such types of organizations can have thousands of roles [18] geographically distributed over multiple locations requiring complex SoD constraints among administrative roles.

Thus, we consider an RBAC system in which the Separation of Duty policy is represented in the form of SMER constraints. The problem addressed in this paper is to find a user-role assignment (UA relation) that enforces these constraints (and hence, the given SoD policy) using the minimum number of users. The permission-role assignment (PA) relation is implicitly included in the SMER constraint specification. It may be noted that, if there are more number of users than roles in a system, the user-role assignment obtained as a solution to the current problem can also be used to guide user assignment resulting in better utilization. Thus, a solution to the problem of finding optimal user assignment to roles in the presence of SMER constraints can both supplement as well as complement efforts in developing role mining techniques.

While we informally introduced the problem in [15] and provided a genetic algorithm based solution, no formal analysis was done. The main contributions of the current paper are as follows

- We formally define the minimum user requirement problem under multiple t-t SMER constraints (called t-t SMER-MIN-USER problem) and show that the problem is NP complete.
- We model the general t-t SMER-MIN-USER problem using graphs and provide a greedy algorithm toward obtaining its solution.

The rest of this paper is organized as follows. In Section 2, we give an overview of RBAC and SMER constraints. We formally define the minimum user finding problem in Section 3. In Section 4, we identify the complexity class of the defined problem. The problem is modeled using graphs in Section 5. We present algorithms based on this modeling to solve the problem and analyze them in

Section 6. Experimental results are presented in Section 7. Finally, we draw conclusions and provide directions for future research in Section 9.

2   Preliminaries

The Role Based Access Control (RBAC) model has the following components [17].

Definition 1. *RBAC is an access control model comprising of the following components:*

- *U, R, OPS, OBJ respectively the set of users, roles, operations and objects*
- *P (the set of permissions)* $\subseteq \{(ops, obj)|ops \in OPS \wedge obj \in OBJ\}$
- *PA* $\subseteq P \times R$, *a many-to-many permission-to-role assignment relation*
- *UA* $\subseteq U \times R$, *a many-to-many user-to-role assignment relation*
- *RH* $\subseteq R \times R$ *is a partial order on R called the role hierarchy or role dominance relation, also written as* $\succeq$
- *assignedusers(r)* $= \{u \in U | (u, r) \in UA\}$, *the mapping of role r onto a set of users*
- *assignedpermissions(r)* $= \{p \in P | (p, r) \in PA\}$, *the mapping of role r onto a set of permissions*
- *A set of constraints CO*

Since we consider separation of duty constraints that do not change with sessions, we have not included the notion of sessions in the above definition. Besides SoD, other types of constraints like cardinality constraints and prerequisite constraints [3] are also supported in RBAC. However, in this paper, we assume that the set CO consists only of SoD constraints specified in the form of SMER constraints [14].

In an RBAC system, the SMER constraints are used to conveniently express an SoD policy. A tuple of the form $\langle RS, t \rangle$ represents a t-m SMER constraint where $RS = \{r_1, ..., r_m\}$ is a set of roles while m and t are integers satisfying $1 < t \leq m$. If no user is a member of t or more roles in $\{r_1, ..., r_m\}$, a t-m SMER constraint $\langle \{r_1, ..., r_m\}, t \rangle$ is said to be satisfied. A canonical form (of cardinality t) of an SMER constraint is a form where $m = t$. It is written as t-t SMER constraint. Li et al. [14] have previously shown that a set of t-t SMER constraints can be used to represent a t-m SMER constraint. Hence, we consider CO to be a collection of t-t SMER constraints only.

3   Problem Definition

In this section, we define the problem of finding the minimum number of users in an RBAC system under multiple t-t SMER constraints.

Definition 2. t-t *SMER-MIN-USER problem (t-t SMUP). Given a set R of roles and a set CO of SMER constraints, find the minimum number of users m such that, for a set of users U where* $|U| = m$ *and a user role assignment relation UA,* $\forall r \in R, \exists u \in U$, *where* $(u, r) \in UA$, *satisfying all the t-t SMER constraints.*

It may be noted that the value of t need not be the same for all the constraints in CO. An example is given below to explain the problem defined above.

Example 1. Let there be an RBAC system with $R = \{r_1, r_2, r_3, r_4, r_5\}$ and $CO = \{co_1, co_2, co_3, co_4, co_5\}$, where $co_1 = \langle\{r_1, r_3\}, 2\rangle$, $co_2 = \langle\{r_1, r_2\}, 2\rangle$, $co_3 = \langle\{r_1, r_4\}, 2\rangle$, $co_4 = \langle\{r_2, r_3, r_4\}, 3\rangle$, $co_5 = \langle\{r_2, r_3, r_5\}, 3\rangle$. The problem is to determine the minimum number of users such that each role is assigned to at least one user while satisfying all the 7 SMER constraints. A minimal set of users U with $|U| = m = 3$ is $U = \{u_1, u_2, u_3\}$. The corresponding UA matrix gives the optimal user assignment. One possible UA matrix with this minimal set of users is shown in Table 1.

Table 1. UA matrix for an instance of t-t SMUP

	r_1	r_2	r_3	r_4	r_5
u_1	1	0	0	0	1
u_2	0	1	0	1	0
u_3	0	0	1	0	0

4   Complexity Class of t-t SMUP

In this section, an analysis of the complexity class of the problem is presented. Since t-t SMUP is an optimization problem, we first define a decision version of the problem.

Definition 3. *Decision t-t SMUP (t-t D-SMUP). Given a set CO of SMER constraints, a set R of roles, and an integer $m \geq 0$, does there exist a set of users U and a user-role assignment relation UA such that, $\forall r \in R$, $\exists u \in U$, where, $(u, r) \in UA$, satisfying the constraints in the set CO, where $|U| \leq m$?*

We show that t-t D-SMUP is an NP-complete problem. Proving that a problem is NP-complete consists of the following three steps [9].

- show that the given problem α is in NP.
- select a known NP-complete problem β.
- construct a polynomial time algorithm γ to reduce β to α.

The known NP-complete problem β used here is the "chromatic number problem" defined below [6]:

Definition 4. *Chromatic number problem (CNP). The chromatic number of a graph G with set $V(G)$ of vertices and set $E(G)$ of edges, is the smallest number of colors $\chi(G)$ needed to color the vertices of G so that no two adjacent vertices have the same color.*

A coloring in which no two adjacent vertices have the same color is called proper coloring and the graph is said to be properly colored. An optimal proper coloring of a graph G is a proper coloring with $\chi(G)$ number of colors.

Definition 5. *Chromatic number decision problem (CNDP). Given a graph G and a positive integer q, is G q-colorable?*

We first establish the following lemma.

Lemma 1. *CNDP $\leq_P$ t-t D-SMUP.*

Proof. The reduction algorithm takes an instance of CNDP and produces an instance of *t-t* D-SMUP in polynomial time as follows:

- $R = V(G)$,
- for an edge $(r_i, r_j) \in E(G)$, there will be an entry $\langle \{r_i, r_j\}, 2 \rangle$ in the set CO of constraints,
- $U = C$, where C is the set of colors assigned,
- $UA = CA$, where CA is the color-to-node assignment relation,
- $m = q$

For a given instance of *t-t* D-SMUP which is reduced from an instance of CNDP, next we prove that the following two cases will always hold:

- if the given instance of *t-t* D-SMUP is a "Yes"-instance, the corresponding CNDP instance is also a "Yes"-instance.
- if the given instance of *t-t* D-SMUP is a "No"-instance, the corresponding CNDP instance is also a "No"-instance.

We prove the first case by contradiction. Assume that for a "Yes"-instance of reduced *t-t* D-SMUP the answer to the associated instance of CNDP is "No". That is, while R and CO can be realized using m users, the graph G is not q-colorable. Given CA is the color-to-node assignment relation, there is an edge between at least two nodes of the same color, which implies that for the corresponding UA relation with m users, $\exists r_i, r_j \in R$, such that $assignedusers(r_i) \cap assignedusers(r_j) \neq \phi$ and $\langle \{r_i, r_j\}, 2 \rangle \in CO$. Thus, the constraint is violated. But, the instance of *t-t* D-SMUP is a "Yes"-instance, which contradicts.

Next, we prove the second case. We assume that for a reduced "No"-instance of *t-t* D-SMUP the answer to the associated instance of CNDP is "Yes". This implies that, there exists a coloring CA using q number of colors such that, no two adjacent nodes are assigned to the same color. This corresponds to the fact that for the reduced instance of *t-t* D-SMUP, $\forall r_i, r_j \in R$ if $\langle \{r_i, r_j\}, 2 \rangle \in CO$, $assignedusers(r_i) \cap assignedusers(r_j) = \phi$. But, the mentioned *t-t* D-SMUP instance is a "No"-instance, which contradicts. Hence, the corresponding CNDP instance which was reduced to the given instance of *t-t* D-SMUP is also a "No"-instance. □

Given a user-to-role assignment relation UA and a set CO of SMER constraints, the Satisfaction Checking problem [14] is defined as the problem to determine whether UA satisfies CO.

Theorem 1. *Decision t-t SMUP is NP-complete.*

Proof. The theorem is proved in 3 steps:

- The algorithm to solve satisfaction checking problem for SMER constraints, which is proved to be in P by Li et al. [14], can act as a certificate of the result of t-t SMUP being correct. Hence, the decision t-t SMUP is in NP.
- Let us select the known NP-complete problem β as the chromatic number problem.
- From Lemma 1, t-t D-SMUP is NP-hard.   □

5   Modeling t-t SMUP Using Graphs

In this section, we formalize the modeling of t-t SMUP using graphs. We observe that any UA relation with minimum number of users will have just one user assigned to a particular role, i.e., $\forall r \in R, |assignedusers(\ r)| = 1$. This is because, a second user assigned to the role r will never contribute to a reduction in the total number of users in the UA relation. Hence, we are only concerned with such types of UA relations in the rest of the section.

Firstly, we introduce a graph based representation of the user-to-role assignment relation UA with a single user assigned to a particular role. Given a set of roles R, a user-to-role assignment relation UA and a set $CO = \{co_1, ..., co_n\}$ of n SMER constraints where, $co_1 = \langle \{r_1, ..., r_{t_1}\}, t_1 \rangle, ..., co_n = \langle \{r_1, ..., r_{t_n}\}, t_n \rangle$ with $t_1, ..., t_n \geq 2$, the graph representation of UA is as follows.

If $RPDU$ denotes the set of all possible pairs of roles having distinct users assigned and $RPCO$ denotes the set of all possible pairs of roles (r_i, r_j), where $r_i, r_j \in \{r_1, ..., r_{t_k}\}$ and $i \neq j$ for $1 \leq k \leq n$ for each $co_k \in CO$, a UA relation satisfying CO can be represented using a properly colored [6] undirected graph G with the set of vertices $V(G) = R$, the set of edges $E(G) = RPCO \cap RPDU$, the set of colors $C = U$ and the color-to-vertex assignment relation $CV = UA$. Thus, the graph G is constructed with roles of the system as nodes and a pair of roles is connected using an edge if the pair is present in any of the constraints in CO and has different users assigned to them in UA.

We take an example to illustrate this representation. The UA matrix in Table 1 of Example 1 can be represented using the graph in Figure 1. It should also be noted that the number of SMER constraints possible for a set R of roles is $\sum_{i=2}^{|R|} \binom{|R|}{i}$.

Definition 6. *UA graph. Given a set R of roles, set CO of SMER constraints and a graph G, we call G a UA graph if a proper coloring of G with $V(G) = R$ and $E(G) \subseteq RPCO$, where each constraint co_k in CO has a pair of roles in $E(G)$, represents a possible UA relation with $U = C$, where U is the set of users and C is the set of colors used to color G, and $UA = CV$, where CV is the color-to-vertex assignment relation.*

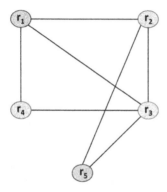

Fig. 1. Graph representation of the UA relation in Example 1

For example, Figure 1 is a *UA graph* with its optimal proper coloring representing the *UA* relation of Example 1.

Before going into further details, we redefine the graph construction process from a set of *t-t* SMER constraints CO. The construction is named as the *Graphical UA Construction*.

Definition 7. *(Graphical UA Construction (GUAC)). Given a set of roles R and a set of n t-t SMER constraints $CO = \{co_1, ..., co_n\}$ where $co_1 = \langle\{r_1, ..., r_{t_1}\}$, $t_1\rangle, ..., co_n = \langle\{r_1, ..., r_{t_n}\}, t_n\rangle$ with $t_1, ..., t_n \geq 2$, GUAC is defined as the construction of a graph from the set CO of SMER constraints. The construction consists of the following steps.*

1: Represent roles $r_i \in R$ as the vertices $V(G)$ of the graph G.
2: Select an arbitrary pair of roles r_i and r_j from $\{r_1, ..., r_{t_k}\}$ of each co_k, where $1 \leq k \leq n$.
3: Represent each selected pair of Step 2 as an edge in $E(G)$ of the graph G.

It must be noted that, the same pair of nodes can be selected from more than one constraints. This implies that the number of edges in a graph constructed using the above definition will have $|E(G)| \leq n$.

We clarify this construction with an example. The graph in Figure 2 is an instance of properly colored GUAC construction of the set R and CO of Example 1. The edges (r_1, r_3), (r_1, r_2), (r_1, r_4), (r_3, r_4), (r_3, r_5) are the edges representing presence of the constraints co_1, co_2, co_3, co_4, co_5. It should be noted that the graph in Figure 1 represents a valid UA matrix but is not a valid GUAC graph, because, the number of edges in the graph is greater than the number of constraints in the instance. Hence, graphs constructed using GUAC will not cover each and every possible UA relation of the instance.

It is obvious that, $\prod_{i=1}^{n} \binom{t_i}{2}$ possible graphs can be constructed using GUAC. The set of all possible graphs constructed using this construction is denoted by SG. Our claim is that, every graph from the set SG is a valid *UA graph*. A proof using mathematical induction for its correctness is formalized next.

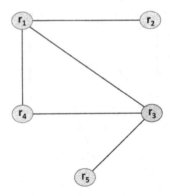

Fig. 2. GUAC construction for the set of roles R and the set of constraints CO of Example 1

Theorem 2. *Optimal proper coloring of a graph constructed using GUAC on a set R of roles and set CO of constraints is a valid* UA *graph.*

Proof. Let $P(k)$ be the proposition that an GUAC construction on R and CO with $|CO| = k$ is a valid *UA graph*. The basis step is to prove $P(1)$ is true. Given a t-t SMER constraint $\langle \{r_1, ..., r_t\}, t\rangle$, we can assign a single user u_1 to at-most $t - 1$ roles among $\{r_1, ..., r_t\}$. The remaining 1 role can be assigned with another user u_2. Hence, the system with $|CO| = 1$ can be fully realized with 2 users. The graph G_1 constructed using GUAC in this case will contain only one edge between any two of the roles mentioned in the constraint. Hence, $\chi(G) = 2$ (which represents m), which implies that the basis step is true.

For the inductive hypothesis, we assume that $P(k)$ holds for a positive integer $k \leq \sum\limits_{i=1}^{|R|} \binom{|R|}{i}$. That is, we assume that optimal proper coloring of a graph G_k constructed using GUAC on R and CO with $|CO| = k$ is a valid *UA graph*. Under this assumption, it is to be shown that $P(k + 1)$ is true, i.e., the graph G_{k+1} constructed using GUAC on R and CO with $|CO| = k + 1$ is a valid *UA graph*. Given G_k, constructing G_{k+1} consists of only one step, which is, selecting an edge (u_{k+1}, v_{k+1}) from the $k+1^{th}$ constraint co_{k+1} and adding it to G_k. That is, $V(G_{k+1}) = V(G_k)$ and $E(G_{k+1}) = E(G_k) \cup e_{k+1}$, where $e_{k+1} = (u_{k+1}, v_{k+1})$. The edge e_{k+1} can be chosen in the following ways.

- The edge inserted in G_k is a new edge, i.e., $e_{k+1} \notin E(G_k)$.
- The vertex u_{k+1} has an edge connected to it and the vertex v_{k+1} is isolated in G_k, i.e., $u_{k+1} \in e_1 \cup e_2 \cup ... \cup e_k$ and $v_{k+1} \notin e_1 \cup e_2 \cup ... \cup e_k$.
- The vertex v_{k+1} has an edge connected to it and the vertex u_{k+1} is isolated in G_k, i.e., $v_{k+1} \in e_1 \cup e_2 \cup ... \cup e_k$ and $u_{k+1} \notin e_1 \cup e_2 \cup ... \cup e_k$.
- The edge e_{k+1} is already present in G_k, i.e., $e_{k+1} \in E(G_k)$.
- Both u_{k+1} and v_{k+1} have an edge connected to it but the edge e_{k+1} is not present in G_k, i.e., $u_{k+1}, v_{k+1} \in e_1 \cup e_2 \cup ... \cup e_k$ and $e_{k+1} \notin E(G_k)$.

As the edges from G_k are kept intact, G_{k+1} is a super-graph of G_k. G_{k+1} keeps satisfying all the k constraints, and the newly inserted edge e_{k+1} ensures that at least one role among the roles mentioned in co_{k+1} will have a distinct user assigned to it, satisfying the $k + 1^{th}$ constraint. Thus, $P(k + 1)$ is proved to be true. □

It is implied from the above theorem that the proper coloring of the undirected graphs constructed using the GUAC construction method is a valid UA representation. For a given R and CO, a number of *UA graphs* are possible, and for each such graph, there can be a number of possible proper colorings. Our goal is to find a valid *UA graph* which requires the minimum number of colors (each color corresponds to one user) to color, i.e., we are in search of a *UA graph* with the lowest chromatic number. So, next, we proceed to prove that at least one graph with the lowest chromatic number exists in the set SG of graphs constructed using GUAC. To do so, we prove that a graph representing an optimal UA relation will contain only one edge from each constraint. However, the edges representing the constraints may overlap, i.e., an edge may represent the presence of more than one constraints. We formalize the notion and prove it in the next theorem.

Theorem 3. *At least one UA graph G with the lowest chromatic number exists in the set SG.*

Proof. To prove the stated theorem, we show that a *UA graph* G_l with the lowest chromatic number will have only one edge representing the presence of one constraint. And, we know from Definition 7 of GUAC graphs that the set SG contains all such possible graphs. Hence, we would proof that $G_l \in SG$. Let G be a graph constructed using GUAC, i.e., it contains only one edge corresponding to each constraint. Let G' be a graph such that $E(G') = E(G) \cup (r_i, r_j)$ and $V(G') = V(G)$, i.e., G' contains one edge more than the graph G. Let the edge (r_i, r_j) be the second edge representing the presence of the constraint $co_k \in CO$. This means that there are two edges from the constraint co_k in G'. Now, due to insertion of a new edge in the properly colored graph G resulting in the formation of the graph G', an optimal proper coloring of G' may differ with an optimal proper coloring of G in the following ways.

- r_i and r_j may have different colors assigned to them in G. In this case, there will not be any change in the coloring of G'. Hence, $\chi(G') = \chi(G)$.
- r_i and r_j may have the same color assigned to them in G. In this case, color assignment of r_i or r_j or of both have to be changed depending on the other nodes connected to it. Furthermore, there can be two cases.
  - The assigned color after the change is an existing color, i.e., the color is already used for some other node or nodes. In this case, the optimal coloring of G' will differ from that of G. But, the chromatic number will remain the same. That is, $\chi(G') = \chi(G)$.
  - The assigned color after the change is a new color. In this case, the chromatic number of G' will increase. That is, $\chi(G') > \chi(G)$.

It can be seen that in all the cases, $\chi(G')$ will never be less than $\chi(G)$, which implies that a second edge (r_i, r_j) from any constraint co_k will not help in reducing the number of users in the optimal UA relation. Hence, it can be claimed that all the UA graphs outside the set SG will have chromatic numbers greater than or equal to that of the graphs in SG. Therefore, it can be concluded that a UA graph G with the lowest number of colors, which corresponds to the minimum number of users, is indeed an element of the set SG. □

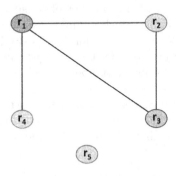

Fig. 3. Approximated optimal GUAC graph constructed for Example 1 using the greedy algorithm

Table 2. CON matrix for the set of SMER constraints in Example 1

	r_1r_2	r_1r_3	r_1r_4	r_1r_5	r_2r_3	r_2r_4	r_2r_5	r_3r_4	r_3r_5	r_4r_5
co_1	0	1	0	0	0	0	0	0	0	0
co_2	1	0	0	0	0	0	0	0	0	0
co_3	0	0	1	0	0	0	0	0	0	0
co_4	0	0	0	0	1	1	0	1	0	0
co_5	0	0	0	0	1	0	1	0	1	0

6   Solving *t-t* SMUP

In this section, we present and analyze algorithms to solve *t-t* SMUP using the modeling described in Section 5. It can be inferred from Theorems 2 and 3 that identifying the graph with minimum chromatic number from the set SG of all possible GUAC graphs will solve *t-t* SMUP. The solution, thus, consists of two steps, first is to construct GUAC graph(s) and second is to find the chromatic numbers of the constructed graph(s) and choose the graph G with minimum $\chi(G)$. The second step can be resolved using any known "efficient" (approximate) algorithm [9] for finding chromatic number with acceptable error bounds. For the first step, we first present a recursive brute force algorithm (Algorithm 1) to construct all possible GUAC graphs. We then provide a heuristic algorithm (Algorithm 2) for constructing *a single* GUAC graph having potentially the least value of chromatic number out of all possible GUAC graphs. The corresponding coloring represents the optimal user assignment under *t-t* SMER constraints.

Algorithm 1. Recursive brute force algorithm to construct all possible GUAC graphs.

```
 1: procedure BFGUAC(CON, i, incompGraph)
 2:     k ← no. of rows in CON
 3:     e ← no. of columns in CON
 4:     if i < k then
 5:         for l ← 1, e do
 6:             if CON(i + 1, l) = 1 then
 7:                 reconGraph ← incompGraph
 8:                 reconGraph(l) ← 1
 9:                 allGraphs ←
10:     .           bfGUAC(CON, i + 1, reconGraph)
11:             end if
12:         end for
13:     else
14:         allGraphs ← allGraphs ∪ incompGraph
15:         return allGraphs
16:     end if
17: end procedure
```

The procedure bfGUAC of Algorithm 1 takes 3 inputs as parameters. The input variable CON is a matrix of '0' and '1', each row of which is the *edge representation* of an SMER constraint. It represents such a constraint using a binary string of length $\frac{n \times (n-1)}{2}$, where n is the number of roles in the system, i.e., $n = |R|$. Each bit represents one of the possible edges of the combined graph G (as described in the last section), in the order, $(r_1 r_2), ..., (r_1 r_n), ..., (r_{n-2} r_{n-1})$, $...(r_{n-2} r_n), ..., (r_{n-1} r_n)$. The jth bit of a constraint co_i is 1 if the jth edge of the above order can be chosen from the SMER constraint to construct the GUAC graph G, and 0 otherwise. Each column represents a possible edge of an GUAC graph. Therefore, $CON(x, y) = 1$ if for the xth constraint $co_x = \langle \{r_1, ..., r_{t_x}\}, t_x \rangle$, $r_i, r_j \in \{r_1, ..., r_{t_x}\}$ where r_i, r_j are the roles in the yth edge of the sequence and $CON(x, y) = 0$ otherwise. The parameter i is an integer variable which denotes that currently the ith constraint is under process. Parameter $incompGraph$ is an array of binary strings where each bit denotes a possible edge of a graph in the sequence of the *edge representation*. The bit is 1 if the edge is present in the graph and 0 otherwise. The procedure has to be called initially with the parameters i set to 0 and $incompGraph$ set to an array of zeros of size of the number of possible edges in the instance. The procedure returns a set $allGraphs$ of arrays where each array represents a possible GUAC graph. We observe that the worst case time complexity of the algorithm is $O(e^k)$, where e is the number of possible edges and k is the number of constraints.

Other than the time complexity of the brute force algorithm in generating the GUAC graphs, there is another disadvantage. The number of graphs generated using GUAC is very high and is upper bounded by $O(e^k)$. In the second step, we have to compute the chromatic numbers of all these graphs and find the

Algorithm 2. Greedy algorithm to construct the graph with approximately minimum chromatic number.

```
 1: procedure CHOOSEBESTGUACGRAPH(CON)
 2:     k ← no. of rows in CON
 3:     e ← no. of columns in CON
 4:     CoveredCon ← 0
 5:     while coveredCon < k do
 6:         maxOnes ← 0
 7:         maxEdge ← 0
 8:         for i ← 1, e do
 9:             ones ← 0
10:             for j ← 1, k do
11:                 if CON(i, j) = 1 then
12:                     ones ← ones + 1
13:                 end if
14:             end for
15:             if maxOnes < ones then
16:                 maxOnes ← ones
17:                 maxEdge ← i
18:             end if
19:         end for
20:         graphEdges(maxEdge) ← 1
21:         CoveredCon ← CoveredCon + maxOnes
22:         for i ← 1, k do
23:             if CON(i, maxEdge) = 1 then
24:                 for j ← 1, e do
25:                     CON(i, j) ← ×
26:                 end for
27:             end if
28:         end for
29:     end while
30:     return graphEdges
31: end procedure
```

minimum among them. The chromatic number problem itself is a hard problem, and hence, computing chromatic numbers for such exponential number of graphs becomes a difficult task. Therefore, we propose a greedy heuristic to construct only one GUAC graph - the one which is likely to have the least chromatic number out of all possible GUAC graphs. Finding chromatic number of one single graph would than give a solution to t-t SMUP.

It is known that the inequality $\chi(G) \leq \left\lfloor \frac{1+\sqrt{1+8e}}{2} \right\rfloor$ [6] holds, where e is the number of edges in a graph G and $\chi(G)$ is the chromatic number of the graph. It implies that, for a graph G, the upper bound for $\chi(G)$ increases with the the number of edges e in it. It should be noted that decreasing the upper bound increases the possibility that the value of $\chi(G)$ will reduce.

Keeping the above observations in mind, we design a heuristic which will approximate the optimal graph G by reducing the number of edges in it. To construct an GUAC graph we need to cover each constraint by selecting an edge from it. Hence, we select the edge in each iteration which covers the maximum number of uncovered constraints. The iterations continue until each constraint is covered. We present the procedure ChooseBestGUACgraph using this heuristic in Algorithm 2. The procedure takes a matrix of SMER constraints CON as parameter. Representation of CON is the same as that in the procedure bfGUAC. The procedure ChooseBestGUACgraph returns an array $graphEdges$ representing the graph with minimum chromatic number. The graph representation in $graph$-$Edges$ is the same as that in the arrays $incompGraph$ and $allGraphs$.

We assume that a minimal set of SMER constraints would be given as input. If the role set of any constraint c is a subset of the role set of another constraint c', the constraint c' will not be included in the given set of constraints CO, since any UA relation satisfying c will automatically satisfy c'. However, if the set CO of constraints is not minimal, a preprocessing step can be introduced that will remove all the constraints whose role sets are supersets of some other constraint in CO. This processing can be done in polynomial time.

Next, we demonstrate the steps of the presented greedy algorithm for the instance in Example 1. The elements of the set of all possible edges of the graph written in a sequence for this system are $(r_1 r_2), ..., (r_1 r_5), ..., (r_3 r_4), (r_3 r_5), (r_4 r_5)$. The input matrix CON where each column corresponds to an edge in the above sequence and each row corresponds to a constraint is shown in Table 2. The while loop in the procedure ChooseBestGUACgraph will run for the following 4 iterations.

1: The edge $(r_2 r_3)$ covers the maximum number (two) of constraints, so,
   $graphEdges \leftarrow [0000100000]$.
2: Next, the edge $(r_1 r_2)$ covers constraint co_2, so now,
   $graphEdges \leftarrow [1000100000]$.
3: The edge $(r_1 r_3)$ covers co_1, so now, $graphEdges \leftarrow [1100100000]$.
4: The last uncovered constraint co_3 is covered by the edge $(r_1 r_4)$, so finally,
   $graphEdges \leftarrow [1110100000]$.

Hence, the graph formed will consist of 4 edges as shown in Figure 3. Chromatic number of this graph is 3.

In the procedure ChooseBestGUACgraph, counting the number of constraints covered by a particular edge cover takes k iterations. There are e such edges in the worst case, hence, finding the edge which covers the maximum number of uncovered constraints is in $O(ek)$. Marking the constraints as covered is also in $O(ek)$. The above steps continue for k iterations in the worst case, hence, the worst case overall time complexity is $O(ek^2)$.

2-2 SMUPs are the instances of t-t SMUP where the set CO contains only 2-2 SMER constraints. It is an important special case of t-t SMUP since, it has been shown in [14] that, although more restrictive than necessary, 2-2 SMER constraints are sufficient to enforce any SoD constraint. For 2-2 SMER constraints, there will be only one possible GUAC graph, which the greedy algorithm will also identify. Hence, going through the first step mentioned above is not required. Instead, minimum user requirement for 2-2 SMER constraints can be computed by directly using the solution for the chromatic number problem [7] or that for any other equivalent problem for which solutions are known to exist within a constant factor.

Next, we present an upper bound on the approximated value of m using the proposed greedy algorithm. The presented bounds are based on some of the known upper bounds for chromatic number [6]. If m_{greedy} is the value of m approximated using the algorithm ChooseBestGUACgraph and κ is the maximum number of constraints which can be covered by a single edge, the following upper bound for m_{greedy} can be derived.

Theorem 4. *For an RBAC system with a set of SMER constraints CO and $k = |CO|$, $m_{greedy} \leq \frac{1}{2} + \sqrt{2(k - \kappa) + \frac{1}{4}}$.*

Proof. Let e be the number of edges in the approximated optimal properly colored graph G_{opt}. Then, $|E(G_{opt})| \leq k - \kappa + 1$, where $|E(G_{opt})|$ is the number of edges in the graph G_{opt}, because the greedy algorithm will surely select the edge which is covering κ number of constraints. There is at least one edge between two colors in G_{opt}, otherwise the same color could be used for both the classes. As, $\chi(G_{opt}) = m_{greedy}$ and $k - \kappa \geq |E(G_{opt})| \geq \frac{1}{2} m_{greedy}(m_{greedy} - 1)$, solving this equation for m_{greedy} we obtain the claimed inequality.   □

Table 3. Minimum user count (mean|mode) for different number of roles having only $3 - 3$ SMER constraints

Roles	Number of constraints												
	5	10	20	30	40	50	100	150	200	250	300	350	400
5	2.05|2	3|3	NA	NA	NA	NA	NA	NA	NA	NA	NA	NA	NA
10	2|2	2.25|2	2.5|2	3|3	3.05|3	3.15|3	4.4|4	NA	NA	NA	NA	NA	NA
15	2|2	2.4|2	2.5|2	3.1|3	2.9|3	3.1|3	3.8|4	4.2|4	4.8|5	5.2|5	5.4|5	6.2|6	7.4|8
20	2|2	2|2	2.6|3	2.8|3	3.1|3	3.12|3	4|4	4|4	4.2|4	4.6|5	4.8|5	5|5	5.4|5

Table 4. Minimum user count (mean|mode) for different number of roles having only $5 - 5$ SMER constraints

Roles	Number of constraints												
	5	10	20	30	40	50	100	150	200	250	300	350	400
5	NA	NA	NA	NA	NA	NA	NA	NA	NA	NA	NA	NA	NA
10	2.05|2	2|2	2|2	2.05|2	2.05|2	2.05|2	2|2	2.6|3	3|3	3.8|4	NA	NA	NA
15	2|2	2|2	2|2	2.1|2	2.1|2	2.4|2	2.8|3	2.8|3	3|3	3|3	3|3	3|3	3.2|3
20	2|2	2|2	2.1|2	2|2	2.2|2	2|2	2.8|3	3|3	3|3	3|3	3|3	3.2|3	3|3

7   Implementation and Experimental Results

The procedure ChooseBestGUACgraph has been implemented in Matlab environment on an Intel Core 2 Duo (processor speed of 3GHz) machine with 2GB of RAM running Linux. Matgraph toolbox [19] is used to compute chromatic number. Experiments were initially carried out with random data sets comprising of 3-3 and 5-5 SMER constraints. Finally, random data sets having mixed *t-t* SMER constraints were used. Twenty different runs were carried out for each combination of parameters and the overall result is reported in this section. Both mean and mode of the twenty values so obtained are included in the result.

Tables 3 and 4 show the minimum user requirement for 3-3 and 5-5 SMER constraints, respectively. While the number of constraints is varied from 5 to 400, the number of roles is varied from 5 to 20 . The results show that the minimum user count for a given number of roles increases with increase in the number of constraints. It may be noted that, the GUAC graph G tends to become more sparse when the number of roles increases, keeping the number of constraints constant. This is because, the maximum number of possible edges of the GUAC graph G (which equals the number of constraints) remains the same. As a result, the minimum user count decreases as the number of roles increases, keeping the number of constraints fixed.

It can also be observed from the tables that, the minimum user count decreases when the value of t is changed from 3 to 5 keeping the number of roles and the number of constraints fixed. This is due to an increase in the overlap among the edges selected from the constraints to form the GUAC graph G, with increase in the value of t. It may be noted that for n number of roles, there can be at most $\binom{n}{t}$ possible t-t SMER constraints. Hence, the cells in the tables which are 'Not Applicable' are marked as NA.

Table 5. Execution time (in seconds) required to compute the minimum user count for different number of roles having only $3 - 3$ SMER constraints

Roles	\multicolumn{13}{c}{Number of constraints}
	5	10	20	30	40	50	100	150	200	250	300	350	400
5	0.05	0.08	NA	NA	NA	NA	NA	NA	NA	NA	NA	NA	NA
10	0.20	0.39	0.81	1.30	2.04	2.78	7.30	NA	NA	NA	NA	NA	NA
15	0.58	1.02	2.22	4.68	5.97	9.68	24.65	44.45	61.28	82.38	112.26	151.22	239.93
20	1.04	2.39	6.00	9.58	40.30	19.42	60.95	105.50	141.56	215.76	262.31	312.23	441.52

Table 5 and Figure 4 present the variations in the time required to compute the minimum user count for different number of roles and different number of 3-3 and 5-5 SMER constraints, respectively. It is observed that the execution time increases with the number of users and constraints. This is because, the number of columns (representing the number of possible edges of an GUAC graph) of the matrix CON increases with the number of roles. Furthermore, the number of rows of the matrix also increases with the number of constraints, which causes the procedure ChooseBestGUACgraph to run for more number of iterations. It is also observed that the execution time required generally decreases with an increase in the value of t. This is due to the fact that the number of possible edges that can be chosen for each constraint increases, which leads to more overlap in the chosen edges and causes the procedure to run for less number of iterations.

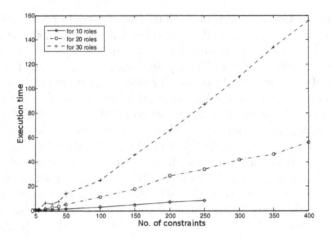

Fig. 4. Variation of the execution time (in seconds) required to find the minimum user count for different number of roles having only $5 - 5$ SMER constraints

Table 6. Minimum user count (mean|mode) for different number of roles having mixed t-t SMER constraints

Roles	Number of constraints										
	10	20	50	100	200	300	400	500	600	700	800
10	2|2	2.2|2	2.4|2	3.05|3	3.35|3	3.8|4	4.55|4	4.6|5	5.15|5	5.7|5	6.7|6
20	2|2	2|2	2|2	2|2	2|2	2.2|2	2.2|2	2.25|2	2.35|2	2.65|3	2.6|3
30	2|2	2|2	2|2	2|2	2|2	2|2	2|2	2|2	2|2	2.2|2	2|2

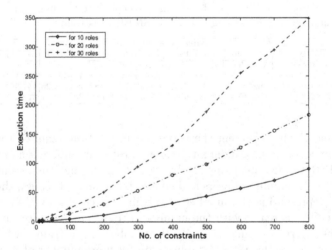

Fig. 5. Variation of the execution time (in seconds) with the number of mixed t-t SMER constraints for 10, 20 and 30 roles

Table 6 and Figure 5 respectively show the overall variations of minimum user requirement and execution time for 10, 20 and 30 roles with mixed t-t SMER constraints. The minimum user count is seen to decrease with an increase in the number of roles. The results also show that, the minimum user count increases as the number of constraints is increased, keeping the number of roles fixed. The execution time slowly increases with an increase in the number of constraints, keeping the number of roles fixed. Further, there is an increase in execution time when the number of roles increases, keeping the number of constraints fixed.

We also compared the current approach with the method proposed in [15]. While the minimum user count value is almost the same in the two approaches, there is a significant improvement in execution time. It has been observed that for mixed set of t-t SMER constraints, instances with 10 roles and 10 SMER constraints took the least time to execute for both the approaches. However, the approach proposed in [15] took 16.64 *seconds* to execute and the current approach took less than one *second*. For the data set containing 20 roles and 100 SMER constraints, the current approach took less than six *seconds* as compared to 58.5 *minutes* by the approach proposed in [15]. Similar improvements in execution time has also been observed for other instances used in [15].

8   Related Work

Since long, the concept of separation of duty (SoD) has existed in physical systems. The term "two-man rule" was often used to refer to this policy. In computer systems, this principle is adopted to achieve a high level of security especially for critical operations. The concept of SoD was first introduced by Clark and Wilson [4] as a procedure to control fraud and error in commercial systems. It was stated that, in a computer system, external consistency can be ensured by separation of all operations into subparts and imposing a requirement that each subpart should be executed by a different individual. Mutual exclusion of roles for efficiently handling SoD constraints in RBAC was first introduced by Kuhn [13]. It has been proved by Li et al. in [14] that a set of Statically Mutually Exclusive Roles (SMER) constraints can be used to equivalently represented a given SoD constraint. Furthermore, they have shown that verifying whether a given RBAC state satisfies a set of SoD constraints is intractable, however, it requires polynomial time to verify if an RBAC state satisfies a given set of SMER constraints.

While in [14] an approach to convert a set of SoD policies into a set of SMER constraints has been proposed, in this work we study the impact of SMER constraints on the minimum user requirement in an RBAC system.

It has also been recognized in the literature that mutually exclusive roles are most commonly used constraints in RBAC [17]. Hence, using SMER constraints to enforce SoD policies in RBAC system has been recognized as an efficient method.

Substantial work has been done in workflow management where the problem of assigning users to roles and roles to tasks is considered [2], [21]. A language to express workflow authorization constraints as clauses in a logic programming language was introduced by Bertino et al. [2]. Algorithms to plan users for a workflow were also proposed in [2]. However, planning of users using minimum number of users was not considered. Also, the SMER constraints, which have been shown to be effective in imposing SSoD constraints [14], are not supported by that framework.

A model (R^2BAC) to support workflow and the "workflow satisfiability problem" (WSP) was proposed by Wang and Li [21]. For a particular workflow, WSP checks whether a valid plan is possible for a given access control state [5]. However, R^2BAC neither supports the general SSoD constraints mentioned in [14] nor the SMER constraints. It is to be noted that, there are considerable differences between the problem of user planning with minimum number of users and the WSP problem.

The work presented in the current paper has been shown to be effective in deciding the minimum number of users required to enforce a given set of t-t SMER constraints while designing an RBAC system. We have also shown how it can be extended for handling other constraints and can be adapted for workflow problems.

9   Conclusion and Future work

We have considered the problem of finding minimum number of users required and corresponding user-role assignment to deploy an RBAC system with a set of t-t SMER constraints. The problem is shown to be NP-complete. A solution to this problem is to find the minimum chromatic number from a set of graphs constructed by choosing a possible pair of roles as an edge from each constraints for each graph. We have proposed a greedy algorithm to identify the graph with minimum chromatic number. We have discussed a possible application of the current work in planning users for workflows. Possible approaches to solve the current problem along with a few other constraints have also been presented.

A workflow system is planned in two phases of which the first phase involves planning or deployment of users in the system. There has been some work on user planning in this context in the presence of various separation of duty constraints. However, user planning using minimum number of users is not considered. In future, we plan to design algorithms for the same. We also intend to derive tighter bounds for the problem considered in the current paper and come up with algorithms with tight approximation ratios. Furthermore, we would like to study other variants of this problem, considering various other constraints considered in an RBAC system.

References

1. Bell, D.E., Lapadula, L.J.: Secure computer system: Unified exposition and multics interpretation. Electronic Systems Division, Air Force Systems Command, Hanscom Field, Bedford, MA 01731 (1976)
2. Bertino, E., Ferrari, E., Atluri, V.: The specification and enforcement of authorization constraints in workflow management systems. ACM Transactions on Information and System Security 2(1), 65–104 (1999)
3. Chen, F., Sandhu, R.S.: Constraints for role-based access control. In: Proceedings of the 1st ACM Workshop on Role-Based Access Control, pp. 39–46 (1996)
4. Clark, D.D., Wilson, D.R.: A comparison of commercial and military computer security policies. In: Proceedings of the 1987 IEEE Symposium on Security and Privacy, pp. 184–194 (1987)
5. Crampton, J., Gutin, G., Yeo, A.: On the parameterized complexity and kernelization of the workflow satisfiability problem. ACM Transactions on Information and System Security, 16(1), 4:1–4:31 (2013)
6. Diestel, R.: Graph Theory. Springer (2005)
7. Ferraiolo, D.F., Kuhn, D.R., Chandramouli, R.: Role-Based Access Control. Artech House (2007)
8. Frank, M., Buhman, J.M., Basin, D.: Role mining with probabilistic models. ACM Transactions on Information and System Security, 15(4), 15:1–15:28 (2013)
9. Garey, M.R., Johnson, D.S.: Computers and intractability: A guide to the theory of np-completeness. W. H. Freeman (1979)
10. Harika, P., Nagajyothi, M., John, J.C., Sural, S., Vaidya, J., Atluri, V.: Meeting cardinality constraints in role mining. IEEE Transactions on Dependable and Secure Computing (to appear, 2014)
11. Harrison, M.A., Ruzzo, W.L., Ullman, J.D.: Protection in operating systems. Communications of the ACM 19(8), 461–471 (1976)
12. Jin, X., Krishnan, R., Sandhu, R.: A unified attribute-based access control model covering DAC, MAC and RBAC. In: Cuppens-Boulahia, N., Cuppens, F., Garcia-Alfaro, J. (eds.) DBSec 2012. LNCS, vol. 7371, pp. 41–55. Springer, Heidelberg (2012)
13. Kuhn, D.R.: Mutual exclusion of roles as a means of implementing separation of duty in role-based access control systems. In: Proceedings of the Second ACM Workshop on Role-based Access Control, pp. 23–30 (1997)
14. Li, N., Tripunitara, M.V., Bizri, Z.: On mutually exclusive roles and separation-of-duty. ACM Transactions on Information and System Security 10(2), 1–36 (2007)
15. Roy, A., Sural, S., Majumdar, A.K.: Minimum user requirement in role based access control with separation of duty constraints. In: 12th International Conference on Intelligent Systems Design and Applications, pp. 386–391 (2012)
16. Sandhu, R.S., Bhamidipati, V., Munawer, Q.: The ARBAC97 model for role-based administration of roles. ACM Transactions on Information and System Security (TISSEC) 2(1), 105–135 (1999)
17. Sandhu, R.S., Coyne, E.J., Feinstein, H.L., Youman, C.E.: Role-based access control models. IEEE Computer 29(2), 38–47 (1996)
18. Schaad, A., Moffett, J., Jacob, J.: The role-based access control system of a European bank: a case study and discussion. In: Proceedings of the sixth ACM Symposium on Access Control Models and Technologies, pp. 3–9 (2001)

19. Scheinerman, E.R.: Matgraph: A MATLAB Toolbox for Graph Theory (2012),
    http://www.ams.jhu.edu/~ers/matgraph
20. Vaidya, J., Atluri, V., Guo, Q.: The role mining problem: finding a minimal descriptive set of roles. In: Proceedings of the 12th ACM Symposium on Access Control Models and Technologies (SACMAT), pp. 175–184 (2007)
21. Wang, Q., Li, N.: Satisfiability and resiliency in workflow authorization systems. ACM Transactions on Information and System Security 13(4), 40:1–40:35 (2010)

Temporal RBAC Security Analysis Using Logic Programming in the Presence of Administrative Policies

Sadhana Jha[1], Shamik Sural[2], Jaideep Vaidya[3], and Vijayalakshmi Atluri[3]

[1] Advanced Technology Development Centre
[2] School of Information Technology,
Indian Institute of Technology, Kharagpur, India
{sadhanajha,shamik}@sit.iitkgp.ernet.in
[3] Management Science and Information Systems Department,
Rutgers University, USA
jsvaidya@business.rutgers.edu, atluri@rutgers.edu

Abstract. Temporal Role Based Access Control (TRBAC) is an extension of the role based access control (RBAC) model in the temporal domain. It is used by organizations needing to enforce temporal constraints on enabling and disabling of roles. For any chosen access control model, decentralization of administrative authority necessitates the use of a separate administrative model. Even with the use of an administrative model, decentralization often leads to an increased concern for security. Analysis of security properties of RBAC has been extensively done using its administrative model (ARBAC97). However, TRBAC security analysis in the presence of an administrative model so far has received limited attention. This paper proposes a method for performing formal security analysis of TRBAC considering a recently proposed administrative model named AMTRAC, which includes all the relations of ARBAC97 as well as an additional set of relations (named REBA) for administering the role enabling base of a TRBAC system. All the components of TRBAC and AMTRAC are specified in Prolog along with the desired safety and liveness properties. Initially, these properties are verified considering the non-temporal relations only, followed by handling of the temporal relations as well. Experimental results show that the method is both effective as well as scalable.

Keywords: TRBAC, AMTRAC, Prolog, Security Analysis.

1 Introduction

Providing secure and restrictive access to its resources is one of the main concerns for any organization. Role-based access control (RBAC) [14] has emerged as an effective means for specifying and meeting security goals in organizations with diverse access control requirements. It is based on the central notion of *roles*. Roles are created to perform a job functions and are associated with a set

A. Prakash and R. Shyamasundar (Eds.): ICISS 2014, LNCS 8880, pp. 129–148, 2014.

of permissions. Users are assigned to roles based on their organizational responsibilities. The Temporal RBAC (TRBAC) model [1] allows temporal constraints on when the roles can be used. It restricts roles to be either in the *enabled* or the *disabled* state. Transition from the enabled to the disabled state is termed as *enabling* of role and the reverse as *disabling* of role.

Administration of a large RBAC or TRBAC system is a challenging task and to address this, administrative models such as ARBAC97 [12] for RBAC and AMTRAC [16] for TRBAC have been proposed. An administrative model brings decentralization in administration by allowing a chief security officer to delegate the authority of management to other administrative officers. It incorporates certain relations that allow administrators to change the state of the system. The use of administrative models restricts the set of possible states which an access control system can transit to. However, decentralization also leads to increased possibility of intentional or unintentional violation of security, resulting in unauthorized information flow. Hence, it is imperative that a comprehensive understanding and analysis of these models be done before they are deployed in practical situations.

Access control models including RBAC and TRBAC provide a multitude of features. While this enables specifying different kinds of access control policies, analysis of the level of security provided by the access control model is tedious and error-prone, if not impossible, when attempted manually. It is more so, when security administration is distributed and state changes could be made by different administrators based on the administrative roles they are allowed to invoke. Automated security analysis is also complicated and requires appropriate tools for solving computationally hard problems. Since state transition in an RBAC or TRBAC system can take place only through the set of administrative relations defined in its administrative model, consideration of administrative models is necessary for analyzing the security properties. Till date, there is limited work on TRBAC security analysis. Additionally, none of the existing approaches consider a comprehensive administrative model.

In this paper, we present a methodology for TRBAC security analysis using Prolog in the presence of a recently proposed administrative model named AMTRAC [16]. Essentially, a security analysis problem can be considered as a searching problem in which the analyzer searches for an instance in which the desired security property does not hold. We use Prolog for security analysis since it has been shown to be able to handle such type of problems quite efficiently. Moreover, the inbuilt capability of handling lists makes it suitable for representing the temporal elements of a TRBAC system. However, effective modeling of temporal components and administrative functions so that security analysis can be done efficiently is a non-trivial task as Prolog does not directly support all such features.

Security analysis in the current context is primarily concerned with the verification of safety and liveness properties. A safety property can be stated as *"Does user u get permission p at time instant t?"* while a liveness property could be *"Is there a time instant t, when none of the roles in the system is in the enabled state?"*. Thus, safety property checks for the presence of an enabled user at a particular point of time and liveness property checks for the presence of an enabled role over the entire set of time periods defined by all the periodic events of the system under consideration. For analysis, both the TRBAC system as well as the corresponding AMTRAC relations are specified in Prolog. Security properties are also defined using Prolog syntax. These specifications are given as input to the *SWI* interpreter[1], which returns true or false depending on whether the system specifications meet the given security properties. It may be noted that, for analysis, we do not use *temporal logic* extension of Prolog, rather first order form is used along with a representation of the temporal aspects of TRBAC.

The rest of the paper is organized as follows. Section 2 contains preliminaries about RBAC, TRBAC, AMTRAC and Prolog. In Sections 3 and 4, we explain how safety and liveness analysis can be done for TRBAC under the AMTRAC administrative model using Prolog. Section 5 presents the results of experimental evaluation of the proposed approach. Section 6 discusses some of the previous work done in this field. Section 7 concludes the paper along with suggestions for prospective future work.

2   Preliminaries

In this section, we provide a brief introduction of the RBAC and TRBAC access control models (Section 2.1), their administrative models (Section 2.2), and Prolog (Section 2.3). This would help in understanding the key concepts used in the rest of the paper.

2.1   RBAC and TRBAC

RBAC [14] is an access control model in which role represent job functions within an organization. Permissions are assigned to roles instead of directly to users. Users get appropriate permissions by becoming members of corresponding roles. The basic components of RBAC include a set of users (U), a set of roles (R), a set of permissions (P), a user-role assignment (UA), a role-permission assignment (PA) and a role- role relation called role hierarchy (RH). These components collectively determine whether a particular user has permission to access a certain resource. RBAC, thus, effectively controls which users have access to which resource.

However, for many applications, which need to make access control decisions based on temporal information, RBAC is not adequate. For such applications, TRBAC, a temporal extension of RBAC, has been proposed. It includes a Role Enabling Base (REB) for defining periodic enabling and disabling of roles expressed as periodic events along with temporal dependencies among roles specified using role triggers. Periodic events (PE) are of the form {I, P, p:E}, where *I* represents the interval for which a periodic event is valid, *P* represents a periodic expression based on the notion of calendars [1] and *p:E* represents a prioritized event expression [1]. For example, (*[01/01/2014, 01/01/2020], all.years +*

---
[1] http://www.swi-prolog.org/

all.months + *all.weeks* + *{1,2,3,4,5}.days* + *{10}.hours* ▷ *8.hours, H: Enable r*)
conveys that the role r is enabled with high (H) priority for a duration of eight
hours starting from the tenth hour of the first, second, third, fourth and fifth
day of every week of every month of every year, during the period 01/01/2014
till 01/01/2020. A role trigger (RT) is of the form $E_1, E_2, ... E_n, C_1, C_2, ... C_m \longrightarrow$
$p{:}E$ *after* $\triangle t$ where, $E_i s$ and $C_j s$ represent event expressions and role status
expressions [1], respectively. $p{:}E$ and $\triangle t$ represent a prioritized event expression
and delay, respectively. For example, (*Enable a, Enabled b* → *Enable c*) conveys that, enabling of role a triggers enabling of role c provided that role b is
already enabled. Thus, periodic events and role triggers collectively determine
which roles in a system are enabled or disabled at various points in time.

2.2 ARBAC97 and AMTRAC

An administrative model defines the set of valid state transition rules for an access control system. ARBAC97 is the first comprehensive administrative model
for RBAC. It has three components, namely, URA97, PRA97 and RRA97.
URA97 includes two relations, namely, *can_assign* and *can_revoke* to modify
the UA of an RBAC system. These relations respectively provide authority to
an administrator to assign new users to a role and to revoke existing users from
a role. PRA97 includes two relations, namely, *can_assignp* and *can_revokep* to
modify the PA of an RBAC system. These relations respectively provide authority to an administrator to assign new permissions to a role and revoke existing
permissions from a role. RRA97 includes a relation named as *can_modify* to
modify the RH of an RBAC system. It allows an administrator to insert new
edges into the hierarchy and delete existing edges from the hierarchy. It also
allows them to create new roles as well as delete existing roles within a role
range. The components of ARBAC97, thus, can be used to change the state
of an RBAC system. To change the state of a TRBAC system, along with the
relations defined in ARBAC97, an additional component named as REBA (Role
Enabling Base Assignment) has been introduced in AMTRAC. REBA includes
a set of eighteen relations. These relations are partitioned into four different categories. While, the first and second categories of relations allow an administrator
to modify an existing periodic event and role triggers, the third and the fourth
category relations allow an administrator to add or delete new periodic events
and role triggers to or from the REB of a TRBAC system. Thus, REBA can be
used to make various possible modifications to the REB of a TRBAC system.

2.3 Introduction to Prolog

A Prolog program describes relations defined by means of *clauses*. A clause
can be either a *fact* or a *rule*. A *fact* represents a predicate expression that
makes a declarative statement about the problem domain. For example, consider
an authorization system having *Alice, Charles* and *Tom* as its users. Each of
the three users is associated with a password through the relation named as
username_password. The set of facts representing this can be written as follows:

username_password(Alice, 123456)
username_password(Charles, 123abc)
username_password(Tom, a2gh45)

A *rule* is a predicate expression that uses logical implication (:-) to describe a relationship among facts. For example, for the authorization system mentioned above, a rule to check whether the combination of *username* and *password* entered by a user is valid or not can be written as follows:

valid_username_password_combination (U, P):- username_password(U, P) → *write('Valid username password combination'); write('Invalid username password combination')*

A program logic expressed in the syntax of Prolog is executed using an interpreter. The interpreter is provided with a query to check whether certain conditions hold or not. For instance, for the authorization system specified above, a query to check whether *Alice* and *123456* is a valid *username-password* combination can be written as:

valid_username_password_combination(Alice, 123456)

The interpreter, when provided with the given query, tries to find whether in the presence of the provided set of facts and rules, it can derive that *Alice* and *123456* form a valid *username-password* combination. If it is able to do so, then it returns *true*; else, returns *false* as output. Thus, we have seen how a Prolog interpreter can be employed to check for the presence of certain conditions in a system.

3   System Modeling in Prolog

To check whether a TRBAC state continues to remain in the safe state in presence of a set of administrative relations, the initial state of a TRBAC system as well as the set of administrative relations are provided as *facts* to the interpreter. Meaning of the security properties is defined in the form of *rules*.

3.1   Modeling TRBAC Using Prolog

In this section, we show how different components of a TRBAC system can be modeled in the form of *facts* of a Prolog program. While modeling a TRBAC system, the following assumptions are made: i) Initially, all roles are in the disabled state, ii) If an enabled role needs to be disabled, the corresponding role trigger is removed from the REB, iii) If a role r_1 triggers another role r_2, then disabling of r_1 causes automatic disabling of r_2, iv) All event expressions are of the same priority and v) Triggers are fired without any delay.

To represent *users*, *roles* and *permissions*, facts of the form *user(string)*, *role(string)* and *per(string)*, respectively are used. In these facts, *string* denotes the name of a user, role or permission. To represent that u_i is a user, a fact of the form $user(u_i)$ is added to the specification, to represent that r_i is a role, a fact of the form $role(r_i)$ is added and to show that p_i is a permission, a fact of the form $per(p_i)$ is added to the program. The *UA*, *PA* and *RH* relations of a TRBAC system are represented by facts of the form $user\_role(string,\ string)$, $role\_per(string,\ string)$ and $role\_per(string,\ string)$, respectively.

A fact of the form $user\_role(u_i,\ r_j)$ represents that the user u_i is a member of the role r_j. A fact of the form $role\_per(r_i,\ p_j)$ represents that the permission p_j is assigned to the role r_i . A fact of the form $role\_H(r_i,\ r_j)$ represents that role r_i is senior to role r_j.

An REB is represented by adding facts corresponding to periodic events as well as role triggers. To express a periodic event, a fact named *periodic_ event* is used and it is of the form:

$periodic\_ event([Integer_i,\ Integer_j],\ [[Year],\ [Month],\ [Week],\ [Day],\ [Hour],$ $[Duration]],\ role)$

$Integer_i$ and $Integer_j$ represent the *begin* and *end* of the interval component of a periodic event. Variables *Year*, *Month*, *Week*, *Day* and *Hour* represent components of the year, month, week, day and hour calendar of a periodic expression. The variable *Duration* represents the component of the duration calendar of a periodic expression. The variable *role* is used to represent the role that will get enabled through a periodic event (assumption has been made that PEs and RTs are used only for role enabling).

Even though Prolog provides sufficient flexibility to represent every form of periodic expression, for the sake of brevity, we constrain the different values that the variables of a periodic_event fact could take. These constraints are as follows:

- $Integer_i$ and $Integer_j$: 4-digit integers such that $Integer_i \leq Integer_j$
- YEAR: all $\backslash_-$
- MONTH: all $\backslash_-$ $\backslash k, 1 \leq k \leq 12$
- WEEK: all
- DAY: all $\backslash_-$ $\backslash k, 1 \leq k \leq 7$
- HOUR: all$\backslash_-$ $\backslash k, 1 \leq k \leq 23$
- DURATION: $1 \leq k \leq 23$

Using the above definition of a periodic event, to represent a periodic event of the form $([2000,\ 2014],\ <all.years\ +\ all.months\ +\ \{1,\ 2,\ 3\}.days\ +\ 10.\ hours\ \triangleright$ $8.\ hours\ >,\ Enable\ r1\ )$, a tuple of the form $periodic\_ event([2000,\ 2012],\ [[all],$ $[all],\ [\_],\ [1,\ 2,\ 3,\ 4,\ 5],\ [10],\ [8]],\ r1)$ needs to be added to the Prolog program.

A role trigger is represented by a relation named as *trigger*. This relation is of the form $trigger(role_{i_1},\ role_{i_2},\ role_{i_3},\ role_{i_4})$, where each $role_{i_k}, 1 \leq k \leq$ 4 could be either a valid role name or an anonymous variable represented as '$\_$'(without quotes). $role_{i_1}$ represents the role present in the event expression of a role trigger, $role_{i_2}$ and $role_{i_3}$ represent the roles present in the role status expression of a role trigger and $role_{i_4}$ represents the role present in the head of a trigger. For example, a role trigger of the form *Enable r_1, Enabled r_2, Enabled r_3 → Enable r_4* could be represented by adding a fact of the from *trigger(r_1, r_2, r_3, r_4)* and a role trigger of the form *Enable r_1, Enabled r_2 → Enable r_3* could be represented as *trigger(r_1, r_2, _, r_3)*. It may be noted that, for simplicity, we restrict the form a role trigger can take, i.e., the body of the trigger can have at-most one event expression and two role status expressions, the head of a trigger can have at-most one event expression. However, Prolog itself does not impose such restrictions and could be efficiently used to represent more complex forms of role triggers.

3.2   Modeling of AMTRAC in Prolog

This sub-section gives details on modeling of the relations of AMTRAC in Prolog. We divide AMTRAC relations into three categories. The first category consists of those relations that add new elements to the components of a TRBAC system. The second category of relations removes elements from the TRBAC system components and the third category modifies the existing elements of a TRBAC system components. We refer to these categories of relations as additive relations, removal relations and modification relations, respectively.

Modeling of Additive Relations: Under this category of relations, fall *can_assign*, *can_assignp* and *insert_Edge* of ARBAC97 and also the *addRT* and *addPE* relations of REBA.

- Modeling of *can_assign*
  To model can_assign, a fact of the form *canassign(arole, role, role)* is used, where *arole* represents an administrative role and *role* denotes a regular role. If a TRBAC system has a *canassign* relation of the form (ar_1, r_1, r_2), then this can be represented in Prolog by adding a fact of the form *canassign(ar_1, r_1, r_2)*. Now the facts that an interpreter can derive from a *canassign* fact are given by the rules:

  can_assign(A, R1, R2) :- canassign(A, R1, R2)
  can_assign(A, R1, R2) :- canassign(A, R3, R2), can_assign(A, R1, R3)
  assigned_user(U, R) :- user_role(U, R)
  assigned_user(U, R) :- member_user_through_hierarchy(U, R)
  user_assigned(U, R) :- assigned_user(U, R)
  user_assigned(U, R) :- can_assign(A, R1, R), assigned_user(U, R)

  The first two lines help the interpreter to find the set of *canassign* relations through which a member of *R1* can be assigned to *R2*. The third and the fourth lines define that a user *U* is a member of role *R* if either there is a tuple of the form *(U, R)* in *user_role* or if *U* gets membership of the role through hierarchy. The fourth and the fifth statements convey that a user *U* is assigned to role *R*, either directly through UA or RH, or it may get assigned due to the presence of a *canassign* fact that allows *A* to assign *U* to *R*.

- Modeling of *can_assignp*

  To model can_assignp, a fact of the form *canassignp(arole, role, role)* is used, where *arole* represents an administrative role and *role* denotes a regular role. If a TRBAC system has a *canassignp* relation of the form (ar_1, r_1, r_2), then this can be represented in Prolog by adding a fact of the form *canassignp(ar_1, r_1, r_2)*. Now the facts that an interpreter can derive from a *canassignp* fact are given by the rules:

  can_assignp(A, R1, R2) :- *canassignp(A, R1, R2)*
  can_assignp(A, R1, R2) :- *canassignp(A, R3, R2), can_assignp(A, R1, R3)*
  assigned_per(R, P) :- *role_H(R, P)*
  assigned_per(R, P) :- *member_per_through_hierarchy(R, P)*
  per_assigned(R, P) :- *assigned_per(R, P)*
  per_assigned(R, P) :- *can_assignp(A, R1, R), assigned_per(R, P)*

  The first two lines help the interpreter to find the set of *canassignp* relations through which permissions of *R1* can be assigned to *R2*. The third and the fourth line define that a permission *P* is associated with a role *R*, if, either there is a tuple of the form *(R, P)* in *role_per* or if *P* is associated with some other role *R3* such that, *R3* is junior to *R*. The fourth and fifth statements convey that a role *R* gets a permission *P*, either directly through PA or RH, or it may get it through the execution of some *canassignp*, which allows *A* to assign *P* to *R*.

- Modeling of *insert_Edge*

  RRA97 allows an administrator to insert new edges into the role hierarchy and also to delete existing edges from the hierarchy. To model insertion of edge, the *InsertEdge* relation is used. It is of the form *insertEdge(arole, role, role)*, where *arole* represents an administrative role and *role* denotes a regular role. If a TRBAC system has an *insertEdge* relation of the form (ar_1, r_1, r_2), then this can be represented in Prolog by adding a fact of the form *insertEdge(ar_1, r_1, r_2)*. Now the facts that an interpreter can derive from a *insertEdge* fact are given by the rules:

  direct_senior(R1, R2):- *role_H(R1, R2)*
  direct_senior(R1, R2):- *role_H(R1, R3), direct_senior(R3, R2)*
  new_senior(R1, R2):- *insertEdge(R1, R2)*
  new_senior(R1, R2):- *insertEdge(R1, R3), new_senior(R3, R2)*
  senior(R1, R2) :- *direct_senior(R1, R2)*
  senior(R1, R2) :- *new_senior(R1, R2)*

  The first two lines help the interpreter to find the set of roles senior to a role *R2* due to initial role hierarchy. The third and the fourth lines help the interpreter to find the set of roles senior to a role *R* due to the hierarchy introduced by the *insertEdge* relation. The fourth and fifth statements convey that the role *R1* is senior to the role *R2* if either *R2* is senior due to initial hierarchical structure or due to the modified hierarchical structure.

– Modeling of *addPE* (R_{16})

The relation R_{16} adds a new periodic event to an REB. The fact used to model R_{16} is of the form *addPE(perodic_ event)*, where *periodic_ event* is a new periodic event such that its format satisfies all the constraints specified in Section 3.1. To add a new periodic event of the form (*[2000, 2014], all.years + 1, 2, 3.days ▷ 2.days, Enable r*), a fact of the form *addPE([2000, 2014], [[all], [_], [_], [1, 2, 3], [_], [2]], r)* is added to the prolog specification. The new facts that an interpreter can derive due to the presence of an *addPE* fact are given by:

effective_ periodic_ event(I, P, R) :- *periodic_ event(I, P, R)*
effective_ periodic_ event(I, P, R) :- *addPE(I, P, R)*

The above statements convey to the interpreter that the set of effective periodic events in a system is the set of periodic events present in the initial state of a TRBAC system along with the set of periodic events added through *addPE*.

– *Modeling of addRT* (R_{17})

The relation R_{17} adds new role trigger to a system. The fact used to model R_{17} is of the form *addRT(trigger)*, where *trigger* is a new role trigger such that its format satisfies all the constraints specified in Section 3.1. To add a new role trigger of the form *Enable r, Enabled s → Enabled t*, a fact of the form *addRT(r, s, _, t)* is added to the Prolog specification. The new facts that an interpreter can derive due to the presence of an *addRT* fact are given by:

effective_ trigger(R1, R2, R3, R4) :- *trigger(R1, R2, R3, R4)*
effective_ trigger(R1, R2, R3, R4). :- *addRT(R1, R2, R3, R4)*

Through these statements, the interpreter is asked to consider the facts written as *trigger* or *addRT* as the set of effective triggers in the system.

Modeling of Removal Relations: Under this category of relations, come *can_ revoke*, *can_ revokep* and *delete_ Edge* of ARBAC97 and also the *removeRT* relation of REBA.

– Modeling of *can_ revoke*, *can_ revokep* and *delete_ Edge* of ARBAC97 and *removeRT* (R_{18}) of REBA. These relations are specified as rules and are respectively of the form:
can_ revoke(A, R) :- *retractall(user_ assigned(U, R))*
can_ revokep(A, R) :- *retractall(per_ assigned(R, P))*
deleteEdge(A, R1, R2):- *retarctall(role_ H(R1, R2))*
removeRT(trigger) :- *retract(trigger)*

The *can_ revoke(A, R)* rule asks the interpreter to remove all the assigned users U from the role R. The *can_ revokep(A, R)* asks the interpreter to remove all the permissions assigned to the role R. A *deleteEdge(A, $R1$, $R2$)* relation asks the interpreter to remove the hierarchy edge between the roles $R1$ and $R2$, and the rule *removeRT(trigger)* asks the interpreter to remove the role trigger *trigger* from the REB of a system.

Modeling of Modification Relations of REBA: We finally show modeling of those relations that modify an existing element of the REB. Under this category of relations, come R_1 to R_{15} of REBA. To model these relations, two rules are used: one for modifying the periodic events and the other for modifying the role triggers. Modification in a periodic event can be essentially achieved by first removing the obsolete periodic event and then adding the modified periodic event to the REB. Similar is the case for modification in a role trigger. To modify a periodic event, a rule of the following form is used.

modify_ periodic_ event(new_ periodic_ event, old_ periodic_ event) :-
     retract(old_ periodic_ event), assertz(new_ periodic_ event)

Here, *new_ periodic_ event* is the required new periodic event and the *old_ per iodic_ event* represents the periodic event that will get removed from the REB.

The above definition conveys to the interpreter to remove the old periodic event from the set of facts and to add *new_ periodic_ event* to the set of facts. Consider a periodic event of the form ([*2000*, *2012*], <*all.years + all.months ▷ 2.days*>, *Enable r*). If an administrator needs to modify the periodic expression to <*all.years + all.months + all.weeks ▷ 2.days*>, then the *modify_ periodic _ event* will be of the form:

modify_ periodic_ event(periodic_ event([2000, 2012], <all.years + all.months ▷ 2.days>, Enable r), periodic_ event([2000, 2012], <all.years + all.months + all.weeks ▷ 2.days>, Enable r).

To modify a component of a role trigger, a rule of the following form is used:

modify_ trigger(old_ trigger, new_ trigger) :-
     retract(old_ trigger), assertz(new_ trigger)

This definition conveys to the interpreter to remove the *old_ trigger* from the set of facts and to add *new_ trigger* into the REB. Consider a trigger of the form *Enable r1 → Enable r2*. Suppose, an administrator wants to modify it to the form *Enable r1 → Enable r3*. To model this requirement, *modify_ trigger* will be of the form:

modify_ trigger([r1, _, _, r2], [r1, _, _, r3])

4   Analysis of Security Properties

In the previous section, we showed how the different relations of AMTRAC can be modeled using Prolog syntax. In this section, we show how these relations affect the security properties of a TRBAC system. We consider both safety as well as liveness analysis in this paper.

4.1 Safety Analysis

As mentioned in Section 1, a safety property for a TRBAC system could be defined as "*whether a user u gets a permission p at some time instant t.*" In Prolog, to define this property, we use a rule named as *safety*. The *safety* rule can be defined as follows:

safety(U, P, T) :- user_ assigned(U, R), per_ assigned(R, P), enabled_ role(R, T)

In the above rule, the predicate *user_ assigned(U, R)* and *per_ assigned(R, P)* respectively return the set of users and the set of permissions assigned to a role R. The predicate *enabled_ role* is used to check whether the role R is enabled at some time instance T or not. A formal definition of this predicate can be written as:

enabled_ role(R, T):- pe_ enabled_ role(R, T); trigger_ enabled_ role(R, T)

The above defined predicate returns *true* if a role R is enabled at time T either through a periodic event or due to a role trigger. To check whether there is some periodic event which causes enabling of a role R at time T, the predicate *pe_ enabled_ role* is used. It is of the form:

pe_ enabled_ role(R, T) :- valid_ periodic_ event(X, Y, R),
element_ at(IBEGIN, X ,1), element_ at(EBEGIN, X ,2),
element_ at(DAYLIST, Y ,4), element_ at(HOURCALLIST, Y ,5),
element_ at(DURCALLIST, Y ,6), element_ at(HOURCAL, HOURCALLIST ,1),
element_ at(DURCAL, DURCALLIST ,1), element_ at(QUERYYEAR, T ,1),
element_ at (QUERYDAY, T ,3), element_ at(QUERYTIME, T ,4),
Z = HOURCAL + DURCAL, write('Z is '), write(Z), nl,
number_ in_ range(IBEGIN, QUERYYEAR, EBEGIN)→ (member(QUERYDAY,
DAYLIST)→ (number_ in_ range(HOURCAL,QUERYTIME, Z) → (write('Role
enabled'));(write('Not enabled'),nl));
(write('query day not in daylist')));(write('query year not in range'))

In the above definition, the predicate *valid_ periodic_ event* refers to the periodic events initially present in the REB as well as the new periodic events that can be added to the REB through the execution of *addPE* relations.

To check whether a role is enabled through some role trigger or not, the predicate *trigger_ enabled_ role* is used. It is of the form:

trigger_ enabled(R, T) :- enabled(R), pe_ enabled_ role(R, T)

The above predicate conveys that a role R is enabled if both the predicates, i.e., *enabled(R)* and *pe_ enabled_ role(R, T)* return *true*. The predicate *enabled(R)* checks whether all the role status expressions and event expressions specified in the role trigger expression of R are satisfied or not. It is of the form:

enabled(R):- valid_trigger(X, Y, Z, R), nl, periodic_event(I, P, X),
periodic_event(First_I, First_P, Y), periodic_event(Second_I, Second_P, Z),
element_at(Ibegin_ PE_Event ,I, 1), element_at (IEnd_PE_Event,I, 2),
element_at(DayListPE_Event,P, 4), element_at(HourCal_PE_Event, P, 5),
element_at(DurCal_PE_Event, P, 6), element _at(Ibegin_ First_ Enabled,
First_I, 1), element_at(IEnd_First_Enabled,First_I, 2),
element_at(Day ListPE_ FirstEnabled,First_P, 4), element_at(HourCal_First_
Enabled, First_P, 5), element_at(DurCal_First_Enabled, First_P, 6),
element_at(Ibegin _Second_Enabled, Second_I, 1),
element_at(IEnd_Second_Enabled,Second_I, 2),
element_at(DayListPE _SecondEnabled,Second_P, 4),
element_at(HourCal_Second_En- abled, Second_P, 5),
element_at(DurCal_Second_Enabled, Second_P, 6),
intersection (DayListPE_Event, DayListPE_FirstEnabled, L),
intersection(L, DayListPE_Second- Enabled, W),
find_ largest(HourCal_PE_Event, HourCal_First_Enabled, HourCal_
Second_Enabled, Max1, Max2),
find_smallest(DurCal_PE_Event, DurCal_First_Enabled, DurCal_Second_
Enabled, Min1, Min2), nl,
find_largest(Ibegin_PE_Event, Ibegin_First_Enabled, Ibegin_ Second_Enabled,
Max_Ibegin1, Max_Ibegin2), find_smallest(IEnd_PE_Event, IEnd_First_
Enabled, IEnd_Second _Enabled, Min_Iend1, Min_Iend2),
assertz(periodic_event ([Max_Ibegin2, Min_Iend2],[[all], [all], [all], W, Max2,
Min2], R))

Assume there is a role trigger of the form *Enable r_1, Enabled r_2, Enabled r_3* → *Enable r_4*, and a query is made whether r_4 is enabled at some time instance t or not. Then, *enabled*(r_4) checks whether both the roles r_2 and r4 are enabled at time t or not.

After defining the safety rule, we next describe how analysis of a TRBAC system can be done in presence of the different administrative policies. To show the effect, we use the TRBAC system whose user policies are shown in Figure 1 and administrative policies are shown in Figure 2.

To perform safety analysis, we define certain desired safety properties for the system as shown in Table 1. To check whether a condition defined in Table 1 holds or not, individual safety queries for each of them are provided to the interpreter. The set of queries provided to the interpreter is shown in Table 2.

There are certain constraints associated with the values of T that can be used in the safety queries defined in Table 2. For the first query, the value of T should be selected in such a way that it lies in the time duration defined by the periodic expression of any periodic event. For the second query, the value of T can be any time instance between morning *0000* hrs to *1600 hrs* and for the last query, the value of T should be a time instance when, out of the two roles *Manager* and *TeamLeader*, only one is enabled.

users = {Alice, Bob, Charles, John, Tom}
roles = {Manager, Engineer, HR, TeamLeader}
permissions = {Access, Read, Edit}

UA = {(Alice, Manager), (Bob, Engineer), (Charles, Engineer), (John, HR), (Tom, TeamLeader)}
PA = {(Manager, Access), (Engineer, Read), (HR, Edit), (TeamLeader, Access)}
RH = {(Manager ⋡ Engineer)}

PE1 : ([2000, 2020], all.years + all.months + all.weeks + {1, 2, 3, 4, 5}.days + 10.hours ▶ 8.hours , Enable Manager)

PE2: ([2000, 2020], all.months + all.weeks + {5, 6}.days + 10.hours ▶ 8.hours, Enable Engineer)

PE3: ([2000, 2012], all.months + all.weeks + {1, 2, 3, 4, 5}.days + 16.hours ▶ 8.hours, Enable TeamLeader)

RT1: Enable Manager, Enabled TeamLeader → Enable HR

Fig. 1. User policies for the example TRBAC system

Table 1. Safety conditions for the example TRBAC system

1. *Tom* should never get *Edit*
2. *Tom* must not get *Access* between 0000 hrs to 1600 hrs
3. *John* should be able to use *Edit* only if both the roles *Manager* and *TeamLeader* are enabled

For all the behavior defined in Table 1, a safety query is posed to the interpreter. If the condition holds, then the interpreter returns *true*; else, returns *false*. For all the defined conditions, the expected answer is *false*, and if the interpreter returns *true* for any of the queries, then the system is said to be in *unsafe* state. To show the effect of the administrative relations, initially, queries are posed in absence of the administrative relations, and then, in the presence of the administrative relations. As mentioned earlier, for the first query, any value of T representing a valid periodic time can be used. So we use the periodic time [*2012, 1, 3, 10*] for executing the first query. Similarly, for the second query, we can use any periodic time not lying in the range *1600* hrs to *0000* hrs. W consider the periodic time [*2010, 4, 3, 13*] as the value of T. For the third query, we use the periodic time [*2010, 2, 3, 13*], since during this periodic time, only the *Manager* role is enabled. It may be noted that, all the periodic times satisfying the constraints specified earlier could also be used as the value of T.

aroles = {CSO, SSO, SO}

can_assign = {(CSO, TeamLeader, Manager), (CSO, Manager, HR)}

modify_role_trigger = (trigger(Enable Manager, Enabled TeamLeader → Enable HR), trigger(Enable Manager → Enable HR))

addRT(Enable Engineer → Enable HR)

Fig. 2. Administrative roles and Administrative relations of AMTRAC which affects safety property of a TRBAC system

Table 2. Safety conditions of the example TRBAC system

1. safety(Tom, Edit, T).
2. safety(Tom, Access, T).
3. safety(John, Edit, T).

When the interpreter is posed with all the three queries, it returns *false* for each of them, signifying that the system is in *safe* state. Next, the same set of queries is posed to the interpreter in the presence of the administrative relations defined in Figure 2. Now, the interpreter returns *true* for all the three queries. Consecutive execution of the *can_assign* relations assigns *Tom* to the roles *Manager* and *HR*, making *Edit* permission available to him. Execution of the administrative relation *addRT* causes enabling of the role *TeamLeader* whenever the role *Engineer* gets enabled. This causes *Tom* to get the *Access* permission between 1000 hrs to 1800 hrs on Saturdays and Sundays. Execution of the *modify_role_trigger* relation causes enabling of the role *HR* whenever the role *Manager* gets enabled, making permission *Edit* available to *John* even when the role *TeamLeader* is not enabled. Thus, it is seen how execution of the different administrative relations can result in undesired transition of the state of a TRBAC system and how a Prolog interpreter can be suitably used to identify such unsafe conditions.

4.2   Liveness Analysis

Liveness analysis checks for the presence of a *dead state*, i.e., it searches for a time instance when none of the roles is enabled. In Prolog, to check for the liveness of a system, we use the predicate *liveness(t)*. It is of the form:

$$liveness(T) :- enabled\_role(R, T)$$

When a query is made for a certain time instance T, the interpreter tries to find a role R for which *enable_role(R, T)* returns *true*. If the interpreter is able to find such a role, then it returns *true* conveying that system is not dead at the given time instance. A liveness query for a system gets affected only if modification is done in the periodic event. Modification in the role triggers will never bring a system to a dead state. This is because a trigger enables a role at t only if some other role gets enabled at t by a periodic event. So, even if removal of the trigger prevents enabling of the triggered role, it cannot prevent enabling of the role which triggers it. So, we consider only those administrative relations which modify the periodic event of a TRBAC system.

Effect of Modifying Periodic Event on Liveness. Modification in any of the components of a periodic event could result in a dead state for the system. Consider the REB shown in Figure 1. If a *modify_ periodic_ event* relation that modifies the periodic time of *PE1* to {[*2000, 2015*], <*all.years + all.months + all.weeks + 1, 2, 3, 4, 5.days + 10.hours ▷ 8.hours*>} is added, then this will bring the system to the dead state from the start of the year *2016*. If a liveness query of the form *liveness*([*2016, 1, 1, 1*]) (the time represented is the 1st hour of the 1st day of the 1st month of 2016), then the system returns *false* for this query, conveying that, the system is in a dead state at the given time. Similarly, it can be shown that if a *modify_ periodic_ event* relation of the form (*periodic_ event*([*2000, 2020*], *all.years + all.months + all.weeks + 1, 2, 3, 4, 5.days + 10.hours ▷ 8.hours, Enable Manager*), *periodic_ event*([*2000, 2020*], *all.years + all.months + all.weeks + 1, 2, 3, 4, 5.days + 13.hours ▷ 8.hours, Enable Manager*)) is executed, then on weekdays, the system will go to a dead state from 1000 hrs to 1300 hrs. Similarly, it can be observed that if a *modify_ periodic_ event* relation of the form (*periodic_ event*([*2000, 2020*], *all.years + all.months + all.weeks + 5, 6.days + 10.hours ▷ 8.hours, Enable Engineer*), *periodic_ event*([*2000, 2020*], *all.years + all.months + all.weeks + 5, 6.days + 10.hours ▷ 8.hours, Disable Engineer*)) is executed, then the system will come to a dead state on the sixth day of every week of every month between the years 2000 to 2020.

5   Experimental Results

To study the performance of the proposed modeling methodology, we have implemented a simulator that takes the number of roles, users, permissions, administrative roles, time intervals, periodic events and role triggers as input and generates a TRBAC system satisfying the input. The number of user-role assignments and also the number of permission-role assignments are kept at 20% of the sizes of the respective cartesian products. A uniform distribution is used to determine the user-role assignment and permission-role assignment entries that are included in the relations. A second script is written to translate the output generated by the simulator program into its corresponding Prolog specifications. For implementation, Java(7.0.1-17), on a Windows 7 system with 64-bit i5 processor @ 2.50GHz and 4GB RAM is used. SWI interpreter 6.6.1 is used for analysis.

Effect of the number of roles on the analysis time is shown in Figure 3. The data set used for the analysis consists of 2000 users, 300 permissions, 4 administrative roles, 10 time expressions, 50 periodic events and 30 role triggers. From the figure, it can be seen that a linear increase in the number of roles causes a close to linear growth in analysis time. This is due to the fact that, a Prolog interpreter works based on the principle of backtracking. A linear increase in the number of roles causes a linear increase in the set of facts having role as one of its parameters.

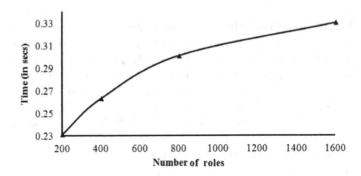

Fig. 3. Effect on analysis time due to variation in number of roles

Figure 4 shows the effect of number of users on the analysis time. The data set used for analysis consists of 300 roles, 300 permissions, 15 time expressions, 50 periodic events, 30 role triggers and 4 administrative roles. It can be observed that, even though the rate of increase in analysis time is linear with increase in the number of users, the rate of growth of time is quite low as compared to the rate of growth of time with number of roles as shown in Figure 3. This is because, when a safety query is specified, the interpreter needs to check only for the user specified in the query, thus making the result of the query independent of other users.

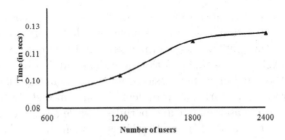

Fig. 4. Effect on analysis time due to variation in number of users

Effect of the number of periodic events and role triggers is shown in Figure 5 and Figure 6, respectively. The rate of growth is quite close to linear for these components of TRBAC as well. However, it can be observed that the analysis time itself is slightly higher as compared to the analysis time needed for the other

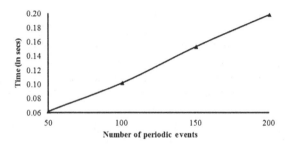

Fig. 5. Effect on analysis time due to variation in number of periodic events

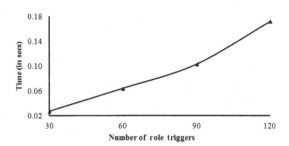

Fig. 6. Effect on analysis time due to variation in number of role triggers

components. This is due to the complex nature of the definitions of periodic events and role triggers.

We also analyzed the effect of each individual administrative relation on the analysis time. It was observed that all the relations have similar effect on the analysis time. This is due to the similarity in format of the relations. The data set used for the analysis consists of 500 users, 200 roles, 300 permissions, 2 administrative roles, 70 periodic events and 20 role triggers. For this data set, it took approximately 0.2 secs to execute a safety query. The combined effect of all the relations of AMTRAC was also studied. For a data set comprising of 1500 users, 300 roles, 300 permissions, 15 time expressions, 120 periodic events, 30 role triggers and 4 administrative roles, the interpreter took 0.232 secs in presence of the AMTRAC relations and 0.141 secs when the AMTRAC relations were not there, to answer a safety query. This is due to the increased number of facts and rules in the presence of the AMTRAC. Even then the total time required is quite encouraging and shows that our modeling and analysis methodology is quite efficient.

6   Related Work

The role-based access control (RBAC) model [14] was proposed to cater to the basic access control needs of commercial organizations. Subsequently, several extensions have been developed that incorporate context related information into the basic RBAC model. In [1], a model named TRBAC (Temporal RBAC) has been introduced for handling temporal constraint on enabling and disabling of RBAC roles. To put additional temporal restrictions on users getting a permission, GTRBAC (Generalized Temporal Role Based Access Control) model has been proposed in [4]. For considering the user location before giving access to resources, the LRBAC (Location-Aware Role Based Access control) model has been proposed in [10]. Other notable work that incorporate temporal as well as spatial information into RBAC include [2], [11].

The need for decentralization in administration has led to the development of administrative models for various access control models. In [12], ARBAC97 is proposed which includes appropriate relations for modifying user-role assignment (URA97), role-permission assignment (PRA97) and role hierarchy (RRA97). Other administrative models for RBAC are presented in [13] and [9]. While a limited number of administrative rules for making modifications to TRBAC is proposed in [18], very recently, a complete administrative model for TRBAC, named as AMTRAC has been proposed [16] . It includes REBA (Role Enabling Base Assignment), which comprises of the relations used for making changes to the role enabling base (REB) assignment of TRBAC, along with all the relations defined in ARBAC97. REBA has a set of eighteen relations for modifying the various components of REB.

Several attempts have been made to develop methods for verifying the security provided by the policies of RBAC and its variants. In [15], petri-net based modeling for the verification of RBAC policies is proposed. It first represents RBAC using a petri-net based framework and then uses it to verify the correctness of a set of underlying security policies. In [17], formal analysis of STRBAC is done using *Alloy*, which is a formal language based on first-order logic. In [7], security analysis of TRBAC using timed automata is proposed. Roles are represented using a user timed automata, while administrative commands are captured in a controller automata. Security properties are specified using Computation Tree Logic (CTL) and verified with the help of a model checking tool named *Uppaal*. In [8], a method for GTRBAC security analysis is proposed where CTL is used to specify a set of safety and liveness properties, which are then verified using the model checking approach.

Apart from performing simple security analysis of RBAC and its variants, various contributions have been made in the field of security analysis using administrative models. In [6], security analysis of RBAC in the presence of AR-BAC97 has been done by reducing the security analysis instance of RBAC into a corresponding security analysis instance of $RT[\leftarrow, \cap]$ [5] and then further reducing the instance so obtained into *Datalog* clauses. In [3], security analysis of user-role assignment of RBAC using URA97 of ARBAC97 is performed and both model checking and logic programming approaches are compared. It has been shown that the logic programming approach outperforms the model checking approach when the number of roles increases significantly. In [18], security analysis of TRBAC is done by using certain administrative rules. However, no formal administrative model has been considered. While security analysis of RBAC has been done based on the administrative models, use of formal administrative models for TRBAC security analysis is yet to be addressed. This is one of the factors for non-deployment of TRBAC at enterprise level even though it has the ability to support a much richer set of features than the RBAC model.

7   Conclusions and Future Work

In this work, we have introduced a methodology for performing security analysis of TRBAC using Prolog. Initially, the components of a TRBAC system and the relations of AMTRAC are modeled using Prolog syntax. To represent the initial content of the TRBAC components, facts are added and the desired security properties, i.e., safety and liveness are defined in the form of rules. Next, the effect of different components of TRBAC and AMTRAC on the analysis time is studied. It has been shown that a linear increase in the number of any of the TRBAC components causes a linear increase in the analysis time. Although each component asserts linear effect on the analysis time, impact of periodic events and role triggers is the most due to their complex nature.

Further work remains to be done to build an even more comprehensive understanding of the security properties of a TRBAC system. In this work, we have made certain simplifying assumptions for representing the administrative relations. However, in practice, some of these might not be feasible. In the future, we plan to perform analysis in the presence of unconstrained forms of administrative relations. A similar problem exists with representing temporal information. Therefore, we plan to provide a more realistic representation of time. This, in turn, will necessitate the use of alternative tools for analyzing problems with access control specifications.

References

1. Bertino, E., Bonatti, P.A., Ferrari, E.: Trbac: A temporal role-based access control model. ACM Transactions on Information and System Security, 191–233 (2001)
2. Bertino, E., Catania, B., Damiani, M.L., Perlasca, P.: Geo-rbac: A spatially aware rbac. In: Proc. of the 10th ACM Symposium on Access Control Models and Technologies, pp. 29–37. ACM (2005)
3. Jha, S., Li, N., Tripunitara, M., Wang, Q., Winsborough, W.: Towards formal verification of role-based access control policies. IEEE Transactions on Dependable and Secure Computing, 242–255 (2008)
4. Joshi, J.B., Bertino, E., Latif, U., Ghafoor, A.: A generalized temporal role-based access control model. IEEE Transactions on Knowledge and Data Engineering, 4–23 (2005)
5. Li, N., Mitchell, J.C., Winsborough, W.H.: Design of a role-based trust management framework. In: Proc. of the IEEE Symposium on Security and Privacy, pp. 114–130. IEEE (2002)
6. Li, N., Tripunitara, M.V.: Security analysis in role-based access control. ACM Transactions on Information and System Security, 391–420 (2006)

7. Mondal, S., Sural, S.: Security analysis of temporal-rbac using timed automata. In: Proc. of the 4th International Conference on Information Assurance and Security, pp. 37–40. IEEE (2008)
8. Mondal, S., Sural, S., Atluri, V.: Towards formal security analysis of gtrbac using timed automata. In: Symposium on Access Control Models and Technologies, pp. 33–42. ACM (2009)
9. Oh, S., Sandhu, R.: A model for role administration using organization structure. In: Proc. of the 7th ACM Symposium on Access Control Models and Technologies, pp. 155–162. ACM (2002)
10. Ray, I., Kumar, M., Yu, L.: LRBAC: A location-aware role-based access control model. In: Bagchi, A., Atluri, V. (eds.) ICISS 2006. LNCS, vol. 4332, pp. 147–161. Springer, Heidelberg (2006)
11. Ray, I., Toahchoodee, M.: A spatio-temporal role-based access control model. In: Barker, S., Ahn, G.-J. (eds.) Data and Applications Security 2007. LNCS, vol. 4602, pp. 211–226. Springer, Heidelberg (2007)
12. Sandhu, R., Bhamidipati, V., Munawer, Q.: The arbac97 model for role-based administration of roles. ACM Transactions on Information and System Security, 105–135 (1999)
13. Sandhu, R., Munawer, Q.: The arbac99 model for administration of roles. In: Proc. of the 15th Annual Conference on Computer Security Applications, pp. 229–238. IEEE (1999)
14. Sandhu, R.S., Coyne, E.J., Feinstein, H.L., Youman, C.E.: Role-based access control models. IEEE Computer, 38–47 (1996)
15. Shafiq, B., Masood, A., Joshi, J., Ghafoor, A.: A role-based access control policy verification framework for real-time systems. In: 10th International Workshop Object-Oriented Real-Time Dependable Systems, pp. 13–20. IEEE (2005)
16. Sharma, M., Sural, S., Vaidya, J., Atluri, V.: Amtrac: An administrative model for temporal role-based access control. Computers & Security (2013)
17. Toahchoodee, M., Ray, I.: Using alloy to analyze a spatio-temporal access control model supporting delegation. IET Information Security, 75–113 (2009)
18. Uzun, E., Atluri, V., Sural, S., Vaidya, J., Parlato, G., Ferrara, A.L., Parthasarathy, M.: Analyzing temporal role-based access control models. In: Proc. of the 17th ACM Symposium on Access Control Models and Technologies, pp. 177–186. ACM (2012)

A Formal Methodology for Modeling Threats to Enterprise Assets

Jaya Bhattacharjee, Anirban Sengupta, and Chandan Mazumdar

Centre for Distributed Computing
Dept. of Computer Science and Engineering, Jadavpur University, Kolkata, India
{jaya.bhattacharjee31,anirban.sg,chandan.mazumdar}@gmail.com

Abstract. Enterprises usually execute business processes with the help of Information Technology (IT) services which, in turn, are realized by IT assets. Enterprise IT assets contain vulnerabilities that can be exploited by threats to cause harm to business processes and breach security of information assets. Hence, detection of threats is crucial for ensuring business continuity and protection of enterprise information security. Existing threat detection mechanisms are limited in scope owing to absence of methodologies for modeling different categories of threats uniformly. This paper presents a formal methodology that can model diverse types of threats to enterprise assets. The methodology provides sufficient flexibility to enterprises for defining threshold values of threat parameters that suit their specific needs and help them to compute probability of occurrence of threats.

Keywords: Asset, Formal Model, Impact, Likelihood of Occurrence, Threat.

1 Introduction

The primary components of an enterprise are business processes and information assets [1]. An information asset, which is generated by a business process, may be used as input by another business process. Today's enterprises frequently utilize Information Technology (IT) services for executing business processes, for example online telephone bill payment, ATM service, etc. IT services are realized with the help of IT assets like Hardware, Software, and Network devices, and human beings who operate them. However, assets usually contain inherent weaknesses, or vulnerabilities, that can be exploited by threats to cause disruption to IT services. This, in turn, may hamper the business processes of an enterprise and result in security breaches of critical/private information assets of enterprises and/or their customers. The increase in interconnectivity between assets of an enterprise further complicate matters and it has been reported that rising incidents of security breaches are a serious cause for concern [2,3].

Information security threat can be defined as a cause of destruction, modification and/or disclosure of assets [4]. Threats can be classified as: Natural (volcanic eruption, earthquake, etc.), Environmental (chemical contamination, power disruption, etc.) and Human-induced threats (malware, eavesdropping, sabotage,

A. Prakash and R. Shyamasundar (Eds.): ICISS 2014, LNCS 8880, pp. 149–166, 2014.
© Springer International Publishing Switzerland 2014

etc.) [1,5]. Assets of an enterprise may be exposed to a wide range of threats. For example, computers in a building can be destroyed by fire that may originate from a coffee vending machine kept within the enterprise premises. Again, the same computers can be subjected to virus attack that spreads via an infected USB device. Hence, it is essential to detect the various types of threats that may harm enterprise assets in order to design and implement appropriate protective measures. As is obvious from the discussion in the next section, existing threat detection methodologies usually identify limited types of threats. While some of them concentrate on malware detection, others may try to predict cyclone patterns. Such specialized methodologies are not suited to the needs of a general purpose enterprise. On one hand, implementation of several specialized methods is a costly affair which is also difficult to maintain. On the other, use of different techniques by each of the implemented methods (graphical approach, filtering technique, pattern-matching system, etc.) renders them extremely difficult to be integrated into a single framework. Moreover, integration may give rise to conflicts that are difficult to resolve and produce incorrect results.

The reason for this anomaly in the domain of threat detection lies in the absence of a methodology that can model different categories of threats uniformly. This paper attempts to address this research gap by proposing a formal model that can be used to specify different classes of threats to enterprise assets. This model can be used to develop generic threat detection methodologies which will prove to be beneficial for general purpose enterprises.

Rest of this paper is organized as follows. Section 2 presents a survey of related work. Section 3 classifies threats and defines their components. Section 4 describes a formal methodology for modeling threats to enterprise assets. While, Section 5 discusses the utility of the proposed methodology, Section 6 illustrates the same with the help of a case study. Finally, Section 7 concludes the paper.

2   Related Work

Different threat detection methodologies have been developed in recent years. In [6] threat is formally modeled using Predicate / Transition (PrT) nets which are highlevel Petri nets. The model addresses system functions, security threats, and security features using PrT nets. Existence of threats is verified against the functions before (and after) the security features are applied. The model uses STRIDE [7] threat classification system to generate *threat-nets* that represent interrelated threats to system functions.

STRIDE approach has been followed by several other methodologies [8,9]. Beckers et. al. [8] proposed a semi-automated technique for identifying privacy threats during the requirements analysis of software systems. The relations between stakeholders, technology, and personal information in the system-to-be are identified, along with the insiders who can breach privacy of stakeholders.

Schaad and Borozdin [9] presented a threat modeling approach for analyzing initial software architecture. They developed a tool for automated threat analysis of software architecture diagrams using STRIDE approach [7].

In [10], a quantitative technique has been proposed to systematically identify privacy requirements, by iteratively analyzing the risks associated with identified threats and attacks. Attack trees are constructed which can be used to identify critical privacy threats to enterprise resources.

The methodology proposed in [11] uses threat trees for performing risk assessment of Internet voting systems. Attacks to hardware and network are decomposed hierarchically into sub-actions. Threat trees are constructed by considering the dependencies among these sub-actions.

Ayed et. al. [12] presented a threat monitoring technique based on filtering and pattern-detection of various events associated with SOA (Service Oriented Architecture). Their approach is to extract threat descriptions from a pre-defined repository and apply appropriate detection techniques at run-time in order to identify potential problems.

In [13], threats to power-sector organizations have been categorized as natural, accidental, malicious, and emerging threats, and their possible impacts have been identified. Using this classification scheme, quantitative trend analyses of a set of representative power blackouts have been performed to figure out the principal threats and the changing trend of threats over time.

Yeh and Chang [14] used empirical data from Taiwanese enterprises to identify the gaps between manager perceptions of information security threats and the security countermeasures adopted by them. They presented a methodology for identifying security baseline depending on the severity values of threats.

Alhabeeb et. al. [15] proposed a dynamic scheme for classifying deliberate threats to enterprise information systems. The scheme considers the following factors: attackers prior knowledge about the information systems, loss of security information, and the criticality of the information systems that might be affected by a threat.

Wu and Ye [16] proposed an information security threat assessment model based on Bayesian Network (BN) and Ordered Weighted Averaging (OWA) aggregation operators. Expert knowledge is integrated to define the conditional probability matrix of reasoning rules in BN; this is used as a basis for the establishment of the threat assessment model. The subjective opinions of experts, regarding the threat level of target information systems, are integrated using the group-decision method of OWA operators; this is considered as the prior information of the threat level of target information systems. Finally, subjective and objective security threat levels are integrated to derive threat assessment results.

As is obvious from the above discussion, none of the existing methods can model diverse kinds of threats to enterprise assets. They either cater to the needs of specific industry sectors, or attempt to model individual threat parameters. Hence, it is difficult for general purpose enterprises, with varying security needs, to implement existing threat models. The problem gets compounded during acquisitions and mergers of enterprises with distinct, sometimes conflicting, security requirements. This paper tries to address these shortcomings by proposing a formal methodology that models threat components uniformly, and addresses information security needs of various types of enterprises.

3 Threat Categories

As stated in Section 1, security standards [1,5] usually classify threats as: Natural, Environmental and Human-induced threats. Disasters caused by nature, which may occur within the vicinity of an enterprise or its assets (human resources, backup media stored in a remote location, etc.), are referred to as natural threats. This includes earthquake, flood, tsunami, thunderstorm, cyclones, volcanic eruptions, etc. Natural threats may cause the following types of impact:

(i) Destruction of IT assets and enterprise premises;
(ii) Financial loss to enterprise business; and
(iii) Death or injury to employees and third party staff of an enterprise.

Environmental threats may occur due to accidents or unexpected changes in environment. Forest fires, chemical contamination, power fluctuations, etc. are examples of environmental threats. Impacts of such kind of threats include:

(i) Destruction or modification of IT assets and enterprise premises;
(ii) Financial loss to enterprise business;
(iii) Loss of reputation, or image, of an enterprise caused by disruption of business processes; and
(iv) Death or injury to employees and third party staff of an enterprise.

Human-induced threats are those that are caused directly or indirectly by human beings. This includes both employees of an enterprise as well as third party staff. Such threats can be attributed either to human errors or purposeful malicious intent. Examples include sabotage, unauthorized system access, spoofing, eavesdropping, malware infection, etc. Human-induced threats may have one or more of the following impacts:

(i) Destruction of enterprise premises;
(ii) Destruction or modification of IT assets;
(iii) Disclosure of sensitive information;
(iv) Financial Loss to enterprise and/or its customers; and
(v) Death or injury to employees and third party staff of an enterprise.

Each of the categories of threats described above comprise of the following attributes: (i) Agent; (ii) Motive; (iii) Resource; and (iv) Result. *Agent* refers to the instrument that causes the threat, namely nature, environment, or human beings. *Motive* is the intent that causes an agent to give rise to a threat. It is obvious that nature and environment do not have any motive behind causing threats. It is only deliberate threats caused by human beings that have malicious intent behind them. Some of these motives are [1]:

(i) challenge, ego, rebellion, status, and monetary gain in case of *hackers*;
(ii) destruction of information, illegal information disclosure, monetary gain, and unauthorized data alteration for *computer criminals*;
(iii) blackmail, destruction, exploitation, revenge, political gain, and media coverage for *terrorists*;
(iv) competitive advantage and economic espionage in case of *state players* and *intelligence companies;* and
(v) curiosity, ego, intelligence, monetary gain, and revenge for *enterprise insiders* (disgruntled, malicious, dishonest, or terminated employees).

Threat agents usually require *resources* to commence an unwanted activity. Types of resources [17] are: (i) financial resource; (ii) manpower; (iii) knowledge or expertise; (iv) tools, techniques, and infrastructure; and (v) time. Human-induced threats can usually be initiated only when one or more of these resources are available. However, in case of natural and environmental threats, only "time" may play an important role. For example, duration of floods can determine the extent of damage caused; similarly, the eruption of a volcano may be time-dependent and occur only after prolonged intervals. It may be noted that availability of resources may vary with the *type* of human agent. For example, a state player will generally have greater resources at its disposal than a disgruntled employee.

The *result* of realization of threat (or occurrence of attack) is physical and/or logical harm to enterprise assets and business processes. This has been enumerated above as *impact* of different categories of threats.

In the next section, these threat attributes have been combined to define a formal model of threats to enterprise IT assets.

4   Threat Model

The threat attributes detailed in Section 3 can be combined to derive a formal model of threat t as

$$t \equiv \{Agt, LOC, Imp\} \tag{1}$$

where, Agt is the threat agent, LOC defines the likelihood of occurrence of threat t, and Imp refers to the impact that will occur in case threat t is realized. The methodology for computing these parameters are described in the following subsections.

4.1   Likelihood of Occurrence of Threat

Probability of threat realization is measured with the help of Likelihood of Occurrence (LOC) of threat [17]. LOC of threat t is derived as a function of five parameters, namely

(i) past occurrences of threat t;
(ii) proximity of assets to areas that are exposed to threat t;

(iii) existence of motive of agent causing threat t;
(iv) resource availability for threat agent; and
(v) efficacy of controls implemented (if any) to mitigate threat t.

Thus,

$$LOC(t) = f(p_t, a_t, mvn_t, res_t, e_c) \tag{2}$$

where, p_t denotes past occurrences of threat t, a_t denotes proximity of assets to threat-prone areas, mvn_t denotes the existence of motive of corresponding threat agent, res_t denotes resource availability for threat agent, and e_c denotes control efficacy.

p_t represents previous incidents that have occurred due to threat t. This includes incidents both in the recent past as well as distant past. It is computed based on

(i) no. of occurrences of threat t; and
(ii) time (year) when t occurred.

For example, if a 5-year period is considered, and if t has occurred twice during the previous year, 3 times during the year before, and so on, then

$$p_t = 2*5 + 3*4 + ...,$$

with greater weight having been assigned to incidents that have occurred more recently. A ceiling value may be fixed for no. of incidents and this may vary from one incident to another. For example, if no. of incidents during a period is 5 or more, a value of 5 may be assigned, for 4 incidents the value may be 4, etc., with a value 0 for 0 occurrences of the incident. Similarly, the period of measurement may also be assigned weights. For example, weight for current year is 5, weight for the previous year is 4, and so on, with a value of 1 being assigned for a period greater than 4 years. The period may be taken as "month" instead of "year" depending on the specific type of threat. Thus,

$$p_t = ceil(\sum(count(t) * weight(period)) / \sum weight(period)) \tag{3}$$

It can be seen that
$$max(p_t) = ceil((5 * 5 + 5 * 4 + 5 * 3 + 5 * 2 + 5 * 1) / (5 + 4 + 3 + 2 + 1)) = ceil(75/15) = 5.$$

A value of 1 is assigned to p_t for zero occurrences of incidents. So, $min(p_t) = 1$.

Hence,

$$p_t \varepsilon \{1, 2, 3, 4, 5\} \tag{4}$$

Proximity of assets to threat-prone areas (a_t) is determined on a 3-point scale. The areas where natural and environmental threats exist can be categorized into "danger zone" (most threat-prone), "striking zone" (less prone to threats), and "safe zone". If asset "a" is within the "danger" zone, then a value of 3 is to be assigned to a_t; if it is within "striking" zone, a value of 2 is assigned; anything beyond has value 1.

In case of human-induced threats that are logical in nature (theft of documents, tampering with software, illegal processing of data, malware infection, etc.), *reachability* and *access* are used as the basis for computation of a_t. While *reachability* determines whether the threat agent can physically reach the asset being considered [18], *access* signifies the authorization (read, write, execute, modify, append, delete) of the threat agent over the asset. In order to cause harm to an asset, an agent must have both *reachability* as well as *access* to that asset. Hence, a_t can be determined as follows:

a value of 3 is assigned to a_t if threat agent has both *reachability* and *access* to asset "a";

a_t has value 2 if threat agent has either *reachability* or *access* to asset "a"; and

a_t has value 1 if threat agent has neither *reachability* nor *access* to asset "a".

The minimum value of a_t is kept at 1, and not 0, to make provision for cases where, owing to some alternate routes (covert channel, etc.), reachability or access of threat agent to the asset might exist, but remain undetected.

In case of human-induced physical threats (destruction of equipment, theft of media, sabotage, etc.), the value of a_t is determined based on the physical reachability of threat agent to the asset being considered. Hence,

a_t has value 3 if threat agent can physically reach the asset location;

a_t has value 2 if threat agent can physically reach the building housing the asset, but not the asset location; and

a_t has value 1 if threat agent does not have physical reachability to the building housing the asset.

It may be noted that if "proximity to threat-prone area" is not applicable for a particular threat, then a value of 1 is assigned to a_t (the reason being the same as stated above).

Hence,

$$a_t \varepsilon \{1, 2, 3\} \tag{5}$$

As stated in Section 3, *motive* is related to human threat agents; it indicates the purpose or intent of the agent for causing threat. Malicious intent may exist in case of disgruntled employees, state enemies, or hackers. Since it is difficult to measure the amount of malice that exists in a threat agent, this can be best modeled as a binary variable as follows:

$$mvn_t = \begin{cases} 1 \text{ , when motive for realization of threat t is present} \\ 0 \text{ , when motive for realization of threat t is absent} \end{cases} \tag{6}$$

Resources may be required for the realization of a threat. It was stated earlier that while, human-induced threats may need different types of resources, in case of natural and environmental threats, the only resource that may be required is *time*. Like motive, it is difficult to estimate the exact amount of resources that are available to an adversary at any particular moment. A feasible solution is to model res_t as a binary variable. Thus,

$$rest_t = \begin{cases} 1 \text{ , when } \textit{sufficient} \text{ resources for realizing threat t are present} \\ 0 \text{ , when } \textit{sufficient} \text{ resources for realizing threat t are not present} \end{cases}$$
(7)

Usually, security controls are implemented by enterprises to mitigate threats. Thus, LOC of a threat may decrease if relevant and effective security controls are present in an enterprise. For example, installation and continuous update of anti-virus software in computers can diminish the probability of virus infections. There are several wellknown control repositories like ISO/IEC 27002:2013 [4], NIST SP 80-53 [19], and COBIT5 [20] standards. Analysis of these standards show that security controls can be classified as managerial, technical, and legal controls. *Managerial controls* are those that rely on the definition and enforcement of security policies and procedures (access control policy, acceptable use policy, information handling procedure, etc.). Since, policies and procedures are vetted and approved by the top management of an enterprise, these are termed managerial controls. *Technical controls* comprise of security tools, techniques, and infrastructure (firewall, anti-virus software, intrusion detection system, etc.). *Legal controls* refer to the laws, regulations and statutes (IT Act, Privacy Law, Data Protection Law, Cryptographic regulations, etc.) that are enforced by authorities to maintain security in enterprises. It is mandatory for an enterprise to identify applicable laws and regulations and ensure compliance with the same.

Implementation of Information Security Management System (ISMS) in an enterprise entails establishment (Plan phase), implementation (Do phase), maintenance (Check phase), and continual improvement (Act phase) of security controls [21]. Thorough study of security standards reveal the sets of activities that need to be performed in order to ensure efficacy of different classes of controls during Plan, Do, Check, and Act phases of ISMS; these are listed in Table 1. The efficacy of controls depends on these four categories of ISMS activities.

Control efficacy for a single control c_i is given by

$$e_{ci} = Est + Imt + Mnt + CIm$$
(8)

where, efficacy e_{ci} is computed as summation of establishment (Est), implementation (Imt), maintenance (Mnt), and continual improvement (CIm) of control c_i.

Since, establishment and implementation of a control are of utmost importance, and the question of maintenance or improvement does not arise without the former phases, it is suggested that maximum values of Est and Imt may be taken as 0.3, while those for Mnt and CIm can be 0.2; minimum value for each of the parameters is 0.Thus,

$\max(e_{ci}) = \max(Est) + \max(Imt) + \max(Mnt) + \max(CIm) = 0.3 + 0.3 + 0.2 + 0.2 = 1$;
$\min(e_{ci}) = \min(Est) + \min(Imt) + \min(Mnt) + \min(CIm) = 0$;

Hence,

$$0 \le e_{ci} \le 1$$
(9)

Table 1. Control activities during Plan, Do, Check, Act phases of ISMS

	Managerial	Technical	Legal
Establish(Plan)	Identify require-ments and define relevant policy and procedure	Identify require-ments and select relevant techniques, and infrastructure	Identify relevant legal, statutory, and regulatory require-ments
Implement(Do)	Document, Approve, and Communicate policy and procedure	Procure, install, and configure tools and infrastructure	Document, Approve, and Communicate policies and proce-dures pertaining to laws and regulations
Maintain(Check)	Review policy and procedure	Review configura-tion, effectiveness, and relevance of tools and infrastructure	Review relevance and implementation of laws and regulations
Continually Improve(Act)	Update, Approve, and Communicate policy and procedure	Update configuration / version of tools and infrastructure	Update, Approve, and Communicate policies and proce-dures pertaining to laws and regulations

Assignment of exact values to each of the components of e_{ci} depends on the judgment of the security administrator or threat assessor. This subjectivity has been introduced considering the fact that perception regarding threats and control efficacy vary between enterprises and hence, some scope for customization is desirable. However, Table 1 may serve as a guideline on which assignment of values of Est, Imt, Mnt, CIm may be based. For example, if all activities pertaining to "Plan" phase have been performed for a technical control, then a value of 0.3 can be assigned to parameter "Est"; similarly, during "Act" phase, if a managerial control has been updated and improved, but this has not been communicated to relevant stakeholders, then a value less than 0.2 (say 0.1) should be assigned to parameter "CIm". It is important to note that if "Imt" value for a particular control is 0 (that is, the control has not been implemented), then values for "Mnt" and "CIm" will automatically be 0 (since there is nothing to "maintain" or "continually improve" in this case).

Often multiple controls are needed to mitigate a threat. The value of e_c, pertaining to *all* controls corresponding to a threat, is obtained as follows:

$$e_c = \sum w_i e_{ci} \tag{10}$$

where, w_i is the relative weight of control c_i such that $\sum w_i = 1, and\, i = 1, ..., n\, for\, "n"\, controls.$

Hence, from Equations 9 and 10,

$$0 \leq e_c \leq 1 \tag{11}$$

It is important to assign proper relative weights (w_i) to security controls. The following guidelines can be followed for assigning relative weights:

(i) If the implemented controls corresponding to a threat belong to different categories, then *legal controls* should be assigned the maximum weight followed by *managerial* and *technical controls*. The relative weights of managerial and technical controls can be equal;

(ii) If the implemented controls corresponding to a threat belong to the same category, then it is advisable to assign equal relative weights to the controls.

In case of natural and environmental threats, LOC(t) is computed as follows:

$$LOC(t) = \begin{cases} ceil((RoundOff(\log_3(p_t + a_t + res_t)))/(2 * e_c)), when\, e_c > 0 \\ ceil((RoundOff(\log_3(p_t + a_t + res_t)))/(2 * 0.2)), when\, e_c = 0 \end{cases}$$
(12)

It may be noted that 0.2 is taken as denominator in the second equation of (12) as this is marginally less than the minimum perceivable positive value of e_c which is 0.3 (e_c has value 0.3 when a single control has been *established* or *implemented* only; since, maintenance, or continual improvement, cannot exist without implementation of a control). Divisor 2 is used in Equation 12 to scale down the value of LOC. By Equations 4, 5, 6, 7 and 12, the maximum and minimum values of LOC(t) for natural and environmental threats are as follows:

$$LOC(t)_{max} = ceil((RoundOff(\log_3(5 + 3 + 1)))/2 * 0.2) = 5(when\, e_c = 0)$$
$$LOC(t)_{min} = ceil((RoundOff(\log_3(1 + 1 + 0)))/2 * 1) = 1$$

LOC(t) for human-induced threats is computed as:

$$LOC(t) = \begin{cases} ceil((RoundOff(\log_3(p_t + a_t + mvn_t + res_t)))/(2 * e_c)), when\, e_c > 0 \\ ceil((RoundOff(\log_3(p_t + a_t + mvn_t + res_t)))/(2 * 0.2)), when\, e_c = 0 \end{cases}$$
(13)

By Equations 4, 5, 6, 7 and 13, the maximum and minimum values of LOC(t) for human-induced threats are:

$$LOC(t)_{max} = ceil((RoundOff(log_3(5 + 3 + 1 + 1)))/2 * 0.2) = 5(when\, e_c = 0)$$
$$LOC(t)_{min} = ceil((RoundOff(log_3(1 + 1 + 0 + 0)))/2 * 1) = 1$$

Thus,

$$LOC(t)\varepsilon\{1, 2, 3, 4, 5\}$$
(14)

5   Threat Impact

The impacts (Imp) caused by the realization of different categories of threats have been detailed in Section 3. Those can be summarized as follows:

(i) Destruction, including physical loss of assets, logical (availability) loss, and impact on legal and contractual aspects of enterprises;

(ii) Modification, including integrity loss of assets, availability loss, and impact on legal and contractual aspects;

(iii) Disclosure (Exposure), consisting of loss of confidentiality of assets, and legal and contractual impact;

(iv) Financial loss; and

(v) Death, comprising of loss of lives of human beings, animals, and/or plants.

It is not prudent to pre-assign specific values to impacts of threats. Different enterprises may perceive criticality of impacts differently, depending on the significance of those impacts on their business processes. For example, while defence-sector organizations may consider disclosure of information to be a serious concern, the entire business of an e-commerce organization may revolve on maximizing information dissemination. In case of the latter, loss of availability of product information may be a serious concern.

Keeping this anomaly in mind, it is sensible to model threat impact subjectively, considering the five impact categories stated above.

Thus, it follows that by Equation 1, a threat, say Eavesdropping, whose LOC value is 4, and which results in disclosure of information, can be modeled as:

$$Eavesdropping \equiv \{Human-being, 4, Disclosure of information\}$$

This methodology can be used for modeling diverse kinds of threats to enterprise assets.

6   Utility of Proposed Methodology

The methodology proposed in Section 4 can be used to formally model threats to enterprise assets. Its uniqueness lies in the fact that, unlike existing models, it can address different kinds of threats uniformly. The function "Likelihood of Occurrence" of threats (LOC) has been defined to cover all such factors that can contribute to the realization of threats. Besides, the methodology is not overtly prescriptive and allows enough flexibility for enterprises to define specific means by which control efficacy can be determined. The numbers in parentheses in Table 2 represent a sample assignment of (maximum) values to the components of security controls that adheres to the restrictions imposed by Equations 8 and 9. An enterprise can define values that suit its needs and address its security requirements.

Another utility of the proposed methodology is that it can be used to compute values of likelihood of occurrence of threats, past occurrence of threats, proximity of assets to threat agents, and control efficacy over different periods of time. These data can then be used to analyze trends of the parameters and correlate them with one another. This will help an enterprise to understand the impact of various parameters on likelihood of occurrence of threats, and design and implement protective measures accordingly. This is illustrated by an example in the following section.

Table 2. Example illustrating assignment of maximum efficacy values to components of security controls

	Managerial	Technical	Legal
Establish(Plan)	Identify requirements (0.2); define relevant policy and procedure (0.1)	Identify requirements (0.2); select relevant tools, techniques, and infrastructure (0.1)	Identify legal requirements (0.1); identify statutory requirements (0.1); identify regulatory requirements (0.1)
Implement(Do)	Document policy and procedure (0.1); approve policy and procedure (0.1); communicate policy and procedure (0.1)	Procure tools and infrastructure (0.1); install tools and infrastructure (0.1); configure tools and infrastructure (0.1)	Document policies and procedures pertaining to laws and regulations (0.1); approve policies and procedures (0.1); communicate policies and procedures (0.1)
Maintain(Check)	Review policy and procedure (0.2)	Review configuration, effectiveness (0.1); review relevance of tools and infrastructure (0.1)	Review relevance of laws and regulations (0.1); review implementation of laws and regulations (0.1)
Continually Improve(Act)	Update policy and procedure (0.1);Approve policy and procedure (0.05); Communicate policy and procedure (0.05)	Update configuration / version of tools and infrastructure (0.2)	Update policies and procedures pertaining to laws and regulations (0.1); approve policies and procedures (0.05); communicate policies and procedures (0.05)

7 Case Study

A case study is presented in this section that applies the proposed methodology to model natural, environmental and human-induced threats to assets of a sample enterprise (say ABC Ltd.). Trends in LOC of sample threats and actual occurrence of incidents in ABC Ltd. are also analyzed with respect to changes in efficacy of security controls.

Table 3 shows the occurrences of incidents in ABC Ltd. and their impacts, corresponding to specific threats, from 2007 to 2014.

Applying Equation 3 to values of Table 3, past occurrences of threats are obtained as follows:

$p_{t1} = (1 * 5 + 1 * 2 + 1 * 1) / 18 = 1$

$p_{t2} = (1 * 4 + 1 * 1) / 16 = 1$

$p_{t3} = (1 * 4 + 2 * 3 + 2 * 2 + 1 * 1 + 3 * 1 + 2 * 1 + 1 * 1) / 18 = 2$

$p_{t4} = (2 * 5 + 4 * 2) / 14 = 2$

$p_{t5} = (1 * 5) / 5 = 1$

Table 3. Natural, environmental and human-induced threats in ABC Ltd

ThreatID	Threat	Threat Type	Number of Occurrences	Year	Impact
t1	Flood	Natural	1	2007	Destruction
t1	Flood	Natural	1	2011	Destruction
t1	Flood	Natural	1	2014	Destruction
t2	Fire	Environmental	1	2009	Financial Loss and Death
t2	Fire	Environmental	1	2013	Financial Loss
t3	Unauthorized Access to Server Sv1	Human-induced	1	2007	Disclosure of information
t3	Unauthorized Access to Server Sv1	Human-induced	2	2008	Disclosure of information
t3	Unauthorized Access to Server Sv1	Human-induced	3	2009	Disclosure of information
t3	Unauthorized Access to Server Sv1	Human-induced	1	2010	Disclosure of information
t3	Unauthorized Access to Server Sv1	Human-induced	2	2011	Disclosure of information
t3	Unauthorized Access to Server Sv1	Human-induced	2	2012	Disclosure of information
t3	Unauthorized Access to Server Sv1	Human-induced	1	2013	Disclosure of information
t4	Corruption of human resource file	Human-induced	4	2011	Modification
t4	Corruption of human resource file	Human-induced	2	2014	Modification
t5	Unauthorized manipulation of business application software Sw1	Human-induced	1	2013	Modification

Table 4. Proximity of assets to threat agents, resource availability and motive of threat agents

Threat ID	Threat Agent	Asset proximity to threat agent	a_t	res_t	mvn_t
t1	Nature	Striking zone	2	1	Not applicable
t2	Environment	Danger zone	3	1	Not applicable
t3	User u1	Reachable from u1	2	0	0
t4	Internal employee u2	Reachable from u2;u2 has execute, read, write permission	3	1	1
t5	Internal employee u3	Reachable from u3;u3 has execute permission	3	1	1

Table 4 lists the proximity of assets of ABC Ltd. to threat agents, availability of resources and presence (or absence) of motives for threats shown in Table 3.

Control efficacies of relevant security controls implemented in ABC Ltd. are shown in Table 5.

By Equation 10, efficacy of controls corresponding to threat t1 is $e_c(t1) = 0.5 * 0.25 + 0.2 * 0.25 + 0.8 * 0.25 + 0.3 * 0.25 = 0.5$ (Assuming equal weightage for implemented controls).

By Equation 12, LOC of threat t1 is
$LOC(t1) = ceil((RoundOff(/log_3(1 + 2 + 1))/2 * 0.5) = 1$ Similarly,
$e_c(t2) = 0.7 * 0.25 + 0.2 * 0.25 + 0.8 * 0.25 + 0.3 * 0.25 = 0.5$
$LOC(t2) = ceil((RoundOff(/log_3(1 + 3 + 1))/2 * 0.5) = 2$

$e_c(t3) = 0.8 * 0.5 + 0.4 * 0.5 = 0.6$
$LOC(t3) = ceil((RoundOff(/log_3(2 + 2 + 0 + 0))/2 * 0.6) = 1$

$e_c(t4) = 0.4 * 0.33 + 0.2 * 0.33 + 0.6 * 0.33 = 0.4$
$LOC(t4) = ceil((RoundOff(/log_3(2 + 3 + 1 + 1))/2 * 0.4) = 3$

$e_c(t5) = 0.4 * 0.33 + 0.3 * 0.33 + 0.6 * 0.33 = 0.4$
$LOC(t5) = ceil((RoundOff(/log_3(1 + 3 + 1 + 1))/2 * 0.4) = 3$

Table 5. Security controls and their efficacies

Threat ID	Security Control	Control Efficacy
t1	Physical protection against flood	0.5
t1	Information backup	0.2
t1	Incidents reporting	0.8
t1	Business continuity management and disaster recovery	0.3
t2	Protection against fire (fire detector and extinguisher)	0.7
t2	Information backup	0.2
t2	Incidents reporting	0.8
t2	Business continuity management and disaster recovery	0.3
t3	Firewall	0.8
t3	Access control	0.4
t4	Access control	0.4
t4	Information security awareness and training	0.2
t4	Application and operator log maintainance	0.6
t5	Access control	0.4
t5	Segregation of duites	0.3
t5	Application and operator log maintainance	0.6

Hence, threats to assets of ABC Ltd. can be modeled as follows:

$Flood \equiv \{Nature, 1, Destruction\}$

$Fire \equiv \{Environment, 2, Financial Loss/Death\}$

$Unauthorized\ Access\ to\ Server\ Sv1 \equiv \{Human-being, 1, Disclosure of information\}$

$Corruption\ of\ human\ resource\ file \equiv \{Human-being, 3, Modification\}$

$Unauthorized\ manipulation\ of\ business\ application\ software\ Sw1 \equiv \{Human-being, 3, Modification\}$

Now, LOC and p_t values for threat t3 (Unauthorized Access to Server Sv1) are calculated for the periods 2007 - 2011, 2008 - 2012, 2009 - 2013, and 2010 - 2014 using the values listed in Tables 3 and 4. It is assumed that values of a_{t3}, res_{t3}, and mvn_{t3} have remained unchanged during these periods. Also, control efficacy $e_c(t3)$ has gradually improved over the years. These are detailed in Table 6 below.

Table 6. p_t, a_t, res_t, mvn_t, e_c and LOC values for threat t3 from 2007 to 2014

	p_{t3}	a_{t3}	res_{t3}	mvn_{t3}	$e_c(t3)$	LOC(t3)
2007-2011	2	3	1	1	0.2	5
2008- 2012	2	3	1	1	0.3	4
2009-2013	2	2	0	0	0.3	2
2010- 2014	1	2	0	0	0.6	1

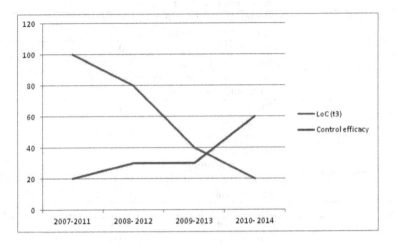

Fig. 1. Likelihood of occurrence of threat t3 vs. efficacy of corresponding controls (2007-2014)

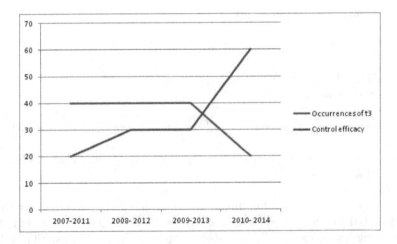

Fig. 2. Actual occurrences of threat t3 vs. efficacy of corresponding controls (2007-2014)

Analysis of trends in LOC and actual occurrence of incidents corresponding to threat t3 in ABC Ltd., with respect to changes in efficacy of security controls, are shown in Fig. 1 and Fig. 2, respectively. It can be observed that both LOC(t3) and p_{t3} have gradually decreased over the years as $e_c(t3)$ has increased. This is a positive result for the enterprise with respect to its security investment. If, on the other hand, LOC(t3) showed an increase despite an increase in $e_c(t3)$, it would mean that the controls have not been able to mitigate threat t3, and this would be a cause for concern for ABC Ltd.

8 Conclusion and Future Work

This paper presents a formal methodology for modeling threats to enterprises and their assets. It has been shown that the proposed methodology is generic enough to cover different kinds of threats. It also provides sufficient flexibility wherein enterprises can define threshold values for various parameters and customize the methodology to suit their specific needs. This allows an enterprise to implement a single uniform technique that can cater to its security needs and identify the probability of occurrence of threats. Additionally, an enterprise can use the values of threat parameters to assess risks [1,17] that can breach security of its assets.

Future work is geared towards development of algorithms for the detection of threats based on the methodology proposed in this paper. The algorithms will enable implementation of the methodology and integration of the same with existing risk assessment methods. Authors also intend to develop a tool that will utilize the proposed methodology to model threats, predict probability of occurrence of threats, and perform trend analyses of threat parameters.

Acknowledgment. This research was partially supported by grants allocated by the Department of Electronics and Information Technology, Govt. of India.

References

1. ISO/IEC: ISO/IEC 27005:2011 Information technology - Security techniques - Information security risk management. 2 edn., Switzerland (2011)
2. Deloitte: Irish information security and cybercrime survey (2014),
   https://www2.deloitte.com/content/dam/Deloitte/ie/Documents/Risk/
   cybercrime_survey_risk_2013_deloitte_ireland.pdf
3. Government, U.K.: 2013 information security breaches survey (2013),
   https://www.gov.uk/government/uploads/system/uploads/attachment_data/
   file/191671/bis_13_p184es_2013_information_security_breaches_survey_
   executive_summary.pdf
4. ISO/IEC: ISO/IEC 27002:2013, Information technology - Security techniques - Code of practice for information security management. 2 edn., Switzerland (2013)
5. BSI: Threats Catalogue - Elementary Threats (2008),
   www.bsi.bund.de/grundschutz

6. Tu, M., Sanford, M., Thomas, L., Woodraska, D., Xu, W.: Automated security test generation with formal threat model. IEEE Transactions on Dependable and Secure Computing 9(4), 526–540 (2012)
7. Swiderski, F., Snyder, W.: Threat modeling. Microsoft Press, US (2004)
8. Beckers, K., Faßbender, S., Heisel, M., Meis, R.: A problem-based approach for computer-aided privacy threat identification. In: Preneel, B., Ikonomou, D. (eds.) APF 2012. LNCS, vol. 8319, pp. 1–16. Springer, Heidelberg (2014)
9. Schaad, A., Borozdin, M.: TAM:automated threat analysis. In: Proc. 27th Annual ACM Symposium on Applied Computing, pp. 1103–1108. ACM, New York (2012)
10. Luna, J., Suri, N., Krontiris, I.: Privacy-by-design based on quantitative threat modeling. In: Proc. 7th International Conference on Risks and Security of Internet and Systems (CRiSIS), pp. 1–8. IEEE Press, New York (2012)
11. Pardue, H., Yasinsac, A., Landry, J.: Towards internet voting security: A threat tree for risk assessment. In: Proc. 5th International Conference on Risks and Security of Internet and Systems (CRiSIS), pp. 1–7. IEEE Press, New York (2010)
12. Ayed, D., Asim, M., Jones, D.L.: An event processing approach for threats monitoring of service compositions. In: Proc. 8th International Conference on Risks and Security of Internet and Systems (CRiSIS), pp. 1–10. IEEE Press, New York (2013)
13. Bompard, E., Huang, T., Wub, Y., Cremenescu, M.: Classification and trend analysis of threats origins to the security of power systems. International Journal of Electrical Power and Energy Systems 50, 50–64 (2013)
14. Yeh, Q.J., Chang, J.T.: Threats and countermeasures for information system security. Information and Management 44(5), 480–491 (2007)
15. Alhabeeb, M., Almuhaideb, A., Le, P.D., Srinivasan, B.: Information security threats classification pyramid. In: Proc. IEEE 24th International Conference on Advanced Information Networking and Applications Workshops, pp. 208–213. IEEE Press, New York (2010)
16. Wu, K., Ye, S.: An information security threat assessment model based on bayesian network and owa operator. Appl. Math. Inf. Sci 8(2), 833–838 (2014)
17. Bhattacharjee, J., Sengupta, A., Mazumdar, C.: A formal methodology for enterprise information security risk assessment. In: Proc. 8th International Conference on Risks and Security of Internet and Systems (CRiSIS), pp. 1–9. IEEE Press, New York (2013)
18. Sengupta, A., Mazumdar, C., Bagchi, A.: Formal methodology for detection of vulnerabilities in an enterprise information system. In: Proc. 4th International Conference on Risks and Security of Internet and Systems (CRiSIS), pp. 74–81. IEEE Press, New York (2009)
19. Ross, R., Katzke, S., Johnson, A., Swanson, M., Stoneburner, G., Rogers, G.: Recommended Security Controls for Federal Information Systems, NIST Special Publication 800-53. 3 edn., Maryland (2009)
20. ISACA: COBIT5 A Business Framework for the Governance and Management of Enterprise IT, Illinois (2012)
21. ISO/IEC: ISO/IEC 27001:2013, Information technology - Security techniques - Information security management systems - Requirements. 2 edn., Switzerland (2013)

A Novel Approach for Searchable CP-ABE with Hidden Ciphertext-Policy

Mukti Padhya and Devesh Jinwala

mukti.padhya@yahoo.in, dcjinwala@gmail.com

Abstract. Ciphertext policy attribute based encryption (CP-ABE) is a technique in which a user with secret key containing attributes is only able to decrypt the message if the attributes in the policy match with the attributes in secret key. Therefore, CP-ABE is suitable for some interesting applications such as cloud computing which requires both security assurances and access control over encrypted data simultaneously. However, we observed that all existing CP-ABE schemes entail a limitation that, if an authorized user wants to search for an encrypted file having particular keywords, then he has to first download and then decrypt the file before searching for particular keywords. When applied to an application involving a cloud, because the number of files on the cloud is likely to be huge, all these process results in large overhead for user.

Therefore, to overcome this limitation, we proposed a new searchable CP-ABE scheme in this paper, that allows the authorized user to check whether the ciphertext contains specific set of keywords or not, using his own token without decrypting the message. The label and keywords attached with ciphertext and secret key respectively, do not reveal any information about the data unless given the authorized token. In addition, our proposed scheme provides receiver anonymity also. The security analysis shows that privacy in this new solution is achieved with an overwhelmingly large probability. Equipping CP-ABE scheme with keyword-searching capability reduces the searching time of ciphertext having particular keywords. To the best of our knowledge ours is the first efficient collusion resistant searchable CP-ABE scheme with hidden ciphertext policy which uses few and fixed number of pairing operation in key word search as well as decryption algorithm.

Keywords: Public-Key Encryption with Fine-grained Keyword Search, Ciphertext Retrieval, CP-ABE, Bilinear Pairings, Hidden Access Structure, Recipient Anonymity.

1 Introduction

The traditional PKC suffers from the complexity in key assignment and certificate management issues, therefore PKC is not efficient in a multicast setup as also for bulk encryption/decryption [1]. In short, the traditional PKC schemes cannot establish a specific access control policy on to restrict who should be allowed to decrypt this data, which is required characteristic for new emerging applications, such as cloud computing etc.

A. Prakash and R. Shyamasundar (Eds.): ICISS 2014, LNCS 8880, pp. 167–184, 2014.
© Springer International Publishing Switzerland 2014

To overcome these limitations, Shamir introduced the concept of identity based encryption (IBE)[2] which uses user's identity such as an email-id or his designation as the public key, thereby eliminating the need for certificate storage, its distribution and revocation. The interest in IBE was further piqued when Boneh and Franklin [3] proposed a practical implementation of IBE. Since then several recent works aimed at constructing different types of fine grained encryption schemes. Other works by Sahai and Waters led to further investigation in the field of Fuzzy IBE and ABE[4].

ABE was further classified as: Key Policy Attribute Based Encryption (KP-ABE) introduced by Goyal et. al. [5] and Ciphertext-Policy Attribute-based Encryption (CP-ABE) given by Bethencourt et. al [6].

In KP-ABE, a ciphertext is associated with a set of attributes S and a user's key is described by monotonic tree access structure T. A user could decrypt a message if the access structure T has the set of attributes S' common to S. In KP-ABE, the encryptor exerts no control over who has access to the data he encrypts, except by his choice of descriptive attributes for the data. Rather, the encryptor must trust that the key-issuer issues the appropriate keys to grant or deny access to the appropriate users [6].

On the other hand, in CP-ABE, ciphertext is associated with tree access structure T and secret key is associated with set of attributes S. Any user who satisfies the access structure T can access the information. Thus, data owner can define access policy for ciphertext to control which ciphertext can be decrypted by whom.

There have been various attempts published in the literature to improve the basic CP-ABE scheme too [7-15]. However, these [7-15] approaches do not provide *receiver anonymity*. This means that after encryption, a user is required to send the access tree along with ciphertext, which is then used to match the attributes defined in the secret key. In addition to protecting the privacy of plaintexts using CP-ABE in multicast scenario, privacy of ciphertext-policy and privacy of credentials is also required in situations where requests for service, credentials, access policies and resources are extremely sensitive. In addition, in some situations encryptor's policy may reveal private information about himself, in which case he would like to protect his privacy against both intended and non-intended recipients of the message. Ideally, an authorized user also should not learn anything about the structure of the policy or which of his credentials were necessary for decryption. To overcome the lack of receiver anonymity, various authors propose different approaches in [16-26].

However, we observed that all existing CP-ABE schemes to improve ciphertext access control, basically just can guarantee the data security, policy and credential security or processing efficiency, but did not take into account how users can safely search and retrieved the encrypted data or file containing specific keywords which stored in cloud storage. To the best of our knowledge, there is no reported searchable CP-ABE scheme. Searchable encryption (SE) is a cryptographic primitive that allows user to store his encrypted data on an untrusted server, while giving the authorized user, ability to search for an encrypted file having particular keywords without revealing any information about the data. Equipping CP-ABE scheme with keyword-searching capability makes authorized user's task more easier in such a way that authorized user can efficiently search for an encrypted file having particular keywords by just checking whether label attached with ciphertext and keywords associated with user's token are matched or not. If both keyword and label are matched then user will retrieve and decrypt that particular file only, instead of downloading and decrypting number of files available on cloud before searching file for particular keywords.

To solve this problem we propose a new searchable CP-ABE access control scheme so that one can check whether ciphertext contain specific set of keywords or not, using his own token without decrypting message. In previous searchable encryption schemes [28-33] server only can test whether one keyword was present in the ciphertext, in contrast to that our proposed scheme can test whether multiple keywords were present in the ciphertext or not. Our proposed scheme is collusion resistant and also provides receiver anonymity by hiding access policy. In policy hiding CP-ABE schemes, the encryptor conceals access policy and hence the decryption will be carried out without knowledge of ciphertext policy. In turn, an intermediate adversary cannot obtain any information about the ciphertext policy. Hence, neither authorized user nor un-authorized can try to "gaming" the system i.e., changing their behavior to gain access to a message, or inferring which messages are important based on their policies.

1.1 Our Contributions

1) We extend the notion of ciphertext policy attribute based encryption to searchable CP-ABE with hidden ciphertext policy. We proposed a novel collusion resistant searchable CP-ABE scheme with hidden ciphertext policy. Our proposed scheme allows the user to check whether a particular set of keywords are labeled to ciphertext or not, without revealing anything about data itself. A user can not test for keyword W for which he does not have a token. In addition, a user gains no knowledge about plaintext by observing the label and keyword attached with ciphertext and token respectively.

2) Delegation of search ability is also possible in our scheme, which makes it attractive towards some interesting applications as mentioned in [27]. For example, an email user may want the server to deliver his/her emails according to some keywords attached on the emails. The user generates some tokens for the keywords and sends them to the server. The server may test whether there are these keywords in the emails. If the test outputs true, the mail will be sent to the user according to the rule.

3) Requiring (a) that the client should not learn information about which of her credentials or the server's credentials are usable, and (b) the server should not learn information about which of the client's credentials are usable, preserve the privacy of the other party's credential set and makes our proposed scheme secure against probing attacks.

In our scheme access policy can be expressed using AND gate with negative attributes and wildcard, so that it is possible to express the access policy effectively. Each attribute in the access policy can take multiple values. In addition, the proposed approach uses a fixed number of pairing operations during the decryption as well as keyword search. Hence, our construction achieves constant computation cost.

4)   Furthermore, in our proposed scheme, the secret key and token consists of 4 group elements, irrespective of the number of attributes. Therefore, authorized user cannot try to decrypt the message with different subsets of his credentials. Even the user cannot extract the individual secret attribute keys from this single secret key component. Hence, different users cannot pool their secret keys in order to decrypt a ciphertext. In addition, for the clauses that authorized user satisfy, he gains no knowledge of which of his attributes were used to satisfy those clauses

5)   We prove that our proposed searchable CP-ABE scheme with hidden policy is secure against adaptive chosen keyword attack and also satisfies the indistinguishability of messages under the DBDH assumption.

1.2   Organization of the Rest of the Paper

The rest of the paper is structured as follows. In section 2, we discuss the related work in the area. In section 3, we describe the preliminaries and the notations that we use throughout the rest of the paper. In section 4, we describe our proposed approach. The security games used to prove the security of our proposed scheme is described in section 5. In section 6, we give construction of our proposed scheme. Security analysis and complexity analysis of our proposed scheme are given in section 7 and section 8 respectively. Last section concludes the paper and references are at the end.

2   Related Work

Boneh et al. [27] proposed the concept of Public key Encryption with Keyword Search (PEKS) to address the problem of searching on encrypted data. Although PEKS schemes provide some approaches to search over the encrypted data by keyword, they cannot support flexible access control policies on encrypted data. Early works mostly only support single-keyword search [28-33]. To grant multiple users the search capabilities and access privileges, user authorization should be enforced.

Therefore, the authors of [34] proposed a searchable CP-ABE scheme. In their scheme data owner encrypts the sensitive data under an access policy before outsourcing sensitive data in the public cloud and builds a corresponding secure index for keywords. Only authorized users whose credentials satisfy the access policy can retrieve this encrypted data through keyword search and decrypt the ciphertext.

The another approach for searchable CP-ABE scheme is proposed by authors of [35].In their scheme the data owner encrypts the index of each file with an access policy created by him/her, which defines what type of users can search this index. The authors of [36], combine the traditional CP-ABE algorithm and a homomorphic encryption algorithm to achieve a searchable ciphertext CP-ABE access control scheme. In their scheme, message is encrypted under homomorphic encryption methods and the key of homomorphic encryption is encrypted using CP-ABE. Then, they combined the both cipher to produce the final ciphertext document. Thus, the ciphertext of homomorphic key is used to realize the CP-ABE access control, the ciphertext of message is used to realize the search operation in the ciphertext data.

In the scheme proposed in [37], a keyword is encrypted with an attribute-based access policy, which can be searched when the users' attributes satisfy the policy. The authors of [38] give Public-Key Encryption with Fine-grained Keyword Search using predicate encryption which can test whether multiple keywords or disjunction/conjunction of keywords were present in the ciphertext or not.

However, all the existing searchable CPABE schemes either encrypt keyword or key of homomorphic encryption under an access policy using CP-ABE encryption function. Therefore, to search any data or file labeled with particular "keyword", authorized user has to first decrypt the ciphertext of keyword or homomorphic key. Thus, all existing searchable encryption schemes does not give the authorized user, ability to search for an encrypted file having particular keywords without revealing any information about the data.

By analyzing the above literature improvement ideas, we propose a searchable encryption of CP-ABE access control scheme with hidden ciphertext policy; which provides the authorized users ability to search for an encrypted file having particular keywords by just checking whether label attached with ciphertext and keywords associated with user's token are matched or not. If both keyword and label are matched then user will retrieve and decrypt that particular file only, instead of downloading and decrypting number of files available on cloud before searching file for particular keywords. In addition, in our proposed scheme label attached with ciphertext and keywords associated with user's token do not reveal any information about data.

3   Preliminaries

In this section, we first give background information on bilinear maps and definitions of computational hardness assumptions. Next we define an access structure and use it in our security definitions. However, in these definitions the attributes will describe the users and the access structures will be used to label different sets of encrypted data.

3.1   Ciphertext-Policy Attribute Based Encryption

Definition I. (Bilinear map). The security of the CP-ABE system is based on the algebraic group called bilinear groups, which are group with bilinear map. Assume G1,G2 and G3 are three multiplicative cyclic group of some prime order p. A bilinear map e: G1 × G2 → G3 is a deterministic function, which takes as input one element from G1, one element from G2, and output an element in group G3, which satisfies the following criteria

    a) Bilinearity : For all $x \in G1$, $y \in G2$, $a,b \in Z_p$, e (x^a, y^b)=e $(x,y)^{ab}$.
    b) Non degeneracy: e (g1, g2) $\neq$ 1 where g1 and g2 are generator of G1 and G2 respectively.
    c) *e* must be computed efficiently.

Definition II. (Discrete Logarithm Problem). Given two group elements g and h, find an integer a $\in Z_p$ such that h= g^a whenever such integer exist.

Definition III. (DBDH assumption). The Decision Bilinear Diffie-Hellman (DBDH) problem in group G of prime order p (according to the security parameter) is a problem, for input of a tuple (g,g^a,g^b,g^c,R) where, a,b,c $\in Z_P$ be chosen at random and g is a generator of G then to decide R= $e(g,g)^{abc}$ or not. An algorithm A has advantage $\in$ in solving DBDH problem in G if $Adv_{DBDH}(A):=|Pr[A(g,g^a,g^b,g^c,e(g,g)^{abc})=0]-Pr[A(g,g^a,g^b,g^c,e(g,g)^R)=0]| \geq \in (\kappa)$, where $e(g,g)^z \in GT \setminus \{e(g,g)^{abc}\}$. We say that the DBDH assumption holds in G if no PPT algorithm has an advantage of at least $\in$ in solving the DBDH problem in G.

Definition IV. (Access Structure). Let U ={ $att_1,att_2,..,att_n$} be a set of attributes. For $att_i \in$ U, S_i = { $v_{i,1}$, $v_{i,2},\ldots, v_{i,ni}$ } is a set of possible values, where ni is the number of possible values for att_i . Let L = $[L_1, L_2,..,L_n]$ $L_i \in S_i$ be an attribute list for a user, and W = $[W_1,W_2,..,W_n]$ $W_i \in S_i$ be an access policy. The notation L|= W express that an attribute list L satisfies an access policy W, namely $L_i = W_i$ (i=1,2..,n). The notation L| $\neq$ W implies L not satisfying the access structure W.

4   Proposed Approach

Proposed CP-ABE scheme consists of different polynomial algorithms as follows.

1. **Setup(1^λ):** The setup algorithm will take implicit security parameter λ and output public parameter MPK and master key MSK.

2. **KeyGen(MSK, L):** The key generation algorithm run by TA, takes as input the master secret key of TA, the set of attributes L for user and then generates the secret key SK_L.

3. **GenToken(MSK,K):** The gentoken algorithm takes as input a master secret key MSK ,the set of keywords K to be searched and give output a token TK for the set of keywords K.

4.**Delegate(SK_L,K):** The delegate algorithm takes as input an authorized user's secret key SK_L for some set of atributes L and a set of keywords K to be searched . It output a token TK for the set of keywords K.

5. **Encrypt(MPK, M, W):** The encryption algorithm takes as input the message M, public parameter MPK and access policy W over the universe of attributes. Generate the output CT such that only those users who had valid set of attributes which satisfy the access policy can only able to decrypt. Assume that the CT implicitly contains access policy W.

6. **Encrypt_KS(MPK, CT, KW):** for a public key MPK, set of key words KW, Encrypt_KS() algorithm produces a searchable encryption of given set of keywords

KW and attached it with ciphertext CT = Encrypt(MPK, M, W) to produce final ciphertext CT_{TW}.

7.KS(CT_{TW}, TK): given a ciphertext labeled with set of keywords KW i.e. CT_{TW} = Encrypt_KS(MPK, CT, KW) and a token TK= GenToken(MSK,K), the key word search algorithm KS() outputs 'yes' if KW=K and 'no' otherwise.

8. Decrypt(CT,SK_L) : The decrypt algorithm run by user takes input the ciphertext CT contains access policy W and the secret key SK_L containing attribute set L. If L satisfies the access policy then algorithm decrypt the CT and give M otherwise gives "ϕ".

5   Security Game

Formally, we define security against an active attacker A using the following games between a challenger and the attacker (the security parameter λ is given to both players as input).

5.1   CPA (Chosen Plaintext Attack) Security Game

The game proceeds as follows:

Init. The adversary sends the two different challenge access structures W_0 and W_1 to the challenger.

Setup. The challenger runs Setup(1^k) to obtain a public key MPK and a master secret key MSK. It gives the public key MPK to the adversary A and keeps MSK to itself.

Phase 1. The adversary A adaptively queries the challenger for secret keys corresponding to an attribute list L, where (L$\not\models W_0$ and L $\not\models W_1$) or (L $\models W_0$ and L $\models W_1$) .The challenger answers with a secret key SK_L for these attributes.

Challenge. The adversary submits two equal length messages M_0 and M_1. Note that if the adversary has obtained SK_L where (L $\models W_0$ and L $\models W_1$) then $M_0 = M_1$. The challenger chooses β randomly from {0,1} and runs Encrypt(MPK, M_β,W_β). The challenger gives the ciphertext CT*= Encrypt(MPK,M_β,W_β) to the adversary.

Phase 2. Same as Phase 1.If $M_0 \neq M_1$ then adversary can not submit L such that L $\models W_0$ and L $\models W_1$

Guess. The adversary A outputs its guess $\beta' \in$ {0, 1} for β and wins the game if $\beta = \beta'$.

The advantage of the adversary in this game is defined as $|Pr[\beta = \beta'] - 1/2|$ where the probability is taken over the random bits used by the challenger and the adversary.

Definition: A ciphertext-policy attribute-based encryption scheme is ciphertext policy hiding (or secure) if all polynomial time adversaries have at most a negligible advantage in this security game.

5.2   CKA (Chosen Keyword Attack) Security Game

We need to ensure that an $KS(CT_{TW}, TK)$ does not reveal any information about keywords KW labeled with ciphertext CT_{TW} unless token TK is available. We define security against an active attacker who is able to obtain token TK for any set of keywords K of his choice. Even under such attack the attacker should not be able to distinguish an encryption of a keyword KW_0 from an encryption of a keyword KW_1 for which he did not obtain the token. The game proceeds as follows:

Setup. The challenger runs Setup(1^λ) to obtain a public key MPK and a master secret key MSK. It gives the public key MPK to the adversary A and keeps MSK to itself.

Phase 1. The adversary A adaptively queries the trusted authority to generate token corresponding to set of keywords K of his choice. The authorized party answers with a token TK for this key-word set.

Challenge. At some point, the attacker A sends the challenger two words KW_0; KW_1 on which it wishes to be challenged. The only restriction is that the attacker did not previously ask for the token corresponding to a keyword KW_0 or KW_1. The challenger chooses β randomly from $\{0,1\}$ and runs Encrypt_KS(MPK, CT, KW_β) The challenger attached CT*= Encrypt_KS(MPK, CT, KW_β) with ciphertext CT = Encrypt(MPK, M, W) to produce final ciphertext CT_{TW} and gives it to the adversary.

Phase 2. Same as Phase 1 but adversary cannot ask for the token corresponding to a keyword KW_0 or KW_1.

Guess. The adversary A outputs its guess $\beta' \in \{0, 1\}$ for β and wins the game if $\beta = \beta'$.

The advantage of the adversary in this game is defined as $|Pr[\beta = \beta'] - 1/2|$ where the probability is taken over the random bits used by the challenger and the adversary.

Definition: A ciphertext-policy attribute-based encryption with keyword search is semantically secure against an adaptive chosen keyword attack if all polynomial time adversaries have at most a negligible advantage in this security game.

6   Construction : Searchable CP-ABE

In this section, we propose a searchable CP-ABE scheme. Here Z_p= group of large prime order p. Group G and G1 are cyclic multiplicative group of prime order p. Without loss of generality, we assume that there are n categories of attributes U={$att_1, att_2, ..., att_n$} in universe. Every user has n attributes with each attribute belonging to a different category. Assume S_i={$v_{i,1}, v_{i,2}, ..., v_{i,ni}$} be the set of all possible values for att_i where ni=1 . Assume L=[$L_1, L_2, ..., L_n$] be a set of attributes for user, where $L_i \in S_i$ and W=[$W_1, W_2, .., W_k$] is an access structure, where $W_i \subseteq S_i$. The set of attributes L =[$L_1, L_2, ..., L_n$]= ($v_{1,j1}, v_{2,j2}, ..., v_{i,ji}, ..., v_{n,jn}$), where ji $\in \{1, ..., 1\}$satisfies the ciphertext policy W if and only if $v_{i,ji} \in W_i$ for $1 \leq i \leq n$. In addition, we also assume that there are m categories of keywords U_{KW} = {$y_1, y_2, ..., y_m$} in universe.

Assume $kv_i=\{kv_1,kv_2,\ldots,kv_m\}$ for $1<i<m$, be the set of all possible values for keyword $\{y_1,y_2,\ldots.,y_m\}$. Let K be the set of keywords attached with user's token and KW be the set of keywords labeled with ciphertext. The set of keywords K $=[K_1,K_2,\ldots,K_p]=\{y_1,y_2,\ldots.,y_p\}$, attached with the token, matches with set of keywords KW=[$KW_1,KW_2,\ldots,KW_q$] labeled with ciphertext if and only if p=q and $y_i \in KW_i$ for $1 \leq i \leq q$,where p,q $\in$ m. The searchable CP-ABE scheme consists of the following algorithms:

Setup(1^λ): This algorithm run by trusted authority (TA) and based on the implicit security parameter λ, the setup algorithm will choose a bilinear group (G,G1) of prime order p and generator g$\in$ G.

 Step 1: A trusted authority generates a tuple G=[p,G,G1,g $\in$ G, e] $\leftarrow$Gen(1^λ) .

 Step 2: For each attribute v_i where $1 \leq i \leq n$, the authority generates random value $\{v_{i,t} \in_R Z_p\}$ $1 \leq t \leq n_i$ and computes $\{T_{i,t} = g^{v_{i,t}}\}$ $1 \leq t \leq n_i.$

 Step 3: For each keyword y_i where $1 \leq i \leq m$, the authority generates random value $\{kv_i \in_R Z_p\}$ and computes $\{T'_i = g^{kvi}\}$

 Step 4: Compute $Y = e(g,g)^\alpha$ where $\alpha \in_R Z_p$

 Step 5: The public key MPK consists of $<Y,g,G,G1 ,e ,\{\{T_{i,t}\}$ $1 \leq t \leq n_i\}1 \leq i \leq n ,$ $\{T'_i\}$ $1 \leq i \leq m >$

The master key MSK is $< \alpha,\{\{v_{i,t} \in_R Z_p\}$ $1 \leq t \leq n_i\}$ $1 \leq i \leq n,$ $\{kv_i \in_R Z_p\}$ $1 \leq i \leq m >$Add/delete/update of attributes and keywords possible after setup by updating the corresponding secret values of that attributes.

KeyGen(MSK, L) *:* The key generation algorithms takes as input the master secret key MSK, a set L of attributes and do the following.

Let $L=[L_1,L_2,\ldots,L_n]=\{$ $v_{1,j1}, v_{2,j2}, \ldots, v_{i,ji}, \ldots, v_{n,jn}\}$,where ji $\in \{1, \ldots, 1\}$ be the attribute list for the user who obtain the corresponding secret key.

 Step 1: The trusted authority picks up random value r $\in_R Z_p$ and computes $D0 = g^r$, $D1= g^{r+\alpha}$.

 Step2: The trusted authority picks up random values $\mu_i \in_R Z_p$ for $1 \leq i \leq n$ and computes

$$D2 , D3 = [\Pi (g^{v,ji + \mu_i})^r , \Pi (g^{\mu_i})^r] \text{ for } 1 \leq i \leq n$$

The secret key is $SK_L = <D0 , D1, D2 , D3 >$

In each invocation of KeyGen algorithm to generate private key, new random numbers r and μ_i will be used. Thus, collusion resistance in our scheme is achieved by two layers of random masking in generation of private key. Random numbers r and μ_i tie each component of private key of single user together so no two users can combine their secret keys to decrypt the secret message. Similarly, randomness is used in GetToken() algorithm also while generating token for keyword search. Thus no two users can combine their token to search for any particular keyword.

GetToken(MSK,K): The GetToken algorithms takes as input the master secret key, a set K of keywords to be searched and do the following.

Let K =[$K_1, K_2, ..., K_p$]= {$y_1, y_2, ..., y_p$}, be the set of keywords for the user who obtain the corresponding token.

Step 1: The trusted authority picks up random value rt $\in_R Z_p$ and computes T0= g^{rt}, T1= $g^{rt+\alpha}$.

Step 2: The trusted authority picks up random values $\mu_i \in_R Z_p$ for $1 \leq i \leq p$ and computes

$$T2, T3 = [\Pi (g^{kvi+\mu i})^{rt}, \Pi (g^{\mu i})^{rt}] \text{ for } 1 \leq i \leq p$$

The token is TK_K= <T0, T1, T2, T3 >

Delegate(SK_L,K): The delegation algorithm takes in a secret key SK_L of authorized user and set of keywords K. The secret key is of the form SK_L= <D0, D1, D2, D3 >. The algorithm chooses random rt $\in_R Z_p$ and $\mu_i \in_R Z_p$ for $1 \leq i \leq n$. Then it creates a delegated token as

Step 1: The authorized user who have secret key SK_L, computesT0= D0, T1=D1.

Step 2: Then authorized user computes

$$T2, T3 = [\Pi(g^{kvi+\mu i})^{rt}, \Pi (g^{\mu i})^{rt}] \text{ for } 1 \leq i \leq n$$

TK_K= <T0, T1, T2, T3 >

The resulting token TK_K is a token for the set of keywords K. Since the algorithm re-randomizes the key, a delegated token is equivalent to one received directly from the authority.

Encrypt(MPK,M,W) :This algorithm is run by sender. Based on MPK, message M and access policy W=[$W_1, W_2, ..., W_k$] where $W_i \subseteq S_i$. It selects s$\in_R Z_p$ and calculates ciphertext CT as follows.

C1=M Y^s

C2=g^s

The encryptor picks up random values $\beta_{i,j} \in_R Z_p$ for $1 \leq i \leq n$ and $1 \leq j \leq l$, and it also computes

$$C_{i,j}=(g^{vi,j+\beta i,j})^s, \quad C4= \Pi (g^{\beta i,j})^s$$

where $\beta_{i,j} \in_R Z_p$

Here, $v_{i,j}= v_{i,j}$ (if $v_{i,j}$ is positive attribute in W)

$\quad = 1$ (if $v_{i,j}$ is negative attribute in W)

$\quad = v_{i,j}$ (if $v_{i,j}$ is wild-card attribute in W)

If v_i is wild-card attribute then $\beta_{i,j}= \beta_{i,1}$ for $1 \leq j \leq l$

CT= < C1, C2, {{$C_{i,j}$}$1 \leq j \leq l$}$1 \leq i \leq n$,C4>.

Encrypt_KS(MPK, CT, KW): This algorithm is run by sender. Based on public key MPK and set of key words KW=[KW_1,KW_2,...KW_n], Encrypt_KS() algorithm produces a searchable encryption of given set of keywords KW as follows
It selects sd $\in_R Z_P$ and calculates $C_{TW}1= Y^{sd}$, $C_{TW}2=g^{sd}$

The encryptor picks up random values $\beta_i \in_R Z_P$ for $1 \leq i \leq n$, and it computes
$$C_{TW}3= \Pi\, (g^{\,kvi + \beta i})^{sd} \quad C_{TW}4= \Pi\, (g^{\,\beta i})^{sd}$$
Then sender attached < $C_{TW}1$, $C_{TW}2$, $C_{TW}3$,$C_{TW}4$> with ciphertext CT = Encrypt(MPK, M, W) to produce final ciphertext CT_{TW}.

KeyWord_Search(CT_{TW},TK_K): The recipient tries to search keyword using his token TK_K associated with the set of keywords K and ciphertext CT_{TW} labeled with set of keywords KW as follows

$$= \frac{C_{TW}1\; e(C_{TW}2,\; T0\, T3)\; e(C_{TW}3,\; T0)}{e(C_{TW}2,\; T1\, T2)\; e(C_{TW}4,T0)}$$

Correctness. Let TK_K and CT_{TW} be as above. If the set of keywords K=[K_1,K_2,...,K_p]= $\{y_1,y_2,....,y_p\}$ matches with the label KW=[KW_1,KW_2,...KW_n] attached with the ciphertext, then

$$\frac{C_{TW}1\; e(C_{TW}2,\; T0\, T3)\; e(C_{TW}3,\; T0)}{e(C_{TW}2,\; T1\, T2)\; e(C_{TW}4,T0)} =$$

$$= \frac{Y^{sd}\; e(g^{sd},g^{rt}\Pi(g^{\mu i})^{rt})\; e(\Pi(g^{kvi + \beta i})^{sd},g^{rt})}{e(g^{sd},\; g^{\alpha+rt}\, \Pi\, (g^{kvi + \mu i})^{rt})\; e(\Pi\, (g^{\,\beta i})^{sd},g^{rt})}$$

$$= \frac{e(g,g)^{\alpha sd}\; e(g^{sd},\, g^{rt})\; e(g^{sd},\, \Pi\, (g^{\mu i})^{rt})\; e(\Pi(g^{kvi + \beta i})^{sd},\, g^{rt})}{e(g^{sd},g^{\alpha+rt})\; e(g^{sd},\, \Pi\, (g^{kvi + \mu i})^{rt})\; e(\Pi\, (g^{\beta i})^{sd},\, g^{rt})}$$

$$= \frac{e(g,g)^{\alpha sd}\; e(g,g)^{rt\, sd}\; e(g,\, g)^{rt\, sd\Sigma kvi + \beta i}\; e(g,g)^{rt\, sd\Sigma \mu i}}{e(g,g)^{rt\, sd}\; e(g,g)^{\alpha sd}\; e(g,g)^{rt\, sd\Sigma\, kvi + \mu i}\; e(g,g)^{rt\, sd\, \Sigma \beta i}}$$

$$= \frac{e(g,\, g)^{rt\, sd\, \Sigma kvi}\; e(g,\, g)^{rt\, sd\, \Sigma \beta i}\; e(g,g)^{r\, sd\Sigma \mu i}}{e(g,g)^{rt\, sd\Sigma kvi}\; e(g,g)^{rt\, sd\Sigma\, \mu i}\; e(g,g)^{rt\, sd\, \Sigma \beta i}}$$

$$=1$$

If output of KeyWord_Search() is 1 then K=KW that means set of keyword attached with user's token is matched with set of keywords labeled with ciphertext.

Decrypt(CT, SK$_L$): The recipient tries to decrypt CT, without knowing the access policy W by using his SK$_L$ associated with the attribute list L as follows

Step 1: $C' = \Pi\, C_{i,ji} = \Pi(g^{\,vi,ji + \beta i,j)})^s$, for $1 \leq i \leq n$

Step 2: The decryption algorithm outputs

$$\frac{C1\, e(D_0,\ C'\ C2)\, e(C2,\ D3)}{e(C2,\ D_2\ D1)\, e(D_0,\ C4)}$$

If the user attribute set L satisfies the hidden access policy W of the ciphertext, the user can recover the message M correctly.

6.1   Recipient Anonymity

We now show how the proposed CP-ABE scheme provides recipient anonymity by employing prime order bilinear groups. Suppose the adversary is given an arbitrary access policy $W' = [W'_1, W'_2, .., W'_k]$ where $W'_i \subseteq S_i$ and a ciphertext CT = < C1, C2, $\{C_{i,j}\}1 \leq i \leq n, 1 \leq j \leq l, C4$> which is an output of the encryption algorithm Encrypt. Let CT is encrypted under an access policy $W = [W_1, W_2, .., W_k]$ .The adversary then performs the DDH-test as follows

$$\frac{C1\, e(g,\ C2\ C')}{e(C2,\ g^{\alpha}\, \Pi\, T_{i,ji'})\, e(g, C4)} \quad = \quad \frac{M\, (g,g)^{\alpha s}\, e(g,\ g^s\, \Pi\, (g^{\,vi,ji + \beta i,j)s})}{e(g^s,\ g^{\alpha}\, \Pi\, (g^{\,vi,ji'}))\, e(g,\ \Pi\, (g^{\,\beta i,j)s}))}$$

There are two possible cases.

If W' = W, for all i, $1 \leq i \leq n$, $W'_i = W_i$ and hence $v_{i,ji'} = v_{i,ji}$ Therefore,

$$\frac{C1\, e(g,\ C2\ C')}{e(C2,\ g^{\alpha}\, \Pi\, T_{i,ji'})\, e(g,\ C4)} \quad = \quad \frac{M\, (g,g)^{\alpha s}\, e(g,\ \Pi^{\,vi,ji + \beta i,j)s})\, e(g,\ g^s)}{e(g^s,\ g^{\alpha})\, e(g^s, \Pi^{\,vi,ji'}))\, e(g,\ \Pi\, (g^{\,\beta i,j)s})}$$

$$= \quad \frac{M(g,g)^{\alpha s}\, e(g,\ g)^{s\Sigma\, vi,ji}\, e(g,g)^{s\Sigma\beta i,j}\, e(g,\ g^s)}{(g,g)^{\alpha s}\, e(g,\ g)^{s\Sigma\, vi,ji'}\, e(g,g)^{s\Sigma\beta i,j}}$$

$$= \quad M\, e(g,\ g^s) \qquad\qquad (1)$$

Suppose W' ≠ W. Then, there exists at least one k, $1 \leq k \leq n$ such that $W'_i \neq W_i$. Without loss of generality, we can assume that $W'_i = W_i$, for all i, $1 \leq i \leq n$ except i = k. Then $v_{i,ji'} = v_{i,ji}$, for all i, $1 \leq i \leq n$, except i = k. Therefore,

$$\frac{C1\, e(g,\ C2\ C')}{e(C2,\ g^{\alpha}\, \Pi\, T_{i,ji'})\, e(g,\ C4)} \quad = \quad \frac{M\, (g,g)^{\alpha s}\, e(g,\ \Pi\, (g^{\,vi,ji + \beta i,j)s})\, e(g,\ g^s)}{e(g^s,\ g^{\alpha}\, \Pi g^{\,vi,ji'})\, e(g,\ \Pi(g^{\beta i,j)s}))}$$

$$= \quad \frac{M(g,g)^{\alpha s}\, e(g,\ g)^{s\Sigma\, vi,ji}\, e(g,g)^{s\Sigma\beta i,j}\, e(g,\ g^s)}{(g,g)^{\alpha s}\, e(g,\ g)^{s\Sigma\, vi,ji'}\, e(g,g)^{s\Sigma\beta i,j}}$$

$$= \frac{M \, e(g,g)^{s \, vk,jk} \, e(g, \, g^s)}{e(g,g)^{s \, vk,jk'}} \qquad (2)$$

In both the cases (1) and (2) the DDH-test gives a random element of G1 so that the adversary cannot determine whether the ciphertext CT is encrypted under the access policy W' or not. Thus, our scheme *preserves* recipient anonymity.

7 Security Analysis

In this section we discuss the security analysis for the proposed CP-ABE scheme with single authority approach. We give the proof in generic group model using the DBDH hardness assumption.

7.1 Security Analysis : CPA Security Game

Theorem: The anonymous CP-ABE construction satisfies the indistinguishability of messages under the DBDH assumption.

Proof: We assume that the adversary A has non-negligible advantage ϵ to break the privacy of our scheme.

Then we can construct an algorithm B that breaks that DBDH assumption with the probability ϵ

Let $(g, g^a, g^b, g^c, Z) \in G \times G1$ be a DBDH instance $a,b,c,z \in_R Z_p$ and g is the generator for group G.

Init. The adversary A gives B the challenge access structure W_0 and W_1. B chooses d randomly from the set $\{0, 1\}$ and set $W_d=[W_{d,1},W_{d,2},\ldots,W_{d,n}]$.

Setup. To provide a public key MPK to A , B sets $Y=e(g,g)^{ab}$, implies $\alpha= ab$. B selects random value $\{v_{i,t} \in_R Z_P \}$ for $1 \leq i \leq n$, $1 \leq t \leq ni$ and computes $\{T_{i,t} = g^{v_{i,t}} \}$ $1 \leq t \leq ni$ for each attribute v_i.

The simulator, B sends the public parameters $MPK = <Y,g,G,G1 ,e ,\{\{T_{i,t}\} \, 1 \leq t \leq n_i \}1 \leq i \leq n , \{ T'_i \} \, 1 \leq i \leq m >$ to A.

Phase 1. A submits an attribute list $L = [L_1, L_2, \ldots, L_n]$ in a secret key query. We consider only the case where $L \not\models W_0 \wedge L \not\models W_1$. The reason for this is if $L \models W_0 \wedge L \models W_1$, then the challenge messages $M_0=M_1$. Therefore, B simply aborts and takes a random guess.

For KeyGen query L, B choose $u \in Z_p$ and set $r = u$ and computes the secret keys as follows

$D_0= g^r = g^u$
$D_1= g^{r+\alpha} = g^{ab+u}$
$D2 , D3 = [\Pi (g^{vi,ji + \lambda i})^u , \Pi (g^{\lambda i})^u]$ for $1 \leq i \leq n$
$SK = <D0, D1, D2, D3 >$

For another secret key query by attacker with attribute list L', the calculated r and λ_i is different and therefore collusion attack is not possible.

Challenge. A submits two messages M_0, $M_1 \in G1$ if $M_0 = M_1$, B simply aborts and takes a random guess. The simulator flips a fair binary coin d, and returns the encryption of M_d. The encryption of M_d can be done as follows:

$$C1 = M_d (e(g,g)^{ab})^c = M_d Z, C2 = g^c$$

B generates, for W_d, the ciphertext components $\{\{C_{i,j}\} \ 1 \leq j \leq l\} \ 1 \leq i \leq n$ and C4 as follows

$$C_{i,j} = (g^{v_{i,j} + \beta_{i,j}})^c \quad C4 = \Pi (g^{\beta_{i,j}})^c$$

and then attached it with output ciphertext of Encrypt_ks() algorithm and sends resultant ciphertext CT_{TW} to A.

Phase 2. Same as Phase 1.

Guess. From the above considerations, the adversary can decide that $Z = e(g,g)^{abc}$ when d = d' and can decide that $Z \in_R G1$ otherwise. Therefore, A breaks the DBDH problem with the probability ϵ.

7.2   Security Analysis : CKA Security Game

Theorem: The searchable CP-ABE secure against an adaptive chosen keyword attack under the DBDH assumption.

Proof: We assume that the adversary A has non-negligible advantage ϵ to break the privacy of our scheme.

   Then we can construct an algorithm B that breaks that DBDH assumption with the probability ϵ

   Let $(g, g^a, g^b, g^c, Z) \in G \times G1$ be a DBDH instance a,b,c,z $\in_R Z_p$ and g is the generator for group G.

Setup. To provide a public key MPK to A , B sets $Y = e(g,g)^{ab}$, implies $\alpha = ab$. B selects random value $\{kv_i \in_R Z_p\}$ for $1 \leq i \leq m$ and computes $\{T'_i = g^{kv_i}\}$ for each keyword kv_i.

   The simulator, B sends the public parameters
   $MPK = <Y,g,G,G1,e,\{\{T_{i,t}\} \ 1 \leq t \leq n_i\} 1 \leq i \leq n, \{T'_i\} \ 1 \leq i \leq m >$ to A.

Phase 1. A submits set of keywords K in a token query. For Gen Token query K, B choose $u \in_R Z_p$, $\mu_i \in_R Z_p$ and set r = u and computes the token as follows

   $T0 = g^r = g^u$
   $T1 = g^{r + \alpha} = g^{ab+u}$
   $T2, T3 = [\Pi (g^{kv_i + \mu_i})^u, \Pi (g^{\mu_i})^u]$ for $1 \leq i \leq n$
   $TK = <T0, T1, T2, T3 >$

For another token query by attacker with set of keywords K', the calculated r and μ_i is different and therefore collusion attack is not possible.

Challenge. A submits two words KW_0; KW_1 on which it wishes to be challenged. We consider only the case where $K \not\models KW_0 \wedge K \not\models KW_1$. The reason for this is if $KW_0 = KW_1$ OR ($K \models KW_0 \wedge K \models KW_1$), then B simply aborts and takes a random guess. The simulator flips a fair binary coin d, and returns the encryption of KW_d. Based on public key MPK and set of key words $KW_d=[KW_{d,1},KW_{d,2},...KW_{d,n}]$, Encrypt_KS() algorithm produces a searchable encryption of given set of keywords KW_d as follows

$$C_{TW}1= (e(g,g)^{ab})^c = Z, \quad C_{TW}2= g^c$$

The encryptor picks up random values $\beta_i \in_R Z_p$ for $1 \leq i \leq n$, and it also computes

$$C_{TW}3= \Pi \ (g^{\ kvi + \beta i})^c \quad C_{TW}4= \Pi \ (g^{\ \beta i})^c$$

Where β_i is random number.
Then attached $< C_{TW}1, C_{TW}2, C_{TW}3, C_{TW}4 >$ with ciphertext CT = Encrypt(MPK, M, W) to produce final ciphertext CT_{TW} and sends it to A.

Phase 2. Same as Phase 1.

Guess. From the above considerations, the adversary can decide that $Z = e(g,g)^{abc}$ when d = d' and can decide that $Z \in_R G1$ otherwise. Therefore A breaks the DBDH problem with the probability ϵ.

8   Complexity Analysis

Let n be the number of all attributes in universe, m be the number of all possible values for each attribute and $N' = mn$ represent the number of all possible combinational values for all attributes. The notation |G| is the bit length of the element which belongs to G. Let the notation kG and kCe (where $k \in Z>0$) be k-times calculations over the group G and pairing, respectively. N is the order of bilinear group. In our scheme it is a big prime number. G1 and GT are bilinear groups. Size of public key (MPK), Master key (MSK), secret key of user (SK) and ciphertext (CT) in our proposed CP-ABE scheme is

MPK	MSK	SK	Token
(N'+M'+1)|G1| + |GT		(N'+M'+1)|Z_N|	4 |G1|	4 |G1|

The expected computational time based on the input parameters for our proposed scheme is

Enc.	Enc. With Keyword search	Keyword search	Dec.
(N' + 2)G1 + GT	(N' + 5)G1 + 2GT	4 Ce + 4 GT	4 Ce + 4 GT

The figures in the table show the maximum value. The results given in above tables clearly indicate that size of the secret key, size of the token and number of pairing operation in key word search and decryption algorithm will remain constant irrespective of number of attributes in ciphertext policy. Thus, our scheme is efficient in terms of computational overhead.

In addition, if we compare our scheme with existing CPABE schemes then only [21],[26] schemes offers recipient anonymity, constant secret key size as well as constant pairing operation same as ours scheme. However, [21],[26] schemes did not provide keyword search capability as ours scheme. Similarly, [7-15] schemes did not provide recipient anonymity as well as keyword search capability. To the best of our knowledge, ours is the first scheme providing all properties viz. collusion resistance, recipient anonymity, keyword search capability, constant secret key size and constant pairing operation simultaneously.

9   Conclusion

In this paper, we propose the first efficient collusion resistant searchable CP-ABE scheme with hidden ciphertext policy and present a concrete construction from bilinear pairings. The proposed scheme allows user to search and retrieve the needed data/file having particular keywords without revealing any information about the data. Our proposed keyword search scheme simultaneously supports fine-grained access control over encrypted data, provides recipient anonymity and also allows delegation of search ability. Our approach can test whether multiple keywords were present in the ciphertext or not and one can express ciphertext policy using AND gate with positive, negative and wildcard attributes. Our proposed scheme is secure against CPA and CKA security game. We had given security proof in generic model using DBDH assumption, one can extend the given scheme for full security model.

References

1. Rivest, R., Shamir, A., Adleman, L.: A method for obtaining digital signatures and public-key cryptosystems. Communications of the ACM 21(2), 120–126 (1978)
2. Shamir, A.: Identity-based cryptosystems and signature schemes. In: Blakely, G.R., Chaum, D. (eds.) CRYPTO 1984. LNCS, vol. 196, pp. 47–53. Springer, Heidelberg (1985)
3. Boneh, D., Franklin, M.: Identity-Based Encryption from the Weil Pairing. SIAM Journal on Computing 32(3), 586–615 (2003)
4. Sahai, A., Waters, B.: Fuzzy identity-based encryption. In: Cramer, R. (ed.) EUROCRYPT 2005. LNCS, vol. 3494, pp. 457–473. Springer, Heidelberg (2005)
5. Goyal, V., Pandey, O., Sahai, A., Waters, B.: Attribute Based Encryption for Fine-Grained Access Control of Encrypted Data. In: ACM Conference on Computer and Communications Security –ACM CCS, pp. 89–98. ACM (2006)
6. Bethencourt, J., Sahai, A., Waters, B.: Ciphertext-policy attribute-based encryption. In: Proceedings of IEEE Symposium on Security and Privacy, pp. 321–334. IEEE Society Press, Los Alamitos (2007)
7. Cheung, L., Newport, C.: Provably secure Ciphertext police ABE. In: Proceedings of the 14th ACM Conference on Computer and Communications Security –CCS, pp. 456–465. ACM Press, New York (2007)

8. Herranz, J., Laguillaumie, F., Ràfols, C.: Constant Size Ciphertexts in Threshold Attribute-Based Encryption. In: Nguyen, P.Q., Pointcheval, D. (eds.) PKC 2010. LNCS, vol. 6056, pp. 19–34. Springer, Heidelberg (2010)
9. Okamoto, T., Takashima, K.: Fully Secure Functional Encryption with General Relations from the Decisional Linear Assumption. In: Rabin, T. (ed.) CRYPTO 2010. LNCS, vol. 6223, pp. 191–208. Springer, Heidelberg (2010)
10. Lewko, A., Okamoto, T., Sahai, A., Takashima, K., Waters, B.: Fully Secure Functional Encryption: Attribute-Based Encryption and (Hierarchical) Inner Product Encryption. In: Gilbert, H. (ed.) EUROCRYPT 2010. LNCS, vol. 6110, pp. 62–91. Springer, Heidelberg (2010)
11. Daza, V., Herranz, J., Morillo, P., Ràfols, C.: Extended access structures and their cryptographic applications. Applicable Algebra in Engineering, Communication and Computing 21(4), 257–284 (2010)
12. Zhou, Z., Huang, D.: On Efficient Ciphertext-Policy Attribute Based Encryption and Broadcast Encryption. In: Proceedings of the 17th ACM Conference on Computer and Communications Security, pp. 753-755. ACM (2010)
13. Attrapadung, N., Libert, B.: Functional Encryption for Inner Product: Achieving Constant-Size Ciphertexts with Adaptive Security or Support for Negation. In: Nguyen, P.Q., Pointcheval, D. (eds.) PKC 2010. LNCS, vol. 6056, pp. 384–402. Springer, Heidelberg (2010)
14. Chen, C., Zhang, Z., Feng, D.: Efficient Ciphertext Policy Attribute-Based Encryption with Constant-Size Ciphertext and Constant Computation-Cost. In: Boyen, X., Chen, X. (eds.) ProvSec 2011. LNCS, vol. 6980, pp. 84–101. Springer, Heidelberg (2011)
15. Doshi, N., Jinwala, D.: Constant Ciphertext Length in CP-ABE. IACR Cryptology ePrint Archive (2012)
16. Waters, B.: Ciphertext-Policy Attribute-Based Encryption: An Expressive, Efficient, and Provably Secure Realization. In: Catalano, D., Fazio, N., Gennaro, R., Nicolosi, A. (eds.) PKC 2011. LNCS, vol. 6571, pp. 53–70. Springer, Heidelberg (2011)
17. Katz, J., Sahai, A., Waters, B.: Predicate Encryption Supporting Disjunctions, Polynomial Equations, and Inner Products. In: Smart, N.P. (ed.) EUROCRYPT 2008. LNCS, vol. 4965, pp. 146–162. Springer, Heidelberg (2008)
18. Nishide, T., Yoneyama, K., Ohta, K.: Attribute-Based Encryption with Partially Hidden Encryptor-Specified Access Structures. In: Bellovin, S.M., Gennaro, R., Keromytis, A.D., Yung, M. (eds.) ACNS 2008. LNCS, vol. 5037, pp. 111–129. Springer, Heidelberg (2008)
19. Balu, A., Kuppusamy, K.: Privacy Preserving Ciphertext Policy Attribute Based Encryption. In: Meghanathan, N., Boumerdassi, S., Chaki, N., Nagamalai, D. (eds.) CNSA 2010. CCIS, vol. 89, pp. 402–409. Springer, Heidelberg (2010)
20. Yu, S., Ren, R., Lou, W.: Attribute-Based Content Distribution with Hidden Policy. In: 4th Workshop on Secure Network Protocols – NPSec, pp. 39–44 (2008)
21. Doshi, N., Jinwala, D.: Hidden Access Structure Ciphertext Policy Attribute Based Encryption with Constant Length Ciphertext. In: Thilagam, P.S., Pais, A.R., Chandrasekaran, K., Balakrishnan, N. (eds.) ADCONS 2011. LNCS, vol. 7135, pp. 515–523. Springer, Heidelberg (2012)
22. Emura, K., Miyaji, A., Nomura, A., Omote, K., Soshi, M.: Ciphertext- Policy Attribute-Based Encryption Scheme with Constant Ciphertext Length. In: Bao, F., Li, H., Wang, G. (eds.) International Journal of Applied Cryptography – IJACT, vol. 2(1), pp. 46–59 (2010)
23. Müller, S., Katzenbeisser, S.: Hiding the Policy in Cryptographic Access Control. In: Meadows, C., Fernandez-Gago, C. (eds.) STM 2011. LNCS, vol. 7170, pp. 90–105. Springer, Heidelberg (2012)

24. Hsiao, H., Lei, C.: A Hidden Access Control Scheme Allowing Negative Constraints. Master Thesis, Electrical Engineering Department, National Taiwan University (2008)
25. Balu, A., Kuppusamy, K.: Ciphertext policy Attribute based Encryption with anonymous access policy. CoRR abs/1011.0527 (2010)
26. Rao, Y.S., Dutta, R.: Recipient Anonymous Ciphertext-Policy Attribute Based Encryption. In: Bagchi, A., Ray, I. (eds.) ICISS 2013. LNCS, vol. 8303, pp. 329–344. Springer, Heidelberg (2013)
27. Boneh, D., Di Crescenzo, G., Ostrovsky, R., Persiano, G.: Public key encryption with keyword search. In: Cachin, C., Camenisch, J.L. (eds.) EUROCRYPT 2004. LNCS, vol. 3027, pp. 506–522. Springer, Heidelberg (2004)
28. Chang, Y.C., Mitzenmacher, M.: Privacy preserving keyword searches on remote encrypted data. In: Ioannidis, J., Keromytis, A.D., Yung, M. (eds.) ACNS 2005. LNCS, vol. 3531, pp. 442–455. Springer, Heidelberg (2005)
29. Curtmola, R., Garay, J.A., Kamara, S., Ostrovsky, R.: Searchable symmetric encryption: improved definitions and efficient constructions. In: Proceedings of the 13th ACM Conference on Computer and Communications Security, pp. 79–88. ACM (2006)
30. Goh, E.: Secure Indexes. In: IACR Cryptology ePrint Archive 2003/216 (2003), doi 10.1.1.2.5433
31. Yang, Z., Zhong, S., Wright, R.N.: Privacy-preserving queries on encrypted data. In: Gollmann, D., Meier, J., Sabelfeld, A. (eds.) ESORICS 2006. LNCS, vol. 4189, pp. 479–495. Springer, Heidelberg (2006)
32. Hwang, Y.H., Lee, P.J.: Public key encryption with conjunctive keyword search and its extension to a multi-user system. In: Takagi, T., Okamoto, T., Okamoto, E., Okamoto, T. (eds.) Pairing 2007. LNCS, vol. 4575, pp. 2–22. Springer, Heidelberg (2007)
33. Curtmola, R., Garay, J., Kamara, S., Ostrovsky, R.: Searchable symmetric encryption: Improved definitions and efficient constructions. Journal of Computer Security 19(5), 895–934 (2011)
34. Wang, C., Li, W., Li, Y., Xu, X.: A Ciphertext-Policy Attribute-Based Encryption Scheme Supporting Keyword Search Function. In: Wang, G., Ray, I., Feng, D., Rajarajan, M. (eds.) CSS 2013. LNCS, vol. 8300, pp. 377–386. Springer, Heidelberg (2013)
35. Sun, W., Yu, S., Lou, W., Hou, Y.T., Li, H.: Protecting Your Right: Attribute-based Keyword Search with Fine-grained Owner-enforced Search Authorization in the Cloud. In: IEEE INFOCOM. IEEE (2014)
36. Xiong, A., Gan, Q., He, X., Zhao, Q.: A Searchable Encryption Of Cp-Abe Scheme In Cloud Storage. In: 10th International Computer Conference on Wavelet Active Media Technology and Information Processing –ICCWAMTIP, pp. 345–349. IEEE (2013)
37. Liao, Z., Wang, J., Lang, B.: Ciphertext-policy Hidden Vector Encryption for Multi-User Keyword Search. In: 3rd International Conference on Internet & Cloud Computing Technology – ICICCT (2013)
38. Zhang, M., Wang, X., Yang, X., Cai, W.: Efficient Predicate Encryption Supporting Construction of Fine-Grained Searchable Encryption. In: 5th International Conference on Intelligent Networking and Collaborative Systems–INCoS, pp. 438–442. IEEE (2013)

Towards a More Democratic Mining in Bitcoins

Goutam Paul[1], Pratik Sarkar[2], and Sarbajit Mukherjee[3]

[1] Cryptology and Security Research Unit,
R. C. Bose Centre for Cryptology & Security,
Indian Statistical Institute, Kolkata 700 108, India
goutam.paul@isical.ac.in
[2] Department of Computer Science and Technology,
Indian Institute of Engineering Science and Technology,
Shibpur, Howrah 711 103, India
iampratiksarkar@gmail.com
[3] Department of Computer Science,
Utah State University, Logan, UT, 84322
sab.mukh90@gmail.com

Abstract. Bitcoin is a peer-to-peer electronic cash system that uses a decentralized architecture. It has enjoyed superiority compared to other cyptocurrencies but it has also attracted attackers to take advantage of the possible operational insecurity. All the Bitcoin miners independently try to find the winning block by finding a hash lower than a particular target. On 14th June 2014, a particular mining pool was able to take control of 51% of Bitcoins processing power, thus extracting the maximum amount of profit for their work. In this paper, we introduce a new defense against this 51% attack. We modify the present block header by introducing some extra bytes and utilize the Timestamp more effectively in the hash generation and suggest an alternative to the existing Proof-of-Work scheme. The proposed approach does not rely on finding a hash value lower than the target, rather it awards the miner involved in generating the minimum hash value across the entire distributed network. Fraudulent activities easily get caught due to effective use of the Timestamp. The new scheme thus introduces fair competition among the miners. Moreover, it facilitates the generation of Bitcoins at a fixed rate. Finally, we calculate and show how the new scheme can lead to an energy-efficient Bitcoin.

Keywords: Bitcoins, Electronic Cash System, Miners, Proof-of-Work.

1 Introduction

In Bitcoin, electronic payments are performed by generating transactions that transfer Bitcoin coins (BTCs) among Bitcoin users. Users are referenced in each transaction by means of virtual pseudonyms referred to as Bitcoin addresses. Each address corresponds to a unique public/private key pair. These keys are used to transfer the ownership of BTCs among addresses [1]. Users transfer coins to each other by issuing a transaction [17]. Two types of information are

A. Prakash and R. Shyamasundar (Eds.): ICISS 2014, LNCS 8880, pp. 185–203, 2014.

processed in the Bitcoin system: transactions and blocks [14]. Transfer of value across the system is referred to as transactions, whereas blocks are used to store these transactions and maintain a synchronization among all nodes in the network. A transaction is formed by digitally signing a hash of the previous transaction where the coin was last spent along with the public key of the future owner and finally incorporating the signature in the transaction.

The transactions need to be verified. Any peer can verify the authenticity of a BTC transaction by checking the chain of signatures. Rather than depending on a centralized authority, for this purpose, the Bitcoin system relies on a network of miners who collectively work towards implementing a replicated ledger for keeping track of all the accounts in the system. Each node in the Bitcoin network maintains a replica of this ledger. The replica is constantly updated with time so that the validity of the transactions can be verified against them.

All valid transactions, included in a block, are forwarded to all users in the network to check the correctness of the block by verifying the hash computation. If the block is deemed to be valid, the users append it to their previously accepted blocks. Since each block links to the previously generated block, the Bitcoin block chain grows upon the generation of a new block in the network. Bitcoin relies on this mechanism to resist double-spending attacks. For malicious users to double-spend a BTC, they would not only have to redo all the work required to compute the block where that BTC was spent, but also recompute all the subsequent blocks in the chain [2].

2   Proof-of-Work and Its Weaknesses

In this section, we present a brief description of the Proof-of-Work [8], abbreviated as PoW, and then discuss the various weaknesses associated with the PoW protocol along with some practical examples. In the absence of any centralized payment system, Proof-of-Work is a protocol used to artificially impose transaction costs. The main goal is to "charge" the requester of a service with the efforts to provide a solution to a puzzle, which would be much harder to do than to be verified.

Nakamoto [25] proposed an innovative use of this principle by utilizing it as a core component in the design of a fully decentralized peer-to-peer cryptocurrency called Bitcoin. To prevent double-spending of the same BTC, Bitcoin relies on a hash-based Proof-of-Work (PoW) scheme to generate blocks containing the valid transactions. The goal here is to generate a hash value which must be lesser than a specified target, which is adjusted with time (see Figure 3). The hash basically contains the Merkle hash of all valid and received transactions which the user wants to include in a block, the hash of the previous block, a Timestamp and a nonce value chosen by the user. If such a nonce is found, users then include it along with other entities, that were needed to generate the hash, in a new block and distribute it publicly in the network. Thus the PoW can be publicly verified by other users knows as miners. Upon successful generation of a block, a miner is granted a fixed amount of BTCs, known as coin-based transaction, plus the transaction fees from all the transactions that have been included in the block. This provides an incentive for users to continuously mine Bitcoins. But still there are some important weaknesses associated with the PoW scheme in Bitcoins.

2.1   Rich Gets Richer, Poor Gets Poorer

Here we identify, how due to the existing protocol, there is an unfair competition among the miners. Bitcoin network purely relies on trustless consensus. Thus if a situation arises when a mining pool controls majority of the voting power, then it could cause havoc.

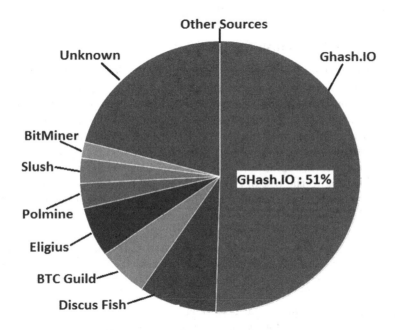

Fig. 1. GHash.io mining pool controlling about 51% of the total processing power (from [18])

A group of miners having 'rich' computational resource may set up a mining pool in such a way that it may control more than 50% of the network's computing power. In such a case that mining pool has the liberty to either modify the ordering or exclude the occurrence of transactions by launching a 51% attack [24]. With the combined mining power, the pool may indulge in double spending by simply reversing transactions that they send. Thus having the required computational power, the pool may be able to validate series of blocks in the block chain by just unscrambling the encrypted series of numbers attached to every Bitcoin transaction. It may also prevent other valid transactions from being confirmed or reject every block found by competing miners. They cannot directly affect the BTCs stored in the user wallets but they would have the power to make certain addresses unusable. And that allows them to impose any mining fee they like. The mining pool keeps on earning maximum profit and thus the use of the term 'Rich gets richer' sounds appropriate.

On 14th June, 2014, a particular mining pool, namely GHash.io [12,18], was able to take control of 51% of Bitcoins processing power, thus extracting the maximum amount of profit for their work. Figure 1 shows the amount of Bitcoin processing power held by each major mining pool on 14th June, 2014. The 'Unknown' group represents the individual users who are not associated with any mining pools, while others, for example, BitMinter, Eligius etc, are different mining pools associated with solving the PoW puzzle. Thus, it can be easily seen that the pools dominate the process of mining.

2.2   Block Races and Selfish Mining

Another problem that may be associated with the PoW protocol is that of 'race attack'. It can be viewed as an attack originated due to double–spending. Such problems arise from transactions that occur within a short interval of time. Thus it becomes tougher to confirm their verification. On the other hand the the PoW protocol requires time (on an average 10 minutes) to verify a block [22]. So within the verification time a Bitcoin exchange might be completed. In this type of attack, an attacker simultaneously sends an illicit transaction log to the seller and another log to the rest of the peers in the Bitcoin network, where the original owner gets back his currency. But by the time the seller realizes that he has received a fraudulent amount, the transaction may have already been carried out.

'Selfish Mining' can also be another possible attack. It was first introduced by Ittay Eyal and Emin Gun Sirer in [20] In this attack, when a miner solves the PoW puzzle and verifies a new block, he keeps it with himself. Thus by not distributing it over the network, he doesn't allow others to work on the next block. Instead, the miner starts working on the next puzzle that would verify the block which would follow his unreleased block. Thus if a mining pool is set up, they might use their overall computational power to keep verifying blocks. Finally when other miners find a new fair-mined block, the selfish miners releases their verified chain of blocks, which might be of several blocks. Their blocks would automatically be added to the main Bitcoin chain and the selfish miners would always gain, since the longer chain always wins. The rest of the miners didn't have the notion of those hidden blocks and that resulted in wastage of hashing power.

2.3   Illegal Usage of Machines for Mining

In Bitcoin mining, an algorithm or a puzzle is needed to be solved, that has increasing complexity related to the number of Bitcoins in circulation. Attackers try to exploit this mechanism of mining by illegally using computational resources, for example, by infecting a huge number of machines [21] in the network with malware, thus building a malicious botnet, that would be able to mine Bitcoins. The attack may be executed by a fake and infected version of legitimate software, packaged with malware or it may happen while clicking on malicious shortened URLs spammed through Email or social Media platforms. Once infected, the computational resources of the victim are used in the mining process.

Another form of attack which recently occurred was the illegal use of supercomputers of research groups for mining Bitcoins. It was first reported in Harvard [28], where a mining operation had been set up on the Odyssey cluster of the Harvard research network. Similar incidents occurred in Imperial College of London [27] and in the research labs of USA [10].

2.4   Wastage of Computing Power

The PoW problem is generally solved using ASIC machines which have been specially designed for this purpose.

Each PoW problem generally requires 10^8 GH/s (Gigahashes/second) to be solved, which can be seen from the chart in Figure 2. Such enormous requirement of computing power attracts illegal use of supercomputers and large computing power machines for Bitcoin mining.

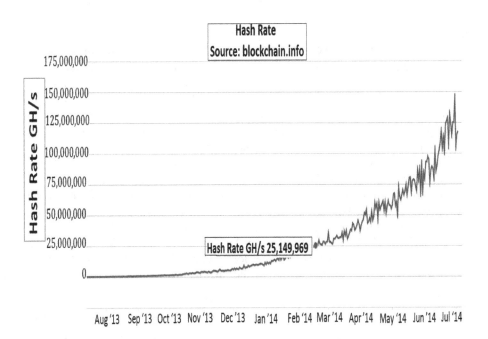

Fig. 2. Chart showing the hash-rate required in solving the PoW puzzle (from [16])

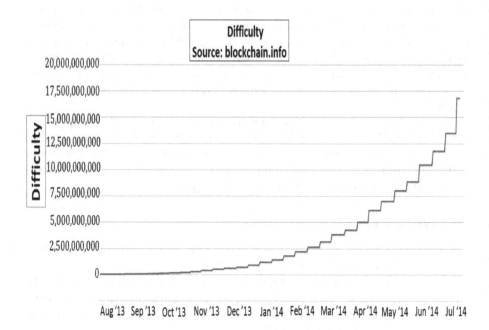

Fig. 3. Graph showing the variation of difficulty in the system (from [15])

According to "Bitcoin Watch" [23], the whole Bitcoin network hit a record-breaking high of 1 exaFLOPS a year earlier. FLOPS would basically mean the number of Floating-point Operations a computer can do Per Second, or how fast it can solve math problems. An exaFLOPS is 10^{18} math problems per second. The most powerful supercomputer in the world, Sequoia, can manage a mere 16 petaFLOPS, or just 1.6 percent of the power geeks around the world have brought to bear on mining Bitcoin. The world's top 10 supercomputers can muster 5 percent of that total, and even the top 500 can only muster a mere 12.8 percent. The new ASIC machines used by the miners are built from scratch and are only used to mine Bitcoins. Thus they can't serve any other purpose. So the total power spent on Bitcoin mining could theoretically be spent on something else, like real world problems that exist naturally. From Figure 2 and Figure 3, we see that the Hash-rate and Difficulty level is exponentially increasing. This would require more computation power for solving the PoW puzzle and in turn would waste more computing power in the future.

2.5   No Guarantee of Coin Generation at a Fixed Rate

The most important aspect of this discussion is the rate at which the Bitcoins are generated. The graph in [13] shows that the time required for confirmation of a transaction usually takes around 5-20 minutes, which is against the policy where each transaction verification should take on an average 10 minutes. If more miners join in the race to find the puzzle for verifying the block, more hashes would be generated and tested within the same time-span. But according to the Bitcoin protocol, the network self-regulates the speed of generation of Bitcoins after a certain time-span (after every 2016 blocks) by checking the number of days required to generate x many hashes. If the time-span is found out to be too short, then the difficulty level of PoW puzzle is increased. and so it becomes harder to find out the required hash in the next round. Thus if a mining pool is set up which could control more than 50% of the computational power, then such rules can be broken.

The problem lies in the self–regulation of the network. If the network members detect that the last hash generation took too much time, then the difficulty level will be adjusted down, and in the next round, the hashes will be easier to be found out. This actually means that if all peers in the network agree on only using 1% of their available computing power, thus also only 1% of electricity and 1% of the electricity bill they have right now, the entire Bitcoin system would still continue to work exactly as before. Everybody would still get the same payout in amount of Bitcoins received, and the self-regulating nature of the network means that exactly the same total amount of Bitcoins would be generated as before. But the fees involved in mining has increased the greed of the miners and they are wasting more and more computing power for mining which results in the exponential rise of the target difficulty. The graph in Figure 3 shows how the target difficulty is managed by the system.

3   Existing Alternative Proposals and Their Disadvantages

In this section, we provide a brief discussion of the alternative strategies that have been proposed to tackle the weakness associated with the PoW protocol. We also point out some weaknesses associated with those schemes.

3.1   Proof-of-Burn

The idea of proof-of-burn [7] is that the miner should show that they have burned some coins in order to generate new coins. Coins can be burnt by sending them to verifiable unspendable addresses. Only those users who have burnt coins in the past can generate new coins in future and gain the transaction and block generation fees. The metric for mining coins is the burning of coins. This system successfully reduces the computing power for mining but it also wastes Bitcoins in the process.

3.2   Proof-of-Stake

The proof-of-stake concept was first introduced by an user QuantumMechanic in [11]. Each active user can show his stake in the system by proving the number of Bitcoins held by him in his addresses. The larger the number of Bitcoins held by an user, the larger will be his stake. Each user holding $y\%$ of stake can mine only $y\%$ of the proof-of-stake coin. Proof-of-stake has been used in Peercoin [29]. As this concept is based on the amount of stake held by an user, it poses a threat of centralization. If an user gains more than 50% of the system Bitcoins then he can monopolize the system and perform double spending or deny service to rest of the users. Thus, the number of Bitcoins held by an user cannot be used as a metric for the Bitcoin security system.

4   Our Proposal

In this section, we describe our proposed scheme. We first describe in short the various resources needed to present our algorithm. Section 4.2 provides an in-depth description of our proposed algorithm.

4.1   Resources Needed

Peer-to-Peer Network. The Bitcoin users are connected in a peer to peer network [6]. They broadcast the details of transactions and blocks over the network using TCP communication.

Timestamp Server. The original Bitcoin paper [25] proposed the idea of a Timestamp server. After that the Bitcoin blockchain contains Timestamped transactions and blocks. This Timestamp helps to prove the existence of the data.

Bitcoin Address. A Bitcoin user has an account, where each account is associated with one or more Bitcoin addresses [1]. A Bitcoin address is an 27-43 length alphanumeric string that represents an address for payments of Bitcoins. Each address has a corresponding private key which is required in order to spend the coins at that address. The address and the private key is a pair of ECDSA [4] keys, where the address is the public key and the private key of the address is the private ECDSA key.

4.2   Description of Our Algorithm

Each user generates a hash, based on which the miner of the next block is decided. The user whose hash is of minimum value amongst all the users in the system, will generate the next block. He will receive the transaction fees for all the transactions that are verified in his block and it will be added to the blockchain as the next block. He will also initiate a coinbase transaction to his public address and award himself with a specified amount of Bitcoins. This award to himself is an additional incentive for verifying the blocks. This scheme deals with the algorithm for generation, broadcast and verification of the hash. It is divided into 3 phases, *hash generation phase, hash broadcast phase* and *hash verification stage*. These 3 phases together run for 10 minutes and give the true minimum hash of the system. We call this duration as the *time frame* which is maintained by the Bitcoin system time. By true minimum, we mean the actual minimum hash amongst all the hashes that has been generated by the miners, and broadcasted in the system. At the end of the algorithm, the miner who has generated the true minimum hash will form the block.

Phase 1: Hash Generation Phase. In this phase the user/miner verifies the transactions and forms a Merkle root tree [5] from those transactions. He generates a block from those transactions with a block header as described in Table 2. He computes the minimum possible hash from the block header by changing the value of the Nonce. This phase continues for 2 minutes and this time is maintained by the Timestamp T (refer to section 4.1) in the hash message. Any message that has been generated after this 2 minutes will be discarded.

Table 1. Present Block Header used in the Bitcoin network. (from [3])

Name	Byte Size	Description
Version	4	Block Version Number.
Previous Hash	32	This is the hash of the previous block header.
Merkle Root	32	The hash based on all the transactions present in the current block.
Time	4	Current Timestamp in seconds (unix format).
Target Bits	4	Target value in compact form.
Nonce	4	User adjusted value starting from 0.

Table 2. Proposed Block Header in our design

Name	Byte Size	Description
Version	4	Block Version Number.
Previous Hash	32	This is the hash of the previous block header.
Merkle Root	32	The hash based on all the transactions present in the current block.
Time	4	Current Timestamp in seconds (unix format).
Bitcoin Address	20	Hash of the Public key of the receiving address.
Nonce	4	User adjusted value starting from 0.

Block Header: We recommend to modify the present 80 bytes block header (Table 1) of the Bitcoin block structure and replace it with the newly proposed block header of 96 bytes (Table 2). The user uses 5 fields similar to the previous block header and includes an additional field (Table 3), i.e. his own public address that is currently being used. The 4 bytes 'Target Bits' field in the header is not required, since in the newly proposed design there is no specific target for the miner to fulfill. The public address of the user which is used during the hash generation, is required to compute the hash. The scheme inserts a new 20 bytes of Bitcoin address U_p field to the block header.

The hash (H) is generated from the 7 fields mentioned in Table 3.

Table 3. Items used by the User to generate the Hash

Version (V)	Previous Block Hash (H_p)	Timestamp (T)	Bitcoin Address (U_p)	Hash of Merkle Tree of verified transactions (H_t)	Nonce (R)	Padding (P)

1. *Version (V)* - The first 4-bytes of the block header describes the block version number V used by the miner. It is the Block version information, based upon the software version creating this block. In our scheme, we use the similar idea of Version number as given in [3] and [9].

2. *Previous Block Hash (H_p)* - In the Bitcoin system, the blocks in the blockchain are chained to each other where each block contains the hash of the previous block. In the proposed scheme, the chaining system has been retained in order to track the previous block. The previous block hash is denoted by H_p and is of 32 bytes size. In our scheme, Previous Block Hash is used in the same sense as given in [3] and [9].

3. *Timestamp (T)* - It denotes the 4-bytes Timestamp of the starting of hash generation by the user. It is updated after every second and is denoted by T. It is used to check whether a user has broadcasted any hash that has been generated before the hash generation period started or after it has expired. If such fraud has occurred, then the hash can be discarded, if its T field value does not lie within the 2 minutes of the generation phase. The timestamp for the start of the hash generation phase is updated every 10 minutes by the system and is available publicly in the Bitcoin network. So fraudulent activity concerning the starting timestamp for the hash generation phase is not taken into account.

4. *Bitcoin Address (U_p)* - The Bitcoin address U_p is the 160-bit (20 bytes) hash of the public portion of a public/private ECDSA key-pair. In our scheme, we use the similar Bitcoin Address as originally proposed by Nakamoto [25]. A key-pair is generated for each address which will be used by the user for mining and transaction purposes. The address helps to track the user, who has the minimum hash value and grants him the right to form and append the next block in the block chain. A more detailed description of this address can be found in 'Address' page of Bitcoin Wiki [1].

5. *Hash of Merkle Tree of verified transactions (H_t)* - The user verifies all the transactions, that occurred in the last 10 mins and are available in his pool. He forms a Merkle tree [5] from the transactions that have been verified. The 32 bytes root (H_t) of the Merkle tree is used for hash generation, since the broadcasted hash (H_t) of the root of Merkle Tree is a proof that the user has not changed any of the transactions that he verified during the hash generation phase.

6. *Nonce (R)* - The user chooses a 4 bytes nonce R which will help him to generate the hash. In the hash calculation, the 4 fields - H_p, T, U_p and H_t are fixed for a particular user at any time during hash generation, and hence cannot be modified by the user to manipulate and generate different hashes.

So the user can only alter the value of R to generate various hashes, within the hash generation period. He keeps a record of the hashes that he has generated within this time period. He then broadcasts the minimum among the generated hashes to the network after the hash generation period expires and hopes his generated hash turns out to be the minimum among all the hashes submitted by the active users in the Bitcoin network. Thus in this proposed scheme, the minimum hash generation is purely based on **luck**.

7. *Padding (P)* - It involves addition of some extra bits at the end of the input concatenated string, in order to make it 128 bytes and then it can be divided into two blocks of 64 bytes each.

The total length T_L of concatenation fields is given by:

$$T_L = 4\ (V) + 32\ (H_p) + 32\ (T) + 4\ (U_p) + 20\ (H_t) + 4\ (R) = 96\ bytes. \quad (1)$$

Thus, the number of bytes required for padding is:

$$P = 128 - 96 = 32\ bytes. \quad (2)$$

The hash H is a 32 bytes SHA-256 hash of the 128 bytes string containing the concatenation of the above fields. In our scheme, we use the similar hash function as originally proposed by Nakamoto [25] [3]. The equation can be stated as:

$$H = SHA(SHA(V||H_p||T||U_p||H_t||R||P)). \quad (3)$$

Hash Message: Each individual miner will generate a hash message M which will contain two parts - block header and hash H. The hash will be compared and the block header can be used for the verification of the hash. Each miner/node will generate his own message during the generation phase and broadcast it to the network.

For completeness and ease of reference, we provide the algorithm [26] here in our notation. Let, N_i denotes a variable which represents the ith node in the network. The value of i varies from 1 to the total number of nodes connected in the network. E.g. N_1 denotes the first node and so on. N_i contains two fields M_{min} and STATE. M_{min} contains the message with the minimum hash value. M_{min} may be generated by the current node N_i or it may have been received by the node from its neighbors. STATE field shows the current state of the node. The state can vary between AVAILABLE, ACTIVE, PROCESSING or SATURATED. Initially all the nodes are AVAILABLE. They become ACTIVE when they successfully generate a hash at the end of the hash generation phase, and storing that hash in their M_{min} field by calling the 'Initialize(M)' function, where M denotes the hash message generated by the node. All the nodes simultaneously call the Initialize() function with their own hash messages as shown in Algorithm 1. Hence, at the end of the generation phase, each node is in ACTIVE state and its M_{min} field contains the hash message generated by it.

Once the *Hash Generation* phase is over and each node is ready with its message M, the next 8 minutes is used for

Procedure Initialize (Hash Message M);
for all Nodes in the network **do**
  $N_i.M_{min}$ = M, where M_{min} is the minimum hash message at each node;
  $N_i.STATE$ = ACTIVE;
end for

Algorithm 1. Hash Message Generation Phase at each node in the network

- broadcasting the messages containing the hashes,
- finding the minimum hash amongst all,
- verifying the minimum hash selected,
- detecting dishonest behaviors in the system which involves checking the Timestamp (T) value of the generated hashes.
- granting the mining rights of the next block to the rightful user, who generated the minimum hash.

Phase 2: Hash Broadcast Phase. After the hash has been generated, it is broadcasted to all the active nodes in the network. Now among those hashes, the minimum needs to be found out in the distributed environment. We propose to use a modified version of the distributed algorithm [26] for finding out the minimum.

In the hash broadcast phase, the hash value at each node would be broadcasted out and the minimum hash message value would be found out in the system. Each active leaf starts the broadcasting stage by calling LeafSending() function and sending its M_{min} value to its only neighbor, referred now as its 'parent', and becomes PROCESSING (Note: messages will start arriving within finite time to the internal nodes). The internal node calls the Receiving_Active(M) function on receiving a message M from its neighbors. It calls Process_Message(M) to compute the minimum among the current minimum hash value it is holding and the one that it has received and stored it in M_{min}. It waits until it has received a message M from all its neighbors but one, and then sends its M_{min} message to that neighbor that will now be considered as its 'parent' and becomes PROCESSING. If a PROCESSING node receives a message from its parent, it calls Receiving_Processing(M) function and becomes SATURATED. Algorithm 2 describes the above procedure.

The algorithm implies that (Lemma 2.6.1 in [26]) exactly two PROCESSING nodes will become SATURATED; furthermore, these two nodes are neighbors and are each others' parent. All the other nodes will be in the PROCESSING state. They will start the hash verification stage by making their minimum hash message public. If there has been any discrepancy in hash broadcasting by dishonest nodes, then it will be resolved in hash verification stage. Other nodes will understand that the hash verification stage has started when they will see that one message has been publicly broadcasted. We present the hash comparison method that has been used in this phase.

————————ACTIVE————————-

Procedure LeafSending()
for all Active Leaf Nodes in the network **do**
  parent $\Leftarrow$ Neighbors;
  send $N_i.M_{min}$ to parent;
  N_i.STATE = PROCESSING;
end for

Procedure Receiving_Active(M)
for all Active Internal Nodes in the network **do**
  $N_i.M_{min}$ = Process_Message(M);
  Neighbors:= Neighbors - sender;
  if number of Neighbors = 1 **then**
    parent $\Leftarrow$ Neighbors;
    send $N_i.M_{min}$ to parent;
    N_i.STATE = PROCESSING;
  end if
end for

————————PROCESSING————————-

Procedure Receiving_Processing(M)
for all Processing Nodes in the network **do**
  N_i.STATE = SATURATED;
  $N_i.M_{min}$ = Process_Message(M);
  Announce M;
  Start Verification stage;
end for

Procedure Process_Message(M)
for all Nodes in the network **do**
  if $N_i.M_{min}.H < M.H$ **then**
    return $N_i.M_{min}$;
  else
    return M ;
  end if
end for

Algorithm 2. Distributed Algorithm for computing minimum hash value

Hash Comparison: Two hashes are compared from the most significant bit (MSB) to the least significant bit (LSB). They are compared from left to right until one bit differs among them. The one with the lower changed bit is the smaller hash. If two hashes are of same value then the header message containing the lower Timestamp will be considered the minimum one. Let us consider an example. Here we have two 32-bytes hashes H_1 and H_2 in hexadecimal format.
$H_1 : 1312af178c253f84028d480a6adc1e25e81caa44c749ec81976192e2ec934c64$,
$H_2 : 1312afaf42fc31103f1fdc0151fa7471187349a4714df7cc11ea464e12dcd4e9$.

The first 3 bytes (underlined) of both the hashes are same. But the 4th bytes are different. The 4th byte (bold) of H_2 is bigger in hexadecimal format, so H_1 is considered as the smaller hash.
$H_1 : 1312af\mathbf{17}8c253f84028d480a6adc1e25e81caa44c749ec81976192e2ec934c64$,
$H_2 : \overline{1312af}\mathbf{af}42fc31103f1fdc0151fa7471187349a4714df7cc11ea464e12dcd4e9$.
We have $H_1 < H_2$, since $17 < af$.

Phase 3: Hash Verification Phase. It is possible that the true minimum hash might not have been broadcasted properly by dishonest nodes and hence a hash value, bigger than the true minimum value is chosen at the end of the hash broadcast phase. Thus, the hash verification stage is required to verify, and if necessary, find the true minimum hash of the system. The message that has been publicly broadcasted by the two saturated nodes will be verified by the others nodes. If any node has a hash value lesser than the hash of that broadcasted message, then he can claim for his hash. His message will also be verified by the other nodes. If the new minimum hash value message is found to be legitimate, then its corresponding user will be the winner of the block. If the hash broadcast and verification stage is completed in less than 8 minutes then the miner will form the block and the system will wait for the 8 minutes period to expire until it can again allow the mining of a new block. The T value will check that miners cannot mine during this extra period, to prevent any unnecessary advantage.

Block formation: The user who has been identified as the generator of the minimum hash will form the block. He will incorporate the transactions in the block and the block header into the block chain. The user being the miner of the block will also initiate a coinbase transaction in the block in order to generate new Bitcoins and award himself with those coins as well as with the transaction fees from each verified transaction.

4.3   Message Complexity

The total number of active nodes that are participating in the mining process is denoted by n. We utilized the saturation stage broadcasting [26] for our minimum hash finding. During the hash broadcast phase, exactly one message is transmitted on each edge, except the two saturated nodes (from equation 2.24 of [26]). The two saturated nodes exchange two messages. So the total number of messages transmitted are:

$$n - 1 + 1 = n. \tag{4}$$

Thus, the message complexity of the scheme is $O(n)$. The time frame of 8 minutes of hash broadcasting can be easily increased by allowing the Bitcoin system to change the time frame. Increasing the time frame will accommodate more users to join in the mining process in the future and still allow generation of Bitcoins at a fixed rate.

4.4 Security Issues

In this section, we discuss salient security features of our scheme.

The node with the highest computing power in the system does not gain any advantage on other nodes for generating the lowest hash of the system. Each node is unaware of the hash generated by the other active nodes in the system. The value of the timestamp changes every second, so the nodes cannot manipulate the result of the hash after 2 minutes by only manipulating the nonce. If two nodes generate the same lowest hash, then the node whose timestamp value is less will win, i.e., the node who generated the lowest hash first will win. Thus, nodes with larger computing power can generate more hashes in those 2 minutes but it does not guarantee their win.

The verification of the hashes is performed using the original Bitcoin procedure of verifying newly mined blocks. Even if the true minimum hash of the system may not be transmitted by the dishonest nodes during broadcasting, it can be claimed and then verified by the peer nodes during the hash verification stage. The dishonest nodes may dominate the system, but during verification, the hash and the block header is made public. A hash will be discarded only if the hash value does not match with the hash of the header fields or it is bigger than some other hash, which has been verified. So evil nodes cannot affect the verification stage.

5   Comparison with Proof-of-Work Protocol and Its Existing Alternatives

In this section, we try to draw a comparison between the original PoW scheme and our proposed scheme on the basis of certain factors:

- Message Complexity of the scheme,
- Primary Concern of the scheme,
- Possibility of the 51% Majority Attack,
- Hash Rate (per miner),
- Competition among miners to generate a new block,
- Time to generate.

We also try to compare our existing scheme with proof-of-stake protocol that has been implemented in new type of Cryptocurrency known as PeerCoin [29]. The comparison has been shown in Table 4.

From the comparison shown in the table, the superiority of our scheme lies in the fact that it defends well against the 51% Majority Attack, which is currently the primary concern among the Bitcoin community. It also provides a fair

Table 4. Comparison between Proof-of-Work, Proof-of-Stake and Our Scheme

	Message Complexity	Main Concern	51% Attack Possible?	Hash Rate (per miner)	Competition	Time to generate
Proof of Work	Only one miner is chosen as winner. So low message complexity	Large Computations required	Yes	Very Large	Unfair competition among miners	Variable time
Proof of Stake	Every miner involved (having stakes) in exchanging messages. High message complexity	Initial distribution of stakes	Yes	Large	Unfair competition among stake holders	Variable time
Our Scheme	Every miner involved in exchanging messages. High message complexity	Flooding of messages in system	No	Small	Fair, competition purely based on luck	10 mins

competition among the miners, since the generation of block in this scheme is purely based on luck. It will not matter if some miner or some mining pool has machines with very high computation power capable of solving large problems within a few seconds. All that matters, is the generation of the minimum hash in the network among all miners. No miner would know what hash value other miners are generating. Even if they try to modify their generated hash value by observing the hash values broadcasted in the network, they would eventually get caught due to the presence of the Timestamp field in the block header. Since they would be considered to be fraud by generating a hash value beyond the Hash generation phase. Thus this scheme is purely based on luck and proves its effectiveness against the primary weakness of PoW protocol.

6   Towards Greener Bitcoins

The PoW protocol uses ASIC machines for mining and hence consumes a lot of energy during the process. Here we show that our scheme reduces the energy consumption by at least 5 times than that of the PoW protocol, using the same ASIC machines. Table 5 from Bitcoin Wiki [2] shows the hash power and energy usage of the machines. The PoW protocol requires these machines to meet the target, else generation would require more than 10 minutes. Also we have shown earlier in Figure 3 that the difficulty level is rising gradually, thus increasing the hashing power requirement.

Let us give an approximate calculation of the energy usage by these ASIC machines. We are stating an example of the average energy usage by these machines from one of the reputed sources of Bitcoin news [19]. The Bitcoin network has an

Table 5. Bitcoin Mining Hardware Comparison (from [2])

ASIC Unit	Hash Power (GH/s)	Energy Usage (kW)	W / GH	Unit Price
Cointerra TerraMiner IV	2000	2200	1.10000	$5,999
KnC Neptune	3000	2200	0.73333	$9,995
Hashcoins Zeus	3500	2400	0.68571	$10,999
Extolabs EX1	3600	1900	0.52778	$9,499
Minerscube	15000	2475	0.16500	$9,225

average hash-rate of 110 million GH/s. The average energy efficiency has been assumed to be 0.7333 W/GH. The network needs 0.7333 x 110 million Watts = 80,666 kW per hour. This equates to 80,666 kW x 24 hrs/day x 365.25 days/year = 707,120,500 kWh/year.

Thus the PoW protocol requires, on an average, 2.54 million GJ/year. Our protocol generates hashes for 2 minutes in an interval of 10 minutes. So only one-fifth of the total time is required for hashing. Assuming the same network hash-rate of 110 million, the network needs 80,666/5 = 16,133 kW. Our scheme consumes energy of the order of 16,133 kW x 24hrs/day x 365.25 days/year = 141,423,631 kWh/year= 0.508 million GJ/year. Since the scheme is totally uniform for different miners and does not require to meet any computation-intensive target, it can use lower hash rate machines for coin generation which will further reduce energy consumption. Thus, it is a greener approach than PoW.

7 Conclusion

In this paper, we have analyzed the major weaknesses of the existing Proof-of-Work protocol of Bitcoins and proposed an alternative solution. Thus in the proposed scheme, having a large computing power doesn't essentially mean that the user has an upper hand in generating the next block. The block generation is now purely based on luck, where the miner having the minimum hash value in the system during a span of 10 minutes, would be declared as winner. The effective use of Timestamp during the hash generation phase, where only a couple of minutes are allowed for hash generation, is shown to eliminate the chances of any fraudulent activities in the system. It has removed the difficulty target which will allow the miners to generate new Bitcoins using less computing power thus mining in a more environment friendly way. This new scheme generates the coins at a fixed rate, which has not been addressed by any other methods, even though it is one of the fundamental requirements for the Bitcoin system.

Acknowledgments. We thank the anonymous reviewers whose feedback helped in improvement of the technical as well as the editorial quality of our paper. We are also grateful to the Project CoEC (Centre of Excellence in Cryptology), Indian Statistical Institute, Kolkata, funded by the Government of India, for partial support towards this project.

References

1. Bitcoin–Wiki. Address, https://en.bitcoin.it/wiki/Address
2. Bitcoin–Wiki. Bitcoin Wikipedia, https://en.bitcoin.it/wiki/Main_Page
3. Bitcoin–Wiki. Block hashing algorithm,
   https://en.bitcoin.it/wiki/Block_hashing_algorithm
4. Bitcoin–Wiki. ECDSA,
   https://en.bitcoin.it/wiki/Elliptic_Curve_Digital_Signature_Algorithm
5. Bitcoin–Wiki. Merkle Tree,
   https://en.bitcoin.it/wiki/Protocol_specification#Merkle_Trees
6. Bitcoin–Wiki. Network, https://en.bitcoin.it/wiki/Network
7. Bitcoin–Wiki. Proof of Burn, https://en.bitcoin.it/wiki/Proof_of_burn
8. Bitcoin–Wiki. Proof of Work Protocol,
   https://en.bitcoin.it/wiki/Proof_of_work
9. Bitcoin–Wiki. Protocol specification,
   https://en.bitcoin.it/wiki/Protocol_specification
10. Bitcoin Magazine. Government bans Professor mining bitcoin supercomputer,
    http://bitcoinmagazine.com/13774/government-bans-professor-
    mining-bitcoin-supercomputer/
11. Bitcoin Talk. Proof of stake instead of proof of work,
    https://bitcointalk.org/index.php?topic=27787.0
12. Bitcoinx. Mining pool giant GHash.io reaches 50% of bitcoin hashing power,
    http://www.bitcoinx.com/mining-pool-giant-ghash-io-reaches-
    50-of-bitcoin-hashing-power/
13. Blockchain. Average Transaction Confirmation Time,
    http://blockchain.info/charts/avg-confirmation-time?timespan=
    2year&showDataPoints=false&daysAverageString=1&show_header=
    true&scale=0&address=
14. Blockchain. Blocks, https://en.bitcoin.it/wiki/Block
15. Blockchain. Difficulty,
    http://blockchain.info/charts/difficulty?timespan=1year&showDataPoints
    =false&daysAverageString=1&show_header=true&scale=0&address=
16. Blockchain. Hash Rate,
    http://blockchain.info/charts/hash-rate?timespan=1year&showDataPoints=
    false&daysAverageString=1&show_header=true&scale=0&address=
17. Blockchain. Transactions, https://en.bitcoin.it/wiki/Transaction
18. Business Insider. Today, Bitcoin's Doomsday Scenario Arrived,
    http://www.businessinsider.in/Today-Bitcoins-Doomsday-Scenario-
    Arrived/articleshow/36516972.cms#ixzz34amw9VI2
19. CoinDesk. Under the Microscope: Economic and Environmental Costs of Bitcoin
    Mining,
    http://www.coindesk.com/microscope-economic-environmental-costs-
    bitcoin-mining/
20. Eyal, Ittay and Sirer, Emin Gün Sirer. Majority is not enough: Bitcoin mining is
    vulnerable. CoRR, abs/1311.0243 (2013)
21. Forbes. Brilliant But Evil: Gaming Company Fined $1 Million For Secretly Using
    Players' Computers To Mine Bitcoin.
    http://www.forbes.com/sites/kashmirhill/2013/11/19/brilliant-but-evil-
    gaming-company-turned-players-computers-into-unwitting-bitcoin-
    mining-slaves/

22. Frequently Asked Questions. Transactions,
    `https://bitcoin.org/en/faq#why-do-i-have-to-wait-10-minutes`.
23. Gizmodo. The World's Most Powerful Computer Network Is Being Wasted on
    Bitcoin, `http://gizmodo.com/the-worlds-most-powerful-computer-network-is-being-was-504503726`
24. Learn Cryptography. 51% Attack, `http://learncryptography.com/51-attack/`
25. Nakamoto, S.: Bitcoin: A peer-to-peer electronic cash system (May 2009)
26. Santoro, N.: Design and Analysis of Distributed Algorithms. Wiley Series on Parallel and Distributed Computing, pp. 71–76. Wiley Interscience (2006)
27. The Guardian. Student uses university computers to mine Dogecoin,
    `http://www.theguardian.com/technology/2014/mar/04/dogecoin-bitcoin-imperial-college-student-mine`
28. The Harvard Crimson. Harvard Research Computing Resources Misused for Dogecoin Mining Operation,
    `http://www.thecrimson.com/article/2014/2/20/harvard-odyssey-dogecoin/`
29. Wikipedia. Proof-of-stake — Wikipedia, The Free Encyclopedia,
    `http://en.wikipedia.org/w/index.php?title=Proof-of-stake&oldid=615023202`

Authentication Schemes - Comparison and Effective Password Spaces

Peter Mayer[1], Melanie Volkamer[1], and Michaela Kauer[2]

[1] Center for Advanced Security Research Darmstadt,
Technische Universität Darmstadt, Germany
[2] Institute of Ergonomics, Technische Universität Darmstadt, Germany

Abstract. Text passwords are ubiquitous in authentication. Despite this ubiquity, they have been the target of much criticism. One alternative to the pure recall text passwords are graphical authentication schemes. The different proposed schemes harness the vast visual memory of the human brain and exploit cued-recall as well as recognition in addition to pure recall. While graphical authentication in general is promising, basic research is required to better understand which schemes are most appropriate for which scenario (incl. security model and frequency of usage). This paper presents a comparative study in which all schemes are configured to the same effective password space (as used by large Internet companies). The experiment includes both, cued-recall-based and recognition-based schemes. The results demonstrate that recognition-based schemes have the upper hand in terms of effectiveness and cued-recall-based schemes in terms of efficiency. Thus, depending on the scenario one or the other approach is more appropriate. Both types of schemes have lower reset rates than text passwords which might be of interest in scenarios with limited support capacities.

Keywords: Usable Security, Authentication, Graphical Passwords.

1 Introduction

Text passwords are the most common means of authentication. Despite this ubiquity, they have been the target of much criticism. User-created passwords are highly predictable. Most users compose their passwords solely of lower case characters, use simple dictionary words or put numbers and special characters at easy foreseeable places [16,28]. Furthermore, users have on average 25 accounts, but only seven passwords [16,19]. This password reuse raises serious concerns when considering that many websites transmit and store passwords in the clear instead of encrypted and cryptographically hashed [3]. Password managers are in many cases also no solution: They introduce a single point of failure; the security of password managers depends on the strength of the master password; and there are portability issues.

These deficits of text passwords motivated many researches to find alternatives. One alternative is graphical authentication. Like text passwords, graphical

A. Prakash and R. Shyamasundar (Eds.): ICISS 2014, LNCS 8880, pp. 204–225, 2014.

authentication schemes are knowledge-based. Their primary goal is to exploit the vast visual memory of the human brain. Visual memory is superior to memory of abstract information such as text [23]. Many different graphical authentication schemes have been proposed and studies have been conducted to assess their security and usability (e.g. [6,8,35]). While graphical authentication is in general promising there are also drawbacks like efficiency when authenticating. Therefore, it is important to understand how different schemes perform wrt. to usability (including efficiency, effectiveness, satisfaction but also memorability) and security in comparison to each other. Most past studies only provide information in comparison to text passwords; and as the experimental settings differ from study to study, this data cannot be used to compare the different schemes and approaches to each other. The authors of prior comparative studies either studied only cued-recall-based or recognition base schemes. Also, to our knowledge, most studies base their configurations of the graphical authentication schemes on the theoretical password space. This is a severe limitation of such studies and renders a comparison an impossible task, because alternative schemes that force or persuade users to choose more secure (and therefore potentially less memorable) passwords are compared side by side with schemes that let the users choose their passwords freely (and therefore potentially very insecurely).

Therefore, more basic research is necessary to enable the comparison and to support decision makers in selecting the most appropriate authentication scheme for their scenario. In this paper we present the first usability study of multiple graphical authentication schemes and text passwords that uses the most recent literature available on the effective password space of the tested schemes as baseline for the security configuration. Furthermore, this study is among the first to compare schemes based on recognition and schemes based on cued-recall in the same experimental setting. The selected graphical schemes are: PassPoints, PCCP, Faces and Things. Participants were asked to login five times over a period of 42 days. 337 participants took part. The evaluated usability measures are derived from the measures used in prior literature and therefore allow a comparison to existing research. The results of the experiment are:

- Usability-wise: The results demonstrate that recognition-based schemes have the upper hand in terms of effectiveness and cued-recall-based schemes in terms of efficiency. We also show that with only one exception the graphical schemes in our study have significantly lower reset rates than text passwords. In addition, we found evidence that male participants like the graphical schemes better after longer times of usage, while female participants find text passwords easier to use. Yet, female participants are more willing to use graphical password schemes than male participants.
- Security-wise: The analysis of the actual password space shows how difficult the prediction of effective password spaces is and that further research is necessary to better judge on the security level of some schemes. The estimates from our study can serve as baseline for configurations in future studies.

– Comparison to prior studies: Our study provides evidence that no significant quantitative difference between the performance of male and female participants exist, as the results of prior studies could not be replicated. However, significant differences in the attitude towards the schemes exist.

2   The Password Space

The password space of an authentication scheme is the set of all passwords and therefore closely related to the guessing resistance of the scheme. The larger the password space, the more guesses (on average) are necessary to find the right password. However, it is important to distinguish between the theoretical and the effective password space. While the theoretical password space includes all possibly selectable passwords for a scheme, the effective password space comprises only the subset of passwords which are likely to be actually chosen. Often the effective and theoretical password spaces are different. The only definitive exception in this regard are system assigned random passwords. Yet, these are not applicable in many scenarios as such passwords are usually more difficult to remember. Assessing the effective password space can be difficult, because a sufficiently large sample of passwords is needed to derive any meaningful information on frequently appearing values [21].

Multiple metrics have been proposed to compare and predict the password spaces of different schemes. The measure most often used to assess the size of the effective password space is the Shannon entropy of recorded password samples [28]. It is also the basis for the recommendations in the NIST Electronic Authentication Guideline and has been used in research of text passwords (e.g. [22,28]) as well as graphical passwords (e.g. [9]). However, it has been found, that neither the NIST estimates nor Shannon entropy provide truely reliable estimates and represent more a "rule of thumb" than an accurate metric, especially since sample sizes in typical usability studies are far smaller than what would be desirable [21,33]. Kelley et al. [21] proposed *guess-number calculator* and Bonneau [2] proposed *α-guesswork* as more robust and reliable metrics, but for none of these two empirical values for graphical passwords are available. Thus, in the the absence of viable alternatives, Shannon entropy is used as measure to configure the schemes in this study.

3   Graphical Passwords

Like text passwords, graphical passwords are knowledge-based authentication. Today's research distinguishes between three types of graphical password schemes, named after the way they strain the users' memory: purely recall-based schemes, cued-recall-based schemes, and recognition-based schemes. We decided against including purely recall-based schemes like *Draw-A-Secret* (DAS) [20] in our study, since such schemes have been shown to be insecure [24]. In the following we briefly describe the cued-recall-based and recognition-based schemes we included in the study.

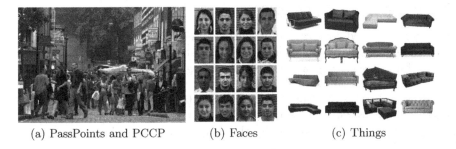

| (a) PassPoints and PCCP | (b) Faces | (c) Things |

Fig. 1. The interfaces of PassPoints and PCCP (marker of the click point not visible during normal operation), Faces, and Things

3.1 Cued-Recall-Based Schemes

Graphical authentication schemes based on cued-recall use the graphical elements as cues to support the users' recall. Wiedenbeck et al. proposed *PassPoints* [35] whose basic working principle is the definition of click-points on an image. The image only serves as a cue for the user, the actual password is composed of the coordinates of the click-points. During authentication, the same image as during enrollment is displayed and the user has to select her/his click-points in the right order. Even with the image as cue, perfect cursor positioning cannot be expected from the user. Therefore, a tolerance margin around each click-point compensates small imprecisions by the user.

To avoid click-point patterns in PassPoints, Chiasson et al. proposed an improvement called *Cued Click-Points* (CCP) [4]. Instead of multiple click-points on one image, in CCP users create multiple click-points, each on a different image. During authentication one image is shown after the other and depending on where on the image the user clicks, either the correct next image of her/his password is shown (when the right click-point was selected) or an image for which s/he has not created a click-point before (when the input was incorrect). In the latter case, authentication has to be finished regardless, but the legitimate user can detect her/his error. To counter so called hot-spots (points that have been noticed to be chosen significantly more often than other click-points), Chiasson et al. proposed *Persuasive Cued Click-Points* (PCCP) [4]. In the authentication phase, they employ persuasive technology by means of an additional viewport during enrollment. While the system offers the possibility to shuffle the viewport, the authors found that the number of hot-spots is significantly reduced and the distribution of click-points in PCCP does not significantly differ from a random distribution [4]. PassPoints and PCCP have an extensive coverage in research literature enabling estimates for the effective password space. Therefore, the two schemes were selected for the usability study. Figure 1(a) shows the interface of the two schemes.

3.2 Recognition-Based Schemes

In recognition-based authentication schemes users need only to recognize their password among a variety of choices, which substantially decreases the required mental effort. *Passfaces* is the most popular recognition-based scheme [26] and is commercially available. During enrollment, the system assigns the users several facial images as their passwords. During authentication, as many grids of facial images as there are faces in the user's password are displayed one after another. In each grid, the user has to identify the image belonging to her/his password. Thus the whole authentication consists of multiple rounds, one for each face in the password.

The same technique as used in Faces was also attempted with objects other than faces [11,18]. Due to its strong coverage in the literature we included a Passfaces-like scheme in the study, which is subsequently referred to as *Faces* (see Fig. 1(b)); as well as a scheme using objects, which is subsequently referred to as *Things* (see Fig. 1(c)).

4   Related Work

In the following we briefly discuss selected related work. Chiasson et al. present in [4] a comparison of the three graphical cued-recall-based authentication schemes PCCP, CCP and PassPoints. They cover usability and security aspects with results from eight user studies. Their results indicate no significant differences in success rates between the three schemes. The timings they recorded are 6-8 seconds for PassPoints and 8-15 seconds for PCCP. The configurations in all studies are based on the theoretical password space.

Hlywa et al. present a comparison of multiple Passfaces-like recognition-based graphical authentication schemes in two web-studies [18] in which recognition-based schemes are configured to password-level security. The schemes used in the study of Hlywa et al. differ only in the type of images. One scheme used faces (similarly to Faces), one scheme used everyday objects (similarly to Things) and one scheme used houses. Both of their studies used configurations similar, but not identical, to those in our experiment. One study used 4 by 4 grids, but instead of a password length of 7 rounds Hlywa et al. used 5. Their other study used a different approach to the grid size, but was configured to use the same password space, namely 2^{28}. In both studies system-assigned passwords were used. They report significantly faster login times for their objects participants than for their faces participants in both studies.

Stobert and Biddle compared in [29] the performance of text passwords as well as recall-based and recognition-based graphical passwords. Their results indicate, that recognition-based passwords had a higher memorability, but their usability was limited by longer login times. Our methodology differs from the one employed by Stobert and Biddle in two key aspects. Firstly, we consider already proposed schemes (some of them used in the wild), while Stobert and Biddle specifically designed a new scheme to compare the different types of memory

Table 1. Configurations (H_{exp} = expected Shannon entropy in bits)

Scheme	Configuration	H_{exp}
Text	8 characters length, policy based on basic8survey [22]	~ 27.19
PassPoints	4 click-points, 600x400 px resolution of image, 9x9 px tolerance margin [9]	$\lesssim 26$
PCCP	3 click-points, 570x380 px resolution of images, 19x19 px tolerance margin	~ 27.7
Faces	7 grids of 16 images each, facial images	~ 28
Things	7 grids of 16 images each, object images, semantically grouped	~ 28

retrieval. Secondly, we base the security configurations of the schemes we use on the effective password space, rather than the theoretical password space.

Schaub et al. analysed and described the design space for graphical passwords on smartphones [27]. To test their design metric, they conducted a non-longitudinal lab-based user study with five different graphical password schemes and PINs. Their schemes' configurations are based on the theoretical password space rather than the effective password space. Also, their usability metrics use different definitions. Therefore, the comparability to this study is very limited.

5   Configuration of the Schemes

For the configuration of the schemes we decided to focus solely on the effective password space. Other attacks such as spyware, shoulder surfing and social engineering, (e.g. mentioned by [31]) were not considered in our study.

Most major websites use password policies resulting in a minimum of about 20 to 28 bits of entropy (or password spaces of 2^{20} to 2^{28} respectively) [17]. Thus, configuring the authentication schemes' effective password spaces to lie within these two values is a close approximation to a lower bound to what would actually be seen in the wild. However, we wanted to narrow down the range for our study. To do so, we analysed Komanduri et al. research on password policies for text passwords and their resulting effective password spaces [22]. They present only one policy whose effective password space lies between 20 and 28 bits of entropy, namely their *basic8survey* policy, for which they report an entropy of 27.19 bits. Therefore, we decided to use this value as baseline and configure the password spaces of all schemes to lie between 2^{27} and 2^{28} or as closely to that target as possible. Table 1 lists all schemes with their configurations. A justification for each scheme is given below in the respective subsections.

5.1   Text Password

The basic8survey policy of Komanduri et al. only states "Password must have at least 8 characters" and does not offer any scenario to the participants [22]. For this policy they reported 27.19 bits of entropy. We used this policy as starting point. We slightly modified it due to some design considerations: Most importantly we made the policy look more like as if it could be from one of the major websites investigated in [17] and additionally enforced a fixed length of 8 characters. Our password policy was included in the introductory text for the scheme and stated the following rules:

1. The passwords are case sensitive. For instance, "EXAMPLE" and "Example" are two different passwords. When choosing a password, remember the capitalization you use.
2. The password must be exactly 8 characters long.
3. Try to not use passwords that are easy to guess, for example "password".
4. Even though it is not a requirement, try to add a number or special character to your password.
5. Choose a new password, that you are not using for any other service.

The first statement is merely a further explanation of the scheme and not a policy rule, it is often found in policies on the Internet. The first actual policy rule regards the password length and is taken from Komanduri et al. [22], but was changed to a fixed length of eight characters. This was done as all graphical schemes can only be configured in such a restricted way. Rules 3 and 4 were added as incentive for the participants to not create "just study passwords" whose main purpose was to be not forgotten. This decision was made in conjunction with the decision to include priming in the study methodology. The last rule was intended to motivate the participants to deal with a new password throughout the study, just as the participants of the other groups would have to. Additionally, the system enforced to choose passwords not mentioned in the policy (e.g. "password" as mentioned in the third rule could not be chosen).

5.2   Cued-Recall-Based Schemes

The alphabet A of the cued-recall-based schemes is the number of distinct click-points on the image. This number is determined by the size of the image divided by the tolerance margin. The theoretical password space P can be calculated from the number of click-points c required by the system: $P = |A|^c$.

PassPoints. The empirical entropy estimates of Dirik et al. in [9] seem to be the only findings for PassPoints passwords allowing an estimation of the effective password space. Therefore, we decided to adopt their PassPoints configuration and use an image with a resolution of 400x600 px. However, we follow prior studies, which argue to use 9 px for the tolerance margin instead of 10 px as an uneven number can be centered around one pixel while it is is unclear how this should be done for an even margin [4]. Regarding the image, we decided to use the people image used by Dirik et al. as the sole image for our PassPoints implementation, as it scored best in their evaluation. They report an observed entropy of 6.5 bits for a click-point on that image. The authors remark that these values are only valid for multiple click-points if independence between the click-points in the password is assumed and that the actual entropy should be assumed to be lower. Seemingly no data on the magnitude of dependence between click-points in PassPoints passwords is available in published literature. Therefore, we decided to use four click-points, as the resulting entropy value of 26 bits (password space of 2^{26} respectively) is closer to the target than any other number of click-points.

PCCP. According to Chiasson et al. the distribution of click-points in PCCP does not significantly differ from a random distribution [5]. Therefore, it can be assumed that the theoretical and the effective password space are approximately identical. We decided to use three click-points on 570x380 px images with a 19 px tolerance margin for the PCCP implementation, which results in an expected entropy of 27.7 bits and thus meets the entropy target. The tolerance margin of 19 px was chosen, as this value achieved better usability ratings than viable alternatives [34]. The image size was chosen as a multiple of the tolerance margin and determined in conjunction with the number of click-points to model the target entropy values of 27 to 28 bits as good as possible. Priority was given to image size, as it was shown that larger images lead to less clustering in PCCP [30]. As the images used in previous studies by Chiasson et al. could not be made available for our study due to copyright concerns, all images for the implementation were taken from the same source as the image for PassPoints. The viewport size of 75 px was adopted from [5]. We decided to restrict user choice by omitting the possibility to shuffle the viewport for the following reason: Chiasson et al. report that most participants either do not shuffle at all or they shuffle a lot in order to circumvent the persuasion mechanism. The latter case negates the security advantage of PCCP over PassPoints.

5.3   Recognition-Based Schemes

Recognition-based schemes suffer from predictability issues if users are allowed to choose their passwords themselves [7]. Consequently, commercial implementations assign random passwords to the users. Furthermore, to our knowledge, no entropy estimates for the configurations of Things and Faces are available. Thus, we decided to assign random passwords to the participants for both recognition-based schemes as recommended by [10,13,18]. Then, the theoretical and effective password space P from the alphabet A (comprised of the images in one grid) and the number of required authentication rounds r is: $P = |A|^r$. To reach the entropy target of 27 to 28 bits, we decided to use a 4x4 grid and 7 rounds, i.e. a password space of $16^7 = 2^{28}$.

Faces. All images used were taken from the Face of Tomorrow project which were also used by other studies regarding facial recognition in authentication [13,18]. We ensured that all grids had images with similar backgrounds and that faces used in one grid were of people from the same ethnicity.

Things. The Things scheme used semantically grouped images, following the work of Weinshall and Kirkpatrick [32]. They found that pictures should not be too similar to one another or users would start confusing them and consequently advise to select "pictures with a clear central subject or action and [...] differences within the group" [32]. Therefore, this criteria was applied to all images gathered for the Things scheme. All images were informally reviewed to fulfill this criteria by colleagues uninvolved in the selection.

6   User Study Methodology

Due to the high relevancy of web-authentication, it was decided to conduct an online web-based study. Each participant had to complete five sessions over a period of about 42 days. The intervals between the sessions prolonged, namely they were: 1 day, 3 days, 7 days, 30 days. The first part of each session comprised the interaction of the participants with their assigned authentication scheme: either creation or authentication. Creation was divided into five phases: (1) the participants entered their user name, (2) an introductory text was shown, (3) the participants created their passwords or the system-assigned passwords were generated, (4) participants could review their new passwords, and (5) a short training to familiarize the participants with their new scheme and to confirm the password. Authentication had two phases: first the participants entered their user name, then they entered their password. A short questionnaire, investigating the participants' impressions regarding the usability and security of their assigned scheme, concluded each session. The participants had a 24 hour window to complete each session. Participants were informed of their sessions by email and reminders were sent out if they had only 5 hours left in their 24 hour window. If at any point during authentication or creation a participant could not remember her/his password, s/he could reset it via an automated procedure on the website. To motivate participation throughout the whole study, a raffle was held for all participants who completed all five sessions. The study was available in English and German. The methodology of this usability study conforms to all requirements of our university's ethics committee. Only the data relevant to our analysis was recorded and participants could request deletion of their data at any time. No additional scenario was presented to the participants, they were fully primed in terms of the password schemes. Fahl et al. have shown that this procedure is scientifically sound [14]. Additionally, Bonneau found that security motivations such as registered payment information has no greater impact than demographic factors [2].

6.1   Participants

Participants were assigned to their schemes using stratified sampling of three factors: the participants sex, the language the participant enrolled in and a 5-point Likert value of the participant's self-assessed experience in password security. The participant's sex was chosen as factor due to previous literature suggesting differences in performance between male and female users [6]. The language the participant enrolled in was chosen as a factor to prevent bias originating from the translation of the questionnaires as well as the instructions explaining the study's procedure and the operation of the authentication schemes to the participants. The self-assessed experience in password security was chosen as a factor due to an evaluation of questions regarding the participants' real life passwords, which is not part of this paper.

Participants were recruited internationally in various ways, including, but not limited to, flyers and posters on campus, mailing lists, forums and social networks. All participants had to enroll on the study's website using a registration form. No paid services such as Amazon's Mechanical Turk or CrowdFlower were used. Overall 337 participants registered for our study and confirmed their email address. Of those 250 were male and 87 female. Participants registered in both languages available in the study, namely 262 participants used German texts and 75 used English texts. The age range was 14 to 67 years (mean = 27.6, median = 25). Almost half the participants (46.5%) reported to have experience in the field of password security (scores of 4 or 5 on a 5-point Likert scale).

6.2   Recorded Measures

The recorded usability measures are aligned along the ISO 9241-11 criteria effectiveness, efficiency and satisfaction.

Effectiveness. The first measure regarding effectiveness is the *success rate*. To retain the highest degree of comparability to past research, we follow the best practices of Biddle et al. in [1] and report success rates after the first and after the third attempt. Additionally, this study includes overall success rates (no limit on the attempts), as this is the most frequently reported measure in the literature. In this study success rates are defined as follows: the rate of participants having successfully authenticated after a certain amount of attempts (one, three, no limit) to the total number of participants using the scheme. The second effectiveness measure is the password *reset rate*. It describes the average number of resets per participant which is a more comparable measure than absolute values due to different numbers of participants assigned to the different schemes. We also report *dropout rates*, which is the number of participants dropped out in relation to the total number of participants assigned to a scheme. Note that the dropout is a rather unreliable measure of effectiveness, especially considering the narrow 24 hours time frame participants had to complete each session.

Efficiency. The first efficiency measure recorded during our study is the *interaction time* in seconds. It only counts the time for the actual interaction with the system and not the time the participants' browsers need to load the images. This prevents unpredictable bias due to different Internet connection speeds. The second measure of efficiency is the *number of attempts needed*, which represents the efficiency measure for each session. This measure complements the interaction times, which are the efficiency measure for each attempt. In order to assess the overall efficiency of the schemes, the two aforementioned measures (interaction times and number of attempts) are combined to calculate *expected average total authentication times*. This measure is what comes closest to traditional authentication timings which measure the time for the overall login procedure (from login request to completed login). However, it has to be stressed that this is an approximation of what is to be expected for the average participant. Yet, it offers a much better comparability between the schemes than the traditionally reported timings, which often depend on the schemes' implementations (i.e. loading times, etc.). The *time needed to read the instructions* is the total time across all sessions to account for participants who had to reset their password and read through the instructions again. These times are also reported in seconds. This measure serves as an indicator regarding the learnability of the schemes. In order to spot implementation issues and gather information on possibly necessary improvements of the schemes' implementations, the analysis also examines *system times*. These predominantly include the time the system needs to load the necessary contents (in particular the images) from the study server. The system times complement the interaction times to detect usability issues caused by the technical side of our implementations.

Satisfaction. *Questionnaires* at the end of each session captured the participants' satisfaction with their assigned scheme. The questions concerned the participants' attitude and impressions regarding the usability and security of their scheme. The majority is implemented using a 5-point Likert scale (5 represents strong agreement and 1 represents strong disagreement).

7   Results

In the following we describe the results of our usability study. The first section concerns itself with the validity of the security assumption (i.e. whether the target entropy values were reached). Then we present the usability results along the lines of the criteria effectiveness, efficiency and satisfaction of ISO 9241-11.

7.1   Validity of the Security Assumptions

In order to check the validity of our assumptions regarding the effective password spaces, we calculated empirical entropy values for all schemes. As we already explained in section 2, due to the small password samples the estimates reported below should only be seen as approximations of the actual differences in the effective password spaces of the schemes. The values of the recognition-based schemes, whose passwords were randomly assigned to the participants, can serve as an indication regarding this deviation. Table 2 shows for each scheme the expected entropy values derived from published research and the empirical values calculated for the passwords of our study.

Text Passwords.   Table 2 shows the entropy estimates calculated from the study text passwords according to [28] and the value reported by Komanduri et al. for their *basic8survey* policy. With an entropy of 27.41 bits the text passwords created by the participants of our study are very close to the target of 27.19 bits.

PassPoints.   Table 2 lists the entropy values calculated from the PassPoints passwords according to Dirik et al. in [9] as well. Entropy values are calculated

Table 2. Target and empirical entropy values in bits

	Target	Calculated
Text	27.19	27.41
PassPoints (upper bound)	26.00	24.17
PCCP	27.69	17.35
Faces	28.00	26.52
Things	28.00	26.79

for each click-point position in the password (analogously to the character positioning in text passwords). These values come very close to those of Dirik et al. but undercut them. Also, the value is calculated under the assumption that the choice of all click-points is independent from the other click-points chosen in the same password. This is not a reasonable assumption [9], but still the target entropy is not reached.

PCCP. The calculated empirical entropy of the PCCP passwords in our study is 17.35 bits and thus far below the target value of 27.69 bits. This result deviates considerably from what was expected.

7.2 Usability Evaluation

The following three sections present the results of the usability evaluation. Most of our data is not normally distributed and/or has heterogenous variances. Therefore, we use robust alternatives to standard tests as suggested by Field [15], Erceg-Hurn and Mirosevich [12] and Wilcox [36] in favor of data transformations. In detail, the used tests were Fisher's Exact Test (FET), the ANOVA-type statistic tests (ATS) developed by Brunner et al. and implemented in the R packages WRS by Wilcox and nparLD by Noguchi et al. [25] as well as Cliff's test (Cliff) as described by Wilcox in [36]. All multiple comparisons use Holm-Bonferroni corrected α-levels. Also, in order to cope with the outliers in the timing data (where participants would leave the session open and return after some time to continue the session), we used robust measures of location in favor of the mean. The standard errors are also calculated with regards to these robust measures of location. Readers unfamiliar with these statistical methods can find further information in appendix A if desired. All factors and their interactions not mentioned in the results were analyzed, but left out since they did not show significant results. Figure 2 shows all effectiveness measures and all efficiency measures. These aspects are discussed in more detail in the following paragraphs.

Effectiveness. The effect of the assigned scheme on the success rates is significant after the first attempt (FET: $p < .001$). Significant differences occur for the pairs Text-PassPoints (FET: $p = .006$), Text-PCCP (FET: $p. = 001$), PassPoints-Faces (FET: $p < .001$), PassPoints-Things (FET: $p < .001$), PCCP-Faces (FET: $p < .001$) and PCCP-Things (FET: $p < .001$). From the results

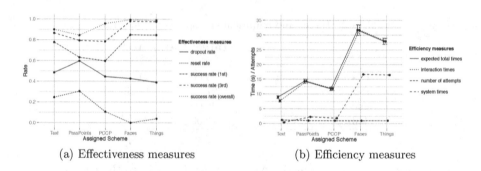

(a) Effectiveness measures   (b) Efficiency measures

Fig. 2. Measured Results

of follow-up Fisher's tests, a bipartition after the first attempt becomes apparent: PassPoints and PCCP (lower group) display both significantly worse success rates than Text, Faces and Things (upper group). After three attempts the effect of the assigned scheme on the success rates is again significant (FET: $p < .001$). The bipartition mostly remains, only the Text group moves somewhat between the upper and the lower group. In detail, significant differences are found for the following pairs: Text-Faces (FET: $p < .001$), Text-Things (FET: $p < .001$), PassPoints-Faces (FET: $p < .001$), PassPoints-Things (FET: $p < .001$), PCCP-Faces (FET: $p < .001$) and PCCP-Things (FET: $p < .001$). For the overall success rates (no limit on the attempts considered), the effect of the assigned scheme on the success rates is also significant (FET: $p < .001$). However, the bipartition is lost. PassPoints scores lowest with significant differences to all schemes except Text. The Text group also shows significant differences to the recognition-based schemes: Text-Faces (FET: $p < .001$) and Text-Things (FET: $p < .001$). In the overall scores, the recognition-based schemes show the best scores. PCCP scores only non-significantly worse. The Text scheme shows significant differences to the recognition-based-schemes, but not to PCCP. Detailed success rates for each session after one attempt, three attempts and overall can be found in appendix B for closer inspection.

As becomes apparent from the reset rates depicted in Fig. 2(a), the variation in the number of password resets is very large: the reset rates vary from 0.3 to 0. A Fisher's test shows that the effect of the assigned scheme is highly significant (FET: $p < .001$). Upon examining the scores of the schemes, a partitioning in three groups becomes apparent. Text and PassPoints show the highest reset rates (0.25 and 0.30). PCCP displays a rate of 0.11 and the recognition-based schemes show the best rates with 0.00 (Faces) and 0.04 (Things).

Figure 2(a) also shows dropout rates for the schemes. The scheme with the highest dropout rate is PassPoints (60%), the one with the lowest is Things (39%). The differences in dropout between the schemes are however not significant. The most important reason for dropout is the 24 hours time frame participants had to return to the study website and complete their session. 53.7% of all dropout can be attributed to this time frame.

Efficiency. From the interaction times plotted in Fig. 2(b) it becomes clear, that for recognition-based schemes it takes much longer to enter the password. A three-way ATS test shows significant main effects for the assigned scheme $(H(4.32, 43.24) = 55.59, p < .001)$ and the session $(H(2.82) = 5.05, p < .001)$. For the assigned scheme, the only non-significant difference is between Faces and Things. The Text group shows the lowest interaction times. The second lowest score is the one of the PCCP group, then follows PassPoints and last are the two recognition based schemes, whose interaction times were twice to three times as high. Regarding the sessions, the only significant differences are between session 2 and 4 and between session 4 and 5. Participants needed longer in the second session, than in the third and fourth, but need the most time in the fifth session. A table with a more detailed breakdown of the interaction times of each session can be found in appendix B.

The second efficiency indicator beside the interaction times is the number of attempts needed. The main effects of the assigned scheme $(H(3.90, 29.27) = 4.98, p = .003)$ and the sessions $(H(2.35) = 5.34, p = .002)$ are significant in an ATS test. The values for the different schemes are depicted in Fig. 2(b). For the assigned scheme, the significant differences occur for the pairs Text-PCCP (Cliff: $p = .004$) and Text-Faces (Cliff: $p = .002$). Concerning the sessions, participants needed more login attempts in the later sessions (4 and 5) than in the earlier sessions. The significant differences for the sessions occur between sessions 2 and 5 $(H(1) = 12.25, p < .001)$, between sessions 3 and 5 $(H(1) = 14.19, p < .001)$ and between sessions 4 and 5 $(H(1) = 14.27, p < .001)$.

While no total authentication times were recorded, expected average total authentication times can be approximated from the average number of authentication attempts and the average interaction times. The two factors "assigned scheme" and "session" are considered in this calculation. As in neither of the two relevant analyses the participants' sex shows a significant effect, its influence can be neglected. The resulting times are depicted in Fig. 2(b) alongside the interaction times. A table with all the values in detail can be found in appendix B. The advantages and disadvantages of some schemes in both analyses more or less annihilate. It is still expected for users of the recognition-based schemes to take twice as long as users of other schemes. However, e.g. the advantage of the Text group over PCCP in the interaction times is eaten up by the higher number of attempts needed in the later sessions. However, this measure should only be seen as an approximation and therefore be treated with caution.

Female participants took on average significantly more time to read the instructions (123.27 sec) than males (97.22 sec) did $(H = 968.71, p = .029)$. This is the only measure for which the participants' sex had a significant main effect. The effect of the assigned scheme is non-significant, as is the interaction. This indicates no significant difference in the learnability between all schemes.

Even if interaction times are low, participants might discard a scheme as unusable, if the system itself takes too long to respond. Figure 2(b) shows the system times for all schemes. An ATS test shows a significant result for the assigned scheme. In fact, all differences except the one between Faces and Things are significant.

Satisfaction. The participants' attitude towards the system was investigated using questionnaires. Figure 3 shows a summary of the average answers to the following 5-point Likert questions: (Q1) The password scheme is easy to use, (Q2) I could remember my password easily, (Q3) Entering my password was fast, (Q4) The creation of my password was easy, (Q5) I think I can remember my password easily, (Q6) I think I can remember my password more easily than passwords I normally use, (Q7) I prefer this new password scheme to my previous passwords, and (Q8) I would recommend this password scheme to others.

	Q1	Q2	Q3	Q4	Q5	Q6	Q7	Q8	
Text	4.25	3.78	4.02	3.71	3.53	2.61	2.45	3.10	1
PassPoints	3.92	4.08	3.28	3.71	3.50	2.90	2.52	3.03	2
PCCP	4.27	4.03	3.74	3.70	3.14	3.33	2.97	3.87	3
Faces	4.29	4.06	3.44	4.00	3.65	3.42	2.77	3.32	4
Things	4.55	4.17	3.77	4.02	3.67	3.39	3.15	3.85	5
Male	4.30	4.05	3.74	3.93	3.56	3.24	2.74	3.38	
Female	4.26	4.08	3.80	3.74	3.58	3.18	3.18	3.87	

Fig. 3. The average answers to a variety of 5-point Likert questions

Participants generally found their assigned authentication scheme easy to use (Q1) and easy to remember (Q2,Q5), but not easier to remember than their current passwords (Q6). PCCP was perceived significantly more difficult to remember ($H(4.68, 97.25) = 3.21, p = .012$). Perception of how fast password entry is differs depending on the assigned scheme (Q3). PassPoints scores lowest. The Text group perceives its scheme as being the fastest. Faces, Things and PCCP are rated equally. Despite the low efficiency apparent from the interaction times, the recognition-based schemes are still perceived to be faster than PassPoints. These differences are significant ($H(3.47, 20.45) = 3.43, p = .031$). Overall, only Things scores favorably in terms of a change towards it, though none of the differences are significant (Q7). While the perceived gain in usability does not seem to be large enough for the participants to happily adopt the new systems, they would generally recommend them to others (Q8).

The analysis of question Q2 also revealed a significant interaction of all three factors (assigned scheme, participants' sex and session). While text passwords always score lowest with the male participants, its rating from the female participants steadily increases up to the point where it scores highest in the last session. Faces preserves its ratings from the male participants over the course of the sessions and scores the highest rating in the fifth session, but is rated lowest by the female participants in all sessions except the fourth where it scores second to last. Thus, the scheme female participants perceive to have the highest memorability in the final session is rated lowest by the male participants and the scheme rated highest by male participants is rated lowest by female participants. These differences seem however to to be purely subjective as they are not mirrored by the actual performance of the participants.

8   Discussion

Configuring the different authentication schemes to the same effective password space is an important aspect of this study's methodology. This goal could only be partially attained. Table 2 shows the target entropy values and the entropy values calculated for the study passwords. For the Text scheme the target has been reached with only a negligible discrepancy. The entropy for the cued-recall-based schemes is lower than expected. The PassPoints entropy estimates for each position in the password (6.15, 6.04, 5.74 and 6.28 bits) are lower than the 6.5 bits found by Dirik et al. in [9]. The individual estimates for PCCP (5.70, 5.85 and 5.80 bits) are even lower than those for PassPoints. The difference in image resolution and tolerance margin size are crucial in this regard. However, such entropy estimates have, to our knowledge, never been reported for PCCP in published literature. Thus, a precise prediction of this loss in entropy was hard if not impossible, especially when considering that user choice was further restricted by omitting the shuffle mechanism. Chiasson et al. stated that there are "no significant differences between PCCP and what is expected to occur by chance" [30]. More research has to be conducted in order to find the relation between their finding and the difference between effective password space and theoretical password space discovered in this study.

The security analysis shows how difficult reliable estimation of the effective password space is. However, empirical determination is the only way to gather reliable data in this regard. The Shannon entropy values reported in this study can provide estimates for future studies. Yet, whenever possible improved metrics such as Bonneau's α-guesswork should be used in favor of Shannon entropy.

The implications of the differences regarding the entropy among the schemes are unclear. At best the differences are small enough to have no effect, although this seems unlikely. At worst, the differences are the same as in other studies, relying on the theoretical password space without any regard to the actual entropy. It is important to keep these findings in mind when interpreting the usability results. Though it has to be mentioned that due to the very small samples we had, all empirically calculated metrics should only be seen as an approximation. This becomes especially clear when regarding the entropy estimates of the recognition-based schemes, which should converge towards 28 bits of entropy in larger samples, due to their random nature.

In the usability evaluation, no scheme emerges as the sole victor of our comparison. The recognition-based schemes have higher effectiveness ratings than all other schemes. This advantage is interesting, as participants of Faces and Things were assigned random passwords and the entropy of the passwords was higher than for the cued-recall-based passwords. The cued-recall-based schemes have better efficiency ratings, where the conceptually more complex scheme PCCP scores even better than its predecessor PassPoints, especially in the later sessions. The interaction times are the only measure in which the Text group scores best. Text passwords scored worse than PCCP in terms of expected average timings when intervals between logins were long, but this might be attributed to the higher entropy in the text passwords.

The satisfaction ratings are mostly similar for all schemes, with two exceptions. Firstly, PassPoints is perceived to be slower than the recognition-based schemes, despite its better efficiency scores. This emphasizes the usability problems participants had with the scheme. Secondly, when participants were asked whether they preferred their new scheme, all schemes except Things score on average below 3 on a 5-point Likert scale. This notably includes the Text scheme. It seems that participants are not very fond of their current text passwords, but the alternative schemes offered to them in this study also do not represent their first choice. Thus, further alternatives need to be evaluated in order to identify the most suitable candidate.

One scheme clearly performs worst in basically all aspects: PassPoints. The adjustment of the security-level according to the findings of Dirik et al. results in low usability ratings overall. Consequently, it is safe to say that PassPoints is unsuitable to function as password scheme on a relevant security-level and can be excluded from future studies. For a meaningful comparison between the remaining schemes and especially when considering one of the schemes for actual implementation in a production environment, the requirements of such an environment play the most important role in judging the scheme's suitability.

The password reset rate of the graphical schemes is significantly lower. Therefore, in situations where recovery of lost passwords is expensive in time or effort, graphical passwords seem to be the better choice. If the user tries to authenticate using her/his text password at least once, then decides to reset the password and the reset procedure takes only about 20 seconds (twice the time of a normal login), even recognition-based graphical schemes have the potential to be more efficient than text passwords due to their superior memorability. However, more research is needed to provide conclusive evidence in this regard, since no reset timings were recorded in this study. For the recognition-based schemes only two resets occurred in the course of this study and success rates are generally higher, coming close to 100% even after longer periods of inactivity. Therefore, they are best suited for applications in which logins are infrequent with long intervals between them. In situations with more frequent logins, PCCP might be the better choice. Success rates are equal to those of traditional text passwords, interaction times are only somewhat elevated and the advantage in password resets remains. The aspect of increased memorability becomes ever more relevant when considering the login policies motivated by the online tracking efforts of companies such as Google or Facebook. The expiration dates in the session cookies of these popular services are usually set years into the future, so users will remain logged in as long as possible. Therefore, the logins of users potentially occur very infrequently on the same device.

Throughout the whole analysis we found no evidence for quantitative differences in the performance of male and female participants. Thus, the results of earlier studies by Chiasson et al. [6] could not be replicated. The only aspect where differences between male and female performance could be found is password creation. Male participants need fewer rounds in the training while spending less time to read the scheme instructions and find creation easier. However, in opposition to what is stated by Chiasson et al., this difference in performance seems not to be dependent on the type of mental work (visual-spatial tasks vs linguistic tasks) as for none of these measures a significant interaction between the assigned scheme and the participants' sex can be found. Yet, the subjective differences in user satisfaction are present and might hinder adoption of graphical passwords especially by male users.

Despite the overall success of this study, it has some limitations that need to be addressed. To configure the effective password space we only considered Shannon entropy. This is one of the most severe limitations of this study. Yet, we argue that it is a necessary compromise we had to make in our first step away from user studies regarding only the theoretical password space. While not optimal, it was the only viable option to approximate the effective password space. For future studies more reliable metrics such as α-guesswork have been proposed in recent literature and should be used instead of Shannon entropy, whenever empirical values allowing estimation of the effective password space are available. Reporting these metrics was unfeasible due to the (for password research) still small sample sizes in this study, but is planned for future work.

A restriction we imposed due to basic design decisions is the fixed length of the passwords for all schemes. For the graphical password schemes this decision was necessary in order to control the theoretical password space. For the text passwords we added the same limitation in order to negate any discrepancies in the usage of the different schemes. However, participants perceive this restriction as unnatural and many wanted more flexibility. However, such flexibility can only be incorporated in a methodology aiming at the same effective password space if studies such as those conducted by Komanduri et al. [22] are available for all schemes in a comparative study. This is obviously not the case for this study, but is an important field for future work.

Also, the decision of comparing schemes with system-assigned passwords to schemes which allow user choice might be considered a limitation of this study. For all the schemes we tried to use implementations, as they might be used for real-world applications. We followed the canonical implementations used in recent studies and distributed as commercial products (user-choice in cued-recall-based schemes and system-assigned passwords in recognition-based schemes).

Last but not least, it has to be noted that the methodology of this study neglects one usability aspect, namely interference of multiple passwords. While it has been shown that its influence is significant, it has been excluded in this study, mainly due to time and recruitment constraints. Future studies should optimally include this aspect.

9   Conclusion

This study compares four graphical authentication schemes and text passwords in a user web-study. It is the first study of its kind to base the security configuration of the tested schemes on the effective password space. An analysis of the security assumptions once again shows how difficult the prediction of effective password spaces is. The estimates reported in this work can serve as baseline for configurations in future studies and represent an individual research contribution.

The results of the usability evaluation show that no scheme emerges as the sole victor of this evaluation, but that all have strengths and weaknesses. Yet, both types of graphical authentication schemes show fewer password resets than the text passwords and in situations were these are costly graphical authentication seems to be the better choice. This is the first time such findings are reported not only inside one category of graphical passwords, but across the cued-recall-based and the recognition-based categories.

The results of Chiasson et al. indicating differences between male and female performance in the usage of graphical password schemes could not be replicated in this study. However, this study found significant differences in the attitude of male and female participants. Additional research is needed in order to find more evidence regarding this issue.

References

1. Biddle, R., Chiasson, S., van Oorschot, P.C.: Graphical passwords: Learning from the first twelve years. CSUR 44(4) (August 2012)
2. Bonneau, J.: The Science of Guessing: Analyzing an Anonymized Corpus of 70 Million Passwords. In: Proc. IEEE S&P, pp. 538–552 (2012)
3. Bonneau, J., Preibusch, S.: The password thicket: technical and market failures in human authentication on the web. In: Proc. WEIS 2010 (June 2010)
4. Chiasson, S., Stobert, E., Forget, A., Biddle, R., van Oorschot, P.C.: Persuasive Cued Click-Points: Design, Implementation, and Evaluation of a Knowledge-Based Authentication Mechanism. IEEE Trans. on Dep. and Sec. Comp. 9(2), 222–235 (2012)
5. Chiasson, S., Forget, A., Biddle, R., van Oorschot, P.C.: Influencing users towards better passwords: persuasive cued click-points. In: Proc. BCS-HCI 2008 (September 2008)
6. Chiasson, S., Forget, A., Stobert, E., van Oorschot, P.C., Biddle, R.: Multiple password interference in text passwords and click-based graphical passwords. In: Proc. CCS 2009, pp. 500–511. ACM (November 2009)
7. Davis, D., Monrose, F., Reiter, M.K.: On user choice in graphical password schemes. In: Proc. USENIX 2004, pp. 151–164 (2004)
8. Dhamija, R., Perrig, A.: Deja Vu: A user study using images for authentication. In: Proc. SSYM 2000, pp. 45–58 (2000)
9. Dirik, A.E., Memon, N., Birget, J.C.: Modeling user choice in the PassPoints graphical password scheme. In: Proc. SOUPS 2007, pp. 20–28 (2007)
10. Dunphy, P., Yan, J.: Is FacePIN secure and usable? In: Proc. SOUPS 2007 (July 2007)
11. Ellis, H.D.: Recognizing Faces. Brit. J. of Psychology 66(4), 409–426 (2011)
12. Erceg-Hurn, D.M., Mirosevich, V.M.: Modern robust statistical methods: An easy way to maximize the accuracy and power of your research. American Psychologist 63(7), 591–601 (2008)
13. Everitt, K.M., Bragin, T., Fogarty, J., Kohno, T.: A comprehensive study of frequency, interference, and training of multiple graphical passwords. In: Proc. CHI 2009, pp. 889–898 (2009)
14. Fahl, S., Harbach, M., Acar, Y., Smith, M.: On the ecological validity of a password study. In: Proc. SOUPS 2013, pp. 13:1–13:13 (2013)

15. Field, A., Miles, J., Field, Z.: Discovering Statistics Using R. SAGE Publications Limited (March 2012)
16. Florêncio, D., Herley, C.: A large-scale study of web password habits. In: Proc. WWW 2007, pp. 657–666 (2007)
17. Florêncio, D., Herley, C.: Where do security policies come from? In: Proc. SOUPS 2010 (2010)
18. Hlywa, M., Biddle, R., Patrick, A.S.: Facing the facts about image type in recognition-based graphical passwords. In: Proc. ACSAC 2011, pp. 149–158 (2011)
19. Ives, B., Walsh, K.R., Schneider, H.: The domino effect of password reuse. Comm. of the ACM 47(4), 75–78 (2004)
20. Jermyn, I., Mayer, A., Monrose, F., Reiter, M.K., Rubin, A.D.: The design and analysis of graphical passwords. In: Proc. SSYM 1999 (1999)
21. Kelley, P.G., Komanduri, S., Mazurek, M.L., Shay, R., Vidas, T., Bauer, L., Christin, N., Cranor, L.F., Lopez, J.: Guess again (and again and again): Measuring password strength by simulating password-cracking algorithms. In: Proc. IEEE S&P, pp. 523–537 (2012)
22. Komanduri, S., Shay, R., Kelley, P.G., Mazurek, M.L., Bauer, L., Christin, N., Cranor, L.F., Egelman, S.: Of Passwords and People: Measuring the Effect of Password-Composition Policies. In: Proc. CHI 2011, pp. 2595–2604 (2011)
23. Mulhall, E.F.: Experimental Studies in Recall and Recognition. Am. J. of Psych. 26(2), 217–228 (1915)
24. Nali, D., Thorpe, J.: Analyzing user choice in graphical passwords. School of Comp. Sci. (2004)
25. Noguchi, K., Gel, Y.R., Brunner, E.: nparLD: An R Software Package for the Nonparametric Analysis of Longitudinal Data in Factorial Experiments. J. of Statistical Software 50(12) (September 2012)
26. Real User Corporation: The Science Behind Passfaces (July 2004)
27. Schaub, F., Walch, M., Könings, B., Weber, M.: Exploring The Design Space of Graphical Passwords on Smartphones. In: Proc. SOUPS 2013. ACM (July 2013)
28. Shay, R., Komanduri, S., Kelley, P.G., Leon, P.G., Mazurek, M.L., Bauer, L., Christin, N., Cranor, L.F.: Encountering Stronger Password Requirements: User Attitudes and Behaviors. In: Proc. SOUPS 2010 (July 2010)
29. Stobert, E., Biddle, R.: Memory retrieval and graphical passwords. In: Proc. SOUPS 2013. ACM Press, New York (2013)
30. Stobert, E., Forget, A., Chiasson, S., van Oorschot, P.C., Biddle, R.: Exploring Usability Effects of Increasing Security in Click-based Graphical Passwords. In: Proc. ACSAC 2010, pp. 79–88 (2010)
31. Suo, X., Zhu, Y., Owen, G.S.: Graphical Passwords: A Survey. In: Proc. ACSAC 2005 (2005)
32. Weinshall, D., Kirkpatrick, S.: Passwords you'll never forget, but can't recall. In: CHI EA 2004, pp. 1399–1402 (2004)
33. Weir, M., Aggarwal, S., Collins, M., Stern, H.: Testing Metrics for Password Creation Policies by Attacking Large Sets of Revealed Passwords. In: Proc. CCS 2010, pp. 162–175 (2010)
34. Wiedenbeck, S., Waters, J., Birget, J.C., Brodskiy, A., Memon, N.: Authentication Using Graphical Passwords: Effects of Tolerance and Image Choice. In: Proc. SOUPS 2005, pp. 1–12. ACM (2005)
35. Wiedenbeck, S., Waters, J., Birget, J.C., Brodskiy, A., Memon, N.: PassPoints: Design and longitudinal evaluation of a graphical password system. Int. J. of Hum.-Comp. Studies 63(1-2), 102–127 (2005)
36. Wilcox, R.R.: Introduction to Robust Estimation & Hypothesis Testing, 3rd edn. Elsevier Academic Press (February 2012)

A   Statistical Methods

The web-based nature of the study imposes some limitations on the data analysis. Some timing values were highly elevated due to participants probably starting the session and then being distracted by other tasks. Therefore, all timings are analysed using medians, modified one-step M estimators (MOM) or trimmed means instead of means. The modified one-step M estimator of location is a measure of central tendency. It accounts for outliers which are determined using the median absolute deviation. A detailed description of the modified one-step M estimator is beyond the scope of this work, but Wilcox and Keselman wrote an excellent introduction to measures of central tendency[1].

All data collected throughout the study turned out to be non-normally distributed. Consequently, traditional parametric statistical procedures could not be applied as even small deviations can cause a severe drop in power of F-statistic tests [36]. The widely used non-parametric Mann-Whitney and Kruskal-Wallis tests were not sufficient for the three-factor design of this study (assigned scheme, sex of the participant and session). Furthermore, even for lower factor analyses they can prove unsatisfactory. The Mann-Whitney test can only control the Type I error rate under the assumption, that the groups have identical distributions [36]. The Kruskal-Wallis test performs only well, if its null hypothesis is true. Otherwise its statistical power is uncertain[2].

Following the advice of Erceg-Hurn and Mirosevich [12] and Wilcox [36], the following statistical methods are applied to scale data. In two-way designs, where the data has no longitudinal factor (e.g. time taken to read instructions), Wilcox advises a two-way ANOVA using modified one-step M estimators and a percentile bootstrap. He provides the R procedure m2way to conduct the analysis. Using a similar method is also suggested by Field [15]. Any follow-up tests are conducted using a similar method with a percentile bootstrap and the MOM for two groups (pbMOM). For all three-factor analyses the rank-based ATS described below is used.

All ordinal data is analysed using rank-based methods. This type of data comprises all Likert-scale questions. As outlined above classical rank-based methods are unsatisfactory. Therefore, instead of the Mann-Whitney test Cliff's test is used for the analysis. It performs well with small samples, can handle tied values and has a slight advantage over alternatives if many tied values appear [36]. Wilcox provides the R procedure cidv2 to conduct this test. Following the recommendations of Erceg-Hurn and Mirosevich in [12], the Kruskal-Wallis test is substituted by the rank-based ANOVA-type statistic (ATS), which allows for heteroscedastic data and tied values [36]. Wilcox provides the R procedure bdm to conduct such a test. The non-longitudinal data with two independent variables is analysed using the R procedure bdm2way provided by Wilcox, analogously to the

---

[1] Wilcox, R.R., Keselman, H.J.: Modern Robust Data Analysis Methods: Measures of Central Tendency. Psychological Methods 8(3), 254274 (2003)

[2] Wilcox, R.R.: Modern Statistics for the Social and Behavioral Sciences: A Practical Introduction. CRC Press (Jul 2011)

procedure bdm. Follow-up analyses are conducted using Cliff's test. Wilcox provides no ATS procedures for longitudinal data. However, Noguchi et al. adapted the ATS method and published their nparLD package for R in 2012 [25]. All longitudinal data is analysed using their procedures.

All tests for independence were conducted using Fisher's exact test due to the robustness in cases with small contingency values. All multiple comparisons use Bonferroni-Holm corrected α-levels. The p-values are given to the third decimal place, if a p-value would be rounded to a value not representable with three decimal places the term $p < .001$ is used.

B   Detailed Effectiveness and Efficiency Values

Table 3 gives a more detailed breakdown of the success rates for each scheme over the course of the five sessions. The influence of the sessions become apparent. The most obvious example are the values for PCCP in the fifth session, where the success rate after the first attempt is about half of the overall success rate.

Table 3. The authentication success rates for each session after the first attempt (1st), after the third attempt (3rd) and overall (∞); sessions S2-S5

	S 2			S 3			S 4			S 5		
	1st	3rd	∞	1st	3rd	∞	1st	3rd	∞	1st	3rd	∞
Text	0.74	0.86	0.86	0.85	0.92	0.95	0.86	0.94	0.97	0.65	0.71	0.81
PassPoints	0.55	0.82	0.86	0.73	0.83	0.88	0.71	0.87	0.95	0.53	0.63	0.66
PCCP	0.59	0.76	0.93	0.65	0.85	1.00	0.65	0.82	0.93	0.47	0.70	0.90
Faces	0.86	0.98	0.98	0.84	0.97	1.00	0.86	1.00	1.00	0.83	0.97	1.00
Things	0.93	0.98	1.00	0.83	1.00	1.00	0.87	1.00	1.00	0.73	0.91	0.94
Male	0.76	0.90	0.94	0.80	0.94	0.97	0.80	0.93	0.98	0.65	0.79	0.86
Female	0.70	0.88	0.92	0.79	0.88	0.96	0.78	0.92	0.98	0.61	0.80	0.91

Table 4 lists all the interaction times and expected average total authentication times. The advantage of the Text group over PCCP in the interaction times is eaten up by the higher number of attempts needed in the later sessions.

Table 4. Interaction times and average total authentication times in seconds

	Interaction times			Expected average				
	S 2	S 3	S 4	S 5	S 2	S 3	S 4	S 5 Overall
Text	9.7	7.6	7.1	8.0	11.7	7.6	8.6	14.7 8.9
PassPoints	13.7	14.1	13.3	15.3	13.7	14.1	13.9	19.3 14.3
PCCP	11.7	12.7	11.5	12.9	11.7	12.7	11.5	12.9 11.8
Faces	37.3	26.4	24.4	31.7	37.3	26.4	24.4	34.7 31.7
Things	29.5	24.7	26.2	32.4	31.2	24.7	26.2	43.2 28.0

A Security Extension Providing User Anonymity and Relaxed Trust Requirement in Non-3GPP Access to the EPS

Hiten Choudhury[1], Basav Roychoudhury[2], and Dilip Kr. Saikia[3]

[1] Dept. of Computer Science, St. Edmund's College, Shillong, India
hiten.choudhury@gmail.com
[2] Indian Institute of Management, Shillong, India
brc@iimshillong.in
[3] National Institute of Technology Meghalaya, Shillong, India
dks@nitm.ac.in

Abstract. Third Generation Partnership Project (3GPP) has standardized the Evolved Packet System (EPS) as a part of their Long Term Evolution System Architecture Evolution (LTE/SAE) initiative. In order to provide ubiquitous services to the subscribers and to facilitate interoperability, EPS supports multiple access technologies where both 3GPP and Non-3GPP defined access networks are allowed to connect to a common All-IP core network called the Evolved Packet Core (EPC). However, a factor that continues to limit this endeavor is the trust requirement with respect to the subscriber's identity privacy. There are occasions during Non-3GPP access to the EPS when intermediary network elements like the access networks that may even belong to third party operators have to be confided with the subscriber's permanent identity. In this paper, we propose a security extension that relaxes this requirement. Contrary to several other solutions proposed recently in this area, our solution can be adopted as an extension to the existing security mechanism. Moreover, it has to be implemented only at the operators level without imposing any change in the intermediary network elements. We also show that the extension meets its security goals through a formal analysis carried out using AUTLOG.

1 Introduction

The Third Generation Partnership Project (3GPP) has standardized the Evolved Packet System (EPS) as part of its Long Term Evolution/System Architecture Evolution (LTE/SAE) initiative. EPS supports the use of multiple access technologies though a common all-IP core network - the Evolved Packet Core (EPC) [5]. This opens up the potential to have a truly ubiquitous network, where communication can be possible among and across 3GPP access networks and non-3GPP access networks. Thus, one can move between 3GPP access networks and non-3GPP networks, like Worldwide Interoperability for Microwave Access (WiMAX), Wireless Local Area Network (WLAN), etc., and still be communicating using EPS.

A. Prakash and R. Shyamasundar (Eds.): ICISS 2014, LNCS 8880, pp. 226–244, 2014.
© Springer International Publishing Switzerland 2014

In 3GPP systems, each User Equipment (UE) is assigned with a unique and a permanent identity by the service provider called the International Mobile Subscriber Identity (IMSI) for identification. Knowledge of IMSI of a subscriber may allow an adversary to track and amass comprehensive profiles about the subscriber, thereby exposing him to various risks and overall, compromising his privacy. Thus, this identity is a precious information to be restricted to as few entities as possible to ensure user anonymity. In case of communication involving 3GPP and non-3GPP networks, like in any other case, this restriction needs to be ensured.

Non-3GPP access to EPS is classified into two categories, viz., trusted and untrusted. 3GPP does not specify as to which non-3GPP technologies be considered as trusted and which as untrusted; this decision is left to the operator. While using trusted non-3GPP access networks (non-3GPP AN), the UE connects directly with the EPC using the access network. For untrusted non-3GPP AN, an Internet Protocol Security (IPSec) tunnel is established between the UE and the EPC [4]. This tunnel provides end-to-end secure channel between the UE and EPC, thereby relaxing the need for trusting the (untrusted) access network with signaling/user data exchanged over it. The idea behind such relaxation in trust requirement is to enhance the reach of 3GPP system beyond 3GPP access networks, as it will simplify the requirement for agreements/pacts between 3GPP and non-3GPP operators.

While the non-3GPP access in EPS is aimed at enhanced 3GPP access across varied access networks, this also opens up certain vulnerability regarding assurance of anonymity. The Authentication and Key Agreement (AKA) protocol, used to provide access security to non-3GPP access to EPS, has occasions where the intermediary network elements like the non-3GPP AN (trusted or untrusted) has to be confided with the IMSI of the subscriber, and that too, by transmitting the IMSI over insecure radio link. Sharing of IMSI with an intermediary implies implicit trust on the latter, and would thus require trust relationships amongst the 3GPP and non-3GPP service providers, something that provisions of non-3GPP access envisaged to relax. Such trust relationship requirements restrict the wider premise of cross network accessibility, limiting the access only amongst the ones sharing such relationships. In addition, the transmission of IMSI over insecure radio link enhances the vulnerability, even in cases where the non-3GPP network is a trusted one.

In this paper, we propose a security extension to the AKA protocol using an end-to-end approach, whereby the knowledge of IMSI is restricted only to the UE and its Home Network (HN), the latter being the one assigning the same; i.e., the knowledge of IMSI is restricted to only the assigned and the assigner. This truly federates the requirement of trusting the intermediary network elements like the non-3GPP AN with the IMSI. The main contributions of the security extension proposed in this paper are: it enhances user anonymity as he moves across the network, and it allows setting up of a conducive platform for flexible on-demand use of access network resources without worrying about the trust relationships. It can be implemented with certain changes at the level of the operator and does not need any intervention in the intermediary networks which might belong to other network providers; this will ease deployment of the extension as it can be implemented over existing system. To the best of our knowledge, there are no other proposal for enhancement of EPS-AKA which talks about restricting the knowledge of IMSI only to the UE and HN, thereby relaxing the requirement to trust the intermediary Serving Network (SN).

This paper is organized into seven sections: Section 2 provides a brief overview of access security for non-3GPP Access to the EPS, Section 3 highlights the vulnerability to identity privacy which can compromise user anonymity, Section 4 reviews some indicative work done in this area from the literature, Section 5 presents our proposed extension and its details, Section 6 provides a brief description of the results that we have obtained from a formal analysis of our proposal, and Section 7 concludes this paper.

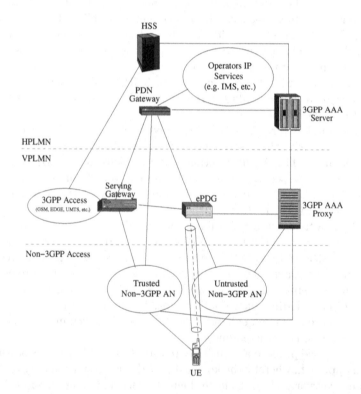

Fig. 1. Security architecture for non-3GPP access to the EPS

2   Access Security for Non-3GPP Access to the EPS

Fig. 1, depicts a simplified view of the security architecture for Non-3GPP access to the EPS. The 3GPP Authentication Authorization Accounting Server (3GPP

AAA Server) is located at the Home Public Land Mobile Network (HPLMN) - the home network of the UE. Its primary responsibility is to authenticate the subscriber, based on authentication information retrieved from the Home Subscription Server (HSS). The authentication signaling may pass via several AAA Proxies. The AAA Proxies, used to relay AAA information, may reside in any network between the Non-3GPP AN and the 3GPP AAA Server. The Packet Data Network Gateway (PDN GW) provides the UE with connectivity to the external packet data networks by being the point of exit and entry of traffic for the UE. The Serving Gateway (SGW), located at the Visitor Public Land Mobile Network (VPLMN) - the serving network, routes and forwards user data packets to and from that network. As mentioned earlier, a tunnel is set up between the UE and EPC for untrusted non-3GPP access; this IPSec tunnel is established between the Evolved Packet Data Gateway (ePDG) and the UE when the latter resides in an untrusted non-3GPP network.

The AKA protocol adopted to provide access security for trusted/untrusted Non-3GPP access to EPS is Extensible Authentication Protocol for Authentication and Key Agreement (EAP-AKA) [4]. The EAP server for EAP-AKA is the 3GPP AAA Server residing in the EPC. We provide an overview of the use of EAP-AKA for trusted and untrusted Non-3GPP access in the following sub-sections:

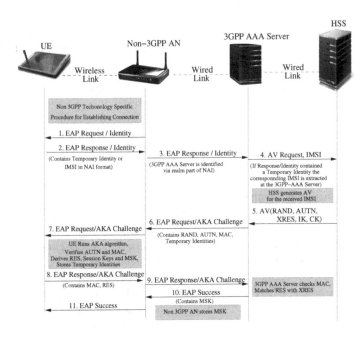

Fig. 2. Message flow during authentication in trusted non-3GPP access to the EPC

2.1   Trusted Non-3GPP Access

In trusted Non-3GPP access, the UE connects with the EPC directly through the Non-3GPP AN. For access security, the UE and the 3GPP AAA Server executes EAP-AKA protocol between them. At the end of a successful EAP-AKA, necessary key materials for secured communication between the UE and the non-3GPP AN are established. The message flows involved in the process is shown in Fig. 2.

At first, the UE establishes a connection with the Non-3GPP AN using a Non-3GPP AN technology specific procedure. The non-3GPP AN initiates the EAP-AKA procedure by sending an EAP Request/Identity message to the UE (Fig 2, Message 1). The UE responds with an EAP Response/Identity message back to the non-3GPP AN that contains the identity of the UE in Network Access Identifier (NAI) format [2] (Fig 2, Message 2). The transmitted identity may either be a temporary identity allocated to the UE in the previous authentication or, in case of the first authentication, the IMSI. This message is then routed towards the proper 3GPP-AAA Server through one or more AAA proxies identified with the help of the realm part of the NAI (Fig 2, Message 3). In case the NAI received from UE contains a temporary identity, the 3GPP AAA Server extracts the corresponding IMSI using a procedure explained in Section 2.3. The 3GPP-AAA server provides the IMSI to the HSS (Fig 2, Message 4) to procure authentication data for mutual authentication between the UE and the 3GPP-AAA server. The authentication data comprises of an Authentication Vector (AV) and contains a random part RAND, an authenticator token AUTN used for authenticating the network to the UE, an expected response XRES, a 128-bit Integrity Key IK, and a 128-bit Cipher Key CK.

$$AV = (RAND; AUTN; XRES; IK; CK) \qquad (1)$$

The AUTN includes a sequence number SQN, which is used to indicate freshness of the AV. On receiving the AV from HSS (Fig 2, Message 5), the 3GPP-AAA Server derives new keying materials, viz. Master Session Key (MSK) and Extended Master Session Key (EMSK) using the IK and CK contained in the AV. Fresh temporary identities (fast re-authentication identity, pseudonym) may also be generated at this stage, using the mechanism explained in Section 2.3. The temporary identities are then encrypted and integrity protected with the keying material. The 3GPP-AAA server sends the RAND and AUTN contained in AV, a Message Authentication Code (MAC) generated using the freshly generated keying materials, and the encrypted temporary identities to the non-3GPP AN via an EAP Request/AKA-Challenge message (Fig 2, Message 6). The non-3GPP AN forwards these to the UE (Fig 2, Message 7). The UE runs UMTS algorithm [3] to verify the correctness of AUTN so as to authenticate the access network. If the verification fails, the authentication is rejected. If it is successful, the UE computes RES, IK and CK and derives the keying materials MSK and EMSK using these keys, and thereafter checks the received MAC with these keying materials. If encrypted temporary identities are received, the same are stored for future authentications. The UE then computes a new MAC value covering the

EAP message with the new keying material. This newly computed MAC value is sent via EAP Response/AKA-Challenge message to the Non-3GPP AN (Fig 2, Message 8), which in turn, forwards this message to 3GPP-AAA Server (Fig 2, Message 9).

The 3GPP-AAA Server checks the received MAC and compares XRES (received earlier from the HSS as part of AV) to the received RES. If all checks are successful, the 3GPP-AAA Server sends an EAP Success message to Non-3GPP AN through a trusted link (Fig 2, Message 10). The keying material MSK is also send with this message to the Non-3GPP AN; the latter stores this to set up secure communication with the authenticated UE. The Non-3GPP AN informs the UE about the successful authentication by forwarding the EAP Success message (Fig 2, Message 11). This completes the EAP-AKA procedure that is required to register the UE with the Non-3GPP AN, at the end of which the UE and the non-3GPP AN share keying material derived during the exchange.

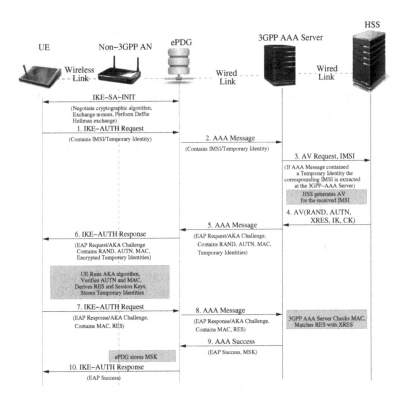

Fig. 3. Message flow during authentication in untrusted non-3GPP access to the EPC

2.2   Untrusted Non-3GPP Access

In case of untrusted Non-3GPP access, the UE does not connect directly to the EPC, but connects via the ePDG. The UE first establishes IPSec tunnel with the ePDG using Internet Key Exchange version 2 (IKEv2) protocol [22], and then performs the EAP-AKA explained in Section 2.1 using this tunnel. The message flows involved in such case is shown in Fig. 3.

The UE and the ePDG exchange a pair of messages (IKE-SA-INIT) to establish an IKEv2 channel in which the ePDG and UE negotiate cryptographic algorithms, exchange nonce and perform a Diffie Hellman exchange. With the IKEv2 secure channel in place, the UE sends its identity (compliant with NAI format, containing the IMSI or a temporary identity) to the ePDG (Fig 3, Message 1), which can only be decrypted and authenticated by the end points (i.e., the UE or the ePDG). The ePDG sends an authentication request message containing the UE identity to the 3GPP-AAA server (Fig 3, Message 2). For communication between ePDG and AAA-Server, the EAP-AKA messages are encapsulated in AAA messages. The 3GPP-AAA server fetches the AVs from the HSS (Fig 3, Message 4) as discussed in Section 2.1, and forwards the EAP message containing RAND, AUTN, MAC and encrypted temporary identities to ePDG (Fig 3, Message 5), the latter forwards this message further to the UE (Fig 3, Message 6). All messages between ePDG and UE are interchanged using IKE-AUTH messages. The UE checks the authentication parameters in the message received from ePDG and responds to the authentication challenge as in case of trusted non-3GPP access (Fig 3, Message 7). The ePDG forwards this response to the 3GPP-AAA server (Fig 3, Message 8). The 3GPP-AAA server performs the usual checks, and once successful, sends an EAP Success message and the keying materials to the ePDG (Fig 3, Message 9). The ePDG forwards the EAP Success message to the UE over the secure IKEv2 channel (Fig 3, Message 10). This completes the EAP-AKA exchange whereby the UE and the ePDG share keying material to be used for secure communication.

2.3   Temporary Identity Generation

An encrypted IMSI based technique is used to generate the temporary identities. Advanced Encryption Standard (AES) in Electronic Codebook (ECB) mode of operation is used for this purpose. A 128-bit secret key Kpseu is used for the encryption [4]. A specific Kpseu for generation of temporary identities is used for only a given interval determined by the operator. On expiry of this interval, a fresh Kpseu is used to generate the identities. This ensures the freshness of the key. Each key has a key indicator value associated with it, and this value is send along with the temporary identity, when the latter is used by UE for identity presentation. This allows the 3GPP-AAA server to use the correct Kpseu for linking the presented identity to the corresponding IMSI. The 3GPP-AAA Server should store a certain number number of old keys for interpretation of the received temporary identities that were generated using those old keys. The number of old keys maintained in the 3GPP-AAA server is operator specific, but it must at least be one, else a just-generated temporary identity may immediately become invalid due to the expiration of the key.

3   Identity Privacy Vulnerability

In order to ensure identity privacy to the subscribers, the 3GPP-AAA Server generates and allocates temporary identities to the UE in a secured way (as discussed in Section 2). These temporary identities, instead of IMSI, are mostly presented by the UE for identity presentation. Two types of temporary identities are allocated to the UE, viz., a re-authentication identity and a pseudonym. The re-authentication identity is used for identity presentation during a fast re-authentication [4] and the pseudonym is used during an EAP-AKA. The UE does not interpret the temporary identities, it just stores and uses them during the next authentication. In-spite of the above, EAP-AKA has vulnerabilities whereby the permanent identity, i.e. the IMSI, might get compromised. Following are the scenarios when IMSI may get compromised during trusted non-3GPP access:

- The IMSI is transmitted in clear text through the radio link for identity presentation during the very first authentication
- A subscriber having a temporary identity from the 3GPP-AAA Server may not initiate any new authentication attempt for quite some time. If the user initiates an authentication attempt using an old temporary identity after the key used to generate the same has been removed from storage at the 3GPP-AAA Server, the latter will not be able to recognize the temporary identity. In cases when both fast re-authentication identity as well as pseudonym are not recognized, the 3GPP-AAA Server will request the UE to send its permanent identity. In response to such a request, the UE may have to transmit its IMSI to the Non-3GPP AN in clear text through the wireless link making the permanent identity accessible to eavesdroppers.
- A corrupt Non-3GPP AN may utilize the received IMSI for various kind of malicious activities or may pass this identity to an unreliable party.
- A malicious/fake Non-3GPP AN may also take advantage of the above situation by creating a spurious EAP Request/Identity message and by requesting the UE for its IMSI through this message; in response to which the unsuspecting UE that does not have a mechanism to authenticate the request at that time, will transmit its IMSI in clear text through the radio link.

In case of untrusted non-3GPP access, there are no threats against identity privacy from passive attackers like eavesdroppers due the IPSec tunnel set up between the UE and the ePDG. However, there exist the following threats from active attackers when sending the IMSI in the tunnel set-up procedure:

- The protected channel is encrypted but not authenticated at the time of receiving the user identity (IMSI). The IKEv2 messages, when using EAP, are authenticated at the end of the EAP exchange. So an attacker may pose as a genuine ePDG and may request the UE for the IMSI. Although the attack would eventually fail at the time of authentication, the attacker would have managed to see the IMSI in clear text by then.

– The IMSI would be visible to the ePDG, which in roaming situations may be in the VPLMN. Such a vulnerability limits the home operator in interoperating with a VPLMN that belongs to an untrusted third party operator.

4   Related Work

In mobile networks, the need to protect the identity privacy of a subscriber even from intermediary network elements like the visitor access network is well established. Herzberg et al. [19] pointed out that in an ideal situation no entity other than the subscriber himself and a responsible authority in the subscriber's home domain should know the real identity of the user. Even the authority in the visited network should not have any idea about the real identity. Towards this, several schemes have been proposed with each of them following a varied approach.

Many of the proposed schemes employ public key infrastructure [29][26][20] [28][18][36], but due to their processor intensive nature, such solutions are not the best of solutions for 3GPP based mobile systems, as the UE may not have high processing and power capability.

The combination of both public key and symmetric key crypto system are also explored in many of the schemes. Varadharajan et al. [31] proposed three schemes using this hybrid approach. However, Wong et al. [33] found that they are vulnerable to several attacks. Another hybrid scheme was proposed by Zhu et al. that uses both public and symmetric key crypto systems [40]. However, in Zhu et al.'s scheme certain security weaknesses were detected, due to which several other improvements were proposed [25][34][7][37]. Recently, Zeng et al. demonstrated that because of an inherent design flaw in the original in Zhu et al.'s scheme, the latter and its successors are unlikely to provide anonymity [38].

Off late, several other schemes were proposed by various researchers [24][17] [14][39][8][13][16][15][12][27][21][23][35]. However, none of these schemes are in line with EAP-AKA. For a mobile operator that already has a big subscriber base, changing over to a completely new authentication and key agreement protocol is a big challenge. Therefore, an ideal scheme for enhanced identity privacy in Non-3GPP access to the EPS would be the one that can be easily configured into the existing authentication and key agreement protocol (i.e., EAP-AKA). At the same time, an ideal scheme should also be restricted only to the operator. Intermediary network elements that may even belong to third party operators should not be expected to participate equally.

5   Our Proposed Security Extension

In this section, we explain our security extension for EAP-AKA that overcomes the existing identity privacy vulnerabilities mentioned in Section 3 and relaxes the need to trust an intermediary network element with the IMSI during Non-3GPP access to the EPS. The knowledge of the IMSI of a subscriber is restricted to the UE and the HSS, and in no situation is revealed to any third party; thus conforming to the requirement stated by Herzberg et al. [19]. This extension is implemented only at Subscriber Identity Module (SIM) of the UE, and the HSS; and does not envisage any change at the intermediate network elements like the Non-3GPP AN and the AAA servers. The SIM and the HSS can be upgraded to support this extension, thereby easing migration challenges in the face of current wide scale deployment. As only the UE and HSS needs to be aware of this extension, the migration can also be taken up in a phased manner, or can be offered as a value added service for ensuring anonymity. This work is in continuation of the authors' earlier proposal for UMTS [9] and LTE [11]. The following sub-sections explain the working of this security extension. A summary of all the functions used in the security extension (working details of which are explained later in this section) is presented in Table 1.

Table 1. Functions used in the extension.

Function	Details
f_i	Generates a $DMSI$ from a given RIC.
f_{Embed}	Embeds a 32 bit RIC into a 128 bit $RAND$.
$f_{Extract}$	Extracts the 32 bit RIC from a 128 bit $ERAND$.
f_n	Encrypts RIC_{Padded} to find $ERIC$.
f_d	Decrypts $ERIC$ to find RIC_{Padded}.
f_{PRNG}	Generates a 128 bit pseudo random number.

5.1 DMSI: Pseudonym for IMSI

Our scheme replaces the transmission of the IMSI with a pseudonym - Dynamic Mobile Subscriber Identity (DMSI). A fresh DMSI is generated as and when the need for transmission of IMSI as per the original protocol arises. Being untraceable to the IMSI, the transmission of short-lived DMSI does not compromise the permanent identity of the user, thereby ensuring anonymity. As the IMSI never gets transmitted, the same also remains unknown to all intermediary network components and thereby remains restricted to UE and HSS.

5.2 Generating DMSI

The DMSI is generated from the most recent value of RAND (Equation 1) received at UE during a successful EAP-AKA procedure, and owes its existence

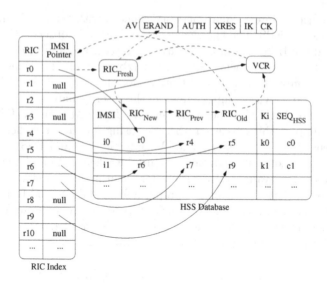

Fig. 4. RIC Index with modified HSS database

to a random number, called the Random number for Identity Confidentiality (RIC) that remain embedded in the RAND (we call this Embedded RAND or ERAND). The HSS maintains a pool of RICs, some of which may be in-use (i.e., assigned to certain UEs) while the others not-in-use at any point in time (Fig. 4). During each run of the EAP-AKA protocol, a not-in-use RIC is randomly selected from the pool of RICs, and is securely transmitted, embedded into the RAND, to the UE. The UE extracts the RIC from the most recently received RAND to generate the next DMSI, which is then used as a pseudonym for the IMSI of the UE. Thus, DMSI is a function of RIC as is shown later in Equation 8:

$$DMSI = f(RIC) \tag{2}$$

The extension ensures that the selected RIC is sufficiently random, and has no correlation with a previously selected RIC. A mapping between the selected RIC and the IMSI of the UE is maintained at the HSS (explained later in this section); this allows the HSS to uniquely identify the UE with the corresponding RIC, and thereby the DMSI.

5.3   Management of RIC

The size of RIC is decided by the operator, and this decides on the size of the RIC pool at HSS. A RIC of size b bits provide a pool of n unique RIC values:

$$n = 2^b \tag{3}$$

As for example, a 32 bit RIC size will ensure a pool of 2^{32}, i.e., approximately 4.29 billion unique RIC values which should be sufficient for the HSS to support a reasonable number of subscribers. The RIC pool is maintained at the HSS database as the RIC-Index (Fig. 4). This is a sorted list of the possible $n = 2^b$ RIC values. Each entry in the RIC-Index has an associated pointer the RIC-Pointer. If the particular RIC value is assigned to a UE, i.e., the RIC is in-use, this pointer will point to the corresponding IMSI in the HSS database. If the RIC is not assigned to any UE, i.e., not-in-use, the RIC-Pointer will be null.

A fresh value of RIC, randomly chosen from the pool of not-in-use RICs from the RIC-Index, is allotted to the UE during the run of EAP-AKA. This is stored as RIC_{Fresh} at the HSS database, and is cryptographically embedded into the RAND part of AV using the long term secret key Ki shared between the HSS and the UE resulting in a new random number called the Embedded RAND (ERAND):

$$ERAND = f_{Embed}Ki(RIC_{Fresh}, RAND) \qquad (4)$$

The AV thus get modified as follows:

$$AV = (ERAND; AUTH; XRES; IK; CK) \qquad (5)$$

This ERAND is now used by the 3GPP-AAA server, instead of the RAND as in the original protocol, to challenge the UE. Since the size of RAND and ERAND is same, this change will be transparent to the 3GPP-AAA server. Example algorithms to embed a 32 bit RIC into a 128 bit RAND and to extract the embedded RIC form the ERAND is proposed in [10]. Only the UE, having the knowledge of the long term shared key Ki, will be able to extract RIC from ERAND.

$$RIC = f_{Extract}Ki(ERAND) \qquad (6)$$

Few, say m, RICs associated with an IMSI the fresh RIC (say RIC_{Fresh}) and $m - 1$ previously generated RICs are stored at the HSS database against that IMSI in the fields RIC_{New}, RIC_{Prev}, RIC_{Old}, etc. When a new RIC is allotted, it is stored in RIC_{New}, the previous value at RIC_{New} moved to RIC_{Prev}, the previous value of RIC_{Prev} to RIC_{Old}, and so on, the oldest of the previous m RICs being released back to the RIC-Index as not-in-use i.e., the RIC that is released will have the IMSI-Pointer reset to null against it in the RIC-Index. This ensures robustness of the protocol against the loss of an ERAND during transit to the UE. The storage of m RICs ensures that a mapping between the RIC that is currently stored at the UE and the corresponding IMSI is always maintained at the HSS. As for any other critical information such as the subscriber's security credentials, billing details, etc., it is the responsibility of the operator to ensure a robust backup mechanism against database crash.

The choice of m is left to the operator. For illustration, if we consider the RIC size to be 32 bits, and $m = 4$, i.e., 2^2 RICs are stored against each IMSI, it would still allow one to provide for 2^{30}, which is approximately 1.073 billion subscribers; this number is more than 5 times the approximately 200 million subscriber base of the largest cellular operator in India as of January, 2014 [30].

Thus, if s is the maximum number of subscribers that the operator wants the proposed extension to handle, then

$$s = n/m \tag{7}$$

n being the total number of possible RICs in the entire pool and m the number of RICs maintained against each IMSI in the HSS's database. The HSS maintains a field SEQ_{HSS} against every IMSI to verify the freshness of a DMSI it receives from an UE and to prevent replay attacks.

5.4   Handling Collision at RIC-Index

Whenever a RIC needs to be embedded into a RAND at the HSS, a new RIC (RIC_{Fresh}) is selected from the pool of not-in-use RICs. In order to select RIC_{Fresh}, a b bit random number (say RN) is generated using a standard Pseudo Random Number Generator. This RN is then searched for in the RIC-Index. If the IMSI-Pointer against RN in the RIC-Index is found to be null, RN is selected as RIC_{Fresh} and the null value is replaced with the address of the record in the HSS's database where the IMSI is stored. However, a collision may occur in this process if the IMSI-Pointer against RN in the RIC-Index is not null, i.e., if that particular RIC value is in-use. For collision resolution, a b bit variable called Variable for Collision Resolution (VCR) is maintained at HSS (Fig. 4). The VCR always contains a not-in-use RIC. Thus, when RN results in a collision, the value at VCR can be used instead. At the very outset, during initialization of the HSS's database, a b bit random number (say RN_0) is stored in the VCR and the IMSI-Pointer against it in the RIC-Index is set to the address of VCR. Whenever there is a collision, the b bit value stored in the VCR is selected as RIC_{Fresh}, its value searched in RIC-Index and the IMSI-Pointer against it set to the address at HSSs database where the IMSI is stored. Once the value of VCR is used for RIC_{Fresh}, the former will have to be replaced with a new not-in-use RIC value. The oldest of the m RIC values in the HSS database against the IMSI in question is then not released to the pool on not-in-use RICs, but is stored at VCR, and the IMSI-Pointer against its value in RIC-Index set to the address of the VCR. This ensures that VCR always contains a not-in-use RIC value to take care of the collisions.

5.5   Resolving Identity to IMSI in AV Request

Under normal operation of EAP-AKA, the UE uses a temporary identity in NAI format [2] to present its identity to the network. The realm part of the temporary identity (NAI format) allows the intermediate AAA proxy servers to guide the request to the appropriate 3GPP-AAA server. When a request for an AV reaches the 3GPP-AAA server along with the temporary identity of the subscriber, the 3GPP-AAA Server resolves the temporary identity to its corresponding IMSI using the procedure discussed in Section 2.3. The AV request is then forwarded to the HSS along with the resolved IMSI. However, in situations enumerated in

Section 3 where the IMSI needs to be transmitted by the UE, the DMSI in NAI format is now transmitted instead:

$$DMSI = MCC\|MNC\|RIC\|ERIC \tag{8}$$

MCC stands for the Mobile Country Code, MNC stands for the Mobile Network Code, and ERIC is created by encrypting a padded RIC (say RIC_{padded}) with the Advanced Encryption Standard (AES) algorithm, taking the long term secret key Ki as parameter. Thus, the ERIC, whose use is explained later, is:

$$ERIC = f_n Ki(RIC_{padded}) \tag{9}$$

where,

$$RIC_{padded} = RIC\|SEQ_{UE}\|R \tag{10}$$

SEQ_{UE} is the value of a 32 bit counter maintained at UE with its value incremented whenever a new DMSI is created for identity presentation, and R is a $128 - (32 + b)$ bit random number. SEQ_{UE} ensures the freshness of DMSI and prevents replay attack at HSS, and inclusion of R pads the RIC_{padded} to 128 bits, a requirement for AES cipher. R also introduces sufficient amount of randomness to harden cryptanalysis of the cipher text.

As before, the realm part allows the intermediate AAA proxy servers to guide the request to the appropriate 3GPP-AAA server, which forwards the DMSI to the HSS along with a request for AV, as it would have done for a received IMSI. Thus, the onus of resolving the DMSI is passed on to the HSS. On receiving the AV request, the HSS resolves the DMSI, which it does by locating RIC part of the received DMSI. It then uses the RIC-Index to find the corresponding RIC-Pointer (Fig. 4), and thereby the IMSI and the long term key Ki. The next step is to decrypt the ERIC part using AES and Ki:

$$RIC_{padded} = f_d Ki(ERIC) \tag{11}$$

The RIC contained in RIC_{padded} is then compared with the RIC part of the DMSI, a success ensures that the DMSI was created by UE having key Ki, and not by a malicious agent. The sole purpose of including ERIC in DMSI is to ensure this protection. A SEQ_{UE} value in RIC_{padded} greater than SEQ_{HSS} ensures the freshness of the request. If any of these checks fail, the request is rejected, else the SEQ_{UE} is copied into SEQ_{HSS} for future reference and a fresh AV is generated as in Equation 5 to respond to the AV request. Fig. 5 and Fig. 6 depicts the message flow under this proposed extension for trusted and untrusted non-3GPP access to EPS.

6   Formal Analysis of Security Requirements

We performed a formal analysis of the proposed scheme through an enhanced BAN logic [6] called AUTLOG [32]. A similar analysis is performed by 3GPP in [1]. The security goals for this analysis are listed in the following subsection.

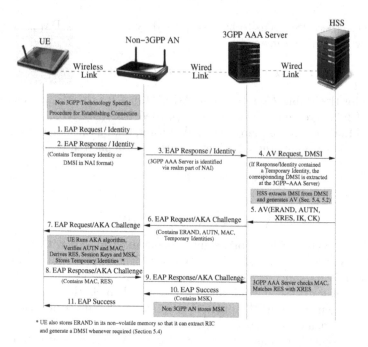

Fig. 5. Message flow during authentication under proposed extension in trusted non-3GPP access to the EPC

6.1   Security Goals

$IMSI$ should be a shared secret between the UE and the HSS. The same should not be disclosed by the UE to any third party including the AN.

$$\textbf{G1: } UE \text{ believes } UE \xleftrightarrow{IMSI} HSS$$

$$\textbf{G2: } UE \text{ believes } \neg(AN \text{ sees } IMSI)$$

When ever temporary identities (i.e., re-authentication identities and pseudonyms) fail to protect the permanent identity (due to reasons discussed in Section 3), a backup mechanism is followed according to our proposed extension, so that identity privacy may still be ensured to the subscriber. According to this mechanism (Section 5), a $DMSI$ created with the RIC that is extracted from the most recent $RAND$ received at the UE is transmitted in lieu of the $IMSI$. During every successful run of the EAP-AKA protocol, if the UE receives a fresh RIC, it can easily protect its permanent identity following this mechanism.

$$\textbf{G3: } UE \text{ believes } UE \text{ has } RIC$$

$$\textbf{G4: } UE \text{ believes } fresh(RIC)$$

It should not be possible for anyone except the HSS (that has access to the RIC-Index) to map a $DMSI$ with its corresponding $IMSI$.

$$\textbf{G5: } UE \; believes \; \neg(DMSI \equiv IMSI)$$

The formal analysis of our extension established the achievement of the above security goals.

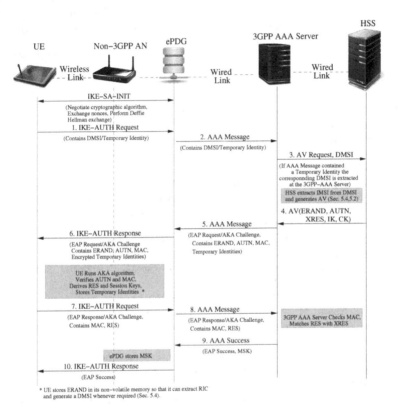

Fig. 6. Message flow during authentication under proposed extension in untrusted non-3GPP access to the EPC

7 Conclusion

A factor that complicates and restricts non-3GPP access to the EPS is the trust requirement on intermediary networks (like non-3GPP AN and ePDG) to take care of subscriber's identity privacy. In this paper, we have proposed an extension to the EAP-AKA protocol to resolve the user anonymity related issues in non-3GPP access to EPS. The main contribution of this paper is to enable total confidentiality of the permanent identity - the IMSI - of the subscriber from eavesdroppers as well as from intermediary network components; this would allow access to 3GPP based networks from diverse non-3GPP based access networks without detailed requirements of trust amongst them. As an additional feature, the proposed changes are transparent to the intermediary network components and can be implemented over the existing subscriber base with limited changes in the HSS and the UE, i.e. only at the operator's level. Being a symmetric key based approach, as followed in EPS-AKA, it takes care of the constraint of the limited computational power of UE; unlike the schemes using public key cryptography. We have also carried out a formal security analysis of our proposal using AUTLOG, and have shown that the extension proposed here conforms to the necessary security requirements.

References

1. 3GPP: Formal Analysis of the 3G Authentication Protocol. TR 33.902, 3rd Generation Partnership Project (3GPP) (2001),
   http://www.3gpp.org/ftp/Specs/html-info/33902.htm
2. 3GPP: Numbering, addressing and identification. TS 23.003, 3rd Generation Partnership Project (3GPP) (2011),
   http://www.3gpp.org/ftp/Specs/html-info/23003.htm
3. 3GPP: 3G Security; Security architecture. TS 33.102, 3rd Generation Partnership Project (3GPP) (2012), http://www.3gpp.org/ftp/Specs/html-info/33102.htm
4. 3GPP: 3GPP System Architecture Evolution (SAE);Security aspects of non-3GPP accesses. TS 33.402, 3rd Generation Partnership Project (3GPP) (2012),
   http://www.3gpp.org/ftp/Specs/html-info/33402.htm
5. 3GPP: Architecture enhancements for non-3GPP accesses. TS 23.402, 3rd Generation Partnership Project (3GPP) (2012),
   http://www.3gpp.org/ftp/Specs/html-info/23402.htm
6. Burrows, M., Abadi, M., Needham, R.M.: A logic of authentication. Proceedings of the Royal Society of London. A. Mathematical and Physical Sciences 426(1871), 233–271 (1989)
7. Chang, C., Lee, C., Chiu, Y.: Enhanced authentication scheme with anonymity for roaming service in global mobility networks. Computer Communications 32(4), 611–618 (2009)
8. Chen, C., He, D., Chan, S., Bu, J., Gao, Y., Fan, R.: Lightweight and provably secure user authentication with anonymity for the global mobility network. International Journal of Communication Systems 24(3), 347–362 (2011)
9. Choudhury, H., Roychoudhury, B., Saikia, D.K.: End-to-end user identity confidentiality for umts networks. In: 2010 3rd IEEE International Conference on Computer Science and Information Technology (ICCSIT), vol. 2, pp. 46–50. IEEE (2010)
10. Choudhury, H., Roychoudhury, B., Saikia, D.: Umts user identity confidentiality: An end-to-end solution. In: 2011 Eighth International Conference on Wireless and Optical Communications Networks (WOCN), pp. 1–6. IEEE (2011)
11. Choudhury, H., Roychoudhury, B., Saikia, D.: Enhancing user identity privacy in lte. In: 2012 IEEE 11th International Conference on Trust, Security and Privacy in Computing and Communications (TrustCom), pp. 949–957. IEEE (2012)
12. Feng, T., Zhou, W., Li, X.: Anonymous identity authentication scheme in wireless roaming communication. In: 2012 8th International Conference on Computing Technology and Information Management (ICCM), vol. 1, pp. 124–129. IEEE (2012)

13. He, D., Bu, J., Chan, S., Chen, C., Yin, M.: Privacy-preserving universal authentication protocol for wireless communications. IEEE Transactions on Wireless Communications 10(2), 431–436 (2011)

14. He, D., Chan, S., Chen, C., Bu, J., Fan, R.: Design and validation of an efficient authentication scheme with anonymity for roaming service in global mobility networks. Wireless Personal Communications 61(2), 465–476 (2011)

15. He, D., Chen, C., Chan, S., Bu, J.: Analysis and improvement of a secure and efficient handover authentication for wireless networks. IEEE Communications Letters 16(8), 1270–1273 (2012)

16. He, D., Chen, C., Chan, S., Bu, J.: Secure and efficient handover authentication based on bilinear pairing functions. IEEE Transactions on Wireless Communications 11(1), 48–53 (2012)

17. He, D., Ma, M., Zhang, Y., Chen, C., Bu, J.: A strong user authentication scheme with smart cards for wireless communications. Computer Communications 34(3), 367–374 (2011)

18. He, Q., Wu, D., Khosla, P.: The quest for personal control over mobile location privacy. IEEE Communications Magazine 42(5), 130–136 (2004)

19. Herzberg, A., Krawczyk, H., Tsudik, G.: On travelling incognito. In: First Workshop on Mobile Computing Systems and Applications, WMCSA 1994, pp. 205–211. IEEE (1994)

20. Horn, G., Preneel, B.: Authentication and payment in future mobile systems. In: Quisquater, J.-J., Deswarte, Y., Meadows, C., Gollmann, D. (eds.) ESORICS 1998. LNCS, vol. 1485, pp. 277–293. Springer, Heidelberg (1998)

21. Jiang, Q., Ma, J., Li, G., Yang, L.: An enhanced authentication scheme with privacy preservation for roaming service in global mobility networks. In: Wireless Personal Communications, pp. 1–15 (2012)

22. Kaufman, C., Hoffman, P., Nir, Y., Eronen, P.: Internet key exchange protocol version 2 (ikev2). The Internet Engineering Task Force Request for Comments (IETF RFC) 5996 (2010)

23. Kuo, W.C., Wei, H.J., Cheng, J.C.: An efficient and secure anonymous mobility network authentication scheme. Journal of Information Security and Applications (2014)

24. Lee, C., Chen, C., Ou, H., Chen, L.: Extension of an efficient 3gpp authentication and key agreement protocol. Wireless Personal Communications, 1–12 (2011)

25. Lee, C., Hwang, M., Liao, I.: Security enhancement on a new authentication scheme with anonymity for wireless environments. IEEE Transactions on Industrial Electronics 53(5), 1683–1687 (2006)

26. Lin, H., Harn, L.: Authentication protocols for personal communication systems. ACM SIGCOMM Computer Communication Review 25(4), 256–261 (1995)

27. Liu, H., Liang, M.: Privacy-preserving registration protocol for mobile network. International Journal of Communication Systems (2012)

28. Park, J., Go, J., Kim, K.: Wireless authentication protocol preserving user anonymity. In: Proceedings of the 2001 Symposium on Cryptography and Information Security (SCIS 2001), vol. 26, pp. 159–164. Citeseer (2001)

29. Samfat, D., Molva, R., Asokan, N.: Untraceability in mobile networks. In: Proceedings of the 1st Annual International Conference on Mobile Computing and Networking, pp. 26–36. ACM (1995)

30. Trai: Highlights on telecom subscription data as on 07 july 2014. Press release, Telecom Regulatory Authority of India (2014)

31. Varadharajan, V., Mu, Y.: Preserving privacy in mobile communications: a hybrid method. In: 1997 IEEE International Conference on Personal Wireless Communications, pp. 532–536. IEEE (1997)
32. Wedel, G., Kessler, V.: Formal semantics for authentication logics. In: Martella, G., Kurth, H., Montolivo, E., Bertino, E. (eds.) ESORICS 1996. LNCS, vol. 1146, pp. 219–241. Springer, Heidelberg (1996)
33. Wong, D.: Security analysis of two anonymous authentication protocols for distributed wireless networks. In: Third IEEE International Conference on Pervasive Computing and Communications Workshops, PerCom 2005 Workshops, pp. 284–288. IEEE (2005)
34. Wu, C., Lee, W., Tsaur, W.: A secure authentication scheme with anonymity for wireless communications. IEEE Communications Letters 12(10), 722–723 (2008)
35. Xie, Q., Hu, B., Tan, X., Bao, M., Yu, X.: Robust anonymous two-factor authentication scheme for roaming service in global mobility network. Wireless Personal Communications 74(2), 601–614 (2014)
36. Yang, G., Wong, D., Deng, X.: Anonymous and authenticated key exchange for roaming networks. IEEE Transactions on Wireless Communications 6(9), 3461–3472 (2007)
37. Youn, T., Park, Y., Lim, J.: Weaknesses in an anonymous authentication scheme for roaming service in global mobility networks. IEEE Communications Letters 13(7), 471–473 (2009)
38. Zeng, P., Cao, Z., Choo, K., Wang, S.: On the anonymity of some authentication schemes for wireless communications. IEEE Communications Letters 13(3), 170–171 (2009)
39. Zhou, T., Xu, J.: Provable secure authentication protocol with anonymity for roaming service in global mobility networks. Computer Networks 55(1), 205–213 (2011)
40. Zhu, J., Ma, J.: A new authentication scheme with anonymity for wireless environments. IEEE Transactions on Consumer Electronics 50(1), 231–235 (2004)

A Usage-Pattern Perspective for Privacy Ranking of Android Apps

Xiaolei Li[1], Xinshu Dong[2], and Zhenkai Liang[1]

[1] National University of Singapore, Singapore
{xiaolei,liangzk}@comp.nus.edu.sg
[2] Advanced Digital Sciences Center, Singapore
xinshu.dong@adsc.com.sg

Abstract. Android applies a permission-based model to regulate applications (apps). When users grant apps permissions to access their sensitive data, they cannot control how the apps utilize the data. Existing taint-based techniques only detect the presence of exfiltration flow for the sensitive data, but cannot detect how much sensitive data are leaked. Users need more intuitive measures to inform them which apps are going to leak more of their private information. In this paper, we take an alternative approach for identifying apps' internal logic about how they utilize the sensitive data. We define such logic as a sequence of operations on the sensitive data, named as the *data usage pattern*. We build a static analysis tool to automatically extract data usage patterns from Android apps. Our evaluation shows that our approach effectively and efficiently identifies the key operations and thus ranks Android apps according to different usage patterns.

Keywords: Android, Privacy, Static analysis, Information flow analysis.

1 Introduction

The Android system relies on a permission-based model to protect sensitive resources on mobile devices. However, the existing permission-based model relies heavily on users' perception of the permissions. A recent study shows that the Android permissions are insufficient for users to make correct security decisions [6]. Users have little idea about how an application (app) would use the granted permissions. For example, to use the advertised features of an app, users may simply grant the dangerous permission to access their locations. In fact, the app may directly leak the location information to an external third-party domain, or carelessly open new interfaces for other apps to escalate their privileges to access it [3]. Although several existing mechanisms have been proposed to analyze the permission usage in Android apps by detecting what and where permissions are used, they do not provide comprehensive information for users to understand how one app utilizes sensitive data after being granted permission to access. Instead, we need a solution which is both technically comprehensive and sufficiently intuitive to end users. Such a solution should help users to make wise choices to protect their privacy when they are installing new apps.

One well-explored direction in understanding the permission usage is to apply data flow analysis on Android apps [2,4,7,8,13,16,17]. However, most of them only determine whether a flow to leak sensitive resources exists or not, but lack precise description

A. Prakash and R. Shyamasundar (Eds.): ICISS 2014, LNCS 8880, pp. 245–256, 2014.
© Springer International Publishing Switzerland 2014

regarding the internal data processing logic, i.e., whether the data usage leaks a lot of information or only a little. Thus, they are unable to inform users of the difference between an app that sends the raw user location to third parties, and another app that only provides a yes/no answer to whether the user is presently at a certain museum or not. Therefore, a desirable approach should deliver more insight to users regarding how their sensitive data are processed and to what extent they are leaked to other parties.

Quantitative information flow (QIF) is an emerging technique for quantifying the information leakage. Various information-theoretic metrics have been proposed, such as through one particular execution path [14] or publicly observable states [9]. Ideally, QIF could be a suitable tool to evaluate how apps use sensitive resources and how much of such information is leaked. Unfortunately, the performance and scalability of existing QIF algorithms and tools are rather limited in practice. In addition, the Android's event-driven paradigm heavily involves asynchronous system callbacks and user interaction, which makes it even more difficult to apply existing QIF mechanisms. Considering the huge number of Android apps and their frequent updates, we need a more efficient and scalable approach.

Our Approach. In this paper, we propose a lightweight and efficient approach to ranking apps based on how they use sensitive resources. In particular, we take the location data of the mobile device as a starting point. Meanwhile, the technique is also applicable to other data types, such as the device ID and the phone number. The idea is to summarize the sequence of key operations on the location data into a *data usage pattern*, which represents the app's internal logic of the location data usage. By comparing the usage patterns for different apps, we group apps with similar functionality and rank them according to their potential leakage of the location information.

Compared to existing data flow analysis techniques that only detect the presence of sensitive data flows, we focus on identifying the important operations on the sensitive data in such flows, which reflect to what extent the data are leaked. Specifically, we propose PatternRanker, which statically analyzes how an app utilizes the location data by analyzing its Dalvik bytecode, and extracts a general and comprehensive pattern representing the location data usage by identifying key operations on the location data. We collect all the possible operations by leveraging static program slicing and taint-based techniques, and then generate the data usage patterns through pre-defined heuristics. The applicability of the data usage pattern is not limited to app ranking. It can also efficiently assist further analysis, such as accelerating existing QIF solutions by applying their current mechanisms on our extracted patterns instead of on the raw logic of apps. We evaluate PatternRanker on 100 top location-related apps, and our experiments show that PatternRanker effectively extracts the data usage pattern for ranking apps. PatternRanker also achieves an average analysis time of 27s per app, which is sufficiently small for analyzing real-world apps.

To sum up, our work has the following contributions:

- We propose a lightweight and scalable approach to ranking apps' threats to user privacy based on the usage pattern of sensitive information.
- We build a static tool to automatically analyze how Android apps utilize the sensitive data and identify the key operations.

– We evaluate a set of 100 top location-related Android apps, and demonstrate the effectiveness of our approach in ranking these apps and classifying them into different categories according to different data usage patterns.

2 PatternRanker Design

Key Design Decisions. We rank one app based on data operation analysis, instead of its leaking bits. For example, Android provides standard APIs *distanceBetween/distanceTo* for apps to calculate the distance between two points. However, some apps implement their own methods to complete the same task through complex mathematical computation (including *toRadians*, *sin* and *cos*). It is extremely difficult to measure which set of math operations may leak more bits of the raw data. It is also improper to conclude that one is safer for leaking fewer bits of the raw data in one particular run, because they are semantically equal even though they may get slightly different results at runtime. Therefore, considering practicality for analyzing real-world apps, we aim to rank apps through identifying the data usage patterns, more specifically, a sequence of key operations on the sensitive data along one flow reflecting the semantic effectiveness whether they preserve the raw data or not, instead of finding a metric of calculating number of bits that one app may leak.

Therefore, we aim to define a pattern to represent how an app operates on the location data, including not only a present flow from pre-defined sources to sinks, but also the key operations in the flow. The data usage pattern indicates two aspects: through which channel and to what degree the sensitive data are leaked. We use the pattern as our ranking metric. For two different usage patterns, we assign a higher rank to the one that leaks less information in the flow, and a lower rank to the one that has only simple data propagation from a source to a sink. We also consider various sink channels for ranking. For example, it gains a higher rank to share the sensitive data with a trusted service than an uncertain domain.

Assumption. The Android system provides well-defined Java interfaces for Android apps to access resources. It also supports NDK that allows developers to design their apps as native code. However, the native code is usually designed for performance improvement in CPU-intensive scenarios like game engines and physics simulation, instead of Android-specific resource access. Hence, the native code is out of the scope in our analysis. In this section, we detail our design of the data usage pattern and a static approach to automatically extracting it.

2.1 Pattern Definition

We focus on analyzing the types of operations on sensitive data in a data flow. To represent how close the output of one operation is to the raw sensitive data, we attach an attribute *Capacity* to the sensitive data during their propagation. Higher value means the output is closer to the original sensitive data. Thus we define the *Pattern* as a sequence of key bytecode operations, which aims to expressively identify the changes of the capacity in one data flow. The sensitive data enter at the source point with the maximum capacity. During the data flow, an operation may reduce the output's capacity. We also aim to use the pattern to indicate the influence of the sensitive data on the control flow, i.e., whether a code branch is conditionally triggered by the sensitive data. Thus we classify the operations into five categories: **Source**, **Sink**, **Branch**, **Capacity-preserving** and **Capacity-reducing**. Next we explain them in detail.

Source/Sink/Branch. The existing work Susi [15] has given a concrete definition for Android sources and sinks. For sources, we only consider the sources related to the location permission. Additionally, the Android system supports callbacks (e.g., *onLocationChanged*) to pass sensitive data (e.g., GPS). We also consider these sensitive callbacks as sources. In addition to standard sinks, such as network APIs, we treat system state-related APIs (e.g., *setRingerMode*) and IPC channels (e.g., *startActivity*) as sinks. To avoid duplicate analysis on known trusted services and advertising libraries, we also treat these interfaces as sinks. Branch operations refer to the bytecode operations which are essential for exploring execution paths, such as if-* and goto.

Capacity-Preserving/Reducing. Different operations on the sensitive data may generate outputs with different capacities. According to the capacity of the output, we classify the operations into capacity-preserving (the output has the same capacity as the input) and capacity-reducing (the output has lower capacity than the input). When summarizing the operation sequence for one pattern, we ignore capacity-preserving operations because the sensitive data have only direct flow without any change of the capacity. Our goal is to identify those key operations that reduce the capacity of one flow. Next, we illustrate our idea through a simple snippet of sequential operations below.

```
1  invoke-virtual {v0, v1}, Landroid/location/LocationManager;-> getLastKnownLocation(
       Ljava/lang/String;)Landroid/location/Location;
2  move-result-object v2
3  ...
4  invoke-virtual {v2, v3}, Landroid/location/Location;-> distanceTo(
       Landroid/location/Location;)F
5  move-result v4
6  move v4, v5
7  cmpg-float v5, v5, v6
8  if-gtz v5, :cond_1
9  :cond_1
10 ...
11 invoke-virtual {v7, v8}, Landroid/media/AudioManager;->setRingerMode(I)V
```

In the above code, we can easily identify its source and sink as Line 1 and Line 11. Line 1 accesses the current location and moves it to v2 (Line 2). Line 4 calculates the distance between the current location with another point, marked as capacity-reducing operation (CRO). The result is moved to v4 and then to v5. Then Line 7 compares the distance with one value, and sets the comparison result in v5. Line 8 uses the comparison result as a condition to trigger a code branch that contains the sink API. The pattern for this code snippet is shown as follows.

```
1  E(SOURCE): invoke-virtual, Landroid/location/LocationManager;-> getLastKnownLocation(
       Ljava/lang/String;)Landroid/location/Location;
2  E(CRO): invoke-virtual, Landroid/location/Location;-> distanceTo(
       Landroid/location/Location;)F
3  E(CRO): cmpg-float
4  E(BRANCH): if-gtz
5  E(SINK): invoke-virtual, Landroid/media/AudioManager;->setRingerMode(I)V
```

It is challenging to precisely distinguish whether an operation is capacity-preserving or capacity-reducing because it varies in different contexts due to two main scenarios: *Uncertain Operand* and *Uncertain Method*. Whether one opcode preserves the capacity depends on its operands. For example, `add-int vx,vy,vz` calculates `vy+vz` and puts the result into `vx`. Supposing `vy` is the raw sensitive data, it depends on `vz` whether the result `vx` maintains the same amount of sensitive information. The operand may come from an external source, such as *SharedPreferences*, external storage, network and Android-specific IPC channels, which is difficult for static analysis to determine. Fortunately, most above uncertain scenarios are rare to happen among the popular apps that we have studied. Thus we treat them as constant values. Similarly, if it invokes an external method that is out of our analysis code base, we are uncertain about what kinds of operations will be possibly performed on the sensitive data. In this case, we treat the external method invocation as capacity-preserving (the worse case) by default. To reduce the overestimation, we semantically model frequently used libraries, such as String, Math and parts of Android APIs.

2.2 Ranking Metric

Our ranking is based on two factors: 1) through which channel the data are leaked; 2) to what degree the data are leaked. Note that one app may contain multiple patterns. Here we demonstrate the metric for ranking one pattern. We use the lowest one to represent the rank for the whole app. According to the various sinks, we classify patterns into two main categories: *In-App Usage* with a higher rank and *Sharing* with a lower rank.

For the category of in-app usage, we further classify into two subcategories: capacity-reducing pattern with a higher rank and capacity-preserving pattern with a lower rank. In a capacity-preserving pattern, the sink in the flow outputs the same amount of information as the raw sensitive data, while a capacity-reducing pattern only infers less amount of information. However, it is difficult to justify two capacity-reducing patterns, for it is improper to claim that two capacity-reducing operations (e.g., *subString*) leak less information than one. In future work, we will consider more metrics as references to compare two capacity-reducing patterns, such as how many bits of information are leaked generally in multiple runs, by applying symbolic execution-based mechanisms [11, 12] on our extracted patterns to efficiently simulate multiple runs of the program and evaluate the impact of these extracted key operations on the sensitive data. For now, as a first step, we only target on identifying these key operations from large-scale real-world Android apps, and thus give a rough classification while leaving further analysis as future work.

For the category of sharing, considering the scenario that it is more acceptable for users to share even the raw location data to trusted services, such as Google Map service, than to share one bit of information with untrusted domains, we further group them into three subcategories according to various sharing domains, from high rank to low rank which are *Known Trusted Services*, *Advertising Libraries* and *Uncertain Parties*. We use a whitelist to maintain the known trusted services and advertising libraries. We give the lowest rank to those apps that transfer the location data to uncertain third party domains through network APIs, WebView APIs, SMS APIs and IPC channels. Usually, apps use dedicated libraries for common services and advertising (e.g., Google

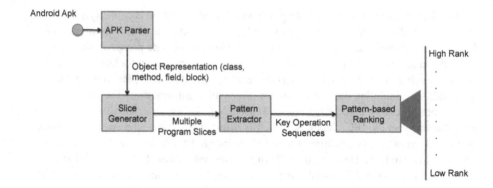

Fig. 1. The Architecture of PatternRanker

map), instead of re-implementing their own through raw Android interfaces (e.g., network APIs). The uncertain channels are mostly used to share content and resources with apps' own third party servers or can only be determined at runtime. Therefore, even though more information (e.g., the recipient's network address, phone number and package name) via these uncertain channels can be mined by applying backward analysis or dynamic instrumentation, they still fall into the uncertain subcategory. Instead, we simply categorize the sharing domains through a whitelist-based filter for common trusted services and advertising libraries collected from large-scale real-world apps.

2.3 PatternRanker Architecture

Figure 1 illustrates the overall architecture. *APK Parser* parses the Android apk into appropriate object representations, such as Smali classes, methods and fields. *Slice Generator* uses slicing technique to generate all the program slices that start from accessing the location data. *Pattern Extractor* extracts the pattern by identifying the key operations in each slice. We design a *Pattern-based Ranking* to rank the apps based on various patterns. Next we explain each component in detail.

Apk Parser. We design static analysis directly on Android disassembled Smali code, which overcomes limitations of the Dalvik-to-Java bytecode transformation [5]. The apk is parsed into Smali files and represented as multiple Smali classes. Each Smali class object is represented as a set of methods and fields. Each method can be further decomposed into several sequential blocks according to its internal branches. Therefore, inside one block, the instructions are sequential without any control flow. The block is treated as a minimum unit for our further analysis.

Slice Generator. We first identify the source points in the app and then perform bottom-to-top analysis. To explore all possible flow paths, we consider field-sensitive flow and Android-specific callbacks into the API hierarchy. To support field-sensitive flow analysis, if the sensitive data is put into one field of a Java object in one method, say M, we also mark all the methods reading that field as top methods of M. Specially, the Android's event-driven paradigm supports asynchronous invocation, such as *Handler*,

Thread and *AsyncTask*. We also bridge the data flow for these scenarios. However, we do not preserve the data flow if it flows outside the app, such as file system, network and IPC channels. From bottom to top, we analyze each method in the call chain. Intuitively, we start tracking the sensitive data from the source point and propagate the taint tags to its top methods.

Now we explain how we analyze inside one method. The method is composed of multiple blocks. We start tainting the sensitive data from the first block with the per-register and per-field granularity. At the beginning of our analysis for each block, we allocate a set of tracked registers and a set of tracked fields. Inside one block, the execution is sequential and the taint tags are propagated according to pre-defined simple propagation rules for each bytecode instruction (e.g., `move` instruction and common math operations). During the tainting, we dynamically update the tracked register set and field set. Specially, if one method invocation involves any tainted input, we dive into the callee method to figure out its internal logic. Note that to support field-sensitive analysis, the input/output of one method include not only the parameters and the return value, but also all the object fields that may be accessed inside it. For efficiency, we do not dive into any method in the publicly known libraries, such as Android SDK, advertising/analytics libraries and other known third-party services. After finishing one block, we go further to its next blocks. The tracked register set and field set are used as the initial sets for its next blocks. To record the control flow, if a branch operation involves a tainted operand, then all the sinks in its branch are treated to be related with sensitive data leakage. However, it may cause overtainting problem to simply taint all the next blocks if the branch condition is tainted. Thus to mitigate this problem, we only maintain the control flow relationship among blocks when the next block of one branch operation has only one reachable path determined by this branch condition.

Pattern Extractor. After we get the program slices, we post-process them to extract patterns. Each slice is treated as sequential operations. We identify whether an opcode is capacity-preserving or capacity-reducing through pre-defined heuristics. Specially, we treat all external methods as capacity-preserving. To reduce false positive, we semantically mark certain Math/String APIs and location-related Android APIs as capacity-reducing, such as *distanceTo/distanceBetween*. For common math operations, `cmp-*`, `cmpl-*`, `cmpg-*`, `rem-*`, `and-*`, `or-*`, `neg-*` are capacity-reducing operations, while `add-*`, `mul-*`, `div-*`, `rsub-*`, `sub-*`, `shl-*`, `*-to-*` are capacity-preserving operations. It is a capacity-reducing operation if it satisfies the following property: even if the sensitive operand is operated with a constant, the result value is still generally unable to recover the sensitive value, such as `and-int`. Specially, we treat `*-to-*` as capacity-preserving, which indicates the data conversion, such as `double-to-int`. Although the conversion may lose the accuracy of the raw data, it semantically behaves like a `move` operation.

Pattern-Based Ranking. As described in Section 2.2, our ranking system is based on two factors: through which channel and to what degree the data are leaked inside one pattern. Thus, we classify the extracted patterns by checking their sinks (indicating the leaking channel and the possible receiver) and their capacities (indicating whether one pattern contains any capacity-reducing operation). As shown in Figure 2, we first

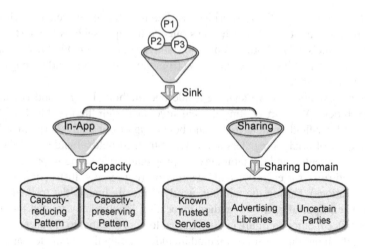

Fig. 2. Pattern-based Ranking Schema

classify the apps into two main categories: in-app usage and sharing, by checking the sinks of the patterns. For the category of sharing, we further classify them into three subcategories based on different sharing domains by grouping various sinks. For the category of in-app usage, we group them into two subcategories: capacity-reducing pattern and capacity-preserving pattern, by checking whether the capacity of sensitive data at the sink point is smaller than that at the source point.

3   Evaluation

We implement a standalone tool via Java, which directly works on disassembled Smali code. It leverages the existing tool SAAF [10] to disassemble Android apks and parse the Smali files into appropriate object representations, such as blocks and fields. We implement the slice generator and pattern extractor. We collected 100 top location-related Android apps from the official Android market (i.e., Google Play) as our sample set, and ran our PatternRanker prototype in a Debian system on a server of Intel Xeon E5-2640@2.50GHz with 64G memory. Next, we show our evaluation results in detail.

3.1   App Analysis on Location Usage

Specifically, we found that 28 apps in our sample set have capacity-reducing patterns for in-app usage. Sharing is an appealing feature on the mobile platform, especially as the social networking becomes popular. From our observation, a common usage for location data is to share the raw location data with trusted services and advertising libraries. According to our ranking design, we list them in the following categories from high rank to low rank, shown as Figure 3. One app may include multiple patterns. Here the statistics for each category shows the number of apps having that pattern.

1) In-App Usage: Capacity-reducing Pattern. We identified that 28 apps have capacity-reducing patterns. 15 of them do the distance calculation operation, among which 10 use the default *distanceTo/distanceBetween* Android APIs and the rest 5 implement distance calculation by themselves using Math libraries. Next we take two examples to demonstrate the extracted patterns from them.

Auto Profile Switcher app, with 1,000 - 5,000 downloads, allows users to configure several profiles, such as *home* and *work*. It automatically switches the profile based on the current location. The extracted pattern for it is shown below. They implement the distance calculation through Math library. The pattern indicates that the app makes a complex mathematical computation on the location data and compares the result with a special value via `cmpg-float`. Through manual analysis, we observed that this special value is read from local storage implemented as *SharedPreferences*. This information can be obtained automatically by applying backward dependency analysis on key operands, which we consider as future work. In the end, the comparison result determines the invocation of a sink API *setRingerMode*.

```
1  E(SOURCE): invoke-virtual, Landroid/location/LocationManager;-> getLastKnownLocation(
           Ljava/lang/String;)Landroid/location/Location;
2  E(CRO): invoke-virtual, Landroid/location/Location;->getLatitude()D
3  E(CRO): invoke-virtual, Landroid/location/Location;->getLongitude()D
4  E(CRO): invoke-static/range, Ljava/lang/Math;->toRadians(D)D
5  E(CRO): ...
6  E(CRO): invoke-static/range, Ljava/lang/Math;->atan2(DD)D
7  E(CRO): cmpg-float
8  E(BRANCH): if-gtz
9  E(SINK): invoke-virtual, Landroid/media/AudioManager;->setRingerMode(I)V
```

Another example shows the internal logic of how the GPS data affect the display. *GPS Speedometer* is a functional speedometer app with 50,000 - 100,000 downloads. It displays the user's location and travel history. One capacity-reducing pattern extracted from this app is shown below. The sink is a display API *setText*. However, the pattern shows that the GPS data go through multiple comparisons and branch opcodes to finally decide the string to be displayed. Through manual analysis, we observed that the app essentially compares the current bearing with a set of constant values and then decides to display a string from `N, NE, E, ES, S, SW, W, NW`.

```
1  E(SOURCE): Lcom/ape/apps/speedometer/SpeedometerMain;-> onLocationChanged(
           Landroid/location/Location;)
2  E(CRO): invoke-virtual, Landroid/location/Location;->getBearing()F
3  E(CRO): cmpl-double
4  E(BRANCH): if-gez
5  E(CRO): cmpg-double
6  E(CRO): ...
7  E(BRANCH): if-gez
8  E(SINK): invoke-virtual, Landroid/widget/TextView;-> setText(Ljava/lang/CharSequence;)V
```

2) In-App Usage: Capacity-preserving Pattern. Information display is one important feature for apps to rich their functionality and convenient users. 25 apps displayed GPS-related information, such as position and signal strength of satellites, accuracy, speed, acceleration and altitude. We observed the following UI-related sinks: *TextView(19), Canvas(7), Toast(3), RemoteViews(2), EditText(1), Notification(1)*.

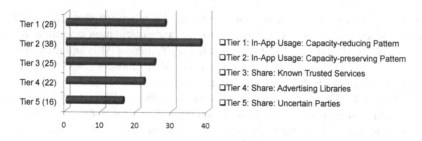

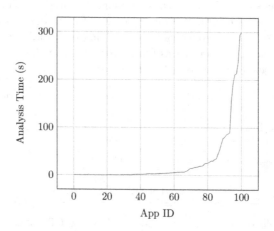

Legend:
- Tier 1: In-App Usage: Capacity-reducing Pattern
- Tier 2: In-App Usage: Capacity-preserving Pattern
- Tier 3: Share: Known Trusted Services
- Tier 4: Share: Advertising Libraries
- Tier 5: Share: Uncertain Parties

Fig. 3. Ranking Results of Extracted Patterns

Fig. 4. Analysis Time Distribution

30 apps logged the GPS data locally. 13 of them directly sent the data to the `LogCat`, which is a public channel for all the installed apps with the `READ_LOGS` permission. However, through manual analysis on the path condition, we found most of them only logged the GPS data in debug mode. This can be verified through the dynamic instrumentation framework [18]. We also observed other logging channels: *database(10), Bundle(4), Java/IO(8)* and *SharedPreferences(6)*.

3) Share: Known Trusted Services. From our statistic in this category, 25 apps used Google map service while the rest 9 used other third-party services.

4) Share: Advertising Libraries. In-app advertising has become an important revenue-generating model for mobile apps. Many of them requested the GPS location for providing targeted advertisement. We observed 22 apps include advertising/analytics libraries potentially accessing the location data from 18 different advertising providers. Commonly one app includes multiple advertising libraries to increase its ads revenue.

5) Share: Uncertain Parties. We also observed that 8 apps share the GPS via IPC channels. For the rest uncertain scenarios, we observed the following sinks: *org/apache/*/HttpPost(5), java/net/DatagramSocket(1), WebView→loadDataWithBaseURL (1)* and *sendTextMessage (1)*. We manually analyzed the WebView and SMS scenarios. In the app *GPS QIBLA LOCATOR*, it uses the WebView API to load an iframe with a URL composed of a fixed third party domain and the geolocation as the parameters.

Mobile Chase-GPS Tracker registers an *onLocationChanged* listener, inside which it composes an SMS message using the location information and sends it to a phone number stored in the *SharedPreferences*.

3.2 Analysis Time

Figure 4 shows the distribution of analysis time for all the apps. Note that the analysis time excludes the apk parsing that can be pre-processed. The average of analysis time is about 27s per app. 35% of apps finished within 1 sec, due to the simple flow of the location data in them. Within one minute, we achieved 87% coverage. Comparing with other analysis tools [1, 19] at the scale of minutes or larger for real-world apps, the average analysis time of our approach is sufficiently small for ranking a large number of Android apps.

4 Conclusion

To provide users with more intuitive measures to understand how apps treat their privacy, we build a tool PatternRanker to automatically extract the data usage pattern to express it. Comparing to existing taint-based techniques that focus on detecting the presence of one flow, our approach effectively identifies the key operations in the flow. Our experiments on the real-world apps demonstrate its effectiveness and efficiency for ranking a large number of apps.

Acknowledgments. We thank anonymous reviewers for their valuable feedback. We thank Prateek Saxena for his comments on an early presentation of this work. This research is partially supported by the research grant R-252-000-519-112 from Ministry of Education, Singapore. Xinshu Dong is supported by the research grant for the Human Sixth Sense Programme at the Advanced Digital Sciences Center from Singapore's Agency for Science, Technology and Research (A*STAR).

References

1. Arzt, S., Rasthofer, S., Fritz, C., Bodden, E., Bartel, A., Klein, J., Le Traon, Y., Octeau, D., McDaniel, P.: FlowDroid: Precise Context, Flow, Field, Object-sensitive and Lifecycle-aware Taint Analysis for Android Apps. In: PLDI (2014)
2. Chan, P.P., Hui, L.C., Yiu, S.M.: DroidChecker: Analyzing Android Applications for Capability Leak. In: WISEC (2012)
3. Davi, L., Dmitrienko, A., Sadeghi, A.-R., Winandy, M.: Privilege Escalation Attacks on Android. In: Burmester, M., Tsudik, G., Magliveras, S., Ilić, I. (eds.) ISC 2010. LNCS, vol. 6531, pp. 346–360. Springer, Heidelberg (2011)
4. Enck, W., Gilbert, P., Chun, B.G., Cox, L.P., Jung, J., McDaniel, P., Sheth, A.N.: TaintDroid: an Information-Flow Tracking System for Realtime Privacy Monitoring on Smartphones. In: OSDI (2010)
5. Enck, W., Octeau, D., McDaniel, P., Chaudhuri, S.: A Study of Android Application Security. In: USENIX SECURITY (2011)

6. Felt, A.P., Ha, E., Egelman, S., Haney, A., Chin, E., Wagner, D.: Android Permissions: User Attention, Comprehension, and Behavior. In: SOUPS (2012)
7. Gibler, C., Crussell, J., Erickson, J., Chen, H.: AndroidLeaks: Automatically Detecting Potential Privacy Leaks in Android Applications on a Large Scale. In: Katzenbeisser, S., Weippl, E., Camp, L.J., Volkamer, M., Reiter, M., Zhang, X. (eds.) Trust 2012. LNCS, vol. 7344, pp. 291–307. Springer, Heidelberg (2012)
8. Grace, M., Zhou, Y., Wang, Z., Jiang, X.: Systematic Detection of Capability Leaks in Stock Android Smartphones. In: NDSS (2012)
9. Heusser, J., Malacaria, P.: Quantifying Information Leaks in Software. In: ACSAC (2010)
10. Hoffmann, J., Ussath, M., Holz, T., Spreitzenbarth, M.: Slicing Droids: Program Slicing for Smali Code. In : SAC (2013)
11. Jeon, J., Micinski, K.K., Foster, J.S.: SymDroid: Symbolic Execution for Dalvik Bytecode. Technical Report CS-TR-5022, Univ. of Maryland (2012)
12. Kim, J., Yoon, Y., Yi, K., Shin, J.: ScanDal: Static Analyzer for Detecting Privacy Leaks in Android Applications. In: MOST (2012)
13. Lu, L., Li, Z., Wu, Z., Lee, W., Jiang, G.: CHEX: Statically Vetting Android Apps for Component Hijacking Vulnerabilities. In: CCS (2012)
14. McCamant, S., Ernst, M.D.: Quantitative Information Flow as Network Flow Capacity. In: PLDI (2008)
15. Rasthofer, S., Arzt, S., Bodden, E.: A Machine-learning Approach for Classifying and Categorizing Android Sources and Sinks. In: NDSS (2014)
16. Sbîrlea, D., Burke, M.G., Guarnieri, S., Pistoia, M., Sarkar, V.: Automatic Detection of Inter-application Permission Leaks in Android Applications. Technical Report TR13-02, Rice University (2013)
17. Wu, L., Grace, M., Zhou, Y., Wu, C., Jiang, X.: The Impact of Vendor Customizations on Android Security. In: CCS (2013)
18. Yan, L.K., Yin, H.: DroidScope: Seamlessly Reconstructing the OS and Dalvik Semantic Views for Dynamic Android Malware Analysis. In: USENIX SECURITY (2012)
19. Yang, Z., Yang, M., Zhang, Y., Gu, G., Ning, P., Wang, X.S.: AppIntent: Analyzing Sensitive Data Transmission in Android for Privacy Leakage Detection. In: CCS (2013)

Privacy Leakage Attacks in Browsers by Colluding Extensions

Anil Saini[1], Manoj Singh Gaur[1], Vijay Laxmi[1],
Tushar Singhal[1], and Mauro Conti[2]

[1] Malaviya National Institute of Technology, Jaipur, India
{anil.cse,gaurms,vlgaur,tushar.singhal}@mnit.ac.in
[2] University of Padua, Italy
conti@math.unipd.it

Abstract. Browser Extensions (BE) enhance the core functionality of the Browser and provide customization to it. Browser extensions enjoy high privileges, sometimes with the same privileges as Browser itself. As a consequence, a vulnerable or malicious extension might expose Browser and system resources to attacks. This may put Browser resources at risk of unwanted operations, privilege escalation etc. BE can snoop on web applications, launch arbitrary processes, and even access files from host file system. In addition to that, an extension can even collude with other installed extensions to share objects and change preferences. Although well-intentioned, extension developers are often not security experts. Hence, they might end up writing vulnerable code. In this paper we present a new attacks via Browser extensions. In particular, the attack allows two malicious extensions to communicate and collaborate with each other in such a way to achieve a malicious goal. We identify the vulnerable points in extension development framework as: (a) object reference sharing, and (b) preference overriding. We illustrate the effectiveness of the proposed attack using various attack scenarios. Furthermore, we provide a proof-of-concept illustration for web domains including Banking & shopping. We believe that the scenarios we use in use-case demonstration underlines the severity of the presented attack. Finally, we also contribute an initial framework to address the presented attack.

Keywords: Cyber Attacks, Browser Attacks, Script-based Attacks, Malicious Scripts, Extension-based Attacks, Browser Vulnerabilities.

1 Introduction

Modern web Browsers support an architecture that allows third-party extensions to enhance the core functionality of the Browser [3]. For example, Firefox provides millions of free extensions to customize and enhance the look and feel of the Browser and enrich rendering of multimedia web content. Firefox provides extensions code to run with full chrome (chrome is the entities making up the user interface of a specific application or extension) privileges including access to

A. Prakash and R. Shyamasundar (Eds.): ICISS 2014, LNCS 8880, pp. 257–276, 2014.
© Springer International Publishing Switzerland 2014

all Browser components, OS resources such as file system and network services, Browser DOM (Document Object Model) [2], and all web page elements. Consequently, malicious and benign vulnerable extensions are significant security threats. The authors have shown that malicious extension could spy on users and install malwares [5,13].

The Browser extension system provides XPCOM (Cross Platform Component Object model) interface APIs that allow one extension to communicate with the objects of other extensions. These interfaces if exploited by malicious extensions could lead to critical attacks. For example, consider two legitimate extensions with the following functionalities: the first extension (X) has the functionality to capture information from any web page whereas the second extension (Y) is able to communicate with network channel. Individually, the functionality of these extensions looks benign, and their information flow, when analysed, cannot be considered as malicious. However, if X is able to communicate sensitive information to Y, this flow could be considered as malicious. Both X and Y can send critical information captured from a web page to the attacker through the network channel. Since attack is the combined activities of two extension, it will not be detected by a method that analyzes individual extension statically or dynamically.

The current research for detecting malicious flow in extensions is primarily focused on an assumption that a single extension can only be used as a source of attack. The paper demonstrates the weakness of this assumption, shows how two legitimate extensions with benign functionality can communicate with each other to deploy critical attacks. Several methods have been proposed to detect malicious or vulnerable extensions [12,14,16]. In this paper, we focus on two of the more popular ones: VEX [12], and SABRE [14]. These methods are able to detect the vulnerable points or tainted JavaScript objects in a Browser extension. Unfortunately these methods check tainted objects or flow originating within an extension only. In particular, these methods do not examine whether the source has originated from some other extension. This is the primary reason why these methods are not effective for resulting from colluding extensions.

In this paper, we discuss the weaknesses of Firefox extension system in handling JavaScript objects. This will lead to some vulnerable points, which an attacker can exploit. We also present a proof-of-concept of the attacks showing how a reference of the JavaScript object of one extension can be invoked by another extension for *accessing* and *sharing* critical information. This suspicious nature is difficult to capture with the known detection approaches [12] [14]. We have addressed the exploitable coding features in two important XPCOM interfaces [7], and JavaScript Wrapper method offered by Firefox. We have demonstrated our finding on different web domain applications and showed how two legitimate extensions can collude with each other to achieve malicious goals in a Browser.

The rest of the paper is organized as follows. In Section 2, we describe a background of XPCOM framework and interfaces. A discussion on how colluding extensions can carry out a malicious activity through inter-extension communication is discussed in Section 4. In Section 5, we present the implementation and evaluation of attacks. Section 6 presents few suggestion about the mitigation techniques. Section 7 surveys the related work and Section 8 presents our conclusion and describes future work.

2   Background and Assumptions

In this section, we present XPCOM framework in brief highlighting the components that are subject to be exploited.

XPCOM Framework: XPCOM is a cross platform component object model, similar to Microsoft COM [24], which provides a set of core components, classes related to file and memory management, threads, basic data structures (strings, arrays, variants), etc. The interaction of Firefox components and its extension are shown in Figure 1. The extensions in Firefox Browser interact with Browser components through XPCOM framework, which provides variety of services within the Browser, such as file system access, process launching, network access, Browser components and APIs access. The JavaScript in extension uses XPconnect [8] to invoke XPCOM components. XPConnect act as a bridge between JavaScript and XPCOM. The user interface of Firefox extension is programmed using XUL (XML User Interface Language). Firefox extensions can randomly change the user interface of the Browser via a technique known as overlays [9] written in XUL. CSS are used to add the presentation and visual styles to the Firefox extension.

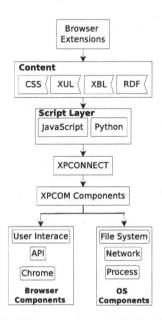

Fig. 1. XPCOM Architecture View in Firefox Extension System

Extension Development: Firefox supports a variety of languages such as XUL (XML User Interface Language), JavaScript and CSS (Cascading Style Sheets) for extension development. It is quite very easy for an attacker to develop malicious extensions for deploying attacks on to Browsers. In [18, 20], we have presented various weaknesses in Firefox extensions that can be used for malicious purpose and few attacks against a number of popular Firefox extensions. An inexperienced user might install a Browser extension by accident, without knowing the consequences.

Assumptions: In this paper, we assume that colluding extensions are installed in the Browser of the victim. The attacker may supply extensions either using social engineering techniques or adding them to Mozilla Add-ons database, may be at different times to evade detection of collusion. As, individually, an extension is benign, it could be added to Mozilla Firefox add-on store. Also, user believing that it is safe to download from this database, may download and install the extensions. Throughout this paper we discuss about extensions or Browser extensions that are compatible with Firefox Browser.

3   XPCOM Interfaces

An interface in Mozilla is a definition of a set of functionalities that could be implemented by XPCOM components. Each component implements the functionality as described by interfaces. A single component might implement multiple interfaces, and multiple components might implement the same interface. XPCOM components are typically implemented natively, which means that they generally do things that JavaScript cannot do itself. However, there is a way in which you can call them by creating an instance of an interface. We can call any of the functions provided by the component as described by the interfaces it implements. For example, a File interface describes properties and functions that can be performed on files. A file would need properties for its name, modification date and its size. Functions of a file would include moving, copying and deleting it. The File interface only describes the characteristics of a file, it won't provide any implementation. The implementation part of the File interface is provided by components. The component will have code which can retrieve the file's name, date and size. In addition, it will have code which copies and renames it. Thus, we can use a component by accessing it using the functions we know from the interface.

In Mozilla, interfaces are usually preceded by *nsI* or *mozI* so that they are easily recognized as interfaces. For example, the `nsIFile` is the interface for interacting with a File System, `nsICookie` is used for accessing JavaScript or HTTP cookies. In this paper, We focus on two interfaces: (i) `nsIObserver`, and (ii) `nsIPrefService`. We will discussed these interfaces in details in Section 4.

3.1   Interface Security Risks

To enhance the Browser functionality and get customizable features, Firefox provides extentions to execute with full Browser privileges. To gain system access

(OS, Network and Browser components), an extension uses XPCOM interface that provides APIs to communicate with Web applications, Browser, and Operating System (OS) components. Figure 2 illustrates the privileges associated with a JavaScript code. The JavaScript-based Extensions (JSEs) and Chrome JavaScript can access the Browser and the OS components by invoking methods described in interfaces whereas the Web Application JavaScript cannot call XPCOM interface. Additionally privileges gained through XPCOM interfaces are not restricted by any Browser policy. For example, the web applications are bound with same origin policy (SOP) [25] but extensions can override this and access cross-domain components. These unbounded restricts makes an extension potential source of Browser attacks.

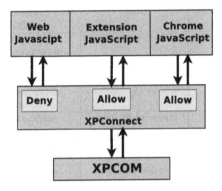

Fig. 2. Scripting Permissions on Firefox extension

Unrestricted access, powerful privileges, and ease in development make these interfaces very popular among extension developers. As these developers are often not security experts, there is strong possibility of bugged/vulnerable code that is liable to exploitation by malicious extensions. We have considered some of the critical functionalities provided by interface methods that may pose security risks in Browsers. We classified security risk in terms of attack vector that defines the key attack areas used by an attacker i.e. *likelihood of attack*. An attack vector represents different domains of Browser system targeted by an attacker through XPCOM interfaces. We categorize the actions performed by an attacker into different attack vectors as shown in Table 1 that also lets the interface used to invoke the resources, the severity of an attack action (critical, high, moderate and low). For example, the information accessed from password fields, cookies is always critical to user and hence rated critical. Interfaces which allows to access arbitrary files and processes on host system are also very critical because using them an attacker can launch a malware process and alter user files. Mozilla and Chromium define the security severity ratings [10] [11] based on the information flows among various resources.

Table 1. Attack Vectors for Extension-based Attacks

S.no	Attack Class	Resources Accessed Exploited	Interface Used	Rating
1.	Accessing Password from Web page	DOM	`nsIDOMNode,` `nsIDOMElement`	Critical
2.	Launching arbitrary local application	Invoke Process	`nsIProcess`	Critical

3.	Cross-domain access and violation	Network Channel	`nsIXMLHttpRequest,`
			`nsIHttpChannel,`
			`nsITransport`
				High

4.	Profile Attack [20]	File System	`nsIFile,`
			`nsILocaFile,`
			`nsIOutputStream`
				Critical

5.	Accessing Confidential hata	DOM	`nsDOMNode,` `nsIDOMElement`	High

6.	Stealing Local Files	File System(OS)	`nsIInputStream,`
			`nsIFileInputStream,`
			`nsILocalFile,`
			`nsIFile`
				High

7.	Accessing Browser history	Browser Components	`nsIBrowserHistory,` `nsIGlobalHistory`	Moderate
8.	Accessing Stored passwords	Password Manager	`nsILoginManager,` `nsILoginManagerStorage`	Moderate
9.	Accessing events	Keyboard & Mouse events	`nsIEventListenerService`	Moderate

10.	Session stealing	Cookie manager	`nsICookieManager,`
			`nsICookie,`
			`nsICookie2,`
			`nsICookieService`
				Critical

11.	Accessing Bookmarks	Bookmark Service	`nsINavBookmarksService`	Low
12.	Setting Browser preferences	Preference System	`nsIPrefService,` `nsIPrefBrach`	High
13.	Setting Extension preferences	Preference System	`nsIPrefService,` `nsIPrefBrach`	High
14.	Accessing Page Information(Images/text)	DOM	`nsIDOMNode,` `nsIDOMElement`	Low
15.	Turn on/off private browsing mode	Browser Component	`nsIPrivateBrowsingService`	Moderate
16.	Access to windows registry system	Windows Registry	`nsIWindowsRegKey`	High

4   Extension Communication

Sometimes the Browser needs to send a message from one component to another component leading to inter component communication. For example, a Browser might want to notify another component that a task is completed by a particular component. This may lead to several different actions to be performed by the other component. Browser extension system provides us this feature so that a user can access different components. XPCOM offers an easy way to achieve this functionality using observers and the observer service interfaces. Also, Browser does not provide any isolation among multiple extensions running simultaneously in same address space. So if an extension X is accessing some information through component C_1 and notifies to extension Y. Extension Y may have transitive access on information which was accessed by C_1. An attacker can exploit of this inter-extension communication to deploy privacy leakage attacks.

4.1   Communication Interface: nsIObserverService

Observers are objects that are notified on occurrence of an event. Using them is a good way for objects to pass messages to each other without the objects having explicit knowledge of one another. Firefox provides an interface called nsIObserverService to allow a client listener to register and unregister a nsIObserver object. This service provides methods used to dynamically add or remove an observer from a notification topic. It also provides APIs to notify registered listeners and a way to enumerate registered client listeners. To register for any event, an object first must implement the nsIObserver interface, only after the observer service implementing nsIObserverService can notify an object of registered events by means of this interface. Listing 1.1 shows an example code for implementing nsIObserver that is registered to receive notifications for the topic myTopicID. Lines 1-3 create an object myObserver which listens notification on a string myTopicID with a weak reference. Line 5 creates an object observerService of nsIObserverService interface. The function in lines 6-9 is called when notification occurs. Once a notification occurs, the myObserver is used for receiving the notification on string topic. The first parameter subject is notification specific interface pointer whose action is being observed, topic is the string on which the notification occurred, and data is auxiliary data describing the resultant change or action. Lines 10-11 add the observer on myTopicID, which is observed by myObserver in line 7 and the lines 13-14 are used to unregister myTopicID.

```
1  observer = new myObserver();
2  function myObserver() {
3  this.register();
4  }
5  var observerService = Components.classes[" @mozilla.org/
       observer-service;1"].getservice(components.interface.
       nsIObserverService);
6  myObserver.prototype = {
7  observer: function(subject, topic, data) {
8
9  // extension statements here....
10  },
11  register: function() {
12  observerService.addObserver(this, "myTopicID", false);
```

```
13
14  },
15  unregister: function() {
16  observerService.removeObserver(this, "myTopicID");
17  }
18  }
```

Listing 1.1. Code for Registering an Observer

Modes of Operation: In this section, we have presented two modes of operation using which one extension can share reference of an object with other extension. So, one extension can access an object of other and call functions from that reference. This reference can be used for invoking functions. For example, if an one extension X has a method to access the cookie information, and another extension Y has a method to send information to a remote site. Exploiting to the method of Y, X can send this information on the remote site. Data leakage can be enacted in following ways.

- **Mode 1:** In this mode, X use an object of Y that defines myStr. X creates an observer on myStr. Y passes a reference of an object Obj through wrappedJSObject using notifyObservers() method to X. Now X object call method of Y with Obj's reference using sub variable. As illustrated in Figure 3, X is calling anyMethod() of Y using Obj's reference. The code snippet and interaction flow of two extensions is shown in Figure 3.

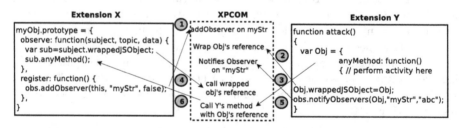

Fig. 3. Mode-1 showing how Extension X can use an object of Extension Y using notifyObserver method

- **Mode 2:** We show one more way to set colluding interaction between two extensions. In this mode, Y can use an object of X that has created an observer on myString. X passes a reference to an object myObj through wrappedJSObject to Y. In this case, the enumerateObserver() is used by Y to enumerate all observers registered for topic myString. Subsequently, Y can access the reference of the object passed by X, and can call method of X with myObj's reference. The code snippet and interaction flow between two extensions are illustrated in Figure 4.

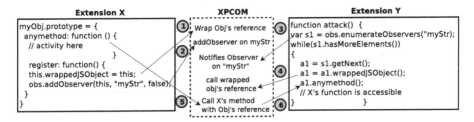

Fig. 4. Mode-1 showing how Extension X can use an object of Extension Y using notifyObserver() method

4.2 Preferences Interface: nsIPrefService

Preferences API allows an extension to read and write strings, numbers, booleans, and references to files to the preferences store. It is relatively easy to use, while providing a number of useful development features, including support for default preferences, preference overrides via user.js, and locking. The preferences API is part of XPCOM components and interfaces. Firefox supports; (1) nsIPrefService interface, which allows to manage the preferences files and also facilitates access to the preference branch object, (2) nsIPrefBranch that can be used for direct manipulation of preferences data. For example, in the Home Page Scheduler, the default home page URL and all the scheduled home pages need to be saved somewhere so that each time the user opens Firefox the data is available. Firefox provides you with the Preferences System for these tasks. We can see all of the currently stored preferences in Firefox using *about:config* into the location bar. This page will show you a listing of all the current preferences and their values, such as, *Browser.startup.homepage* tells the Browser what page to load when the user wishes to visit their home page.

From the attacker's perspective, these preferences can be set or modified for achieving malicious goals. For example, an attacker, through a malicious extension added to victim's Browser can set a malicious page as a home page. He can also modify the critical preferences of security tool such as *noscript* [19], change Browser's privacy settings allowing access to private data etc. In Firefox, an extension has privilege to change the preferences of Browsers as well as any other extension. In this paper, we will show how two preference management interfaces (nsIPrefService and nsIBranch) can be used by attacker to set or reset the stored preferences. We describe two potential attack points that can be exploited by an attacker through preferences system.

- **Changing Browser's Preferences:** Browser has many security related preferences, such as, enable/disable cookies/JavaScript, privacy settings etc. An attacker can set or reset critical Browser preferences through an extension having privileges to override the default preferences values. For example, we can disable the Firefox pop-up blocking by setting *dom.disable_open_during_load* preference value to *true*. Figure 5 shows an example for changing preference of the Browser.

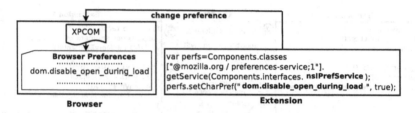

Fig. 5. Changing privacy settings of web Browser

- **Changing Extension's Preferences:** Some extensions use preferences for customizing itself. For example, *noscript* provides the preference to set whitelisting URLs so that it can be bypassed. An extension can change these preferences without user's notice. We have implemented an extension for bypassing *noScript*(a security tool provided by Firefox) using `nsIprefService`. Our extension is able to change critical preferences of *noScript*. We have added a malicious domain(eg. malicious.com) in *noScript* using *capability. policy.manoscript.sites* preference string, so that it bypasses all its security checks provided by *noScript* for that domain. The code snippet of our extension is shown in Figure 6.

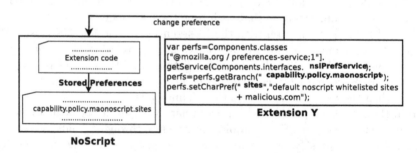

Fig. 6. Changing Preference of NoScript Extension

5   Browser Attacks and Evaluation

We have presented two techniques for achieving privacy leakage as follows:

- Object collusion technique using sharing of object references.
- Collusion through Preference technique by changing Browser and extension preferences.

In Object Collusion technique, we demonstrate the impact of collusion-based attack on three major web domains; Banking, Online Shopping, and domains that offer Download credits. Using proposed techniques, we present a modified version of attack that is derived from MitB (Man-in-the-Browser) attack, a well known Banking Trojan [15]. The major goals of this attack are; (1) Stealing user assets, such as, login credentials, (2) Modifying current web bank transaction on the fly, and (3) Modifying web pages contents on the fly without victim's notice. The potential attack vector for MitB attack is through malicious Browser extension. Once installed into Browser as an extension, this gets activated when user visits target web sites, such as Bank websites. In collusion through preference technique we demonstrate the impact of insecurely configured Browser and extension preferences. We have analysed only security relevant preferences of Browser and popular security extensions.

5.1   Object Collusion Technique

This technique demonstrates a new way of launching the MitB attack using two legitimate extensions, so that even a client side solutions [12] [14] won't be able to detect malicious flow and vulnerability by analyzing these extensions individually. We have randomly selected ten legitimate Firefox extensions from Mozilla add-on database and modified these by adding inter-communication functionality discussed in Section 4. These modified extensions are installed on different versions (3, 9, 12 and 25) of Firefox. We then apply test case scenarios of selected web sites of three domains.

Object Collusion Attack Scenario-1: The first attack scenario for collusion-based attack consists of two benign extensions. First X can read the critical information from a Web page whereas the second Y has functionality to communicate over network channel. Figure 7 shows various steps taken by two extensions to achieve malicious goal of privacy leakage.

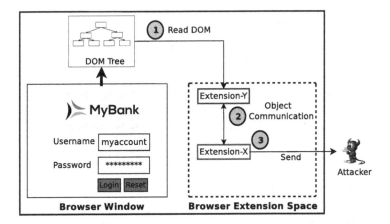

Fig. 7. Scenario-1 showing how credentials can be stolen

- Y takes user credential from Browser DOM tree and send its object's reference to X.
- X then use this reference to access the DOM information from Y and send it over network channel to attack domain.

The code snippet of two extensions are shown in Figure 8.

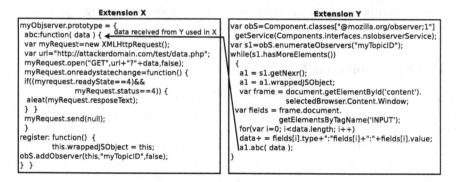

Fig. 8. Code snippet for Scenario-1

Object Collusion Attack Scenario-2: This scenario will demonstrate the modification of web page information on the fly. We illustrate this scenario through an example of the web sites that offer an user to buy download credits (torrents, file hosting, warez sites, etc.). These web sites allow you to create an $userID$ with credentials and payment details. We have implemented two extension to steal user credits in a way the credit provider server does not notice. Figure 9 shows various steps taken by two extension in collusion to modify current user details. At the time of account creation, our attack modifies the user details without victim's notice.

- X will read the information from web page DOM.
- X will wrap the reference of an object carry web page information accessible to extension Y.
- Y will modifies the user details and finally when victim user click on submit button, the modified information is sent to the credit server, and with this our account will be created on the server with download credits.

The code snippet of two extensions is shown in Figure 10.

Object Collusion Attack Scenario-3: In this scenario, we demonstrate how an attacker can dynamically add new fields on the current page. We have considered on-line shopping websites as an example to demonstrate this attack. Suppose a victim user wants to buy some item he has selected from a shopping web site. We have implemented an attack using two extensions having following functionalities; first it modifies the shipping address and mobile number of

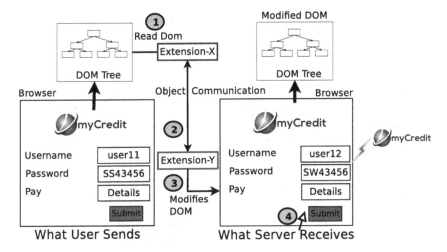

Fig. 9. Scenario-3 showing how a new field can be added and sent to attacker domain

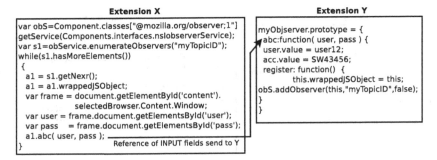

Fig. 10. Code snippet for Scenario-2

purchaser and second it adds new field to steal payment details of victim user. Figure 11 shows various steps taken by two extension to create this attack. As a victim provides various details such as name, shipping address, mobile no etc.

- Y in reads all information from page DOM and at the same time it adds new field to web page asking for payment details.
- Y wrap the reference of an object carry web page information accessible to X.
- X modifies the user details.
- When victim user clicks on submit button, the modified information is sent to the credit server, payment information is sent to attacker server.

The X remains legitimate because it modifies the information captured from sensitive source but this information is not sent to sink, instead this information is captured by Y. The code snippet of two extensions is shown in Figure 12.

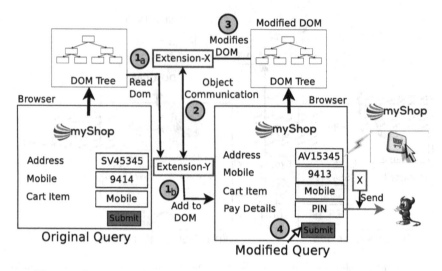

Fig. 11. Scenario-2 showing how transactions can be modified on the fly

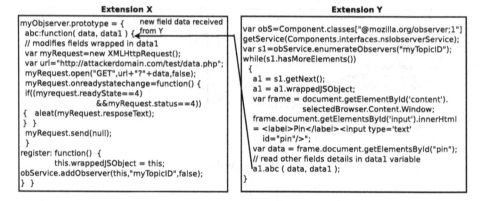

Fig. 12. Code snippet for Scenario-3

5.2 Results for Colluding Objects Technique

Table 2 summarizes the experimental results for Object Collusion attack. We have tested the attack using three different attack scenarios and found following:

- Scenario-1 is 100% successful against shopping and Download credit domain whereas only few bank websites allow the extensions capture credential information. Our attack is able to capture username from banking login page but the password is hashed. In one-third of 50 banking websites our attack scenario is able to extract both username and password from bank login page.
- Second attack scenario is 100% successful for all the web sites that we tested. Every website allowed our extension to modify the typed content on the fly.

This scenario is critical for every shopping and buy credit domains that are tested. We have not applied this attack on banking domains.

- The third attack scenario is successfully executed on 78% is of shopping domains and 80% of buy credit domains. Other domains did not allowed to add extra field on the page and if field is successfully added they won't allow to proceed further. The web domains maintain session with every text field using *type=hidden* for HTML input tag. When a new field is added to web page, the session is changed and this effectively mitigates the attack. We have not applied this attack on banking domains.

Table 2. Results for Attack scenarios executed on web domains

	Banking Domains(50)	Shopping Domains(50)	Buy Credit Domains(50)
	Success	Success	Success
Scenario - 1	22%	100%	100%
Scenario - 2	Not Applied	100%	100%
Scenario - 3	Not Applied	78%	80%

5.3 Collusion through Preference Changes Evaluation

This technique demonstrates how mis-configured preferences can result in critical Browser attacks. We have selected five security relevant preferences of Browser and three popular Browser security extensions; (1) noscript, (2) web of trust, and (3) adblock. We have implemented one extension, which is able to change the selected preferences. Our extension is installed on different versions (3, 9, 12 and 25) of Firefox. This extension modifies the selected preferences with insecure values and for each preference we have evaluated Browser security. Table 3 shows the five critical Browser preferences and preferences of three security extensions modified by our extension.

5.4 Effectiveness of Colluding Attacks over MitB

We have implemented our extensions in such a way that even a client side solutions [12, 14] would not be able to detect malicious flows and vulnerabilities. VEX and SABRE check the suspicious flow pattern from injectable sources to executable sinks. VEX uses static analysis technique to check whether an information flow is from sensitive source to sink. Our extensions contains either sensitive source or sink flow but not both. However, the legitimate functionality of an extension may cause such flows but that will be discarded by current framework of both the methods. Since a single extension has no suspicious flow and vulnerability detected it will be passes as legitimate by VEX. We have checked our extension against another solution framework called SABRE. It uses dynamic technique to check malicious flow from sensitive source to sink, which is not found while an extension scanned individually.

Table 3. Results showing Browser security leaks using preferences

Preference	Risk after modifying preferences
Critical Browser Preferences	
security.csp.enable	enable/disable the content security policy of Browser
dom.disable_open_during_load	Allows allows pop-up windows on Browser if set to true
dom.popup_allowed_events	Adding entries to this list may allow unwanted pop-ups
extensions.update.url	Adding malicious url using this preference will change extension update source
Browser.safebrowsing.malware.enabled	Do not download malware blacklists & do not check downloads if set to false
noscript Extension	
capability.policy.manoscript.sites	Adding url to this preference will bypass all the security checks provided by noScript
adblock Extension	
extensions.adblockplus.whitelistschemes	Using this preference an attacker can add and remove whitelisting rules
Web of Trust Extension	
weboftrust.norepsfor	Adding malicious domain using this preference will bypass the malicious domains

6 Mitigation Techniques

In this section, we propose possible mitigation techniques for aforementioned collusion attacks caused.

– **Sandboxing:** We explored SpiderMonkey, a JavaScript engine for Mozilla Firefox Browser, and found few weaknesses in handling the JavaScript objects. SpiderMonkey creates top-level object called JSRuntime object that represents an instance of the JavaScript engine. A program typically has only one JSRuntime, though it may have many threads. JSRuntime is the area where all the memory of the extension is global. The JSRuntime is the universe in which JavaScript objects live; they can't travel to other JS-Runtimes. The JSContext is a child of the JSRuntime. A context can run scripts, contains the global object and the execution stack. Once created, a context can be used any number of times for different scripts. Objects may be shared among JSContexts within a JSRuntime. There's no fixed association between an object and the context in which it is created. Since, the memory is common for all extensions, and hence objects of one extension are accessible to other extension as well. We suggest a sandbox environment for extensions so that their memory spaces are isolated from each other, and any communication should be through Browser kernel. Sandboxing through visualization shall mitigate such attacks. Alternately, binding between object and the its context be strengthened and violation of the binding be not allowed by default.

Few modern Web Browser components run in a sandbox environment with restricted privileges. Browser critical component, such as, the rendering engine runs in a sandbox with restricted privileges and no direct access to the local file system or other OS level components. For example, in Chrome architecture rendering engine runs in a sandbox and has no direct access to the local file system. When uploading a file, rendering engine uses Browser kernel API for file upload. Apart from Sandbox environment, the web Browser provides isolation among web programs and modularizes their execution by assigning each web program or Browser tab to the specific operating system process within the Browser. Browser provides single and shared space for all the extensions. In some Browsers the extensions are isolated from other Browser components but not from other extensions, and thus, runs is same address space. If each extensions runs in separate address space just link web page tabs in Chromium Browser, their objects are isolated from each other and cannot communicate directly.

- **Improving Client Side Solutions:** We have analyzed two popular client side solutions, VEX [12] and SABRE [14] that are effective against vulnerable and malicious extensions. We found that these solutions are meant for analyzing single extension at a time, and hence remain ineffective if a malicious flow originates from two inter-communicating extensions. To mitigate such attacks, VEX (static analysis) should consider the objects created by *nsIObserverService* as sensitive source as they can pass on sensitive information to other extensions.

- **Reported Solutions for MitB and Similar Attacks:** Several solutions to protect against the MitB problem have been suggested. These third-party solutions can be adapted to mitigate information stealing from Browser. These solution need to incorporate in Browser analysis of installed extensions before these are accepted for extension by Browsers [1, 4, 6].

7 Related Work

Recently, the authors in [18] considered a more practical approach and demonstrate examples of possible attacks on Firefox extensions. They discussed the possible vulnerability is in existing Firefox extensions, which could be exploited to launch concrete attacks such as remote code execution, password theft, and file system access. Liu et al. [17] scrutinize the extension security mechanisms employed by Google Chrome against "benign-but-buggy" and malicious extensions, and evaluate their effectiveness. They propose changes to Chrome to make malware easier to identify. The work by Ter Louw et al. [21] highlighted some of the potential security risks posed by Firefox extensions. They proposed runtime monitoring of XPCOM calls for detecting suspicious activities in extensions. To the best of our knowledge, no one considered yet an attack caused due to inter-communication between objects of two extensions, where individual extension performs legitimately but their combined functionality could lead to an attack. We have found this weakness in Firefox Browser and implemented proof-of-concept for the same.

The analysis of MitB attack was first introduced by P. Guhring [15], in which he presented the detailed description of the problem, identified the various points of attacks, the methods of attack and also suggested possible countermeasures for the MitB attack. A comprehensive review on the Browser extensions based MitB Trojan attack, poses a serious and growing threat to the online banking customers has been presented by Utakrit in [23]. In this the author has analysed the MitB attack for online banking transactions and suggested some mitigation techniques. In [22], Dougan and Curran have presented a comprehensive study on the MitB attacks, its variants Trojans. The author has examined the attack with reference to its control structure, data interaction techniques, and the methods for bypassing security. The MitB attacks can be detected by client side solutions, such as [12] [14] if it uses Browser extensions as an attack vector.

8   Conclusion and Future Work

This paper presents a new security risks and exploits present in Firefox's XP-COM interfaces. We have presented collusion between extensions, and showed how two legitimate extensions collude to achieve malicious goals. Our attacks are undetectable by existing popular client site methods used for detecting malicious flow and vulnerability in extensions. We have demonstrated our finding by meeting malicious goal using two legitimate extensions on three critical web domains; banking, online shopping, and Buy credit domains. We also provided the proof-of-concept explaining how the multiple extensions can collaborate with each other for compromising the Browser.

In future, we shall examine these security issues and devise effective countermeasures to improve the existing solutions. In this work, we suggested some possible approaches to mitigate this attack. In future work, we will implement these techniques and improve the Browser against such dangerous attacks. Also, we hope that Mozilla Firefox will consider these issues and come with secured policy to provide users a secure browsing environment.

Acknowledgments. Mauro Conti is supported by a Marie Curie Fellowship funded by the European Commission under the agreement n. PCIG11-GA-2012-321980. This work has been partially supported by the TENACE PRIN Project funded by the Italian MIUR (20103P34XC), and by the Project "Tackling Mobile Malware with Innovative Machine Learning Techniques" funded by the University of Padua.

References

1. Defeating man-in-the-browser. how to prevent the latest malware attacks against consumer corporate banking, http://download.entrust.com/resources/download.cfm/24002/
2. Document object model, https://developer.mozilla.org/en/docs/DOM
3. Mozilla developer network-extensions, https://developer.mozilla.org/en/docs/Extensions
4. Protection against man-in-the-middle attacks, http://www.ca.com/ /media/Files/whitepapers/protection-from-mitm-mitb-attacks-wp.pdf
5. Security issue on amo, http://blog.mozilla.com/addons/2010/02/04/please-read-security-issue-on-amo/
6. Understanding man-in-the-browser attacks and addressing the problem, http://ru.safenet-inc.com/uploadedFiles/About_SafeNet/Resource_Library/Resource_Items/WhitePapers-SFDCProtectedEDP/Man%20in%20the%20Browser%20Security%20Guide.pdf
7. Xpcom interface, https://developer.mozilla.org/en-US/docs/XUL/Tutorial/XPCOM_Interfaces
8. Xpconnect, https://developer.mozilla.org/en/docs/XPConnect
9. Xul overlays, https://developer.mozilla.org/en-US/docs/XUL_Overlays
10. Adam, B.: Severity guidelines for security issues. The Chromium Project, http://dev.chromium.org/developers/severity-guidelines
11. Adamski, L.: Security severity ratings. MozillaWiki (2008)
12. Bandhakavi, S., Tiku, N., Pittman, W., King, S.T., Madhusudan, P., Winslett, M.: Vetting browser extensions for security vulnerabilities with vex. Commun. ACM 54(9), 91–99 (2011)
13. Caraig, D.: Firefox add-on spies on google search results, http://blog.trendmicro.com/firefox-addo-spies-on-google-search-results/
14. Dhawan, M., Ganapathy, V.: Analyzing information flow in javascript-based browser extensions. In: Proceedings of the 2009 Annual Computer Security Applications Conference, ACSAC 2009, pp. 382–391 (2009)
15. Guhring, P.: Concepts against man-in-the-browser attacks
16. Hedin, D., Birgisson, A., Bello, L., Sabelfeld, A.: Jsflow: Tracking information flow in javascript and its apis. In: Proceedings of the 29th Annual ACM Symposium on Applied Computing, SAC 2014, pp. 1663–1671. ACM, New York (2014)
17. Liu, L., Zhang, X., Yan, G., Chen, S.: Chrome extensions: Threat analysis and countermeasures. In: NDSS (2012)
18. Liverani, R.S., Freeman, N.: Abusing firefox extensions. In: Defcon17 (2009)
19. Maone, G.: Noscript
20. Saini, A., Gaur, M.S., Laxmi, V.: The darker side of firefox extension. In: Proceedings of the 6th International Conference on Security of Information and Networks, SIN 2013, pp. 316–320. ACM (2013)
21. Ter Louw, M., Lim, J.S., Venkatakrishnan, V.N.: Extensible Web Browser Security. In: Hämmerli, B.M., Sommer, R. (eds.) DIMVA 2007. LNCS, vol. 4579, pp. 1–19. Springer, Heidelberg (2007)

22. Kevin, C., Timothy, D.: Man in the browser attacks. International Journal of Ambient Computing and Intelligence (IJACI) 4 (2012)
23. Utakrit, N.: Review of browser extensions, a man-in-the-browser phishing techniques targeting bank customer. In: 7th Australian Information Security Management Conference, p. 19 (2009)
24. Kindel, C., Williams, S.: The component object model: A technical overview
25. Zalewski, M.: Browser security handbook. Google Code (2010)

CORP: A Browser Policy to Mitigate Web Infiltration Attacks

Krishna Chaitanya Telikicherla, Venkatesh Choppella,
and Bruhadeshwar Bezawada

Software Engineering Research Center,
International Institute of Information Technology (IIIT),
Hyderabad - 500032, India
KrishnaChaitanya.T@research.iiit.ac.in, Venkatesh.Choppella@iiit.ac.in,
Bezawada@mail.iiit.ac.in

Abstract. Cross origin interactions constitute the core of today's collaborative Word Wide Web. They are, however, also the cause of malicious behaviour like Cross-Site Request Forgery (CSRF), clickjacking, and cross-site timing attacks, which we collectively refer as *Web Infiltration attacks*. These attacks are a rampant source of information stealth and privacy intrusion on the web. Existing browser security policies like Same Origin Policy, either ignore this class of attacks or, like Content Security Policy, insufficiently deal with them.

In this paper, we propose a new declarative browser security policy — "Cross Origin Request Policy" (CORP) — to mitigate such attacks. CORP enables a server to have fine-grained control on the way different sites can access resources on the server. The server declares the policy using HTTP response headers. The web browser monitors cross origin HTTP requests targeting the server and blocks those which do not comply with CORP. Based on lessons drawn from examining various types of cross origin attacks, we formulate CORP and demonstrate its effectiveness and ease of deployment. We formally verify the design of CORP by modelling it in the Alloy model checker. We also implement CORP as a browser extension for the Chrome web browser and evaluate it against real-world cross origin attacks on open source web applications. Our initial investigation reveals that most of the popular websites already segregate their resources in a way which makes deployment of CORP easier.

Keywords: Web Browser, Security, World Wide Web, Cross-site request forgery, Access control policy.

1 Introduction

When the World Wide Web was invented in 1989 [1], it only had a set of static pages interconnected via hyperlinks. With the addition of images in 1993[2], a request to a website could cascade a set of requests to multiple other sites. There is something unnerving about such *cross-origin* (or *cross-site*) HTTP requests triggered without explicit user interaction. With the advent of forms and scripts

A. Prakash and R. Shyamasundar (Eds.): ICISS 2014, LNCS 8880, pp. 277–297, 2014.

in 1995[3], cross-site interactions became a real security threat. For example, as shown Figure 1, a genuine website, say *G.com*, could now be compromised by an attacker who injects malicious content like an image tag pointing to attacker's site, say *A.com*. This is an example of a cross-site scripting (XSS) attack. A victim requesting the infected page could end up unwittingly participating in exfiltration, i.e., the leakage of private data to *A.com*.

Despite several proposals like whitelisting[4], input sanitization[5], static analysis[6], browser sandboxing[7], XSS vulnerabilities continue to be pervasive on the web. Browsers as early as 1995[8] introduced the Same Origin Policy (SOP)[9], which was designed to prevent scripts from accessing DOM, network and storage data belonging to other web origins. The earlier problem of cross-origin requests through automatic form submissions or content inclusion was, however, left unanswered by SOP. Content Security Policy (CSP), introduced in 2010[10] improves on SOP in mitigating the exfiltration problem by disabling inline scripts, restricting the sources of external scripts.

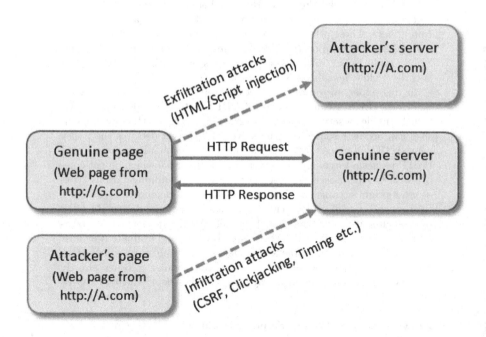

Fig. 1. Exfiltration vs. Infiltration attacks

1.1 Proposed Approach

Our work begins by seeking a common thread between CSRF, clickjacking and cross-site timing attacks with the goal of understanding the limitations of CSP in addressing these attacks. We label these attacks as *Web Infiltration attacks*. The root of web infiltration is a request initiated from an evil page to a genuine but unsuspecting server, (Figure 1). In web infiltration attacks, a victim who is already logged in to a genuine site, *G.com*, unwittingly visits an attacker's site, *A.com* in a separate browser instance (or tab). The web page obtained from *A.com* triggers state-changing requests to *G.com* either through an automatic form submission initiated by a script or via an <img> tag, or through other similar vectors. The request to *G.com* goes from the victim's browser and uses the victim's credentials. *G.com* is unable to discriminate between genuine and forged requests. Web infiltration is complementary to exfiltration. Exfiltration is caused by XSS and can be controlled by CSP. Infiltration, on the other hand, can not be controlled by CSP.

We propose a novel approach to prevent web infiltration, based on the following observations:

- **Observation 1:** Irrespective of how a network event (HTTP request) is initiated, a web server responds with a resource. Therefore, any network event, e.g., loading an image can infiltrate and potentially change the server's state e.g., delete a resource.
- **Observation 2:** The prevention and detection techniques for web infiltration attacks that we have investigated are triggered too late. They apply either after an HTTP request leaves the browser [11,12] or after the browser has already received the response [13,14].
- **Observation 3:** Client side state information (cookies) of a website is shared across all tabs of a browser or multiple instances of the same browser, even though its access by other websites is restricted by Same Origin Policy.
- **Observation 4:** Website developers or administrators segregate the paths of various resources on the server, as a good engineering practice.

From *Observation 1*, we infer that a policy which monitors the initiator of web interactions is required. From *Observation 2*, we infer that every request must be subjected to the policy before it leaves the browser. From *Observation 3*, we infer that the policy should be available to and enforced by all tabs of the browser. From *Observation 4*, we infer that segregation of resource paths can be used as an important factor in the design of the policy.

Based on the above inferences, we propose a simple security policy, *Cross-Origin Request Policy (CORP)*, to prevent web infiltration attacks. The policy is a 3-way relation defined over the sets browser *event types*, *origins*, and the set of *resource paths* derived from the server's origin. CORP may therefore be seen as a policy that controls *who*, i.e., which site or origin, can access *what*, i.e., which resource on a cross-origin server, and *how*, i.e., through which browser event. CORP is declarative; it can be added as an HTTP response header of the landing page of a website. To implement the policy, web administrators need to segregate resources on the server based on the intended semantic effect of the resource. For example, all public resources could be in the path */public*, while all state changing resources could be sequestered in a different path. Thus the semantics of resources is mapped to paths. Fortunately, as discussed in Section 5, most website administrators already segregate resources along the lines proposed by the policy.

A web browser enforcing CORP would receive the policy and store it in memory accessible to all tabs or browser instances similar to the cookie storage mechanism. Assume that tab t_A contains a page p_A from a server s_A. Along with the p_A, the browser also receives a CORP policy $c(s_A)$ from s_A. Assume that the browser now opens a page p_B received from s_B in tab t_B and p_B attempts to make a cascading cross-origin request to s_A. The cross-origin request from p_B to s_A will be intercepted and allowed only if it complies with the permissions $c(s_A)$.

Threat Model: We follow the threat model classifications proposed by Akhawe et al. [15], which defines the capabilities of web, network and gadget attackers. Throughout the paper, we take into consideration only the threats that come under the capabilities of a web attacker. A web attacker has root access on at least one web server and can generate HTTP requests against any web server. However, the attacker has no special network privileges, which means threats like man-in-the-middle cannot be realized and HTTP headers generated by the browser or server cannot be tampered.

Contributions: Our contributions in this paper are as follows: (1) We have identified a class of web infiltration attacks that include CSRF, clickjacking and cross-site timing attacks and designed a uniform browser policy to mitigate all of them. (2) We have formalized our proposal in Alloy [16], a finite state model checker, and verified that it is sound. (3) We have built two websites - one playing the role of a genuine website and the other a malicious website (a test suite) triggering malicious calls to the first. We have collected a large number of attack vectors from literature and incorporated them into the test suite. (4) We have implemented our proposal as an extension for Google Chrome web browser. We have evaluated the extension by configuring CORP on the genuine site and verified that infiltration attacks by the malicious site are blocked by the extension. (5) We have configured CORP on three popular open source web applications in our test environment to verify the effectiveness and ease of deployment on real world websites. (6) We have also analyzed home page traffic of over 15,000 popular websites and confirmed that the burden on web administrators to deploy CORP will be minimum.

Organization of the Paper: The rest of the paper is organized as follows: Section 2 gives an overview of web infiltration attacks. Section 3 gives an overview of related work done in preventing these attacks. Section 4 explains the design of CORP. Section 5 describes the implementation of CORP as a Chrome extension and the experimental methodology to evaluate its effectiveness and Section 6 concludes with a discussion of future work.

2   Web Infiltration Attacks

In this section, we examine three common attacks: CSRF, clickjacking and cross-site timing. Each of these is an instance of a web infiltration attack.

2.1 Understanding CSRF

CSRF is a highly exploited web based vulnerability and is consistently listed in the OWASP Top Ten [17]. In a typical CSRF attack, a malicious site instructs a victim's browser to send an HTTP request to an honest site. This malicious request is sent on behalf of the victim, thereby disrupting the integrity of the victim's session.

In the example below, it is assumed that a user is logged in at a genuine site *G.com* and then opens an attacker's site *A.com* in a new browser tab. The page from the attacker's site contains the HTML shown in Listing 1.1.

```
<img src="http://G.com/user/delete.php">
```

Listing 1.1. Basic CSRF attack via image tag

As soon as the attacker's page is loaded, the image tag triggers a cascading HTTP request to *G.com*, which deletes the user's profile on the site. Though servers do not generally accept state changing requests using HTTP GET, generating HTTP POST requests using HTML forms is trivial. Irrespective of the origin from which a request has initiated, browsers attach authentication credentials i.e., cookies to every request made to the destination origin. Due to this, browsers do not distinguish between a request triggered by a genuine and a malicious web page[1]. Also, in most cases servers do not have information about the origin which triggered the request (see Section 3.1 for details).

2.2 Understanding Clickjacking

Clickjacking was first reported in web browsers in 2008 [18]. It is also known as UI-redressing and has gained popularity in the modern attacker community. In this, attackers lure users to visit a malicious page and trick them to click on invisible targets e.g., buttons, which belong to a cross origin web page. Typically, attackers embed target cross origin content in iframes, reduce their opacity to zero and position them above seemingly genuine buttons. End users will not have any suspicion or indication that their click is hijacked, but the attacker will be able use their click for malicious purposes. Clickjacking differs from CSRF in the fact that along with the click, user's credentials as well as CSRF tokens (if present) are submitted[2]. This makes clickjacking more dangerous than CSRF.

There are many online scams/spams, especially on social networks, which use clickjacking and make money. Facebook recently sued an ad network that used clickjacking and stole personal information of users, thereby making up to $1.2 million a month [19].

---

[1] This is an instance of the "Confused Deputy Problem", where the browser is the confused deputy.

[2] This is an instance of the "Confused Deputy Problem", where the user is the confused deputy.

2.3   Understanding Cross-Site Timing Attacks

Bortz et al. [12] explained that the response time for HTTP requests can expose private information of a web user e.g., detecting if a user has logged in at a particular site, finding the number of items in the user's shopping cart etc. Though there are several ways to time web applications, as shown by Bortz et al., we examine a class of timing attacks called *cross-site timing attacks*, which rely on cross origin HTTP requests. In these attacks a genuine user is tricked to open a malicious page, which tries to load resources e.g., images, html pages etc. from a site being targeted. On measuring the time taken for the loading of the resources, sensitive information such as the login status of a user can be extracted. Two recent works by Stone and Kotcher et al., showed how SVG filters [20] and CSS shaders [21] can be used as vectors for cross-site timing. Technically, cross-site timing attacks can be classified as CSRF attacks with the exception that the traditional defenses for CSRF i.e., tokens do not generally work for these. Typically, attackers target authenticated resources [22], which do not have CSRF tokens e.g., private profile pictures, script files etc. This means, majority of websites are vulnerable to cross-site timing attacks. We have analyzed popular social networks and email providers and found at least one way of detecting the login status of a user. We found that apart from authenticated resources, even authenticated URLs can also be used as a vector for login detection. Listing 1.2 shows the case where the script tag makes a cross origin HTTP request to a non-existing page on a target site to detect login status of the user.

```
<script src="http://example.com/user/nonExistingPage.php"
    onload=notLoggedIn() onerror=loggedIn()>
```

Listing 1.2. Login detection by fetching cross origin authenticated resources

Once the login status of a user is known, as explained by Bortz et al., spammers can perform invasive advertising and targeted phishing i.e., phishing a site which a user frequently uses, rather than phishing randomly.

Apart from these, we have identified an attack scenario that uses login detection, which we call *Stealth mode clickjacking*. Developers usually protect sensitive content using authentication. So in most cases, for a clickjacking attack to be successful, the victim should be logged in at the target site. Moreover, if the victim is not logged in and clicks on the framed target, authentication will be prompted, thereby raising suspicion. Using login detection techniques, an attacker can redesign the attack by ensuring that clickjacking code executes only if the victim is logged in at the target site, thereby removing any scope of suspicion. We observe that it is easy to compose such attacks with a comprehensive knowledge of the web.

We observe that CSRF, clickjacking and cross-site timing attacks have a common root, which is a cross origin HTTP request triggered by a malicious client to a genuine server without any restrictions. We attempt to mitigate these attacks by devising a uniform browser security policy explained in detail in Section 4.

3   Related Work

In this section, we briefly describe existing defenses against each of CSRF, click-jacking and cross-site timing attacks.

3.1   Approaches to Mitigate CSRF

In the case of CSRF, there are several server side (Secret tokens, NoForge, Origin header etc.) and client side defences (RequestRode, BEAP, CsFire etc.) to prevent the attack.

Secret Tokens: This is one of the most popular approaches used by developers. In this, the server generates a unique random secret and embeds it into web pages in every HTTP response. The server checks if the secret received from the browser is the same as the one it generated earlier and accepts the request if the check succeeds. Since the token is not available to the attacker, request forgery cannot happen. CSRF Guard [11] and CSRFx [23] are a few server side frameworks which implement this technique. Though this technique is robust, most websites, including high profile ones, often miss them. Also, using social engineering techniques tokens can be stolen thereby re-enabling request forgery.

NoForge: NoForge [24] is a server side proxy which inspects and modifies client requests. It modifies responses such that future requests originating from the web page will contain a valid secret token. It takes countermeasures against requests that do not contain a valid token. The downside of this approach is, since it is a server side proxy, it will not be able to add tokens to dynamic content generated by JavaScript in the browser.

SOMA: Same Origin Mutual Approval (SOMA) [25] enforcing constraints on HTTP traffic by mandating mutual approval from both the sites participating in an interaction. Websites send manifest files that inform a browser which domains the site can communicate with. The domains whitelisted in the manifest expose a service which replies with a "yes" or "no" when queried for a domain name. When both the sites agree for the communication (via the manifest and the service), a cross origin request is allowed. Though SOMA enforces strict restrictions on cross origin interactions, it involves an additional network call to verify the permissions of a request. Moreover, it does not provide fine-grained control such as restricting only a subset of cross origin requests for a domain.

Origin Header: Barth [26] et al., proposed adding an *Origin* header to HTTP request headers, which indicates the origin from which each HTTP request initiates. It was an improvement over its predecessor - the Referer header, which includes path or query strings that contain sensitive information. Due to privacy constraints, the Referer header is stripped by filtering proxies [27]. Since the Origin header sends only the *Origin* in the request, it improves over Referer in terms of privacy. Majority of modern browsers already implemented this header. Using the origin information, the server can decide whether it should allow a particular cross origin request or not. However, origin header is not sent (set to *null*) if the request is initiated by hyperlinks, images, stylesheets and window navigation (e.g., *window.location*) since they are not meant to be used for state changing operations. Developers are forced to use *Form GET* if they want to check the origin of a GET request on the server. Such changes in application code require longer time for adoption by developer community.

Request Rodeo: Request Rodeo [28] is a client side proxy which sits in between web browser and the server. It intercepts HTTP responses and adds a secret random value to all URLs in the web page before it reaches the browser. It also strips authentication information from cross origin HTTP requests which do not have the correct random value, generated in the previous response. The downside of this is, it does not differentiate between genuine and malicious cross origin requests. Also, it fails to handle cases where HTML is generated dynamically by JavaScript, since this dynamic content has come after passing through the proxy.

BEAP: Browser Enforced Authenticity Protection [29] is a browser based solution which attempts to infer the intent of the user. It considers attack scenarios where a page has hidden iframes (clickjacking scenarios), on which users may click unintentionally. It strips authorization information from all cross origin requests by checking referer header on the client side. However, it also strips several genuine cross origin interactions, which are common on the web.

CsFire: CsFire [30,31] builds on Maes et al. [32] and relies on stripping authentication information from HTTP requests. A client side enforcement policy is constructed which can autonomously mitigate CSRF attacks. The core idea behind this approach is - Client-side state is stripped from all cross-origin requests, except for expected requests. A cross-origin request from origin A to B is expected if B previously delegated to A, by either issues a POST request to A, or if B redirected to A using a URI that contains parameters. To remove false positives, the client policy is supplemented with server side policies or user supplied whitelist. The downside of this approach is that without the server supplied or user supplied whitelist, CsFire will not be able to handle complex, genuine cross origin scenarios and the whitelists need to be updated frequently.

ARLs: Allowed Referrer Lists (ARLs) [33] is a recent browser security policy proposed to mitigate CSRF. ARLs restrict a browser's ability to send ambient authority credentials with HTTP requests. The policy requires developers identify and decouple credentials they use for authentication and authorization. Also, a whitelist of allowed referrer URLs has to be specified, to which browsers are allowed to attach authorization state. The policy is light weight, backward compatible and aims to eradicate CSRF, provided websites meet the policy's requirement. However, expecting all legacy, large websites to identify and decouple their authentication/authorization credentials may be unrealistic, since it could result in broken applications and also requires extensive regression testing. Our proposal, CORP, which uses whitelists like CSP and ARLs, does not require complex/breaking changes on the server. Details of the approach are explained in Section 4.1.

3.2 Approaches to Mitigate Clickjacking

There are several proposals to detect [34,35], prevent [36,37] Clickjacking and intelligent tricks [38,39] which bypass some of them. Browser vendors and W3C have incorporated ideas from these proposals and are working towards robust defense for clickjacking. Below are two important contributions in this direction:

X-Frame-Options (XFO) Header: The X-Frame-Options HTTP response header [13], was introduced by Microsoft in Internet Explorer 8, specifically to combat clickjacking. The value of the header takes two tokens-DENY, which does not allow content of the frame to render, and SAMEORIGIN, which allows content of the frame to render only if its origin matches with the origin of the top frame. XFO was the first browser based solution for clickjacking.

CSP User Interface Security Directives: Content Security Policy (CSP) added a set of new directives- *User Interface Security Directives for Content Security Policy* [14] specifically to focus on User Interface Security. It supersedes XFO and encompasses the directives in it, along with providing a mechanism to enable heuristic input protections.

Both XFO and CSP, though promise to prevent clickjacking, leave CSRF wide open. Also, these solutions get invoked just before the frame is rendered, which is too late in the request/response life-cycle. Due to this, several bypasses such as *Double Clickjacking* [38], *Nested Clickjacking* [39] and *Login detection using XFO* [22] arise.

3.3 Approaches to Mitigate Cross-Site Timing Attacks

Bortz et al. [12] proposed that by ensuring a web server takes constant time to process a request might help in mitigating cross-site timing attacks. However, it is unlikely to get wider acceptance in web community as it involves complex server side changes. A popular recommendation by security researchers is to disable *onload/onerror* event handlers for cross origin requests, but this affects genuine cases. As of date, cross-site timing attacks are still unresolved.

4   Cross Origin Request Policy

In this section, we first explain the core idea behind Cross Origin Request Policy (CORP) and its importance in mitigating web infiltration attacks. Next, we explain the model of a browser which receives CORP and enforces it. Finally, we explain the directives which make the policy, with examples.

4.1   Core Idea Behind CORP

Based on our clear understanding of various types of web infiltration attacks (Section 2), we realize the need for a mechanism which enables a server to control cross origin interactions initiated by a browser. Precisely, a server should have fine-grained control on *Who* can access *What* resource on the server and *How*. By specifying these rules via a policy on the server and sending them to the browser, requests can be filtered/routed by the browser such that infiltrations attacks will be mitigated. This is the core idea behind CORP. Formally speaking, *Who* refers to the set of origins that can request a resource belonging to a server, *What* refers to the set of paths that map to resources on the server, *How* refers to the set of event-types that initiate network events (HTTP requests) to the server. We identify HTML tags such as <img>, <script>, <iframe> etc., and window events such as redirection, opening popups etc., as event-types (explained in Section 4.3). Therefore, CORP is a 3-way relation defined over the sets *Who*, *What* and *How*, as shown in Equation (1).

$$CORP \subseteq Origin \times ResourcePath \times EventType \tag{1}$$

Equation (2) shows an example of a policy which is a subset of the 3-way relation.

$$Origin = \{O_1, O_2, O_3\}$$
$$ResourcePath = \{P_1, P_2, P_3\}$$
$$EventType = \{Img, Script, Form\}$$
$$CORP, C_p = \{(O_1, P_1, Img), (O_2, P_2, Form), (O_2, P_3, Script)\} \tag{2}$$

Let us say a website belonging to the origin O_0 sets this policy and a CORP-enabled browser receives it. Then, only the cross origin requests that satisfy the tuples in the policy will be allowed by the browser and rest will be blocked. E.g., A webpage belonging to the origin O_1 will be allowed to request for images only under the path P_1, from a server belonging to the origin O_0 (refer to the first tuple in Equation (2)). Similarly, a webpage belonging to the origin O_1 will not be allowed to submit a form to the server belonging to O_0, since it is not defined in the policy.

4.2   Browser Model with CORP

Figure 2 shows the model of a browser which supports CORP. It shows the difference between exfiltration and infiltration attacks, thereby explaining how CORP differs from CSP. The figure shows a genuine server G, with origin http://G.com, an attacker's server A, with origin http://A.com and a browser with two tabs - *t1* and *t2*. A general browsing scenario, which is also the sufficient condition for a cross origin attack, where a user logs in at *G.com* in *t1* and (unwittingly) opens *A.com* in *t2* is depicted in the model.

Setting the Policy: Once a user requests the genuine site *G.com* by typing its URL in the address bar of *t1*, an HTTP request is sent from *t1* to *G*. In response, along with content, CORP is sent via HTTP response headers by G (shown by arrows 1 and 2 in the figure). The tab *t1* receives the policy and sends

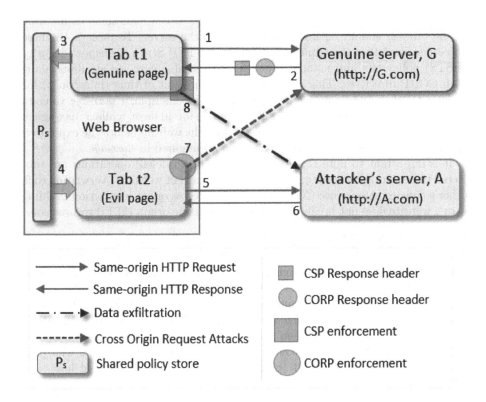

Fig. 2. Browser model showing exfiltration & infiltration and how they are mitigated by CSP & CORP

it to a shared policy store P_s where P_s ensures that CORP is available to every tab or instance (arrows 3 and 4 in the figure) of the browser. Now, when a user unwittingly visits a malicious page from A in $t2$ (arrows 5 and 6 in the figure), every HTTP request initiated by the page in $t2$ to G will be scrutinized and restrictions in *CORP* will be enforced (location 7 in the figure). Requests from $t2$ to G will be allowed only if they comply with the configuration in the policy. As per the guidelines in Section 4.3, web administrators will be able to configure rules in a way that web infiltration attacks will be prevented. It is sufficient to configure CORP on the login page/home page of a website. It is not a per-page policy like CSP and adding CORP on every page only overrides the policy.

Deleting the Policy: As users visit multiple websites, their browsers keep accumulating CORP policies and therefore, a mechanism to delete the policies is required. In CSP and HTML5 CORS, policies will be stored in the browser only till the participating websites remain open in browsers. The same mechanism cannot be used in CORP, because if a CORP-enabled website is closed accidentally by a user while being logged in and the policy is destroyed, malicious websites will be able to trigger infiltration attacks. To prevent this, it is important for the policy to be persistent in the browser. At the same time, its life-time in the browser should be under the control of the server. To meet both these objectives we follow the expiry mechanism of HTTP Strict Transport Security (HSTS) policy [40] and mandate the server to send a *max-age* attribute along with CORP directives. This attribute sets the amount of time (in seconds) for which CORP should be active in the browser. For example, a *max-age* value of 2592000 seconds ensures that the policy is active for 30 days, while a max-age of 0 deletes the policy immediately. If a user visits the website before the expiration time, the timer will be reset to the new time configured in *max-age*.

It is important to note that policy's set, get and delete operations are subjected to same origin checks on the browser, to prevent websites overwriting each other's policies. Also, since CORP aims to filter cross origin interactions, adding it to a website does not break the site's existing same origin HTTP transactions.

CORP and CSP - How They Differ: *CORP* and *CSP* together complement *SOP* and help in fixing *exfiltration* and *Infiltration*. *CSP* was designed to enforce restrictions on HTTP traffic leaving a genuine webpage, as shown by location 8 in Figure 2. *CORP* was designed to enforce restrictions on HTTP traffic sent by a malicious web page to a genuine server (location 7 in the figure). Also, *CSP* expects origins as directive values as they are sufficient to control exfiltration. *CORP* specifies a 3-way relation defined over the sets event-types, paths and origins. In a nutshell, *CORP* configured on a website *A.com* defines who (i.e., which origins) can probe what (i.e., which resource) on *A.com* and how (i.e., which event).

4.3   Abstract Syntax of CORP

Listing 1.3 shows the abstract syntax of *CORP*.

```
policy ::= rule *...
rule  ::= pattern permission
pattern ::=  origin-list eventType-list path-list
permission ::= ALLOW | DENY
origin-list ::= origin +... | ANY
eventType-list ::= eventType +... | ANY
path-list ::= path +... | ANY
origin ::= RFC 6454
eventType ::= img | media | style
                  | font | script | iframe
                  | form-action | xhr | hyperlink
                  | window | object
path ::= RFC 2396
```

Listing 1.3. Abstract syntax of CORP

For path, an additional pattern "resourcePath/*" is allowed to simplify the configuration of CORP. The wild card '*' in the pattern provides a way to refer to any resource under a specific resource path. E.g., Access to all paths under "admin" directory can be controlled using the pattern "/admin/*".

Order of Precedence for CORP Rules: CORP rules are processed from top to bottom, till the default rule is reached. When a cross origin request is made by a website against a CORP-enabled site, the request is scrutinized by the first rule in the policy. If a match is found, the first rule is executed and rest of the rules are not evaluated. Else, the request is scrutinized by the next rule and the process continues till the last rule.

The last (default) rule is set to "* * * Allow", which means "Allow everything". If a server sends an empty policy, it is the same as not configuring CORP at all. In such cases, the default rule is evaluated and all cross origin requests are allowed. This approach ensures that CORP does not break existing cross origin interactions on a website. Also, it enables web administrators to incrementally build stricter rules and tighten the security of their servers. We demonstrate a few example policies in the following discussion.

Example Policies

- **Deny All:** A banking site may want to completely block all cross origin requests to its site. It may achieve this by setting the simple policy shown in Listing 1.4.

```
*    *    *    DENY
```

Listing 1.4. Block all cross origin requests

- **Selective Content:** A photo sharing site may want to respond only to authenticated cross origin requests involving scripts, images (from any site) and block any other authenticated cross origin request. It may set the policy shown in Listing 1.5.

```
*      img      /img              ALLOW
*      script   /scripts   ALLOW
*      *        *                        DENY
```

Listing 1.5. Allow access to selective content

- **Partners Only:** An e-commerce website might expose state-changing web services and expects only its partner sites, say *P1.com, P2.com*, to do a form submission to its services. It can set the policy shown in Listing 1.6.

```
{P1.com,   P2.com}    form      {/update, /delete}
           ALLOW
*                                *
                                         DENY
```

Listing 1.6. Allow selective access to selective origins

4.4   Security Guarantees Provided by CORP

CORP helps website administrators use browser's capabilities in adding additional security to their sites. The following are the security guarantees provided by CORP:

Fine Grained Access Control. Through CORP, websites can decide *who* (i.e., which set of origins) can trigger cross origin requests to their sites and more importantly *how* (i.e., through which mechanism). Having such a fine grained access control helps web administrators selectively allow/deny cross origin requests, thereby enhancing the security of their site.

Combating CSRF. By binding various event types e.g., <img> to paths serving their corresponding resources e.g., *http://A.com/images/* via CORP, the semantics of request initiators is maintained. The implication of this binding is that active HTML elements can no longer be used as vectors for cross origin attacks. Also, by whitelisting sensitive paths and defining which origins can request them, automated requests triggered by scripts through various techniques can be blocked. If CORP is properly configured, CSRF attacks can be eliminated completely.

Early Enforcement of Clickjacking Defense. As discussed in Section 3.2, XFO and CSP-UI-Security directives are two important proposals to mitigate clickjacking. Figure 3 explains how enforcement of clickjacking defense takes place in XFO/CSP and CORP. The workflow in the figure is similar to the workflow depicted Figure 2. As explained in Section 4.2, consider the normal browsing scenario where a user (victim) opens a genuine site *G.com* in tab *t1* and unwittingly opens an attacker's site *A.com* in tab *t2*. In this case, the evil page (belonging to *A.com*) embeds an iframe and points its *src* to a page belonging to *G.com*, with an intention to hijack the victim's click. The iframe makes an HTTP request to the genuine server (*G*) and gets the HTML response along with HTTP headers. If the page is configured with either X-Frame-Options header or CSP clickjacking directive, browsers enforce XFO/CSP and do not render the HTML response (location 7 in the figure), thereby preventing clickjacking. However, since the request triggered by the iframe has already reached the server *G*, CSRF attack has already taken place. Also, due to this delayed enforcement, Clickjacking bypasses such as *Double Clickjacking* [38], *Nested Clickjacking* [39] and *Login detection using XFO* [22] arise. CORP mitigates these problems by ensuring that clickjacking enforcement take place even before a cross origin request is triggered. If the genuine site *G.com* in *t1* is configured with CORP, the policy will be stored in a shared policy store P_s, which is accessible to all instances of the browser. As soon as the iframe in the evil page (loaded in *t2*) triggers an HTTP request to *G.com*, CORP's enforcement triggers (location 5 in the figure), thereby blocking the request altogether. Since the request is blocked at the browser itself, CSRF is mitigated. The same logic applies to other bypasses for clickjacking. Hence, CORP is the right way to eliminate clickjacking completely. Listing 1.7 shows CORP configuration to mitigate clickjacking.

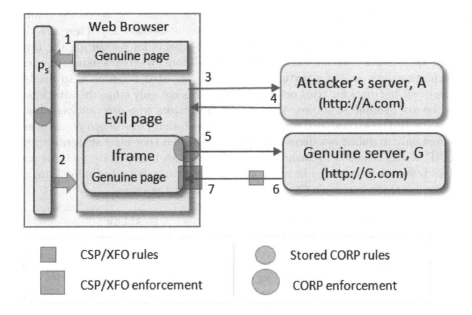

Fig. 3. Browser model showing the enforcement of Clickjacking defense in CSP/XFO and CORP

```
*        iframe      *        DENY
```

Listing 1.7. Defeating clickjacking with CORP

Controlling Social Engineering Attacks. Attackers attempt several social engineering tricks on end users by leveraging popups [41], iframes [42,43] and hyperlinks. Spam emails having hyperlinks that point to sensitive web pages (e.g., delete.php) continue to be a common menace. Today, there are no standard defenses against these attacks as there is no mechanism for a server to instruct *how* a cross origin request should originate to itself. By configuring CORP, website administrators can block requests initiated by frames, popup windows, hyperlinks for all or specific paths. This ensures that end users do not succumb to most of the common social engineering tricks.

```
*        href                    /non-sensitive
         ALLOW
*        {href, window, iframe}  *                DENY
```

Listing 1.8. Controlling social engineering attacks

Listing 1.8 shows a sample CORP configuration, which blocks vectors for social engineering. The configuration allows hyperlinks to navigate only to non-sensitive pages, denies requests which open popups or navigate to any location via *window* object and denies framing.

Defeating Cross-Site Timing Attacks. The vectors for cross-site timing attacks are same as that of CSRF, as discussed in Section 2.3. They use the *onload* and *onerror* event handlers of HTML elements for measuring the time taken for a resource to load under various conditions, thereby leaking sensitive information such as login status. One of the suggested defenses is to disable these event handlers for cross origin requests. This not only stops the attack but also breaks genuine scenarios. Website administrators who are cautious about cross-site timing attacks can configure CORP such that cross origin requests are allowed only to public resources i.e., resources which do not need authentication. CORP blocks requests to authenticated resources such as private pictures and URLs before they leave the browser, thereby defeating cross-site timing attacks. Listing 1.9 shows a sample CORP configuration for the same.

```
*        img        /public/images/*        ALLOW
*        *          *
                                            DENY
```

Listing 1.9. Defeating cross-site timing with CORP

5   Experimentation and Analysis

In this section, we explain about the implementation of CORP as a Chrome extension, its evaluation and the results of our analysis.

5.1   Implementation

We have developed an extension for Google Chrome web browser to implement a prototype of CORP. When a user installs the extension and loads a CORP-enabled website, the extension receives the CORP header, parses it and stores it in browser's memory using *HTML5 localstorage* API. The storage is accessible across tabs of the browser and policies set by multiple websites are stored and retrieved using the *origin* of the site as the key. When a genuine, CORP-enabled site (G) is opened in one tab and an attacker's site (A) makes a cross origin request to G, the extension intercepts every outgoing request from A if it is made to the origin of G and checks the policy associated with it. Only if the request complies with the policy set by G, the extension will allow the request, else it will block it. The *chrome.webRequest.onHeadersReceived* event of Chrome extension API helps in receiving HTTP response headers. The *chrome.webRequest.onBeforeRequest* [44] event helps in the interception process. It is fired before any TCP connection is made and can be used to cancel requests.

5.2   Experiments

We have conducted several experiments to evaluate the soundness of CORP, its ease of deployment and effectiveness.

Validating the Soundness of CORP: We have used Alloy [16], a finite state model finder, to formalize and verify the soundness of our proposal, CORP. We have modelled cross origin web interactions and came up with predicates which show instances of web infiltration attacks. We verified that on configuring CORP, Alloy fails to produce attack instances. Details about the formal model of CORP shall be provided at a different venue.

Evaluating CORP against a Corpus of Attacks: We have built a web application which is vulnerable to web infiltration attacks and a malicious web application which can launch attacks on the vulnerable application. We have referred to the test suite created by De Ryck et al. [31] and added their CSRF attack vectors to the malicious web application. We have also added vectors for clickjacking and timing to the application. As in the general browsing scenario, if a genuine user logs in at the vulnerable application in one tab, opens the malicious application in another tab and interacts with it, malicious requests (GET and POST) will be triggered which affect the vulnerable application adversely. On configuring CORP headers on the vulnerable web application and enabling the extension, all malicious cross origin calls will be blocked.

The chrome extension, vulnerable and malicious web applications can be accessed online and the attacks discussed in the paper can be replayed before and after installing the extension. Source code is available on Github [45].

Configuring CORP on Open Source Web Applications: To understand how CORP performs on real world websites, we have deployed three popular open source web applications (Table 1) and CORP-enabled them. Instead of deploying vulnerable versions of these applications and fixing them with CORP, we chose to deploy latest versions. Our idea is to verify that CORP is at least as good as the previous defenses and additionally conforms to the security guarantees promised in Section 4.4. We first confirmed that these applications implement at least one of the popular defenses against each of the web infiltration attacks (Section 3). As we have seen that these defenses insufficiently deal with infiltration attacks, we started afresh by completely disabling them. Then we started enabling CORP on each of these applications and verified that they are resilient to infiltration attacks. Our analysis shows that the effort required to CORP-enable large applications greatly depends on how resources are organized on the server e.g., all images placed under a single "/images" directory as against being scattered along multiple directories. Table 1 shows the number of rules needed to enable CORP on each of the applications, without reorganizing resources on the server. With proper segregation of resources, the number of rules can be brought down to less than 10 per application.

Table 1. Summary of open source web applications we experimented with

Application	Type	Version	# of source files	Lines of code	# of CORP rules
Wordpress	Blog/CMS	3.9.1	2288	23.9K	14
Moodle	LMS	2.5.6	11950	92.9K	84
Mediawiki	Wiki software	1.15.5-7	1338	99K	11

Analyzing Adherence of Top Websites to CORP: We have analyzed the home page traffic of Alexa [46] Top 15,000 websites, to find if they adhere to CORP by segregating their content based on types. The following content types were considered for analysis - images, css, scripts, html and flash. Figure 4 shows the results of the analysis. We find that more than 70% of sites already have an adherence greater than 60%. This is a positive indicator for the deployment of CORP, showing that website administrators can immediately use CORP on their existing sites and control their susceptibility to infiltration attacks.

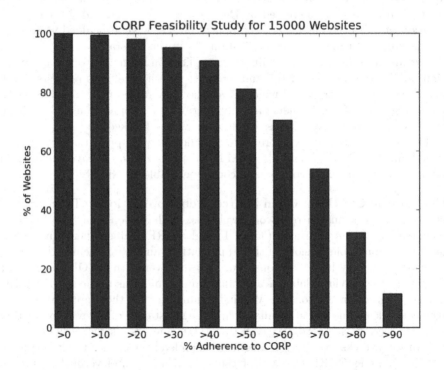

Fig. 4. Bar chart showing adherence of Alexa Top 15,000 websites to CORP

6   Conclusion and Future Work

HTTP works at a level of abstraction that cannot anticipate the semantics of the transaction or of the resource sought by a client. Declarative policies like CSP and CORP fill this semantic gap by conveying to the browser *who* (origins) can access *what* (resources) and *how* (events) as a result of a transaction. We believe that CSP and CORP together solve a large majority of exfiltration and infiltration attacks. The truth of this conjecture will, however, depend on the acceptance of CORP by browser vendors and its widespread adherence by web administrators.

As new web standards emerge, declarative policies like CSP and CORP will need to carry richer semantic intent. Such information could, for example, be used to control other types of browser events like user interactions e.g., "no copy-paste" while visiting Bank.com or force the browser to a canonical configuration e.g., disable browser extensions while visiting Bank.com. As future work, we plan to explore and expand the class of browser event types specifiable by declarative policies and study their impact on usability and security. Browsers for other form factors like mobiles and tablets present other challenges. We plan to experiment the implementation of declarative policies on these platforms.

Acknowledgements. We thank Kaushik Srinivasan and Akshat Khandelwal for their assistance in analyzing the traffic of 15,000 websites; Amulya Sri for her assistance in implementing CORP on open source web applications.

References

1. W3C: History of the World Wide Web. Technical report (1989),
   http://www.w3.org/Consortium/facts#history
2. Pilgrim, M.: Dive into HTML5. Technical report,
   http://diveintohtml5.info/past.html#history-of-the-img-element
3. Berners-Lee, T., Connolly, D.: Hypertext Markup Language – 2.0. Technical Report RFC1866, W3C (1995), http://tools.ietf.org/html/rfc1866
4. Jim, T., Swamy, N., Hicks, M.: Defeating script injection attacks with browser-enforced embedded policies. In: Proceedings of the 16th International Conference on World Wide Web, pp. 601–610. ACM (2007)
5. OWASP: XSS Prevention Cheat Sheet,
   https://www.owasp.org/index.php/XSS_(Cross_Site_Scripting)_Prevention_Cheat_Sheet
6. Vogt, P., Nentwich, F., Jovanovic, N., Kirda, E., Kruegel, C., Vigna, G.: Cross Site Scripting Prevention with Dynamic Data Tainting and Static Analysis. In: NDSS (2007)
7. Jayaraman, K., Du, W., Rajagopalan, B., Chapin, S.J.: Escudo: A fine-grained protection model for web browsers. In: 2010 IEEE 30th International Conference on Distributed Computing Systems (ICDCS), pp. 231–240. IEEE (2010)
8. Wikipedia: Netscape navigator 2 (1995),
   http://en.wikipedia.org/wiki/Netscape_Navigator_2
9. Zalewski, M.: Browser Security Handbook. Technical report (2011),
   https://code.google.com/p/browsersec/wiki/Part2#Same-origin_policy
10. Stamm, S., Sterne, B., Markham, G.: Reining in the web with content security policy. In: Proceedings of the 19th International Conference on World Wide Web, pp. 921–930. ACM (2010)
11. OWASP: CSRF Guard (2007), https://www.owasp.org/index.php/CSRF_Guard
12. Bortz, A., Boneh, D.: Exposing private information by timing web applications. In: Proceedings of the 16th International Conference on World Wide Web, pp. 621–628. ACM (2007)
13. Microsoft: Combating ClickJacking With X-Frame-Options. Blog (March 2010),
    http://blogs.msdn.com/b/ieinternals/archive/2010/03/30/combating-clickjacking-with-x-frame-options.aspx

14. Maone, G., Huang, D.L.S., Gondrom, T., Hill, B.: User Interface Security Directives for Content Security Policy (September 2013), https://dvcs.w3.org/hg/user-interface-safety/raw-file/tip/user-interface-safety.html
15. Akhawe, D., Barth, A., Lam, P.E., Mitchell, J., Song, D.: Towards a formal foundation of web security. In: 2010 23rd IEEE Computer Security Foundations Symposium (CSF), pp. 290–304. IEEE (2010)
16. Jackson, D.: Software Abstractions: Logic. Language, and Analysis. The MIT Press (2006)
17. OWASP: OWASP Top Ten Project, https://www.owasp.org/index.php/Category:OWASP_Top_Ten_Project
18. Hansen, R., Grossman, J.: Clickjacking. Blog (December 2008), http://www.sectheory.com/clickjacking.htm
19. Facebook: Facebook, Washington State AG target clickjackers. Blog (January 2012), https://www.facebook.com/notes/facebook-security/facebook-washington-state-ag-target-clickjackers/10150494427000766
20. Stone, P.: Pixel perfect timing attacks with html5 (2013), http://contextis.com/files/Browser_Timing_Attacks.pdf
21. Kotcher, R., Pei, Y., Jumde, P.: Stealing cross-origin pixels: Timing attacks on css filters and shaders (2013), http://www.robertkotcher.com/pdf/TimingAttacks.pdf
22. Jeremiah, G.: Introducing the 'I Know...' series. Blog (October 2012), https://blog.whitehatsec.com/introducing-the-i-know-series/
23. Heiderich, M.: CSRFx (2007), https://code.google.com/p/csrfx/
24. Jovanovic, N., Kirda, E., Kruegel, C.: Preventing cross site request forgery attacks. In: Securecomm and Workshops, pp. 1–10. IEEE (2006)
25. Oda, T., Wurster, G., van Oorschot, P., Somayaji, A.: SOMA: Mutual approval for included content in web pages. In: Proceedings of the 15th ACM Conference on Computer and Communications Security, pp. 89–98. ACM (2008)
26. Barth, A., Jackson, C., Mitchell, J.C.: Robust defenses for cross-site request forgery. In: Proceedings of the 15th ACM Conference on Computer and Communications Security, pp. 75–88. ACM (2008)
27. AdBlockPlus: HTTP Referer (2008), http://adblockplus.org/blog/http-referer-header-wont-help-you-with-csrf
28. Johns, M., Winter, J.: RequestRodeo: Client side protection against session riding. In: Proceedings of the OWASP Europe 2006 Conference (2006)
29. Mao, Z., Li, N., Molloy, I.: Defeating cross-site request forgery attacks with browser-enforced authenticity protection. In: Dingledine, R., Golle, P. (eds.) FC 2009. LNCS, vol. 5628, pp. 238–255. Springer, Heidelberg (2009)
30. De Ryck, P., Desmet, L., Heyman, T., Piessens, F., Joosen, W.: CsFire: Transparent client-side mitigation of malicious cross-domain requests. In: Massacci, F., Wallach, D., Zannone, N. (eds.) ESSoS 2010. LNCS, vol. 5965, pp. 18–34. Springer, Heidelberg (2010)
31. De Ryck, P., Desmet, L., Joosen, W., Piessens, F.: Automatic and precise client-side protection against CSRF attacks. In: Atluri, V., Diaz, C. (eds.) ESORICS 2011. LNCS, vol. 6879, pp. 100–116. Springer, Heidelberg (2011)
32. Maes, W., Heyman, T., Desmet, L., Joosen, W.: Browser protection against cross-site request forgery. In: Proceedings of the First ACM Workshop on Secure Execution of Untrusted Code, pp. 3–10. ACM (2009)

33. Czeskis, A., Moshchuk, A., Kohno, T., Wang, H.J.: Lightweight server support for browser-based CSRF protection. In: Proceedings of the 22nd International Conference on World Wide Web, pp. 273–284 (2013)
34. Balduzzi, M., Egele, M., Kirda, E., Balzarotti, D., Kruegel, C.: A solution for the automated detection of clickjacking attacks. In: ASIACCS 2010, pp. 135–144. ACM, New York (2010)
35. Maone, G.: Hello ClearClick, goodbye clickjacking! Blog (October 2008), http://hackademix.net/2008/10/08/hello-clearclick-goodbye-clickjacking/
36. Rydstedt, G., Bursztein, E., Boneh, D., Jackson, C.: Busting frame busting: a study of clickjacking vulnerabilities at popular sites. In: IEEE Oakland Web 2.0 Security and Privacy (W2SP 2010) (2010)
37. Huang, L.S., Moshchuk, A., Wang, H.J., Schechter, S., Jackson, C.: Clickjacking: Attacks and Defenses. In: USENIX Security Symposium (2012)
38. Huang, L., Jackson, C.: Clickjacking attacks unresolved. White paper, CyLab (2011), http://mayscript.com/blog/david/clickjacking-attacks-unresolved
39. Lekies, S., Heiderich, M., Appelt, D., Holz, T., Johns, M.: On the fragility and limitations of current browser-provided clickjacking protection schemes. In: Woot 2012, USENIX Security Symposium. USENIX (2012)
40. Hodges: RFC 6797, HTTP Strict Transport Security (HSTS) (November 2012), http://tools.ietf.org/html/rfc6797
41. Telikicherla, K.C.: Analyzing the new social engineering spam on facebook - lady with an axe. Blog post (June 2013), http://bit.ly/FBSpamAxe
42. Nafeez, A.: Stealing Facebook Graph API Access Token: Yet Another UI Redressing Vector (September 2011), http://blog.skepticfx.com/2011/09/facebook-graph-api-access-token.html
43. Kotowicz, K.: Cross domain content extraction with fake captcha, http://blog.kotowicz.net/2011/07/cross-domain-content-extraction-with.html
44. Google: Life cycle of requests in Chrome.webRequest API (2013), http://developer.chrome.com/extensions/webRequest.html
45. Telikicherla, K.C.: CORP repository (October 2013), http://iiithyd-websec.github.io/corp/
46. Alexa: Alexa top sites (October 2013), http://www.alexa.com/topsites

An Improved Methodology towards Providing Immunity against Weak Shoulder Surfing Attack

Nilesh Chakraborty and Samrat Mondal

Computer Science and Engineering Department
Indian Institute of Technology Patna
Patna-800013, Bihar, India
{nilesh.pcs13,samrat}@iitp.ac.in

Abstract. In a conventional password based authentication system, an adversary can obtain login credentials by performing shoulder surfing. When such attacks are performed by human users with limited cognitive skills and without any recording device then it is referred as weak shoulder surfing attack. Existing methodologies that avoid such weak shoulder surfing attack, comprise of many rounds which may be the cause of fatigue to the general users. In this paper we have proposed a methodology known as Multi Color (MC) method which reduces the number of rounds in a session to half of previously proposed methodologies. Then using the predictive human performance modeling tool we have shown that proposed MC method is immune against weak shoulder surfing attack and also it improves the existing security level.

Keywords: Authentication, Human shoulder surfer, Human performance modeling tool, Session password.

1 Introduction

Authentication is an important component of computer security. Among the different authentication schemes, password based authentication is one of the popular schemes for its efficacy and ease of use. However, the scheme fails to give security against *observation attack* while entering password in a public place (like ATM counter). In this attack, the attacker observes the credentials entered by the user and later may use it illegally for login purpose. This attack is also referred as *shoulder surfing attack*.

Now depending upon the nature of shoulder surfing attack and the types of equipment adversary uses, the attack is divided into two categories − *a) Strong Shoulder Surfing Attack*, where an adversary uses some recording device (like conceal camera) to record a user login session [12] [11] and, *b) Weak Shoulder Surfing Attack*, in which attacker relies on limited cognitive capabilities of human users and does not use any recording devices, though s/he might use pencil and paper to note down session information [18]. Now in general strong shoulder surfing resilient schemes such as [29] [12], [11] require more computational skills from users' end than that of weak shoulder surfing resilient schemes [26], [18].

A. Prakash and R. Shyamasundar (Eds.): ICISS 2014, LNCS 8880, pp. 298–317, 2014.

As system used in public domain (like ATM machine) is handled by all type of users so computational complexity during login is required to be less and thus, weak shoulder surfing resilient schemes become effective over strong shoulder surfing resilient one. In addition of giving protection against observation attack, shoulder surfing resilient schemes provide security against attacks such as- keylogger based attack [14], spreading chemicals on keypad to obtain the keystrokes [7], etc.

To avoid weak shoulder surfing attack, Roth et al. [26] proposed a scheme (we call it as Black-White or, BW method) in 2004 which was considered to be secure against weak shoulder surfers till 2012 [28]. Later Kwon et al. [18] proved that, human shoulder surfers − without equipped with any gadgets like recording device, can break the security of BW method by performing following three operations :

1. Covert attention [21] [18]
2. Perceptual grouping [19]
3. Motor operation [2]

In their work [18] authors proposed an improved methodology (termed as Four Color or FC method in this paper) which overcomes the above three step operations attack, performed by skilled human shoulder surfers. In literature, shoulder surfers capable of performing *Covert Attention, Perceptual Grouping* and *Motor Operation* are denoted as *CPM shoulder surfer*. The details of these operations are explained in Section 2. Though FC method is secured against weak shoulder surfing attack but the major problem with this scheme is that a huge number of rounds is required for login. In fact, both BW and FC methods require 16 rounds in a session during login for a PIN of length 4. Thus the user fatigue level becomes high [26] as user needs to face more number of rounds in a session. This may cause human mind inattentive and increase error rate during login [22]. Motivated by this issue we have made two major contributions in this paper.

Contribution 1: We have proposed a new model known as Multi Color or MC model in which user faces 8 rounds for a four digit PIN. Security analysis shows that MC method provides better security against random key selection attack (see Section 4) than of those BW and FC methods.

Contribution 2: We have performed security analysis of our method against CPM shoulder surfers, by using human performance modeling tool as shown by Kwon et al. [18]. We introduce the concept of *hardness factor*, higher value of which shows less vulnerability of a method against weak shoulder surfing attack. We also derive that MC method has higher value of *hardness factor* compared to BW and FC method.

The rest of the paper is organized as follows − in Section 2 we have given a brief overview of the existing work and also discussed some preliminary concepts required to understand our approach. The proposed approach is presented in Section 3. We have performed security analysis in Section 4. Usability analysis of our work is illustrated in Section 5. We conclude and give future direction of our work in Section 6.

2   Overview of Existing Work and Some Preliminary Concepts

Many methods [27], [4], [12], [11] have been proposed since international standard for PIN management, ISO 9564 mandated the fact that PIN entry device should be designed in such a way which can give protection against shoulder surfing attack [1]. Some methodologies such as [12], [11] were developed to resist partially observable shoulder surfing attack. Methods like [4], [29] were proposed to tackle fully observable shoulder surfing attack against strong adversary. However most of these schemes require a lot of computation from the user end.

Schemes proposed to handle weak adversary is relatively easy to use. In 2004 Roth et al. proposed a scheme termed as BW method [26] which is resilient against shoulder surfing attack performed with limited cognitive skill. In this method, the user interface consists of a numeric keypad on which, half of the numeric buttons on the keypad are colored as black and rest are colored as white as shown in Fig 1.

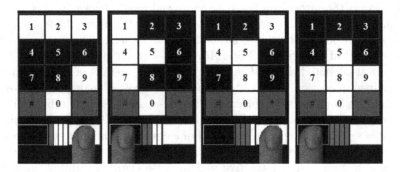

Fig. 1. Above figure shows user response for PIN digit 3. Each time keypad gets partitioned into half of the keys as black and the rest as white. User needs to identify the correct partition in which his/her PIN digit belongs.

The color of the numeric buttons varies in each round. User needs to identify the proper color that appears on his chosen PIN digit by pressing either black or white color button. User chooses a four digit PIN from a set $Q = \{0, 1, 2, ..., 9\}$. User needs to face $r = \lceil log_2|Q| \rceil$ rounds for each PIN digit. So for a l digits (here $l = 4$) long PIN user will face $l \times r$ rounds.

Limitations of BW Method: To explain the limitations of BW method, some prerequisite knowledge is required about the vision and information processing capabilities of human. This will help readers to understand the activities of CPM shoulder surfers and vulnerability of BW method more clearly.

Foveal Vision: It refers to normal vision capability of human while fixing his/her eye at a particular object [23]. For example, in the word $n+1$, by looking at 'n' a person can understand the whole word. This is because while looking at 'n', character '+' and '1' also come into normal vision angle. It has been observed that people having normal (or correct to normal) vision, can notice objects within 2° of visual angle, by fixing eye at a particular position. 1° visual angle is about 3 normal text from the point of eye fixation.

Fig. 2. Above figure shows a foveal and parafoveal vision ranges of human eyes by fixation of eye to a particular point (shown by yellow color +). Inner circle shows the foveal vision range and outer circle shows the parafoveal vision range.

Parafoveal Vision: It signifies the vision region which is hard to see (if not impossible) by fixing eye at a particular point. It starts from the end point of foveal vision region and surrounds within an angle of 5° from the eye fixation point [23]. Readers can assume that, this region starts after 4 to 5 normal text and ends after 8 to 9 texts from there. To gain information from this vision region, human needs saccadic (rapid) eye movements (except skillful video game player). Video game players normally have improved vision capabilities than of normal people [13] and can obtain information from extra foveal vision region even without saccadic movement of eyes. Both foveal and parafoveal vision ranges have been shown in Fig.2.

Covert Attention: Covert attention corresponds to attention not associated with eye movements. Significance of covert attention is, human can store a fair amount of information in visual short term memory (VSTM) [20] from foveal vision range by performing covert attention. By this operation, video game players can obtain the information from both the visual angles (2° and 5°) because of their improved vision skill [5] [13]. Extracted information from the range of foveal vision, helps adversary to perform perceptual grouping which is discussed next.

Perceptual Grouping: Perceptual grouping [19] implies grouping of objects and it depends upon their proximity, similarity, continuation, closure and symmetry. In BW method adversary can group objects (colored numeric buttons) based upon their color from the fovel vision range.

Motor Operation: Motor operation [2] requires a co-ordination between central nervous system and the musculoskeletal (muscular and skeletal) system. Human processes the grouping information by performing covert attention and perceptual grouping which requires effort of human mind. Now if the adversary wants to write down some gained information, his/her hand (comes under musculoskeletal system) must be engaged and thus the co-ordination between hand and mind is required for surreptitious handwriting, without moving the eyes.

Attack on BW Method by CPM Shoulder Surfers: Time required to enter a digit in each round by user is called response time. If the response time of the user allows the attacker to perform the necessary operation to obtain the PIN digit then attacker will proceed successfully. By using CPM-GOMS tool Kwon et al. [18] in their work showed that CPM shoulder surfers can proceed successfully to break the security of BW method. In Fig. 3 we have shown a pictorial presentation of attack scenario on BW method.

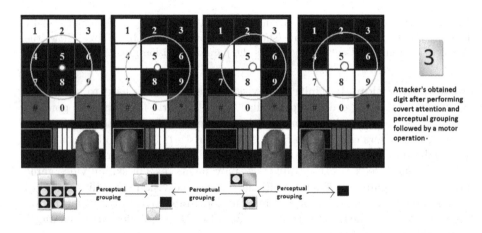

Fig. 3. Above figure shows a foveal vision angle to obtain the perceptual grouping. Parafoveal vision helps attacker to obtain the color chosen by user see (Fig. 2). Based upon the user response attacker discards the group (shown by yellow dot in the picture) from (visual short term memory) VSTM [8] [20] not falling into user color response. Finally attacker obtains a group consisting of single object due to logarithmic decrease of group cardinality in BW method.

In the first round of response of a digit, attacker first groups the black and white objects together. One thing is needed to mention here, while attacker groups those black and white numeric buttons depending on the colors, attacker overlooks the digits on the color buttons. After perceptual grouping attacker sees the user response in the first round corresponding to the first digit and depending upon that attacker discards one of the group from VSTM. For example, if user presses white color button then attacker discards the group of black objects. Reason behind this is, user PIN has appeared on the button belonging to white color group, so only that information is required by the attacker. In the immediate next round attacker keeps his/her eyes on those part of the keyboard interface which forms the previous color group and has been stored in his/her VSTM. Now in this round attacker finds that color black has appeared on some portion of the group stored in VSTM and color white has appeared on the rest. Now again depending upon user response attacker discards some of the objects from VSTM and stores a smaller perceptual group in VSTM at the end of the second round. This will be continued through out the four rounds corresponding a PIN digit of user. In every round, the cardinality of the perceptual group will be decreased and always it will converge to 1 on or before four rounds. After identifying a single object by the end of fourth round attacker will observe the digit written on it. Then s/he performs hand motor operation to write down the digit.

FC Method: In 2013 Kwon et al. [18] proposed a scheme referred as FC Method in which they have used four colors for coloring the numeric keypad. Each numeric button has been divided into two partitions. So there has been a total of 20 partitions (10 numeric buttons each having 2 partitions) which are filled with those 4 colors. The basic principal behind coloring the button are (i) each color will appear in exactly 20/4 (i.e. 5) partitions. (ii) same color will not appear on a button twice. So in each round user will find that his/her PIN digit posses two colors. User can choose any one of those two colors as his response and will press the color button of his/her chosen color. For giving response there exist four color (which are used to color the numeric buttons) buttons on user interface.

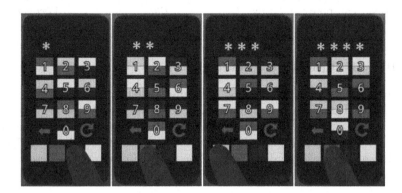

Fig. 4. Above figure shows user response for PIN digit 6. Each time user keypad gets partitioned using four colors. User needs to identify one of the correct color of his/her corresponding PIN digit.

Power of FC Method: There are evidences that human can recognize a visual object in quick time, occurring within $100 - 200$ milliseconds of stimulus presentation and can bring that thing within consciousness in another 100 milliseconds of time [25]. So objects posses similar properties can be perceptually grouped within at most 300 milliseconds. As in BW method attacker needs to perceptually group two different objects (black and white) so it takes 600 milliseconds to perform perceptual grouping. In [18] Kwon et al. showed that login time complexity of BW method in each round, would allow CPM shoulder surfers to get that required time for perceptual grouping operation. Thus security of the BW method was compromised.

In FC method perceptual grouping to identify objects of four colors takes $(4 \times 300$ or) 1200 milliseconds [25] in each round. But time complexity of each round does not allow the CPM shoulder surfers to get that required time for perceptual grouping, in fact in [18] authors showed that CPM shoulder surfers only get 700 milliseconds for perceptual grouping which is much less that the required time limit and thus reduces the chance of attack.

3   Proposed Multi Color Methodology

The main problem of FC method is that it takes 16 rounds for a four digit PIN. Thus the login process becomes lengthy and as a result is more error prone. In the proposed approach our aim is to reduce the login rounds without compromising with the security. In this section first we will discuss the basic feature and the login principal by using our proposed Multi Color (MC) methodology. Next we will describe how each digit of user PIN gets identified by the system uniquely. In MC method we have used a set *COLORS* consisting of five different colors – here *COLORS* = { Red, Green, Pink, Yellow, Sky }. For color blind people the same set can be replaced by *MARKS* = { Black, White, Dot, Vertical strip, Horizontal strip }. User PIN consists of 4 digits denoted as *d1,d2,d3,d4*.

3.1   Basic Feature of MC Method

Each numeric button in MC method is subdivided into three partitions namely *Up, Middle* and *Down*. So for ten numeric buttons from 0 to 9 there are 30 (3×10) partitions over which the five colors will be distributed. So each color will appear exactly in (30/5 or) 6 places. Now there will be a coloring constraint, by following which those colors will be distributed. The coloring constraint is described as follows:

Each color will appear in six partitions in six different numeric buttons. Among those six partitions, each partition will appear exactly twice.

In Fig. 5 we have shown the distribution of five colors in MC method. Each numeric button holds three different colors. Each color is placed on six different numeric buttons holding each partition exactly twice. Five color buttons shown bellow in Fig. 5 are used for giving response by user. To design the login interface

Fig. 5. A prototype model of MC method

Table 1. Useful notations used in algorithms

Notations	Descriptions
$\delta(X)$	Randomly permute elements of set X
B_k	Numeric button associated with digit k
$B_k(p)$	p^{th} partition in B_k
cfPosition(S)	Returns the first element from the set S
getEmpty(B_k)	Returns the partitions in B_k, not filled by any color
equCheck(A,B)	Checks whether set A, B are equivalent or not
colr(B_k(p))	Returns color at p^{th} partition of B_k
getValue(p)	Returns the value associated with a partition p
getColorpos(C,B_k)	Returns the partition where Color C placed in B_k
cardinality(S)	Returns the cardinality of set S
exchangeBackColor(B_X,B_S)	Background color of numeric buttons B_X and B_S exchanged
rand(S)	Choose an element from set S randomly
view(Keypad)	Shows the colored numeric buttons on user interface

we have used Algorithm 1. Readers can refer to Table 1 to understand the meaning of the notations used in Algorithm 1 (and also in Algorithm 2 in Section 3.2) in Table 1.

Algorithm 1 takes the permuted color set $COLORS$ as its one of the inputs. The other input N is a set of integers from $0-9$. At each iteration, for each color $C \in COLORS$ set $FILLED$ holds those partitions where C is already placed twice and can not be placed any more. Set S used in Algorithm 1 stores values of k for which numeric button B_k has already been encountered for a particular color. Variable k, used in the algorithm assures that same numeric button B_k for a particular color C, does not get selected more than once.

Algorithm 1. Color.NumericButtons()

Input: This algorithm will take set $COLORS$ and set N = $\{0, 1, ..., 9\}$ as input.
Output: This algorithm colors ten numeric buttons by following coloring constraint.
$COLORS \leftarrow \delta(COLORS)$ /* randomly permute the color set */
foreach *(C $\in$ COLORS)* **do**

    Initialize: up $\leftarrow$ 0; mid $\leftarrow$ 0; down $\leftarrow$ 0; /* variable up, mid and down are associated with partition Up, Middle and Down respectively */
    FILLED $\leftarrow$ empty ; S $\leftarrow$ empty;
    while *(1)* **do**

        k $\leftarrow$ rand(N-S);   /* selects a random number from the set N-S */
        P $\leftarrow$ getEmpty(B_k); /* holds those partitions in B_k not filled by any color */
        if *(equCheck(P,FILLED) = false AND P $\neq$ empty)* **then**
            pos $\leftarrow$ cfPosition(δ(P $-$ (P$\cap$FILLED)));
            if *(pos $\neq$ empty)* **then**   /* condition false if P $\subseteq$ FILLED */
                B_k(pos) $\leftarrow$ C;
                getValue(pos)++;   /* increases value of up, mid, down */
            end
            if *(up=2)* **then**
                FILLED $\leftarrow$ Up;
            end
            if *(mid=2)* **then**
                FILLED $\leftarrow$ Middle;
            end
            if *(down=2)* **then**
                FILLED $\leftarrow$ Down;
            end

        end
        add digit k to set S
        if *(cardinality(S) = 10)* **then**   /* if color C can not be placed in any numeric button by maintaining the coloring constraint */
            for *(t = 0 to 9)* **do**
                if *(C $\notin$ B_t)* **then**   /* if B_t not posses color C */
                    for *(r = 0 to 9)* **do**
                        pos $\leftarrow$ getEmpty(B_r); /* pos initially holds partitions in B_r not filled by any color */
                        pos $\leftarrow$ cfPosition(δ(pos$-$(pos$\cap$FILLED)));
                        if *(pos $\neq$ empty)* **then**
                            if *(colr(B_t(pos)) $\notin$ B_r)* **then**
                                B_r(pos) $\leftarrow$ colr(B_t(pos)); B_t(pos) $\leftarrow$ C; /* swap colors between the partitions */
                              getValue(pos) ++; break;
                        end
                      end
                    end
                end
                if *(up = 2 AND mid = 2 AND down = 2)* **then**
                    break;
                end
            end
        end
        if *(up = 2 AND mid = 2 AND down = 2)* **then**
            break;
        end
    end
end
return (ColorNumericKeypad);

3.2   Login Procedure and Evaluation of User Response

Using our proposed methodology user will give response twice for each of his/her PIN digit. As user PIN is 4 digit long so user will face $2 \times 4 = 8$ rounds in each session. In the first round user selects one color out of three colors from the numeric button corresponding to the first digit of the PIN and presses the corresponding color button. While choosing the color in the first round, user needs to remember the chosen partition. For the subsequent responses in that session user will look for the numeric button corresponding to his/her PIN digit and will select the color from the same partition.

Fig. 6 and Fig. 7 show user response for first two digits of PIN "d1 d2 d3 d4"(where d1 = 2, d2 = 3, d3 = 4, d4 = 1 taken as an example here). User gives his/her response in the first round by choosing a color from the middle of the numeric button corresponding to his/her first PIN digit 2 and thus user will always select a color from the middle of his/her corresponding PIN digit in that session. User enters his /her response for the first PIN digit in the first and second round, then for the second PIN digit in third and fourth round and so on. With the notion of the above discussion we define session partition next.

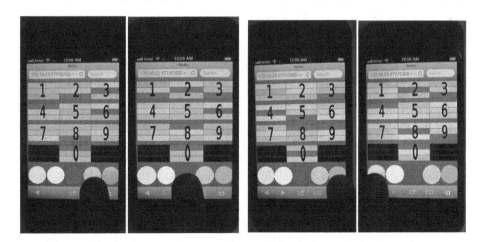

Fig. 6. Above figure shows first and second round responses for digit 2 with *session partition* selected as middle

Fig. 7. Above figure shows third and fourth round responses for digit 3 while *session partition* remains middle

Definition 1 *Session partition: It represents an arbitrary partition $SP \in \{Up, Middle, Down\}$ on the numeric button corresponding to the first PIN digit of the user from where user chooses the first color for giving response in first round. For giving rest of the responses, user will choose the color from same session partition SP corresponding to the numeric button of the PIN digit.*

Validation of User Response: Our scheme ensures that valid responses of genuine user will uniquely be identified. This means by guessing a different PIN an attacker will never be able to access the valid user's account. Total 8 rounds complete the MC method and user has to response in two consecutive rounds for a single PIN digit. So by the end of each even round (2,4,6,8) every single PIN digit of user should uniquely get identified by the system.

To achieve this we have used the following strategy. After giving the first color response by the user, system will track the session partition (for that entire session) with the help of user color response and first PIN digit of the user. Next in each odd (1,3,5,7) round system will record the color "C" appeared on session partition corresponding to the user PIN digit d1,d2,d3,d4 respectively. Then system will look for all other numeric buttons (say "tracked buttons") along with partition (say "tracked partition") where color "C" has appeared. In each even round (2,4,6,8) system will ensure that color "$\overline{C}$", which has appeared on the session partition on the numeric button corresponding to the user PIN digit, will never appear in those "tracked buttons", on the "tracked partitions". Though "$\overline{C}$" may appear in those "tracked buttons" on different partitions. One thing needed to mentioned here that "$\overline{C}$" may same as "C". If user fails to choose the session partition properly then system will return numeric buttons with arbitrary color combination by maintaining coloring constraint in each round and will block the user at the end of the session.

For instance in Fig.6 user has responded with color button "Green" in the first round. System finds that user has identified *session partition* as Middle by identifying the color "Green" on the user PIN digit 2. Next system locates "Green" color in all other "tracked buttons" along with partitions. In the immediate even round (second round) system allocates color "Red" in the session partition Middle, of numeric button 2. System ensures that "Red" color has not appeared on the "tracked partitions" of those "tracked buttons".

Significance of this is, if an attacker guesses a PIN digit wrongly, say 7 and identified session partition as middle in the first round, then also his response will match with the valid response of the user (see Fig. 6). This is because, same color has appeared in both the partitions (middle of numeric button 7 and 2). Now as system ensures that, color appear in middle of numeric button 2 will not appear in the previously tracked partitions (including middle of numeric button 7) in immediate even round (here second round), so attacker finds a different color (green) in middle of numeric button 7 which is not a valid color response, as color "Red" has appeared in middle of numeric button 2. Thus if an attacker proceedes successfully in any of those odd rounds (by guessing a wrong PIN digit or wrong session partition), our system ensures that, in immediate even round followed by an odd round, attacker will give a wrong response if either of PIN digit or session partition is wrong.

We have used Algorithm 2 to evaluate user response. Two array data structures "but" (abbreviation of button) and "poss" (abbreviation of position) are used in that algorithm which will hold the information about "tracked buttons" and the partition information respectively. In Fig.6 user responds by pressing color button "Green" in the first round. So array "but" and "poss" will hold the information about color "Green" that has appeared on the other numeric buttons. Table 2 shows the content of both the arrays for the above described situation. We have presented Algorithm 2 which will evaluate the user response. *The user will only get authenticated if array Resp in Algorithm 2 holds value 1 at all it's indices.* In Algorithm 2 "response" indicates the color entered by user as his/her response.

Table 2. Information stored in "but" and "poss"

index	but	poss
0	1	up
1	4	down
2	5	up
3	7	middle
4	9	down

4 Security Analysis

On discussing the security analysis of MC method first we will show the attack scenario by CPM shoulder surfers against skilled user login. Skilled users [18] are those who can minimize the login duration by suppressing rapid eye movement. We have used CPM-GOMS tool to perform security analysis. To prove the validity of the theoretical analysis we have performed an experimental analysis in support. Both the results show that MC method is more secure than BW and FC method.

Modeling the Security and Usability Trade-Off Using CPM-GOMS Tool for MC Method: Though it is quite feasible for CPM shoulder surfers to perform shoulder surfing attack on BW method but in FC method [18] authors have shown using CPM-GOMS tool that the same attack is infeasible. In our work we have used the same tool to show that our method is even slightly better than FC method. One thing can be noticed that, while performing the experimental analysis for user login and attacker activity we have tried our best to keep both user set and adversary set as mentioned in [18] in terms of their background and ability to perform. This helps us to compare better with the previous technologies.

The reason behind modeling execution time using CPM-GOMS [16] [15] (stands for cognitive perceptual motor and goals, operators, methods, and selection rules) is, it can model overlapping actions by interleaving cognitive, perceptual and motor operators and thus can predict the skilled behavior. Next we will introduce different functionality of CPM-GOMS.

Algorithm 2. Evaluation of user response

Input: This algorithm takes color keypad as input generated by Algorithm 1. **Output:** This algorithm will check user response in each round.

```
for (r=1 to 8) do
    Keypad ← Color.NumericButtons();    /* Keypad holds colored keypad returned by Algorithm 1 */
    if (r = 1) then
        view(Keypad); flag ← 0;
        if (response ∈ B_{d1}) then
            SP ← getColorpos(response,B_{d1});                    /* sets session partition */
            flag ← 1; Resp[r] ← 1; k←0;
            for (i=0 to 9) do
                if (response ∈ B_{d⌈r/2⌉} and i ≠ d⌈r/2⌉) then
                    but[k] ← i; poss[k] ← getColorpos(response,B_{d⌈r/2⌉}); k++;
                end
            end
        else
            SP ← null; Resp[r] ← 0;
        end
    else
        if (SP ≠ null) then                                   /* If SP correctly identified */
            if (r.Isodd() = true) then
                flag ← 1; view(Keypad);
                if (SP = getColorpos(response,B_{d⌈r/2⌉})) then
                    Resp[r] = 1; k←0;
                    for (i=0 to 9) do
                        if (response ∈ B_{d⌈r/2⌉} and i ≠ d⌈r/2⌉) then
                            but[k] ← i;
                            poss[k] ← getColorpos(response,B_{d⌈r/2⌉}); k++;
                        end
                    end
                else
                    flag ← 0; Resp[r] ← 0;
                end
            else
                if (flag = 1) then                            /* If SP correctly identified */
                    pColor ← colr(B_{d⌈r/2⌉}(SP));             /* holds valid color response */
                    for (t=0 to 4) do
                        X ← but[t]; Y ← poss[t];
                        if (colr(B_X(Y)) = pColor) then
                            for (S=0 to 9) do
                                if (poss[t] ≠ getColorpos(pColor, B_S)) then
                                    exchangeBackColor(B_X,B_S); break;
                                end
                            end
                        end
                    end
                    view(Keypad);
                    if (response = pColor) then
                        Resp[r] = 1;
                    else
                        Resp[r] = 0;
                    end
                else
                    view(Keypad); Resp[r] = 0;
                end
            end
        else
            view(Keypad); Resp[r] = 0;
        end
    end
end
```

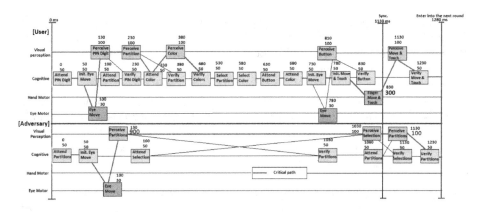

Fig. 8. Modeling and synchronization of MC method. (Each round takes 1280 ms. All rounds finish in 10.24 sec.) Skilled user is modeled.

Descriptive Operators and Functionalists of CPM-GOMS: Every task has been represented by a box with a duration in milliseconds (ms). According to the architecture of production system, cycle time of each cognitive operator is 50 ms [3] which is considered here. The cycle time to visually understand the presence or absence of an object is taken as 100 ms [9] but it may vary with the complexity of visual perception. The eye motor operation is set to 30 ms [17] which follows the conventional eye movement time in all CPM-GOMS models proposed after 1992 [10]. Time required for hand motor is reported as 300 ms in [18] and it has been evaluated empirically in their work. In our observation we also find the same. The reason behind this, in [6] author shows that "touch on screen" may take around 450 ms, though it may vary depending upon the screen distance and width. But estimated 450 ms time includes visual perception (requires 100 ms) of button and cognitive operation "initiation of move and touch" (requires 50 ms). So time required to perform hand motor is 300 ms, which is justifiable. The synchronization point is set after user presses a color button as his/her response.

Basic Idea Behind Overcoming the Attack: The basic idea behind overcoming the attack performed by CPM shoulder surfers is to increase the time required to perform the attack in such a manner so that it exceeds the user login time. If attacker does not get the required time to process the information then s/he will definitely fail. There are enough evidences that human can recognize objects within a time range of $100 - 200$ ms and takes another 100 ms to bring this information into awareness [25], thus perceptual grouping of same type of objects take $100 + 200 = 300$ ms. So in BW method adversary requires around 600 ms for perceptual grouping (300 ms each for recognizing group of black object and group of white object). Now in MC method as we have used five overlapping colors so total time required for perceptual grouping is $300 \times 5 = 1500$ ms. We modeled skilled user login time (see Fig. 8) by CPM-GOMS, which shows that by suppressing saccadic eye movement user can give response in 1280 ms time in each round (which is very close to the actual login time by skilled user 1275 ms in each round discussed in Section 5). So attacker needs to accomplish the attack within 1280 ms. But human performance modeling tool shows due to other activities like, *Attend Partition, Initiate (Init.) Eye Move and so on* s/he only gets at most 900 ms (see Fig. 8) time to perform perceptual grouping which is never been enough to perform the attack. Attacker needs 600 ms more to perform the attack. Thus like FC method [18] and unlike BW method [26] CPM shoulder surfers fail in MC method to perform the attack. With the notion of above discussion we will define "hardness factor" next.

Definition 2 *Hardness factor:* *It is the ratio of actual time needed by CPM shoulder surfers to get the PIN digit and skilled user login time. Higher value of this shows less vulnerability of a methodology against the shoulder surfing attack performed by CPM shoulder surfers.*

In our proposed method user login time (or the time CPM shoulder surfers gets) is 1280 ms. But to perform the attack, it requires $1280 + 600 = 1880$ ms. So hardness factor becomes $1880/1280$ or, 1.468.

Experimental Analysis of Shoulder Surfing Attack: To see whether the theoretical acceptance of the attack model is valid in reality or not we have selected 15 participants (12 male and 3 female) as attacker having average age of approx 24 years and (correct-to) normal eyesight. They all were right handed. As suggested in [18], we have selected only those people who like to play fast video games. Our experimental analysis comprises of two phases − a) *Training Phase* in which we introduced three methods to the attackers and gave a demonstration on how attack can be performed by CPM shoulder surfers on BW method. For each of the methods we employed 5 skilled users (total 15) who we believe, can achieve reasonably faster login time. We also split the participants (who will perform the attack) in 3 groups (each having 5). Then we asked them to learn how the attack can be performed. We allow each group to perform the attack on a single method in each day (first day on BW method, second day on FC method and third day on MC method). There were one to one interaction between the skilled users and participants. It took three days to complete the training phase. Each participant faced around 15 rounds for each of the methods in training phase. Next in b) *test phase* fourth, fifth and sixth day we asked the participants to perform the attack on BW, FC and MC method respectively. The attack was performed against 20 login (by skilled user) sessions for each participant. So we have collected total $(20 \times 15) = 300$ results from the participants for each of the methods. We have used smart phones for login.

We have seen that 68.3% of the attackers have been able to identify all the four digits of PIN for BW method. Three of them were able to do it in 18, 16 and 16 sessions (out of 20 sessions). The duration of each login session was about $15 − 16$ seconds (skilled user login time) in BW method. In the next two days of experiment, (meant for FC and MC method) there was a severe degradation in attackers performance. None of them was able to retrieve all

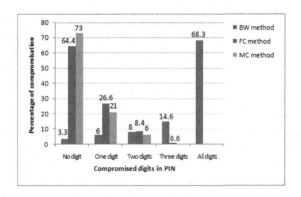

Fig. 9. Above figure shows that CPM shoulder surfers in 68.3% cases can get all PIN digits entered by user using BW method. All digits in the PIN are secure only in 3.3% of cases of BW method and that of 64.4% for FC and 73% for MC method.

four digit successfully in any single session. Many of them even failed to detect a single digit. Fig. 9 shows the performance graph of attacker for BW, FC and MC method. Duration of each session for FC method was $17 - 18$ seconds (skilled user login time) and that of MC method was $10 - 11$ seconds (skilled user login time). While performing the attack by video game players, we have observed that non-video game players can achieve the same capabilities as video game players by several practices [13].

Security against Random Key Selection Attack: In each of the BW and FC methods, attacker can proceed successfully with a probability $1/2$ in each round by randomly guessing the color buttons. Thus security against this kind of attack in both the method are $(1/2)^{16}$ or, 15.25×10^{-6}. In case of MC method attacker might success in the first round with a probability $3/5$ (as 3 colors will appear on user's PIN digit and choosing of anyone is valid for the first round). But in subsequent rounds, the probability of success will get reduces to $1/5$ and thus probability of success by the attacker will be $(3/5) \times (1/5)^7$ or, 7.68×10^{-6}, which is further reduced from both BW and FC method.

5 Usability Analysis

While performing usability analysis we have incorporated total 30 participants (21 male and 9 female) whose ages were between $24 - 45$ years. They all were habituated with touch screen technology and having (correct-to-) normal eye sight. We made three groups and randomly assign ten users to each group. We demonstrated how BW, FC and MC methodologies work and uploaded all three of those in a server so that they can use it to train themselves for login. We have set a global PIN, which is same for all participants for all three methods. During the demonstration we show them by suppressing saccadic eye movement, how one can achieve faster response time and encourage them to do so while login. We also gave all participants 2 days of time to get familiar with the login modules.

During test period we collected the data for one day. We randomly pick each group and assign a random chosen login method to each group so that each group gets one method out of three. No methods were distributed to more than one group. Participant were asked to perform the login using smart phones. Each participant in a group were requested to login ten times using the login methodology allocated to that group. Thus for each methodology we have obtained (10×10) 100 tested data. There after we have performed an analysis regarding login time and percentage of error during login. Fig. 10 shows how login time varies for BW, FC and MC methods $(10.2 - 14.8$ sec for MC method, $17.1 - 24$ sec for FC method and $16 - 22$ sec for BW method). We have taken average login time for each participant to perform statistical significance test. In t test $(t(18) = 0.228, P<0.05)$ [24] shows no significant difference between BW and FC method in terms of login duration. A one way ANOVA test suggest $(F(2,27) = 35.3, P<0.05)$ [24] among BW, FC and MC method, at least one method significantly reduces login duration. So cumulative result of both the test suggests, using MC method one can achieve faster login time.

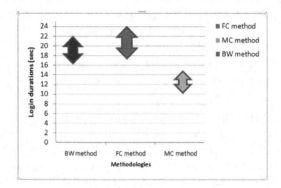

Fig. 10. Above figure shows a comparison of login duration among BW, FC and MC method

Result in Fig.10 shows that login time increases for some users and this is because, few users make a random eye movement during login and do not follow the strategy of "suppression of saccadic eye movement" during login. In this paper we have shown that, by following some smart work user can reduce the login time and thus can avoid the attack while using MC or, FC method. But using BW method no user can avoid such attack and thus this method is vulnerable to shoulder surfing attack performed by CPM shoulder surfers.

Percentage of error occurs during login was estimated as 0.16 for BW method, 0.15 for FC method and that of 0.07 for MC method. Student t test $(t(18) = 0.80, P < 0.05)$ [24] suggests there exists no significant difference between BW and FC method. A one-way ANOVA test shows $(F (2, 27) = 3.45, p < 0.05)$ [24] at least one method among BW, FC and MC method significantly reduces error rate while login. Cumulative result of both the test shows MC method is less prone in terms of login by user.

User Feedback: After performing the usability analysis, we gave all the users a feedback form. Almost all (above 80%) agree that our methodology takes a bit more time (2 − 3 login session) in terms of learning initially. But most of them prefer MC method due to less number of rounds and better security. They also agree that fatigue level using our methodology is much less.

In [18] using CPM-GOMS tool authors showed that skilled user login time using BW method is 960 ms and that of 1080 ms for FC method in each round. They also informed that CPM shoulder surfers require 960 ms to perform the attack on BW method and 1580 ms for FC method (each result was derived using CPM-GOMS tool). Hardness factor greater than 1 suggests a method is secure against CPM shoulder surfers and it increases monotonically. In Table 3 we have presented a summary of comparative analysis among all three methodologies. Pr[SRKS] in Table 3 denotes *probability of success by selecting random keys* for giving response.

Table 3. The outline of comparative features among BW, FC and MC method

	BW method	FC method	MC method
PIN length	4	4	4
Rounds	16	16	8
Hardness factor	1	1.462	1.468
Pr[SRKS]	$1/2^{16}$	$1/2^{16}$	$3/5^8$
Login time	More	More	Less

6 Conclusion and Future Work

Strong shoulder surfing attack resilient schemes (that resist recording attack) often require more computational skills from users end and so they are not very commonly used in public domain. Authentication system used in public domain are often targeted by human shoulder surfers and for those systems a better alternative is to use schemes which can resist attack performed by human adversaries. Schemes which can resist such attack are known as weak shoulder surfing resilient schemes.

In this paper we have presented MC Method which is immune to weak shoulder surfing attack performed without any recording device. Our proposed methodology minimizes user effort during login by a large margin. That is a major advantage we have achieved here. However, to achieve this we have not compromised with the security aspect. On the contrary we are able to increase the security level. These two advantages combined together have made the proposed MC scheme to a powerful scheme. We have also shown the comparative study with two existing techniques and found that the proposed technique performs well with respect to those techniques both in terms of usability and security point of view. In future we will try to extend this shoulder surfing resilient scheme against the adversaries with recording device.

Acknowledgments. This work is partially supported by a research grant from the Science & Engineering Research Board (SERB), Government of India, under sanctioned letter no. SB/FTP/ETA-226/2012. Authors also like to thank Mr. Subho Shankar Basu for providing helpful suggestions.

References

1. Banking–Personal Identification Number (PIN) Management and Security–Part 1: Basic Principles and Requirements for Online PIN Handling in ATM and POS Systems, Clause 5.4 Packaging Considerations, ISO 9564-1:2002 (2002)
2. Allen, G., Buxton, R.B., Wong, E.C., Courchesne, E.: Attentional activation of the cerebellum independent of motor involvement. Science 275(5308), 1940–1943 (1997)
3. Anderson, J.R., Matessa, M., Lebiere, C.A.-R.: A theory of higher level cognition and its relation to visual attention. Human-Computer Interaction 12(4), 439–462 (1997)
4. Bai, X., Gu, W., Chellappan, S., Wang, X., Xuan, D., Ma, B.P.: PAS: predicate-based authentication services against powerful passive adversaries. In: Annual Computer Security Applications Conference, ACSAC, pp. 433–442. IEEE (2008)
5. Bavelier, D., Achtman, R., Mani, M., Föcker, J.: Neural bases of selective attention in action video game players. Vision Research 61, 132–143 (2012)
6. Bi, X., Li, Y., Zhai, S.: FFitts law: modeling finger touch with fitts' law. In: Proceedings of the SIGCHI Conference on Human Factors in Computing Systems, pp. 1363–1372. ACM (2013)
7. Blonder, G.: Graphical passwords. lucent technologies, inc., murray hill, nj. US patent, ed. United States (June 1996)
8. Brady, T.F., Konkle, T., Alvarez, G.: A review of visual memory capacity: Beyond individual items and toward structured representations. Journal of Vision 11(5), 1–34 (2011)
9. Card, S.K., Moran, T.P., Newell, A.: The psychology of human computer interaction hillsdale. LEA, NJ (1983)
10. Carroll, J.M.: HCI models, theories, and frameworks: Toward a multidisciplinary science. Morgan Kaufmann (2003)
11. Chakraborty, N., Mondal, S.: Color Pass: An intelligent user interface to resist shoulder surfing attack. In: IEEE Students' Technology Symposium (TechSym), pp. 13–18 (2014)
12. Chakraborty, N., Mondal, S.: SLASS: Secure login against shoulder surfing. In: Martínez Pérez, G., Thampi, S.M., Ko, R., Shu, L. (eds.) SNDS 2014. CCIS, vol. 420, pp. 346–357. Springer, Heidelberg (2014)
13. Green, C.S., Bavelier, D.: Action video game modifies visual selective attention. Nature 423(6939), 534–537 (2003)
14. Holz, T., Engelberth, M., Freiling, F.: Learning more about the underground economy: A case-study of keyloggers and dropzones. In: Backes, M., Ning, P. (eds.) ESORICS 2009. LNCS, vol. 5789, pp. 1–18. Springer, Heidelberg (2009)
15. John, B.E.: Extensions of GOMS analyses to expert performance requiring perception of dynamic visual and auditory information. In: Proceedings of the SIGCHI Conference on Human Factors in Computing Systems, pp. 107–116. ACM (1990)
16. John, B.E., Gray, W.D.: CPM-GOMS: an analysis method for tasks with parallel activities. In: Conference Companion on Human Factors in Computing Systems, pp. 393–394. ACM (1995)

17. John, B.E., Kieras, D.E.: The GOMS family of user interface analysis techniques: comparison and contrast. ACM Transactions on Computer-Human Interaction (TOCHI) 3(4), 320–351 (1996)
18. Kwon, T., Shin, S., Na, S.: Covert Attentional Shoulder Surfing: Human Adversaries Are More Powerful Than Expected. IEEE Transactions On Systems, Man, and Cybernatics: Systems 44(6) (2013)
19. Lowe, D.G.: Perceptual Organization and Visual Recognition. Tech. rep., DTIC Document (1984)
20. Luck, S.J., Vogel, E.K.: The capacity of visual working memory for features and conjunctions. Nature 390(6657), 279–281 (1997)
21. Posner, M.I.: Orienting of Attention*. Quart. J. Experimental Psychology 32(1), 3–25 (1980)
22. Rabinbach, A.: The human motor: Energy, fatigue, and the origins of modernity. Univ of California Press (1992)
23. Rayner, K., White, S.J., Kambe, G., Miller, B., Liversedge, S.P.: On the processing of meaning from parafoveal vision during eye fixations in reading. In: The Minds Eye: Cognitive and Applied Aspects of Eye Movement Research, pp. 213–234 (2003)
24. Rosenkrantz, W.A.: Introduction to Probability and Statistics for Science, Engineering, and Finance. CRC Press (2011)
25. Treisman, A.M., Kanwisher, N.G.: Perceiving visually presented objects: Recognition, awareness, and modularity. Current Opinion Neurobiol. 8(2), 218–226 (1998)
26. Roth, V., Ritcher, K., Freidinger, R.: A PIN-entry method resilient against shoulder surfing. In: ACM Conf. Comput. Commun. Security, pp. 236–245 (2004)
27. Wiedenbeck, S., Waters, J., Sobrado, L., Birget, J.-C.: Design and Evaluation of a Shoulder-Surfing Resistant Graphical Password Scheme. In: ACM Working Conference Advance Visual Interfaces, pp. 177–184 (2006)
28. Yan, Q., Han, J., Li, Y., Deng, R.H.: On Limitations of Designing Leakage-Resilient Password Systems: Attacks, Principles and Usability. In: 19th Internet Social Network Distributed System Security (NDSS) Symposium (2012)
29. Zhao, H., Li, X.: S3PAS: A scalable shoulder-surfing resistant textual-graphical password authentication scheme. In: 21st International Conference on Advanced Information Networking and Applications Workshops, pp. 467–472 (2007)

Catching Classical and Hijack-Based Phishing Attacks*

Tanmay Thakur and Rakesh Verma

Computer Science Dept., University of Houston, TX, 77204, USA

Abstract. The social engineering strategy, used by cyber criminals, to get confidential information from Internet users is called phishing. It continues to trick Internet users into losing time and money each year, besides the loss of productivity. The trends and patterns in such attacks keep on changing over time and hence the detection algorithm needs to be robust and adaptive. Although, many phishing attacks work by luring Internet users to a web site designed to trick them into revealing sensitive information, recently some phishing attacks have been found that work by either installing malware on a computer or by hijacking a good web site. In this paper, we present effective and comprehensive classifiers for both kinds of attacks, classical or hijack-based. To the best of our knowledge, our work is the first to consider hijack-based phishing attacks. Our techniques are also effective at zero-hour phishing web site detection. We focus on the fundamental characteristics of phishing web sites and decompose the classification task for a phishing web site into a URL classifier, a content-based classifier and ways of combining the two. Both the URL classifier and the content-based classifier introduce new features and techniques. We present results of these classifiers and combination schemes on datasets extracted from several sources. We show that: (i) our URL classifier is highly accurate, (ii) our content-based classifier achieves good performance considering the difficulty of the problem and the small size of our white list, and (iii) one of our combination methods achieves superior detection of phishing web sites (over 99.97%) with reasonable false positives of about 3.5 % and another achieves just 0.22% false positives with more than 83% true positive rate. Moreover, our content-based classifier does not need any periodic retraining. Our methods are also language independent.

1 Introduction

Phishing is a social engineering threat aimed at gleaning sensitive information such as user names, passwords and financial information from unsuspecting victims. Attackers typically lure Internet users to a web site designed to trick them into revealing sensitive information. Many phishing web pages are copies of some version of a legitimate site such as PayPal or eBay. Some offer money or prizes as incentives. Users are typically attracted to phishing pages by sending them

---

* Research partially supported by NSF grants CNS-1319212 and DUE 1241772.

A. Prakash and R. Shyamasundar (Eds.): ICISS 2014, LNCS 8880, pp. 318–337, 2014.

warning or enticing emails, or by posting URL links in: forums, social networking sites, chat and bulletin boards. Recently, some new phishing attacks have surfaced that involve either installing malware on a computer [22] or hijacking a legitimate web site, e.g., Netcraft reported that the asecna.aero site was hacked in an April 2014 report [18]. *Classical phishing attacks* can be defined as the pages asking for sensitive information from users by mimicking a legitimate domain or giving an incentive, warning etc. In contrast, in a *hijack based attack*, phishers hijack a server on a legitimate domain and then put content to steal sensitive information from users. In this attack, the URL and hence the domain is legitimate, but the contents are phishing and not authored by the domain owner.

The urgency for efficient and reliable phishing detection schemes becomes clear upon considering the phishing activity trends in the second quarter of 2013 (April-June 2013, Q2 2013) as published by the Anti-Phishing Working Group (APWG) Reports [2]. The APWG definition of phishing encompasses both social engineering and technical subterfuge to steal consumers' personally identifiable information (PII). Social-engineering schemes include spoofed e-mails that point consumers to counterfeit websites and technical schemes include malware planted onto PCs to steal credentials directly. Given this definition, the APWG reports that the number of unique phishing websites detected in Q2-2013 reached a high of 44,511 in May 2013. Payment Services accounted for a large percent of attacks with the number of phished brands reaching a high of 639 in Q2-2013. United States continued its position as the top country for hosting phishing websites during this time. The percentage of computers infected with banking Trojans and password stealers also rose. For more information on phishing trends, refer to the reports by APWG [2].

Besides the loss of time and productivity, estimates of money lost every year in phishing attacks run from several hundred million to billions of dollars. Hence its detection is an important challenge for researchers. The trends in patterns of the phishing sites keep changing and hence, we need a robust algorithm that is not just specific to the given dataset. Also, the lifetime of phishing sites is very short. "On an average a phishing domain lasts 3 days 31 minutes and 8 seconds" [17]. The algorithm should also be fast enough to catch such pages before they do their job. Finally, the algorithm should rely on fundamental characteristics of phishing web sites. We kept all of this into consideration and designed robust heuristics to tackle the changing patterns of the sites.

As pointed out in [28], "phishing patterns evolve constantly, and it is usually hard for a detection method to achieve a high true positive rate while maintaining a low false positive rate." Existing phishing site detection methods fall into one of the following categories: URL matching against human-verified blacklists, heuristics used with machine learning, password based, or some combination of information extraction with information retrieval. The first category of methods has very low false positives rate, but such methods are not robust against future cases. Sheng et al. [21] show that zero-hour protection of major blacklist-based toolbars has true positive rates in the 15-40 % range. Updating these blacklists typically requires heavy human effort and is a slow process. For example, January 2012 statistics from Phishtank show that the median time to verify that a URL is a phish was two hours. Of course, human-verification can be easily overwhelmed by automatically generated URLs. Heuristics used with machine learning suffer from the need for a clean, labeled training corpus, over-fitting to the training corpus and the need for retraining because of model drift over time. Password-based schemes lack robustness for phishing detection [9]. Information extraction based schemes such as named-entity extraction [28] suffer from the lack of parsable sentences on web sites and also the limits of automatic natural language processing techniques. Moreover, named-entity extraction techniques are also particularly prone to lower-casing problems such as failure to recognize paypal (note the lower case) as a named entity.

Our proposed schemes are built on the following observations. First, the fundamental difference between a phishing and a legitimate site lies in its objective. While a legitimate site typically conveys some information to the reader or elicits some basic information from a user to provide a service, a phishing site is designed to *steal* the victim's information. Second, there are basically two kinds of phishing sites in classical phishing attacks. The first type of sites copy the content of a legal site such as a bank, or a credit card company, or a payment site such as PayPal, etc. The second type consists of sites that do not copy any legal site, but instead entice the user through either an advertisement or a financial lure such as the promise of a prize, gift, etc. These observations play a crucial role in our method. We present a URL classifier based on new and classical features.

A key feature of *hijack-based phishing attacks* is that the browser address bar continues to show a legitimate URL, e.g., see [22] and the Netcraft news item link given above. Hence URL analysis cannot catch such phishing attacks. Therefore, to thwart hijack-based attacks, we present a content-based classifier that combines structural elements of a site together with certain intentional information extracted from the page itself. A key advantage of our content-based classifier is that no training data is required for it. It assumes no knowledge of phishing signatures or specific implementations. Hence, it is suitable as both a zero-hour, stand-alone phishing site detection scheme, and also in combination with other existing methods such as blacklists and white-lists.

Finally, for classical phishing attacks, we present three combination schemes that combine the judgments of the URL classifier and the content-based classifier. Another advantage of our methods is that they are language independent, which we will justify later.

Unlike many other techniques, we also focus on the advantages of SSL certifications and the form content in the web page. SSL is an acronym for an encryption technology called Secure Sockets Layer. Having SSL certificates for websites ensures encrypted communication and hence secure connection between user's web browser and web servers. This helps in transmission of private data without problems of eavesdropping, message forgery or message tampering. If the web page does not have SSL certificates, then it is possible to see each bit of data and taking this advantage; phishers can just take information from here instead of hosting their own phishing site. We call this kind of website unsafe or vulnerable. Our algorithm also helps to detect such vulnerable pages.

Our content-based classifier analyzes the phishing web site's behavior using a copy detection algorithm and a real-time bot that injects random input data of the correct type for the form input fields on the web site. Thus, it can also be used to flood the phishing website with junk information and carry out a denial of service attack on confirmed phishing sites. To the best of our knowledge, this is the first time such an analysis has been conducted for classifying websites.

1.1 Our Contributions and Results

We present new features and techniques that are effective for zero-hour classical phishing web site detection, for hijack-based phishing attacks, and for insecure site detection. Our content-based classifier is based on fundamental characteristics of a phishing site and the innate differences between a phishing site's behavior versus a normal site's behavior. We surveyed the common patterns of phishing websites from a small dataset of 200-300 phishing URLs and used these patterns to detect them.

We evaluate all classifiers and four combination schemes. The best detection rate is 99.97 % with 3.5% false positives. Using search based filtering it went down to 93.37% with reasonable false positives of 0.54%. In contrast, the previous best zero-hour phishing classifier [29] achieved a detection rate of 73% with a slightly lower false positive rate of 0.03% (more detailed comparisons below), all with Internet search. Our results are also competitive against the more recent work of [27], which uses machine learning techniques. In contrast, we make minimal use of machine learning.

The rest of this paper is organized as follows. The next section Section 2 presents relevant related work on phishing detection. Section 4 presents our URL classifier and its performance analysis on several datasets, Section 5 presents the content-based classifier and its performance, and Section 6 presents the datasets, our combination schemes and their performance results. Section 8 presents the results of testing on the datasets including the performance of individual heuristics and a failure analysis. Section 9 concludes.

2 Prior Work and Comparison

Digital identity theft through phishing is primarily a social engineering attack and has attracted a lot of research interest in this context. Different research groups have studied this problem from various perspectives: server-side and browser-side strategies, education/training, and evaluation of anti-phishing tools, detection schemes and finally studies that analyze the reasons behind the success of phishing attacks, e.g., [15,21,7,6,5,3,4,8,1,30]. Naturally, we cannot survey all of these studies due to space limitations. We present below a selection of past work with the understanding that this discussion is not meant to be exhaustive. In this section, we survey prior research directly related to our work on detecting phishing sites and especially those techniques that do not rely on URL analysis since as mentioned earlier, the latest attacks manage to leave the URL unchanged from that of a legal site, which are the focus of this paper. In the following paragraphs, we briefly outline the prior work on phishing categorized by their research objectives.

2.1 Phishing Detection Using Blacklist Approach

The reporting of a page as phishing, then its manual verification is a basic building block of generating blacklists. This could not prove effective alone and gave detection rate of just 15-40% [21]. Updating such blacklists over time is a very time consuming process and requires tedious human effort for manual verification. Also, this strategy will not help in zero-hour phish detection and hence we do not use blacklists in our algorithm.

2.2 Phishing Detection Using Content of Page and Information Retrieval

One approach to detect phishing using web page content is analyzing the structure of the URLs and validating the authenticity of the content of these target web pages. Cantina [31] is one such scheme: a content-based approach to detecting phishing websites, based on information retrieval and text mining algorithms. They tested their methods on a small dataset of 100 websites since analyzing content takes time. Their results exhibit a tradeoff between detection of phishing web sites and the false positive rate for legitimate web sites. There are many other schemes that use some subset of URL features, IP-based features, and content-based features [9,16].

2.3 Zero-Hour Phishing Detection Using Text Analysis

Xiang et al. [29] proposed a scheme for zero-hour phishing site detection, which uses whitelists, text comparison of the web-page against the text content of existing phish sites, and additional verification using a search engine (as in Cantina) if a page is flagged as a potential phish. They also use a sliding window in the back-end to incrementally build a *machine learning* model as new phishing signatures are built. They achieve a 0% false positive rate with a true positive rate of 67.74% using the search-oriented filtering and a 0.03% false positive rate and 73.53% true positive rate without it.

2.4 Phishing Detection Using Machine Learning

In [27], the Cantina+ and zero-hour phishing detection researchers enriched their techniques with machine learning and did bigger experiments with unique and near-duplicate websites and were able to achieve a detection rate of 92% for phishing web sites with false positives ranging from 0.4% to 1.4% depending on the testing scenario: randomized (10% of phishing websites as training data - the sites could be future or historical) versus timed testing (20% of phishing websites as training dataset - the sites came from only historical data).

A research team from Google has presented a machine learning classification technique with hundreds of features to accomplish a large scale automatic classification of phishing web pages [26] by analyzing both the URL and the content of the page and claims to achieve 90% accuracy in classifying web pages with false positives below 0.1%. This classifier is being used to maintain Google's phishing blacklist automatically.

The Google classifier is rebuilt *every day* and if a website is off-line during the training phase it will not be in the model. We also checked their performance on the same testing URLs. Although they have better false positives rate but their detection rate is significantly lower than our classifier (detailed comparisons are in the Results section). We noticed even if the phishing contents are taken down from the website, they mark the URL as phishing. Hence, their analysis is not real time.

Other Phishing Techniques. There are many strategies used in phishing detection. Some of them are based on URL analysis, information extraction, text analysis, etc. For more details on phishing and detection schemes, we encourage the reader to refer the books by [13,14] and [20] and the paper [12] for additional references. For phishing email detection schemes, we refer the reader to [24,23] and references cited therein.

Although there is considerable research on phishing detection but there are very few schemes for zero-hour phishing detection and the existing schemes are not effective for hijack-based attacks. Hence, we propose and evaluate three new classifiers for zero-hour phishing, insecure site detection, and hijack-based attacks. The following section describes the dataset, our methodology and the resulting classifiers in detail.

3 Overview of the Classification Approach and Initial Steps

Phishing websites can be detected by analysis of URL, its redirection, title of the page, text in the body, HTML source, website certification, etc. We implemented our algorithm to check for important and fundamental clues and then take a decision. The fundamental clues are:

- A phishing web site must ask for information.
- It must either impersonate a popular web site or entice the visitor with some incentive (prize, gift, etc.)
- It will have a low search rank because of its short-lived nature and poor in-degree (incoming links) from other web sites.

Focusing on fundamental clues makes our algorithms robust to the changing trends in the phishing attacks. Our analysis is mainly based on real-time behavior of the pages and on similarity detection and hence we need some preprocessing to get the input data. The structure can be divided in four main parts. First part is preprocessing, second is analysis of URL, third is actual body/behavior analysis and last is filtering with search function.

3.1   Pre-processing Steps

The very first pre-processing step is to remove duplicate URLs and analyze only unique URLs. We check if the original URL or the URL that is reached after opening the page (redirected URL) is already processed. This removes redundancy in the input data and ensures unbiased results.

To ensure that we analyze the real-time content of the given page, we first open the content in a mimicked browser. We verify and remove any pages with 404 or similar errors. We then retrieve the top level domain (TLD) of the given URL. If the page is able to provide all the required information without any error, then we proceed. All errors are reported and the URLs are removed from subsequent analysis.

3.2   Whitelisted Domains

We expect that administrators of good domains will follow professional security practices and ensure the sanctity of the content hosted on their domains. They typically will not allow anybody to put malicious content that will cause their domain reputation to drop. We collected a set of such genuine domains and treat it as our whitelist.

We build our own whitelist. We listed the top 5,000 domains as ranked by Alexa. Many phishers use free hosting domains to launch their phishing attacks. There can be instances in which an administrator takes some time to remove such pages from the hosting domain. To avoid this scenario we removed domains that offer free hosting and free blogging. We studied the distribution of common targets from the json file provided by Phishtank. We discovered that some of the common banking targets are missing from the top rated domains. We added them to our whitelist. Finally, we chopped the whitelist to just 5000 domains.

The Whitelist-domain function checks whether the domain of the given URL or redirected URL is in the whitelist, and then bypasses it as a legitimate page. Google is a top rated domain and it has google document service. We found that phishers also managed to create phishing pages and host it on the google document site. An illustration of such URL is `https://docs.google.com/my-demo-PayPal-phishing-page`. So, we have to be cautious about such cases and hence we allowed all the Google domains except for docs.google.[TLDs]. This function bypasses further complex steps and hence the classification of the web pages can be done faster. However, in principle this step could be omitted or given as an option to the user.

3.3 Sensitive Information Check

This step ensures that the page is really asking for some sensitive information and can be a potential phishing candidate. We check whether the page has a password field anywhere on it. Many phishing pages go offline soon, and our pre-processing step takes care of the errors and exceptions caused by such behavior. But, many domains show a completely different page with fancy 404 messages (e.g., Oh! You broke something; message from `http://commaccounting.co.nz/moodle/blog/a/e84c2591f611f5438a3314460e280865`). This URL hosted phishing content in past but while we were processing it there were no such contents and no errors but a page with this fancy message. Sensitive information check will remove all such pages and mark them as legitimate. Only pages asking for sensitive information advance forward after this step.

4 URL Classifier

4.1 U1: Targets in URL

Cyber criminals put the target (e.g., PayPal, eBay, BankOfAmerica, etc.) in the URL to disguise the URL to the user. According to quarterly reports by APWG (Anti Phishing Working Group), 45-50% phishing URLs contained target names in the URL last year (2013). This strategy is used to fool naive users into believing that they are really visiting the desired page. Many researchers discussed this strategy and use of this feature. We have improved this method over existing techniques. We take the URL, and remove the main domain and TLD from it. We are now left with either subdomain and/or the extended URL. We check targets in such remaining part of the URL and not the complete URL directly. We need an accurate and comprehensive list of targets for this purpose. We analyzed 12,000 URLs from Phishtank and collected the top targets that were targeted more than 0.1% of the time among those 12,000 URLs. As expected, PayPal ranked first with more than 13.6% followed by AOL, which was just 1.1%. Also, phishers try to attack a big population and hence a popular domain. So, we added all the whitelisted domains to the list of targets. This made the list strong and removing the actual domain name with TLD from the input URL helped us to get rid of false positives. Experiments were done to test this function and the result varied from true positive rate of 40% to 50% with almost 0% false positives.

4.2 U2: Misplaced TLDs

This is similar to checking targets in URL, but we check for list of all top level domains (TLDs) that are placed not at the actual TLD location. Phishers use this strategy to disguise URLs. We remove the main domain and actual TLD from the URL and check for the TLDs in the rest of the URL.

4.3   U3: URL Classification Using Machine Learning Approach

4.3.1 Features
The above two methods for URL analysis are modifications on prior research work and observations. In addition, we also implemented single feature classifiers to classify the URL based on the length of just the domain and distribution of the characters independently. We used machine learning algorithm to build a model for those features. The first classifier's feature is the length of the domain of the URL, while the second classifier's feature was the Euclidean distance between the distribution of English characters in the URL and the distribution of English characters in standard English text.

4.3.2 Machine Learning Algorithm
Both classifiers were based on the WEKA library's PART machine learning algorithm. The PART algorithm is a separate-and-conquer rule learner. It creates a partial C4.5 decision tree and chooses the best leaf as a rule for the classifier. The algorithm combines C4.5 and RIPPER rule learning algorithms. We chose to use PART because it performs reliably, and allows us to view the rules that the algorithm generates. Being able to view the rules gives us insight into the classifier, and allows us to, for example, identify reasons for false-positive results.

4.3.3 Dataset, Training and Testing
In order to train both of the classifiers a data set was created that consisted of 20,240 URLs with 10,600 legitimate and 9,640 phishing URLs. The legitimate URL list was taken from the top 12,000 websites provided by Alexa.com accessed on February 11, 2014. The phishing URLs were taken from 12,000 results from Phishtank.com accessed on February 12, 2014. We then took the 12,000 legitimate URLs and removed all common occurrences with the testing data sets bringing the count to 10,600 and thereby ensuring that our training and testing sets were completely unique. We used the same process on the phishing set bringing the count to 9,640. Combining these two sets, we created our final training data set for the URL classifiers. We used a 10-fold cross validation technique to evaluate our two single feature classifiers. The true positive rate of URL length classifier was 76% with false positive rate of 14% while the URL distance classifier was better with about 92% true positive rate and false positives of just 9%.

4.4   Overall URL Classifier

The final URL classifier score is a *logical OR* of the decisions of the (i) Targets in URL (U1) detector (ii) Misplaced TLD (U2) detector and (iii) the Machine-learning based URL classifier (U3), which means a URL is classified as phishing if either of these three judges returns true for phishing and legitimate if none of them returns true.

5   Content-Based Classifier

5.1   C1: More Redirections

To maximize the profit by phishing attacks, phishers use free hosting sites to launch their attacks. Such free hosting sites want to advertise their domains and so they keep many links redirecting to the main site. They also give very less data space and phishers cannot use the big sized data such as images. So, phishers directly use the image links from the actual target site to display it on the phishing page. All of this leads to more external URLs than internal. We count both internal, external URLs and if external URL count is more than internal then we say that the page may be a phish.

5.2   C2: Copy Detection

The goal of Copy Detection is to determine the closeness and similarity of the given page with the target pages. We developed this method since a phisher tries to make the phishing page look very similar to a target page to disguise the malicious intent. We calculate precision, recall and F-score of the closeness of the candidate page with potential target pages. A small experiment with about 100 phishing pages and 100 legitimate pages was conducted to determine the threshold to use for the F-score. If the F-score for the similarity of a candidate page with a legitimate page exceeds the empirical threshold and the URL of the page is not in the whitelist, then it is marked as phishing.

The second part in this function, which is performed sequentially after the closeness check, is to check the copyright name of the page. We have data for 513 login pages of common targets. We know that such big organizations have their own website team and they reserve their own copyrights. Most of the time the copyright name partially matches the part of the domain of the URL. Again, this is a novel idea to the best of our understanding. For example, PayPal phishing site has copyright 1999-2014 PayPal, Facebook has copyright Facebook 2014. Phishing pages copy the targets as much as possible and hence, they show the same copyright message. This definitely fails to match with the domain of the URL and hence we mark such cases as Phishing. In some cases, a legitimate site may have a domain name that does not match with the copyright information. In such cases, there is usually an image in the address bar and image similarity or image text similarity techniques can be used. We leave this extension to future work.

If we do not find any similar candidate of the given page in our dataset then we mark it undetermined. This is justified since our whitelist is not necessarily exhaustive.

5.3   C3: Unsecured Password Handling

It is very important for any page to transmit the passwords in encrypted format. SSL certificates are given to the domains or sites to ensure this secured and encrypted flow of passwords. The best case is when the page having SSL is asking for password fields and submitting it to the page with SSL certificate. Some organizations ask for the password fields without SSL but ensure to transmit the password via a secured SSL channel and to the page having SSL. Use of SSL avoids eavesdropping to a greater extent. As the cost of SSL is high, phishers usually do not use SSL. Above heuristics made us think about the logic of this method.

In this method, we check for the secured flow of the passwords. If there are no password fields then we directly say that the page is legitimate. If the page has unsecured flow, then we mark it as a potentially phishing page.

5.4   B1: Real-Time Form Behavior Analysis

There are many methodologies depending on various heuristics for phishing detection. However, for determining the true false negatives and true false positives, the "best" way is to visit the page from browser and look for signs of phishing pages or actually fill all the input elements and notice where we land.

If we fill all the required fields in the form with all invalid credentials, we expect that the page should give an error message and ask us to re-enter the information. This is the legitimate behavior. But, phishing pages will accept any data filled in the fields and either redirect us to actual target page or give us a message similar to "Thanks for logging in. Please connect after some time." After entering the fake confidential data on the forms, we noticed following behavior.

Legitimate Behavior:

- Keeps on the same domain and/or redirects to SSL certified same domain.
- Gives error message.
- Gives another chance to login or asks to reset password giving "Forgot Password?" link.

Phishing Behavior:

- Accepts the fake credentials and shows page similar to 'successful login'
- Redirects to the target domain (or any other domain than the input URL).
- Asks for more information.

This is very basic behavior and due to space limitations, we cannot list all the (rare) cases of more complex behaviors. We take advantage of such distinguishing behavior of login forms and create our classifier. Logins forms have action-URL. We create a bot to mimic a web browser and parse all the forms on the given page. We bypass the forms which don't ask for sensitive information and process the remaining forms. Action-URL is the biggest hint for observing the form behavior.

Algorithm 1. Behavior Analysis

```
 1: procedure REAL-TIME FORM ANALYSIS(URLs)
 2:     Parse all the forms in the HTML for the input URL
 3:     Extract all the forms requesting input through password fields
 4:     if not a single form for the input-URL then
 5:         return Legitimate
 6:     end if
 7:     Parse the action-URLs
 8:     if domain of the action-URL = the input domain then
 9:         if the web-page of action-URL is SSL certified then
10:             return Legitimate
11:         end if
12:     end if
13:     if domain of the new URL ≠ domain of the input URL then
14:         return Phishing
15:     else if action-URL = given-URL then
16:         legitimateFlag := True
17:     end if
18:     Open the page of the action-URL inside sandbox
19:     if the new page did not ask to login again then
20:         phishingFlag := True
21:     else if new page keeps on same domain & asks for some more sensitive
    information & none of the conditions above satisfies then
22:         create a set URLsToProcessSet of all such action-URLs from the
    page
23:     end if
24:     while URL in URLsToProcessSet do
25:         iterationCounter ← iterationCounter + 1
26:         Follow the similar steps from (step 2) for each URL
27:         Remove the processed URL from URLsToProcessSet
28:     end while
29:     if URLsToProcessSet is empty ‖ iterationCounter > threshold then
30:         if legitimateFlag := True then
31:             return Legitimate
32:         else if phishingFlag = True then
33:             return Phishing
34:         else
35:             return Undetermined
36:         end if
37:     end if
38:     return Undetermined
39: end procedure
```

end

Algorithm 1 simulates human interaction with the Web site to check its behavior. It is a completely novel method to the best of our knowledge.

Sign-up forms have exceptional behavior. As they enable us to create new profile, they accept any syntactically correct email-ID and/or user-name and password. Then they display a message like profile created successfully and may give a form to login. From the bot perspective this is the combination of both phishing and legitimate behavior. Step-15 of Algorithm 1 takes care of such behaviors.

5.5   Overall Content-Based Classifier

The final content-based classifier score is a *logical OR* of the decisions of the (i) More Redirections (C1) detector (ii) Copy Detection (C2) (iii) Unsecured Password Handling (C3) (iv) Real-time Form Analysis (B1) , which means a page is classified as phishing if either of these four judges returns true for phishing and legitimate if none of them returns true.

6   Combination Schemes

If the URL is not bypassed by any of initial steps given above, we have results from the URL classifier and the content-based classifier including each of the components that make up these two classifiers.

For the final decision we study three combination schemes. The first scheme (called *OR scheme* hereafter) takes the logical OR of the results of the URL classifier and the content-based classifier, which means the page is marked as phishing if either of them declares the page to be a phishing page. The second scheme (called *AND scheme* hereafter) computes the logical AND of the URL classifier and the content-based classifiers. The third scheme (called *Potential scheme*) works on the potential of the phishing nature. It calculates how many component functions of the two classifiers classify the page as phishing and keeps the count as potential. If the potential is at least two, then the page is marked as a phishing page.

Fourth scheme (*Content scheme*) is designed to focus more on hijack based attacks, where the URL belongs to the legitimate domain but the contents come from hijackers/ phishers. Content scheme is logical OR of all classifiers excluding the URL classifiers. Table 1 summarizes the combinations.

Table 1. Summary of schemes

Scheme Name	Logical Formula
OR	(U1 OR U2 OR U3) **OR** (C1 OR C2 OR C3 OR B1)
AND	(U1 OR U2 OR U3) **AND** (C1 OR C2 OR C3 OR B1)
Potential	Count of classifiers classifying an URL as 'phish' ≥ 2
Content	C1 OR C2 OR C3 OR B1

6.1 Search Based Filtering

At the very end, if the page is marked as phishing, we check the results of an Internet search. However, this is an optional step in our algorithm (as opposed to some previous work in which it is essential) and we do report the results with and without Internet search.

Search engines have special features which enables them to display highly ranked pages higher in the search results. Login page from legitimate sites would have been accessed by many people and hence, it will be ranked higher. In contrast, as the lifetime of the phishing websites is very low, there is no chance that they can make high page-rank. We take advantage of page-rank system by search engines.

Unlike other systems [31,29], our search based filtering is the simplest. We do not use any TF-IDF, nor the most frequently appearing words in the page, and no natural language processing, we simple input the whole redirected URL to yahoo search engine with its default settings. We take the top 10 results from it. If there are at least two matches for the domain of the input URL with the domains in the result, then we mark this page as legitimate. Otherwise we mark it as undetermined. This function is mainly focused on reducing the false positives rather than phishing detection.

7 Datasets and Extraction of URLs

Our final experiment is tested on 17200 legitimate URLs and 17200 phishing URLs. In mid-November of 2013, we downloaded the top ranked 1 million URLs from Alexa.com. Top ranked 5000 domains are used in our whitelist after some filtering process. DMOZ [19] is open directory with large number of legitimate URLs. We took a random set of 17200 URLs from it as our legitimate dataset.

As we are interested in checking the real-time behavior of a page, we wanted those phishing pages that remain online at least until we test the URL. Since we do not want to test our classifiers on old phishing modus operandi, we do not save the information regarding the URL and/or its contents; we extract fresh phishing URLs each time. We used Phishtank data to extract the phishing URLs. They provide a json file of phishing URLs with some details. We extracted the URLs verified from Phishtank and reported as online. But, after manually checking some of those URLs at random, we found that many of them were 404 pages, or pages with no content, or had some other errors. Thus, the data from Phishtank tends to be noisy and we needed more filtering.

As direct parsing from json file is not sufficient, we developed our own filtering mechanism. We mimicked an internet browser and went to the URLs automatically. Then, we checked for 404 messages from the browser. If we get such a message, we removed the URL from the set. While designing this algorithm, we also found that there were many URLs that took more than 10 seconds to load and gave timeout exception. We checked for all the exceptions possible including connection-timeout, malformed URL, pages with no content, and server errors. We also removed the URLs giving such exceptions. After this filtering, we get the potential phishing pages with high likelihood but no guarantee that the page will have phishing behavior while testing. Thus, we try our best to make the data noise-free, but making the data totally noise free is almost impossible as the lifetime of phishing URLs is too small.

We also made sure to extract the phishing URLs just before running our main algorithm to avoid the problem of the phishing URL going offline. To extract such URLs for the final testing, we used json file from Phishtank dated 15 July 2014. We believe that the latest reported phishing URLs are more likely to still host phishing content when we test our algorithms on them and hence we extract fresh URLs. Finally, we have 17200 phishing URLs and 17200 legitimate URLs. Our whole analysis is based on real-time behavior of the pages and hence we need the preprocessing step to get the input data.

8   Results and Evaluation

8.1   Pre-processing, Whitelisting and Sanitization

We tested our system extensively on 34400 URLs, half of which were potential phishing and half were legitimate. To remove the error pages and offline pages, we have used pre-processing steps as described above.

Out of 17200 legitimate URLs, 14382 URLs gave error free response in timely manner and these URLs are actually tested. Similarly, out of 17200 phishing URLs, 1981 URLs were duplicates and removed from the analysis and 7507 URLs responded without any error and were given to our algorithm. Hence, out of 34400 URLs, 21889 URLs are processed, and tested by our algorithm.

As the dataset is huge, and our system is automated, instead of opening the page in a browser, we create a sandbox and open the page in it. We use python 2.7.6 and different modules of it including urllib2, mechanize, and beautifulSoup. The algorithm requires strong and stable network connection. The average time per URL is slightly over two seconds. It includes the time to reach the server, download the information, library calls such as getTLD and other local computations.

8.2   Analysis of Methods over Input URLs

The page is tested through all of our classifiers (viz. U1, U2, U3, C1, C2, C3, and B1) and the individual results are noted. Figure 1 shows contribution of each classifier separately. From the figure it is clear that if we logically combine the output of the classifiers, we will get a better result. Hence, we have created OR, AND, Potential and Content schemes.

8.3   Summary of Results and Measurements

Our results are now summarized using the following measures with definitions given below. Since we are interested in detecting phishing pages, we consider

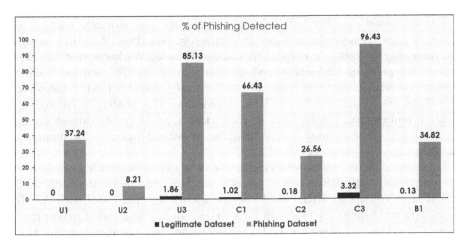

Fig. 1. Statistics for Individual Classifiers on input URLs

this as the "positive condition." We apply the following formulas to present the results of all the schemes.

$$TruePositiveRate(TPR) = TruePositives/ActualPositive$$

$$= TP/(TP + FN)$$

$$FalsePositiveRate(FPR) = FalsePositive/ActualNegative$$

$$= FP/(FP + TN)$$

$$Precision(PR) = TP/(TP + FP)$$

$$F - score = 2 * PR * TPR/(PR + TPR)$$

Table 2. Results of different schemes

	Search Filtering = **OFF**				Search Filtering = **ON**			
Scheme	TPR	FPR	PR	F-score	TPR	FPR	PR	F-score
OR	**99.97%**	3.50%	88.25%	93.75%	93.37%	0.54%	97.84%	95.55%
AND	87.64 %	1.80 %	92.76%	90.13%	82.30%	**0.22%**	98.98%	89.88%
Potential	97.94 %	2.48 %	91.24 %	94.47 %	91.55 %	0.36 %	98.52 %	94.91 %
Content	99.31 %	3.44 %	88.37 %	93.52 %	92.84 %	0.53 %	97.88 %	95.30 %

All the classifiers serve different purposes. URL classifier works only on the given URL and can be considered to be doing static analysis. Even if the system is not connected to the Internet, this scheme will work. Other advantage of this scheme is that this scheme is fastest among our schemes.

Content-based classifier will help to see the live and dynamic content of the web page. Hence, the analysis is completely real-time. Real-time analysis using only content can detect hijack-based attacks. We know that the lifetime of the phishing URLs is very short. And even if the URL started hosting genuine content, unlike our content-based scheme, almost all other detection techniques would still classify the URL as phishing. This analysis is completely dynamic and requires a stable Internet connection. C2 performs the lowest among the classifiers since we used a very small list of potential targets for similarity checking.

Language independence of the classifiers can be elaborated with the help of a few simple facts [10]. URLs of web pages in any language are created with valid ASCII characters. Our URL based classifiers work on analysis of such ASCII characters and hence they can work for web page in any language. Content classifiers C1, C3 and B1 check for the HTML code and more specifically redirection tags. Those tags have a specific syntax and cannot be changed according to the language of the web page. C2 tries to check similarity of pages by directly matching the words in it. It is a check for a perfectly matching set of characters and no processing is required in terms of finding the meaning or context of the words. Hence, all the classifiers and hence the system can withstand the phishing attack in any language.

Combination of these schemes makes our detection technique more accurate, robust, reliable and real-time. Table 2 shows that the performance of AND scheme is optimal and the search-based filtering will have negligible effect on the TPR as well as FPR and hence PR and F-Score.

8.4   Direct Comparison

Each browser, nowadays, has an integrated phishing detector. Also, extensions (sometimes called plugins) like Netcraft [18] and Web of Trust [25] are available to provide more security to the users. Anti-virus programs like *McAfee* install extra layer of protection from phishing URLs to the browser. The only way to compare our model with such detection systems is to manually visit each of the URLs from our TestingSets and see the visible response on the web browser. This is very tedious and difficult way to get the results for each of the URLs. We also tried to get tools for phishing detection from other researchers, but they either didn't have any public API or we didn't get response from them.

The work done by Xiang et al. [29] cannot be directly compared to our work as the datasets are different. However, their TPR of 67.74% is very less than our TPR with modest FPR.

Fortunately, Google has an API for phishing detection called Google Safe Browsing API [11]. We fed the same dataset to the API simultaneously with our experiments and recorded the results. We found that, Google's safe browsing (GSB) is good in maintaining the FPR close to zero, but it failed in detecting the phishing sites. Direct comparison is shown in Table 3.

Table 3. Direct comparison of different schemes

Scheme	Search Filtering = OFF				Search Filtering = ON			
	TPR	FPR	PR	F-score	TPR	FPR	PR	F-score
GSB	51.46 %	0.03 %	99.80 %	67.91 %	-	-	-	-
OR	99.97%	3.50%	88.25%	93.75%	93.37%	0.54%	97.84%	95.55%
AND	87.64 %	1.80 %	92.76%	90.13%	82.30%	0.22%	98.98%	89.88%
Potential	97.94 %	2.48 %	91.24 %	94.47 %	91.55 %	0.36 %	98.52 %	94.91 %
Content	99.31 %	3.44 %	88.37 %	93.52 %	92.84 %	0.53 %	97.88 %	95.30 %

8.5   Security Analysis

The determined phisher who reads our work can try and thwart detection as
follows. Copying a legal web-site's content is *almost* a necessary step to lure
victims (the only other mechanism is to offer some kind of incentive to people,
which may not attract many victims since these strategies are quite dated now,
e.g., the Nigerian emails). Assume that the phisher can thwart the URL analysis
or take the scenario of a hijack based attack. In this case they must proceed as
follows to thwart the content-based analysis.

First, they must ensure that the number of external links is smaller than the
number of internal links. Second, they must change the behavior of the website
to that of a legal one to avoid detection, which means that the site should show
an error message or two and then keep the user on the same page with asking
credentials again. Next they must obtain an SSL certificate and lastly they must
insert enough junk text into the web site to thwart copy detection and make an
invisible/hidden copyright field whose name matches with the domain of their
URL while showing a copyright of the target being copied. There are a couple of
problems with this approach. First, this means that the phisher cannot be lazy
and use some kind of kit for building the site. Thus the work of the phisher is
increased significantly and the cost-benefit ratio becomes less attractive. Second,
a user that is redirected to the same page after entering valid credentials may
smell a rat very quickly after a few attempts to get into what seems like the legal
site and thus the time left for the phisher to carry out any exploits on the user's
accounts will be diminished. Responsible user will report the URL as phishing
and the URL would be blacklisted sooner. Even if all the phisher does is sell
those credentials in some underground network, those credentials will be usable
for a shorter period and such credentials will be worth less and less over time.
Third, this requires considerable sophistication from the phisher and obviously
our schemes can be made even more sophisticated as well.

9   Conclusions and Future Work

We have considered the problem of detecting phishing web sites and presented
a comprehensive solution that is robust and uses novel techniques in the URL

classifier (e.g., character frequencies, Euclidean distance) and in the content-based classifier (e.g., similarity detection using F-score and real-time web page behavior) apart from some other simplifications and improvements over existing methods. It performs competitively with the best previous methods. Furthermore, we address the important problem of hijack-based phishing attacks (as far as we know for the first time) through the content-based classifier and the problem of zero-hour phishing detection as well. The content-based classifier has the advantage of not needing any retraining and the URL classifier also requires minimal training, which is fast and efficient.

One direction for future work is to combine it with a malware detector to detect and thwart sites that do not try to steal sensitive information but install malware on the web site visitor's machine. Another useful direction would be to expand the size of the whitelist, which would help the copy detector in catching more phishing sites.

Acknowledgments. We would like to thank the reviewers for their constructive comments.

References

1. Abu-Nimeh, S., Nappa, D., Wang, X., Nair, S.: A comparison of machine learning techniques for phishing detection. In: Proc. Anti-phishing Working Group's 2nd Annual eCrime Researchers Summit, pp. 60–69. ACM (2007)
2. Anti-Phishing Working Group. Phishing activity trends report - h1 2011. In: APWG Phishing Trends Reports (2011)
3. Basnet, R., Mukkamala, S., Sung, A.: Detection of phishing attacks: A machine learning approach. Soft Computing Applications in Industry, 373–383 (2008)
4. Bergholz, A., Beer, J.D., Glahn, S., Moens, M.-F., Paaß, G., Strobel, S.: New filtering approaches for phishing email. Journal of Computer Security 18(1), 7–35 (2010)
5. Bergholz, A., Chang, J., Paaß, G., Reichartz, F., Strobel, S.: Improved phishing detection using model-based features. In: Proc. Conf. on Email and Anti-Spam (CEAS) (2008)
6. Chandrasekaran, M., Narayanan, K., Upadhyaya, S.: Phishing email detection based on structural properties. In: NYS CyberSecurity Conf. (2006)
7. Fette, I., Sadeh, N., Tomasic, A.: Learning to detect phishing emails. In: Proc. 16th int'l conf. on World Wide Web, pp. 649–656. ACM (2007)
8. Gansterer, W.N., Pölz, D.: E-mail classification for phishing defense. In: Boughanem, M., Berrut, C., Mothe, J., Soule-Dupuy, C. (eds.) ECIR 2009. LNCS, vol. 5478, pp. 449–460. Springer, Heidelberg (2009)
9. Garera, S., Provos, N., Chew, M., Rubin, A.: A framework for detection and measurement of phishing attacks. In: Proc. 2007 ACM Workshop on Recurring Malcode, pp. 1–8 (2007)
10. Google- Webmaster Central Blog. Working with multilingual websites (2010)
11. Google Developers. Safe browsing api – google developers (2013)
12. Hong, J.: The state of phishing attacks. Commun. ACM 55(1), 74–81 (2012)
13. Jakobsson, M., Myers, S.: Phishing and countermeasures: understanding the increasing problem of electronic identity theft. Wiley-Interscience (2006)

14. James, L.: Phishing exposed. Syngress Publishing (2005)
15. Ludl, C., McAllister, S., Kirda, E., Kruegel, C.: On the effectiveness of techniques to detect phishing sites. In: Hämmerli, B.M., Sommer, R. (eds.) DIMVA 2007. LNCS, vol. 4579, pp. 20–39. Springer, Heidelberg (2007)
16. Ma, J., Saul, L.K., Savage, S., Voelker, G.M.: Learning to detect malicious urls. ACM TIST 2(3), 30 (2011)
17. McGrath, D.K., Gupta, M.: Behind phishing: An examination of phisher modi operandi. In: LEET (2008)
18. Netcraft. Netcraft extension - phishing protection and site reports (2014)
19. Netscape Communications Corporation. Open directory rdf dump (2004)
20. Ollmann, G.: The phishing guide. Next Generation Security Software Ltd. (2004)
21. Sheng, S., Wardman, B., Warner, G., Cranor, L., Hong, J., Zhang, C.: An empirical analysis of phishing blacklists. In: Proc. 6th Conf. on Email and Anti-Spam (2009)
22. Stone-Gross, B., Cova, M., Cavallaro, L., Gilbert, B., Szydlowski, M., Kemmerer, R.A., Kruegel, C., Vigna, G.: Your botnet is my botnet: analysis of a botnet takeover. In: ACM Conference on Computer and Communications Security, pp. 635–647 (2009)
23. Verma, R., Hossain, N.: Semantic feature selection for text with application to automatic phishing email detection. In: Lee, H.-S., Han, D.-G. (eds.) ICISC 2013. LNCS, vol. 8565, pp. 455–468. Springer, Heidelberg (2014)
24. Verma, R., Shashidhar, N., Hossain, N.: Detecting phishing emails the natural language way. In: Foresti, S., Yung, M., Martinelli, F. (eds.) ESORICS 2012. LNCS, vol. 7459, pp. 824–841. Springer, Heidelberg (2012)
25. Web of Trust. Safe browsing tool — wot (web of trust) (2014)
26. Whittaker, C., Ryner, B., Nazif, M.: Large-scale automatic classification of phishing pages. In: Proc. of 17th NDSS (2010)
27. Xiang, G., Hong, J., Rose, C.P., Cranor, L.: Cantina+: A feature-rich machine learning framework for detecting phishing web sites. ACM Trans. Inf. Syst. Secur. 14, 21:1–21:28 (2011)
28. Xiang, G., Hong, J.I.: A hybrid phish detection approach by identity discovery and keywords retrieval. In: Proceedings of the 18th International Conference on World Wide Web, pp. 571–580. ACM (2009)
29. Xiang, G., Pendleton, B.A., Hong, J., Rose, C.P.: A hierarchical adaptive probabilistic approach for zero hour phish detection. In: Gritzalis, D., Preneel, B., Theoharidou, M. (eds.) ESORICS 2010. LNCS, vol. 6345, pp. 268–285. Springer, Heidelberg (2010)
30. Yu, W., Nargundkar, S., Tiruthani, N.: Phishcatch-a phishing detection tool. In: 33rd IEEE Int'l Computer Software and Applications Conf., pp. 451–456 (2009)
31. Zhang, Y., Hong, J., Cranor, L.: Cantina: a content-based approach to detecting phishing web sites. In: Proc. 16th Int'l Conf. on World Wide Web, pp. 639–648. ACM (2007)

PMDS:
Permission-Based Malware Detection System

Paolo Rovelli[1] and Ýmir Vigfússon[1,2]

[1] School of Computer Science
Reykjavik University
Menntavegi 1, Reykjavik 101, Iceland
[2] Department of Mathematics and Computer Science
Emory University
400 Dowman Drive, Atlanta GA 30322, USA

Abstract. The meteoric growth of the Android mobile platform has made it a main target of cyber-criminals. Mobile malware specifically targeting Android has surged and grown in tandem with the rising popularity of the platform [3, 5, 4, 6]. In response, the honus is on defenders to increase the difficulty of malware development to curb its rampant growth, and to devise effective detection mechanisms specifically targeting Android malware in order to better protect the end-users.

In this paper, we address the following question: do malicious applications on Android request predictably different permissions than legitimate applications? Based on analysis of 2950 samples of benign and malicious Android applications, we propose a novel Android malware detection technique called Permission-based Malware Detection Systems (PMDS). In PMDS, we view requested permissions as behavioral markers and build a machine learning classifier on those markers to automatically identify for unseen applications potentially harmful behavior based on the combination of permissions they require. By design, PMDS has the potential to detect previously unknown, and zero-day or next-generation malware. If attackers adapt and request for fewer permissions, PMDS will have impeded the simple strategies by which malware developers currently abuse their victims.

Experimental results show that PMDS detects more than 92–94% of previously unseen malware with a false positives rate of 1.52–3.93%.

Keywords: Android, Permissions, Malware Detection System, Machine Learning, Data Mining, Heuristics.

1 Introduction

Mobile devices are being adopted at an exponential rate: mobile phone subscriptions have increased from 700 million in 2000 to 7 billion by the end of 2014, representing more than 96% of the world's population, with the market penetration in developing world projected to reach 90% by the same time [1]. The number of smartphones in use worldwide have surpassed one billion-unit for

A. Prakash and R. Shyamasundar (Eds.): ICISS 2014, LNCS 8880, pp. 338–357, 2014.
© Springer International Publishing Switzerland 2014

the first time ever in second half of 2012 [7], and already in 2013 did the total number of smartphones shipped exceed that of feature phones [8].

The convenience of interactive mobile devices has enticed their users, who now carry a wealth of sensitive information around with them: personal data, bank information and account details, GPS location, contacts, text messages and emails [9–13]. The value of these data has attracted cyber-criminals who invest time and money in exploiting vulnerable mobile platforms, commonly through malware.

Google's Android platform has become the most targeted mobile operating system, likely for two key reasons [14]. On one hand, Android is a ubiquitous platform, with more than 1.9 billion installed-base devices [2]. On the other hand, Android applications are easy to reverse-engineer and can be readily modified or repackaged. Since attackers focus their energy on targets that have the highest return on investment, popular platforms like Android with accessible inner workings are doomed to attract special attention from cyber-criminals.

In anticipation of malicious behavior, the fundamental Android design includes various security and authentication mechanisms. One of the fundamental mechanisms is application permissions, where newly installed applications will ask the user for approval on what types of access will be required for the program to work. The mechanism enables granular control of restrictions into what specific operations can be performed by the particular application.

Yet the old adage that security is only as strong as the weakest link continues to apply: many families of Android malware prey on unsuspecting users by camouflaging themselves as regular applications that need elevated privileges to the system. Often times, legit applications are "repackaged" with a Trojan payload that preys on unsuspecting users or steals the ad revenue from the host application [18, 19]. Researchers from the App Genome project reported that 11% of the Android applications in two alternative China-based markets were repackaged, and another study has reported an alarming 5-13% repackaging rate among six different third-party markets [20]. The effectiveness of the permissions mechanism is compromised if the user fails to notice unusual requests for permissions.

In this paper, we focus on a basic question: *to what extent can Android malware be detected and thereby thwarted by solely focusing on the permissions they request?* We compare 1450 malware samples to 1500 benign applications from the Google Play Store and analyze differences and patterns between the two groups. We found correlation between the group of permissions required by an application with its behavior, that is whether the application was benign or malicious. Using this link, we propose a novel Android malware detection technique, called Permission-based Malware Detection Systems (PMDS). PMDS uses a machine learning classifier to automatically identify (potentially) dangerous behavior of previously unseen applications based on the combination of permissions they require. Through a machine learning approach, PMDS has the potential to detect previously unknown and zero-day or next-generation malware.

The contributions presented in this paper are the following.

- We propose PMDS: a simple, novel approach to categorize the behavior of an Android application and consequently to detect malware.
- We present a low-overhead cloud-based architecture for PMDS, detailing both the client-side and a server-side applications, which uses the previously presented Android malware detection technique.
- We demonstrate the feasibility of our system through cross-validation on 2950 real-world samples, showing that PMDS was able to detect 92–94% of previously unseen Android malware at 1.52%–3.93% false positive rate.

2 Background

Android is an operating system, primarily designed for touchscreen mobile devices, including smartphones and tablets, the core of which is built on top of a modified version of the Linux kernel. Every application on Android is run as a different user in its own, separate Linux process [38]. Above the Linux kernel layer, Android provides native user-space libraries, such as *OpenGL* and *WebKit*, and the Dalvik Virtual Machine (VM): an open source Virtual Machine optimized to run Java applications on mobile devices. On top of the Android system architecture there are the applications, which run on an application framework composed of Java-compatible libraries based on Apache Harmony.

Android applications are distributed and installed using the Android PacKage (APK) file format: an archive file built on the ZIP file format and carries the *.apk* file extension. Since each Android application runs in its own process with its own instance of the Dalvik VM, all application code runs in isolation from other applications.

Furthermore, each application in the Android architecture has access only to the components it requires to complete its work, and none other. Consequently, an application that wishes to access particular system components must request specific permission. The design creates a secure operating environment in which applications cannot access parts of the system unless they are explicitly granted privileges [38, 39].

An application that requires special privileges must explicitly declare those in an *AndroidManifest.xml* file, an entry file bundled within APK packages that provides semantic-rich information about the application itself and its components.

Furthermore, Android applications (as well as libraries) can enforce their own, custom permissions. These custom permissions are also declared in the *Android-Manifest.xml* file together with the system ones. [40, 39]

Because each permission is related to an action, the permissions required by an application can be seen as an indicator of its *possible*[1] future behavior and thus the risk manifested by granting the privileges to the program at hand.

---

[1] It is important to note that the declaration of certain permissions in the *Android-Manifest.xml* file does not necessarily imply their use at runtime.

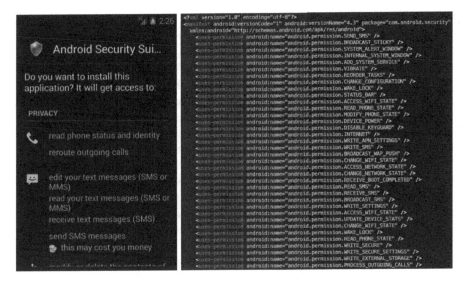

Fig. 1. Example of a malicious application (*Trojan-Banker://Android/ZitMo.B*) which requires for a specific group of permissions. On the right the permissions are required during the installation process, while on the left the *AndroidManifest.xml* file in which the required permissions are declared.

We note that not every piece of malware asks for a dangerous combination of permissions. Some rely on exploiting vulnerabilities in other services to escalate privileges, and may not require for any special permissions at all [14]. Zhou *et al.* showed that bundling exploits was the exception rather than the norm in modern Android malware. Our focus will be on malware that specifically requests permissions to undertake undesirable behavior.

3   Design and Implementation

The key goal of our study is to understand whether the group of permissions required by an application correlates with its ultimate behavior as either benign or malicious. If there is a correlation, how can it be leveraged to automatically identify potentially dangerous behavior of previously unseen applications? In this section we describe design decisions and implementation of a detection framework architecture that exploits a classifier based on application permissions.

3.1   Design

A malware detection framework for Android can be architected in a variety of ways. A proactive approach would be to embed detection for all users into an Android marketplace, such as Google Play Store or an alternative third-party market, and perform a scan when developers upload their code. However, such changes are dramatic and should only be issued after the methods have been thoroughly validated. Here, we instead describe a proof-of-concept architecture focused on protecting individual clients.

By taking a client-centric view, the next issue is to address the trade-off between overhead and accuracy. On one end of the spectrum, the detection logic could reside entirely on the mobile device, with updates periodically issued from an Internet service. This option requires more processing and in turn consumes more battery from the device. It also leaves open a window of vulnerability between updates during which malicious applications could be installed without warning. On the opposite end, one could outsource detection entirely to a cloud service, leaving a bare bones client-side framework that focuses solely on mitigation when malicious applications are detected. This strategy allows more elaborate and powerful detection programs to be run in the cloud where resources are less constrained. However, communication with a remote service incurs higher latency and may degrade user experience if the application cannot start until it has been scanned, or security if the application starts before the response from the scan has been received from the cloud server.

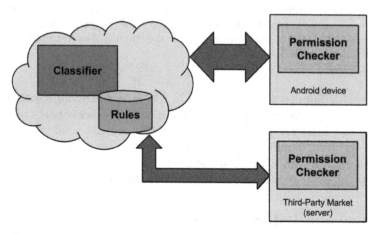

Fig. 2. The Permission-based Malware Detection System (PMDS) architecture. The clients, whether they are Android devices or Android marketplaces, have a "Permission Checker" that extracts permissions by an application and sends them to a server-side application where the application is evaluated as benign or malicious.

Taking these factors into consideration, PMDS is implemented as a cloud system. Such system has several additional advantages. An important one is that the cloud service is no longer subjected to the Android architecture design and its limitations, allowing more accurate analysis that are poised to improve detection rates. As mentioned above, the second main advantage is that fewer resources are spent on the device itself, which in turn will improve the battery lifetime compared to an on-device scan.

As shown in Figure 2, the Permission-based Malware Detection System (PMDS) is composed of a client-side application, whose task is to extract the permissions of an application and send them to the server-side component. The server is the core of our technology, as it is tasked with classifying the behavior of the given application instance as either benign or malicious and, then, signaling the results to the client-side application as quickly as possible. In order to do so, we will rely on machine learning classifiers that we discuss below.

As with other malware detection systems, the client-side component can implement two strategies: it can provide an interface that enables the user to perform a manual scan of installed programs (on-demand scan), or it can be used to automatically scan recently obtained applications (on-install scan). Anecdotal evidence suggests that people are not vigilant about virus and malware scans, making time between scans larger than needed, so we focus on on-install scans.

However, the standard Android platform is designed to disallow applications from interacting with the installation process. Specifically, when an application is installed from Google Play Store or another third-party market, our malware scanner is limited to registering and then handling an event telling us that a new application has been installed, rather than interrupting the process. In light of this limitation, our on-install scanner will be able to detect a malicious application only after it has been installed, creating a race condition between execution of the new program and the scan. If the scan is fast enough, PMDS will detect and remove a malicious application before it is launched and thus before it can do harm. Our implementation is guided by the concern that lookups must produce a prompt response, meaning that we strive to minimize server-side computation time and network latency. On a positive note, the asynchronous notifications about newly installed applications implies that no particular delay is added to the installation process, thereby minimizing user interruption.

Finally, we must be mindful of two additional concerns when designing a cloud system for mobile devices. First, one cannot trust that mobile devices is connected to the global Internet at all possible times. We will make the assumption that applications are generally installed from markets on the Internet, and that the connection will remain up for a short amount of time following the installation. In fact, our analysis below confirms that most applications require Internet access to function properly. The second concern is that applications should strive to minimize network traffic. The communication protocol we implemented is designed to communicate the required information efficiently, as described below.

3.2   Implementation

Server-Side Application. The server-side application is the crux of our Permission-based Malware Detection System (PMDS) as it is the component responsible for classifying an application's behavior as either benign or malicious.

In our prototype of the server-side application, we use Python to automatically extract the permissions declared by an application in its *AndroidMani-fest.xml* file of the APK package (see Figure 3). We piggyback on the Android Asset Packaging Tool (*aapt*) which is a part of the Android SDK. The *aapt* program is versatile, in particular the *"aapt dump permissions"* command lists the permissions declared by an application:

```
$ aapt dump permissions MyPkg.apk | sed 1d | awk '{print \$NF}'
```

After extracting the permissions, the program automatically save the information in the Weka's Attribute-Relation File Format (ARFF) [43, 44].

Our prototype then uses Weka [33] to train multiple classifiers in order to detect new and unseen malware.

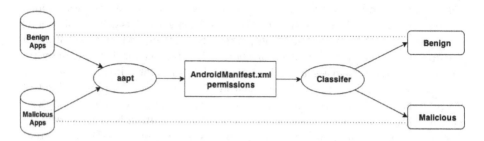

Fig. 3. To create the classifier's dataset, the permissions declared in the *AndroidManifest.xml* file of an application are automatically extracted using the Android Asset Packaging Tool (*aapt*). Then, the classifier automatically labels the application behavior, as either benign or (potentially) malicious, according to the combination of permissions the application requires.

Android applications can enforce their own custom permissions, as mentioned earlier, which appears as noise in the classifier. In PMDS, we omit custom permissions and collect only the system permissions available in the Android API documentation, for a total of 130 permissions [41]. The permissions requested by an application is represented as a binary vector of Boolean values, one for each permission, where *TRUE* stays for the presence of that particular permission while *FALSE* stays for its absence. In our database, we also store the application behavior, saved as either *benign* or *malicious*.

```
FALSE,FALSE,FALSE,FALSE,FALSE,TRUE,FALSE,TRUE,FALSE,TRUE,TRUE,TRUE,
TRUE,...,FALSE,FALSE,FALSE,malicious
```

As an optimization, we store permissions in a fixed-length array rather than an extensible map. Modifying the permission types, such as by adding new permissions, or order can compromise the integrity or prediction quality of the classifiers. The optimization allows us to compress the data for each application into no more than a bit for each permission.

In order to automatically and properly label the behavior of previously unseen applications (as either benign or malicious), we train a representative classifier from each of four modern approaches for classifiers. We chose the following machine learning algorithms: C4.5 Decision Tree, K*, RIPPER and Naïve Bayes, and evaluate their performance in Section 4.

C4.5 Decision Tree-Based Learning. We used the J48 open source Java implementation of the Ross Quinlan's C4.5 *Decision Tree-based learning algorithm* which is available in Weka. The C4.5 algorithm builds decision trees from a set of training data using information entropy as a distance measure. The decision trees are then used as predictive models for mapping observations about an item – its features – and conclusions about the item's target value – its class label. [34, 32, 33]

K* Lazy Learning. On the other hand, K* is a *Lazy (Instance-based) learning algorithm* developed by Cleary and Trigg. The K* algorithm classifies an instance by comparing it to a database of pre-classified examples and using entropy as a distance measure. The biggest drawback is that evaluation is comparatively slow and can grow with data, in exchange for faster training times. [35]

RIPPER Rule-Based Learning. RIPPER (Repeated Incremental Pruning to Produce Error Reduction) is a *Rule-based learning algorithm* developed by William W. Cohen. The RIPPER algorithm classifies an instance according to a sequence of Boolean clauses linked by logical AND operators, which together imply the membership of the instance to a particular class. [31]

Naïve Bayes Learning. Finally, Naïve Bayes is a simple *Bayesian learning algorithm* developed by John and Langley. The Naïve Bayes probabilistic algorithm is based on applying Bayes' theorem with strong (naïve) independence assumptions. In other world, for this algorithm, the presence (or absence) of a particular feature is unrelated to the presence (or absence) of any other feature of a class. [36]

3.3   Client-Side Application

The client-side component is responsible for extracting the permissions declared by an application and send them to the server-side application.

Retrieving the list of applications currently installed on an Android device – irrespective of whether they are user or system applications (see Section 2) – can be achieved by *PackageManager* class. The interface further enables the caller to retrieve various extra information related to each application, including the permissions they require [42].

Recall that Android explicitly prohibits tampering with the installation process of an application from Google Play Store. PMDS instead registers a handle for the event that a new application has been installed. A custom on-install scanner will scan the executable, but notably malware can only be detected *after* the application has been installed. However, the detection is designed to be faster than an average user is at opening the newly installed application.

We "hook" our scanner to the installation process by creating and registering a *BroadcastReceiver* handler for the *PACKAGE_ADDED* and *ACTION_PACKAGE*

```
final PackageManager pm = getPackageManager();
final List<ApplicationInfo> listOfInstalledApps =
pm.getInstalledApplications(PackageManager.GET_META_DATA);

// Retrieve each installed app info:
for ( final ApplicationInfo ai : listOfInstalledApps ) {
  final String appName = pm.getApplicationLabel(ai).toString();
  final String appPackage = ai.packageName;
  List<String> appPermissions;

  final PackageInfo pi = pm.getPackageInfo(appPackage,
  PackageManager.GET_PERMISSIONS);

  if ( (pi != null) && (pi.requestedPermissions != null) ) {
    Collections.addAll(appPermissions, pi.requestedPermissions);
  }

  ...
}
```

Fig. 4. Assembling a list of installed applications on Android. The *getInstalledApplications()* method of the *PackageManager* class returns a list of *ApplicationInfo* objects. Each of these objects represents an installed application.

_REPLACED broadcast actions. The first action is broadcast every time a new application package has been installed on the device, while the latter is called every time a new version of an application package has been installed, thus replacing an existing version that was previously installed.


```
<receiver android:name="com.example.onInstallBroadcastReceiver"
          android:exported="false">
  <intent-filter android:priority="1000">
    <action android:name="android.intent.action.PACKAGE_ADDED" />
    <action android:name=
     "android.intent.action.ACTION_PACKAGE_REPLACED" />
    <data android:scheme="package" />
  </intent-filter>
</receiver>
```

Fig. 5. XML. Example of *BroadcastReceiver* that handles the on-install event, thanks to the *PACKAGE_ADDED* and *ACTION_PACKAGE_REPLACED* broadcast actions.

When the BroadcastReceiver is triggered, the permissions required by the installed APK package are extracted by the client-side component and sent to the server-side application.

```
public class onInstallBroadcastReceiver
               extends BroadcastReceiver {

  /**
   * Receiving an Intent broadcast.
   *
   * @param context  the Context in which the receiver is running.
   * @param intent   the Intent being received.
   */
  @Override
  public void onReceive(Context context, Intent intent) {
    String action = intent.getAction();

    if ( action.equals( Intent.ACTION_PACKAGE_ADDED ) ||
         action.equals( Intent.ACTION_PACKAGE_REPLACED ) ) {
      // Retrieve the installed/updated package:
      final String appPackage =
      intent.getData().getEncodedSchemeSpecificPart();

      // [...] Scan the APK package [...]
    }
  }
}
```

Fig. 6. Java. Example of *BroadcastReceiver* handler for the on-install event, corresponding to the XML code in Figure 5.

The use of `BroadcastReceiver` allows us to minimize the use of the CPU and, therefore, the battery consumption. Since PMDS uses only the 130 system permissions available in the Android API documentation [41] on the server side, we can also optimize the packet exchange so that the client-side application needs transmit only a data sequence of 130 bits that indicates each permission requested by the application. The server-side application will answer with a single bit, predicting that the application intention is either malicious or benign. Note that other layers, such as TCP, the HTTPS protocol and other chatty formats, add additional space overhead on top of the protocol.

4   Evaluation

Since it is the core of our Permission-based Malware Detection System (PMDS), our evaluation is focused on determining the efficiency of the server-side classifier.

4.1   Dataset and Analysis

We use a dataset of 2950 samples, divided into 1500 unique benign samples (*i.e.* no updated versions of the same applications are included) and 1450 malicious ones. The benign samples were collected from the Google Play Store [46], while all the malicious samples were taken from both the Android Malware Genome Project [14] and Contagio Mobile [45]. We disregard applications that do not request additional permissions.

Figure 7 shows the most frequently requested permissions by the samples in our dataset, both benign and malicious, ordered by decreasing popularity. The *INTERNET* privilege was the most required permission for both benign and malicious applications, in concord with Zhou and Jiang's study [14]. On the other hand, our dataset shows significant difference between the groups in certain permissions, such as: *READ_PHONE_STATE, ACCESS_WIFI_STATE, READ_SMS, WRITE_SMS, SEND_SMS, RECEIVE_SMS, READ_CONTACTS* and *CALL_PHONE*.

4.2   Experimental Set-Up

In order to evaluate the accuracy of each machine learning classifier, we use the standard tenfold cross-validation. Cross-validation is a model validation method that divides data into two segments: one used to train the machine learning algorithm and one used to test it. Tenfold cross-validation takes 90% of the dataset for training and 10% for testing, and then repeats the procedure 10 times with different parts used for training and testing, and then outputs the average accuracy across the runs. In this way, we are testing the classifiers against previously unseen data (i.e. data not used for training the classifiers), which in our case represent zero-day or next-generation malware.

In order to evaluate the results of the performed experiments, we use the following standard evaluation measures: *True Positive* (TP) – the number of applications correctly classified as malicious, *True Negative* (TN) – the number of applications correctly classified as benign, *False Positive* (FP) – the number of applications mistakenly classified as malicious, and *False Negative* (FN) – the number of applications mistakenly classified as benign. Furthermore, we define the normalized term *True Positive Rate* (TPR) to mean the fraction of truly benign samples that were characterized as such (*i.e.* $TPR = \frac{TP}{TP+FN}$), and the term *False Positive Rate* ($FPR = \frac{FP}{FP+TN}$). We also define *Accuracy* (ACC) to mean the fraction of applications correctly classified out of the total amount of applications (*i.e.* $ACC = \frac{TP+TN}{TP+TN+FP+FN}$) and, finally, with the term *Error Rate* (ER) we mean the fraction of applications mistakenly classified out of the total amount of applications (*i.e.* $ER = \frac{FP+FN}{TP+TN+FP+FN}$). To illustrate the efficacy of a solution, we will use *Receiver Operating Characteristic (ROC) curves*, graphical plots of the TPR versus the fraction of false positives out of the total actual negatives (*i.e.* $\frac{FP}{TN+FP}$), at various threshold settings.

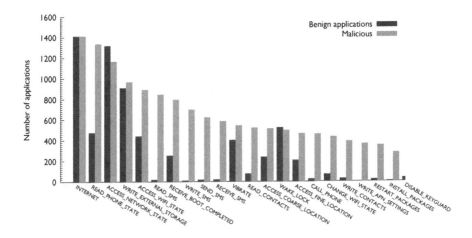

Fig. 7. Most frequently requested permissions by the Android applications in our dataset. The blue bars show the number of times the specific permissions have been requested by benign applications, while the orange bars show the number of times they have been requested by malicious applications.

4.3   Standard Machine Learning Classifiers

Table 1, and Figures 8 and 9, show the results obtained in our first batch of experiments, where we used the four representative machine learning algorithms (C4.5, K^*, RIPPER and Naïve Bayes).

Table 1. Experimental results using four different classifiers: a *Decision Tree-based learner* (C4.5), a *Lazy Instance-based learner* (K^*), a *Rule-based learner* (RIPPER) and a *Bayesian learner* (Naïve Bayes). The classifiers automatically label the behavior of previously unseen applications as either benign or malicious.

	TP	TN	FP	FN	TPR	FPR	ACC	ER
C4.5	1340	1456	44	110	92.41 %	3.03 %	94.78 %	5.22 %
K^*	1338	1478	22	112	92.28 %	1.52 %	95.46 %	4.54 %
RIPPER	1338	1465	35	112	92.28 %	2.4 %	95.02 %	4.98 %
Naïve Bayes	1155	1450	50	295	79.66 %	3.45 %	88.31 %	11.69 %

As evident on the figures, the overall best results were obtained using K^*, with which we achieved a detection rate of 92.28% and a false positives rate of 1.52% – the minimum across all experiments. We achieved the highest detection rate (92.41%) using C4.5, while the highest accuracy (95.02%) using RIPPER. Naïve Bayes produced the least competitive results, both in terms of the detection rate and the false positive rate.

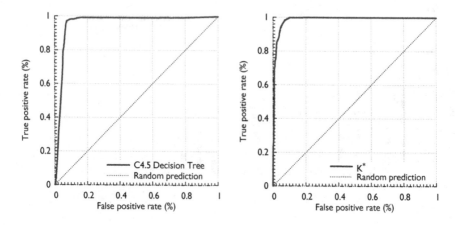

Fig. 8. The Receiver Operating Characteristic (ROC) Curve of our C4.5 (left) and K^* (right) classifiers, respectively

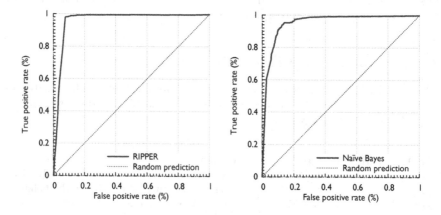

Fig. 9. The Receiver Operating Characteristic (ROC) Curve of our RIPPER (left) and Naïve Bayes (right) classifiers, respectively

4.4   Boosted Machine Learning Classifiers

The machine learning literature is endowed with a methodology called *boosting* that converts rough and moderately inaccurate classifiers into stronger combined classifiers by systematically reducing bias. We subjected three of the four classifiers that had been trained to Adaptive Boosting (AdaBoost), a *machine learning meta-algorithm* developed by Yoav Freund and Robert Schapire. AdaBoost uses a boosting approach in which multiple classifiers (possibly through parameterization) are trained, and their output is joined into a weighted sum that can provide more accurate prediction [37].

We boosted the previously evaluated machine learning algorithms with AdaBoost, and show the results in Table 2, and Figures 10 and 11.

Table 2. Experimental results using AdaBoost in conjunction with the previous machine learning algorithms (i.e. C4.5, RIPPER and Naïve Bayes)

	TP	TN	FP	FN	TPR	FPR	ACC	ER
C4.5	1366	1443	57	84	94.21 %	3.93 %	95.22 %	4.78 %
RIPPER	1353	1442	58	97	93.31 %	4 %	94.75 %	5.25 %
Naïve Bayes	1345	1362	138	105	92.76 %	9.52 %	91.76 %	8.24 %

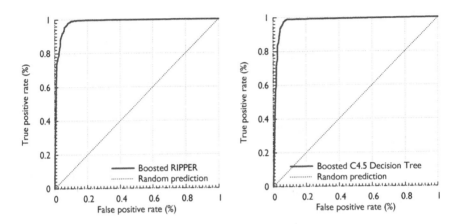

Fig. 10. The Receiver Operating Characteristic (ROC Curve) of our AdaBoost classifier using RIPPER (left) and C4.5 (right) as base classifiers respectively

In these experiments, we note that Naïve Bayes had the largest relative improvement in detection rate and false positives rate through boosting. The best results were obtained from the boosted version of the C4.5, with which we achieve a detection rate of 94.21% and a false positive rate of 3.93%. The improved detection rate over the best non-boosted method thus comes at the price of higher false positive rate.

We note that False Positive Rate (FPR) must be minimized since malware detection engines are primarily engineered to filter out potentially harmful content. The FPR is low but not zero, and may potentially be reduced through the use of a whitelisting mechanism.

4.5 Improvements

Future work will address areas where improvement is needed. First, some permissions declared by Android applications imply different privileges; this delegation of privilege is not captured by the PMDS prototype.

For example, the *READ_EXTERNAL_STORAGE* permission, which allows an application to read from the External Storage, is implicitly granted by the system if the targeted API level is equal or lower than 3 or if the application

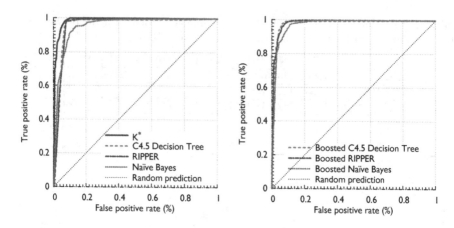

Fig. 11. Comparison of the Receiver Operating Characteristic (ROC Curve) across various base classifiers (left) and the AdaBoost variants (right)

requires the *WRITE_EXTERNAL_STORAGE* permission, which allows an application to write to the External Storage. Furthermore, the *READ_EXTERNAL_STORAGE* permission is enforced only from API level 19, from which point this permission is not longer required to read files in the application-specific directories.

Another example is the *READ_CALL_LOG* permission, which allows an application to read the user's call log. If an application targets API level equals or lower than 15, this particular permission is implicitly granted by the system if the application requires also the *READ_CONTACTS* permission, which allows an application to read the user's contacts data. PMDS needs to be carefully designed to capture the nuances of privilege delegation.

It is possible that an application uses some permissions – and accordingly to performs some system actions – without explicitly declaring them in its *AndroidManifest.xml* file. Our PMDS prototype ignores this dilemma, but future work should account for implied permissions in order to provide more precise correlation between the group of permissions required by applications and their behavior.

5   Related Work

While many traditional malware detection methodologies are based on signatures, there is a growing trend towards apply machine learning and data mining techniques to detect unknown malicious code. The approaches taken thus far, however, have been mostly concentrated on malware for the Microsoft Windows platform [23–30].

Some prior works explore the possibility of detecting Android malware using permissions. These projects, however, are predominantly based on heuristics and do not deploy machine learning techniques. In the closest project, Huang *et al.* [16] ask the same research question as us: can malicious applications be detected using permissions? In order to retrieve the permissions, the authors disassemble the APK packages, identify the Android system functions invoked, and then reconstruct the permissions being used. To evaluate their detection model, the authors use a dataset of 124,769 benign applications and 480 malicious ones, and 4 machine learning algorithms, respectively: *AdaBoost, Naïve Bayes, Decision Tree* and *Support Vector Machine*. The authors use several other features (*e.g.* the number of particular file formats and both the number of under-privileged and over-privileged permissions) in addition to the permissions to improve their detection mechanism. The authors claim that their experiments show that a single classifier is able to detect about 81% of malicious applications. Our evaluation of PMDS suggest that the method achieves comparatively higher detection rate.

Other related works that take advantage of permissions are VetDroid [22], the fingerprinting schemes DroidRanger [17], DroidMOSS [20], and work on generative models for risk scores based on requested permissions of Sarma *et al.* [21].

VetDroid [22] is a dynamic behavioral profiler framework which use the permissions to reconstruct sensitive behaviors in Android applications. VetDroid is able to reconstruct some malicious behaviors of Android applications, to ease malware analysis, and to find information leaks and vulnerabilities. The authors use a dataset of 600 malware, collected from the Android Malware Genome Project [14], and 1,249 free applications collected from the Google Play Store. While both VetDroid and PMDS try to correlate permissions to behavior, VetDroid is a tool to provide better behavior understanding and to help analysis (the output of the system is a report), rather than a complete detection system.

DroidRanger is a permission-based behavioral fingerprinting scheme to detect new samples of known Android malware families [17]. The authors propose a two layer scheme. Applications are first filtered based on the Android permissions required and then sieved through a heuristics-based filter. The authors use a dataset of 182,823 applications collected from 5 different marketplaces to evaluate their detection model. They claim that their experiments show that DroidRanger detects 119 infected applications in their dataset, with a false negative rate of 23.52% in the first version and of 5.04% in the second version. The authors focus only on the most used Android permissions of 10 Android malware families whereas PMDS investigates the whole vector. The works also differ in that PMDS leverages machine learning algorithms for its detection whereas DroidRanger takes a heuristic-based approach. A subset of the authors of DroidRanger also created DroidMOSS [20], which is focused entirely on detecting repackaged applications and uses fuzzy hashing to detect the changes made from the original legitimate program.

Sarma *et al.* propose the use of probabilistic generative models to compute a risk score depending on the permissions required by an application [21]. The authors use a dataset of 158,062 benign applications collected from the Android Market and 121 malicious ones. The authors claim that, for a very low warning rate of 0.05%, they were able to identify the 50% of the malware. Furthermore, using a different weight when training, they claim to achieve 71% of detection rate and 2.4% of warning rate. PMDS, in contrast, achieved 94% detection rate in our evaluation – comprised of nearly $10\times$ more malicious applications and $10\times$ fewer benign ones – while retaining a lower warning rate. We believe the two approaches are also complementary and could potentially be fused to provide an even more effective detection system.

6   Conclusion

In the wake of the exponential growth of the Android mobile platform there is rapid proliferation of Android malware. In this paper we have proposed a new detection technique for Android malware, called Permission-based Malware Detection System (PMDS). Our work focuses exclusively on how well permissions in Android are indicative of undesirable behavior. We built a client-server architecture for PMDS, the crux of which is a server-side machine learning classifier that automatically identifies (potentially) dangerous behaviors of previously unseen applications based on the combination of permissions they require.

Our experimental results shows the feasibility of using well-established classifiers in order to provide heuristic detection on unknown and zero-day or next-generation malware which are not detected by standard detection systems. PMDS was able to detect more than 92–94% of previously unseen malware with a false positive rate of 1.52–3.93%. Our approach shows that a simple permission-based mechanism may be used alongside classic detection algorithms to thwart the rampant mobile malware and thus raise the security bar in the mobile space.

Acknowledgments. We thank Gianfranco Tonello of TG Soft for support, Marjan Siriani for helpful comments and the anonymous reviewers for constructive feedback. Our work was supported in part by grants from Emory University, and grant-of-excellence #120032011 from the Icelandic Research Fund.

References

1. The International Telecommunication Union. The World in 2014: ICT Facts and Figures (2014),
   http://www.itu.int/en/ITU-D/Statistics/Documents/facts/
   ICTFactsFigures2014-e.pdf
2. Gartner Forecast: PCs, Ultramobiles, and Mobile Phones, Worldwide, 2011-2018, 2Q 2014 (2014),
   http://www.gartner.com/document/2780117
3. Svajcer, V.: Sophos Mobile Security Threat Report (2014)
4. Panda Security: Annual Report PandaLabs 2013 (2013),
   http://press.pandasecurity.com/wp-content/uploads/2010/05/
   Quarterly-Report-PandaLabs-April-June-2013.pdf
5. F-Secure: F-Secure Mobile Threat Report Q3 2013 (2013),
   http://www.f-secure.com/static/doc/labs_global/Research/
   Mobile_Threat_Report_Q3_2013.pdf

6. G Data SecurityLabs: G Data Mobile Malware Report H2 2013 (2013),
   https://blog.gdatasoftware.com/uploads/media/
   GData_MobileMWR_H2_2013_EN.pdf
7. Strategy Analytics: Global Smartphone Installed Base by Operating System for 88
   Countries: 2007 to 2017 (2012),
   http://www.strategyanalytics.com/default.aspx?mod=
   reportabstractviewer&a0=7834
8. IDC: More Smartphones Were Shipped in Q1 2013 Than Feature Phones, An Industry First According to IDC (2013),
   http://www.idc.com/getdoc.jsp?containerId=prUS24085413
9. Leavitt, N.: Malicious code moves to mobile devices. IEEE Computer 33(12), 16–19
   (2000)
10. Foley, S.N., Dumigan, R.: Are handheld viruses a significant threat? Communica-
    tions of the ACM 44(1), 105–107 (2001)
11. Dagon, D., Martin, T., Starner, T.: Mobile Phones as Computing Devices: The
    Viruses are Coming! IEEE Pervasive Computing 3(4), 11–15 (2004)
12. Hypponen, M.: State of cell phone malware in 2007. USENIX (2007),
    http://www.usenix.org/events/sec07/tech/hypponen.pdf
13. Lawton, G.: Is it finally time to worry about mobile malware? Computer 41(5),
    12–14 (2008)
14. Zhou, Y., Jiang, X.: Dissecting Android Malware: Characterization and Evolution.
    In: IEEE Symposium on Security and Privacy (SP), pp. 95–109. IEEE (2012),
    http://www.malgenomeproject.org
15. Spreitzenbarth, M., Freiling, F.: Android Malware on the Rise. University of Er-
    langen, Germany, Tech. Rep. CS-2012-04 (2012)
16. Huang, C.-Y., Tsai, Y.-T., Hsu, C.-H.: Performance evaluation on permission-based
    detection for android malware. In: Pan, J.-S., Yang, C.-N., Lin, C.-C. (eds.) Ad-
    vances in Intelligent Systems & Applications. SIST, vol. 21, pp. 111–120. Springer,
    Heidelberg (2012)
17. Zhou, Y., Wang, Z., Zhou, W., Jiang, X.: Hey, You, Get Off of My Market: Detect-
    ing Malicious Apps in Official and Alternative Android Markets. In: Proceedings
    of the 19th Annual Network and Distributed System Security Symposium (2012)
18. Chen, K., Liu, P., Zhang, Y.: Achieving accuracy and scalability simultaneously
    in detecting application clones on Android markets. In: Proceedings of the 36th
    International Conference on Software Engineering, ICSE 2014, pp. 175–186. ACM,
    New York (2014)
19. Crussell, J., Gibler, C., Chen, H.: Attack of the clones: Detecting cloned applica-
    tions on android markets. In: Foresti, S., Yung, M., Martinelli, F. (eds.) ESORICS
    2012. LNCS, vol. 7459, pp. 37–54. Springer, Heidelberg (2012)
20. Zhou, W., Zhou, Y., Jiang, X., Ning, P.: Detecting repackaged smartphone appli-
    cations in third-party Android marketplaces. In: Proceedings of the Second ACM
    Conference on Data and Application Security and Privacy, CODASPY 2012, pp.
    317–326. ACM, New York (2012)
21. Sarma, B.P., Li, N., Gates, C., Potharaju, R., Nita-Rotaru, C., Molloy, I.: Android
    permissions: a perspective combining risks and benefits. In: Proceedings of the 17th
    ACM Symposium on Access Control Models and Technologies, pp. 13–22. ACM
    (2012)
22. Zhang, Y., Yang, M., Xu, B., Yang, Z., Gu, G., Ning, P., Wang, X.S., Zang, B.:
    Vetting undesirable behaviors in android apps with permission use analysis. In:
    Proceedings of the 2013 ACM SIGSAC Conference on Computer & Communica-
    tions Security. ACM (2013)

23. Siddiqui, M., Wang, M.C., Lee, J.: A Survey of Data Mining Techniques for Malware Detection using File Features. In: Proceedings of the 46th Annual Southeast Regional Conference on XX, pp. 509–510. ACM (2008)

24. Ye, Y., Wang, D., Li, T., Ye, D.: IMDS: Intelligent Malware Detection System. In: Proceedings of the 13th ACM SIGKDD International Conference on Knowledge Discovery and Data Mining, pp. 1043–1047. ACM (2007)

25. Schultz, M.G., Eskin, E., Zadok, F., Stolfo, S.J.: Data Mining Methods for Detection of New Malicious Executables. In: IEEE Symposium on Security and Privacy (SP), pp. 38–49. IEEE (2001)

26. Kolter, J.Z., Maloof, M.A.: Learning to Detect and Classify Malicious Executables in the Wild. The Journal of Machine Learning Research 7, 2721–2744 (2006), JMLR.org

27. Tabish, S.M., Shafiq, M.Z., Farooq, M.: Malware Detection using Statical Analysis of Byte-Level File Content. Proceedings of the ACM SIGKDD Workshop on CyberSecurity and Intelligence Informatics, pp. 23–31. ACM (2009)

28. Kiem, H., Thuy, N.T., Quang, T.M.N.: A Machine Learning Approach to Anti-virus System. In: Proceedings of Joint Workshop of Vietnamese Society of AI, SIGKBS-JSAI, ICS-IPSJ and IEICE-SIGAI on Active Mining, Hanoi-Vietnam, pp. 61–65 (2004)

29. Firdausi, I., Lim, C., Erwin, A., Nugroho, A.S.: Analysis of machine learning techniques used in behavior-based malware detection. In: Second International Conference on Advances in Computing, Control and Telecommunication Technologies (ACT), pp. 201–203. IEEE (2010)

30. Dua, S., Du, X.: Data mining and machine learning in cybersecurity. Taylor & Francis (2011)

31. Cohen, W.W.: Fast effective rule induction. In: ICML, vol. 95, pp. 115–123 (1995)

32. Quinlan, J.R.: C4.5: programs for machine learning, vol. 1. Morgan Kaufmann (1993)

33. Holmes, G., Donkin, A., Witten, I.H.: Weka: A machine learning workbench.iN: Proceedings of the Second Australian and New Zealand Conference on Intelligent Information Systems, pp. 357–361. IEEE (1994)

34. Witten, I.H., Frank, E.: Data Mining: Practical machine learning tools and techniques. Morgan Kaufmann (2005)

35. Cleary, J.G., Trigg, L.E.: K*: An Instance-based Learner Using an Entropic Distance Measure. In: ICML, pp. 108–114 (1995)

36. John, G.H., Langley, P.: Estimating continuous distributions in Bayesian classifiers. In: Proceedings of the Eleventh Conference on Uncertainty in Artificial Intelligence, pp. 338–345. Morgan Kaufmann (1995)

37. Freund, Y., Schapire, R.E.: A desicion-theoretic generalization of on-line learning and an application to boosting. In: Vitányi, P.M.B. (ed.) EuroCOLT 1995. LNCS, vol. 904, pp. 23–37. Springer, Heidelberg (1995)

38. The Android Open Source Project: Application Fundamentals,
    http://developer.android.com/guide/components/fundamentals.html

39. The Android Open Source Project: System Permissions,
    http://developer.android.com/guide/topics/security/permissions.html

40. The Android Open Source Project: App Manifest,
    http://developer.android.com/guide/topics/manifest/manifest-intro.html

41. The Android Open Source Project: Android Permissions,
    http://developer.android.com/guide/topics/security/permissions.html

42. The Android Open Source Project: PackageManager,
    http://developer.android.com/reference/android/content/pm/
    PackageManager.html
43. The University of Waikato: Attribute-Relation File Format (ARFF),
    http://www.cs.waikato.ac.nz/ml/weka/arff.html
44. The University of Waikato: ARFF, http://weka.wikispaces.com/ARFF
45. Mila: Contagio Mobile, http://contagiominidump.blogspot.it
46. Google: Google Play Store, https://play.google.com/store

Efficient Detection of Multi-step Cross-Site Scripting Vulnerabilities

Alexandre Vernotte[1], Frédéric Dadeau[1,2], Franck Lebeau[3],
Bruno Legeard[1,4], Fabien Peureux[1], and François Piat[1]

[1] Institut FEMTO-ST, UMR CNRS 6174 – Route de Gray, 25030 Besançon, France
{avernott,fdadeau,blegeard,fpeureux,fpiat}@femto-st.fr
[2] INRIA Nancy Grand Est – BP 239, 54506 Vandoeuvre-lès-Nancy, France
frederic.dadeau@inria.fr
[3] Erdil – 9, Avenue des Montboucons, 25000 Besançon, France
franck.lebeau@erdil.com
[4] Smartesting R&D Center – 2G, Avenue des Montboucons, 25000 Besançon, France
bruno.legeard@smartesting.com

Abstract. Cross-Site Scripting (XSS) vulnerability is one of the most
critical breaches that may compromise the security of Web applications.
Reflected XSS is usually easy to detect as the attack vector is immediately executed, and classical Web application scanners are commonly
efficient to detect it. However, they are less efficient to discover multi-step
XSS, which requires behavioral knowledge to be detected. In this paper,
we propose a Pattern-driven and Model-based Vulnerability Testing approach (PMVT) to improve the capability of multi-step XSS detection.
This approach relies on generic vulnerability test patterns, which are
applied on a behavioral model of the application under test, in order
to generate vulnerability test cases. A toolchain, adapted from an existing Model-Based Testing tool, has been developed to implement this
approach. This prototype has been experimented and validated on real-
life Web applications, showing a strong improvement of detection ability
w.r.t. Web application scanners for this kind of vulnerabilities.

Keywords: Vulnerability Testing, Model-Based Testing, Vulnerability
Test Patterns, Web Applications, Multi-step Cross-Site Scripting.

1 Introduction

Code injection security attacks, and more particularly cross-site scripting (XSS),
are part of the most prevalent and dangerous cyber-attacks against Web appli-
cations reported these last years; see, for example, OWASP Top Ten 2013 [29],
CWE/SANS 25 [20] and WhiteHat Website Security Statistic Report 2013 [28].
In this latter, XSS appears to represent 43% of all the serious vulnerabilities
discovered in a large panel of Web applications. As another example, Claudio
Criscione reports at GTAC 2013 that nearly 60% of security bugs detected in
Google software are XSS vulnerabilities[1].

---

[1] https://developers.google.com/google-test-automation-conference/2013/
presentations#Day2Presentation7 [Last visited: July 2014]

A. Prakash and R. Shyamasundar (Eds.): ICISS 2014, LNCS 8880, pp. 358–377, 2014.
© Springer International Publishing Switzerland 2014

An XSS vulnerability occurs each time an application stores (with more or less persistence) a user input and displays it into a Web browser without proper sanitization (without removing or replacing any character that may contribute to an unwanted behavior). Therefore, it is possible to inject a piece of code and see this code executed by the Web browser, potentially causing severe damage to visitors (often without them knowing). XSS attacks is easy to put into practice, and presents a great number of variants. It is also an entry point for many exploits (session hijacking, credentials stealing, etc.). The difficulty of handling XSS issues is mainly due to the complexity of the application logics. Indeed, developers need to think about a systematic protection of the displayed data, what is an error-prone exercise, since a given user input may be subsequently displayed in a large variety of places in the application. It is thus mandatory to detect XSS-related issues at the earliest, by performing vulnerability testing at the application level. XSS vulnerabilities can be classified into four categories[2]:

(i) **DOM-based XSS** when the injected data stay within the browser (and modify the DOM "environment"),
(ii) **Reflected XSS** when the untrusted injected data are directly displayed/executed right after being injected,
(iii) **Stored XSS** when the injected data is stored by the application and retrieved later in another context (e.g., in a user's profile),
(iv) **Multi-step XSS** (a special breed of stored XSS) when it requires that the user performs several actions on the applications (mainly navigation steps) to display/execute the attack vector.

While the first three categories are usually well-identified and easily detected by automated penetration testing tools, such as Web application vulnerability scanners [2], the last one remains a challenging issue [10]. On the one hand, manual vulnerability testing is becoming more and more difficult as Websites are growing in size and complexity: indeed, as the result of an attack cannot be seen immediately, the penetration tester has to dig into the application logics to understand where a given user input is supposed to be sent back to the client. On the other hand, current automated vulnerability discovery techniques can test for a large percentage of technical vulnerabilities, but are often limited in accessing large parts of the Web application, because they lack any knowledge about the functional behaviour and the business logics of the application.

Recently, vulnerability test patterns have been introduced to describe a testing procedure for each class of vulnerabilities [25]. However, such a process remains manual, and using vulnerability test patterns for testing automation is still a challenge. In addition, the current automated vulnerability testing tools (i.e. Web application scanners) often display false positive and false negative results, raising alarms when there is no error or missing potential weaknesses, respectively. Hence, it is the cause of a useless and costly waste of time.

The approach presented in this paper aims to improve the accuracy and precision of multi-step XSS testing, by proposing a testing approach driven by

---

[2] https://www.owasp.org/index.php/Top_10_2013-A3-Cross-Site_Scripting_ (XSS) [Last visited: July 2014]

automated *vulnerability test patterns* composed with a *behavioral model* of the system under test. These patterns describe generic test scenarios that assess the robustness of the Web application w.r.t. a given kind of vulnerability. To achieve that, it relies on the information contained in the behavioral model, especially the location of the possible user inputs and their associated resurgences, to check that user inputs are correctly sanitized before being displayed on a Web page. As a major result, this approach increases the efficiency of penetration testers for detecting vulnerabilities such as multi-step XSS. The main contribution of this paper relates to the proposal of a pattern-driven and model-based approach to generate vulnerability tests for Web applications. More precisely, this concerns:

- The formalization of vulnerability test patterns using generic test purposes to drive the test generation engine, including a combinatorial unfolding of untrusted injected data taken from standard databases, such as the OWASP collection of attack vectors[3].
- The separation of the behavioral model for Web application vulnerability testing between a generic part (whatever the application under test is) and an ad-hoc part, which is specific to the targeted application under test.
- The full automation of the testing process, including test generation, test execution and verdict assignment.

The paper is organized as follows. Section 2 introduces the principles of XSS-based attacks, and illustrates them on a running example of a vulnerable Web application named WackoPicko. Section 3 describes the contribution of the paper, namely our pattern-driven and model-based vulnerability testing approach. It especially defines the content of the behavioral model and the expressiveness of the test pattern language, which are the key artefacts of the approach. Experience reports are provided and experimental results are discussed in Sect. 4. Finally, the related work is presented in Sect. 5, while conclusion and future works are given in Sect. 6.

2   Challenges of Detecting Multi-Step Cross-Site Scripting Vulnerabilities

This section introduces the challenge of detecting multi-step XSS vulnerabilities, and illustrates this issue on a running example of a vulnerable Web application. More precisely, this section aims to explain and exemplify the difficulties faced by mainstream automated penetration testing tools (i.e. commercial or open-source Web scanners) for accurately detecting multi-step XSS vulnerabilities. Based on these conclusions, we finally expose the research questions we are addressing to efficiently detect such multi-step XSS vulnerabilities.

---

[3] https://www.owasp.org/index.php/XSS_Filter_Evasion_Cheat_Sheet [Last visited: July 2014]

2.1   Running Example: The WackoPicko Web Application

First of all, in order to illustrate multi-step XSS vulnerability and to evaluate the accuracy and precision of our approach, we use the Web application called WackoPicko[4], which is a deliberately-unsecured Web application developed by Adam Doupé [10]. The objective of this test bed, developed using PHP/MySQL, is to provide a realistic but vulnerable environment. Like education-oriented vulnerable Web applications such as DVWA (Damn Vulnerable Web Application[5]) or WebGoat[6], WackoPicko can aid security professionals to learn, improve or test their skill in vulnerability discovery on a realistic Web application, with nowadays features (e.g., posts, comments) and realistic workflows. It can also be used to test Web security testing tools, like vulnerability scanners for instance.

Basically, WackoPicko allows users to authenticate themselves, share pictures, comment pictures, and possibly buy pictures. WackoPicko presents realistic features (authentication, shopping, ...) that can be found in many Websites, along with more complex workflows (e.g., uploading a picture, commenting the picture). It embeds several vulnerabilities, notably SQL Injection, Cross-Site Scripting, Cross-Site Request Forgery and Local/Remote File Inclusion, which are ranked by the OWASP project among the most frequently used attacks.

2.2   Multi-step XSS Principles and Illustration

The main characteristic of a multi-step vulnerability is that the attack vector is injected in one page, saved (e.g., in a database), and then echoed later in another page or another application. Hence, detecting such a vulnerability involves being able to perform a sequence of actions starting from attack vector injection until vulnerability checking. For instance, using the WackoPicko example, such a sequence appears when a user adds a comment to a picture. The corresponding workflow, depicted in Fig. 1, is now described.

(a) Comment setting   (b) Comment preview   (c) Comment display

Fig. 1. Nominal workflow of picture comment using WackoPicko

---

[4] https://github.com/adamdoupe/WackoPicko [Last visited: July 2014]

[5] http://www.dvwa.co.uk/ [Last visited: July 2014]

[6] https://www.owasp.org/index.php/Category:OWASP_WebGoat_Project [Last visited: July 2014]

0. Prerequisites. This preliminary step consists in logging the user on the application, and browsing the application until viewing a particular picture.

1. Setting a comment. In this step (see Fig. 1(a)), the user sets his new comment in the text area, and clicks the *Preview* button. By clicking the button, the client (i.e. the browser) sends a *POST* request to the Web server.

2. Preview of the comment. This step (see Fig. 1(b)), consists of visualizing the comment before validation by the user. When the server receives the *POST* request, it stores the new comment in the *comments_preview* table of its database. Then, the server sends back to the browser a new page that displays a preview of the comment. The user may accept or reject its comment with the respecting *Create* and *Cancel* buttons. By clicking the *Create* button, the browser sends a *POST* request to the server.

3. Displaying the comment. The final step (see Fig. 1(c)) consists in displaying a validated comment. When the server receives the previous *POST* request, it concretely relates the comment to the picture, making this comment available every time the picture page is displayed.

A malicious attack can consist of injecting a piece of code (for instance the vector `<script>alert("XSS")</script>`) in the text area, previewing, creating, and visualizing the result. What makes this attack a multi-step XSS attack is the fact that only the picture page is vulnerable to XSS: the injected vector is properly sanitized on the comment preview page and it thus requires an extra step from the user (validating the comment) to detect the vulnerability. The corresponding workflow, depicted in Fig. 2, shows that the attack vector injected as picture comment (see Fig. 2(a)) is next interpreted as Javascript code (and not as a harmless string) and the alert window is displayed (see Fig. 2(c)).

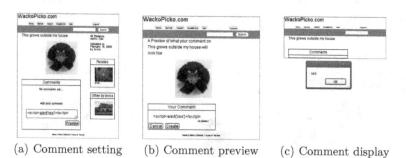

(a) Comment setting   (b) Comment preview   (c) Comment display

Fig. 2. Multi-step XSS attack workflow of picture comment using WackoPicko

It should be noted that the comment preview page is not vulnerable to XSS attack (see Fig. 2(b)): there is no alert message since the attack vector is treated as a standard string in which special characters are encoded. Indeed, the source code of the page embeds the harmless HTML-encoded attack vector (`&lt;script&gt;alert("XSS")&lt;/script&gt;`). This prevents the `<script>` tag from being interpreted by the browser.

2.3 Research Questions

As illustrated in the previous section, whereas it is mostly easy to automatically detect reflected XSS, multi-step XSS are far more difficult to discover. Indeed, the untrusted data are not immediately displayed/executed after they are injected, and several navigation steps to display/execute the attack vector are required to record the breach. Current vulnerability detection techniques highly struggle with this problem, mostly because it requires knowledge of the logic of the application under test to navigate from an injection point to its output page. Hence, within our work, we aim to address the following research questions:

RQ1. To what extend does the knowledge of the business logic of the application help to increase the accuracy of the detection for multi-step XSS?

RQ2. To what extend is it possible to automatize generic test patterns dedicated to such Web application vulnerabilities?

RQ3. To what extend test execution and verdict assignment can be fully automated?

RQ4. To what extend is it possible to improve the overall efficiency of the process with respect to manual penetration testing activities and state of the practice by means of automated penetration testing techniques and tools?

To achieve this goal, the proposed testing approach consists to combine formalized test patterns with a behavioral model focused on the business logic for vulnerability testing of Web applications. Formalized test patterns provide penetration testing scenarios, and the model provides the minimal but necessary required information, namely: states/pages and transitions/navigation combined with logical application data and dataflow information. The next section introduces this testing approach, called Pattern-driven and Model-based Vulnerability Testing (PMVT).

3 Pattern-Driven and Model-Based Vulnerability Testing for Multi-step XSS

This section introduces a Pattern-driven and Model-based Vulnerability Testing (PMVT) approach, which is a generic solution for Web application vulnerability testing. We first describe the principles of the approach, before giving information on the different artefacts that it involves, namely a behavioral model and test purposes implementing a vulnerability test pattern.

3.1 Principles of the PMVT Approach

The PMVT process, depicted in Fig. 3, is composed of four activities:

① The *Test Purposes* design activity consists of formalizing a test procedure from vulnerability test patterns that the generated test cases have to cover. These Test Purposes can be generic to be applied for a category of application. We show later that the Test Purpose for multi-step XSS is generic whatever the Web application is.

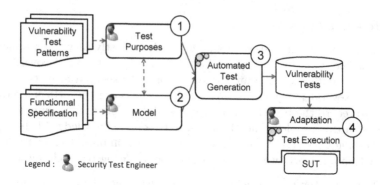

Fig. 3. Pattern-driven and Model-based Vulnerability Test process

② The *Modeling* activity aims to design a test model that captures the behavioral aspects of the application under test to generate consistent (from a functional point of view) sequences of stimuli.

③ The *Test Generation* activity consists of automatically producing abstract test cases, including expected results, from the artifacts defined during the two previous activities.

④ The *Adaptation, Test Execution and Observation* activity aims to (*i*) translate the generated abstract test cases into executable scripts, (*ii*) to execute these scripts on the application under test, (*iii*) to observe the responses and to compare them to the expected results in order to assign the test verdict and automate the detection of vulnerabilities.

All these activities are supported by a dedicated toolchain, based on an existing Model-Based Testing (MBT) software named *CertifyIt* [18] provided by the company Smartesting[7]. CertifyIt is a test generator that takes as input a test model, written with a subset of UML (called UML4MBT [3,8]), capturing the behavior of the application under test. A UML4MBT model consists of (*i*) UML class diagrams to represent the static view of the system (with classes, associations, enumerations, class attributes and operations), (*ii*) UML object diagrams to define the data and entities (used to compute test cases) that exist at the initial state, and (*iii*) statechart diagrams (annotated with OCL constraints) to specify the dynamic view of the application under test. Such UML4MBT models have a precise and unambiguous meaning, so that those models can be understood and computed by the *CertifyIt* technology. This precise meaning makes it possible to simulate the execution of the models and to automatically generate test cases by applying the strategies given by the test purposes. Each generated test case is typically an abstract sequence of high-level actions from the UML4MBT models. These generated test cases contain the sequence of stimuli to be executed, but also the expected results (to perform the observation activity and automate the verdict assignment), obtained by resolving the associated OCL constraints. The next sections describe each of the activities and illustrate them using the WackoPicko running example.

---

[7] http://www.smartesting.com [Last visited: July 2014]

3.2 Formalizing Vulnerability Test Patterns into Test Purposes

A Vulnerability Test Patterns (vTP) is a normalized textual document describing the testing objectives and procedures to detect a particular flaw in a Web application. Hence, there are as much vTP as there are types of application-level flaws. Our approach is based on the vTP provided during the ITEA2 research project DIAMONDS[8] [26]. For instance, Fig. 4 presents an excerpt of the vTP defined for the multi-step XSS vulnerability. At this stage, Vulnerability Test Patterns are still textual. The PMVT approach takes such textual vTP as starting point by translating them into formal directives, called Test Purposes, in order to be able to automate testing strategy implementation and execution.

Name	multi-step XSS
Description	This pattern can be used on an application that does not check user inputs. An XSS attack can redirect users to a malicious site, or can steal user's private information (cookies, session, ...).
Objective(s)	Detect if a user input can embed attack vector enabling an XSS attack.
Prerequisites	N/A
Procedure	Identify a sensible user input, inject the attack vector $<script>alert(xss)</script>$.
Observation/ Oracle	Go to a page echoing the user input, check if a message box 'xss' appears.
Variant(s)	- attack vector variants: character encoding, Hex-transformation, comments insertion - procedure variants: attack can be applied at the HTTP level; the attack vector is injected in the parameters of the HTTP messages sent to the server, and we have to check if the attack vector is in the response message from the server
Known Issue(s)	Web Application Firewalls (WAF) filter messages send to the server (black list, clac regEx, ...); variants allows to overcome these filters
Affiliated vTP	Stored XSS
Reference(s)	CAPEC: http://capec.mitre.org/data/definitions/86.html WASC: http://projects.Webappsec.org/w/page/13246920/CrossSiteScripting OWASP: https://www.owasp.org/index.php/Cross-site_Scripting_(XSS)

Fig. 4. Vulnerability Test Pattern of multi-step XSS attack

A *test purpose* is a high-level expression that formalizes a testing objective to drive the automated test generation on the behavioral model. It has been originally designed to drive model-based test generation for security components, typically Smart card applications and cryptographic components [6]. Within PMVT context, a test purpose formalizes a given vTP in order to drive the vulnerability test generation on the behavioral model. Basically, such a test purpose is a sequence of significant *steps* that has to be exercised by the test case scenario in order to assess the robustness of the application under test w.r.t. the related vulnerability. Each step takes the form of a set of operations/behaviors to execute, or specific state to reach.

Figure 5 shows the WackoPicko test purpose formalizing the vTP presented in Fig. 4. This automatically generated test purpose specifies that, for all sensible pages echoing user inputs and for each user input of a given page, a test has to perform the following actions: (*i*) use any operation to reach a page showing

---

[8] http://www.itea2-diamonds.org [Last visited: July 2014]

```
for_each instance $page from
"Page.allInstances()->select(p:Page|not(p.all_outputs->isEmpty()))" on_instance sut,
for_each instance $param from "self.all_outputs" on_instance $page,

use any_operation any_number_of_times to_reach
 "WackPick.allInstances()->any(true).webAppStructure.ongoingAction.all_inputs->exists(d:Data|d=self)"
on_instance $param

then use threat.injectXSS($param)

then use any_operation any_number_of_times to_reach
 "WackPick.allInstances()->any(true).webAppStructure.ongoingAction.oclIsUndefined()
and WackPick.allInstances()->any(true).webAppStructure.current_page=self" on_instance $page

then use threat.checkXSS()
```

Fig. 5. Test purpose formalizing the vTP of multi-step XSS attack (Figure 4)

the XSS-sensitive user input, (*ii*) inject an attack vector in this user input, (*iii*) use any operation to reach a page echoing the user input, and (*iv*) check if the attack succeeded. It should be underlined that the structure of this test purpose, addressing multi-step XSS vulnerability, is fully generic. Moreover, since pages and user inputs are automatically retrieved from OCL constraints from the UML4MBT test model, this automated generation of test purpose can therefore be applied for any Web application.

3.3   Test Model Specification

As for every Model-Based Testing (MBT) approach, the modeling activity consists of designing a test model that will be used to automatically generate abstract test cases. Our approach, based on Smartesting technology, requires a model designed using the UML4MBT notation. To ease and accelerate this modeling activity, which is known to be time consuming, we have developed a Domain Specific Modeling Language (DSML), called *DASTML*, that allows to model the global structure of a Web application: the available pages, the available actions on each page, and the user inputs of each action potentially used to inject attack vectors. It solely represents all the structural entities necessary to generate vulnerability test cases. The transformation of a DASTML instantiation into a valid UML4MBT model is automatically performed by a dedicated plug-in integrated to the Smartesting modeling environment. The DASTML Domain Specific Modeling Language is composed of four entities:

Page. Page entities represent the different pages that compose the Web application under test. We follow the comparison technique proposed in [11], meaning that we may consider two physical pages as the same if they exactly provide the same action and navigation entities. On the contrary, we may consider a single physical page as two distinct pages if there is at some point a variation in the action and navigation entities. We also distinguish the initial page from the others by using a boolean attribute *is_init*.

Navigation. Navigation entity is typically a link or a button that takes the
user to another page, without altering the internal state of the application
nor triggering any function or service of the application.

Action. Action entities have pretty much the same form as navigation entities,
but there are two main differences. First, an action entity may carry data
(in case of a Web form for instance). Second, an action entity can alter the
internal state of the application (e.g., any user interaction that has modify
the database is considered as an action). In addition, the *is_auth* attribute
allows to distinguish authentication actions from the others. This way, we
can easily refer to it when the attacker has to log on the Web application.

Data. Data entity, defining any user input, is composed of a key and a value.

The metamodel of DASTML is depicted in Fig. 6. Entities interact with each
other based on multiple relations. *Navigate_to* and *navigate_from* provide the
source page and the target page of a navigation entity. Identically, *has_action*
and *sends_users_to* provide the source page and the target page of an action
entity. An action may be associated to one or more data (in case of a Web form
for instance), with relation *has_data*. Data have a (*reflects*) relation to link them
to one or more output page (in this way, for each user input, the page where it
is rendered back is known, what is crucial for XSS vulnerability testing).

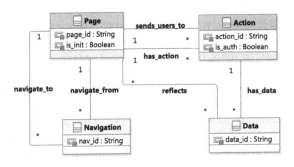

Fig. 6. Metamodel of the DASTML Domain Specific Modeling Language

The code fragment, introduced in Fig. 7, is an instantiation of DASTML to
model the WackoPicko running example. In this DASTML model, the entry point
is the "HOME" page, where users can navigate to the "LOGIN" page. There,
users can authenticate themselves (see the *:auth* suffix on the "LOGIN" action),
and if valid credentials are provided, they reach the "HOME_LOGGED_IN"
page. At some point, users may visit a picture page. This page has a "COM-
MENT_PICTURE" action that requires a user input called "CP_CONTENT",
which abstract value is "CONTENT1". This input is rendered back on two pages:
"PICTURE_CONFIRM_COMMENT" and "PICTURE". Finally, the completion
of the action redirects users to the "PICTURE_CONFIRM_COMMENT".

```
PAGES {
    "HOME" : init {                              "RECENT_PICTURES" {
        NAVIGATIONS {                                NAVIGATIONS {
            "GO_TO_LOGIN" -> "LOGIN"                     "SHOW_PICTURE" -> "PICTURE"
        }                                            }
    }                                            }

    "LOGIN" {                                    "PICTURE" {
        ACTIONS {                                    ACTIONS {
            "LOGIN" : auth ("USERNAME" = "                   "COMMENT_PICTURE" ("
USER1" ,                                     CP_CONTENT" = "CONTENT1"
                        "PASSWORD" = "                  => { "
PWD1" )                                     PICTURE_CONFIRM_COMMENT" , "PICTURE" })
                -> "HOME_LOGGED_IN"                      -> "PICTURE_CONFIRM_COMMENT" ,
        }                                            }
    }                                        }
                                             "PICTURE_CONFIRM_COMMENT" {
    "HOME_LOGGED_IN" {                           ACTIONS {
        NAVIGATIONS {                                "CONFIRM_COMMENT" -> "PICTURE
            "GOTO_RECENT_PICTURES"           "
                -> "RECENT_PICTURES" ,           }
            "GOTO_GUESTBOOK"                     }
                -> "GUESTBOOK"               }
        }
    }
}
```

Fig. 7. DASTML instantiation for the WackoPicko application

3.4   Test Generation

The *test generation* activity, which aims to produce test cases from both the behavioral model and the test purpose, is composed of three phases.

The first phase aims to transform the model and the test purposes into elements computable by the test case generator *CertifyIt*. Notably, test purposes are transformed into *test targets*, which a sequence of *intermediate objectives* used by the test generation engine [7]. The sequence of steps of a test purpose is mapped to a sequence of intermediate objectives of a test target. Furthermore, this first phase unfolds the combination of values between iterators of test purposes, such that one test purpose produces as many test targets as possible combinations.

The second phase consists to automatically derive *abstract test cases* by computing the test targets on the behavioral model. This phase is computed by the test case generator *CertifyIt*. An abstract test case is a sequence of completely valuated *operation calls* (i.e. all parameters are instantiated). An operation call represents either a stimulation or an observation of the application under test. Each test target automatically produces one test case verifying both the sequence of intermediate objectives and the model constraints. Note that an intermediate objective (i.e. a test purpose step) can be translated into several operation calls.

Finally, the third phase allows to export the abstract test cases into the execution environment. Within PMVT approach, this consists of (*i*) automatically creating a JUnit test suite, in which each abstract test case is exported as a JUnit test case, and (*ii*) automatically creating an interface, which defines the prototype of each operation of the application under test. The implementation of these operations, which aims at linking abstract keywords/operations to concrete actions, is in charge of the test automation engineer (see next subsection).

Figure 8 presents an abstract test case for the WackoPicko example, generated from the multi-step XSS attack test purpose introduced in Fig. 5, and the test model derived from the DASTML instantiation presented in Fig. 7.

```
1    sut.goToLogin()
2    sut.login(LOGIN_1,PWD_1)
3    was.finalizeAction()
4    sut.checkPage() = HOME_LOGGED_IN
5    sut.goToRecentPictures()
6    sut.checkPage() = RECENT_PICTURES
7    sut.goToPicture(PICTURE_ID_1)
8    sut.checkPage() = PICTURE
9    sut.submitComment(P_COMMENT_CONTENT_1)
10   threat.injectXSS(PICTURE_COMMENT)
11   was.finalizeAction()
12   sut.checkXSS()
13   sut.checkPage() = PICTURE_COMMENT_PREVIEW
14   sut.validateComment())
15   sut.checkXSS()
16   sut.checkPage(PICTURE)
```

Fig. 8. Abstract test case for the WackoPicko application

Basically, this test case consists to (i) log on the application using valid credentials (steps #1, #2, #3 and #4), (ii) browse the application to a picture (steps #5, #6, #7 and #8), (iii) submit a comment with an attack vector on a given user input (steps #9, #10, #11, #12 and #13), (iv) browse to a page echoing the injected data and check if there exists an application-level flaw (steps #14, #15 and #16), using the *checkXSS()* observation that allows to assign a verdict to the test case.

3.5   Adaptation and Test Execution

During the modeling activity, all data used by the application (pages, user input, attack vector, etc.) are modeled at an abstract level. As a consequence, the test cases are abstract and cannot thus be executed as they are. The gap between stimuli (resp. keywords) of the abstract test cases and the concrete API (resp. data) of the application under test must be bridged. To achieve that, the test case generator *CertifyIt* generates a file containing the signature of each operation. The test automation engineer is in charge of implementing each operation of this interface. Since Web applications become richer and richer (notably due to more and more complex client-side behaviors), actions and observations of the application are executed on the client-side Web GUI by using the HtmlUnit framework[9]. The different attack vector variants are extracted from the OWASP XSS Filter evasion cheat sheet[10], which provides about one hundred variants for XSS detection. This way, our approach only focuses on producing abstract vulnerability test cases, and each one is concretized and automatically executed with each possible attack vector variant.

Finally, regarding the test verdict assignment, we introduce the following terminology: *Attack-pass* when the complete execution of a test reveals that the application contains a breach, *Attack-fail* when the failure of the execution of the last step reveals that the application is robust to the attack.

---

[9] http://htmlunit.sourceforge.net/ [Last visited: July 2014]
[10] https://www.owasp.org/index.php/XSS_Filter_Evasion_Cheat_Sheet [Last visited: July 2014]

4   Experimental Results on Real-Life Applications

The execution of the hundred test cases generated for the vulnerable WackoPicko example (derived from the abstract test case introduced in Fig. 8 and using the hundred OWASP XSS attack vector variants), has shown that 80% of the executed test cases are attack-pass. The remaining 20% have been run with variants designed to unveil a particular XSS vulnerability, for which WackoPicko example is not sensitive. Hence, these results fit the manual experiments we conducted on WackoPicko and gave a first validation of our approach, i.e. our approach is suitable for effective detection of multi-step XSS vulnerabilities on early 2000's simple Web applications. However, to complete and confirm these first results, further experimentations have been conducted to do comparison with other techniques like vulnerability scanners and penetration testing.

4.1   Overview of the *stud-e* Web Application

We notably applied the PMVT approach on a real-life Web application, named *stud-e*, and conducted this industrial use case in partnership with the development team. This case study is an e-learning Web-based application that is currently used by more than fifteen thousands users per year in France. It provides three profiles: *students*, *teachers*, and *administrators*. Students can access and download material of their courses, practice quizzes and exercises, participate to their exams and review their scores, interact with their teachers through embedded emails and forums. Teachers can grant course material, elaborate quiz and exercises, manage their courses, group courses into modules, define exams, give scores to exams, tutor their students. Administrators are in charge of student registrations, teacher management, privilege definition and parameter settings. This application uses *infinite-urls*, meaning that every page is accessed through a unique timestamped identifier. It also uses a custom url-rewriting mechanism. A lot of effort has been put into security-related matters: all non-user data are encrypted (e.g., session data, database keys, etc.), data retrieved from the database are sanitized, and user input validation occurs both at client-side and server-side. That is why *Stud-e* is representative of an important class regrouping sensitive Web applications (e.g., banking area) that emphasizes security protection and encryption, which is a struggle for current vulnerability detection techniques.

Because the application uses infinite-urls, exhaustive testing of the Website based on its url is impossible. Hence, we applied a risk assessment approach to identify potential threats, business assets, vulnerabilities, and attack scenarios. These pieces of information were gathered while interviewing real users about the attack scenarios they feared the most. As a result, two possible attack scenarios arise. The first attack scenario focuses on a *dishonest teacher* who wants to steel/suppress educational material, for its own needs or for revenge. In this first case, the threat is a dishonest teacher, the targeted business assets are the educational materials. The second scenario focuses on a *dishonest student* who wants to cheat by influencing its scores. In this second case, the threat is a dishonest student, the targeted business assets are the exams and related scores.

Both attack scenarios are particularly complex. For instance, the *dishonest teacher* scenario involves browsing 9 pages and performing 38 user actions (clicks, field filling, etc.), and features a great number of intermediate pages and actions. In this scenario, the test engineer has to browse 6 pages and perform 8 user actions between the injection page and the observation page. These features make the detection of multi-step XSS vulnerabilities very hard for current techniques.

4.2 Experimental Results

We were able to successfully apply the PMVT approach to *stud-e* despite all its security features. It took approximately 3 hours to produce the DASTML instantiation of the Web application including pages, actions and data. The test generator computed the 14 expected vulnerability test cases in 15 minutes. Five (5) more hours were spent for adaptation activity to write the HtmlUnit implementation of the operations corresponding to the abstract actions. Finally, it took about 2 seconds to execute one test with a particular variant. Hence, it requires approximately 50 minutes, to execute the entire set of tests (2s × 14 tests × 106 variants = 2968 s).

Two vulnerabilities has been discovered. The first one was introduced for the sake of this study, whereas the second concerned a unintended multi-step XSS vulnerability. Tests executions did not produce any false positive, thanks to the short risk assessment phase and the precision of the test targets. They did not produce any false negative either, even though 20% of executions were marked as *attack-fail*: it means that *stud-e* is robust to the variants used in each *attack-failed* test execution. It takes the entire variants list to assess the presence of a certain vulnerability. Compared to the two identified attack scenarios, the sequence embedding the second multi-step XSS vulnerability was both shorter and simpler (only one profile was involved). This discovery led to a update of the source code of the Web application. Notice that this discovery was due to the systematic identification of user input fields and their respecting echoing page, which produces test cases with many relevant checks all along the test case.

4.3 Comparison Studies

To do comparison with other approaches, we conducted two vulnerability detection campaigns on the *stud-e* application: one using Web Application Scanners (WAS), one following a penetration testing protocol. Experiments with five WASs (IBM AppScan, NTOSpider, w3af, skipfish, and arachni) showed that these tools are not suitable for this kind of Web application. Most of them (w3af, skipfish, arachni and NTOSpider) were not able to authenticate to the application.

The protection mechanism of *stud-e*, which we described earlier, constitutes a solid barrier for scanners since their modus operandi relies on storing all found URL to fuzz each of them without respect of logical workflow (aside from the authentication process).

An additional protection mechanism, which makes *stud-e* almost impossible to crawl, is the use of a frame set. If the request does not originate from the frame that contains the link or the form responsible for the request, the server refuses the request and the user gets thrown back to the authentication page. Hence, only IBM AppScan was able to get past through the authentication page and access the authenticated area. However, we had to define a "multi-step operation sequence" in order to reach an injection page. No XSS vulnerability has been found during the scan.

Experiments with penetration testing were not straightforward. The use of tools (like intrusive proxies) demonstrates to be inefficient, mainly for two reasons. Firstly, none of these tools are able to replay a full test sequence. Their replay feature only allows to replay one HTTP request to the server, and this is not relevant for the purpose of detecting multi-step XSS vulnerabilities. Secondly, they work at the HTTP level, which is not suited for *stud-e*. Indeed, this application embeds a protection mechanism, which makes the crafting of relevant HTTP requests very difficult. Each request to the server embeds control parameters, dynamically generated on each page. Without the knowledge of the Javascript code behavior and the knowledge of the control parameter, crafting a correct HTTP request is merely impossible.

Hence, after failing at using intrusive proxies, we finally execute the tests by hand. For the *dishonest student* attack scenario, it took approximatively 1 minute to execute the entire scenario. Knowing that this scenario has three tests, and that each test must be executed 106 times (because of the 106 attack vector variants), the total execution time required to test the scenario is approximately 5 hours (1 min × 3 tests × 106 variants = 318 min). For the *dishonest teacher* attack scenario, it took approximatively one minute and a half to execute the entire scenario. Knowing that this scenario has 11 tests, and that each test must also be executed 106 times, the total execution time required to test the scenario is approximatively 29 hours (1.5 min × 11 tests × 106 variants = 1749 min to compute all the execution configurations).

4.4 Experimentation Summary

After a short risk assessment phase that lead to identify two threat scenarios, the PMVT approach has been experimented with a focus on them. It successfully detected 2 multi-step XSS vulnerabilities (now corrected by the development team) on a large and real-life Web application. We spent 10 hours to deploy the whole process. In comparison with a manual penetration testing approach, we have shown the efficiently of PMVT, which makes it possible to save about 19 hours in regard to manual testing attempt. The experiments using 5 Web Application Scanners have also shown that, due to specific characteristics of the *stud-e* application (defensive programming), no scanner succeeded to find any of the vulnerabilities. To conclude, these encouraging experimental results enable to successfully validate the relevance and efficiency of our approach.

5   Related Work

Due to the prevalence of XSS vulnerabilities, many research directions are investigated to prevent XSS exploits or to detect XSS flaws.

Examples of *prevention* are defense mechanisms installed on the server (Web application firewalls for instance) and/or on the client's browser that examines incoming data and sanitizes anything considered malicious. Lots of solutions have been elaborated to protect against XSS, based on Web proxies [16], reversed proxies [30], dynamic learning [4], data tainting [21], fast randomization technique [1], data/code separation [12], or pattern-based HTTP request/response analysis [19]. XSS prevention is efficient against multi-step XSS vulnerabilities because it is enough to scan user inputs to spot malicious vectors. But it comes with another challenge, which is the capacity of identifying script code as being malicious. Again, it takes some knowledge of the application's behavior to separate harmless scripts sent by the server from malicious scripts injected by miscreants. In addition, it does not solve the main problem of developers who are unaware of the severity of XSS and good practices that help enforcing security. Worse, it might invite them to solely rely on third party security tools like Web Application Firewalls and foster poor-secured Web applications to proliferate.

Contrary to prevention approach, *detection* is an offensive strategy. It is a testing activity consisting of impersonating a hacker and performing attack scenarios using manual, tool-based (intrusive proxies, ...) or automated techniques (Web Application Vulnerability Scanners, ...), in a harmless way (without compromising the application or the server where it is hosted). Usually, XSS detection is done post-development, by a third-party security organization. It can also be done prior to the application's deployment, and therefore may be seen as an acceptance test criterion. Related work on XSS detection can be classified into two categories: static analysis security testing (SAST), or dynamic analysis security testing (DAST). The first category encompasses the use of code-based techniques while the second category consists of executing and stimulating the system in order to detect vulnerabilities.

A majority of the techniques found in the literature propose to deal with XSS using SAST techniques. Kieyzun et al. [15] propose a vulnerability detection technique addressing SQL injections (SQLi) and XSS-1 (reflected) as well as XSS-2 (stored) vulnerabilities, based on dynamic taint analysis. Wassermann and Su [27] use string-taint analysis for cross-site scripting vulnerabilities detection. This technique combines the concepts of tainted information flow and string analysis. Shar et al. [23] present an automated approach that not only detects XSS vulnerabilities using a combination of the concepts of tainted information flow and string analysis, but also statically removes them from program source code. The same authors designed another approach [24] that aims to build SQLi and XSS detectors by statically collecting predefined input sanitization code attributes. All these approaches are SAST techniques, meaning that program source code has to be disclosed one way or another. The underlying concept behind each is taint analysis [22] which consists of keeping track of the values derived from user inputs throughout the application internals.

Although code analysis appears quite effective for detecting multi-step XSS, a major problem is that program source code is not always available. Moreover, these techniques are bound to a specific programming language, while there exists a tremendous number of languages to develop a Web application (PHP, .NET, JSP, Ruby, J2E, and so on). Hence, several dynamic application security testing (DAST) techniques have been proposed regarding the detection of vulnerabilities such as XSS.

In [17], Korscheck proposes a workflow-based approach to deal with multi-step XSS vulnerabilities, by using manually recorded traces to model a Web application and then injecting malicious data by replaying the traces. User traces reduce the test design cost while still carrying enough information to handles logical barriers, but it hardly handles the Web application evolution.

In [14], the authors present a multi-agent black-box technique to detect stored-XSS vulnerabilities in Web forms. It is composed of a Web page agent parser (i.e. a crawler), a script injection agent to perform the attacks, and a verification agent to assign a verdict. This approach solely relies on an automatic Web crawler, which may miss consequent parts of the Web application, and therefore miss potentially vulnerable injection points.

Blome et al. [5] propose a model-based vulnerability testing that relies on attacker models, which can be seen as an extension of Mealy machines. The approach is based on a list of nominal and attack vectors, a configuration file that contains system-specific information, and an XML file, describing the attacker model. This approach addresses lots of vulnerabilities but multi-step XSS is not addressed. It would imply to model a complex heuristic to inject and observe this particular vulnerability type. Also, attacker models are specific to one Web application, and it requires great effort from test engineers to design these artifacts for every test campaign.

The approach presented in [13] consists of modeling the attacker behavior. It also requires a state-aware model of the application under test, annotated using input taint data-flow analysis, to spot possible reflections. Concrete application inputs are generated with respect to an Attack Input Grammar, which produces fuzzed values for reflected application input parameters. This technique tackles multi-step XSS detection. However, it requires a great effort from test engineers to deploy the approach: the model inference process needs to be rightly tuned. Also, it cannot handle client-side oriented applications (using Ajax).

Buchler et al. [9] formalize the application under test using a secure ASLan++ model, where all traces fulfill the specified security properties. The goal is to apply a fault injection operator to the model, and use a model checker to report any violated security goal. For each violated security goal corresponds an abstract attack trace which is concretized semi-automatically using a pivot language. This approach has been able to find reflected XSS vulnerabilities, but has not been used to discover multi-step XSS. Also, having test engineers provide a formalized representation of a Web application is something we consider highly handicapping.

6   Conclusion and Future Works

This paper introduced an original approach, called Pattern-driven and Model-based Vulnerability Testing (PMVT), for the detection of Web application vulnerabilities. This approach is based on generic test patterns (i.e. independent from the Web application under test) and a behavioral models of the application under test. The behavioral model describes the functional and behavioral aspects of the Web application. The generic test patterns define abstract vulnerability scenarios that drive the test generation process. The proposed approach thus consists of instantiating the abstract scenarios on the behavioral model in order to automatically generate test cases, which target the vulnerability described in the initial test pattern. To experiment and evaluate the PMVT approach, a full automated toolchain, from modeling to test execution, has been developed and experimented, using real-life Web applications, to detect multi-step cross-site scripting vulnerabilities, which are nowadays one of the most critical and widespread Web application attacks.

A thorough experimentation on a real-life e-learning Web application has been conducted to validate the approach, and a comparison with existing automated testing solution, such as vulnerability scanners, has shown its effectiveness to generate more accurate vulnerability test cases and to avoid the generation of false positive and false negative results. These benefits directly stem from the combination of the behavioral model, capturing the logical aspects of the application under test, and the test patterns, driving with precision the test generation process. Moreover, the automation of the test generation and test execution makes it possible to adopt an iterative testing approach and is particularly efficient to manage security regression tests on updated or corrected further versions of the application under test.

Besides these research results, the experiments showed possible improvements of the method and the toolchain. The main drawback of our approach echoes the one of traditional MBT process. Indeed, although we reached a first level of simplification using the dedicated DASTML Domain Specific Modeling Language, the needed effort to design the model is still high. We are working on to integrate another simplification level by using user traces (as proposed in [17]) to infer the model: users would browse a Web Application and record their actions, then an algorithm would translate the results into a DASTML instantiation. This improvement may also automate the adaptation of the generated abstract test cases since the user traces could naturally provide the link between the abstract stimuli/data of the model and the corresponding concrete ones. We are also investigating the extension of the approach in order to address more vulnerability classes, both technical (such as cross-site request forgery, file disclosure and file injection) and logical (such as integrity of data over applications business processes). This extension requires to define generic test patterns ensuring the automated coverage of these vulnerabilities. Finally, another research direction aims at experimenting and extending the current approach to address Web applications on mobile devices.

Acknowledgment. This work is supported by the French FSN project DAST (see the project Website at dast.univ-fcomte.fr [Last visited: July 2014]).

References

1. Athanasopoulos, E., Pappas, V., Krithinakis, A., Ligouras, S., Markatos, E.P., Karagiannis, T.: xJS: practical XSS prevention for web application development. In: Proc. of the USENIX Conference on Web Application Development (WebApps 2010), pp. 147–158. USENIX Association, Boston (2010)
2. Bau, J., Bursztein, E., Gupta, D., Mitchell, J.: State of the Art: Automated Black-Box Web Application Vulnerability Testing. In: Proc. of the 31st Int. Symp. on Security and Privacy (SP 2010), pp. 332–345. IEEE CS, Oakland (2010)
3. Bernard, E., Bouquet, F., Charbonnier, A., Legeard, B., Peureux, F., Utting, M., Torreborre, E.: Model-based Testing from UML Models. In: Proc. of the Int. Workshop on Model-Based Testing (MBT 2006). LNI, vol. 94, pp. 223–230. GI, Dresden (2006)
4. Bisht, P., Venkatakrishnan, V.N.: XSS-GUARD: Precise dynamic prevention of cross-site scripting attacks. In: Zamboni, D. (ed.) DIMVA 2008. LNCS, vol. 5137, pp. 23–43. Springer, Heidelberg (2008)
5. Blome, A., Ochoa, M., Li, K., Peroli, M., Dashti, M.: Vera: A flexible model-based vulnerability testing tool. In: 6th Int. Conference on Software Testing, Verification and Validation (ICST 2013), pp. 471–478. IEEE CS, Luxembourg (2013)
6. Botella, J., Bouquet, F., Capuron, J.-F., Lebeau, F., Legeard, B., Schadle, F.: Model-Based Testing of Cryptographic Components – Lessons Learned from Experience. In: Proc. of the 6th Int. Conference on Software Testing, Verification and Validation (ICST 2013), pp. 192–201. IEEE CS, Luxembourg (2013)
7. Bouquet, F., Grandpierre, C., Legeard, B., Peureux, F.: A test generation solution to automate software testing. In: Proc. of the 3rd Int. Workshop on Automation of Software Test (AST 2008), pp. 45–48. ACM Press, Leipzig (2008)
8. Bouquet, F., Grandpierre, C., Legeard, B., Peureux, F., Vacelet, N., Utting, M.: A subset of precise UML for model-based testing. In: Proc. of the 3rd Int. Workshop on Advances in Model-Based Testing (AMOST 2007), pp. 95–104. ACM Press, London (2007)
9. Buchler, M., Oudinet, J., Pretschner, A.: Semi-Automatic Security Testing of Web Applications from a Secure Model. In: 6th Int. Conference on Software Security and Reliability (SERE 2012), pp. 253–262. IEEE, Gaithersburg (2012)
10. Doupé, A., Cova, M., Vigna, G.: Why Johnny Can't Pentest: An Analysis of Black-Box Web Vulnerability Scanners. In: Kreibich, C., Jahnke, M. (eds.) DIMVA 2010. LNCS, vol. 6201, pp. 111–131. Springer, Heidelberg (2010)
11. Doupé, A., Cavedon, L., Kruegel, C., Vigna, G.: Enemy of the State: A State-aware Black-box Web Vulnerability Scanner. In: Proc. of the 21st USENIX Conference on Security Symposium (Security 2012), pp. 523–537. USENIX Association, Bellevue (2012)
12. Doupé, A., Cui, W., Jakubowski, M.H., Peinado, M., Kruegel, C., Vigna, G.: deDacota: toward preventing server-side XSS via automatic code and data separation. In: Proc. of the 20th ACM SIGSAC Conference on Computer and Cummunications Security (CCS 2013), pp. 1205–1216. ACM, Berlin (2013)
13. Duchene, F., Groz, R., Rawat, S., Richier, J.L.: XSS Vulnerability Detection Using Model Inference Assisted Evolutionary Fuzzing. In: Proc. of the 5th Int. Conference on Software Testing, Verification and Validation (ICST 2012), pp. 815–817. IEEE CS, Montreal (2012)

14. Gálan, E.C., Alcaide, A., Orfila, A., Alís, J.B.: A multi-agent scanner to detect stored-XSS vulnerabilities. In: 5th Int. Conference for Internet Technology and Secured Transactions (ICITST 2010), pp. 1–6. IEEE, London (2010)
15. Kieżun, A., Guo, P.J., Jayaraman, K., Ernst, M.D.: Automatic creation of SQL injection and cross-site scripting attacks. In: 31st Int. Conference on Software Engineering (ICSE 2009), pp. 199–209. IEEE, Vancouver (2009)
16. Kirda, E., Jovanovic, N., Kruegel, C., Vigna, G.: Client-side cross-site scripting protection. Computers & Security 28(7), 592–604 (2009)
17. Korscheck, C.: Automatic Detection of Second-Order Cross Site Scripting Vulnerabilities. Diploma thesis, Wilhelm-Schickard-Institut für Informatik, Universität auf Tübingen (December 2010)
18. Legeard, B., Bouzy, A.: Smartesting CertifyIt: Model-Based Testing for Enterprise IT. In: Proc. of the 6th Int. Conference on Software Testing, Verification and Validation (ICST 2013), pp. 391–397. IEEE CS, Luxembourg (2013)
19. Mahapatra, R.P., Saini, R., Saini, N.: A pattern based approach to secure web applications from XSS attacks. Int. Journal of Computer Technology and Electronics Engineering (IJCTEE) 2(3) (June 2012)
20. MITRE: Common weakness enumeration (October 2013), `http://cwe.mitre.org/` (last visited: February 2014)
21. Nentwich, F., Jovanovic, N., Kirda, E., Kruegel, C., Vigna, G.: Cross-Site Scripting Prevention with Dynamic Data Tainting and Static Analysis. In: Proc. of the Network and Distributed System Security Symposium (NDSS 2007), pp. 1–12. The Internet Society, San Diego (2007)
22. Sabelfeld, A., Myers, A.C.: Language-based information-flow security. Journal on Selected Areas in Communications Archive 21(1), 5–19 (2006)
23. Shar, L.K., Tan, H.B.K.: Automated removal of cross site scripting vulnerabilities in web applications. Information and Software Technology 54(5), 467–478 (2012)
24. Shar, L.K., Tan, H.B.K.: Predicting SQL injection and cross site scripting vulnerabilities through mining input sanitization patterns. Information and Software Technology 55(10), 1767–1780 (2013)
25. Smith, B., Williams, L.: On the Effective Use of Security Test Patterns. In: Proc. of the 6th Int. Conference on Software Security and Reliability (SERE 2012), pp. 108–117. IEEE CS, Washington, DC (2012)
26. Vouffo Feudjio, A.G.: Initial Security Test Pattern Catalog. Public Deliverable D3.WP4.T1, Diamonds Project, Berlin, Germany (June 2012), `http://publica.fraunhofer.de/documents/N-212439.html` (last visited: February 2014)
27. Wassermann, G., Su, Z.: Static detection of cross-site scripting vulnerabilities. In: Proc. of the 30th Int. Conference on Software Engineering (ICSE 2008), pp. 171–180. IEEE, Leipzig (2008)
28. Whitehat: Website security statistics report (October 2013), `https://www.whitehatsec.com/assets/WPstatsReport_052013.pdf` (last visited: February 2014)
29. Wichers, D.: Owasp top 10 (October 2013), `https://www.owasp.org/index.php/Category:OWASP_Top_Ten_Project` (last visited: February 2014)
30. Wurzinger, P., Platzer, C., Ludl, C., Kirda, E., Kruegel, C.: SWAP: mitigating XSS attacks using a reverse proxy. In: 5th Int. Workshop on Software Engineering for Secure Systems (SESS 2009), pp. 33–39. IEEE, Vancouver (2009)

CliSeAu: Securing Distributed Java Programs by Cooperative Dynamic Enforcement

Richard Gay, Jinwei Hu, and Heiko Mantel

Department of Computer Science, TU Darmstadt, Germany
{gay,hu,mantel}@mais.informatik.tu-darmstadt.de

Abstract. CliSeAu is a novel tool for hardening distributed Java programs. CliSeAu takes as input a specification of the desired properties and a Java bytecode target program, i.e. the format in which Java programs are usually provided. CliSeAu returns hardened Java bytecode that provides the same functionality as the original code, unless this code endangers the desired properties. By monitoring the components of a distributed system in a decentralized and coordinated fashion, our tool CliSeAu is able to enforce a wide range of properties, both effectively and efficiently. In this article, we present the architecture of CliSeAu, explain how the components of a distributed target program are instrumented by CliSeAu, and illustrate at an example application how CliSeAu can be used for securing distributed programs.

1 Introduction

Dynamic enforcement mechanisms establish security at run-time by monitoring a program's behavior and by intervening before security violations can occur [1–3]. Dynamic enforcement mechanisms are often tailored to a particular purpose. For instance, authentication mechanisms ensure the authenticity of users, access-control mechanisms ensure that only authorized accesses can be performed, and firewalls ensure that only authorized messages can pass a network boundary. Besides such special-purpose security mechanisms, there are also dynamic enforcement mechanisms that can be tailored to a range of security concerns.

Our novel tool CliSeAu belongs to this second class of dynamic enforcement mechanisms. Given a Java bytecode target program and a policy that specifies a user's security requirements, CliSeAu enforces that the requirements are met.

In this respect, CliSeAu is very similar to two well known tools, SASI [4] and Polymer [5], and there are further similarities. Firstly, all three tools aim at securing Java bytecode.[1] Secondly, like in Polymer, security policies in CliSeAu are specified in Java. Thirdly, like Polymer, CliSeAu bases enforcement decisions on observations of a target program's actions at the granularity of method calls. Fourthly, like in Polymer, the possible countermeasures against policy violations include termination of a target program, suppression or replacement of policy-violating actions, and insertion of additional actions. Finally, all three tools

---

[1] There is a second version of SASI for securing x86 machine code.

A. Prakash and R. Shyamasundar (Eds.): ICISS 2014, LNCS 8880, pp. 378–398, 2014.

enforce policies by modifying the target program's code. Like SASI, CLISEAU performs this modification statically before a program is run.

A distinctive feature of CLISEAU is the support for enforcing security properties in distributed systems in a coordinated and decentralized fashion. CLISEAU generates an *enforcement capsule* (brief: *EC*) for each component of a distributed program. The granularity of encapsulated components is chosen such that each of them runs at a single *agent*, i.e. at a single active entity of a given distributed system. The local *ECs* at individual agents can be used to make enforcement decisions in a decentralized fashion. Decentralizing decision making in this way avoids the bottleneck and single point of failure that a central decision point would be. Moreover, localizing enforcement decisions increases efficiency by avoiding communication overhead. Purely local, decentralized enforcement, however, has the disadvantage that a smaller range of security properties can be enforced than with centralized enforcement decisions [6]. CLISEAU overcomes this disadvantage by supporting communication and coordination between *ECs*. If needed, enforcement decisions can be delegated by one *EC* to another. There are a few other tools that support decentralized, coordinated enforcement, and we will clarify how they differ from CLISEAU when discussing related work.

Another distinctive feature of CLISEAU is the technique used for combining *ECs* with components of a target program. Parts of the *EC* code are interwoven with the target program using the in-lining technique [4], which is used by SASI and Polymer. Other parts of the *EC* code are placed in a process that runs in parallel with the modified target program. This ensures responsiveness of an *EC*, even if its target program is currently blocked due to a pending enforcement decision or has been terminated due to a policy violation.

The enforcement of security properties with CLISEAU is both effective and efficient. In this article, we illustrate the use of CLISEAU at the example of distributed file storage services. As example policy, we use a Chinese wall policy [7]. This is a prominent example of a security policy that cannot be enforced in a purely local, decentralized fashion [6] and, hence, the communication and coordination between *ECs* is essential for enforcing this policy. We also provide results of an experimental evaluation using three different distributed file storage services as target programs. Our evaluation indicates that the performance overhead caused by CLISEAU is moderate. Preliminary reports on further case studies with CLISEAU in the area of social networks, version control systems, and e-mail clients can be found in the student theses [8], [9], and [10], respectively.

In summary the three main novel contributions of this article are the description of the architecture and implementation of CLISEAU (Sections 3 and 5), the explanation of how CLISEAU combines *ECs* with the components of a target program (Section 4), and the report on the case study and experimental evaluation with distributed file storage systems (Sections 6 and 7).

CLISEAU's source code is available under MIT License at http://www.mais.informatik.tu-darmstadt.de/CliSeAu.html.

2   Scope of Applications for CliSeAu

Programs are often developed without having a full understanding yet of the security concerns that might arise when these programs are used. Moreover, even if security aspects have been addressed during program development, a user of the program might not be convinced that this has been done with sufficient rigor. Finally, security requirements might arise from a particular use of a program, while being irrelevant for other uses. In general, it is rather difficult for software engineers to anticipate all security desires that forthcoming users of a program might possibly have. Moreover, being overly conservative during system design regarding security aspects is problematic because security features might be in conflict with other requirements, e.g., regarding functionality or performance and, moreover, can lead to substantial increases of development costs.

Hence, there is a need for solutions that harden programs for given security requirements. This was our motivation for developing CLISEAU as a tool that enables one to force properties onto existing, possibly distributed programs.

CLISEAU can be used by both software developers and software users. In order to apply CLISEAU, one must be able to express security requirements by a Java program (see Section 6 for more details on how this works) and the architecture of the distributed target program must be static.

The class of properties that can be enforced with CLISEAU falls into the class of safety/liveness properties [11,12]. These are properties that can be expressed in terms of individual possible runs of a system, such that a property is either satisfied or violated by an individual program run. Security requirements that can be expressed by properties within this spectrum are, for instance, "A file may only be read by a user who is permitted to read this file." (confidentiality), "Only programs that are authorized to write a given channel may send messages on this channel." (integrity), and "A payment may only be released if different users from two given groups have confirmed the payment." (separation of duty). Security properties that are outside this spectrum are now commonly referred to as hyper-properties [13] and include, for instance, many information flow properties, as already pointed out in [14]. The limitation to properties falling into the safety/liveness spectrum is shared by many other generic tools for dynamic enforcement, including the aforementioned tools SASI and Polymer.

In order to enforce a given property, a dynamic enforcement mechanism needs certain capabilities. Firstly, it must be able to anticipate the next action of the target program. Secondly, it must be able to block this action until it is clear whether this action is permissible. Thirdly, it must be able to unblock the action – if the action is permissible – and to impose suitable countermeasures on the target program – if the next action would lead to a violation of the desired property. As mentioned before, CLISEAU encapsulates each component of a target program by an *EC*. Each of these *EC*s runs at a single agent and can observe, block, and unblock the method calls of the target's component that this *EC* supervises. An *EC* can also impose countermeasures on the supervised component. The implementation technique that CLISEAU uses for combining

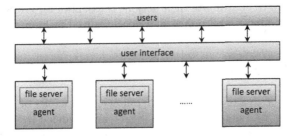

Fig. 1. Architecture of a distributed file service

a target program with the enforcement code ensures that each *EC* has these capabilities (see Section 4 for details on this technique).

Consider, for instance, a file storage service that provides large storage capacities to users. The functionality of a file storage service includes the uploading and downloading of files by users as well as the controlled sharing of files among users. A well known example of such a file storage service is DropBox.[2]

Figure 1 depicts the architecture of a distributed realization of a file storage service. The service is deployed on a collection of distributed machines, each of which hosts a file server program. Users interact with an interface that mitigates their input to the appropriate servers and that communicates the outputs of each file server to the respective users. The mapping of files to servers might be based on criteria like, e.g., geographic proximity in order to ensure low latency. The concrete mapping of files to servers might be hidden from the user.

CLISEAU can be used to secure such a distributed file storage service by encapsulating each file server program with an *EC*. Each *EC* is tailored to a security policy that captures the user's security requirements. An individual *EC* could be tailored, e.g., to a policy requiring that users access files stored at the supervised server only if they are authorized to do so. Moreover, an individual *EC* could also be used to control the sharing of files stored at the given server. However, there are also security requirements that cannot be enforced locally by an individual *EC*. This is the case when the *EC* does not have sufficient information to decide whether an action is permissible or not. For instance, if one wants to limit how much data a user shares within a particular time period then an *EC* needs to know how much data stored at other servers has been shared by this user. Another example are conflicts of interest, where if a user has accessed some file *A* then he must not access some other file *B* afterwards, even if in principle she is authorized to access both files. In order to decide whether file *B* may be accessed, an *EC* needs to know whether the user has already accessed file *A* at some other server. Conflicts of interest must be respected, e.g., within companies that work for other companies who are competitors.

In our case study and experimental evaluation, we show how CLISEAU can be used to prevent conflicts of interests, expressed by a Chinese Wall policy, in a distributed file storage service. The ability of CLISEAU's *EC*s to communicate

---

[2] `https://www.dropbox.com/`

with each other and to coordinate their actions is essentail for CliSeAu's ability
to enforce such a Chinese wall policy in a decentralized fashion.

3   Design of CliSeAu

CliSeAu is designed in a modular fashion, following principles of object-oriented
design [15,16]. The *ECs* generated by CliSeAu are modeled by UML diagrams
that capture different views on CliSeAu. Design patterns employed in the design
of CliSeAu include the factory pattern and the strategy pattern [16]. Objects
are used to capture the actions of a target program as well as an *EC*'s reactions
to such actions.

An *EC*'s reaction to an action is captured by a *decision object*, which corresponds to a particular decision of how to influence the behavior of the target.
For example, decisions could range over a fixed set of decision objects that represent the *permission* or the *suppression* of a program action, the *insertion* of
additional program actions, or the *termination* of the program. Decision objects
can also be more fine-grained and specify further details such as the reason why
a decision is made or how the program should be terminated.

An action of a target program is represented by an *event object*, which corresponds to a particular method call by the target program. The fields of such an
object capture information about the method call, like actual parameters or the
object on which the method is called. How much detail about a method call is
stored in the corresponding object, can be chosen by a user of CliSeAu. This
allows the user to abstract from details of a method call that are not relevant
for her security requirements. For instance, one might represent the program
action of sending a particular file by an event object that captures the name of
the file and the identifier of the receiver in fields, while abstracting from other
information like the name of the protocol by which the file shall be transferred.

In the following, we call an action of the target program (i.e., a method call)
security relevant if its occurrence might result in a security violation. We also
call an action security relevant if whether this actions occurs or doesn't occur
affects whether possible future events are deemed security-relevant or not. When
applying CliSeAu, one can specify the subset of a program's actions that are
security relevant. CliSeAu exploits this information to choose which of a program's actions need to be guarded or tracked.

The abstraction from a target program's security-irrelevant actions and from
security-irrelevant details of security-relevant actions both reduce conceptional
complexity. This simplifies the specification of security policies and improves
performance. Memory is needed only for storing the security-relevant details of
security-relevant actions and only security-relevant actions needed to be supervised by CliSeAu.

In the following, we show different views on CliSeAu's *ECs*, focusing on the
ECs' activities (Section 3.1), the high-level architecture (Section 3.2), and the
parametric low-level architecture (Section 3.3). We conclude this section with
the architecture of CliSeAu itself (Section 3.4).

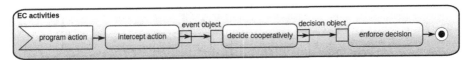

Fig. 2. Activities of an *EC* (UML activity diagram)

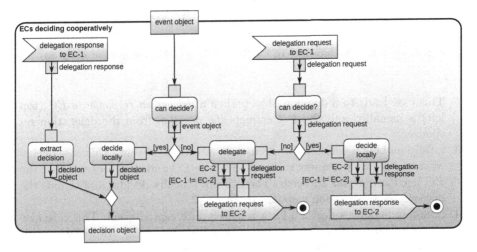

Fig. 3. Cooperative deciding by *ECs* (UML activity diagram)

3.1   Activity View of an *EC*

At runtime, an *EC* performs three main activities (Figure 2): *intercepting* the next security-relevant actions of the program, *deciding* about such actions, and *enforcing* the decisions. Intercepting consists of observing the execution of a target program, blocking security-relevant actions until a decision about them has been made, and capturing the respective next security-relevant action by an event object. Enforcing consists either of enabling the currently blocked action of the target program or, alternatively, of forcing a countermeasure on the target.

The *ECs* generated by CLiSeAu can cooperate with each other when making decisions. We capture the individual activities belonging to cooperative deciding in detail in Figure 3. Essentially, four cases can be distinguished:

1. locally making a decision for a locally intercepted event. This case occurs when an event object (top box) is given to the deciding activity by the intercepting activity of Figure 2 and the check whether the *EC* itself *can decide* succeeds. Then the *EC decides locally* and returns the result as a decision object (bottom box).
2. remotely making a decision for a locally intercepted event. This case also occurs when an event object is given to the deciding activity. However, in this case, the check whether the *EC* can decide fails and the *EC delegates* the decision-making to an *EC-2* by signalling a *delegation request to EC-2*.

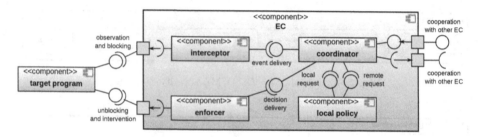

Fig. 4. High-level architecture of CLiSeAu's *ECs* (UML component diagram)

This case leads to a decision object when a *delegation response to EC* (top left) is signalled and the *EC extracts the decision* from the delegation response.

3. locally making a decision for a remotely intercepted event. This case occurs when a delegation request is signalled to the *EC* and the check whether the *EC* itself *can decide* succeeds. Then the *EC* locally decides and signals the decision as a delegation response to an *EC-2*.

4. remotely making a decision for a remotely intercepted event. This case also occurs when a delegation request is signalled to the *EC*. However, in this case, the check whether the *EC* itself can decide fails and the *EC-2* delegates the decision-making to an *EC-2* by signalling a delegation request to *EC-2*.

Note that the cooperative deciding activity ends when the *EC* delegated the decision-making for an event object. That is, the activity does not block until a response is signalled, which enables the *EC* to cooperate with remote *ECs* in the meantime.

3.2   High-Level Architecture of *ECs*

The high-level architecture of the *ECs* generated by CLiSeAu follows the concept of *service automata* [6], according to which a service automaton is an *EC* that features a modular architecture consisting of four particular components: the interceptor, the coordinator, the local policy, and the enforcer. Each of the components is responsible to perform particular activities of the *EC* (see Section 3.1) and uses particular interfaces to interact with the other components of the *EC*. The UML component diagram in Figure 4 visualizes the high-level architecture of CLiSeAu's *EC*.

In CLiSeAu, the *interceptor* is a component that performs the activity of intercepting attempts of the program to perform security-relevant actions. Furthermore, its purpose is to generate event objects. The component requires an interface to the program by which it *observes and blocks* the program's attempts to perform actions. How this interface is established by combining the *EC* with the target program is the focus of Section 4. The component also requires an interface for the *event delivery*.

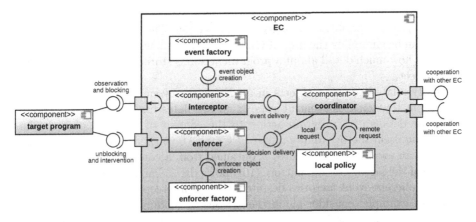

Fig. 5. Low-level architecture of an *EC* (UML component diagram)

The *enforcer* of CLiSeAu is a component that enforces decisions. The component provides an interface for the *delivery of enforcement decisions*. It requires an interface for *unblocking and intervening* the program execution.

The *local policy* of CLiSeAu is a component that performs the activities of (i) checking in which cases it can make a local decision, (ii) making local decisions, (iii) delegating the decision-making for events, and (iv) extracting decision objects from delegation responses. The component provides an interface for processing *local requests* – in the form of events capturing local program actions – as well as *remote requests* – in the form of delegation requests or delegation responses.

The *coordinator* of CLiSeAu is a component that connects the components within one *EC* as well as *ECs* with each other. The component provides an interface for the delivery of events that are to be decided. It requires interfaces for the delivery of enforcement decisions, the delivery of local requests, and the delivery of remote requests. For the *cooperation with other ECs*, an *EC* provides one interface and requires one interface of each other *EC*.

3.3 Parametric Low-Level Architecture of *ECs*

CLiSeAu provides a generic *EC*, that is, an *EC* that is parametric in the security policy that the *EC* enforces. The parametricity of CLiSeAu's *ECs* is manifested in two kinds of entities: data structures (event objects, decision objects, delegation requests, and delegation responses) as well as active components. The refined architecture of *ECs* in Figure 5 pinpoints the parametric activities to three components (solid white boxes in the figure): the event factory (enabling parametric events), the enforcer factory (enabling parametric countermeasures), and the local policy (enabling parametric deciding and delegation). The remaining components (shaded boxes) are fixed by the *EC*.

Parametric events. An event object corresponds to a particular attempt of the target program to perform a security-relevant action. The concrete type of event objects can be chosen by the user of CLISEAU. That allows the user of CLISEAU to choose how much detail about a program action is stored in the corresponding event object.

Closely related to event objects in an *EC* is the event factory component, a component that creates event objects. It encapsulates functionality that transforms the details of a program action to the content of an event object. The parametric event factory allows a user of CLISEAU to specify how the information that an event object captures is obtained from a concrete program action. The use of the factory design pattern [16] allows the *EC* architecture to integrate varying concrete event factories despite the fixed interceptor component.

For an example, consider again the actions of sending a file. To create the event objects for the action of sending a file, the factory could access the actual parameters to the method call of the action and read the needed information from the arguments. Suppose that two sending actions share the same file name and recipient, but differ in the protocol used for the file transfer (e.g., FTP vs. HTTP) and in the access time-stamp. In this case, the factory could transform the two actions to the same event object, which contains only the fields file name and recipient identifier.

Parametric deciding and delegation. A decision object corresponds to a particular decision of how to influence the behavior of the target program. The concrete type of decision objects can be chosen by the user of CLISEAU. That allows the user of CLISEAU to choose how much technical details about concrete countermeasures must be known when making decisions.

When an *EC* cannot make a decision about an event on its own, it delegates the decision-making to another *EC*. In this process, the *EC*s exchange delegation requests and delegation responses. A delegation request is an object that captures enough information for the delegate *EC* to make a decision or to further delegate the request. Analogously, a delegation response is an object that captures a decision for the receiving *EC*. The concrete types of delegation requests and delegation responses can be chosen by the user of CLISEAU. That allows the user of CLISEAU to choose what information is exchanged between the *EC*s. For instance, a delegation request corresponding to an event object could, in addition to the event object to be decided upon, carry partial information about the delegating *EC*'s state.

The local policy is the active component of an *EC* that encapsulates the *EC*'s functionality for deciding and delegating decision-making. The parametric local policy allows a user of CLISEAU to specify for the respective security policy how decisions shall be made and when cooperation between *EC*s shall take place. The use of the strategy design pattern [16] allows the *EC* architecture to integrate varying concrete local policies despite the fixed coordinator component.

Parametric countermeasures. CLISEAU captures countermeasures, i.e., actions that the *EC* performs to prevent security violations, by *enforcer objects* in the

EC. An enforcer object is an object that encapsulates concrete code whose execution results in actions that prevent the security violations. For instance, an enforcer object can encapsulate code for suppressing an action of the program, for terminating the program, for replacing an action of the program by other actions like the display of an error message, or for allowing an action to execute. The concrete set of possible enforcer objects can be chosen by the user of CLISEAU. This allows one to tailor countermeasures to the concrete target.

Closely related to decision objects and enforcer objects inside an *EC* is the enforcer factory component. An enforcer factory is an object that generates enforcer objects. The factory takes a decision object as input and returns enforcers whose execution could achieve the effect intended by the decision. Being a parametric component, the enforcer factory allows a user of CLISEAU to tailor which decisions result in which countermeasures specificly for the application scenario. For example, for a decision object "permit", the factory could return an enforcer that permits the execution of program actions. For the decision "terminate", the factory could return an enforcer that executes "System.exit(1)".

Instantiation of parameters. The parametric components of an *EC* must be *instantiated*, i.e., substituted by concrete instances of the components, before the *EC* can be used for enforcing a concrete security policy on a concrete target. That is, before one can use CLISEAU, one must define a concrete instance for each parametric component of the *EC*.

When using CLISEAU to enforce a security policy in a distributed target program, one must instantiate an *EC* for each of the target's agents. All *ECs* for the target must share at least the same instantiation of the delegation request and delegation response objects, such the *ECs* can cooperate with each other. The remaining parameters of the *ECs* can be instantiated tailored to the respective agents of the target. For instance, decisions may be enforced differently at the individual agents. In this case, the instantiated *ECs* would comprise different enforcer factories and enforcer objects. However, for a distributed target consisting of replications of one and the same agent, all parameter instances may also be shared among the individual *ECs*.

3.4   Architecture of CliSeAu

Figure 6 shows the high-level architecture of CLISEAU. This architecture consists of three main components. The *configuration reader* consumes as input the instantiations of the *EC* parameters. It passes these parameters to the *EC* instantiator. The *EC instantiator* takes CLISEAU's generic *EC* as well as the parameters of the *EC* and instantiates the *EC* based on the parameters. The *EC combiner* takes an instantiated *EC* as well as the code of an agent and combines the two. This combination establishes the interfaces between the program and the interceptor and enforcer that are described in Section 3.2. The technique for combining the code of an agent with an *EC* is described in Section 4.

When using CLISEAU to enforce a security policy on a distributed target, each agent of the distributed target is combined with an *EC*. This *EC* intercepts

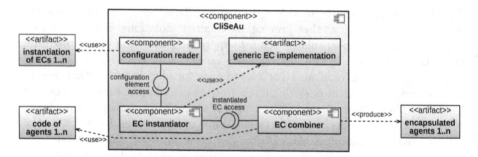

Fig. 6. Architecture of CLiSeAu (UML component diagram)

the security-relevant events of the agent, participates in cooperatively deciding for security-relevant events, and enforces decisions on the agent. To enforce a security policy on a distributed target, CLiSeAu therefore takes instantiations of the *EC* parameters for *each* agent and all agents of the target as input.

The result of applying CLiSeAu to a distributed target with a given instantiation of the *ECs* is a set of encapsulated agents. The *ECs* at the encapsulated agents then together enforce the security policy encoded by the instantiation.

4   Technique for Combining *ECs* with Targets

For combining the components of a distributed target program with *ECs* generated by CLiSeAu, CLiSeAu applies a technique that we describe in the following. The combination of an *EC* with an agent consists of two parts: rewriting the code of the agent as well as creating a separate program that shall, at the runtime of the agent, run in parallel to the agent.

Rewriting the code of the agent serves the purpose of making security-relevant program action's guarded. Being guarded here means that the *EC* makes a check against the policy before the action occurs and runs a countermeasure against the action in case the action would violate the policy. For this rewriting, CLiSeAu takes as input a specification of the security-relevant program actions.

As part of the rewriting, CLiSeAu places code into the agent that corresponds to the *EC* components for intercepting and the acting. That is, the interceptor, the event factory, the event objects, the enforcer, the enforcer factory, the enforcer objects, and the decisions objects are placed into the code of the agent. In the rewritten code of the agent, the code of the interceptor is placed before each security-relevant action and the enforcer is placed "around" the action in the style of a conditional. The remaining components are added to the code of the agent at a place where they can be invoked by the interceptor or enforcer executor.

The separate program that is created by CLiSeAu as part of combining an *EC* with an agent covers the *EC* components for deciding. That is, the separate program contains the coordinator, the local policy, the delegation request/response, and the event and decision objects.[3]

Placing the interceptor and the enforcer executor into the code of the agent as guards of code for security-relevant actions serves the purpose of enabling an efficient enforcement of security policies that are expressed at the level of program actions. Alternatives such as intercepting and enforcing within the operating system may allow the *ECs* to enforce the same security policies but incurs overhead for reconstructing program-level actions from operating system-level actions.

Placing the event factory and the enforcer factory into the code of the agent mainly serves the purpose of efficiency: event objects are supposed to be smaller in size than all agent's data related to a program action (e.g., large data structures on which the action operates); hence, transmitting an event object from the agent to the separate program requires less time. A similar argument applies to the placement of the enforcer factory, because decision objects are smaller in size than the enforcer objects. A beneficial, more technical side-effect of this placement of the factory components is that this placement eliminates or reduces the dependency of the separate program on agent-specific data structures.

Placing the coordinator and the local policy into a separate program serves the purpose of effectiveness and efficiency: the separate program runs in parallel to the agent; hence, it remains responsive even when the agent is blocked due to a pending enforcement decision or has been terminated due to a policy violation. More concretely, even in these cases the separate program can receive delegation requests and make decisions or delegate further with the coordinator and local policy. If a blocked agent would delay the operation of the coordinator and local policy, this would impact the efficiency of the enforcement. Worse, if a terminated agent would prevent the coordinator and local policy from operating, then this could prevent an effective enforcement in cases when cooperation is required to make precise decisions.

5   Implementation

The CLISEAU implementation consists of two parts: an implementation of generic *ECs* following the architecture in Figure 5, called SEAU, and a command-line tool following the architecture in Figure 6, called CLI, for instantiating *ECs* and combining the instantiated *ECs* with target agents. The SEAU implementation consists of Java classes for the fixed components of CLISEAU's *ECs* and Java interfaces and abstract classes for the parametric components. CLI takes as input the instantiation of the SEAU *ECs* in the form of a configuration file and produces instantiated *ECs*. An example configuration is given in Section 6. For modifying the Java bytecode of the agents of a target program according to the technique presented in Section 4, CLI uses AspectJ [17] as a back-end.

---

[3] CLISEAU provides a base implementation of the delegation request/response; one can also supply one's own implementation.

6   Case Study

We have applied CLISEAU to a distributed file storage service. We built the service by ourselves, following the architecture of distributed programs depicted in Figure 1 of Section 2. Our service uses off-the-shelf file servers: DRS [18], AnomicFTPD [19], and Simple-ftpd [20]. Function-wise, our service allows users to upload, download, and share files.

Security-wise, our service only supports user authentication. However, other more specific security requirements may also arise. Consider for instance that the storage service is used in an enterprise setting like in a bank. According to [21], an employee of the bank may not access files from the bank's two client companies that have conflicts of interests. In general, such a requirement is captured by *Chinese Wall policies* [7]: no single user may access files that belong to two companies bearing conflicts of interests.

To enforce a security requirement that is not obeyed in our service, like a Chinese Wall policy, we need to employ some security mechanism. CLISEAU can be used to generate such a mechanism by performing the following steps: (1) define security-relevant actions, event objects, and event factory; (2) define the *ECs*' local policies; (3) define decision objects, enforcer objects, and enforcer factory; (4) assemble the above to a configuration for CLISEAU.

Following these 4 steps, we actually provide an instantiation for CLISEAU. In turn, CLISEAU uses this instantiation to generate *ECs* and combine them with the file servers of our service. In this way, our service is hardened with the enforcement of the Chinese Wall policy. Now we explain in detail how to construct an instantiation for our service with AnomicFTPD as the file servers.

Security-relevant actions, event objects, and event factory. In order to enforce a security requirement on a program, we first identify the program's security-relevant actions. For the Chinese Wall policy that we want to enforce on our service, the actions are method calls whose execution corresponds to users' file accesses. For the AnomicFTPD file server, we find that file download boils down to a call of the method eventDownloadFilePre of an ftpdControl class with a File parameter. Therefore we use the pointcut in Figure 7 (a) (Lines 1-3) to specify that calls of the method eventDownloadFilePre are security-relevant and shall be intercepted.[4] From an intercepted method call, an event object shall be created. Observe that the Chinese Wall policy shall define which company each file belongs to and a COI (conflicts-of-interests) relation on the set of companies. As such, the event object should capture the user who attempts to access a file, the company that the file belongs to, and the involved COI relationships. Figure 7 (a) (Lines 4-5) shows the event object AccessEvent, which has three fields: user, company and COI. In order to construct AccessEvents, we

---

[4] The security-relevant actions depend on the interpretation of "access": users access files by (1) only downloading them or (2) by either downloading or uploading. Figure 7 (a) (Lines 1-3) is defined for case (1). In case (2), we could define a similar specification but with the pointcut extended to match method calls for file uploads.

<table>
<tr><td rowspan="1">(a) actions, events and event factory</td><td>

```
1  pointcut FileAccess(ftpdControl control, File file > boolean):
2     call(boolean eventDownloadFilePre(File))
3        && target(control) && args(file);
4  class AccessEvent implements AbstractEvent {
5     String user, company, COI; }
6  class AccessEventFactory {
7     AccessEvent fromFileAccess(ftpdControl control, File file) {
8        return new AccessEvent(getUser(control),
9           getCompany(file), getCOI(file)); } }
```
</td></tr>
</table>

(a) actions, events and event factory

```
1  pointcut FileAccess(ftpdControl control, File file > boolean):
2     call(boolean eventDownloadFilePre(File))
3        && target(control) && args(file);
4  class AccessEvent implements AbstractEvent {
5     String user, company, COI; }
6  class AccessEventFactory {
7     AccessEvent fromFileAccess(ftpdControl control, File file) {
8        return new AccessEvent(getUser(control),
9           getCompany(file), getCOI(file)); } }
```

(b) local policy

```
class ChineseWallPolicy extends LocalPolicy {
   PolicyResult decideEvent(AccessEvent event) {
      if (locallyResponsibleFor(event)) return getChineseWallDecision(event);
      else return new Delegation(whoIsResponsible(event), event); } }
```

(c) decisions and enforcer factory

```
1  enum BinaryDecision implements AbstractDecision { PERMIT, REJECT }
2  class SuppressionEnforcerFactory implements EnforcerFactory{
3     Enforcer fromDecision(final AbstractDecision d) {
4        BinaryDecision bd = (BinaryDecision) d;
5        switch (bd.decision) {
6           case PERMIT: return new PermittingEnforcer();
7           case REJECT: return new SuppressingEnforcer(); } } }
```

(d) CLiSeAu configuration

```
1  cfg.agents            = srv1, srv2, srv3, ...
2  srv1.code             = AnomicFTPD.jar
3  srv1.address          = srv1.example.com
4  srv1.localPolicy      = ChineseWallPolicy
5  srv1.pointcuts        = FileAccess.pc
6  srv1.eventFactory     = AccessEventFactory
7  srv1.enforcerFactory  = SuppressionEnforcerFactory
8  # parameters for srv2, ...  are defiend similarly  and are omitted here
```

Fig. 7. An instantiation of CLiSeAu

use the AccessEventFactory in Figure 7 (a) (Lines 6-9). In this event factory, the fromFileAccess method uses the actual parameters of the intercepted method call and extracts the needed information to create an object of AccessEvent.

Local policy. Next we define the local policy component of an *EC*. The local policy shall make decisions about security-relevant actions and about delegation of decision-making. For our service, we construct the local policy component named ChineseWallPolicy in Figure 7 (b). ChineseWallPolicy checks whether it should decide upon an input event by the method locallyResponsibleFor. If it is the case, then a decision is computed by the method getChineseWallDecision. Otherwise ChineseWallPolicy delegates the decision-making for the event to a remote *EC* by the method whoIsResponsible. We implement the methods locallyResponsibleFor and whoIsResponsible with the guarantee that accesses to conflicting files are always decided by the same *EC* (i.e., its local policy component). The implementation of getChineseWallDecision checks whether or not a user trying to access a file has already accessed a conflicting file before. A method for deciding delegation requests is defined analogously to decideEvent and thus omitted here.

Decision objects, enforcer objects, and enforcer factory. We choose a decision for enforcing the Chinese Wall policy to be either permitting an access or rejecting the access; the BinaryDecision object in Figure 7 (c) (Line 1) captures this choice of decision. Corresponding to the two decision values are two enforcers: PermittingEnforcer and SuppressingEnforcer, which allows an intercepted method call to execute and suppresses the call, respectively. These two enforcers are provided by CLISEAU. The SuppressionEnforcerFactory of Figure 7 (c) (Lines 2-7) turns a reject decision into a SuppressingEnforcer object and a permit decision into a PermittingEnforcer object.

Configurations. Finally, we provide the configuration in Figure 7 (d) for CLISEAU. The configuration declares which agents exit (Line 1), which programs the agents run (Line 2), and the agents' addresses (Line 3). The configuration also assembles references to the previously described parts of the instantiation (Lines 4-7).

Figure 7 constitutes an instantiation of CLISEAU, which hardens our file storage service with a system-wide enforcement of Chinese Wall policy. CLISEAU allows us to address individually the aspects of an instantiation: how to intercept security-relevant actions, how to decide and possibly delegate, and how to enforce decisions. When using CLISEAU, we can focus on these aspects and, for instance, we need not be concerned about exchanging messages between distributed *ECs* or instrumenting the executables of the program. In particular, the deciding can be defined at a more abstract level (here based on AccessEvents) than the level of program actions (here involving the program-specific data type ftpdControl).

7   Performance Evaluation

Securing a program with CLISEAU necessarily results in some reduction on the program's runtime performance. Our evelution focuses on the run-time overhead of the enforcement.

Experimental setup. We evaluated CLISEAU with the distributed file storage service introduced in Section 6. The service has 3 variants, depending on which file servers are used. In our experiments, the service consisted of 10 file servers, all of which are either DRS [18], AnomicFTPD [19], or Simple-ftpd [20]. We refer to them as *DRS service*, *AnomicFTPD service*, and *Simple-ftpd service*, respectively. We used CLISEAU to enforce the Chinese Wall policy (i.e., no single user may access files bearing conflicts of interest), as described in Section 6.

We conducted all experiments on a 2.5 GHz dual CPU laptop running Gentoo Linux with Kernel 3.6.11, OpenJDK 6, and AspectJ 1.6.12. All servers of each service were run on the same machine. We chose this setup because in our experiments, we are interested in the overhead introduced by the implementation of

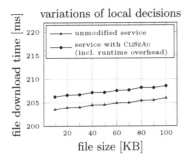
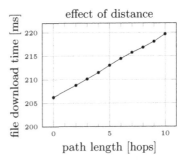

Fig. 8. AnomicFTPD runtime evaluation

CLISEAU. By using local network connections, we factor out the overhead introduced by a real network, as this overhead originates from CLISEAU-independent aspects such as network topology and network load distribution. We leave experiments in real network settings as future work.

Run-time overhead. We evaluated the impact of CLISEAU on the services' runtime performance of file downloads from the perspective of a service user: we measured the duration from the moment the user made a file download request till the moment the user obtained the file. For DRS, we used a modified DRS client to access files and measured inside the client the durations of the accesses; the modification was done to measure the time. For AnomicFTPD and Simpleftpd, we accessed files and measured durations with a self-written FTP client implemented based on the Apache Commons Net library. In both clients, time was taken using the System.nanoTime API method of Java.

For each service, we varied both the size of the requested files and the number of hops taken in the cooperation between the *ECs* for making enforcement decisions. Figures 8–10 show the results, which are averaged over the measurements of 2500 independent experiments.

The diagram on the left-hand side of Figure 8 shows the absolute time required for downloading files of different size from the AnomicFTPD service. With the unmodified service, downloads took from about 203.5 ms to 206 ms, depending on the file size. As Figure 8 (lhs) shows, the time is roughly linear in the file size. On the other hand, the service secured with CLISEAU used time ranging from about 206 ms to 208.5 ms. Still, download time remains linear in the file size (see Figure 8, lhs). As Figure 9 (lhs) shows, the absolute runtime overhead caused by CLISEAU ranged from about 2.5 ms to 2.75 ms. This corresponds to a relative overhead of about 1.3%. We consider this performance overhead reasonable for the security enforcement it is traded for.

We conducted the same experiments on the DRS service and the Simple-ftpd service as on the AnomicFTPD service. Figure 9 shows the results. The absolute overhead is less than 3 ms. For Simple-ftpd and AnomicFTPD, the overhead is roughly constant regardless of the changes in file size. For DRS, the overhead

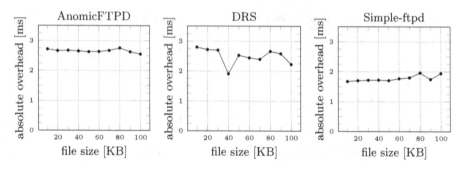

Fig. 9. Absolute runtime overhead for different file sizes

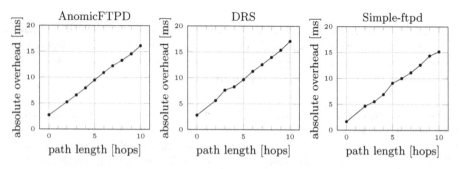

Fig. 10. Absolute runtime overhead for different path lengths (effect of distance)

was relatively more unstable; the reason for this remains unclear to us. Still, the variation stays in a limited range from 1.9 ms to 2.8 ms.

Figure 8 (rhs) shows the absolute time required for downloading files of 10 kilobytes from the AnomicFTPD service when varying the number of hops taken in the cooperation between the *ECs*. We obtained up to 10 hops by letting the local policy implementations to not directly delegate to the responsible *EC* but delegate to a number of other *ECs* before. This setting reflects the cases where responsible *ECs* are not directly reachable from a delegating *EC* or where more than one *EC* share the information for deciding about an event. In our experiments, the download time ranged from about 206 ms to 220 ms, corresponding to overhead between about 2.7 ms and 16.1 ms (see Figure 10, lhs). The overhead grows almost linearly with the number of hops at approximately 1.34 ms per hop. Our experiments with DRS and Simple-ftpd show very similar results; see the diagrams in the middle of and on the right hand side of Figure 10, respectively.

Summary. The *ECs* gengerated by CLISEAU caused moderate runtime overhead for our file storage service: For file download, the overhead was about 3 ms when the *ECs* could make decisions locally. When coopeerative decision-making was needed, the overhead increased linearly with the number of the hops between the *ECs* involved in the cooperation. This linearity is encouraging for deploying CLISEAU-generated *ECs* in a real-world setting like the Internet where a distributed program may have a larger number of agents and thus of hops for cooperation among *ECs*.

8 Related Work

As described in the introduction, CLISEAU follows the line of SASI [4] and Polymer [5]. SASI is a tool for generating *ECs* for Java bytecode programs as well as for x86 executables. The *ECs* generated by SASI either permit the occurrence of a security-relevant action or terminate the target otherwise. CLISEAU also allows one to specify enforcers that use termination as a countermeasure. However, CLISEAU additionally allows one to specify countermeasures corresponding to the suppression, insertion or replacement of security-relevant actions.

Polymer is a tool for generating *ECs* for Java bytecode programs. The policies that a user provides to Polymer can define so-called abstract actions, Java classes whose instances can match a set of program instructions. Furthermore, Polymer allows a policy to be composed from several subordinate policies; in such a composition, the superior policy queries its subordinate policies for their policy suggestions and combines these to obtain its own suggestion. Only when a suggestion is accepted, its corresponding countermeasure is executed. For the countermeasures, Polymer supports the insertion and replacement of actions, throwing a security exception, as well as to termination of the target. Considering a non-distributed setting, Polymer and CLISEAU support the same observable program operations (method calls), the same expressiveness in the decision-making (Java code), and the same kind of countermeasures. Therefore, the class of properties enforceable with CLISEAU is the same as for Polymer. Conceptually, Polymer's abstract actions are very similar to the combination of CLISEAU's event objects and event factories. Polymer's suggestions, in turn bear a similarity to CLISEAU's decision objects. However, in Polymer the layer between suggestions and their corresponding countermeasures serves the purpose of policy composition while CLISEAU's layer between decision objects and countermeasures (as enforcer objects) reduces the dependency between the local policy and technical details of the target program.

Further tools for generating *ECs* for Java bytecode programs include, for example, JavaMOP [22]. A particular characteristic of JavaMOP is the generation of efficient *ECs* for properties on parametric program actions. The focus of Java-MOP's efficiency efforts is enforcing properties on individual Java objects of the target program, which are realized by binding the objects of the target program to individual monitors for the decision-making. In contrast, with CLISEAU, we sacrifice this kind of optimization for the sake of an abstraction layer that maps program entities to entities at the policy-level. The latter shall then be usable by a distributed *EC* in the decision-making for system-wide security requirements.

Tools that are specifically tailored to distributed systems include, for example, Moses [23], DiAna [24], and Porscha [25]. Moses is a tool for dynamic enforcement for distributed Java programs. Technically, Moses is implemented as a middleware that is to be used by the agents of target programs for the coordination among themselves. Moses aims at enforcing properties, called laws, on the co-ordination between agents. The policies of Moses enforce such properties at the level of agent communication by delivering, blocking, or modifying exchanged messages. CLISEAU differs from Moses in two main directions. First, CLISEAU can intercept and intervene not only communication operations of agents but also computation operations of a single agent, like the file accesses in our example of a distributed file storage service. Second, CLISEAU can be applied to arbitrary Java programs and does not rely on the program to be built upon a particular middleware. This allows CLISEAU to enforce security requirements also on programs that have not been designed with an enforcement by CLISEAU in mind, such as the targets of our experimental evaluation (Section 7).

DiAna is a tool for monitoring temporal properties on the state of distributed Java programs. These programs are assumed to be built on a monitoring library. In this sense, DiAna is similar to Moses. DiAna's *ECs* intercept the communication operations between the agents of the target and exchange information among each other by piggy-backing the information on the messages exchanged between the agents. That is, DiAna's *ECs* perform coordinated decentralized monitoring. CLISEAU differs from DiAna in two main directions: first, CLISEAU does not rely on the target to be built upon a particular library and, second, a *EC* generated by CLISEAU is able to intercept and coordinate its enforcement for program actions beyond agent communication.

Porscha [25] is an *EC* for enforcing digital rights management policies on Android smart phones. Porscha *ECs* are placed in the runtime environment of the target. Also, the *ECs* exchange information about the policy that affects the data exchanged by the agents of the target. Porscha and CLISEAU have in common that they support coordinated decentralized enforcement. However, a key difference is that the *ECs* generated by CLISEAU can coordinate their enforcement by themselves, without relying on the intercepted communication actions of agents. That is, the *ECs* communicate and cooperate in a proactive way, regardless of whether and when the agents of a distributed program communicate with each other. This allows the *ECs* to enforce security in the scenario of Section 6, in which cooperation is required also for file access events that do not correspond to data exchange between agents of the storage service.

9   Conclusion

We presented the tool CLISEAU for securing distributed Java programs. CLISEAU uses cooperative dynamic mechanisms to enforce system-wide security requirements and allows to instantiate the mechanism for different programs and security requirements. We showed a case study of CLISEAU on a distributed file storage service and performed experimental evaluation on the example service. The experimental results demonstrate that the enforcement mechanisms provided by CLISEAU incur moderate runtime overhead.

Acknowledgments. We thank Sarah Ereth, Steffen Lortz, and Artem Starostin for their feedback on our research. We are also grateful to Cédric Fournet and

Joshua Guttman for inspiring discussions at early stages of our research project. This work was partially funded by CASED (www.cased.de) and by the DFG (German research foundation) under the project FM-SecEng in the Computer Science Action Program (MA 3326/1-3).

References

[1] Schneider, F.B.: Enforceable Security Policies. Transactions on Information and System Security 3(1), 30–50 (2000)

[2] Fong, P.W.L.: Access Control By Tracking Shallow Execution History. In: IEEE Symposium on Security and Privacy, pp. 43–55. IEEE Computer Society (2004)

[3] Ligatti, J., Bauer, L., Walker, D.: Edit Automata: Enforcement Mechanisms for Run-time Security Policies. IJIS 4(1-2), 2–16 (2005)

[4] Erlingsson, U., Schneider, F.B.: SASI Enforcement of Security Policies: A Retrospective. In: Proceedings of the 2nd NSPW, pp. 87–95. ACM (2000)

[5] Bauer, L., Ligatti, J., Walker, D.: Composing Expressive Runtime Security Policies. Transactions on Software Engineering and Methodology 18(3) (2009)

[6] Gay, R., Mantel, H., Sprick, B.: Service automata. In: Barthe, G., Datta, A., Etalle, S. (eds.) FAST 2011. LNCS, vol. 7140, pp. 148–163. Springer, Heidelberg (2012)

[7] Brewer, D.F., Nash, M.J.: The Chinese Wall Security Policy. In: Proceedings of the IEEE Symposium on Security and Privacy, pp. 206–214 (1989)

[8] Mazaheri, S.: Race conditions in distributed enforcement at the example of online social networks. Bachelor thesis, TU Darmstadt (2012)

[9] Scheurer, D.: Enforcing Datalog Policies with Service Automata on Distributed Version Control Systems. Bachelor thesis, TU Darmstadt (2013)

[10] Wendel, F.: An evaluation of delegation strategies for coordinated enforcement. Bachelor thesis, TU Darmstadt (2012)

[11] Lamport, L.: Proving the Correctness of Multiprocess Programs. IEEE Transactions on Software Engineering 3(2), 125–143 (1977)

[12] Alpern, B., Schneider, F.B.: Defining Liveness. Information Processing Letters 21, 181–185 (1985)

[13] Clarkson, M.R., Schneider, F.B.: Hyperproperties. Journal of Computer Security 18(6), 1157–1210 (2010)

[14] McLean, J.D.: Security Models. In: Marciniak, J. (ed.) Encyclopedia of Software Engineering. John Wiley & Sons, Inc. (1994)

[15] Booch, G., Maksimchuk, R.A., Engle, M.W., Young, B.J., Connallen, J., Houston, K.A.: Object-oriented Analysis and Design with Applications, 3rd edn. (2007)

[16] Gamma, E., Helm, R., Johnson, R., Vlissides, J.: Design Patterns: Elements of Reusable Object-Oriented Software. Addison-Wesley Longman Publishing Co., Inc., Boston (1995)

[17] Kiczales, G., Hilsdale, E., Hugunin, J., Kersten, M., Palm, J., Griswold, W.G.: An Overview of AspectJ. In: Lindskov Knudsen, J. (ed.) ECOOP 2001. LNCS, vol. 2072, pp. 327–353. Springer, Heidelberg (2001)

[18] DRS (1999), http://www.octagonsoftware.com/home/mark/DRS/

[19] AnomicFTPD v0.94 (2009), http://anomic.de/AnomicFTPServer/

[20] simple-ftpd (2010), https://github.com/rath/simple-ftpd

[21] PUBLIC LAW 107 - 204 - SARBANES-OXLEY ACT OF 2002

[22] Chen, F., Roşu, G.: MOP: An Efficient and Generic Runtime Verification Frame-work. In: Proceedings of the 22nd OOPSLA, pp. 569–588. ACM (2007)

[23] Minsky, N.H., Ungureanu, V.: Law-governed Interaction: a Coordination and Control Mechanism for Heterogeneous Distributed Systems. ACM Transactions on Software Engineering Methodology 9(3), 273–305 (2000)

[24] Sen, K., Vardhan, A., Agha, G., Roşu, G.: Efficient Decentralized Monitoring of Safety in Distributed Systems. In: Proceedings of the 26th ICSE, pp. 418–427 (2004)

[25] Ongtang, M., Butler, K.R., McDaniel, P.D.: Porscha: Policy Oriented Secure Content Handling in Android. In: ACSAC, pp. 221–230 (2010)

Automatic Generation of Compact Alphanumeric Shellcodes for x86

Aditya Basu, Anish Mathuria, and Nagendra Chowdary

DA-IICT, Gandhinagar, India
{basu_aditya,anish_mathuria,posani_nagendra}@daiict.ac.in

Abstract. Shellcode can be viewed as machine language code that is injected in the form of string input to exploit buffer overflows. It usually contains non-ASCII values because not all machine instructions encode into ASCII values. Many applications allow arbitrary string input, even though only strings containing characters that are ASCII or a subset of ASCII are deemed valid. Thus a common defense against shellcode injection is to discard any string input containing non-ASCII characters. Alphanumeric shellcode helps attackers bypass such character restrictions. It is non-trivial to construct alphanumeric shellcodes by hand and so tools have been created to automate the process. The alphanumeric equivalent, generated by the existing tools, is much larger than the original shellcode. This paper presents two new encoding schemes to reduce the size of the alphanumeric equivalent. A smaller shellcode is better as it can fit into smaller buffers and is even more useful in case an application restricts the input size. Results show that the size reduction of the encoded shellcode is more than 20% for many shellcodes.

1 Introduction

A common and important class of attack on computer systems is the *code injection attack*. This attack has two phases: a) injection of code (a.k.a. the *shellcode*), and b) execution of the injected code. Typically, code is injected in *placeholders* for data. So, while the target program expects *data*, the attacker instead sends *code* (disguised as data). The attacker then redirects the program execution to the injected code. To do this, the attacker can exploit program vulnerabilities such as buffer overflows [1].

The ASCII ranges $0x30 - 0x39$ (0-9), $0x41 - 0x5a$ (A-Z) and $0x61 - 0x7a$ (a-z) form the alphanumeric character set. Shellcodes typically consist of bytes that are not alphanumeric. To counter shellcode injection, we can inspect each byte of the incoming data and discard any byte that is not an alphanumeric character. Such filtering does not provide adequate protection, as it is feasible to construct shellcodes that consist of only alphanumeric bytes. However, constructing alphanumeric shellcodes by hand is a non-trivial and tedious task. Rix [2] developed a tool to automate the conversion of non-alphanumeric shellcode into alphanumeric shellcode for the x86 architecture. His tool encodes the

A. Prakash and R. Shyamasundar (Eds.): ICISS 2014, LNCS 8880, pp. 399–410, 2014.

non-alphanumeric bytes into alphanumeric bytes and further embeds instructions within the output shellcode, whose purpose is to decode (or recover) the original bytes at runtime. Rix uses the XOR instruction (which is alphanumeric for many combinations of operands on x86) to recover the non-alphanumeric bytes of the shellcode. The XOR instructions use specific hardcoded constants for each non-alphanumeric byte that is encoded. The most important drawback of Rix's approach is that every non-alphanumeric byte of the original shellcode requires separate instructions to be embedded in the modified shellcode. This increases the size of the modified shellcode, which typically is over 4 times the size of the original shellcode (see Table-2, section 4.2).

Jan Wever [3] introduced the looped decoding approach as an alternative to the sequential decoding used by Rix. The encoding scheme used by Wever modifies both alphanumeric and non-alphanumeric bytes of the shellcode. The decoding logic is implemented in the form of a loop, whose size is independent of the size of the encoded shellcode. Using a fixed size decoder helps to reduce the size of the modified shellcode, which is important due to the constraints placed on the shellcode.

The exploit shellcodes typically spawn a shell, copy a file (like *passwd*), expose a port, and so on. Such shellcodes have alphanumeric characters like filenames (e.g. "/bin/sh" or "/etc/passwd") and ports (e.g. 8080) in them, to name a few. Over and above, there are some instructions that are partly or completely alphanumeric. So, if we only patch the non-alphanumeric bytes in the shellcode, then it results in a more compact alphanumeric shellcode encoding. Using a *looped decoder*, as opposed to a sequential decoder, also helps to reduce the size of the final alphanumeric shellcode. In this paper we propose two new encoding schemes: Non-Alpha Touch and Alpha Freedom. The main idea behind the proposed schemes is to patch only the non-alphanumeric bytes (Rix's idea), but using a looped decoder (Jan Wever's idea). The performance of our schemes depends on the number of non-alphanumeric bytes present in the original shellcode. We demonstrate that our schemes yield more compact encodings than *Jan Wever's Encoder*, for many shellcodes (see Table 1, section 4.2).

In the Non-Alpha Touch scheme, a fixed alphanumeric byte (called the *alpha mark*) is inserted before every non-alphanumeric byte in the original shellcode. Each non-alphanumeric byte is replaced with *two* corresponding alphanumeric bytes, which represent the encoded form of the non-alphanumeric byte. At runtime, the decoding loop uses the *alpha mark* to determine the portions of the shellcode which need to be decoded. This scheme uses *three* bytes to encode each non-alphanumeric byte in the original shellcode.

In the Alpha Freedom scheme, we add a tweak to the encoding scheme, which allows the decoding loop to determine the need for decoding without the *alpha mark*. This helps further reduce the number of encoding bytes to *two* for every non-alphanumeric byte in the original shellcode. This is done by constricting the range of allowed alphanumeric values that can be used in the encoded shellcode.

The rest of the paper is organized as follows. Section 2 gives an overview of the previous related work. Section 3 describes the new schemes in detail. Section 4 presents the implementation related aspects of the new schemes and compares their performance with the existing schemes. Section 5 concludes the paper and discusses some future work.

2   Related Work

2.1   Rix — XOR Patching

The Phrack article by Rix [2] is one of the first works on automatic translation of arbitrary shellcode into an alphanumeric shellcode with similar functionality. The main idea behind his tool was categorizing each byte of the shellcode into one of the four categories (explained below) and the fact that the XOR opcode with many operand combinations forms instructions consisting only of alphanumeric bytes (*for* x86). Also, some essential operations like negation can be simulated by: XORing with -1. As -1 is non-alphanumeric, it is obtained by decrementing 0 by 1.

The alphanumeric shellcode generated by the Rix tool can be divided into *three* sections. The first section is the *Initializer*, the second is the *XOR Patcher*, and the third is the *Encoded Shellcode*. The *Initializer* (first section) initializes registers with constants and the memory address of the start of the shellcode. The *XOR Patcher* (second section) performs the actual decoding of the *Encoded Shellcode*. This section consists of XOR instructions to decode the encoded non-alphanumeric values in the *Encoded Shellcode* section. The patching instructions vary based on the category of the byte and the actual byte value to be patched (decoded). For this reason, the *XOR Patcher* is *sequential* in nature and its size partly depends on the number of non-alphanumeric bytes in the original shellcode. Due to size optimizations done by Rix, the actual size of the *XOR Patcher* also depends on the *distribution* of non-alphanumeric bytes across the original shellcode. Once the XOR Patcher section finishes execution, the *Encoded Shellcode* section (third section) is completely *decoded* and the original shellcode is recovered.

Rix's tool works as follows. For each byte B of the input shellcode, it performs exactly one of the four actions listed below.

1. The byte B is alphanumeric. Skip the byte.
2. The byte B is not alphanumeric, but is *less than* 0x80. Then, find a and b, such that $a \oplus b = B$, where a and b are any suitable alphanumeric bytes[1]. Then one of a or b is embedded in the encoded shellcode and the other byte is used in the XOR instruction that recovers the original byte at runtime.
3. The byte B is not alphanumeric, but is *greater than* 0x80, and $(\sim B)$ is alphanumeric. Then embed $(\sim B)$ into the encoded shellcode and add instructions to the XOR patcher to recover the original byte at runtime.

---

[1] Here it is implicitly assumed that the required bytes a and b exist. This can be proved but we omit the proof.

4. The byte B is not alphanumeric, but is *greater than* 0x80, and ($\sim B$) is not alphanumeric. Then, ($\sim B$) is *less than* 0x80. So we do the operation as listed in (2).

Rix encodes the non-alphanumeric shellcode by replacing all *non-alphanumeric bytes* with some chosen *alphanumeric bytes*. The *decoder* recovers the original shellcode by XORing the replaced bytes with some chosen alphanumeric bytes. The latter are hardcoded in the *decoder* itself and so the size of the decoder increases as the number of non-alphanumeric bytes (in the original shellcode) increase. It takes 7 bytes of *decoder* instructions for recovering *each isolated* non-alphanumeric byte of the original shellcode. If a series of non-alphanumeric bytes occur together, then Rix does some size optimizations to reduce the number of the decoder instructions.

2.2   Jan Wever — Looped Decoding

In 2004, Jan Wever released his alpha series of alphanumeric shellcode decoders [3]. To minimize the size of the *decoder*, he came up with the idea of *Looped Decoding*. He encoded the bytes of the original shellcode by replacing *every* byte (including alphanumeric and non-alphanumeric bytes) of the original shellcode with *two* bytes of alphanumeric encoded data. To get back the original byte, he used a left-shift operation, followed by, an ex-or (xor) operation. He created an alphanumeric decoding loop, which when repeatedly run on the encoded shellcode, would decode the corresponding bytes of the encoded shellcode. A significant advantage of *looped decoding* is that the size of decoder is fixed: it is *not* dependent on the size of input shellcode. This property helps to substantially reduces the *total size* of the resultant alphanumeric shellcode. It also helps in predicting the size of the output (runtime decoder + encoded shellcode). One other important benefit of the looped decoder approach is that, unlike Rix, both the *decoder* and the *encoded shellcode* can be independently generated. The decoder can be compiled separately, without any knowledge of the type of shellcode that it needs to decode. The exact encoding and decoding procedures of Jan Wever's scheme are explained in more detail below.

Encoding. To encode a byte, say $0xAB$, from original shellcode, we choose two bytes $0xCD$ and $0xEF$; where $F = B$, E is chosen such that $0xEF$ is alphanumeric, $D = A \oplus E$, and C is again chosen such that $0xCD$ is alphanumeric.

Decoding. To decode the original byte, we first fetch the corresponding bytes $0xCD$ and $0xEF$. We then compute $(CD << 4) \oplus EF$; the least significant byte of the computed value yields the desired byte, $0xAB$.

3   Two New Encoding Schemes

3.1   Non-Alpha Touch (NAT)

In this scheme, we put an *alpha mark* (i.e. alpha byte) before every non-alphanumeric byte of the shellcode. This *alpha mark*, which is chosen to be 'y' in the implementation of this scheme, tells the *runtime looped decoder* to decode the next *two* bytes and recover back the original byte of the shellcode. Another *alpha mark*, chosen to be '*z*', is used to mark the end of the encoded shellcode. After '*z*' is encountered, the loop breaks and control is transferred to the start of the decoded shellcode. The end mark '*z*' can be omitted if the encoded shellcode is NULL terminated. Wever's decoder terminates when it encounters a null character in the encoded shellcode.

We chose the bytes 'y' and 'z' as the alpha marks to simplify the decoder logic. There are no alphanumeric characters after 'z'. So a single compare operation followed by conditional jumps can be used to detect the necessity of decoding.

All the alphanumeric bytes, except 'y' and 'z', are kept intact in the encoded version of the shellcode. The bytes 'y' and 'z', along with all the non-alphanumeric bytes are encoded into 3 bytes: (*i*) Start marker i.e. 'y', (*ii* and *iii*) Encoded bytes using Jan Wever's encoder. During encoding, the most significant nibbles (of CD and EF) are chosen to ensure that the bytes CD and EF are alphanumeric. When choosing C and E, we make sure that the ASCII values of CD and EF are not equal to the values of characters 'y' and 'z'. This ensures that the *decoding loop* will be able to successfully recover the encoded shellcode. Examples of some bytes encoded using NAT are shown in Figure 1.

For the final output to be completely alphanumeric, the *decoding loop* needs to be alphanumeric, along with the encoded shellcode. As the control transfer instructions such as jump and call are not alphanumeric, the decoding loop is not completely alphanumeric. To make the decoder loop alphanumeric, it is first patched using Rix's technique (XOR patching), and then followed by the encoded shellcode. So, the decoding process now becomes a 2-stage process, in which Rix's XOR Patcher, patches our *looped decoder*, which in turn recovers the encoded shellcode.

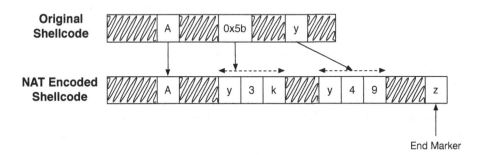

Fig. 1. NAT Encoding Illustrated

Analysis. This scheme introduces *three* alphanumeric bytes in place of a single non-alphanumeric byte of the shellcode. If the size of the original shellcode is n bytes, then the encoded shellcode size using Jan Wever's encoder is $2n$. The size in bytes of the shellcode encoded using Non-Alpha Touch scheme is between

$n + 1$ and $3n + 1$. The plus 1, comes due to additional end *alpha marker*. This alpha marker can be omitted if the encoded shellcode is guaranteed to be NULL terminated, which is required by Jan Wever's implementation. In the worst case, if all bytes need to be patched, then the size of the encoded shellcode will be $3n + 1$ bytes; if none needs to be patched, then the size will be $n + 1$ bytes.

3.2 Alpha Freedom (AF)

With NAT, the size of the encoded shellcode can go up to $3n + 1$ bytes, whereas with Wever's encoding it is exactly $2n$ bytes. To improve the encoding performance of our approach, we need to be able to perform decoding without an explicit *alpha marker*, which could save *one byte* per encoded byte. To this end, we will partition the alphanumeric range into *two* parts. The partitioning process is explained below.

Note that in Jan Wever's encoding scheme, we select the most significant nibble – MSN (of CD and EF), such that both CD and EF are alphanumeric. The corresponding MSN's are C and E, respectively. Let's focus on the byte CD. The possible values of both C and D, individually, are in $\{0, 1\}^4$ (in binary). Now, D is fixed and given to us by calculations, but we are free to choose C, to make CD alphanumeric. As the nibble D can have a possible of 16 values ($\{0, 1\}^4$), we choose a subset of the alphanumeric ASCII characters whose least significant nibbles cover the entire range of all possible 16 values. Let's say we choose the character range as 'K-Z' ($0x4b - 0x5a$). Then, we can always choose the MSN of CD, such that CD lies in the range 'K-Z', effectively partitioning all alphanumeric characters into 'K-Z' and non-'K-Z' space. As before, we set aside 'z' to mark the end of encoded shellcode. The end marker is again optional, as in NAT, if we know that the encoded shellcode is NULL terminated.

We choose a continuous ASCII range of alphanumeric characters to make the *decoding logic* simpler. Effectively, the runtime decoder only needs to check if the current byte lies in the 'K-Z' range or not (along with if it's 'z' or not). If the current byte lies in the 'K-Z' range, then the current byte and the next byte are used to recover the corresponding byte of the original shellcode.

During encoding, if we encounter a byte in the 'K-Z' range or if the byte is 'z', then we need to encode that byte also, even though it is alphanumeric. This is the price that we pay to get rid of the explicit *alpha marker*. Although other ranges are possible, the 'K-Z' range is selected for a specific reason. Many shellcodes have alphanumeric characters in the form of filenames (e.g. "/bin/sh" or "/etc/passwd"), ports (e.g. 8080), etc. The capital letters are not commonly found in such ASCII strings. So by selecting our implicit marker range as 'K-Z', we get a more compactly encoded shellcode as compared to both the Wever's encoding scheme and the NAT scheme.

Examples of some bytes encoded using AF are shown in Figure 2. As in NAT, the decoding loop is not completely alphanumeric. So the decoding loop is first patched using Rix's technique and then followed by the encoded shellcode.

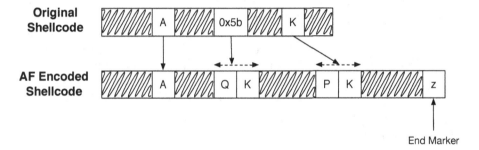

Fig. 2. AF Encoding Illustrated

Analysis. The Alpha Freedom scheme is superior to NAT, in terms of the size of the encoded shellcode. But, it also results in a more complicated decoding logic. For larger shellcodes, this is less of an issue as the encoding performance of AF is much better than NAT. The encoded shellcode size is between $n + 1$ and $2n + 1$, for an unencoded shellcode which is n bytes long.

4   The Implementation

The alphanumeric shellcode generated by our tool consists of three stages. The first is the Rix stage, the second is the scheme specific - *decoder loop* stage, and the third stage is the actual shellcode. The last stage (chronologically the *third* one), contains the actual shellcode which needs to be executed, but in *encoded* form. In essence, *transformations* are performed on the original shellcode to make it completely alphanumeric. Different transformations are made depending on the encoding scheme in use - NAT or AF. Once the transformations are performed on the original shellcode, we get the *encoded shellcode*, which is used in the *last* stage. It is the second stage (*decoder loop*) that, at runtime, undoes all the transformations done on original shellcode, in order to recover back the original shellcode. However, this second stage is again not completely alphanumeric. We transform the second stage using the Rix tool to encode the non-alphanumeric bytes present in the decoder loop. After the transformations are done, the second stage becomes completely alphanumeric. Now comes the first stage which consists of the initializer and XOR patcher sections that are emitted by Rix tool. Combining all the above three stages yields a completely alphanumeric equivalent version of the original shellcode that can be readily executed.

At runtime, the Rix stage (first stage) recovers the decoding loop. The decoding loop in turn recovers the original shellcode by decoding the third stage. At this point, the original shellcode starts executing.

We wrote a *python* script that takes as input any shellcode and converts it into an encoded form (the third stage) using NAT or AF. Both the first and second stages are invariant for any shellcode (for a particular scheme). So, the actual output is readily generated by prepending the precomputed first and second stages to the output of the python script.

We use the GNU portable assembler *as* to compile the assembly code of the scheme specific *decoder loop*. Then we strip the ELF header from the compiled binary. This stripped binary is then passed on to the Rix tool, which generates the first and second stages required for our use. The total size of the first and second stages taken together is 363 *bytes* for NAT and 291 *bytes* for AF.

4.1   Decoding Loop

The general structure of the decoders for both the schemes is the same. The decoder first computes the memory address of the start of the *Encoded Shellcode* and stores the computed address in a register. As the looped decoder iterates over the *Encoded Shellcode*, it keeps on incrementing this computed address, to keep track of the next byte to be decoded.

Next the decoder sets the ECX and the EDX registers to point to the start of the *Encoded Shellcode*. The ECX register is used to read the values from memory, whereas the EDX register is used to write values to the memory. So the ECX register is labelled as the *get* register and the EDX register is labelled as the *set* register. After decoding, a NAT encoded byte shrinks from *three* bytes to a *single* byte, while an AF encoded byte shrinks from *two* byte to a *single* byte. The *get* register is used to keep track of the next byte to be fetched and the *set* register is used to ensure that the decoded shellcode is not fragmented.

The *loop* section performs the actual decoding process. It performs arithmetic operations on the byte pointed by the *get* register, and then based on the result it decides whether the byte needs decoding or not. From the result of these arithmetic operations, the decoder also figures out whether the decoding process needs to *continue* or *stop*. These arithmetic operations performed by the *loop* section are scheme specific. A series of conditional jump instructions are used to branch to the relevant section for processing the byte.

The *alpha_skip* section copies a single byte from the *get* memory location to the *set* memory location, and then increments the *get* and *set* registers by *one*. This section is used to skip decoding for the bytes which were alphanumeric in the original shellcode. Next comes the *non_alpha_combine* or the *non_alpha_collapse* section. This section fetches the relevant bytes from the *get* memory location, performs the decoding using Jan Wever's decoding logic, and writes back the decoded byte to the *set* memory location. Finally, on completion of the decoding process - when $'z'$ (the *end mark*) is encountered, the control jumps to the *end_of_payload* section. In case of the NAT decoder, this section *NULL* terminates the decoded shellcode, whereas in case of the AF decoder, this section marks the beginning of the decoded shellcode. The NULL termination is not strictly necessary and can be skipped. It is present in the NAT decoder only for debugging purposes. Once the NAT decoder NULL terminates the decoded shellcode, the instructions that follow are part of the original shellcode. After the decoder loop terminates, the original shellcode, located immediately after the decoder, starts executing. This is achieved by setting the initial value of the *set* memory location to the end of the decoder.

Listing 1.1 gives the assembly code for the implementation of AF decoder; the total size of the AF decoder is 52 bytes, out of which 27 bytes are alphanumeric. The code for the NAT decoder is omitted for lack of space.

Listing 1.1. AF Implementation

```
 1  #AF Decoder:
 2
 3  00000000 <looped_decoder>:
 4  # ecx is set to the addr of the pop instruction
 5     0:    e8 00 00 00 00    call    5 <anchor>
 6  00000005 <anchor>:
 7     5:    59                pop     %ecx
 8  # compute start address of encoded shellcode
 9     6:    8d 49 2f          lea     0x2f(%ecx),%ecx
10
11  # Alphanumeric way to copy ecx into edx
12  # ecx = edx = pointer to encoded shellcode
13     9:    51                push    %ecx
14     a:    5a                pop     %edx
15
16  0000000b <loop>:
17     b:    30 ff             xor     %bh,%bh
18
19  # Compare M[ecx] with byte 'K'
20     d:    80 39 4b          cmpb    $0x4b,(%ecx)
21  # If less, goto alpha_skip
22    10:    7c 0c             jl      1e <alpha_skip>
23
24  # Compare M[ecx] with 'Z'
25    12:    80 39 5a          cmpb    $0x5a,(%ecx)
26  # If less or equal, goto non_alpha_collapse
27    15:    7e 0f             jle     26 <non_alpha_collapse>
28
29  # Compare M[ecx] with byte 'z'
30    17:    80 39 7a          cmpb    $0x7a,(%ecx)
31  # If less, goto alpha_skip
32    1a:    75 02             jne     1e <alpha_skip>
33    1c:    74 16             je      34 <end>
34
35  0000001e <alpha_skip>:
36    1e:    32 39             xor     (%ecx),%bh    ;
37    20:    88 3a             mov     %bh,(%edx)
38    22:    41                inc     %ecx          ;
39    23:    42                inc     %edx          ;
40    24:    75 e5             jne     b <loop>
41
42  00000026 <non_alpha_collapse>:
```

```
43   26:    32 39        xor    (%ecx),%bh  ;Get CD byte
44   28:    c0 e7 04     shl    $0x4,%bh    ;Compute CD << 4
45   2b:    41           inc    %ecx
46   2c:    32 39        xor    (%ecx),%bh  ;Compute CD << 4 ^ EF
47   2e:    41           inc    %ecx
48   2f:    88 3a        mov    %bh,(%edx)  ;
49   31:    42           inc    %edx        ;
50   32:    75 d7        jne    b <loop>
51   00000034 <end>:
```

4.2   Performance Analysis

Table 1 compares the encoding performance of Wever's encoding with the NAT and AF encodings. Note that the *header size* (Rix stage + looped decoder) is *not* included in the figures mentioned in the table. We tested our implementation on several shellcodes taken from a well-known public repository [4]. Table 2 compares the *total size* of the alphanumeric shellcodes generated by the Rix tool with the NAT and AF schemes.

Table 1. Encoding Performance

| Shellcode | Original Size | | | Wever | NAT | AF |
	Alpha	Non-Alpha	Total	**(in bytes)**		
Exit gracefully	1	6	7	14	20	14
Spawn shell - /bin/sh	20	14	34	68	63	55
Add root user with no password	36	33	69	138	136	110
Execute command after setreuid	39	32	71	142	136	112
Copy /etc/passwd to /tmp	43	54	97	194	206	158
SET_PORT() portbind	47	53	100	200	209	169
Append etc_passwd & exit()	41	66	107	214	240	175
Download + chmod + exec	54	54	108	216	217	173
TCP bind shell	41	67	108	216	245	190
Send /etc/passwd over TCP port	44	67	111	222	246	189
Forks a HTTP Server on port 8800	44	122	166	332	411	301
Password Authentication portbind port 64713	75	91	166	332	351	281
ConnectBack with SSL connection	270	152	422	844	727	588

Table 2. Total Size Comparison

Name	Original Size			Rix	NAT	AF
	Alpha	Non-Alpha	Total			
Exit gracefully	1	6	7	103	383	305
Spawn shell - /bin/sh	20	14	34	192	426	346
Add root user with no password	36	33	69	379	499	401
Execute command after setreuid	39	32	71	350	499	403
Copy /etc/passwd to /tmp	43	54	97	589	569	449
SET_PORT() portbind	47	53	100	571	572	460
Append etc_passwd & exit()	41	66	107	650	603	466
Download + chmod + exec	54	54	108	636	580	464
TCP bind shell	41	67	108	682	608	481
Send /etc/passwd over TCP port	44	67	111	670	609	480
Forks a HTTP Server on port 8800	44	122	166	1178	774	592
Password Authentication portbind port 64713	75	91	166	961	714	572
ConnectBack with SSL connection	270	152	422	1970	1090	879

5 Conclusions and Future Work

Existing approaches to automatically-generated alphanumeric shellcodes work as follows: the shellcodes are placed in encoded form and then recovered at runtime using self-modifying code. The two schemes presented in this paper focus on optimizing this encoded form of the shellcode while trying to keep the decoding logic simple. The schemes produce a more compactly encoded shellcode than the existing schemes. However, the size of the output (decoder + encoded shellcode) is bigger for small shellcodes due to the complexity and size of the decoder.

Our future work will involve improving the performance of the NAT and AF schemes. The size of the complete decoder (*Rix stage* + *Scheme decoder*) can be reduced by re-writing the scheme decoder using more alphanumeric instructions. The current NAT implementation uses fixed alphanumeric characters as the *alpha* and *end* markers. The *alpha* and *end* markers can be chosen at compile time based on the least frequently occurring - alphanumeric character in the shellcode. This will help in reducing the number of unnecessary encodings of alphanumeric characters of the shellcode. This in turn will help in the reducing the overall size of the output. The same can also be done for the *end* marker as well as the implicit marker range of the current AF implementation.

Previous work to automate the process of creating alphanumeric shellcode for the 64-bit architecture (x86-64 or IA64) includes Jan Wever's alpha3 compiler [5]. The alpha3 compiler can produce IA64 alphanumeric shellcode for any given input IA64 binary shellcode. We plan to develop a tool for automating IA64 alphanumeric shellcodes using the schemes presented in the paper (NAT and AF).

The proposed schemes can also be implemented for the ARM architecture. It has been shown that alphanumeric shellcode can be written for the ARM architecture [6], [7]. Some work has also been done to automate the process of generating alphanumeric shellcodes for ARM [8].

Acknowledgments. We thank the anonymous reviewers for their critical and insightful comments on a draft of this paper.

References

1. Aleph One. Smashing the stack for fun and profit. Phrack, 49 (1996), http://phrack.org/issues/49/14.html
2. Rix. Writing IA32 alphanumeric shellcodes. Phrack, 57 (2001), http://phrack.org/issues/57/18.html
3. Wever, B.J.: Writing IA32 restricted instruction set shellcode decoder loops, http://skypher.com/wiki/index.php?title=Www.edup.tudelft.nl/ bjwever/ whitepaper_shellcode.html.php
4. Shellcodes database, http://shell-storm.org
5. ALPHA3 - alphanumeric shellcode encoder, https://code.google.com/p/alpha3/
6. Younan, Y., Philippaerts, P.: Alphanumeric RISC ARM shellcode. Phrack, 66 (2009), http://phrack.org/issues/66/12.html
7. Younan, Y., Philippaerts, P., Piessens, F., Joosen, W., Lachmund, S.: Filter-resistant code injection on ARM. Journal of Computer Virology and Hacking Techniques 7(3), 173–188 (2011)
8. Kumar, P., Chowdary, N., Mathuria, A.: Alphanumeric Shellcode Generator for ARM Architecture. In: Gierlichs, B., Guilley, S., Mukhopadhyay, D. (eds.) SPACE 2013. LNCS, vol. 8204, pp. 38–39. Springer, Heidelberg (2013)

Analysis of Fluorescent Paper Pulps for Detecting Counterfeit Indian Paper Money

Biswajit Halder[1], Rajkumar Darbar[2], Utpal Garain[3], and Abhoy Ch. Mondal[1]

[1] Dept. of Computer Science, University of Burdwan, W.B., India
[2] School of Information Technology, IIT, Kharagpur, India
[3] Indian Statistical Institute, Kolkata, India
{biswajithalder88,rajdarbar.r}@gmail.com, utpal@isical.ac.in,
abhoy_mondal@yahoo.co.in

Abstract. The paper itself forms an important security feature for many security paper documents. This work attempts to develop a machine assisted tool for authenticating the paper of a security document. Image processing and pattern recognition principles form the basis of this automatic method. Paper pulps play a crucial role in characterizing a paper material. These pulps are visible in the UV scanned image of the document. Therefore, the pulps are first identified in the UV scanned image. This identification is done by borrowing ideas from rice grain detection method. Once the pulps are detected, shape and color features are extracted from them. Paper pulps coming from fake documents are significantly different from those of genuine documents in their shapes and colors. Using the shape and color features, a multilayer back propagation neural network is used to discriminate paper pulps as genuine or fake. The proposed method is tested with Indian banknote samples. Experiment shows that consideration of paper pulps is one of the crucial tests for authenticating paper money.

Keywords: Computational Forensics, Security document authentication, Banknote,Paper pulp, Image Processing, Pattern Recognition.

1 Introduction

With the advancement of scanning, copying and printing technologies, counterfeiting of security documents (i.e. deeds, postal stamp, ticket, bank check and draft etc.) has become a serious threat to our society. Counterfeiting of bank notes is playing havoc on economy of many countries [4, 2, 3]. As a result, authentication of banknotes has been an area of utmost concern [5, 6]. Though significant study has been conducted in the field of forensic signature or handwriting authentication, little research has been done for authentication of security paper documents [22]. This work is motivated by this research need. Bank notes consist of several security features in order to prevent their counterfeiting. Printing technique, artwork, security thread, watermark, etc. are significant security marks that are embedded in banknotes [7, 8]. The manual authentication of these security features as so far have been done by the forensic question

A. Prakash and R. Shyamasundar (Eds.): ICISS 2014, LNCS 8880, pp. 411–424, 2014.

document examiners is a time consuming process and an unattractive solution especially when verification of a large number of documents comes into question. An automatic authentication process could provide a viable solution to this problem. A couple of patents on developing automatic method for authentication of currency notes is reported in the literature [9–11] but the technical details of these systems are not readily available because of the commercial reason. This has severely limited us to judge the true potential of the commercial systems. In this area, the reproducible research efforts are still rare in number.

The authors of the paper in [1] proposed a semi-automatic approach for characterizing and distinguishing original and fake Euro notes. Their method is based on the analysis of several areas of a banknote using a Fourier transformed infrared spectrometer with a microscope with an attenuated total reflectance (ATR) objective. They considered four different regions of a note and observed that fake notes were easily identifiable from the analysis of the spectra corresponding to the four regions. However, the authors did not propose any automated scheme for decision-making. Later on, the authors in [12] described another system for authenticating Bangladeshi Bank Notes. They assumed that original currencies under test have the bank name printed in micro letter text. They scanned this part (the region where the bank name should be) using a grid scanner and the textual images are fed in an optical character recognition engine that matches characters with prototypes. Since the fake currencies were assumed not to have the text they show very low matching score. The algorithm is heavily dependent on one feature which makes the system very sensitive. The system would fail miserably if the counterfeiters happen to develop means of duplicating the feature in question. Recently, Roy et. al.[13] presented an authentication method based on detection of printing technique. They tested their method for Indian bank notes where the name of the bank and denomination of the note are printed using intaglio technique. Any deviation from this printing technique was reported as a counterfeiting effort. Later on, they extended their system to consider other security features like artwork, micro print text, security thread, etc. and presented a more robust system for authentication of banknotes [14].

The previous efforts attempted to exploit several security features but the paper material itself was hardly consulted for authenticating the document in question. For any security paper documents including the banknotes, the paper itself plays a crucial role in proving some kind of security to the document [15]. The paper based security is normally achieved by embedding certain special ingredients to the paper material during its manufacturing process. A review on security papers can be found in [16]. Colour optical pulp (or fibre) embedded in the paper is an example. Security fibres may be metallic or photo-chromic. The optical pulp defines a certain kind of characteristics of the paper. They are luminescent under ultraviolet (UV) ray and therefore, visible when the paper is scanned under UV or illuminated light ray. The forensic experts often check the intended paper quality by physical contacts and sometimes, though manually, they check the brightness, illumination and density of the paper pulp in order to authentic the paper of the document in question. This paper attempts to make this process automatic. The preliminary version of this paper was presented in an unreferenced workshop [17]. Here we present an extended and elaborate version of the research.

The salient contribution of this work is to capture the pulp-based paper security feature in a computational way and then associate these features with the notion of genuine and fake documents. The problem has been viewed from the pattern recognition and artificial intelligence principles. Security aspects are represented as feature vectors and the concept of genuine and fake is defined in the feature space. For extracting features, ideas from rice grain detection [18, 19] in images are borrowed as it closely matches with the present problem of detecting fluorescent paper pulps in images. The features suitable for paper pulps are identified in this work. Moreover, as elimination of foreign body is more difficult in UV scanned images than in rice grain images taken by CCD camera, an improved elimination method has been designed for paper pulp detection. Next, the features are extracted and analysed. Classification is done using neural network. Experiment considers Indian banknotes that make use of pulp based paper as a major security aspect. Involvement of real forensic samples is a significant aspect of this study. The experiment shows the importance of paper pulp in detecting fraudulent documents and attests the proposed approach for authenticating banknotes.

2   Proposed Method

The paper used for printing currency notes is a high quality paper made by 100% cotton. Cotton has given whiteness of paper and folding capability. This paper also gives specific identity by its surface finish and crackling sound. During manufacturing process extra features like watermark, security thread and optical fibre (i.e. pulp) are embedded for additional security aspects. The optical fibres or pulps are of specific color and length. For example, in Indian 500 rupee currency note, these fibres are photo-chromic in nature. It spreads randomly on the notes which are illuminated under UV light source. When a banknote is scanned under UV light, the fluorescent paper pulps are visible in the scanned image. Fig. 1(a) shows a banknote and Fig. 1(b) shows the UV scanned image of the banknote. One may see the fluorescent paper pulps visible in the image in Fig. 1(b). The bright spots in the scanned image correspond to the paper pulps present in the note. These pulps play crucial role in authenticating the paper. In a counterfeit note, if the paper is very different from the genuine one, these pulps may not be seen at all. In a high quality counterfeiting, these pulps came as very bright spots and their shapes show significant difference with respect to the pulp marks of the genuine. Therefore, the illumination and shape of these paper pulps are important in characterizing a note paper as genuine or fake.

Our overall approach is divided into a number of stages: (i) detect pulps in a UV scanned banknote, (ii) extract features from the detected pulps, (iii) train a NN classifier based training samples that include both genuine and fake notes.

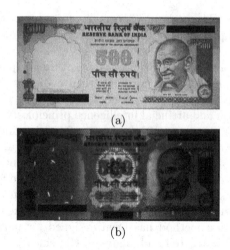

(a)

(b)

Fig. 1. (a) A 500 rupee Indian banknote (b) UV scanned image of the note

Once the classifier is trained, we use this for classification which is configured as 2-class (genuine vs. fake) problem.

2.1   Detection of Paper Pulps

Detection of paper pulps has two stages: identification and verification. During identification phase, detected pulps may be mixed with several foreign (non-pulp) elements mostly coming from background artworks. So removal of foreign particles is done during verification stage.

Identification of Paper Pulps: Paper pulps are identified in a UV scanned image by following a 7-step method as given in Algorithm-1. The UV scanned image is represented in RGB color space. As the pulps are mostly blue in color, we convert the RGB image to CMY (Step-2 of the algorithm) and consider the cyan part of the resultant image at Step-3. Next, median filtering is applied at Step-4 to eliminate small unwanted particles. The centroids obtained at Step-7 indicate individual position of pulps in the image. At this stage, all detected points do not correspond to paper pulps. Many other particles which are same as pulp are identified at this stage. These foreign bodies come from background artwork of the banknote. So the next step is to eliminate these foreign elements and identify only the pulps in the image. This elimination is done by the following process.

Elimination of Non-pulp Elements: The method described in Algorithm-2 eliminates the non-pulp particles from the detected set of pulps. In Algorithm-1, the centroids detected at Step-7 correspond to paper pulps. Here, around each centroid an m-by-m pixel-window is considered on the initial RGB image (Step-1 of

---

Algorithm 1. PULP IDENTIFICATION

Begin
Step 1: Acquire the currency note image (RGB) by UV light
Step 2: Image Complement (RGB − > CMY)
Step 3: Extract cyan image
Step 4: Apply median filter
Step 5: Convert binary image by OTSU thresholding
Step 6: Connected component labelling of background pixels
Step 7: Compute centroid of each component
End

Algorithm-2). The value of m is sufficiently large to completely contain a pulp mark within the window. The gray level co-occurrence matrix (GLCM) [20] is computed for each pixel window at Step-2. For this purpose, we transform the gray image to k ($k < 256$) level image (I). Let $s\equiv$(x,y) be the position of a pixel in I and $t\equiv(\triangle$x,$\triangle$y) be a translation vector. Then the co-occurrence matrix M_t is calculated as,

$$M_t = card(s, s + t) \in R^2 \mid I[s] = i, I[s + t] = j \qquad (1)$$

Where co-occurrence matrix M_t is a (k x k) matrix whose (i,j)-th element indicates the number of pixel pairs separated by the translation vector t (here, $t = 1$) that have the pair of gray levels (i, j). Texture features are extracted at Step-3. An artificial neural network (ANN) is used at Step-4 to discriminate pulp from non-pulp elements. A set of training samples is separately identified for the training this ANN. The features extracted at Step-3 are tagged with pulp and non-pulp identification for training the ANN. In our experiment, the values of m and k are set to 60 and 8 (i.e. the image transforms to 8 levels). These values are fitted empirically. Fig.2 shows the detection of pulp in Fig. 2(a) and then elimination of non-pulp elements to give final result in Fig. 2(b). Fig. 3(a) shows detection of an individual pulp.

Algorithm 2. ELIMINATION OF NON-PULP ELEMENTS

Begin
Step 1: Around each centroid as detected at Step 7 of Algorithm-I, $m \times m$ sub-image is cropped from the initial RGB image.
Step 2: For each such sub-image, compute Gray Level Co-occurrence Matrix (GLCM) [20] under consideration of two adjacent pixels on four directions 0 °, 45 °, 90 °,and 135 ° .
Step 3: Generate texture level four statistical features i.e. contrast, correlation, energy and homogeneity from each co-occurrence matrix.
Step 4: Configure an artificial neural Network (ANN) for discriminating pulps from non-pulp particles.
End

2.2   Feature Extraction from Pulps

Two aspects, namely, shape and color of pulps are considered for feature extraction. Regions of interest are found around the detected pulps. One such example

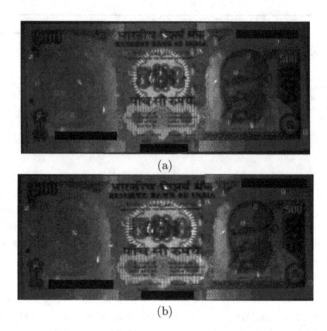

(a)

(b)

Fig. 2. Identification of pulps: (a) detected pulps after execution of Algorithm-1 (b) pulps after elimination of foreign bodies by Algorithm-2

is shown in Fig. 3(b). Feature are extracted from this region of interest. Image analysis techniques used for extraction of features. In total, 10 features are extracted: 4 features coming from shape properties and the remaining 6 features are from color properties of the pulp particles. The four shape features are computed as follows:

(i) Area (f_1): This feature calculates the number of pixels inside pulp identified by a connected component (refer Step 6 of Algorithm-1).

(ii) Rectangular Aspect Ratio (f_2): This feature is given by the ratio of the length and width of the rectangular bounding box of the pulp particle. Fig. 3(c) shows how the rectangular bounding box of a detected pulp is identified.

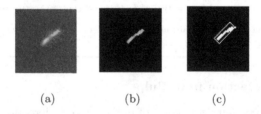

(a)   (b)   (c)

Fig. 3. Rectangular box around a pulp: (a) Pulp detection, (b) Region of interest and (c) identification of the rectangular box around the pulp

(iii) Pulp Aspect Ratio (f_3): The pulp aspect ratio is computed as the ratio of the lengths of the major and minor axes. The length (d_{max}) of the major axis is measured as the distance between the end points of the longest line that could be drawn through the pulp particle. Similarly, the length (d_{min}) of the minor axis is the distance between the end points of the longest line that could be drawn inside the pulp and is perpendicular to the major axis.

(iv) Shape Factor (f_4): This feature is defined as follows: $f_4 = \frac{d_{rms}}{d}$; where, d_{rms} is the root means squared deviation and is defined as, $\sqrt{\frac{(d_{max}-\bar{d})^2+(\bar{d}-d_{min})^2}{2}}$. The mean diameter of the pulp is denoted by $\bar{d}$ and computed as $\frac{(d_{max}-d_{min})}{2}$.

(v) Colour Features: The brightness and illumination of paper pulps give significant clue about the paper quality. They change with the change in paper material. Therefore, features extracted from color space play crucial role in discriminating pulps coming from genuine or fake paper. We consider HSI color space for extracting color features The average Hue, Saturation and Intensity of the pulp pixels give three features f_5, f_6, and f_7. Similarly, their variances are computed and give another three features (f_8, f_9, and f_{10}).

The above features are considered after consulting with the forensic experts. Many of these features they use for manual inspection of the paper in question. It is noted that these features show significant discriminatory power in differentiating genuine and fake samples. This is highlighted in Sec. 3 where experimental results are shown. Fig. 4 shows the discriminatory power of three features, the first one refers to pulp aspect ratio (f_3), the second refers to the average hue (f_5) coming from color space analysis and the third, i.e., shape factor (f_4) coming from shape analysis.

2.3 Training of the Classifier

Initially a neural classifier is configured to discriminate whether a pulp is part of genuine or fake paper. A back propagation neural network (BPNN) is used for this purpose. Multilayer perceptron is used where input layer is consisting of 10 nodes corresponding to 10 features as described in Sec. 2.2. The output layer has just 1 node as the classification problem is binary in nature. Only one hidden layer is used and the number of nodes in the hidden layer is computed as: $N=(\frac{I+O}{2} + \sqrt{y})$; where N=number of nodes in hidden layer; I=number of input features; O=number of outputs; and y=number of patterns in the training set. The multilayer feed forward network model with back propagation (BP) algorithm for training is employed for classification task. A gradient descent method is used to find the optimized set of connection weights that are updated as per the following equation:

$$W_{t+1} = W_t + \alpha \left(\frac{\partial E}{\partial W}\right)\bigg|_{W_t} + \beta\left\{W_t - W_{t-1}\right\} \tag{2}$$

where W_t is weight at the current iteration, W_{t+1} is weight in the next iteration, E is the error term which is calculated as $E=\frac{1}{2}(T - O)^2$; T is Target and

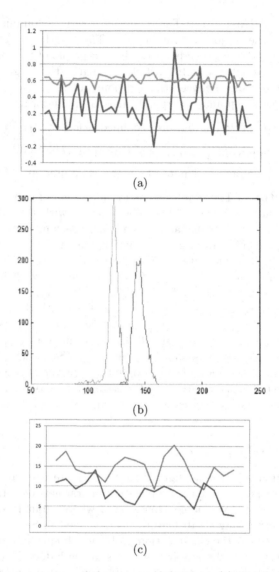

Fig. 4. Discriminatory power of the extracted features: (a) distribution of the pulp aspect ratio (f_3) for pulps from genuine and fake banknotes (blue line is for samples from fake currency); (b) distribution of average hue (f_5) of pulp pixels coming from genuine (green line) and fake (red line) banknote samples; (c) distribution of the shape factor (f_4) for pulps from genuine (green line) and fake banknotes (blue line)

O is Output. The parameters α and β are the learning rate and momentum, respectively. A four-fold cross validation is used for the classification task. The efficiency of the BPNN is evaluated using 3 performance measures i.e. Confusion Matrix, Performance Plot, and ROC plot. The graphical representation of confusion matrix, performance plot and ROC plot in each fold is investigated.

The root-mean-square-error (RMSE) is also studied both at the individual pulp and document (i.e. whole paper currency) levels.

2.4   Authentication of Banknotes

Finally, authentication of banknotes is done based on the pulp level authentication. For example, if p number pulps are detected in a UV scanned image of a banknote, each pulp undergoes checking for its authenticity. The neural network described in Sec. 2.3 is used for this purpose. If majority of the pulps show a particular type (genuine or fake), the banknote turns out of that category.

3   Experiment

3.1   Dataset

The experiment considers 200 samples of banknotes. All of these are not real samples. We got some real samples from the forensic experts who labelled genuine and fake notes. We extracted features from these labelled notes and labelled the feature vectors as genuine or fake. From these feature vectors, later, we synthetically generated other samples so that we get 100 samples for each genuine and fake classes. We assumed the distribution to be Gaussian to generate the synthetic samples. Each real sample is scanned using *VSC5000* UV scanner. The resolution of scanning was set at 200 dpi. It is noted that each genuine currency note image contains about 15 pulps (this number normally varies from 11 to 17). In fake samples, this number does not vary significantly. In 200 banknotes including both the genuine and fake samples, a total of 3124 pulps were detected. The pulps coming from genuine banknotes are labelled as genuine sample and the pulps originated from the fake banknotes are treated as fake samples.

Identification of the pulps above is done following a semi-automatic process. Sec. 2.1 describes a two-stage method for pulp identification. Though the first stage does not require any training, the second stage of this method requires training of a Neural Net. The stage one of the pulp detection algorithm is initially executed for 50 banknotes and extracted pulps are manually tagged as pulp or foreign to train the net. Next, this trained net is used to detect pulps in the remaining 150 notes. It is observed that the net gives about 90% accuracy in discriminating detected pulps as true pulp or foreign element. The errors are then manually corrected to make the dataset suitable for the subsequent experiments.

From each pulp, a 10-dimensional feature vector is extracted. Among 3124 feature vectors, 1602 are labelled as genuine and 1522 are tagged as fake. Tagging of each pulp is quite easy as all the pulps extracted from a banknote take the label of that note. The whole dataset is divided into 4 subsets for conducting a four-fold cross validation test. The numbers of samples in training, validation and test sets are in 2:1:1 ratio.

Table 1. Confidence in Pulp Level

It. No.	Confidence Interval		Classification of pulps					
	Genuine	Fake	Genuine Samples			Fake Samples		
			G	F	C	F	G	C
1	(0.975,1.025)	(-0.0150,0.0150)	47	02	01	45	03	02
2	(0.970,1.029)	(-0.0128,0.0128)	49	01	00	46	01	03
3	(0.969,1.030)	(-0.0182,0.0182)	44	03	03	47	03	00
4	(0.970,1.029)	(-0.0250,0.0250)	48	00	02	43	02	05
Avg.(%)			94%	3%	3%	90.5%	4.5%	5%

It.: Iteration, G: Genuine, F: Fake, C: Confusion, Accu.: Accuracy

Table 2. Pulp Level Authentication

Fold	#Epoch (Best validation at epoch no.)	MSE (Min)	Gradient	Classification accuracy	
				Training	Test
Fold 1	44 (38)	0.00107300	0.00291	94.93%	90.00%
Fold 2	27 (21)	0.00784510	0.00924	92.88%	88.67%
Fold 3	27 (21)	0.07414200	0.03070	90.91%	88.11%
Fold 4	34 (28)	0.06693800	0.04040	89.94%	86.88%
Avg.	33	0.03749952	0.02081	92.16%	88.41%

3.2 Pulp Level Authentication

As mentioned earlier that a neural network is used for discriminating each pulp as genuine or fake. The parameters of the back-propagation neural network are as follows: maximum number of epochs: 1000, minimum MSE value: 0.001, learning rate (α): 0.9, momentum (β): 0.1. Two early stopping conditions were used: (a) total mean squared error (MSE)$\leq$ 0.001 (b) training stopped after 1000 epochs.

At first, recognition of individual pulps is evaluated without mixing genuine and fake pulps together. In evaluating this, we find out two confidence intervals, one for the genuine pulps and the other for the fake pulps. These two confidence intervals are calculated as $1 \pm [\sigma.Z_{\frac{\alpha}{2}}]$ and $0 \pm [\sigma.Z_{\frac{\alpha}{2}}]$, respectively where σ is the standard deviation of pulp recognition accuracy (say, r), i.e. $\sigma = \sqrt{(\frac{r.(1-r)}{n})}$, where n is the total number of pulps; $\frac{\alpha}{2}$ represents the area in each of the two tails of the standard normal distribution curve and $Z_{\frac{\alpha}{2}}$ is the two-tailed normal score for the probability of error α. Following these confidence intervals, Table-1 shows the result for recognition of pulp types at 94% confidence level.

Next all the pulps are mixed together and recognition of their types using the neural net is evaluated. Table-2 reports this result. It is noted that about 88% pulps are accurately classified as genuine or fake by the neural net and this accuracy is achieved at quite low MSE, i.e. 0.037. Fig. 5 graphically shows the behaviour of the neural net. The results are plotted for fold-1. However, similar characteristic curves were observed for other folds. Fig. 5(a) shows the confusion matrix. The ROC plot is shown in Fig. 5(b). As the ROC plot hugs more the left and top edges, it guarantees better accuracy. Fig. 5(c) shows the

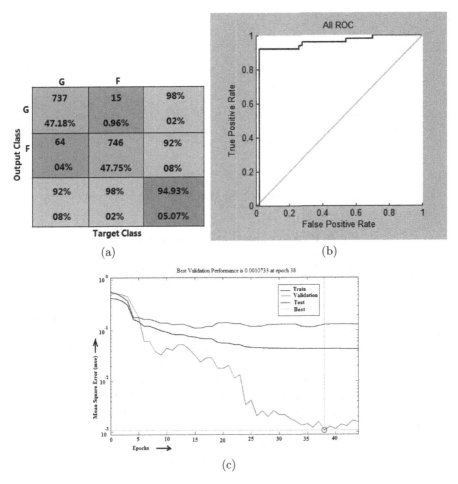

(a)   (b)

(c)

Fig. 5. Behaviour of the neural net in classifying pulps: (a) confusion matrix, (b) ROC plot and (c) performance plot

performance plotted with mean square error (MSE) value against each epoch. The performance plot shows that with the increase of the number of epoch, the MSE value during training gradually decreases and the best validation is achieved at epoch number 38.

3.3   Authentication of Banknotes Using Pulp

Pulp level authentication result is used to authenticate a banknote as described in Sec. 2.4. Let p be the number of pulps detected in the UV scanned image of bank-note after execution of Algorithm-2 (Sec. 2). Each of these p pulps is authenticated using the neural network as reported in Sec. 3.2. The individual authentication scores are then consulted to determine the nature of the banknote.

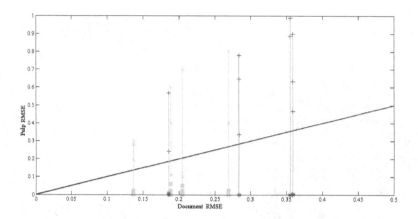

Fig. 6. Banknote classification using paper pulps

In Sec. 3.2, we have checked that the classifier can authenticate the paper pulps with about 88% accuracy. Keeping this accuracy in mind, we decided that at least 75% of the pulps in a banknote should be of similar type (genuine or fake) to label the banknote with that type. If it happens that 75% paper pulps do not show agreement in their class label, the system rejects that banknote and calls for manual intervention. For example, if a banknote normally shows 16 paper pulps, at least 12 pulps should have the same class (genuine or fake) for the system to take decision about the category of the banknote.

The above method was tested for authentication of 200 banknotes divided into 4 groups for conducting a 4-fold cross-validation task. The banknotes of the first two folds participated in training of the neural net. Actually, the pulps inside them are used to train the classifier. The third fold is used for validation purpose. The banknotes in the fourth set are authenticated using the trained classifier. It is observed that out of 200 banknotes 199 samples were correctly classified based on their paper pulp. In one case (which is actually a genuine sample), the system fails to decide as some of its paper pulps are degraded because of the degradation of the paper of the banknote. This banknote is an old one and had been folded at many places. For all other cases, 75% or more paper pulps are rightly authenticated for their class and hence, the system could take accurate decision.

Fig. 6 plots errors in recognizing pulp types as well as document types for eight representative banknotes (genuine samples are marked with green color and red color is used to mark fake samples). The 45° line is shown using the blue color. It is noted that for each banknote there are some pulps for which types are not recognized properly. Misclassified pulps are marked with '×' for genuine and '+' for fake samples. For these pulps RMSE value is higher. However, as the majority of the pulps in a banknote are classified properly, the overall document level (i.e. at banknote level) RMSE value is quite low. Therefore, banknote note types are correctly identified.

4   Conclusion

This paper reports an experiment in the context of machine aided authentication of security paper documents. The role of paper pulps is investigated in order to authenticate a paper in question. To the best of our knowledge, this is one of pioneering efforts for involving paper pulp for developing automatic authentication of security paper documents. Experiments with banknotes strongly attest the viability of the proposed method. As availability of real forensic data in large scale is a hurdle in every country, a small set of real forensic samples is used to develop and verify the system. The future of this research would consider a separate dataset to test the generality of the approach. Though the present study shows the role of paper pulps for banknotes, we advocate that the proposed approach can be used as a part of the whole system for authenticating paper documents. This is because the full authentication should use other security features too. For example, for authenticating banknotes other salient security features like watermark, security thread, background artwork, printing process, etc. are to be validated [14], [21].

Acknowledgments. The authors sincerely acknowledge the help from the questioned document examiners of the Department of Forensic Sciences, Kolkata, India. Initial version of this work was presented in an unreferenced workshop namely, 5th Int. Workshop on Computational Forensics (IWCF), 2012 [17]. The authors sincerely acknowledge the researchers who gave their suggestions/comments on the work.

References

1. Vila, A., Ferrer, N., Mantecon, J., Breton, D., Garcia, J.F.: Development of a fast and non-destructive procedure for characterizing and distinguishing original and fake Euro notes. Analytica Chimica Acta 559(2), 257–263 (2006)
2. Counterfeit Currency in Canada, Publication of Royal Canadian Mounted Police (December 2007)
3. Kaushal, R.: Fake money circulation boosts black economy, India Today (August 5, 2009)
4. Counterfeit Banknotes, Report of the parliamentary office of science and technology, UK (1996), http://www.parliament.uk/briefing-papers/POST-PN-77.pdf
5. Williams, M.M., Anderson, R.G.: Currency Design in the United States and abroad: Counterfeit Deterrence and Visual Accessibility. Federal Reserve Bank of St. Louis Review 89(5), 371–414 (2007)
6. Counterfeit deterrence: Currency design in India and Abroad, The Holography Times 3(6) (2009)
7. Reserve Bank of India,High Level RBI Group Suggests Steps to Check Menace of Fake Notes, Press release number 2009-2010/232 (August 11, 2009)
8. Department of Financial Services, Ministry of Finance, Govt. of India, Counterfeit Notes from ATM, Press release number F No 11/16/2011-FI, 3rd Floor, Jeevan Deep Building, New Delhi, India (July 6, 2012)

9. Mondardini and Massimo, Device for validating banknotes, EPO Patent, No. EP 0537513 (A1) (April 21, 1993)
10. Graves, B.T., Jones, W.J., Mennie, D.U., Sculits, F.M.: Method and Apparatus for Authenticating and Discriminating Currency, US Patent, No. 5,960,103 (September 28, 1999)
11. Slepyan, E., Kugel, A., Eisenberg, J.: Currency Verification, US Patent, No. 6,766,045 (July 20, 2004)
12. Yoshida, K., Kamruzzaman, M., Jewel, F.A., Sajal, R.F.: Design and implementation of a machine vision based but low cost stand-alone system for real time counterfeit Bangladeshi bank notes detection. In: Proc. 10th Int. Conf. on Computer and Information Technology (ICCIT), Dhaka, pp. 1–5 (December 2007)
13. Roy, A., Halder, B., Garain, U.: Authentication of Currency Notes through Printing Technique Verification. In: Indian. Conf. On Computer Vision, Graphics & Image Processing (ICVGIP), India (2010)
14. Roy, A., Halder, B., Garain, U., Doermann, D.: Automatic Authentication of Indian Banknotes. In: Machine Vision and Applications (MVA). Springer (2013) (submitted)
15. Chia, T.H., Levene, M.J.: Detection of counterfeit U.S. paper money using intrinsic fluoresecence lifetime. Optics Express 17(24) (2009)
16. Van Renesse, R.L.: Paper based document security - a review. In: IEEE European Conference on Security and Detection, pp. 75–80 (April 1997)
17. Halder, B., Darbar, R., Garain, U.: Investigating the role of fluorescent paper pulp for detecting counterfeit Banknotes. In: Proc. 5th Int. Workshop on Computational Forensics (IWCF), Tsukuba, Japan (2012)
18. Sun, C., Berman, M., Coward, D., Osborne, B.: Thickness measurement and crease detection of wheat grains using stereo vision. Pattern Recognition Letters 28(12), 1501–1508 (2007)
19. Hobson, D.M., Carter, R.M., Yan, Y.: Characterisation and Identification of Rice Grains through Digital image Analysis. In: Proc. IEEE Instrumentation and Measurement Technology Conference (IMTC), Poland, pp. 1–5 (2007)
20. Haralick, R.M., Shanmugam, K., Dinstein, I.: Textural Features for Image Classification. IEEE Trans. Systems, Man and Cybernetics (SMC) 3(6), 610–621 (1973)
21. BARS 5000 Currency sorter, by BARS GmbH, Siemensstr. 14, D-840 30 Landshut, Germany
22. Garg, G., Sharma, P.K., Chaudhury, S.: Image based document authentication using DCT. Pattern Recognition Letters 22, 725–729 (2001)

A Vein Biometric Based Authentication System

Puneet Gupta and Phalguni Gupta

Department of Computer Science and Engineering,
Indian Institute of Technology Kanpur
Kanpur 208016, India
{puneet,pg}@.iitk.ac.in

Abstract. In this paper, a highly secure and an accurate personal authentication based on palm-dorsa vein patterns is proposed. Hand-dorsa images are acquired in infrared light by using a low cost camera. Acquisition takes place under unconstrained environment in a contact-less manner. Hand-dorsa images are preprocessed to extract the palm-dorsa which is used for vein pattern extraction by using multi-scale matched filtering. Image registration based matching is performed to verify the user identity. Performance of the proposed system is evaluated on a database containing 840 images from 140 different classes. Experimental results indicates that the proposed system performs better that other existing systems.

Keywords: Vein matching, Biometrics, Vein extraction, Hand detection.

1 Introduction

Due to availability of large digital data and cheap hardware, data protection or security is a prime concern which can grant the access to genuine user while restricting the impostor. Tradition systems make use of keys or passwords for system security. But these are not much effective because these can be easily spoofed, forget, lost or stolen. In contrast, modern systems based on biometrics are proliferated which require individual characteristics for recognition because it has following physiological properties: universality, uniqueness, permanence and acceptability [4].

Vein pattern is one such biometric trait which is the created from the subcutaneous blood vessels. Like any other biometric trait, it is highly useful for personal authentication because it: i) is unique; ii) can be easily acquired by cheap sensors; iii) can be instantaneously acquired; iv) is assumed to be stable for longer duration; v) is highly user friendly; and vi) is universal. It is hard to forge as it lies inside the skin and assures liveness. Due to this, vein based biometric systems are considered to be more secure than any other biometric trait based systems. An image containing vein pattern can be acquired by using x-ray and ultrasonic scanners. In addition, it is observed that a vein pattern is visible in infrared (IR) light because veins contain blood which can absorb the

A. Prakash and R. Shyamasundar (Eds.): ICISS 2014, LNCS 8880, pp. 425–436, 2014.

IR light and result in darker intensities near vein pattern. Even though x-ray and ultrasonic scanners (in medical imaging) acquires high quality vein images, these are avoided during acquisition because of high user's inconvenience and slow acquisition time. In contrast, infrared imaging instantaneously acquire the vein images in a contact-less and non-invasive manner. But these have low contrast, poor quality and non-uniform illumination. A vein image can be acquired by either near infrared (NIR) or far infrared (FIR) imaging [20]. In NIR, vein image is acquired by infrared (IR) light by using the fact that blood flowing in vein absorbs IR light. While in FIR, vein image is acquired as a thermal image by using the fact that the vein areas have higher temperature as compared to its surrounding tissues. In comparison to FIR images, NIR images are more robust against environmental conditions (like humidity and temperature) and human body conditions (like skin thickness). Therefore, NIR based vein image are acquired in this paper.

Despite of various advantages of a vein pattern based biometric system, it suffers from various problems which limit its applicability. Spurious vein can be generated or genuine veins can be missed during vein extraction due to (i) skin properties (like thickness and hairs); (ii) environmental conditions (like temperature); (iii) non-uniform illumination; (iv) varying width veins; and (v) area near interphalangeal joints has high illumination. Further, contact-less data acquisition can also results in different pose [11] which can deteriorate the vein matching accuracy. The proposed system is designed to handle these issues. It uses multi-scale matched filtering to suppress the noise and to enhance the variable width veins. It presents a image registration based correlation matching to handle occlusion and spurious vein generation. Also, it detects the hand type (either left or right) present in the image which prunes a large database during matching.

This paper is organized as follows. Some vein pattern based biometric authentication systems are discussed in the next section. The proposed system is explained in the Section 3. Experimental results have been analyzed in Section 4. Conclusions are given in the last section.

2   Literature Survey

Like any other biometric system, a vein pattern based biometric system consists of three stages, which are:

1. **Enhancement:** Spurious veins can be extracted from the acquired vein images due to non-uniform illumination, low local contrast and noises due to hairs and texture on human hand. Thus, various filters like Gabor [13], Steerable [23] and Curvelets [27] filters are applied on vein images. These are formed by using local neighborhoods of vein pattern and thus perform ineffectively for variable width veins. Vein tracking can be used by using the intuition that vein area can be tracked large number of times from several locations while background areas are tracked fewer number of times. Local minima has been used to track the vein structure in [16]. Maximum curvature

information along with vein tracking has been used in [17]. But thin veins are tracked few number of times due to small width. In addition, local shape of a vein is neglected during vein tracking which can result in the generation of spurious veins. Vein images can also be enhanced by using restoration algorithms [24], [25] which tries to minimize the scattering effect produced during IR imaging.

2. **Feature Extraction:** Thresholding algorithms [13], [26] are used to extract the veins from the enhanced vein image. Global thresholding algorithms give wrong results if there is a significant overlap between foreground and background pixel intensities. On the other hand, local adaptive thresholding algorithms can handle such issue and give better vein extraction even if non-uniform illumination are present in the image. Features extracted from the vein pattern are categorized as either local features or global features. Local features [15] consists of geometrical transformation invariant points like minutiae endings and bifurcations. In [18], vein double bifurcation is also used for performance improvement. Various minutiae representations like distances between minutiae pairs [19], minutiae triangulations [12] and spectral minutiae [8] can be used as feature representation to obtain better results. Another category of feature extraction, global features mainly use full vein pattern or vein skeletons.

3. **Matching:** Point to point matching algorithms can be used for local feature matching, either in spatial domain [20], [21] or in frequency domain [9]. Systems which match local features, have poor performance because: 1) sometime noise can generate spurious features; 2) local feature representations like orientation of minutiae cannot be accurately determined; and 3) sometime few genuine local features are extracted. In contrast, global feature matching of shape feature can handle these issues. It has large dimensionality which can be reduced by using invariable moments [14] and machine learning techniques [10]. But such a loss of information reduces the system performance. Better options are the use of pixel-by-pixel matching [1] and correlation matching [3] which match the full vein pattern or vein skeleton.

3   Proposed System

In this section, a vein biometric based authentication system is proposed. Initially, hand-dorsa of user hand is acquired by using the acquisition setup. Palm-dorsa present in the hand-dorsa is used to extract the genuine vein pattern. Vein patterns are matched for authenticating the user. Figure 1 shows the flow-graph of the proposed system.

3.1   Image Acquisition

The proposed acquisition setup consists of a wooden box with a fixed plank attached at its bottom. Plank is of black color and free from pegs. A low cost camera is attached on the top of wooden box such that area of plank can be

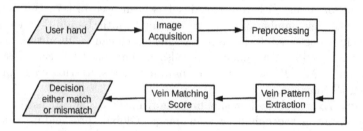

Fig. 1. Flow-graph of the Proposed System

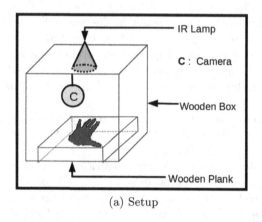

(a) Setup

Fig. 2. Image Acquisition

completely captured. A user hand is placed on the plank without any constraint on finger orientation, in such a way that the hand-dorsa is completely exposed to the camera. An IR filter is attached in front of camera which allow the camera to acquire the IR images. But IR radiation of 3000-12000 nm emitted from the human hand, cannot be perceived by the camera. Thus, an IR lamp of 850 nm is placed inside the box for irradiating the user hand. For illustration, consider Figure 2 which shows the acquisition setup. Since the proposed setup does not contain any other docking device or pegs, it is an unconstrained data acquisition. Also, no direct contact between user hand and camera makes it a completely touch-less system.

3.2 Preprocessing

Most of the areas in the acquired image (let I) contain background which do not contain useful information and hence, such areas should be removed [6]. Hand-dorsa present in I is extracted and it is eventually processed to extract the palm-dorsa and to detect the hand type (either left or right hand).

Algorithm 1. *Preprocessing(I)*

Require: Hand image, I
Ensure: Return $HandType$ and I_I storing hand type and extracted ROI respectively.

1: I_B = global_threshold_algorithm(I) //Binarized image
2: Remove holes and small sized components from I_B.
3: B_h = canny_edge_detector(I_B) //contains contour
4: Find key-points by applying contour tracing algorithm on B_h.
5: Detect $HandType$ (left or right) by using hand geometry constraints on key-points.
6: Find end points of thumb and left finger.
7: Fingers are removed from I_B by using key-points to detect the ROI, I_I.
8: **return** ($HandType$ and I_I)

Since there is a clear separation between intensity of plank and hand area, global thresholding algorithm followed by 8-neighborhood connectivity algorithm [5] is applied on I to extract the hand-dorsa. It may happen that small blobs or holes are present in the hand-dorsa due to hair or texture on the hand-dorsa. Morphological operations [7] are used to remove such noises. Contour (or boundary) of extracted hand, B_h, is detected by using Canny edge detector.

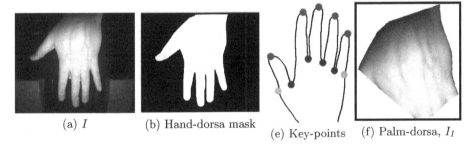

(a) I (b) Hand-dorsa mask   (e) Key-points   (f) Palm-dorsa, I_I

Fig. 3. Various Stages of Preprocessing

Finger areas present in acquired IR image are removed to obtain palm-dorsa area or region of interest (ROI). Two types of key-points are used for this purpose, viz., (i) valley points between alternating fingers which are given by local minima in B_h; and (ii) fingertips which are determined by local maxima in B_h. It is intuitive that the length of hand boundary from the fingertip of ring finger to the fingertip of little finger is less than the length of hand boundary from the fingertip of thumb to the fingertip of index finger. This intuition along with detected key-points is used to determine the hand type. To remove the fingers from the extracted hand, two additional key-points are required which are the end points of thumb and little finger. These are determined by using the fact that end points of a finger are equidistant from its fingertip. By using domain knowledge of hand geometry and extracted key-points, fingers present in the extracted hand are cropped to obtain the ROI. For illustration, consider Figure 3 which shows an acquired image, hand-dorsa area, key-points and extracted ROI. In it, blue, red and green color represent valley points, fingertips and additional key-points respectively. Let I_I represents the extracted ROI from I. Steps required during acquired image preprocessing are given in Algorithm 1.

3.3   Vein Enhancement

I_I contains low contrast, non-uniform illumination and noises due to hairs and texture. Thus, it is enhanced by using matched filtering to account for these issues. A template which looks like a vein is required for effective matched filtering. It has been observed that a vein resembles line shaped structure in a local neighborhood [27] while its cross sectional profile has nearly Gaussian shape [17]. Therefore, a vein shaped filter, G_ϕ, is defined which has two orthogonal directions such that in one direction, it has Gaussian shape of standard deviation σ and mean m while in other direction, it has line shape of length l. It is given by:

$$G_{\phi,s}(x,y) = -e^{\left(p^2/s\sigma_x^2\right)} - m$$

such that

$$p = x\,cos\phi + y\,sin\phi \quad \text{and} \quad |p| \leq 3s\sigma_x$$

$$q = y\,cos\phi - x\,sin\phi \quad \text{and} \quad |q| \leq sl/2$$

where (x,y) represents the pixel location while ϕ and s denotes the orientation and scale respectively. It is applied on I_I to obtain the filter response, that is

$$R_g^s(x,y) = G_{\phi,s}(x,y) \otimes I_I(x,y)$$

where $\otimes$ denotes the convolution operator. Such a matched filter at one scale is unable to detect the variable width veins. Thus, matched filter at multiple scales are evaluated and then consolidated to obtain variable width veins. In addition,

---

Algorithm 2. $Vein\_Enhancement(I_I^R, G_1, G_2)$

Require: Two filters, G_1 and G_2 at different scales along with ROI, I_I.
Ensure: Return M containing vein enhanced image.
1: $R_g^{s1} = G_1 \otimes I_I$
2: $R_g^{s2} = G_2 \otimes I_I$
   /* R_g^{s1} and R_g^{s2} are filter responses at different resolutions while $\otimes$ is the convolution operation */
3: **for** each pixel (x,y) **do**
4:     $M(x,y) = \left(R_g^{s1}(x,y) \times R_g^{s2}(x,y)\right)$
       // Consolidation of filter responses
5: **end for**
6: **return** M

---

it is also beneficial to reduce the effects of noises. Mathematically, consolidated of filter responses at two different scales, s_1 and s_2, is carried out by using:

$$M = \left(R_g^{s_1} \ast R_g^{s_2} \right)$$

where M is the multi-scale matched filter response and $\ast$ represents the element-wise product operation. Algorithm 3 describes the steps involved in vein enhancement.

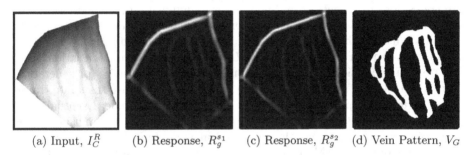

(a) Input, I_C^R (b) Response, $R_g^{s_1}$ (c) Response, $R_g^{s_2}$ (d) Vein Pattern, V_G

Fig. 4. Example of Vein Pattern Enhancement and Extraction

3.4 Vein Extraction

In the enhanced vein image M, there is a clear distinction between vein and non-vein pixels thus, global thresholding algorithm is applied on M to extract the vein pattern. It may happen happen that the extracted vein pattern contains spurious holes or blobs due to noises, which are removed by using standard morphological open and close operations. It is observed that the boundary of I_I can generate spurious vein pattern. Therefore, boundary of I_I is detected by using canny edge detector and is eventually removed from the extracted vein pattern. Let vein pattern extracted from M is denoted by V_G. Steps involved during vein extraction are described in Algorithm 3. An example of vein extraction is shown in Figure 4.

Algorithm 3. $Vein\_Extraction(M)$

Require: M storing the vein enhanced image.
Ensure: Return V_{SG} containing the extracted vein pattern.
1: I_B = global_threshold_algorithm(M) //Binarized image containing vein pattern
2: Remove holes and small sized components from I_B.
3: B = canny_edge_detector(I_I^R) //contains hand contour
4: **for** each pixel (x,y) **do**
5:     $V_{SG}(x,y) = I_B(x,y) \wedge (\neg B(x,y))$
      // where $\neg$ and $\wedge$ are negation and binary AND operation respectively.
6: **end for**
7: **return** V_{SG}

3.5   Vein Matching

Assume that V_G claims the user identity stored corresponding to the template, U_G. It should be remembered that U_G and V_G have same hand type, i.e., either both left or both right hands. The proposed acquisition setup which offers unconstrained imaging can introduce large translation and rotation deformations in the acquired image. But large nonlinear deformations cannot be generated by it. In addition, it is possible that: (i) sometime some part of genuine vein pattern is missed; or (ii) spurious vein pattern can be generated. Reasons behind these are noises, low local contrast and non-uniform illumination [22] in the acquired images. To handle these issues, correlation based matching along with image registration is used in this paper. Fourier-Mellin transform based image registration [2] is used to register V_G with respect to U_G, which accounts for translation, scaling, rotation, occlusion (or missing of some vein areas) and noise (or generation of false veins). In it, rotation and scaling parameters are transformed into translation by using log-polar transformation on spectral magnitude. Eventually, all geometrical parameters required for registration are calculated by using phase correlation. Let R represents the registered image obtained after transforming V_G with respect to U_G. Matching score, s_{uv}, between U_G and V_G, is evaluated by

$$s_{uv} = \frac{\sum_{x,y} R\left(x,y\right) \times U_G\left(x,y\right)}{max\left\{\sum_{x,y} R\left(x,y\right), \sum_{x,y} U_G\left(x,y\right)\right\}} \tag{1}$$

where max is the maximum operator while (x,y) denotes a pixel location. If s_{uv} is greater than the preassigned threshold then V_G and U_G are said to be matched otherwise, not-matched. Algorithm 4 describes the steps required in the proposed vein matching algorithm.

4   Experimental Results

4.1   Database Description

To the best our knowledge, there does not exist any such publicly available database. A database consisting of hand-dorsa images acquired under IR light is created in Biometrics lab, IIT Kanpur to evaluate the performance of the proposed system. It contains 840 images collected from 70 users, each of size 2304×1536 pixels. From each user, it acquires images of both hand, six images per hand. Thus, total twelve images per user are acquired. Different hand refers to a separate class during performance evaluation, thus 140 different classes are considered for experimentation. Correct recognition rate (CRR) and equal error rate (EER) are used for performance evaluation. For testing, the test set is created from one image per class while rest of the images are used as a probe set. Hence, total 700 (1 × 700) genuine matchings and 97,300 (139 × 700) impostors matchings are used for evaluation.

Algorithm 4. $Vein\_Matching(V_G, U_G, th)$

Require: Vein patterns, V_G and U_G, along with a threshold, th, required for matching.

Ensure: Return matching decision in D.

1: Transform V_G such that V_G is registered with respect to U_G and store it in R.

2: $s_{uv} = \dfrac{\sum_{x,y} R(x,y) \times U_G(x,y)}{max\left\{\sum_{x,y} R(x,y), \sum_{x,y} U_G(x,y)\right\}}$

3: **if** $s_{uv} \leq th$ **then**

4:     $D = not\ matched$

5: **else**

6:     $D = matched$

7: **end if**

8: **return** D

4.2 Performance Evaluation

In Table 1, comparison between the proposed vein biometric based authentication system with various existing systems is shown. It indicates that the proposed system has better performance than other systems. Reasons behind this are:

1. The proposed system uses full vein pattern while other systems uses only a subpart of vein pattern. More vein pattern means more features and thus better matching results.

2. It has been observed that matched filtering delivers better performance if the filters required for filtering closely resembles the required shape. Thus, in the proposed system, filters are created by using the most appropriate vein like structure which enhances the performance of the proposed system.

3. Variable width veins and noises due to non-uniform illumination, hairs and texture can result in erroneous vein matching. In the proposed system, these issues are suitably handled by using multi-scale analysis and thus allows better performance of the proposed system.

4. Under unconstrained environment, large rotation and translation can be introduced which degrade the system performance. Such geometric deformations are appropriately eliminated in the proposed system by using image registration.

5. Missing of genuine vein pattern or generation of spurious veins are inevitable and can result in spurious vein generation which further degrades the system performance. These are effectively handled by using correlation based matching.

6. Low performance is observed in [21] because: (i) minutiae features are not accurately localized; (ii) sometime a vein image contains only few genuine minutiae; and (iii) spurious minutiae are extracted which can lead to false matching.

7. System in [14] performs worst than any other system because it uses invariable moments for dimensionality reduction which leads to loss of useful information. Use of such feature descriptors having low discriminatory power, results in spurious vein matching.

8. Since [16] and [17] do not consider local vein shape for vein extraction, false veins can be generated due to hairs and texture on palm-dorsa. Due to the false veins, these systems have lower performance than the proposed system.

In addition, it has been seen that the proposed system has accurately detected the hand type from the acquired image with correct detection accuracy of 100%.

Table 1. Results of Unimodal Hand Geometry Matching

System	Features	Matching Algorithm	ROI Type	CRR	EER
[21]	Minutiae	Haudroff Distance	Subpart	86.42	15.29
[14]	Moments	Support Vector Machine	Subpart	57.57	45.78
[16]	Vein	Correlation	Subpart	96.14	5.31
[17]	Vein	Correlation	Subpart	97.28	4.16
Proposed	Vein	Proposed	Full	**98.71**	**2.43**

5   Conclusions

An accurate personal authentication based on palm-dorsa vein patterns has been presented in this paper. It has acquired hand-dorsa images under unconstrained environment in a contact-less manner from a low cost camera. Palm-dorsa has been extracted from acquired images by using the domain knowledge of hand geometry. Multi-scale matched filtering is applied on it to extract vein pattern. For authentication, vein pattern has been used for matching. But it can be erroneous due to geometrical deformations, occlusion and noises. Thus, image registration based correlation matching has been used. To evaluate the performance of the proposed system, a database containing 840 images from 140 different classes has been used. Experimental results have illustrated that the proposed system exhibit superior performance than other existing systems.

Acknowledgment. Authors are thankful to Saurabh Srivastava who have helped in designing the setup and data acquisition, and to the anonymous reviewers for their valuable suggestions. This work is partially supported by the Department of Information Technology (DIT), Government of India.

References

1. Badawi, A.M.: Hand vein biometric verification prototype: A testing performance and patterns similarity. In: International Conference on Image Processing, Computer Vision, and Pattern Recognition, pp. 3–9 (2006)
2. Chen, Q., Defrise, M., Deconinck, F.: Symmetric phase-only matched filtering of fourier-mellin transforms for image registration and recognition. IEEE Transactions on Pattern Analysis and Machine Intelligence 16(12), 1156–1168 (1994)

3. Cross, J., Smith, C.: Thermographic imaging of the subcutaneous vascular network of the back of the hand for biometric identification. In: International Carnahan Conference on Security Technology, pp. 20–35. IEEE (1995)
4. Flynn, P.J., Jain, A.K., Ross, A.A.: Handbook of biometrics. Springer (2008)
5. Gupta, P., Gupta, P.: Slap fingerprint segmentation. In: International Conference on Biometrics: Theory, Applications and Systems, pp. 189–194. IEEE (2012)
6. Gupta, P., Gupta, P.: A dynamic slap fingerprint based verification system. In: Huang, D.-S., Bevilacqua, V., Premaratne, P. (eds.) ICIC 2014. LNCS, vol. 8588, pp. 812–818. Springer, Heidelberg (2014)
7. Gupta, P., Gupta, P.: An efficient slap fingerprint segmentation and hand classification algorithm. Neurocomputing 142, 464–477 (2014)
8. Hartung, D., Aastrup Olsen, M., Xu, H., Thanh Nguyen, H., Busch, C.: Comprehensive analysis of spectral minutiae for vein pattern recognition. IET Biometrics 1(1), 25–36 (2012)
9. Hartung, D., Olsen, M.A., Xu, H., Busch, C.: Spectral minutiae for vein pattern recognition. In: International Joint Conference on Biometrics, pp. 1–7. IEEE (2011)
10. Heenaye, M., Khan, M.: A multimodal hand vein biometric based on score level fusion. Procedia Engineering 41, 897–903 (2012)
11. Huang, B., Dai, Y., Li, R., Tang, D., Li, W.: Finger-vein authentication based on wide line detector and pattern normalization. In: International Conference on Pattern Recognition, pp. 1269–1272. IEEE (2010)
12. Kumar, A., Prathyusha, K.V.: Personal authentication using hand vein triangulation and knuckle shape. IEEE Transactions on Image Processing 18(9), 2127–2136 (2009)
13. Kumar, A., Zhou, Y.: Human identification using finger images. IEEE Transactions on Image Processing 21(4), 2228–2244 (2012)
14. Li, X., Liu, X., Liu, Z.: A dorsal hand vein pattern recognition algorithm. In: International Congress on Image and Signal Processing, vol. 4, pp. 1723–1726. IEEE (2010)
15. Lin, C.L., Fan, K.C.: Biometric verification using thermal images of palm-dorsa vein patterns. IEEE Transactions on Circuits and Systems for Video Technology 14(2), 199–213 (2004)
16. Miura, N., Nagasaka, A., Miyatake, T.: Feature extraction of finger-vein patterns based on repeated line tracking and its application to personal identification. Machine Vision and Applications 15(4), 194–203 (2004)
17. Miura, N., Nagasaka, A., Miyatake, T.: Extraction of finger-vein patterns using maximum curvature points in image profiles. IEICE Transactions on Information and Systems 90(8), 1185–1194 (2007)
18. Soni, M., Gupta, P.: A robust vein pattern-based recognition system. Journal of Computers 7(11), 2711–2718 (2012)
19. Wang, K., Zhang, Y., Yuan, Z., Zhuang, D.: Hand vein recognition based on multi supplemental features of multi-classifier fusion decision. In: International Conference on Mechatronics and Automation, pp. 1790–1795. IEEE (2006)
20. Wang, L., Leedham, G., Cho, S.Y.: Infrared imaging of hand vein patterns for biometric purposes. IET Computer Vision 1(3), 113–122 (2007)
21. Wang, L., Leedham, G., Siu-Yeung Cho, D.: Minutiae feature analysis for infrared hand vein pattern biometrics. Pattern Recognition 41(3), 920–929 (2008)
22. Wilson, C.: Vein pattern recognition: a privacy-enhancing biometric. CRC Press (2011)
23. Yang, J., Li, X.: Efficient finger vein localization and recognition. In: International Conference on Pattern Recognition, pp. 1148–1151. IEEE (2010)

24. Yang, J., Shi, Y.: Finger–vein roi localization and vein ridge enhancement. Pattern Recognition Letters 33(12), 1569–1579 (2012)
25. Yang, J., Shi, Y.: Towards finger-vein image restoration and enhancement for finger-vein recognition. Information Sciences 268, 33–52 (2014)
26. Yang, J., Shi, Y., Yang, J., Jiang, L.: A novel finger-vein recognition method with feature combination. In: International Conference on Image Processing, pp. 2709–2712. IEEE (2009)
27. Zhang, Z., Ma, S., Han, X.: Multiscale feature extraction of finger-vein patterns based on curvelets and local interconnection structure neural network. In: International Conference on Pattern Recognition, pp. 145–148. IEEE (2006)

Digital Forensic Technique
for Double Compression Based JPEG Image
Forgery Detection

Pankaj Malviya and Ruchira Naskar

Department of Computer Science and Engineering
National Institute of Technology Rourkela
Rourkela–769008, India
malviyapankaj023@gmail.com, naskarr@nitrkl.ac.in

Abstract. In today's cyber world images and videos are the major sources of information exchange. The authenticity of digital images and videos is extremely crucial in the legal industry, media world and broadcast industry. However, with huge proliferation of low-cost, easy–to–use image manipulating software the fidelity of digital images is at stake. In this paper we propose a technique to detect digital forgery in JPEG images, based on "double–compression". We deal with JPEG images because JPEG is the standard storage format used in almost all present day digital cameras and other image acquisition devices. JPEG compresses an image to optimize the storage space requirement. When an attacker or criminal alters some part of a JPEG image by any image–editing tool and rewrites it to memory, the forged or modified part gets doubly–compressed. In this paper, we exploit this double–compression in JPEG images to identify digital forgery.

Keywords: Cyber forgery, Digital forensics, Image tampering, JPEG compression, Image Authentication.

1 Introduction

In todays cyber world digital images and videos act as the most frequently transmitted information carriers. This has been made possible by the huge proliferation of low–cost, efficient devices such as digital cameras for image acquisition and availability of high–speed transmission media such as the internet. Gone are the days when image acquisition was camera film dependent and image formation could only be done by experts in dark rooms. With the advancement of analog to digital converters, every step of digital image acquisition, formation and storage, is now well within the grip of the common man. However, the present day easy availability of low–cost image processing software and desktop tools, having immense number of multimedia manipulating features, pose threat to the fidelity of digital multimedia data. Common image processing operations such as cropping, splicing, blurring etc., made widely available by such software tools, compel us to question the trustworthiness of the digital images and videos.

A. Prakash and R. Shyamasundar (Eds.): ICISS 2014, LNCS 8880, pp. 437–447, 2014.

Digital images and videos being the major sources of evidence towards faithfulness of any event, maintenance of their trustworthiness and reliability is a major challenge in todays digital world. Digital images act as the major electronic evidences for law enforcement across the world. They are the most effective and efficient means to collect digital evidences from crime scenes. It is extremely crucial to preserve such digital evidences against cyber–crime for suitable presentation in court of law as well as for the media world and broadcast industry. The need for investigation and maintenance of the fidelity and reliability of digital images and videos, has given rise to the field of "Digital Forensics" [1,2] in the research community. Over the recent years, researchers have focused on the areas of digital image authentication, detection of tampering, identification of image forgery as well as investigation of image sources.

In most present–day digital cameras the standard format for image storage is JPEG (Joint Photographic Experts Group) [3]. This standard is used due to the fact that JPEG format provides the best compression, hence optimal space requirement for image storage. The statistical as well as perceptual redundancy in natural images, are efficiently exploited in JPEG compression. Moreover, the JPEG format has an adaptive compression scheme that allows saving in varying levels of compression. However, every time we compress an image some space is saved but at the same time some information loss occurs. Also when the image is reconstructed from its JPEG compressed version, it contains degradations compared to the original image. Although the loss of information is disadvantageous while image forgery detection, various JPEG features are advantageous for identification of alteration or modification of JPEG images.

In this paper, we present a digital forensic technique for detection of forgery in JPEG images. To clearly understand the concept behind JPEG forgery investigation technique, proposed in this paper, let us consider a modification attack carried out on JPEG images. To deliver the attack, the attacker first opens the image in an image editing software, manipulates some regions of the image, and finally re–saves the image back in JPEG format. In this entire process, some regions of the image get "doubly–compressed". Hence, degree of compression of the forged part is different from the rest of the image. This difference in degree of compression, although not perceptible to the *Human Visual System* (HVS), has been efficiently utilized in our work to provide evidence of image manipulation.

Rest of the paper is organized as follows. In Section 2 we present the background of digital forensics and its application to JPEG images. In Section 3 we describe in detail, the proposed technique for detection of digital forgery in JPEG images. In Section 4 we present our experimental results. Finally we conclude the paper with directions for future research in Section 5.

2   Related Work

Digital forensics is the branch of science and technology which deals with detection of cyber–crime and forgery by investigation of digital evidences. Here we deal with digital forensics of multimedia data, specifically *digital image foren-sics* [4,2].

In this work we deal with detection of digital image forgery, specifically JPEG images. A digital image forgery may involve a single or multiple images. In a single image forgery, some portion of the image is replaced by some other portion. Hence some objects may be deleted from, modified or repeated in the image. Additionally such image modifications are usually accompanied by smoothening of the object edges by smudging or blurring selected regions of the image. As mentioned previously, in todays scenario, easy availability of user–friendly image processing tools has made such image manipulations extremely trivial, even for novice users.

Many digital forensic methods exploit the statistical characteristics, inher-ently present in natural images (for e.g., very high pixel–value correlation) to identify forged or unnatural images. In natural images, *visual descriptors* are features used to quantify the visual stimulus that the image produces in the HVS. One example of visual descriptors used in [5] to identify natural images, is *color properties* of the image. The authors [5] have used the number of distinct colors comprising the image as well spatial variation of colors in the image. *Reg-ularity in color composition* is another inherent natural image statistical feature, exploited by the authors in [7], by considering that the foreground (objects) and background are highly color–compatible in natural images.

Examples of other natural image statistics used in digital image forensics are shadow texture, surface roughness or smoothness, power spectrum of image [8,9] etc. Wavelet domain coefficients and various moments of the wavelet distribution, such as mean and variance, are also used by some researchers [10,11] as natural image statistics in digital forensics.

In digital image forgeries involving multiple images, portion(s) of one image is maliciously transplanted into another, to give an idea to the viewers that the transplanted portion is a valid part of the latter image. This class of forgery is referred as "copy–move" forgery. One of the earliest digital forensic techniques for copy–move attack, proposed by Fridrich et. al. in [12], is based on the principle of cloning identification. In [12], the authors search for two image regions, having exactly identical pixel values. However standard images consisting of thousands of pixels, it is computationally quite infeasible to carry out a brute–force search to find such identical (image region) pairs. To make the searching efficient, the authors divide the entire image into fixed–sized blocks and then sort the blocks lexicographically. Post-sorting, extraction of identical image blocks from this sorted list is trivial.

While transplanting an image block onto some other region of the image, many times the adversary needs to resize the block, to match the dimension of the region to obscure. One such forgery approach has been presented in [13]. Re–sampling (by an integer factor) induces periodic correlations among original and forged image blocks. Such correlation among signal samples, a phenomenon not prevalent in natural images, is exploited in [13] to detect transplantation of re–sampled image blocks.

The image blocks which are transplanted may also be geometrically transformed by the attacker in many situations, e.g. an image block may be rotated by some angle by the attacker before it is transplanted. In such case, duplicate image regions may be detected by matching *Scale–invariant feature transform* (SIFT) [14] keypoints of the regions. Such forensic approaches to diagnose copy–move forgery having geometrically transformed image blocks, have been proposed in [15,16].

Digital forensic techniques for JPEG forgery detection, based on analysis of *JPEG ghost classification* are proposed in [17] and [18]. *JPEG ghost classification* is a forensic analysis technique that enables detection of multiple JPEG compressions in an image. As discussed previously, when some region in a JPEG image is manipulated by an adversary, it undergoes multiple compressions while re–saving. Multiple JPEG compressions, limited to specific image regions are detectable by investigation of JPEG ghosts. JPEG ghosts differentiate between the different compression ratio in the image while compressing the image more than once. A JPEG ghost is uncovered by comparing original and re–compressed versions of the forged image. The technique of JPEG image forgery detection through analysis of JPEG ghosts is beneficial in situations where some parts of the image is forged and it is very difficult to visually identify the tampering. To understand the details of JPEG forgery detection through classification of JPEG Ghosts, the readers are requested to refer to [17,18].

3   Proposed Work

In a JPEG image, whenever any kind of editing is carried out on the image and it is written back to memory, the image undergoes re–compression. This feature is exploited in the proposed work to detect any illegal modification or tampering in JPEG images. To make the idea clearer, let us consider the 512×512 *Lena* images shown in Fig. 1 (a) and (c), both of which are JPEG images. Now let us consider a modification attack which modifies a region at the center of the original image shown in Fig. 1(a). This central region of size 200×200 pixels, shown in Fig. 1(b), has been extracted, re–saved at a different JPEG quality and transplanted into the original image of Fig. 1(a) to produce the forged image of Fig. 1(c). It is evident from Fig. 1 that the regions saved at different JPEG quality factors, are not perceptibly distinguishable.

Next, we propose a forensic technique to identify such JPEG forgeries with multiple degrees of compression (the degree of compression varying from region to region) within the same image. To detect such forgery of a JPEG image, the following procedure is followed:

1. First, we compress the entire JPEG image iteratively, at varying degrees of compression. We refer to this degree of compression as the JPEG quality factor. The JPEG quality factor may range from 0 to 100. Higher the JPEG quality, higher is the image quality, with quality factor 100 implying no compression of the image at all. With decrease in the value of quality factor,

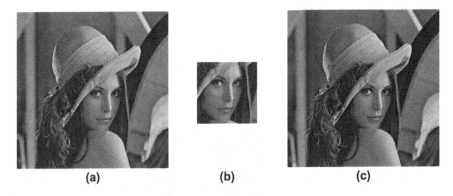

Fig. 1. *Lena* JPEG images: (a) Original 512×512 image; (b) Central 200×200 portion, re–saved at a different degree of compression; (c) Forged image having its central portion modified

the image degradation increases. In our work, we vary the quality factor between [40,90].

2. Let the quality factor of the original JPEG image I be q, which is a constant, and the quality factor used for re–compression be q', which is varied in [40,90] in steps of 1. For each q', we find the squared–error matrix of the image. The squared–error matrix D_1 is defined as:

$$D_1(i,j) = [I(i,j) - I_{q'}(i,j)]^2, \ \forall 512 \leq i,j \leq 512 \tag{1}$$

where image $I_{q'}(i,j)$ is produced by compressing I at quality q'.

3. From each squared–error matrix $I_{q'}$, we again compute the consecutive horizontal pixel–pair differences, row–wise. The absolute pixel–pair differences are computed as:

$$D_2 = \{|I_{q'}(i,j) - I_{q'}(i,j+1)| : 1 \leq i \leq 512, 1 \leq j \leq 511\} \tag{2}$$

where D_2 contains 512×511 elements.

4. We consider D_2 as the vector $[D_2(1), D_2(2), \ldots D_2(512 \times 511)]$. And we consider another vector P of pixel–pair positions in a 512×512 matrix; $P = [1, 2, \ldots 512 \times 511]$.

5. Finally, we plot the vector of absolute differences, D_2 against P. We investigate the variation of the elements of D_2 over the entire 512×512 image matrix, from the D_2 vs. P plot. Our key observation in this paper is that, for forged JPEG images (containing multiple degrees of compression within the same image), for certain values of $q' \in [40, 90]$, the D_2 vs. P plot demonstrates a sudden rise, which remains persistent over a range of P (pixel–pair positions), corresponding to the area or region of image tampering. That is, if 200×200 pixels are tampered, the D_2 values remain persistent for $(200 \times 199 =)39,800$ positions, after the sudden rise.

The D_2 vs. P plot for the *Lena* image in Fig. 1 has been shown in Fig. 2. Fig. 2(a) shows a sudden rise in the plot, which is persistent for the range of

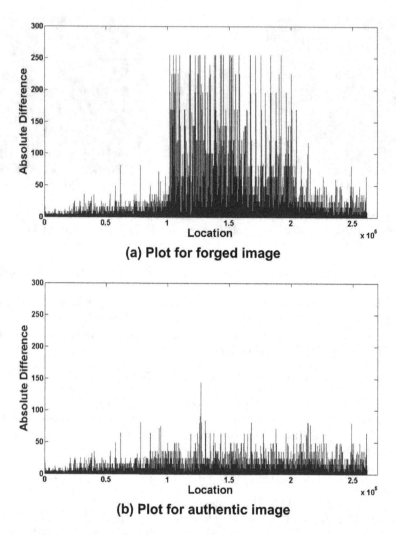

(a) Plot for forged image

(b) Plot for authentic image

Fig. 2. Absolute squared–error pixel–pair differences vs. pixel–pair positions: (a) Plot for forged *Lena* image; (b) Plot for authentic/original *Lena* image

pixels having undergone double–compression due to modification. This feature of JPEG images, provides an evidence of JPEG image forgery, involving double–compression. Authentic JPEG images having no sub–part manipulated (hence doubly–compressed), demonstrate neither such a sudden rise of D_2 values nor its persistence. This is evident from Fig. 2(b), which shows the D_2 vs. P characteristics of the authentic or original JPEG *Lena* image, without any modification or tampering.

Note that, the proposed scheme is a *blind* forgery detection technique, where we need neither the original image nor any information pre–computed from the

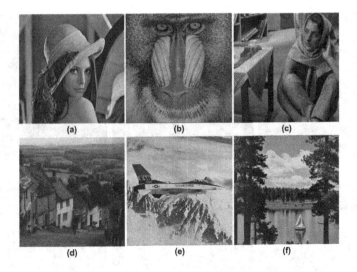

Fig. 3. 512×512 Test Images

original image, for forgery detection. The only information a forensic analyzer has in a *blind* detection scheme is the (possibly) forged image.

4   Results and Discussion

The proposed scheme has been implemented in `MATLAB`. We have utilized the `imwrite` function of the `MATLAB Image Processing Toolbox` to compress images at varied JPEG quality factors. Our test images include standard image processing test images. In this paper we present the results for six test images, shown in Fig. 3.

In our experiments, we have manually induced modification into our test images to test the efficiency of forgery detection by the proposed scheme. To bring about this manual modification attack, we have performed the following steps:

1. We extracted a central 200×200 pixels region from a test image.
2. The extracted portion was re-saved as a separated JPEG image, at a quality factor different from that of the original test image, using the `imwrite` function.
3. The re-compressed portion is transplanted into the original image, at the same central position.

Now, the manually modified or forged images were analyzed by the proposed technique to detect forgery.

As discussed in Section 3, different values of forged image re-compression factor q', give different squared-error matrices $I_{q'}$. The optimal squared-error matrix is determined to be the one, from which the modified image region(s)

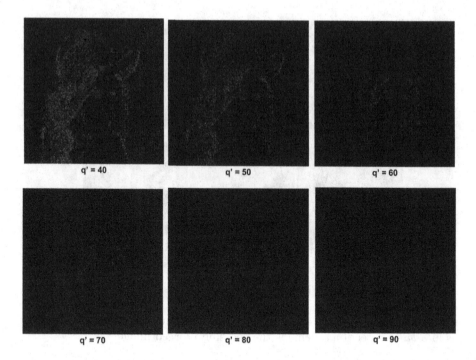

Fig. 4. Squared–error matrices for test image *Lena*, at varying degrees of re–compression q'

is(are) most clearly visible. For all our test images, the re–compression factor q' generating the optimal squared–error matrix, has been found to lie within the range [65,85]. For the *Lena* image, the squared–error matrices for varying degree of re–compression, q', have been shown in Fig. 4. Here, the optimal squared–error matrix, in which the modified image regions are most clear, is generated by $q' = 70$.

For a particular test image, we have investigated double–compression based JPEG forgery by analyzing its D_2 vs. P characteristics, corresponding to the optimal squared–error matrix, for which $q' \in [65,85]$. These plots have been shown in Fig. 5 (a)–(d) for our test images *Lena*, *Mandrill*, *Barbara* and *Goldhill*. The plots in Fig. 5 prove that for modified JPEG images there is a sudden increase in absolute squared–error pixel–pair difference, and this increased value is retained over a range of pixel–pair locations, corresponding to the area of tampering. However this characteristics is inherent in JPEG images containing regions with double–compression. In JPEG images with no modification, such characteristics is absent. This is evident from the D_2 vs. P plots corresponding to our original and authentic test images, as shown in Fig. 6.

Note that the plots corresponding to authentic *Barbara* and *Goldhill* images (Fig. 6 (c) and (d) respectively) demonstrate considerable uniformity in difference values (≈ 0) over the entire range of pixel–pair locations, as compared to

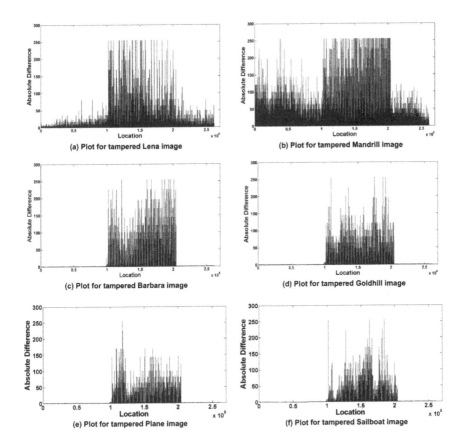

Fig. 5. Absolute squared–error pixel–pair differences vs. pixel–pair locations: (a) Plot for forged *Lena* image; (b) Plot for forged *Mandrill* image; (c) Plot for forged *Barbara* image; (d) Plot for forged *Goldhill* image; (e) Plot for forged *Plane* image; (f) Plot for forged *Sailboat* image

Lena and *Mandrill* (Fig. 6 (a) and (b) respectively). This is due to high correlation among neighboring pixels, present in *Barbara* and *Goldhill* images. Due to minimum inter–pixel correlation in *Mandrill*, the plot of Fig. 6(b) shows the maximum randomness in variation of absolute difference. However, irrespective of inter–pixel correlation among neighboring pixels, a forged JPEG image always demonstrates consistent D_2 vs. P characteristics, as is evident from Fig. 5.

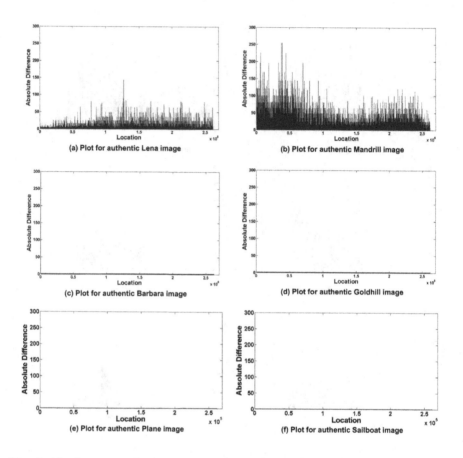

Fig. 6. Absolute squared–error pixel–pair differences vs. pixel–pair locations: (a) Plot for authentic *Lena* image; (b) Plot for authentic *Mandrill* image; (c) Plot for authentic *Barbara* image; (d) Plot for authentic *Goldhill* image; (e) Plot for authentic *Plane* image; (f) Plot for authentic *Sailboat* image

5   Conclusion

In this paper, we have presented a digital forensic technique for detection of JPEG image forgery, which results from modifying the image and re–writing it to memory by an adversary. The proposed technique exploits the feature of "double–compression", inherent in forged JPEG images. Out experimental data prove the forgery detection efficiency of the proposed scheme. Automation of Quality factor determination is the future direction for this research. Utilizing the forensic results and data related to JPEG forgery, recovery of forged JPEG regions may also be investigated in the future.

References

1. Sencar, H.T., Memon, N. (eds.): Digital Image Forensics: There is More to a Picture than Meets the Eye. Springer, New York (2013)
2. Redi, J., Taktak, W., Dugelay, J.L.: Digital Image Forensics: A Booklet for Beginners. Multimedia Tools and Applications 51(1), 133–162 (2011)
3. Wallace, G.: The JPEG still picture compression standard. IEEE Transactions on Consumer Electronics 34(4), 30–44 (1991)
4. Sencar, H.T., Memon, N.: Overview of state-of-the-art in digital image forensics. Indian Statistical Institute Platinum Jubilee Monograph series titled Statistical Science and Interdisciplinary Research. World Scientific, Singapore (2008)
5. Wu, J., Kamath, M.V., Poehlman, S.: Detecting differences between photographs and computer generated images. In: Proceedings of the 24th IASTED International conference on Signal Processing, Pattern Recognition, and Applications, pp. 268–273 (2006)
6. Manjunath, B.S., Ohm, J.R., Vasudevan, V.V., Yamada, A.: Color and Texture Descriptors. IEEE Trans. Circuits and Systems for Video Technology 11(6), 703–715 (2001)
7. Lalonde, J.F., Efros, A.A.: Using color compatibility for assessing image realism. In: Proceedings of the International Conference on Computer Vision (2007)
8. Wang, N., Doube, W.: How real is really a perceptually motivated system for quantifying visual realism in digital images. In: Proceedings of the IEEE International Conference on Multimedia and Signal Processing, pp. 141–149 (2011)
9. Ng, T.T., Chang, S.F.: Classifying photographic and photorealistic computer graphic images using natural image statistics. Technical report, ADVENT Technical Report, Columbia University (2004)
10. Farid, H., Lyu, S.: Higher–order wavelet statistics and their application to digital forensics. In: IEEE Workshop on Statistical Analysis in Computer Vision (2003)
11. Srivastava, A., Lee, A.B., Simoncelli, E.P., Zhu, S.C.: On advances in statistical modeling of natural images. Journal of Mathematical Imaging 18(1), 17–33 (2003)
12. Fridrich, A.J., Soukal, B.D., Lukáš, A.J.: Detection of copy-move forgery in digital images. In: Proceedings of Digital Forensic Research Workshop (2003)
13. Popescu, A.C., Farid, H.: Exposing digital forgeries by detecting traces of re–sampling. IEEE Transactions on Signal Processing 53(2), 758–767 (2005)
14. Lowe, D.: Distinctive image features from scale–invariant key–points. Internaional Journal of Computer Vision 60(2), 91–110 (2004)
15. Pan, X., Lyu, S.: Detecting image duplication using SIFT features. In: Proceedings of IEEE ICASSP (2010)
16. Huang, H., Guo, W., Zhang, Y.: Detection of copy–move forgery in digital images using SIFT algorithm. In: IEEE Pacific–Asia Workshop on Computational Intelligence and Industrial Application (2008)
17. Farid, H.: Exposing digital forgeries from JPEG ghosts. IEEE Transactions on Information Forensics and Security 4(1), 154–160 (2009)
18. Zach, F., Riess, C., Angelopoulou, E.: Automated Image Forgery Detection through Classification of JPEG Ghosts. In: Proceedings of the German Association for Pattern Recognition (DAGM 2012), pp. 185–194 (August 2012)

Preserving Privacy in Location-Based Services Using Sudoku Structures

Sumitra Biswal[1], Goutam Paul[2], and Shashwat Raizada[3]

[1] Independent Researcher, New Delhi 110 095, India
sbiswal2912@gmail.com
[2] Cryptology and Security Research Unit,
R. C. Bose Centre for Cryptology & Security,
Indian Statistical Institute, Kolkata 700 108, India
goutam.paul@isical.ac.in
[3] Applied Statistics Unit,
Indian Statistical Institute, Kolkata 700 108, India
shashwat.raizada@gmail.com

Abstract. With the prevalence of ubiquitous computing and the increase in the number of mobile phone and smartphone users, multiple features and applications are being introduced to facilitate users' daily life. However, users are unaware of the potential danger when the data is collected in return by the service providers. Users and the data associated with them are vulnerable to privacy attacks and threats. The concerning issue has been of interest to many researchers and several techniques have been proposed to counteract such threat and vulnerability issues. This paper proposes a new technique using Sudoku structures and shows how it can ensure users' privacy and degrade the confidence level at the adversary's end for tracking the user. In the proposed scheme, the service providers can be customized for varying needs of the user and in accordance with the types of queries. As a simple yet effective technique, it can create reasonable obfuscation for the adversary while guaranteeing accuracy of service for the users.

Keywords: Anonymity, Location-Based Services, Location Privacy, Obfuscation, Sudoku.

1 Introduction and Motivation

Consider the plight of an undercover cop caught spying in the territories controlled by drug cartel. He has been shot and is injured. However, he runs off and lands up in a place and is unaware of any nearby medical centers. He could call someone or some hospital known to him for his help. But he might be tracked; meanwhile, he cannot afford to disclose his position anyway. It would be ideal if he knew a place nearby. So, how is he supposed to meet his requirement without disclosing his location?

A. Prakash and R. Shyamasundar (Eds.): ICISS 2014, LNCS 8880, pp. 448–463, 2014.
© Springer International Publishing Switzerland 2014

This is where *privacy-preserving* technique comes into scenario. It is critical, not only for the agent but also for every user who wants to get some information via the Location-Based Services (LBS) offered in one's smart phones, without revealing one's personal data that include one's location as well.

Several studies have found that smartphone and mobile phone users access these LBS facilities more often. A recent study by the Pew Internet and American Life Project [1] reveals that about 74% of smartphone users overall accessed LBS. This tremendous and apparently ever increasing growth of mobile phone and smartphone users equipped with LBS, certainly are exposed to irresistible and plethora of applications and services, which they avail at the cost of their private information.

The computation of region for providing LBS is not limited to a single server. The work gets divided amongst many servers and third party services that can be untrustworthy. An adversary might mask itself as one of the trusted third party or hack into one of those intermediary service providers, thereby gaining control over the database to extract private or sensitive data from the users query.

Elaina Zintl [14] reports that according to Privacy Rights Clearinghouse (PRC), smartphones and mobile phones can be used to track the user location, as well as everything they do on it. For example, a device known as *Stingray*, brought up by Harris Wireless Products Group of Melbourne, is a sham cell phone tower that deceits all nearby wireless devices to connect to it.

Similar violations of user privacy have been reported in news media as well. The Red Tape Chronicles [14] finds that the gadget is able to collect data such as the cell phone's unique ID, the dialed numbers and location information without user's knowledge. The Brickhouse Security [14] also states that all the information recorded by the service providers are accessible by the third parties and as well as the Government agencies.

Another report [13] justifies how exposed data can be of threat. Certain companies that try to get rid of old data and upgrade to newer versions, sell off their obsolete systems on eBay and other online websites. However, as most of these companies are unaware of proper way of deletion of data, the system sold still pertain to some amount of private data.

It is therefore pertinent that without forbidding the usage of LBS, we need to develop a technique wherein LBS services are provided without collecting sensitive or privacy oriented user data. This technique would work at a prime level for various kinds of queries like, private query over public data, public query over private data and private query over private data [11]. It should also focus on user location privacy and involve client-server architecture to attain an acceptable level of computational complexity and to ensure privacy of desired level. Our current work focuses on designing such a system exploiting the Sudoku structure. As we will see, a clever way of using multiple Sudoku structures gives the scope for preserving user's privacy in location-based services.

2   Related Works

We find two major approaches to address the problem of location privacy, one involving *anonymity* and the other using *obfuscation*.

The most widely used method to achieve anonymity has been using *pseudonyms*, i.e., assigning false identity to users during query. Beresford and Stajano [12] have come up with methods for tracing the users - their names, the places they most frequently visit and their stay in office building. Despite frequent changes in pseudonyms, it is not difficult to trace out the actual user and their location through queries posed by the users and collected database.

k-anonymity is another important concept brought by Sweeney [3]. This deals with making a user indistinguishable from other $k-1$ users. This k-factor proposed by Sweeney has made major contributions to the field of Privacy-Preserving technique.

Bugra Gedik and Ling Liu [4] have come up with personalization of k-factor to suit users' anonymity level. They believe that "One size fits all" might not be valid in every case. We also understand that a uniform value of k might not satisfy users' environmental variations such as sparse domain or instantaneous change of population density while on the move. In [8], Vitaly also focuses the same aspect as to how it might get useless with respect to the curse of dimensionality.

We also observe from [10] that frequently occurring elements having similar query can make the actual user vulnerable to another major and popular form of attack, called *probabilistic inference attack*. Entropy l-diversity technique certainly gives the efficiency of a database in terms of diversity. However, entropy might not be sufficient to reveal the risk level of adversary attack, especially, probability inference attack.

Hashing combined with k-anonymity, as described in [7], has major influence to serve the issue of private query on private data. However, we believe that it might lead to formation of look-up tables by comparing the value against a certain place. This might violate the *trajectory mode* of privacy [11] (avoidance of linking locations to form trajectory).

Krumm [2,9], finds that adding random noise to obfuscate users' location has also been influential in the field of concern but, the inference attack still lies high on certain entities most probably due to non-uniformity.

Other much relevant and significant techniques of obfuscation based on accuracy of users presence to enhance ones privacy are Location perturbation, Spatial cloaking, Spatio-Temporal cloaking [11]. However, their Quality of Service (QoS) degrades with increasing masks.

Some papers have given novel location privacy preserving mechanisms where the worst case scenarios are well addressed along with the strategies to be adopted by the users to maintain privacy. In [20,21], the use of Markov model to determine the users real identity is well described. Along with, the level of privacy incurred by users and the rate of failure of an adversary are well computed. Further, mechanisms to safeguard user privacy has been described along with how optimal it is to ensure privacy of user. However, the work [21] talks about distortion factor that has impact on QoS rendered to the user. The trade off between privacy and QoS still persists. Further, the choice of imposing maximum quality loss to the user seems unrealistic, since in general use, determining the amount of privacy required cannot be best quantified. Again, the adversary, in the worst case, turns out to be the LBS, there are chances of determining the degree of quality loss manipulation by a user at a given event (position and timestamp). Hence, coalescing such degree of quality loss over a time period can also help in building user profile.

In [22], the various means of attack on location privacy along with parameters that can be source of eroding location privacy have been well described. Of all the points enlisted, the inference attack, availability of quasi-identifier's users' Point of Interests (POIs) have been discussed which are also covered in our work with strategic mechanism as how to make it difficult for adversary to violate trajectory privacy.

Most research works infer that the degree of security and data privacy lies on a threshold value defined by the user or in the prescribed algorithm. The threshold level, when not met, can cause data leakage for adversary attacks.

Thus, to provide the optimum level of security and user privacy, it is required that the data obfuscation be done to such a degree, so as neither to distort it to a high level, nor to release enough data for the adversaries to breech user privacy. It should be designed to increase confidence level at the user end to get accurate response for the query and at the same time degrade the confidence level at the adversary's end to identify the location and identity of the user.

It is also to be noted that our work is not a pure form of k-anonymity. Our work does not have k-factor of users for posing a query. It also does not rely on third parties like anonymizers. In [5], Ghinita et al. proposed the Private Information Retrieval (PIR) framework which is very similar to our mechanism. Both include a grid granularity method of computing entities desired by the querying user. Both do not require trusted third parties. Identification probability and correlation attacks are also significantly reduced in both the methods. However, the difference lies in the cryptographic support extended by PIR, while our work focuses on retrieving information without disclosing user's location. Further, the cost incurred in PIR is comparatively higher than that of Kido's work [15] and our work. As per [6], none of the optimization mechanisms used can break the linear server computation restriction which forms an integral part of the PIR protocol. Hence, though PIR gives so far the best privacy feature to the users in LBS, yet it incurs high cost of communication.

3 Sudoku-Based Privacy Preserving Technique

The technique based on a Sudoku based architecture, can map an entire city over a set of Sudoku grids. A user's location is determined by the block number in the Sudoku grid.

3.1 Why Sudoku?

Sudoku is a class of puzzles consisting of a partially completed rectangular grid of N^2 cells, partitioned into N regions each containing N cells, where $N = n^2$, n being an integer. The grid has to be filled in using a pre-defined set of N distinct symbols (typically, the numbers $1, \ldots, N$), so that each row, column and region contains exactly one of each element of the set. The puzzle was popularized in 1986 by the Japanese puzzle company Nikoli, under the name Sudoku, meaning *single number*.

Sudoku variants are characterized by the size N and shape of their regions. For classic Sudoku, $N = 9$ and the regions are 3×3 squares. If the regions are simply rows and columns, the Sudoku becomes a *latin square*. The general problem of solving $n^2 \times n^2$ Sudoku grids is known to be NP-complete [17]. The number of classic 9×9 Sudoku solution grids is approximately 6.67×10^{21}. It has recently been shown that the arrangement of numbers in Sudoku puzzles have greater Shannon entropy than the number arrangements in a randomly generated 9×9 matrices [16].

The rationale behind using a sudoku-based scheme is as follows.

1. Sudoku is an MDS (Maximal Distance Separable) matrix. There is no number that repeats itself in the same row or column or region.
2. It follows uniform distribution principle. Each number appears scattered evenly in a given pattern.
3. There may be multiple solutions to a sudoku puzzle. Because of the complexity of finding a solution and multiplicity of the solutions, a Sudoku grid satisfies the confidence level rising at the user-end and degrading confidence level at adversary's end.

3.2 Parameters of Our Scheme

Consider that a city is mapped by different servers on the basis of different Sudoku structures. The structure gets repeated to cover the entire city. It is necessary to define certain terms or parameters in this context, in order to describe and evaluate our technique. Let $[1, N]$ denote the set of integers $\{1, \ldots, N\}$.

Definition 1. Grid. *A grid is a basic $N \times N$ Sudoku square, containing the numbers from $[1, N]$.*

Definition 2. Order. *An $N \times N$ Sudoku grid containing the numbers from $[1, N]$ is said to have order N.*

Definition 3. Cell. *A cell is the smallest square in the Sudoku grid, labeled by exactly one number in $[1, N]$.*

Definition 4. Cellsize. *The length of the edge of each cell in meters is called the cellsize.*

Definition 5. Block. *A block refers to the set of cells in the city having the same number from $[1, N]$.*

3.3 Description of the Proposed Technique

Let the order be N. The cellsize of the smaller cells in a given grid can vary within 15 sq.km. Assume that, the order of the Sudoku structure varies from one mapping server to other, as depicted in Fig. 1, Fig. 2 and Fig. 3.

In accordance to service provider 1, suppose the user finds himself in cell numbered 2 and queries the server, "Find the hospitals in cell numbered 2." The benefit here lies in the fact that, the server has to respond to the query irrespective of users position. The response contains hospitals from all the cells which are numbered 2 in the city.

Fig. 1. Service Provider 1 maps city with Sudoku structure of order N=4

Fig. 2. Service Provider 2 maps city with Sudoku structure of order N=9

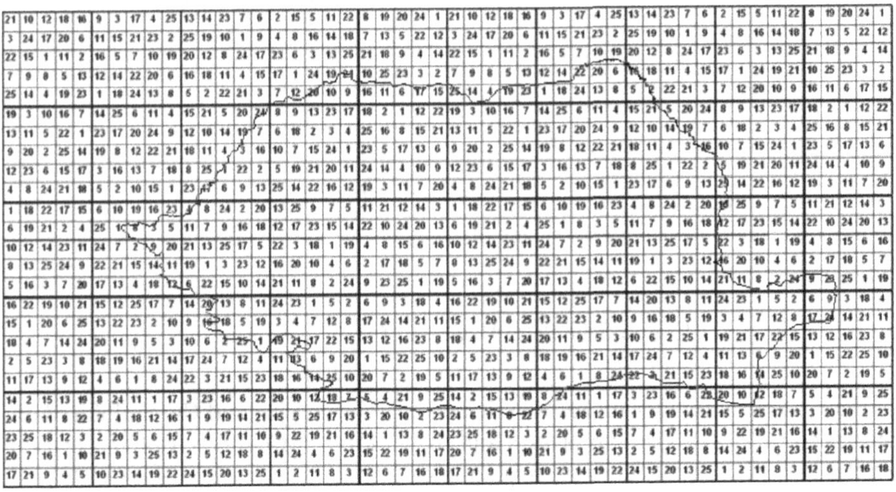

Fig. 3. Service Provider 3 maps city with Sudoku structure of order N=25

In the second step, the user wants a refined answer to his or her query, as all entities are not relevant. Asking the same server would be useless and he cannot afford to give more information to get the reply. So the second step involves taking help of service provider 2 which has mapped the city according to its terms. The procedure repeats but the set of responses generated can vary according to the pattern and structure of the Sudoku.

The refined result involves comparison of the collected sets of response from each server to find the most common entity/entities. Thus, the user can get his/her desired result. Since every server is independent of each other, it is likely that an adversary masking itself as one of those servers cannot affect the location privacy of the user. There are chances that a user might get more than one or two entities in the refined stage which gives the user an option to go for any of those entities, thereby obfuscating the refined response for the adversary.

A major benefit lies in the mining of common entities restricted to the user device. The technique can work more effectively by perceptively collecting the amount of entities used for obfuscation as well as computing cell size for an optimal amount of entities for privacy preservation. However, potential threats exist that two or more servers are hacked by an adversary and sets generated are collided before it reaches the user system. Therefore, it is important that, we aim at encrypting the sets such that unauthorized person cannot interpret the results.

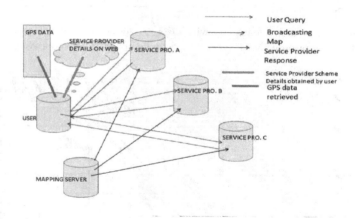

Fig. 4. Schematic Diagram of the Mechanism

Each service provider makes its scheme, i.e., the cellsize and the Sudoku mapping pattern (order, grid structure), and the view port or boundary of application available to the user. The user gets to know his or her location using GPS and then computes the block he/she is in using the details made available by the service providers. The user then makes the desired query to the service provider.

On the service provider side, the mapping server provides the database of entities. The entities received are distributed in various blocks as per the schemes of the service provider. The results matching the query are made available to the user. For optimum result, the user queries other service providers in a similar fashion. At last all the results obtained are analyzed at user end to find the closest answer to the query.

Fig. 4 gives a schematic diagram of the entire system.

The data is stored in a sanitized form, each time a user queries an entity or navigates through a route. Instead of storing the records in the form of timestamp, latitude and longitude and speed, the data stored is of the format - pseudonym, delayed timestamp and block traversed. Hence, the database remains ambiguous to the adversary.

4   Adversary Attack Scenarios

Suppose we are given a city with area X sq.m, let the grid used to map be of order N and cellsize C (in meters).

Number of such grids mapping the city is given by

$$G = X \ / \ (N^2 \cdot C^2).$$

Number of each kind of block available for a city is given by

$$U = G \cdot N = X/(N \cdot C^2).$$

We may consider U as a measure of *ubiquity* [15] that means subjects existing in an entire area. In other words, it is the uniform scattering of users such that the service providers have trouble in spotting them. Since each block represents a user, his/her ubiquity equates to U.

We assume that the adversary gets hold of a server's answering dataset. It is likely that each dataset offers varying number of choices for the user to opt as per suitability. In order to have a generic view of user's block of presence, the adversary intends to look for closely spaced entities.

For a given query, suppose the dataset of k entities is obtained in a block and d_{ij} is the distance between the i-th and the j-th entities. There are two conditions that will enhance adversary complexity.

- **Scattering of Scarce Entities:** If the pairwise distance (d_{ij}) between the entities is greater than or equal to $C\sqrt{2}$, it indicates that the entities are not clustered within the same block, but scattered across all such identical blocks. Thus, they are physically located in different blocks but logically belong to a single block.
- **Scattering of Abundant Amount of Entities:** If d_{ij} is less than $C\sqrt{2}$ for many pairs, it indicates that there is uniform clustering of the entities across the identical blocks.

It has been experimentally observed that the above conditions are valid in most of the responses obtained. This is because all the entities are located at a fair amount of distance from each other. While a user chooses a smaller cellsize for a refined response, the entities are unlikely to deviate from the aforesaid conditions.

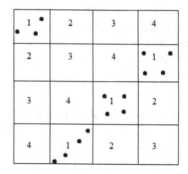

Fig. 5. Scattering of scarce Entities

Fig. 6. Scattering of Abundant amount of Entities

In this technique, there is no third party service made available. There is always higher chances of the third party services being compromised.

An adversary attack may become easier if at least three service providers are compromised. However, since the response generated at each provider is sufficiently large and dynamic, it is highly uncertain to obtain smaller set of entities via data intersection.

Overhead issue at the server end is reduced since no fake user locations are used. While most techniques are based on multiple users communicating with a single service provider, our technique uses single user communicating with multiple service providers [11].

The above measure can sustain as long as the user is static and has not begun his/her journey. Nevertheless, the most prominent mechanism of attack is Inference based Attack wherein the adversary links the movement of the user and builds in a generic profile of user's lifestyle. Such a technique of attack involves formation of a trajectory based on the POIs visited by the user over a specific time period. [18]

For instance, there are four POIs visited by a user over a week at specific timings. The user leaves a certain location, say, POI 1 at 8:00 a.m, follows a particular route except on Sunday. He reaches POI 2 at 8:30 a.m. He follows another route every weekdays starting his/her journey at 9:00 a.m from POI 2 and reaches POI 3. He starts from POI 3 again and follows a route to POI 2 and reaches there by 2:00 p.m. He reaches POI 1 by 3:00 p.m. Then he follows another route to POI 3. He leaves POI 3 at 6:00 p.m every weekday and follows a route to POI 4. He visits POI 4 on weekdays at 6:00 p.m and on weekends at 7:00 a.m. Then he goes to POI 1 and resides there for more than 10 Hours.

Such observations on a consistent basis acquired from the service provider database can provide ample of information to the adversary about his/her daily life. He can deduce that POI 1 is his/her residence, POI 2 is some School/ Educational Institute. POI 3 is his/her workplace and POI 4 is some recreational club (Gym, Sports complex etc). Thus, in order to prevent such specific user based profiling by the adversary, we suggest the following technique.

Step 1: Server End

– Computing centers of regions in a grid as per cellsize.
– Categorizing centroid to blocks.
– Computation of all possible routes between given blocks.

Step 2: User End

– Geocode the destination and find the block as per desired server schemes.
– Query server on basis of source block and destination block.
– Retain all possible routes available from server.
– Follow the appropriate route and change of pseudonym each time a block is crossed with delaying of time involved.

The service provider database in general is complied with certain policies to prevent linking observations. However, in our paper, we do not trust the service provider either. Hence, the data records released from user device are sanitized using mix-zone concepts (pseudonym for every block covered), random delay of time recorded for every move and user location replaced with block numbers (anonymization). In addition, the user's routing query is also anonymized.

Hence, by this method, there is obfuscation of link-based user data thereby providing no ample set for observation and profiling at adversary's end.

5 Experimental Results

In this paper, we focus on the uniformity of the distribution of various entities. We carried out a series of experiments wherein we analyzed results of 20 samples containing varying amount of entities. For implementation, we used C# and SQL.

We observed that, there is uniform distribution of entities across the blocks, provided the population of such entities is fairly large or dense. It is also observed that while we decrement the cellsize, the degree of variation amidst the entities in blocks degrades. As the cellsize approaches a value near the order, ideal uniformity is approached.

Table 1. Grid Order 4 with no. of entities = 1680 and cellsize = 500m

BLOCK	HOSPITALS	RESTAURANTS	ATM_COUNTERS
1	84	236	470
2	6	14	23
3	4	13	27
4	86	237	480

Table 1 shows ones of the simulation results of dense entity population. It can be observed that there is high amount of non-uniformity in blocks 2 and

3. This can lead to tracing out the user location as per user query; provided the condition "Scattering of scarce entities" is not valid (see Section 4). Hence, uniform distribution is envisaged to enhance security of entities so as to prevent user location detection.

Table 2. Grid Order 4 with no. of entities = 1680 and cellsize = 50m

BLOCK	HOSPITALS	RESTAURANTS	ATM_COUNTERS
1	49	124	227
2	51	113	251
3	35	135	252
4	45	128	250

Table 2 shows a relatively uniform distribution of entities, thereby enhancing obscurity. To quantify the (non-)uniformity in the entities, we define a term called *variability* as follows.

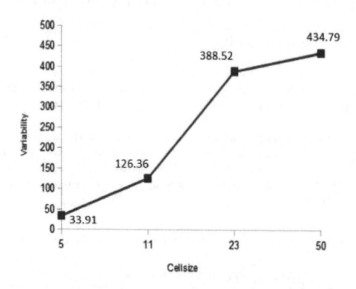

Fig. 7. Degree of Variability vs. Cellsize for Grid Order 4

Suppose there are N blocks and M types of entities. Suppose $n_{i,j}$ is the number of entities of type j in block i, $1 \leq i \leq N$, $1 \leq j \leq M$.

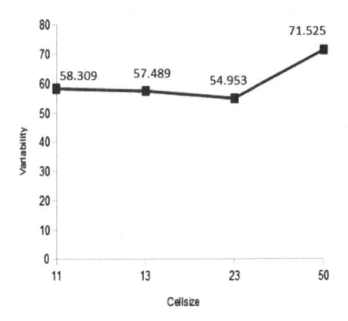

Fig. 8. Degree of Variability vs. Cellsize for Grid Order 9

Definition 6. Variability. *It is the sum of Standard Deviation values computed for each kind of entity across the blocks, i.e.,* $\sum_{j=1}^{M} \sqrt{\frac{1}{N-1} \sum_{i=1}^{N} (n_{i,j} - \overline{n_j})^2}$, *where* $\overline{n_j} = \frac{1}{N} \sum_{i=1}^{N} n_{i,j}$.

Fig. 7 and Fig. 8 show the trend of decreasing variability (degree of variation) with decreasing cellsize. It was also observed that with cellsize approaching the order of the grid, the result tends to be highly favorable. Further, with increasing order, the variability tends to decrease. While in many techniques, the service providers give details of the entities, our method provides pertinent details of entities to geocode. Hence it is a cost reduction technique.

5.1 Comparison with Kido et al.'s Scheme

Following Kido et al. [15], we assume that the average total cost per entity including the packet header equals to 128 bytes and we took a total of 1000 entities. Tables 3, 4, and Figures 9, 10, 11, 12 show the ubiquity model and answering message cost against cellsize.

In Table 5, we compare the techniques that follow similar yet widely diverse methods to enhance location and trajectory privacy.

Table 3. Ubiquity and Message cost for Order 4

CELLSIZE (m)	UBIQUITY	ANSWERING MESSAGE COST (KBytes)
500	1484	33.9968
800	579.6875	35.5456
1000	371	34.4448
2500	59.36	33.984
4000	23.1875	35.0848
5000	14.84	34.8416

Table 4. Ubiquity and Message cost for Order 9

CELLSIZE (m)	UBIQUITY	ANSWERING MESSAGE COST (KBytes)
200	4122.22	14.6944
500	659.956	14.08
800	257.638	13.7088
1000	164.88	15.7696
2500	26.382	14.72
4000	10.305	15.7824

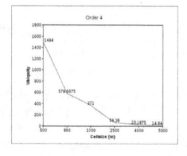

Fig. 9. Order 4 : Cellsize Vs. Ubiquity

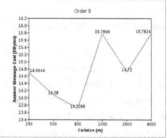

Fig. 10. Order 9 : Cellsize Vs. Ubiquity

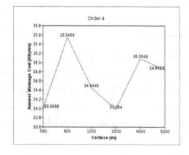

Fig. 11. Order 4: Cellsize Vs. Answer
Message Cost

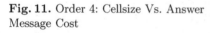

Fig. 12. Order 9: Cellsize Vs. Answer
Message Cost

Table 5. Comparative Features of [15] and Sudoku Query Techniques

Properties	Anonymous Communication technique using Dummies in LBS [15]	Sudoku based Query and Location Privacy technique
Dummy users	Yes	No
Pseudonyms	Yes	Yes
Communication cost for Requiring message	(+ 8 Bytes) with increase of sending position data by one $O(\sqrt{n})^1$ where n is number of position data	Remains constant as no Dummy users position Data generated i.e. 8 Bytes every Query $O(1)$ as each query involves sending only block value.
Communication cost for Answer Message Over 100 queries and each service cost = 128 bytes	PER POSITION DATA: Minimum = 14.7 KB (Average number of services = 114.47) Maximum = 137 KB (Maximum number of services = 1067)	PER CELLSIZE: Order 9 : 13.7 KB - 15.78 KB (approx.) and Order 4 : 33.9 KB - 35.8 KB (approx.) PER BLOCK: Order 9 : 12.672 KB - 17.536 KB (approx.) and Order 4 : 29.44 KB - 37.76 KB (approx.) SQL based query cost is $O(\log n)$ Where n is the number of entities selected
Ubiquity	Increases with increasing number of Dummies	Increases with decreasing cellsize
Trajectory Privacy	Enhanced with help of Dummies and movement algorithms	Enhanced with help of Block values, Pseudonyms and delayed Timestamp

[1] According to [15], the complexity is $O(\log(n))$. It should be $O(\sqrt{n})$, because storage or message required is $N + N = 2N$, that is $O(N)$. Together, they can form $N \cdot N = N^2$ many pairs. With $N^2 = n$, we have $N = \sqrt{n}$.

6   Conclusion

Our paper focuses on adversarial location service provider and extracting service without the involvement of any third party. It also provides mechanism to mitigate the issues of adversary gaining access to location service provider database or user device data logs and records.

Our work for experimentation has involved real time coordinates and positions but has not incorporated any real time metadata or user dataset. In future, we intend to work with real time metadata to improvise the observations. The technique addresses the issues pertaining to the LBS behavior discussed in [22]. Further, with alarming concern of privacy owing to disclosures of NSA surveillance [23], location service providers market has encountered a major setback. Our approach provides a solution for LBS providers as well, such that they do not seek users' location in order to provide the services.

So far, there has been no ideal privacy related approach that guarantees full privacy to the user from an adversary. At any point of time, given enough quasi-identifiers, the users' profiling is possible. Note that cryptographic approach can safeguard user-server interaction from eavesdroppers; however, the computational and communication costs incurred in this case are very high.

The major challenge posed by Location privacy domain is to ensure balance amidst privacy, QoS and cost. In our future work, we intend to improvise our work that addresses this challenge expeditiously.

References

1. Murphy, S.: More SmartPhone Owners Use Location-Based Products [STUDY] (May 11, 2012),
   http://mashable.com/2012/05/11/location-based-services-study
2. Krumm, J.: Inference Attacks on Location Tracks. In: LaMarca, A., Langheinrich, M., Truong, K.N. (eds.) Pervasive 2007. LNCS, vol. 4480, pp. 127–143. Springer, Heidelberg (2007)
3. Sweeney, L.: k-Anonymity: A model for protecting privacy. International Journal on Uncertainty, Fuzziness and Knowledge-based Systems 10(5), 557–570 (2002)
4. Gedik, B., Liu, L.: Protecting Location Privacy and Personalized k-Anonymity: Architecture and Algorithms. IEEE Transactions on Mobile Computing 7(1) (January 2008)
5. Ghinita, G., Kalnis, P., Khoshgozaran, A., Shahabi, C., Tan, K.-L.: Private queries in location based services: anonymizers are not necessary. In: ACM SIGMOD International Conference on Management of Data, pp. 121–132 (2008)
6. Khoshgozaran, A., Shahabi, C.: In Privacy in Location-Based Applications, pp. 59–83 (2009)
7. Raizada, S., Paul, G., Pandey, V.: Nearby-Friend Discovery Protocol for Multiple Users. In: International Conference on Computational Science and Engineering, vol. 3, pp. 238–243 (2009)
8. Shmatikov, V.: k-Anonymity and Other Cluster-Based Methods, https://www.cs.utexas.edu/~shmat/courses/cs380s_fall09/21kanon.ppt
9. Krumm, J.: A Survey of Computational Location Privacy. Personal and Ubiquitous Computing 13(6), 391–399 (2009)
10. Fung, B.C.M., Wang, K., Fu, A.W.-C., Yu, P.S.: Introduction to Privacy-Preserving Data Publishing Concepts and Techniques. Series Editor: Kumar, V. (ed.) Chapman & Hall/CRC Data Mining and Knowledge Discovery Series
11. Mokbel, M.F.: Privacy-Preserving Location Services[Tutorial]. In: IEEE International Conference on Data Mining, IEEE ICDM 2008 (2008)
12. Beresford, A.R., Stajano, F.: Location Privacy in Pervasive Computing. IEEE Pervasive Computing 2(1), 46–55 (2003)
13. Devaney, T.: Hackers grab private data from devices. In The Washington Times (September 05, 2012),
    http://www.equities.com/news/headline-story?dt=2012-09-06&val=454542&cat=finance
14. Zintl, E.: 'Stingray' Device Invades American Privacy (September 13, 2012),
    http://theminaretonline.com/2012/09/13/article23248
15. Kido, H., Yanagisawa, Y., Satoh, T.: An Anonymous Communication Technique using Dummies for Location-based Services. In: Second Int'l Conf. Pervasive Services (ICPS), pp. 88–97 (2005)

16. Newton, P.K., DeSalvo, S.A.: The Shannon entropy of Sudoku matrices. Proceedings of the Royal Society A 466(2119), 1957–1975 (2010)
17. Yato, T., Seta, T.: Complexity and Completeness of Finding Another Solution and Its Application to Puzzles. IEICE Transactions on Fundamentals of Electronics, Communications and Computer Sciences E86-A(5), 1052–1060 (2003)
18. Gambs, S., Killijian, M.-O., del Prado Cortez, M.N.: Show Me How You Move and I Will Tell You Who You Are. Transactions on Data Privacy 4(2), 103–126 (2011)
19. Khoshgozaran, A., Shahabi, C.: Private Information Retrieval Techniques for enabling Location Privacy in Location-Based Services. In: Bettini, C., Jajodia, S., Samarati, P., Wang, X.S. (eds.) Privacy in Location-Based Applications. LNCS, vol. 5599, pp. 59–83. Springer, Heidelberg (2009)
20. Shokri, R., Theodorakopoulos, G., Le Boudec, J.-Y., Hubaux, J.-P.: Quantifying Location Privacy. In: IEEE Symposium on Security and Privacy (SP), pp. 247–262 (May 2011)
21. Shokri, R., Theodorakopoulos, G., Troncoso, C., Hubaux, J.-P., Le Boudec, J.-Y.: Protecting location privacy: optimal strategy against localization attacks. In: ACM Conference on Computer and Communications Security (CCS), NY, USA, pp. 617–627 (2012)
22. Freudiger, J., Shokri, R., Hubaux, J.-P.: Evaluating the Privacy Risk of Location-Based Services. In: Danezis, G. (ed.) FC 2011. LNCS, vol. 7035, pp. 31–46. Springer, Heidelberg (2012)
23. Paganini, P.: Location services, Google is tracking your every move you make (August 24, 2014), http://securityaffairs.co/wordpress/27739/digital-id/location-services-track-you.html

Location Obfuscation Framework
for Training-Free Localization System

Thong M. Doan[1], Han N. Dinh[1], Nam T. Nguyen[1], and Phuoc T. Tran[2]

[1] John von Neumann Institute, Vietnam National University, Ho Chi Minh, Vietnam
[2] University of Information, Vietnam National University, Ho Chi Minh, Vietnam
{thong.doan,han.dinh,nam.nguyen}@jvn.edu.vn,
phuoctran.uit@gmail.com

Abstract. Wi-Fi localization has become an essential service for many aspects of life, especially for indoor-environment where GPS-based technology cannot operate. SIL, a new family of Wi-Fi localization algorithms, has been introduced recently. SIL stands out from the rest of the localization techniques thanks to its training-free property. Capable of performing localization without pre-trained data, SIL resolves the costly training-phase commonly presenting in most other Wi-Fi localization algorithms. SIL can either operate independently or use crowd-sourcing to query and share preprocessed location information. The latter saves the bandwidth cost but poses a security threat of user's location leakage. In this paper, we propose LOF, a framework to secure location anonymity while preserving acceptable-bandwidth-cost for training-free localization algorithms such as SIL.

Keywords: location anonymity, k-Anonymity, distortion, obfuscation, location privacy.

1 Introduction

Many Wi-Fi-based localization techniques have been proposed due to the increasing popularity of Wi-Fi APs (Access Points). Generally, these techniques can be classified into two main categories: training-required and training-free [1]. In the former category, one common step that all algorithms share is the costly training phase. In this step, some known positions in the network are recorded with their associated information. This information map is used to estimate the location in the runtime phase. The biggest challenge of this training step is that it costs a lot of time and physical-labor. Additionally, this step needs to be repeated regularly to adapt to environment changes.

To avoid the costly training phase, SIL-family algorithms [1, 2] are proposed. They are the first training-free algorithms, which exploit the nearby observable access points' names to infer the location. Specifically, SIL utilizes what the APs' names represent (usually the business names or its related information) and aggregates this information to predict the device's current position.

A. Prakash and R. Shyamasundar (Eds.): ICISS 2014, LNCS 8880, pp. 464–476, 2014.

In SIL, querying HTML pages to extract location information is one of the essential components. Nevertheless, this component consumes high bandwidth, which causes significant overhead for SIL. To reduce such overhead, SIL has a choice to retrieve the pre-processed location-information from a third-party, such as a server node or a peer node. Querying the pre-processed information saves considerable bandwidth than self-querying multiple HTML pages to extract the information, as HTML pages are usually large in size. Thus, the overhead is reduced dramatically. However, requesting the location information from the third-party poses users to privacy problems since the third-party can easily find the location of users.

In this paper, we propose LOF – Location Obfuscation Framework. This framework addresses the privacy threat in the training-free Wi-Fi localization while maintaining low and customizable bandwidth overhead. LOF allows users to decide the trade-off between privacy level and the corresponding overhead cost. The foundation of LOF is based on two key ideas: 1) utilizing K-Anonymity to add distortion information in the query sent to the third-party [3-8]; 2) removing customizable amount of important information in the query. By applying LOF into SIL, we aim to preserve the location anonymity while still keeping the bandwidth cost at an acceptable level. Based on experimental results, LOF secures at least 90-percent of anonymity level. Additionally, the bandwidth overhead is nearly costless for performing localization.

2   Related Works

In this section, we study the training-free localizations and their location-privacy threat. Then we review K-Anonymity – a general model for privacy protection.

2.1   SIL – Training-Free Localization

SIL is proposed as a Wi-Fi-based training-free localization framework that aims to remove the need of the expensive training step. To predict the device's current position, SIL utilizes the SSIDs of nearby observable APs to aggregate the related location information via Web search results. In fact, SIL relies on the observation that the names of the APs located at a location often contain information related to that location. For instance, if an AP, named TokyoDeli, is detected, it is a good indicator telling us that our current position is nearby one of the TokyoDeli restaurants. Thus, if SIL can analyze all the SSIDs of observed APs, it can extract the location information linking to the user's current position. Aggregating all the information, SIL can predict the device's location.

Continuing with the previous example, if we can detect another AP with the name McDonald, we can conclude that the current location must be around both McDonald and TokyoDeli restaurants. Thus, if we are able to find a location that is geographically close to both restaurants, we can return it as the predicted address.

Fig. 1 illustrates general framework of SIL. It is composed of three components: SSID Scanning, Geo-Information Retrieving and Address Processing.

In the **SSID Scanning** component, the mobile device will scan for SSIDs from nearby APs. In the **Geo-Information Retrieving** component, based on collected

SSIDs, SIL will gather related information from the Internet and extract a list of potential addresses, called *candidate list*. In the **Address Processing** component, SIL ranks addresses in the *candidate list* and return the correct one to the users. The performance of SIL depends greatly on the algorithm chosen for the Address Processing component. Such algorithms are ISIL and CGSIL [1, 2].

However, both algorithms are experiencing the bandwidth-overhead problem, resulting from the Geo-Information Retrieving component. In details, for each observed SSID, this component is responsible for downloading many HTML files related to that SSID. Based on those files, the component must extract relevant address information from the HTML files. This process is bandwidth-consuming due to the accumulative downloading of HTML files. As a result, it also requires more power. This is especially true for mobile device due to its limitation in data-plan and battery power.

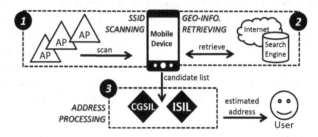

Fig. 1. The General Framework of SIL

To avoid this bandwidth overhead, the authors in SIL recommend using both local cache and third-party help. Specifically, every time SIL extracts the location information from HTML files, it will store that information in cache so that it can reuse the cached data the next time it sees the same SSID. This approach helps reduce downloading the same HTML files. On the other hand, in the third-party optimization, the mobile node will present the SSID to the third-party and ask the third-party to retrieve the location information on its behalf. Note that the third-party can be a dedicated server, other peer nodes or the cloud. The idea of using the third-party as the crowd-source will considerably reduce the bandwidth and operation overhead [2].

However, asking the third-party poses location privacy threat; as the third-party could use the SSIDs embedded in the query to estimate the user location by applying any SIL-family algorithm internally. Thus, to prevent such threat, we propose using **K-Anonymity** [3] and **PIH** (partial information hiding). Specifically, K-Anonymity will add carefully-chosen distortion SSIDs to the requested query; while PIH will remove a percentage of actual SSIDs from the query. The final goal is to obfuscate the information sent to the third-party so that it cannot deduce the user location.

2.2   K-Anonymity

According to [3-8], K-Anonymity is a framework to prevent a third-party from deducing the user location based on the requested data sent to the third-party. K-Anonymity is widely used to protect location privacy [3-8]. One application of K-Anonymity is to prevent location-based identity inference in anonymous spatial queries [4]. Fig. 2 presents an overview of how K-Anonymity is usually deployed.

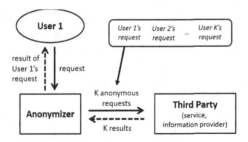

Fig. 2. K-Anonymity Framework

As illustrated in Fig. 2, there are three entities in the framework: the user, an anonymizer and a third-party (service or information provider). In this framework, a user sends his location to the anonymizer. The anonymizer, which is a trusted server, sends the request of the user together with K-1 requests from other users to the third-party. The fundamental idea of K-Anonymity is to ensure the user request is indistinguishable from the K-1 requests. After receiving K requests, the third-party will return all possible results to the anonymizer. Finally, the anonymizer will remove unnecessary results (from other K-1 users) and return the desired result to the user.

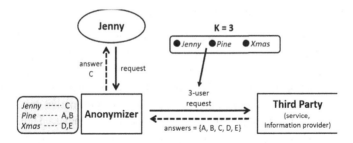

Fig. 3. Example of K-Anonymity with K=3

For instance, in Fig. 3, Jenny sends her request to the anonymizer. Assuming that K=3, the anonymizer generates a package including Jenny's request together with two other users' requests, and sends the package to the third-party. The third-party then returns all possible answers (A, B, C, D, E) for all three requests in the package to the anonymizer. The anonymizer, upon removing unrelated results from the package, will forward the remaining results to the corresponding user. Even though the third-party could predict positions of all three users, it has a possibility of 1/3, or 1/K, to ascertain the position of each user.

In most applications of K-Anonymity, the mobile node cannot localize its location by itself, but must ask a third-party for the location localization instead [3-8]. Additionally, all nodes must trust the anonymizer. Nevertheless, in SIL, the mobile node is capable of performing the localization itself [1, 2] at the cost of bandwidth overhead. Therefore, to reduce such cost, SIL has an option to request a third-party for pre-processed location information, which as a result, leads to the need for concealing the user location information. In other words, if the mobile node downloads and extracts the location information by itself, it can protect its location privacy. However, if the node asks a third-party for the pre-processed location information, it potentially reveals its location information. Hence, LOF is proposed as a feasible solution to preserve location anonymity for SIL while maintaining low and customizable bandwidth overhead. Note that, LOF does not require any trusted anonymizer as in other approaches.

Adopting the idea of K-Anonymity, LOF includes distortion information in the request to mix up the localization information at the third-party side. Additionally, rather than sending the full request information, LOF partially removes some information in the request. To sum up, instead of sending the whole SSID-set to the third-party, LOF sends a partial set to make it insufficient for the third-party to extract user location.

3   Our Approach

In this paper, we propose LOF, a system to protect the user privacy in SIL-family algorithms while maintaining minimal bandwidth overhead.

As mentioned in Section 2.1, to cut down the bandwidth cost, mobile node will request the pre-processed geo-information from a third-party. In our system, we call the third-party as Geo-Information Supporter (GIS).

In the most ideal case, GIS will process all the geo-information and the mobile node just takes it for granted to perform the rest of the localization step. Thus, the processing and bandwidth overhead of SIL could be reduced dramatically as most work is shifted to the GIS. However, in that case, the personal information of the user could be leaked out to the GIS. In other words, the privacy has been violated. On the other hand, if mobile node decides to process all geo-information by itself, it can avoid the privacy concern at the cost of high bandwidth overhead. Thus, the goal of LOF is to introduce a framework that obfuscates the user location information while minimizes the bandwidth overhead.

Note that in SIL, the GIS returns intermediate geo-information result rather than direct location address. The result is utilized to estimate the device's location [1, 2].

3.1   Anatomy of LOF

In SIL, the mobile device sends the set of observable SSIDs to the GIS. In return, the GIS responds with geo-information related to the location. Thus, to prevent privacy leakage, LOF will obfuscate the requested set by: 1) applying K-Anonymity to add distortion information to the set; 2) applying PIH to remove certain important information from the set.

Specifically, by applying K-Anonymity, LOF will send additional noise to GIS to further reduce the chance of exposing the user location to GIS. A set of irrelevant SSIDs, called *disguised SSIDs*, forms the *disguised-set* and is used as the noise.

On the other hand, in PIH, the full set of observable SSIDs, called *original set*, are divided into two subsets. One of them, called *request-set*, is sent to GIS. The other subset, called *process-set*, is self-processed by the device. The reason for the division is to minimize the risk of information leakage when exposing the whole SSID-set to GIS. Also, the division helps reduce the chance for GIS to predict user location based on the received information.

The *disguised-set* (K-Anonymity) and *request-set* (information partition) form the *obfuscated set*, which is sent to the GIS. Note that the GIS has no further knowledge to distinguish the *request-set* from the *disguised-set*. We define:

- $F = \{s_1, s_2, \ldots, s_n\}$ as the *original set*
- $(F_p \cup F_q = F) \wedge (F_p \cap F_q = \emptyset)$
  F_p: *process-set*
  F_q: *request-set*

$$\alpha = \frac{|F_q|}{|F|} \cdot 100\%$$

- $O = \{s_1, s_2, \ldots, s_n\}$ as the *obfuscated set*
- $(D \cup F_q = O) \wedge (D \cap F_q = \emptyset)$
  D: *disguised-set*

$$\beta = \frac{|D|}{|F|} \cdot 100\%$$

$$|O| = \alpha |F| + \beta |F|$$

The device will send O, composed of F_q (based on alpha value – α) and D (based on beta value – β), to the GIS. At the same time, the device self-retrieves and processes geo-information of F_p. The information returned from the GIS and the information self-retrieved by the device are aggregated to localize the position of the device.

Note that the higher value of α, the less work for the device to self-process by simply receiving processed geo-information from GIS. For example, if α is 100%, the bandwidth the device uses is negligible since the device received all geo-information from GIS, which is up to a few kilobytes [2]. However, in general, as α increases, the location anonymity decreases as more information is sent to the GIS. In contrast, the greater β value is, the more *disguised SSIDs* GIS will receive. If β is 200% and the *actual-set* has 10 *original SSIDs*, GIS will receive 20 *disguised SSIDs* in total. In other words, as β increases, the location anonymity increases as less location information is sent to the GIS.

However, the experimental result has shown that not only the size of the *disguised set* (β) contributes to the location anonymity, the way we select the *disguised SSIDs* also does. We will discuss the selection (distribution) of disguised SSIDs in the next section.

3.2   Distribution of Disguised SSIDs

As usual, we tend to select the *disguised SSIDs* randomly. However, according to [2], CGSIL works based on the geo-correlation of the SSIDs. Hence, if the *disguised SSIDs* are in random positions and are not in a close proximity, they will be weakly ranked or eventually filtered out by the three filters of CGSIL, leading to the expose of the actual address in the *request-set*. Therefore, we suggest selecting the disguised SSIDs so that they could be in a close proximity with each other. In general, we have two ways of picking the *disguised SSIDs*, as illustrated in Fig. 4.

- Random Distribution (**RD**): the SSIDs are scattered randomly and have no geo-relation with each other.
- Inter-proximate Distribution (**ID**): the SSIDs are geo-correlated and in close proximity with each other.

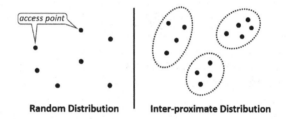

Fig. 4. Distribution of Disguised SSIDs

The effect of each distribution onto privacy leakage is described in Section 5.2.

4   Experiment Setup

4.1   Data Collection

The dataset we use is the same as that of [2]. Specifically, in our experiment, we collected data from four districts including about 60 roads in HCM City. The total street length in our collected data is about 67,500m. On each street, we recorded data at different locations. We collected more than 6,700 locations, which equals to 600 hours of labor. The collected data includes the AP's name. The exact street number addresses were also recorded for the purpose of evaluating the accuracy of our approach.

4.2   Experiment Simulation

For each road in our dataset, we simulate a mobile device applying LOF whenever it performs SIL localization. The locations where the device conducts experiment are 10-15m apart from each other, which is a reasonable distance for a mobile device to perform localization in real time. At each location, the predicted address by SIL and by GIS are recorded for evaluation.

4.3   Privacy Measurement

We define some terminologies used for presenting results in Section 5:

- **Distance error:** the Euclid distance between the actual address and the predicted address.
- **Acceptable error range:** the error range that is acceptable by the users. For example, if the acceptable error range is 500m, that means the users accept the predicted address to be correct if its distance error is 500m.
- **Accuracy:** the accuracy level of CGSIL is calculated as:

$$accuracy = \frac{the\ number\ of\ locations\ yielding\ correct\ address}{the\ number\ of\ all\ locations}$$

- **Normalized anonymity:** the anonymity level secured by LOF is calculated as the complement of the accuracy level and vice versa.

$$normalized\ anonymity = 1 - accuracy$$

- **Bandwidth:** the bandwidth is calculated by the total bytes of 1) the HTML files the device download; 2) the results the device receives from GIS.

For evaluation purpose, we calculate the accuracy when GIS performs localization on the *obfuscated set* with different settings of α and β. Then the accuracy is converted and normalized into the anonymity level to evaluate the efficiency of LOF.

5   Performance Results

In this section, we will first study the effect of α and β onto the anonymity level. Following that we will describe the different distribution (ID or RD) of the disguised SS-IDs in terms of privacy. Then we will examine the correlation between α and β. Note that the SIL algorithm we use in these experiment is CGSIL [2].

5.1   The Effect of α and β on Anonymity and Overhead

In this section, we will discuss the effect of changing the values of α and β onto the prediction accuracy by GIS. Based on the experimented result, we try to figure out the suitable values of α and β for securing the user privacy while minimizing the bandwidth overhead.

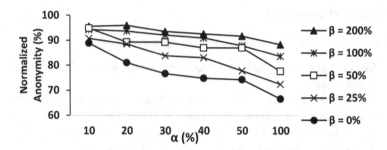

Fig. 5. Anonymity level with fixed β, error range = 500m, with ID SSIDs

In Fig. 5 and Fig. 6 the horizontal axis stands for the values of α while the vertical axis stands for the anonymity level (defined in Section 4.3). Note that in these experiments, the β value is fixed, the α value is varied and the anonymity is measured with error range=500m. The *disguised SSIDs* in Fig. 5 and 6 are distributed as ID and RD distributions respectively.

According to both figures, the anonymity level increases as β increases from 0% to 200%. In contrast, the anonymity decreases as α increases from 10% to 100%. However, in Fig. 5, the anonymity level is stable at 95% when β is 100%, regardless of different values of α. In other words, 95% of the cases, the prediction of user location by the GIS is outside 500-meter radius of the actual address. The same result is achieved in Fig. 6 where the stable anonymity level is 90%. This is due to the fact that the disguised SSIDs are dense enough to distract the concentration of the SSIDs in the *request-set*, leading to the wrong prediction of GIS.

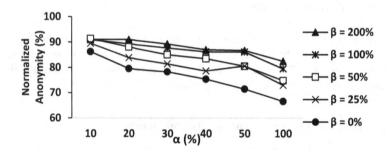

Fig. 6. Anonymity level with fixed β, error range = 500m, with RD SSIDs

To sum up, if we want the bandwidth overhead to be reduced in half, α should be 50% and β should be 100%. In addition, if we want the bandwidth to be negligible, we should set both α and β to be 100%. In either case, the anonymity level is at least 90%.

5.2   The Effect of ID and RD Distributions on Anonymity

In Section 5.1, we have examined the effect of α and β onto the anonymity level. Nevertheless, we still do not know which kind of disguised SSIDs distribution (ID vs. RD)

is more efficient for LOF. Thus, the task of this experiment is to study how different distributions of disguised SSIDs affect the anonymity level.

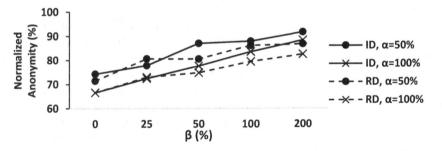

Fig. 7. Anonymity level with fixed α, error range = 500m

In Fig. 7, the horizontal axis stands for the values of α while the vertical axis stands for the accuracy of the prediction. Also, the β value is varied and the α value is fixed at 50% and 100%. As shown in the figure, as β increases, the anonymity level increases. Especially, the slope of the ID line (solid line) is steeper than that of the RD line (dash line). In other words, as β increases, the anonymity in case of ID increases faster than that in case of RD. This implies that ID distribution yields better anonymity level than RD distribution. Because CGSIL works based on the geo-correlation of the SSIDs [2], SSIDs in ID distributions are less likely to be filtered out by CGSIL's filters since the SSIDs are in close proximity to each other. On the other hand, SSIDs in RD distribution have high tendency to be filtered out by the filters.

In summary, we should use ID distribution in LOF to better protect user privacy.

5.3   The Correlation of α and β

So far we have analyzed the effect of α and β onto the anonymity level. These values are configurable in LOF at deployment phase. Therefore, in case the users prefer customized values, they should understand the correlation of α and β. Thus, this section will discuss such relationship.

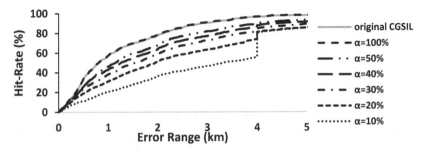

Fig. 8. Hit-Rate of GIS Prediction with β=0%

In Fig. 8 and Fig. 9 show the CDF (cumulative distribution function) of the Hit-Rate for different values of error range. The vertical axis represents the *hit-rate* of GIS; while the horizontal axis represents the error range. We define *hit-rate* as the percentage of cases that the GIS predicts the user location correctly within a given radius error range. For example, in Fig. 8, at error range equal to one kilometer and α equal to 10%, the 20-percent-*hit-rate* means that 20% of the cases, GIS will predict the user position to be within one-kilometer-radius from the actual address correctly. Note that the β value in Fig. 8 and Fig. 9 are 0% and 200% respectively.

As shown in Fig. 8, the curves at different values of α are separated from each other, which means the accuracy strongly depends on α rather than β. In details, the accuracy decreases as α decreases. The result is reasonable because the smaller value α is, the less information GIS acquires to predict the user location, leading to lower accuracy. Note that in the Fig. 8, the curve at $\alpha = 100\%$ ($\beta=0\%$) is the same as the curve of the original CGSIL, since we send the *original set* to GIS without distortion; therefore GIS and the device have the same set of SSIDs, leading to the identical accuracy.

However, when β increases to 200%, all six curves, each of which represents for one value of α, converge to one curve and clearly distinguish themselves from the original CGSIL. It means that, at high value of β, the accuracy seems to be steady and is determined by β rather than α. Since at that time, the amount of *disguised SSIDs* outnumbers (two times) the amount of *original SSIDs*. Thus, the *disguised SSIDs* strongly affect the prediction of the GIS and obfuscate the actual address.

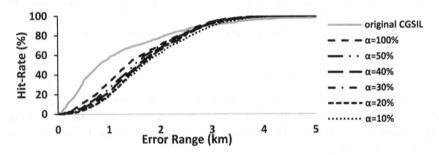

Fig. 9. Hit-Rate of GIS Prediction with $\beta=200\%$

In summary, at low values of β, the anonymity is dependent upon α's value; but, at comparatively high values of β, the anonymity is dependent upon β's value.

5.4   Overhead Analysis

In this section, we study the correlation between the overhead and α value. The bandwidth depends mainly on α rather than β value because α is proportional to the amount of HTML files the device must download and process. Thus, in this experiment, we only analyze the effect of α on the overhead; we fix $\beta=100\%$ (Section 5.1).

In Fig. 10, the vertical axis represents the bandwidth overhead in megabyte, while the horizontal axis represents the α value. According to the figure, the bandwidth decreases as α increases. It is reasonable because the higher α value is, the more information LOF requests to GIS, leading to less work for the device to process. At $\alpha=50\%$, the bandwidth cost is 6MB and at $\alpha=100\%$, the bandwidth cost is negligible.

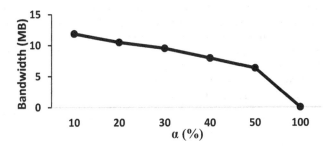

Fig. 10. Bandwidth Overhead with a Variety of α Values

In conclusion, if users prefers 90% of anonymity, they should pick $\alpha=50\%$ and $\beta=100\%$ with the average cost at 6MB per location. However, if users prefer virtually no bandwidth cost, they could pick $\alpha=100\%$ and $\beta=100\%$; in which the anonymity is reduced by 4%.

6   Conclusion

We have proposed LOF, a system to secure the location anonymity for SIL-family algorithms. The system obfuscates the user's actual location from the GIS by adding distortion information into the requested set and removing certain important information from that set also. While securing the user privacy, LOF efficiently keeps the bandwidth overhead at minimal level. In general, if users prefer high anonymity (90%), with low bandwidth cost (6-MB), α should be 50%. However, if users prefer negligible bandwidth cost and 4-percent-reduction in anonymity, α should be 100%. In either case, the β should be 100% or more. For better anonymity level, the suitable distribution for disguised SSIDs should be ID.

Acknowledgement. This research is funded by Viet Nam National University Ho Chi Minh City - John von Neumann Institute, under grant number C2013-42-02 and research fund for contract 16-2014/HDK-JVN.

References

1. Le, T., Doan, T., Dinh, H., Nguyen, N.: Instant Search-based Indoor Localization. In: IEEE Consumer Communications and Networking Conference (CCNC), Las Vegas, Nevada, USA, pp. 143–148 (2013)
2. Doan, T.M., Dinh, H.N., Nguyen, N.T.: CGSIL: Collaborative Geo-clustering Search-based Indoor Localization. Accepted in the 16th IEEE International Conference on High Performance Computing and Communications (HPCC), Paris, France (2014)
3. Le, T.D., et al.: Convert Wi-Fi Signals for Fingerprint Localization Algorithm. In: Proc. IEEE Int. Conf. on Wireless Communication, Networking and Mobile Computing (WiCOM 2011), Wuhan, China, Session 12, pp. 1–5 (2011)
4. Sweeney, L.: k-Anonymity: A Model for Protecting Privacy. International Journal on Uncertainty, Fuzziness and Knowledge-Based Systems, 557–570 (2002)
5. Kalnis, P., Ghinita, G., Mouratidis, K., Papadias, D.: Preventing Location-Based Identity Inference in Anonymous Spatial Queries. IEEE Transactions on Knowledge and Data Engineering 19(12), 1719–1733 (2007)
6. Gedik, B., Liu, L.: A Customizable k-Anonymity Model for Protecting Location Privacy. In: ICDCS, pp. 620–629 (2004)
7. Zhong, G., Hengartner, U.: A Distributed k-Anonymity Protocol for Location Privacy. In: IEEE Int. Conference on Pervasive Computing and Communications (PerCom), pp. 1–10 (2009)
8. Gedik, B., Liu, L.: Protecting Location Privacy with Personalized k-Anonymity: Architecture and Algorithms. IEEE Transactions on Mobile Computing 7(1) (2008)
9. Gkoulalas–Divanis, A., Kalnis, P., Verykios, V.S.: Providing K–Anonymity in Location Based Services. SIGKDD Explorations 12(1)

Author Index

Atluri, Vijayalakshmi 129

Basu, Aditya 399
Bezawada, Bruhadeshwar 277
Bhattacharjee, Jaya 149
Biskup, Joachim 30
Biswal, Sumitra 448
Bugliesi, Michele 89
Butin, Denis 69

Calzavara, Stefano 89
Chakraborty, Nilesh 298
Choppella, Venkatesh 277
Choudhury, Hiten 226
Chowdary, Nagendra 399
Conti, Mauro 257
Cybenko, George 1

Dadeau, Frédéric 358
Darbar, Rajkumar 411
Decroix, Koen 69
De Groef, Willem 89
Dinh, Han N. 464
Doan, Thong M. 464
Dong, Xinshu 245

Fayaz, Seyed Kaveh 9

Garain, Utpal 411
Gaur, Manoj Singh 257
Gay, Richard 378
Gupta, Phalguni 425
Gupta, Puneet 425

Halder, Biswajit 411
Heorhiadi, Victor 9
Hu, Jinwei 378

Jajodia, Sushil 1
Jansen, Joachim 69
Jha, Sadhana 129
Jinwala, Devesh 167

Kauer, Michaela 204
Khan, Wilayat 89

Laxmi, Vijay 257
Lebeau, Franck 358
Legeard, Bruno 358
Li, Xiaolei 245
Liang, Zhenkai 245
Liu, Peng 1

Majumdar, Arun Kumar 109
Malviya, Pankaj 437
Mantel, Heiko 378
Mathuria, Anish 399
Mayer, Peter 204
Mazumdar, Chandan 149
Mondal, Abhoy Ch. 411
Mondal, Samrat 298
Mukherjee, Sarbajit 185

Naessens, Vincent 69
Naskar, Ruchira 437
Nguyen, Nam T. 464

Padhya, Mukti 167
Paul, Goutam 185, 448
Peureux, Fabien 358
Piat, François 358
Piessens, Frank 89
Preuß, Marcel 30

Raizada, Shashwat 448
Ramanujam, R. 50
Reiter, Michael K. 9
Rovelli, Paolo 338
Roy, Arindam 109
Roychoudhury, Basav 226

Saikia, Dilip Kr. 226
Saini, Anil 257
Sarkar, Pratik 185
Sekar, Vyas 9
Sengupta, Anirban 149
Singhal, Tushar 257
Sundararajan, Vaishnavi 50
Sural, Shamik 109, 129
Suresh, S.P. 50

Telikicherla, Krishna Chaitanya   277
Thakur, Tanmay   318
Tran, Phuoc T.   464

Vaidya, Jaideep   129
Verma, Rakesh   318

Vernotte, Alexandre   358
Vigfússon, Ýmir   338
Volkamer, Melanie   204

Wellman, Michael P.   1